POLITICAL AND ECONOMIC ENCYCLOPAEDIA
OF THE PACIFIC

Other recent titles from St James Press include the following:

Political Parties of the World, edited by Alan J. Day (1988), ISBN 0-912289-94-5, $85.00

Elections Since 1945: A Worldwide Reference Compendium, general editor Ian Gorvin (1989), ISBN 1-55862-017-6, $150.000

Trade Unions of the World, 1989–90 (1989), ISBN 1-55862-014-1, $85.00

Religion in Politics: A World Guide, edited by Stuart Mews (1989), ISBN 1-55862-051-6

World Directory of Minorities, compiled by the Minority Rights Group (1989), ISBN 1-55862-016-8, $85.00

POLITICAL AND ECONOMIC ENCYCLOPAEDIA OF THE PACIFIC

ST. JAMES INTERNATIONAL REFERENCE

Edited by
GERALD SEGAL

with contributions by the following:
Douglas Anthony (DA), Richard Boyd (RB),
Peter & Susan Calvert (P&SC), Peter Ferdinand (CIPF),
Jonathan Fryer (JF), Ian Gorvin (IG), James Grayson (JHG),
Hermann Halbeisen (HH), Tom Millar (TBM), William Nester (WN),
Geoffrey Parrinder (GP), Darren Sagar (DS), Richard Sim (RS),
Ralph Smith (RBS), Steve Tsang (ST), Phil Williams (PW)

1989

St J

ST. JAMES PRESS
CHICAGO AND LONDON

POLITICAL AND ECONOMIC ENCYCLOPAEDIA OF THE PACIFIC

Published by Longman Group UK Limited, Westgate House,
The High, Harlow, Essex, CM20 1YR, United Kingdom.
Telephone (0279) 442601
Telex 81491 Padlog
Facsimile (0279) 444501

R
330.99
P759

abdp Association of British Directory Publishers

Published in the USA and Canada by St James Press,
233 East Ontario Street, Chicago 60611, Illinois, USA

ISBN 0-582-05161-4 (Longman)

1-55862-033-8 (St James)

British Library Cataloguing in Publication Data
Segal, Gerald, *1953*−
    Political and economic encyclopaedia of the Pacific.-
    (Longman international reference).
    1. Pacific region. Social conditions
    I. Title
    909'.09823
    ISBN 0-582-05161-4

Printed in Great Britain by
Richard Clay Ltd,
Bungay, Suffolk

INTRODUCTION

Surely there is now little need to make the case for "thinking Pacific". There can be little doubt that parts of the Pacific are developing so quickly that the region will be of increasing importance for international security, world finance and trade, and new ideas about ideology and models of development.

Yet there is a remarkable problem in obtaining information about the politics, economics and security of the Pacific. Most books focus on East Asia and many find it easier to deal with the region on a country-by-country basis. As a result, it is not possible to develop a sense of the Pacific as a region, and it is especially difficult to find information on the international relations of the Pacific. At a time of dramatic and vital changes in the patterns of trade in the Pacific, such a problem must be overcome.

Of course, it is rarely useful to see the Pacific as a single, coherent region.[1] It is often, as in international economics, a curious mixture of sub-regional politics and a major player in global relations. Certainly the politics of individual countries are closely connected with events in neighbouring countries, but they are also increasingly tied up with changes on a worldwide basis.

Organization

As a result, any reference book on the Pacific needs to be tailored to the specific features of the region and its interaction with the world outside. The traditional method of country-by-country analysis will not be sufficient to cover the sub-regional and global connections. A focus on East Asia will not do justice to the links across the water to North America and increasingly even to South America. The coverage of this volume is genuinely Pacific in that it covers politics, economics and security from Vladivostok to Vancouver and Valparaiso. It even includes the Antarctic dimension in the south, but it draws the line at Burma in the west. It covers the immediate hinterland of Mongolia and Laos, and certainly pays attention to the much neglected islands within the basin.

The most distinctive aspect of the organization is the alphabetical order of entries. This has been chosen because there are two broad types of entries. The national entries provide basic material on individual countries and are the largest sections of the book. As a result, these entries are sub-divided in a more-or-less uniform format. Differences reflect the specific features of the country. There are also more specific national entries that cover the leading personalities, parties and issues that deserve broader coverage. The second type of entries is international. They cover bilateral and multilateral issues in the fields of security, economics, ideology, culture and resources.

How to use the book

Given the alphabetical format, it is usually easy to find a specific topic. But anything except the narrowest subject cannot be fully appreciated without reference to other sections of the book. As a result, and most rarely for an encyclopaedia, there is a detailed index that will quickly locate related material; in addition, within the text itself useful cross-references to other entries are picked out in bold at their first mention in any entry.

For example, if the reader is interested in the fate of Hong Kong, the obvious place to start is with the Hong Kong entry. But reference to the Basic Law should also be consulted, as indeed should individual entries for China, Macau, and specific sub-topics for each of those.

---

[1] See Gerald Segal, *Rethinking the Pacific* (Oxford: Oxford University Press, 1990).

Of course, in trying to understand the fate of Hong Kong, or the patterns of politics, economics and security in the Pacific as a whole, the subject matter keeps changing. Our emphasis has been on the post-1945 Pacific, and we expect to be updating material well into the twenty-first century—the so-called "Pacific Century".

Gerald Segal

The Publishers would like to thank Collins Longman Atlases for permission to reproduce the maps on the endpapers of this book.

Note: The abbreviations BCE (Before Common Era) and CE (Common Era) used for dates in this book are the equivalent of BC and AD respectively.

A

AKIHITO, EMPEROR. In January 1989, Emperor Akihito acceded to the Japanese throne. His popularity is reinforced by that of his consort, the erstwhile commoner, Empress Michiko. Since his succession, Emperor Akihito has attempted to treat his subjects as equals by using plain but polite language. He has cut down the number of police guarding him at public functions and has ordered many of them to wear plain clothes so as not to intimidate his subjects. It seems likely that the new Emperor will effect the final transformation of the Imperial Office to that of constitutional monarch.

RAB

ALATAS, ALI. Ali Alatas, aged 57, replaced Mochtar Kusumaatmadja as Foreign Minister of Indonesia in March 1988. Soon after his inauguration as Foreign Minister he pledged to initiate a more "active" foreign policy. He served as a Foreign Affairs Department spokesman in the early 1960s and as Political Counsellor in the Indonesian Embassy in Washington from 1966-1970. Alatas was known to have been close to Adam Malik, serving as his personal secretary from 1975-78 while Malik was Foreign Minister and again from 1978-82 when he was Vice President. He represented Indonesia at the United Nations, first in Geneva (1976-78) and later in New York (1983-88).

DS

ALUMINIUM. Australia is the world's largest producer of bauxite ore, the major aluminium ore, with large deposits in Western Australia, the Northern Territory and Queensland. It is estimated to produce some 35 per cent of the world's bauxite ore and 30 per cent of its alumina. The extensive provision of bauxite and alumina and of cheap coal-based power has led to Australia becoming a major site for aluminium production. There are five aluminium smelters currently operating, the largest being at Tomago, New South Wales. Ambitious expansion plans for smelting have been shelved in the 1980s because of the depressed world market for aluminium and increased electricity costs.

Indonesia is also developing its aluminium industry. A 500mw hydro-power plant costing £1,200 million to build and capable of producing around 225,000 tonnes a year was opened in 1982. The plant was conceived to exploit bauxite reserves on Bintan Island, near Singapore. Financial problems have delayed this project and for the moment alumina from Australia is being imported instead.

Malaysia, producing more than one million tonnes of bauxite a year in the early 1970s, has seen its production decline markedly. It imports about 60,000 tonnes of aluminium every year and the demand is growing. It is examining the possibility of building an integrated bauxite/alumina/aluminium complex in Trengganu, but with the slump in commodity prices it is not clear whether the country will be able to afford the M$2,000 million complex.

High costs and a shortage of cheap energy were the principal reasons obliging the Philippines to abandon plans in 1983 for an aluminium industry producing around 140,000 tonnes per year. New Zealand too was obliged to drop its plans for a second smelter in 1982 when soaring costs obliged Alusuisse and then Pechiney to withdraw from the project. (*See also* **Bauxite**)

RS

AMERICAN SAMOA. *Population*: 37,800, Samoan Polynesians (est. 1988). *Total land area*: 199 sq km. An external (unincorporated) territory of the United States in the central South Pacific, comprising seven islands in an east-west chain. *Main settlement*: Pago Pago. *Seat of government*: Fagatogo.

The islands were probably inhabited by Polynesians at least 3,000 years ago. European contacts were made during the eighteenth and nineteenth centuries. In 1872 the United States obtained from the Kingdom of Samoa the right to build a naval station at Pago Pago. In 1889, the USA, Britain and Germany assumed a tripartite protectorate over the kingdom, guaranteeing its neutrality. In 1899, a convention recognized US paramount interest in islands east of lat. 171°German paramount interest to the west of that line. The high chiefs ceded the eastern group to the USA in 1904, formally accepted by Congress in 1929. The islands were administered by the US Navy until 1951, then by the Department of the Interior. American Samoans are American nationals but not citizens. In 1978 the first governor was elected. In mid-1986 the governments of American Samoa and Western Samoa signed an agreement for joint development of tourism, transport and fishing.

The economy is based on smallholding farmers, fishing (with canning for export), tourism, and US military and civil administrations (38 per cent of the labour force). Tuna accounts for 98 per cent of exports.

TBM

ANDEAN PACT. The Andean Pact or Group, also known as the Cartagena Agreement, which established it in the Colombian city of that name in 1969, aims to accelerate the harmonious development of its member states through economic and social integration. Its members are Bolivia, Colombia, Ecuador, Peru and Venezuela. Chile withdrew its membership in 1977. The Group's headquarters are in Lima, Peru.

Although the organization's goal has been to foster greater regional co-operation, especially in industry, it has been dogged by political problems. For example, in 1980, Bolivia came under heavy criticism from other members for its domestic situation and Ecuador suspended its membership temporarily the following year, after a border dispute with Peru. Trade agreements were for a while hampered by the number of exempted products, but a new trade formula was devised in 1986 to try to encourage liberalization. An agreement was signed with the European Communities in 1983, with the aim of fostering regional co-operation.

Since 1979, there has been an "Andean Parliament", which makes recommendations on regional policy. It has five representatives from each member state and meets in each capital city in turn.

JF

ANTARCTIC TREATY. While most parts of the globe were being claimed by European powers the Antarctic continent remained ignored and unexplored. Uninhabited, permanently frozen and of no obvious economic importance, Antarctica was not a subject of international dispute until the twentieth century. Parts of the continent and adjacent islands have been claimed by various nations, most notably Argentina, Australia, Chile, France, New Zealand, Norway and the United Kingdom.

It was not until the 1950s that the potential importance of Antarctica was recognized. As a result, the 12 nations with an interest in Antarctica signed the Antarctic Treaty in 1961. It effectively established Antarctica as a strict

nature reserve. The treaty further provided for a joint scientific research by the signatory nations with the findings to be jointly shared. The treaty also prohibited all signatories from exploiting living Antarctic resources or from conducting activities that would deplete those resources. The treaty has been upheld and the wild animals and sparse plant life respected.

Unfortunately the Antarctic Treaty did not include the seas surrounding the continent. The economic value of the animal resources there has long been known and exploitation of these began in the nineteenth century. Of special importance were the large herds of whales that gathered in neighbouring waters to feed off the plankton. In 1982 the Antarctic Treaty nations agreed on a protective zone around the continent to preserve marine life, most notably the krill, a shrimplike crustacean.

Originally signed by 12 countries, there are now 20 adherents plus 17 observer members of the Antarctic Treaty. The full signatories are Argentina, Australia, Belgium, Brazil, Chile, China, France, West Germany, East Germany, India, Italy, Japan, New Zealand, Norway, Poland, South Africa, the United Kingdom, the USA, the USSR and Uruguay.

The Antarctic Treaty is due to be renegotiated in 1991. A supplementary agreement concerning the future of mineral exploitation was reached in 1988. (*see* **Antarctica: Minerals Exploitation Agreement**)

RS

ANTARCTICA: MINERALS EXPLOITATION AGREEMENT. An agreement governing the future exploitation of Antarctica's mineral, oil and gas resources was reached on June 2, 1988, at Wellington, New Zealand. The agreement flowed from a decision taken earlier in 1981 by members of the Antarctic Treaty – itself first signed in 1961 and due for renegotiation in 1991 – to reach an agreement regulating the exploitation of minerals. Since then members have observed a non-binding ban on exploration and development.

The Wellington agreement provides for the prospecting of Antarctica's minerals, using such methods as seismic testing, as soon as the agreement is ratified by 16 of the 20 voting members of the Antarctic Treaty. The continent is known to have reserves of antimony, chromium, copper, gold, lead, molybdenum, tin, zinc, uranium, iron, coal, and natural coke. However, while extensive iron reserves have been found near the Prince Charles Mountains of East Antarctica and coal deposits in the Transantarctic Mountains belong to one of the world's largest coalfields, exploitation of minerals is still not yet economically viable and is not expected to become so until the end of the century.

The agreement is significantly qualified by the proviso that any subsequent major project for exploitation or development will require the unanimous approval of all 20 voting treaty signatories. The initial 16 ratifying powers must include the seven nations with territorial claims – Argentina, Australia, Chile, France, New Zealand, Norway, and the United Kingdom – together with the Soviet Union and the United States. The other voting members are Belgium, Brazil, China, West Germany, East Germany, India, Italy, Japan, Poland, South Africa and Uruguay. The treaty also has 17 non-voting observer members. (*See also* **Antarctic Treaty**)

RS

ANWAR IBRAHIM. Anwar is widely regarded as a future **United Malays National Organization** (UMNO) leader and possible Prime Minister of Malaysia. During the 1970s he was a leading student radical and a prominent critic of government policies from a liberal Islamic viewpoint. Prior to the 1982 federal elections he resigned as president of the Malaysian Islamic Youth Movement (Abim) and entered party politics as an UMNO candidate, winning a seat in Penang. He entered the Cabinet in 1983 and became Minister of Education in 1986.

DS

ANZUS PACT. A tripartite security treaty between Australia, New Zealand and the United States was signed on Sept. 1, 1951, in San Francisco, and came into force on April 29, 1952. The treaty is known as the Pacific Security Treaty or, deriving its name from the initials of the signatories, the ANZUS Pact.

The organ of the ANZUS pact is the Council – known as the Pacific Council – set up under Article 7 of the treaty. It is composed of the Foreign Ministers (or their deputies) of the signatory powers. The Foreign Ministers generally meet once a year, but special Council meetings, attended by the deputies, are held in Washington more frequently. The Council has no permanent staff or funds. At the first meeting of the Pacific Council, held in Honolulu on Aug. 4–6, 1952, it was decided to create a military organization. In this organization each of the three signatory countries is represented by a military officer, who attends Council meetings. The military representatives also hold their own meetings on occasion.

Their function is to advise the Council on military co-operation in the Pacific.

The alliance appeared to work fairly harmoniously through most of its history and after the Soviet military intervention in Afghanistan in December 1979, it was agreed that Australia would deploy an aircraft carrier and a task force in the Indian Ocean; that New Zealand would provide air and naval support; and that the USA would increase maritime surveillance, anti-submarine patrolling and military aid to countries in the region. In a memorandum of understanding between the United States and New Zealand of Feb. 26, 1982, the ANZUS Pact was expanded by provisions for procedures for supplying New Zealand with logistic support in the event of an emergency.

This alliance, however, was soon to be thrown into crisis by a shift in the policy of New Zealand resulting from the victory of the New Zealand **Labour Party**, led by **David Lange**, in the election of July 1984. The Labour Party was strongly committed to anti-nuclear policies and decided to ban US nuclear-powered or nuclear-capable ships. The United States, which has maintained a policy of neither confirming nor denying the presence of nuclear weapons on board specific ships, reacted vigorously to this, with Secretary of State George Shultz declaring that it would make the alliance virtually meaningless. The issue came to a head on Feb. 4, 1985, when the government refused a US request for port facilities in New Zealand for the USS *Buchanan*, a US destroyer with a potential nuclear capability.

The United States, perhaps because of concern that this might be a precedent which could be followed in Europe should some of the left-wing opposition parties come to power, reacted very strongly. New Zealand was accused of breaching Article 2 of the ANZUS Treaty in which the partners pledged to develop their capacity to resist armed attack through self-help and mutual aid. In addition, a proposed ANZUS Pact meeting and joint exercises in the Pacific were cancelled. There was also discussion in Washington of other punitive measures including those to stop the flow of military intelligence to New Zealand and economic reprisals.

On Sept. 1, 1985, Prime Minister Lange announced that his government would present a bill to ban nuclear weapons from New Zealand and that port calls by US Navy vessels would not be resumed until such legislation was enacted. The reaffirmation of the non-nuclear policy had considerable public support which stemmed in part from the sensitivity of New Zealanders to nuclear issues that had been generated by the use of the South Pacific as a nuclear testing area. It

3

also reflected the government's conviction that the main danger was not Soviet aggression in the Pacific but the possibility that New Zealand might be entangled in a conflict between the superpowers that was of little intrinsic relevance to it.

Accordingly, the New Zealand Prime Minister stated on Sept. 27, 1985, that his government would "not accept the proposition that the ANZUS alliance requires us to accept nuclear weapons". He also said: "We do not ask the United States to defend New Zealand with nuclear weapons. We do intend to exercise greater self-reliance in our own defence." On Sept. 30 he stated that New Zealand wished to remain in ANZUS and have a good relationship with the United States but would not "surrender our nuclear policy". The policy was directed only against the nuclear elements of ANZUS and the New Zealand government in effect wanted to ensure that the alliance was based only on conventional forces and was not simply another element in the overall US nuclear policy.

The New Zealand bill, presented on Dec. 10, 1985, established a New Zealand zone free of nuclear arms and biological weapons, and implemented the South Pacific **Nuclear Free Zone Treaty** signed in August 1985 by Australia, New Zealand and South Pacific nations which renounced the manufacture, possession or control of nuclear weapons. It was made clear, however, that it was directed against nuclear weapons and not against nuclear-capable ships. Moreover, although the legislation forbids nuclear-armed ships from docking in New Zealand ports, the ships are allowed to pass through New Zealand's territorial waters.

On Jan. 2, 1986, the New Zealand Prime Minister expressed regret at the fact that the United States had curtailed almost all defence co-operation with New Zealand. New Zealand also expressed considerable hope that the issue could be defused. The difficulty for the United States, however, was that the issue had become a very symbolic one. Accordingly, on Aug. 12, 1986, the United States formally suspended all its security obligations to New Zealand under the ANZUS Pact until New Zealand was prepared to restore unrestricted port and air access to US warships and military aircraft.

Since then there has been little movement on either side. Australia ultimately sided with the United States but clearly was not as opposed to New Zealand's policy as was Washington. In some ways this reflected the strategic realities, as the main element in ANZUS has always been the Australia–United States connection. New Zealand has suffered from the disruption in intelli-gence and from the lack of joint exercises. Nevertheless, with no immediate threats to its security, this is a price that the Labour government has been prepared to pay. The result has been that ANZUS, if not quite defunct, has gone into what is virtually a state of suspended animation.

PW

AQUINO, CORAZON. Corazon (Cory) Aquino was inaugurated as President of the Philippines on Feb. 25, 1986, after defeating the incumbent **Ferdinand Marcos** in a presidential election held earlier that month and subsequently organizing a series of ultimately successful non-violent civil disturbance actions in protest at Marcos's refusal to accept defeat.

Cory Aquino was the widow of Benigno Aquino, the country's foremost opposition leader until his assassination at Manila airport in 1983 upon his return from self-imposed exile in the USA. The killing of Benigno (in which the Marcos regime was ultimately implicated) precipitated an outburst of popular resistance to the regime. In late 1985, prompted by what he perceived as opposition disunity, Marcos called an early presidential election. Cory Aquino was chosen as a presidential candidate by the Philippine Democratic Party, People's Power (PDP-Laban) and a number of other groups. Although she had become increasingly involved in the opposition movement since her husband's death, Cory's political authority rested solely on her symbolic status as a martyr's widow. With the persuasion of the Catholic Church, the fractured opposition coalesced behind her and, supported by the majority of the electorate, the Army and the USA, she successfully ousted Marcos.

The initial euphoria of the post-Marcos era masked Aquino's political inexperience, but her fragile coalition soon came under pressure from the legitimate right and the illegitimate left. Nevertheless, Aquino confounded her critics, many of whom predicted her swift overthrow after an initial honeymoon period, by surviving a series of military coup attempts and political crises. What is more, she appears to have consolidated her position despite the apparent failure of her government to address successfully the deep economic and political concerns of the mass of her supporters.

DS

ARMS CONTROL. The Pacific region has been an area where arms control seems to have little relevance or effect. This is particularly true if arms control is considered only in terms of formal agreements limiting or reducing the level of armaments. There have been no negotiations in the Pacific similar in scope or form to the talks that have taken place in Europe on reducing conventional forces. From 1973 to 1988 the member states of NATO and the Warsaw Pact were involved in negotiations to reduce conventional forces in the central region of Europe. These negotiations have been superceded by the Conventional Forces Europe negotiations which are considering reductions in a larger area from the Atlantic to the Urals. In addition, Europe was the main focus of the Intermediate Range Nuclear Forces (INF) Treaty signed by the USA and the Soviet Union in December 1987 which provided for the removal of all nuclear missiles with a range between 500 and 5,000 km. This treaty also had implications for the Pacific region in that initially the Soviet Union sought to maintain 100 SS-20s in the Asian part of the Soviet Union. Eventually however the superpowers agreed that they would reduce to zero this particular category of weapon. If this made a contribution to security in Asia, this was not its prime purpose – the global double zero was simply much easier to verify.

There are several reasons why the European theatre has been a more obvious focus for arms control than the Pacific. The first and most important is that there is both a starkness and a simplicity about the military confrontation in Europe that is absent in Asia. In Asia there are many local and regional conflicts which, although sometimes overlaid by great power competition, have a life and logic of their own. They do not stem so much from regional arms races as from traditional rivalries and hostilities exacerbated by regional ambitions and fears. In the European theatre, in contrast, forces are arrayed against each other along the inner-German border, and it is possible to focus on the military balance between the two alliances. The forces are directed against each other and it is relatively easy to count them, if rather more difficult to reach satisfactory conclusions about what the numbers mean. There is nothing like as direct a military relationship in the Pacific. Although it is possible to assess the balance of naval forces between the superpowers, this is relevant to only one of many military competitions and conflicts in the region. Indeed, there are many difficulties in efforts to assess the balance of power in the region, because at the very least it has to be a triangular assessment involving the superpowers and China. Furthermore, it is difficult to ignore Japan in this equation, especially in view of the fact that it is now the third largest defence spender in the world. In view of all this there is a rather more

obvious and more competitive arms dynamic in Europe than there is in much of the Pacific.

There is also what has been described as a distinctive strategic culture in the Pacific. In Europe there is a long tradition of regulated state behaviour. The Pacific not only lacks such a tradition, but many of the states in the region are suspicious of formal rules regarding them as a continuation of colonialism and a subtle attempt to maintain old patterns of domination and to uphold an unsatisfactory status quo.

The nature of conflicts in the Pacific adds a further inhibition to progress in arms control. Many of the conflicts arise from territorial disputes that have been left over from World War II or that, in some cases, can be traced back for centuries. Arms control can do little about these problems and insofar as an arms control agreement suggests support for the status quo, there is likely to be an asymmetry of attitude among the states involved in particular disputes.

If arms control is more broadly construed, however, as restraint on the level, character, deployment and use of arms, then it has been of relevance in the Pacific. There is an emerging pattern of arms control in the Pacific, based on tacit and informal measures, focusing on conventional rather than nuclear weapons and on confidence building measures and demilitarization. The most important example of tacit and informal arms control playing a part in defusing regional tensions and conflicts has been the Sino-Soviet dispute. In the second half of the 1980s China and the Soviet Union have engaged in a series of tacit arms control measures, such as thinning out troops along their common border and creating what are virtually demilitarized zones. This has been part of the broader detente in Sino-Soviet relations and has both accompanied and reinforced diplomatic efforts to normalize the relationship between the two leading communist powers. Each side has removed between 80,000 and 100,000 troops from the border region over the last five years and Gorbachev's United Nations announcement in December 1988 that the Soviet Union would make substantial unilateral cuts in its military forces has particular relevance to the Far East. Forty per cent of the Soviet reductions will come from the Far East and when these are implemented Soviet forces ranged against China will be about half the size they were in the late 1970s.

A second form of arms control that has relevance to the Pacific region is the establishment of regulatory mechanisms to avoid inadvertent violence. An early example of this, which had global application but was very relevant to the Pacific given the maritime nature of superpower competition, was the 1972 Agreement on Avoiding Incidents at Sea. This established certain conventions which significantly reduced the number of collisions and provocations between Soviet and American vessels. In 1985 in response to the shooting down of a civilian airliner, KAL 007, over Soviet air-space in 1983, the superpowers and Japan agreed on certain improvements in air safety designed to avoid any further incidents of this kind.

The other kind of arms control that has been evident in the Pacific region has been what might be termed institutionalized conflict management. This has been most evident in Korea where the De-militarized Zone (DMZ) has provided something of a buffer and an additional inhibition against another round of warfare. This is not to deny that there have been problems with violations of the DMZ. Moreover, it has not prevented periodic increases in tension between the two Koreas. Its shortcomings, however, should not be allowed to obscure its utility.

None of these measures is very startling or ambitious, but just as military conflict in the Pacific is fragmented and untidy, so arms control has to be of a similar nature. There are, however, more ambitious proposals for Pacific arms control. One of the most ambitious of these has been proposals for Zones of Peace (ZOP) which rest upon the substantially erroneous assumption that strains and tensions are caused by extra-regional powers and if these remain outside the region then harmony will reign. Part of the problem with this in the Pacific is that it is difficult to define extra-regional powers. Even more important is the fact that so many of the region's conflicts are indigenous with very specific local roots.

This did not prevent the members of ASEAN from declaring, in 1971, a Zone of Peace, Freedom and Neutrality (ZOPFAN). The difficulty with this is that it could do little to halt the conflicts in the region. Even so the supporters of this idea, inspired by the South Pacific **Nuclear Free Zone** idea enshrined in the Treaty of Raratonga, suggested in June 1987 that they should establish a nuclear weapons-free zone. The United States, however, was opposed to this idea and it was dropped.

Somewhere between the grandiose schemes for arms control and the very specific measures that have been relevant to the Pacific are the proposals enunciated by the Soviet Union. In the 1970s the Soviet Union proposed as Asian collective security scheme, which was in effect an anti-Chinese measure. This did not get very far. In 1986, however, Mikhail Gorbachev unveiled a new vision for security in Asia. He proposed that security relations be based not on competition and rivalry but on a more co-operative process similar to that of the Helsinki process in Europe. The Soviet agenda is an ambitious one and includes the elimination of all foreign bases in the Pacific, a freeze on the number of nuclear-capable aircraft in the Pacific, the creation of nuclear-free zones on the Korean peninsula and in Southeast Asia, reducing conventional arms to levels of sufficiency, and no first use agreements, as well as the convening of an Asia-Pacific Conference modelled on the Conference on Security and Co-operation in Europe.

The agenda is a long-term one and is designed to limit, hamper and constrain United States power in the region, especially its maritime forces. For this reason, there has not been a very enthusiastic response from the United States – nor indeed from China. Washington has dismissed the proposals as requiring asymmetrical sacrifices by the USA and as an attempt to divide the United States and its allies. Nevertheless, it is not inconceivable that if the improvement in Soviet-American relations in the late 1980s is continued, there might be discussions about more formal arms control arrangements for the Pacific. In the meantime the best prospects for arms control in the region seem to be the low-key informal measures of the kind that have been evident in Sino-Soviet relations. Arms control in the Pacific is not something that can stand alone, rather it can only be part of a broader process of conflict control and military disengagement. In view of the nature of the conflicts in the Pacific, anything else would be both irrelevant and inappropriate.

PW

ASIAN DEVELOPMENT BANK. The Asian Development Bank exists to promote economic development in the region. To this end it has, since it began its operations in 1966, raised loans from private and public sources, and with these funds it has responded to requests for assistance from member governments. It also gives technical assistance with development projects, and can help member governments in the co-ordination of their economic policies.

The Bank has 47 member countries, 32 of which are located within the Asia-Pacific (ESCAP) region and include the developed nations of Japan, Australia and New Zealand. The other members are the advanced nations of Western Europe, Canada and the United States. Members command voting power with regard to the decisions the Bank makes in proportion to the size of their subscription to its capital stock. In practice, Japan with 12.5 per cent and the USA with 12.4 per cent of the voting power have by far the most powerful individual voices. Two-thirds of the voting power lies in the combined hands of the nations of the region.

Whilst the powers of the Bank are vested in the Board of Governors, all but the most important matters such as the admission of new members, alterations to the authorized capital stock and so on, are delegated to a Board of Directors. Eight of the twelve directors represent member countries within the region.

The Bank possesses ordinary capital and a number of Special Funds. The two are kept entirely separate. At the end of March, 1987, subscriptions to the capital stock consisted of US$20,831.4 million authorized capital, US$20,634.5 million subscribed capital and US$2,494.3 million paid-in capital. Capital is also raised in the financial markets of the world, the sum borrowed in 1986 totalling US$813 million. These ordinary capital resources are used to make loans to the more developed countries of the region, and the lending rate is now adjusted periodically (every six months) to reflect changing conditions in the world's money markets. By contrast, the Special Funds are used to provide resources at concessionary rates to the least developed countries of the region. The Asian Development Fund (ADF), itself a consolidated version of two earlier funds, is the main vehicle for concessionary loans. It is replenished periodically by an injection of contributions from member countries, the latest (ADF V) taking place in 1987 and providing US$3,600 million for use for the period 1987–90. The Bank is also able to make technical assistance grants from its smaller Technical Assistance Special Fund, contributions to which totalled US$81.9 million up to 1987.

In recent years, somewhat more than 40 per cent of loans approved have been for agriculture or agriculture-related projects. About one-quarter of loans have been for energy-related projects such as constructing power transmission lines; about 15 per cent have been for social-infrastructure projects in education and health, whilst the remaining 10 per cent or so have been in the transport sector. In all cases, the Bank has favoured schemes that have resulted in the creation of tangible physical assets. It has been unwilling, for example, to provide loans to help members over balance of payments difficulties.

However, since 1985 the Bank has altered its philosophy somewhat, in that it has decided to increase its assistance to the private sector. Loans to private enterprises no longer require a government guarantee, and help may even be forthcoming for the privatization of public sector enterprises. This change mirrors a widespread alteration in attitudes amongst aid-giving countries and in other multi-national agencies.

During the period 1968–86, nearly two-thirds of all loans (by value) made by the Bank were to countries in the Pacific region. It is impossible to estimate the magnitude of the contribution resources provided by the Bank made to the development of the economy of the region over the period. We must suppose it to have been considerable. However, the total volume of loans and the value of its technical aid has stagnated since about 1984. The reasons for this are various, but the tendency would seem to reflect doubts about the ability of the Bank's loans to match the current needs and aspirations of the member nations as regards the next stage in their development, and also the increasing ability of some of the major loan recipients of the past (e.g. Indonesia, Korea and Malaysia) to raise loans commercially. The dead weight of existing debt and the problems it poses has undoubtedly been another factor.

DA

ASSOCIATION OF SOUTH-EAST ASIAN NATIONS (ASEAN).

ASEAN is a regional co-operative organization established on Aug. 8, 1967. Its members include Indonesia, Malaysia, Singapore, Thailand, the Philippines and Brunei (the latter having gained membership in January 1984). The organs of ASEAN are its ministerial conference, which is composed of the Foreign Ministers of the six member countries and which meets annually; a standing committee, which meets when necessary between ministerial meetings; and a secretariat, established in 1976.

ASEAN's formation was facilitated by the election of **Marcos** as President of the Philippines in 1965 and **Suharto**'s displacement of **Sukarno** in Indonesia the following year. Both Marcos and Suharto were more favourably disposed than their predecessors towards the formation of an expansive regional organization. Efforts at the formation of a regional body in the early 1960s (e.g. the Association of Southeast Asia – ASA) had foundered upon the creation of Malaysia in 1963 and the initiation of "Confrontation" between Malaysia and Indonesia. During the 1940s and 1950s initiatives on regional co-operation in Southeast Asia had been externally promoted, the prime example being the US-inaugurated South-East Asia Treaty Organization (**SEATO**), which comprised only two indigenous nations (Thailand and the Philippines).

The declaration signed by the member states upon ASEAN's establishment in 1967 emphasized the primacy of economic, social and cultural collaboration. Joint efforts in political and security-related issues were conspicuous by their absence, the one exception being a nebulous statement emphasizing that "all military bases of foreign powers existed only on a temporary basis and with the express consent of the countries concerned" and were not to be "used for direct or indirect interference in the national independence and freedom of the region's states."

The first summit meeting of the heads of state and government of the ASEAN member countries was held in Bali in February 1976. That it had taken nine years for the leaders to convene formally reflected not only the absence of a collective ASEAN ethos, but also the preoccupation of each member state with internal political and economic concerns. The catalyst for the Bali summit and the resultant commitment to increased co-operation was the 1975 communist victory in Indo-China. In the aftermath of this conquest, ASEAN had invited the Indo-Chinese states into their organization. They had refused, condemning ASEAN as little more than a disguised SEATO. Thus the emergence of a potentially hostile communist compact on Thailand's eastern border created an environment which fostered the belief that the elevation of the collective over the national interest was an indispensable security imperative.

The Bali summit produced two documents: (i) a Treaty of Amity and Co-operation in Southeast Asia; and (ii) a Declaration of Concord. The Treaty expressed the determination of the five parties to "promote active co-operation in the economic, social, cultural, technical, scientific and administrative fields as well as in matters of common ideals and aspirations of international peace and stability in the region". To this end the five nations undertook to "maintain regular contacts and consultations . . . on international and regional matters". The treaty further laid down that "no ASEAN nation shall participate in any activity considered a threat to another member's economic and political stability". Intra-regional differences were to be settled through direct friendly negotiations, and to facilitate this the five nations would "constitute a High Council comprising a representative at ministerial level" from each nation.

The Declaration of Concord provided for co-operation in the pursuit of political stability in the region as well as in member states individually; for member states to take active steps, individually and collectively, towards the establishment of a Zone of Peace, Freedom and Neutrality (ZOPFAN); for economic co-operation by helping each other by "according priority to the supply of the individual country's needs in critical

circumstances in respect of basic commodities . . . by the establishment of large-scale ASEAN industrial plants".

At a second meeting of heads of state and government held in Kuala Lumpur in August 1977, it was emphasized that the ASEAN countries desired "to develop peaceful and mutually beneficial relations with all countries in the region, including Kampuchea, Laos and Vietnam", and that in their view the economic and social advancement of the member states of ASEAN was a "fundamental element in ensuring the political stability of the ASEAN region".

It was noted that an agreement on ASEAN preferential trading arrangements, signed in February 1977, had been ratified by all member countries; that exchanges of preferences on a first batch of 71 products had been agreed upon; and that progress had been made, among other matters, in the development of an ASEAN submarine cable system, studies on the setting up of an ASEAN regional satellite system, the harmonization and modernization of ASEAN national fleets and the promotion of containerisation and joint bulk shipments.

Following the overthrow of the *Khmer Rouge* regime in Kampuchea by Vietnamese forces and its replacement by a pro-Hanoi regime early in 1979, the Foreign Ministers of ASEAN member countries quickly met in Bangkok. They issued a statement deploring "the armed intervention threatening the independence, sovereignty and territorial integrity of Kampuchea", affirming "the right of the Kampuchean people to decide their own future without interference or influence from outside powers", and calling for "the immediate withdrawal of all foreign troops from Kampuchean territory".

From this point onwards ASEAN played a pivotal role in sustaining Vietnam's diplomatic isolation, at the same time encouraging international support for the tripartite rebel Coalition Government of Democratic Kampuchea. However, as the opportunities for a diplomatic settlement of the conflict increased during 1988 and 1989 the ASEAN nations, and in particular Thailand (the "front-line" ASEAN state), and Indonesia (the organization's official interlocutor with Vietnam), were leading participants in the complex negotiations.

A third summit meeting was held in Manila in December 1987, at which the heads of government signed a Declaration of ASEAN Resolve, promising to maintain their "solidarity and co-operation under all circumstances". Stressing ASEAN unity, the declaration stated that "ASEAN regionalism, founded upon political, economic and cultural cohesion, is more vital than ever for the future of Southeast Asia". It committed ASEAN to intensifying its efforts towards finding a political solution in Kampuchea and said that ASEAN would seek an early realization of ZOPFAN as well as a nuclear-free zone in the region.

The leaders also signed four economic agreements: (i) a protocol on the improvement of the ASEAN preferential trading arrangements; (ii) a memorandum of understanding to implement a "standstill and rollback" on non-tariff barriers; (iii) a revised basic agreement on ASEAN industrial joint ventures, creating a pre-approved list of projects receiving tariff preferences of 90 per cent; and (iv) an agreement on the promotion and protection of intra-ASEAN investments.

ASEAN held its 1989 Foreign Ministers' meeting in Brunei in early July. Rusli Noor, a former Indonesian diplomat, was elected as the organization's new secretary general. At a post-ministerial conference, the six member states agreed to attend an exploratory meeting in November to discuss an Australian Asia-Pacific Co-operation proposal.

DS

AUSTRALIA. Population: 16,139,000 (est. December 1988). *Area*: 7,687,000 sq km. *Gross Domestic Product* (1987–88): $A291,887 million (June 1987). *Trade* (1987–88): imports $A40,386 million; exports $A40,537 million. *Main trading partners*: Japan, USA, European Community. *Defence spending* (1987–88): $A7,404 million. *Education spending* (1987–88): $A5,685 million. *Urban population as percentage of total*: 85.7. *Birth rate*: 15.2 per thousand. *Life expectancy*: males 72.3; females 78.8.

Early history. Australia's first settlers came to the island continent from Southeast Asia between 50,000 and 120,000 years ago, and over time built a civilization with over 200 distinct languages and hundreds of dialects, in something like 500 different groupings. The Aborigines did not develop systems of agriculture, but were semi-nomadic societies of hunter-gatherers. Their social organization was based on the extended family; within larger hordes or bands, with elaborate rituals and religious beliefs handed down orally from generation to generation. They had no written language or literature. When white settlers arrived in 1788, the Aborigines probably numbered about 750,000, although this can be only an estimate.

The first European contacts were probably made by Portuguese in the sixteenth century. In 1605 the Dutch explorer Willem Janz saw and named Cape Keer Weer on what is now Cape York Peninsula in Queensland. During the next 22 years other Dutch ships explored parts of the western coastline, and in 1642 Able Tasman landed on the coast of what he called Van Diemen's Land and we now call Tasmania, before going on to New Zealand. In 1688 the English pirate William Dampier landed on the coast of north-west Australia and on a second voyage traversed around 1,000 miles of the coastline, subsequently reporting unfavourably on it and its inhabitants. But the voyage that led to white settlement was that of Captain James Cook in 1768–70, primarily to observe in Tahiti the transit of Venus across the face of the sun, but with instructions to sail south and west in search of the supposed southern continent. Cook charted much of the east coast of "New Holland", including the area known as Botany Bay.

In 1786 the British government decided to establish a penal colony at Botany Bay. The main reason was the heavily overcrowded state of British gaols after the American War of Independence and the refusal of the Americans to accept further British convicts.

The "First Fleet" of 11 vessels sailed from Portsmouth on May 13, 1787, and seven months later made landfall in New South Wales. Botany Bay was found unsuitable, and the settlement was established on a magnificent harbour a few miles to the north, Port Jackson, the township being named after the Secretary of State for Home Affairs, Lord Sydney. The first settlement comprised 1,030 people of whom 736 were convicts, about a quarter of whom were women.

From this inauspicious beginning there developed the six Australian colonies – Tasmania (Van Diemen's Land), Victoria (Port Phillip), Queensland (Moreton Bay), Western Australia (Swan River Colony) and South Australia. Only South Australia, which experimented with the systematic colonization proposals of Edward Gibbon Wakefield, did not base its development on convict labour. Convicts continued to be transported to eastern Australia until 1852, and to Western Australia (from 1850) until 1868. A total of over 160,000 convicts arrived in the colonies, roughly a quarter of them coming from Ireland.

After coming perilously close to starvation, as supply ships foundered and crops failed, the initial settlers developed an economy that took advantage of the vast quantities of grazing land, and the development of fine wool exports from Merino sheep imported from Spain via South Africa. Later in the nineteenth century, the discovery of substantial gold and other mineral deposits, the extensive growing of wheat and the export of meat under refrigeration provided the export income for the importing of consumer durables and the investment capital needed to develop the country. By 1891 the white population had grown to over two million.

There is no record of the change in numbers of the Aboriginal inhabitants during the first century of white occupation. For the most part, Aborigines had no civil or personal rights. Their cultures were not understood. The land with which they identified in a deeply religious sense was expropriated and sacred sites desecrated. The white men's attitude to food production and to ownership of animals was in inevitable conflict with the blacks'. They were intensely vulnerable to imported diseases, especially smallpox, and in Tasmania there was a deliberate campaign to exterminate them.

With the expansion of settlement, the growth of a non-convict white population, and the development of the economy, there came democratic institutions. In 1842 New South Wales was given a two-thirds elected legislature. In 1850 this was extended to Victoria, South Australia and Tasmania, under the Australian Colonies Government Act. Soon all four colonies had bicameral legislatures with an elected lower house. In Western Australia, a small nominated Legislative Council established in 1832 was not made more representative until 1870, and a bicameral responsible government created in 1890. The telegraph linking the colonies to each other and to London was completed in 1872. State-funded railways extended settlement and met the needs of pastoral and agricultural production. Rudimentary social services were established. An influx of migrants from Asia (especially China) and Pacific islands produced legislation to exclude non-whites.

In the last quarter of the century, there was a spasmodic but increasing movement towards unity between the colonies. This was partly for reasons of defence: from the time of the Crimean War (1854-56) there was fear of invasion, exacerbated by the final withdrawal of the imperial garrison in 1870 and the growth of European rivalry in the Pacific. New South Wales developed under free trade, Victoria under a protective tariff – an obvious absurdity between neighbours. A common policy on immigration, especially on coloured immigration, seemed desirable. After extensive negotiations the six colonies joined in a single federal "Commonwealth of Australia" on Jan. 1, 1901, the written constitution being included in an Act of the British parliament and deriving both from the Westminster system and from the American federal model. A new capital was built at Canberra, some 300 km south-west of Sydney, becoming the seat of government in 1927.

The leaders of the new Australia did not see it then as an independent state, but as a single, federated, self-governing colony within the British Empire. The colony of New South Wales had sent troops to help the British position in the Sudan in 1884-85; all Australian colonies contributed to the British forces in South Africa 1899-1902, and Victoria and New South Wales helped to protect British interests in China during the Boxer uprising in 1900. Although it began to build its own defences prior to World War I, partly out of fear of Japan, Australia felt automatically committed to that war, sending overseas from a population of about four million more than 330,000 troops, of which nearly 60,000 died in the war – mainly in the Dardanelles and in France and Belgium. The war brought a sense of nationhood and achievement. It also divided the people over the question of conscription, two referenda on which were lost by the popular vote. Through the vigorous rhetoric of its Prime Minister (W. M. Hughes) and the achievements of its armed forces, Australia obtained a place in the peace negotiations, and signed the treaty and joined the League of Nations in its own right.

Between the two world wars, Australia was substantially inactive in world affairs, although after Japan's invasion of Manchuria in 1931 and of "China proper" in 1937, increasingly apprehensive of Japan. In 1936-37, Prime Minister Joseph Lyons floated the idea of a non-aggression pact in the Pacific, but most nations were becoming preoccupied by the gathering storm in Europe. Australia's dependence on a few primary exports made her vulnerable to falls in international commodity prices, and the depression hit hard, with significant recovery only occurring at the end of the thirties. Australia gradually took on the functions and attitudes of an independent state, with its own foreign service and (from early in World War II) overseas diplomatic posts. While accepting the notion of national autonomy under the Balfour Declaration of 1926, Australia waited until 1942 to ratify the relevant legislation – the 1931 Statute of Westminster – and entered the war against Germany "as a result" of Britain's declaration. Australian forces fought in North Africa, Greece, Crete, Syria, and then were brought home for the defence of the mainland and of New Guinea against the Japanese after the disastrous loss of the Singapore base in which an Australian division was taken prisoner. Fortunately, American air power in the battles of the Coral Sea (May 1942) and Midway (June) inflicted such damage on the Japanese navy that Japan was unable to invade Port Moresby, as planned, or to attack Australia, as hoped. The Australian operations in New Guinea and Borneo were a sideshow for the island-hopping American campaign that culminated in the atomic bombs dropped on Hiroshima and Nagasaki in August 1945. The Royal Australian Air Force took part in the campaign in Europe, and the Navy joined with Britain's in the Atlantic, the North Sea and the Mediterranean. Australia took a leading part in the British Commonwealth Occupation Force in Japan (1946–50).

Australia entered World War II with a United Australia Party (conservative) government led by R.G. Menzies. In 1941 it lost its majority in the House of Representatives and the Labor Party under John Curtin and J.B. Chifley held office until December 1949. The Minister for External Affairs during this period, Dr H.V. Evatt, sought a greater international role for Australia. Unsuccessful in influencing allied wartime policies, he negotiated a treaty with New Zealand in January 1944 (the ANZAC, or Canberra, Pact) under which the two states claimed a special role in the post-war security of the Southwest Pacific and in the welfare of its native peoples. At the conference that established the United Nations, Evatt was a leader of the smaller and middle powers, pressed for a greater UN role in economic and social matters, and helped establish the Trusteeship system.

Post-1945 history. The war had demonstrated the importance of the United States to the security of Australia. Evatt tried but failed to get continental US assurances of protection. The conservative coalition Liberal and Country parties government under Menzies that came to power in late 1949 was more successful. It committed forces alongside those of the USA in Korea in 1950, and demurred at signing a peace treaty with Japan, that would allow it to rearm in self-defence, until a security agreement (the **ANZUS Pact**) was made with the USA and New Zealand (September 1951). The Menzies government, in pursuit of regional security, based its foreign policies on loyalty to its British and American partners, and a pronounced anti-communism, as well as an imaginative if modest aid programme. It sent forces to Malaya (1950 and 1955) to help in the "Emergency" against communist insurgents, signed the South-East Asia Collective Defence Treaty (1954), took a somewhat reluctant and belated part in the defence of Malaysia against Indonesian "confrontation", and a much more enthusiastic and substantial part in the war in Vietnam (1962–72) – Australian forces there eventually reaching a total of 8,000, about half of whom were conscripts. US facilities related to

its nuclear deterrent capacity and electronic and intelligence gathering were established at North West Cape, Pine Gap and Nurrungar. Because of the continuing impact of regional conflict on the tenor of Australian politics, a split in the Labor party on religious and ideological lines, and a general improvement in the economy dating from the high commodity prices during the Korean war, the conservative coalition remained in office until December 1972 – a record 23 years.

The Labor government of E.G. Whitlam broadly continued the foreign policies of its predecessors, though with a tone more sympathetic to the Third World countries and causes and less anti-communist. It quickly established diplomatic relations with the People's Republic of China and other communist governments, withdrew a training remnant from Vietnam, and abolished conscription. An attempt to exert regional leadership in Southeast Asia met a lukewarm response. Tariffs were reduced by a worthy 25 per cent, but an international economic recession added to Whitlam's problems, not the least of which was the lack of a majority in the Senate. In November 1975 his government was dismissed by the Governor-General, Sir John Kerr, on the grounds that it could not in the existing parliamentary situation assure supply, i.e. the provision through legislation of funds to pay public service salaries and other expenses of government.

The interim coalition government led by Malcolm Fraser that replaced Whitlam was given strong support at the subsequent election. Fraser had inherited one major foreign policy problem – the Indonesian claim to Portuguese **East Timor**, prompting an invasion by Indonesian forces. Whitlam had encouraged President Suharto to believe that East Timor should become part of Indonesia. The bloody occupation posed a dilemma for Fraser and his more liberal foreign minister, Andrew Peacock. The resulting ambivalence – publicly opposing the use of force and privately expressing understanding of Indonesia's concerns – pleased no one. Fraser also inherited a Whitlam initiative – negotiations for a treaty of friendship and co-operation with Japan – which he successfully concluded, formally redressing the discrimination suffered by Japanese people and enterprises in trying to enter Australia during the previous century. Fraser combined a strident anti-communism and a combative personal style with a sympathy for black African causes. He came to office at a time of deepening international recession, and increased trade barriers in the European Community, a traditional Australian market. In its own region, Australia was criticized for its restrictive tariffs. The coalition failed to solve the problems of inflation and unemployment, both of which were running at around 10 per cent. There was a record balance of payments deficit. The coalition remained in office until March 1983, when the Labor party under its new leader, the former Trade Union president **R.J.L. (Bob) Hawke**, was elected to power.

Australia under Hawke. In both domestic and foreign affairs, the Hawke government adopted policies that were pragmatic rather than ideological and were often as conservative as his opponents'. Relations with the United States continued to be warm, despite American trade competition. Labor deregulated the financial markets, invited foreign banks into the country, and floated the Australian currency. By involving and balancing the factions within his own party, adopting a process of building consensus with the trade unions and the private sector, and by a personal style attractive to the electorate, Hawke has remained remarkably popular. The opposition developed problems of leadership and ideology, which may be alleviated by the re-election of Peacock in May 1989 as Leader of the Opposition. Labor easily won elections (called early) in 1985 and 1987 and during most of the Hawke period four of the six states have had Labor governments. The government has managed to balance the domestic budget, but the balance of payments on current account has soared to new heights. The manufacturing sector has declined as a proportion of the economy (from 30 per cent 30 years ago to around 16 per cent), and primary exports continue to be affected by world price fluctuations and dumping from American and European producers.

In 1985 New Zealand advised the United States that nuclear-armed or nuclear-propelled warships would not be allowed to enter New Zealand ports. After extensive recriminatory negotiations, the US government suspended the application to New Zealand of provisions made under the ANZUS Pact, including the supply of military information and preferred access to defence technology. Australia supported the USA diplomatically, but has also retained its own direct defence links with New Zealand.

In March 1987, the Defence Minister, Kim Beazley, tabled a White Paper which spelled out a greater sense of self-reliance within Australia's immediate environment, while still maintaining the US alliance. An extensive programme of re-equipment should make the army more mobile, upgrade the navy's surface and submarine fleet and the surveillance capacity of the air force.

One matter overlapping both state and federal jurisdictions is that of Aborigines, since a consti-

tutional change in 1967 gave the federal government joint responsibility. Many Aborigines were frequently fringe dwellers on the outskirts of towns, living in sub-standard accommodation; others were employed in the pastoral industry, and others lived on reserves which were being increasingly penetrated by mining companies. In January 1972 a protest movement encamped outside Parliament House, Canberra, drew attention to their demands for political recognition. The Whitlam government established a Department of Aboriginal Affairs and introduced land rights legislation for the Northern Territory (under federal jurisdiction) which the Fraser government carried through. This provided for the transfer of reserves to Aboriginal ownership together with the establishment of land councils which could resist mining encroachments, and set up an Aboriginal Land Commission to hear Aboriginal claims for traditional but non-reserve land. Several other land councils within the states have been created, and a federation of them to press for land rights. In 1975 the government established the Aboriginal Land Commission to buy land for Aboriginal corporations. It was dissolved in 1980. Vocal groups are agitating for some kind of treaty between the whites and the Aborigines.

Equality of Aboriginal rights has aroused international interest, emphasized by Australia's celebration in 1988 of two centuries of white occupation. Many Aborigines adopted an attitude of hostile or subdued opposition to these celebrations. Attention has been further focused on Aborigines because of the death in custody of several scores of them during the past decade. A Royal Commission was set up to investigate.

The exuberant bicentenary events included an Expo in Brisbane, a re-enactment of the First Fleet, and many thousands of celebrations, large and small, of a historical, sporting and cultural nature around the nation.

The vast natural resources of Australia, in minerals and land as well as a skilled and educated population, and a stable political system, assure it of a continued favourable standard of living. The continuing high level of capital inflow is both evidence of and a factor in this prosperity. But the outflow of interest and other service payments, the low level of domestic research and development, and the uncompetitiveness of much manufacturing industry are clouds on this prosperity and indicate the need for some painful restructuring of the economy.

TBM

AUSTRALIAN DEMOCRATS. Originally a breakaway from the Liberal Party, combining the

Liberal Movement and the Australia Party. The party is especially concerned with humanitarian and environmental issues, and holds the balance of power in the Senate.

TBM

AUSTRALIAN LABOR PARTY (ALP). Based on the trade union movement which developed political aspirations in the late nineteenth century in order to increase social justice and especially to protect working-class interests. The federal parliamentary leader is **R.J.L. (Bob) Hawke**, Prime Minister, a former President of the Australian Council of Trade Unions. State parties form the government in Victoria, South Australia and Western Australia.

TBM

B

BASIC LAW (HONG KONG). The Basic Law of the Hong Kong Special Administrative Region will become Hong Kong's constitutional instrument in 1997. It is being drafted by the 59 members of the Basic Law Drafting Committee, which was appointed by the Chinese National People's Congress (NPC) in June 1985. The Committee published a first draft of this legislation in April 1988 and a second draft in February 1989 for public comment in Hong Kong, and will submit the final version to the NPC for enactment in 1990.

The Basic Law provides a definition of the Chinese principles of "one country, two systems" and "Hong Kong people administering Hong Kong". In practice, it recreates a British Crown colony system of government without the colonial trappings in Hong Kong after June 1997. The NPC will interpret the Basic Law.

ST

BATMÖNH, JAMBYN. Mongolian statesman, born in 1926. Since 1984 he has been Chairman of the Presidium of the People's Great *Hural* (President of Mongolia) and general secretary of the **Mongolian People's Revolutionary Party**; between 1974 and 1984 he was Chairman of the Mongolian Council of Ministers.

IG

BAUXITE. The principal ore of aluminium. The annual production of bauxite, in thousands of tonnes, is as follows: Australia, 34,400; China, 2,000; USA, 856; Indonesia, 830; Malaysia, 492. (*See also* **Aluminium**)

RS

BAYKAL-AMUR MAINLINE (BAM – Baykalo-Amurskaya Magistral). A railway running for 3,145 km through the far eastern part of the Soviet Union from Ust'Kut (north-west of Lake Baykal, at the end of a branch line of the Trans-Siberian Railway) to Komsomolsk-na-Amure, where it links up with a line to the Pacific. Work on laying the line began in 1974 and was declared completed in 1984, but the BAM is not due to become fully operational until the latter part of 1989 (*see also* **Trans-Siberian Railway**).

IG

BEAGLE CHANNEL. The islets of Picton, Lennox and Nueva, situated at the eastern entrance to the Beagle Channel, believed since the nineteenth century to be Chilean, were disputed by Argentina, and in 1977 an arbitral award by the International Court of Justice in favour of Chile was rejected by Argentina, and war averted by the offer of mediation by the Vatican. Following the restoration of civilian rule in Argentina, the mediation proposals (confirming the islands as Chilean but establishing maritime boundaries confirming under the "Two Ocean" principle that the meridian of Cape Horn would remain the boundary between the Argentinian and Chilean spheres of influence and hence the eastern political boundary of the Pacific) were ratified by both states and confirmed by referendum in Argentina.

P&SC

BHUMIBOL ADULYADEJ, KING (KING RAMA IX). King Bhumibol succeeded to the throne of Thailand in June 1946 following the death of his brother, King Ananda Mahidol. As King, Bhumibol is head of state and head of the armed forces. Under the terms of the 1978 Constitution, he exercises legislative power through the National Assembly, executive power through the Council of Ministers and judicial power through the courts. He is advised by a Privy Council.

The King's 60th birthday (the highly auspicious date on which, according to the Buddhist religion, he completed his fifth cycle) was celebrated throughout Thailand on Dec. 5, 1987. Further celebrations took place on July 2, 1988, on which date King Bhumibol became the longest reigning monarch of the Chakri dynasty.

DS

"BOAT PEOPLE", VIETNAMESE. Since the collapse of Saigon and the Republic of Vietnam in April 1975, over 1.5 million people are estimated to have left the country as refugees in one sense or another. Approximately 150,000 left as a direct result of the Communist takeover: of these 130,000 departed with the American evacuation, and another 20,000 are thought to have escaped (mainly by sea) down to the end of 1977. The main flood of migration began in 1978-79, when an acceleration of "socialist transformation" in the South coincided with the deterioration in Sino-Vietnamese relations. About 160,000 people of Chinese origin crossed the land border into China by the end of 1978. (After March 1979 that border was heavily fortified.)

The main form of emigration was by boat into the South China Sea, where many refugees were picked up, and many others probably died at sea. It has been estimated that in the 10 years 1979–88 at least one million Vietnamese "boat people" touched land in Southeast Asia. That total excludes those picked up at sea and taken directly to other countries. Most of those arriving in the ASEAN countries were resettled elsewhere, mainly in Australia, Canada, the United States, and some European countries, but in 1989 there was still a backlog of 140,000 Vietnamese refugees not yet resettled. By then a new increase in numbers was causing concern, and on March 13, 1989 the ASEAN countries decided collectively to end the policy of making all Vietnamese eligible for resettlement in third countries.

Another feature of the new wave of emigration in 1988–89 was the growing number of Vietnamese leaving northern Vietnam by boat for Hong Kong, creating a mood of crisis there and leading to a series of diplomatic exchanges between the British and Vietnamese governments. Both Hong Kong and the ASEAN countries introduced a distinction between genuinely "political" refugees and those (thought to be the majority) who had left merely for "economic" reasons. There was talk of forcible repatriation, but Vietnam refused to take people back unless they returned "voluntarily". These problems were discussed, with only limited progress, at an international conference on Indochinese refugees in Geneva in June 1989.

Under international pressure the Vietnamese authorities themselves introduced an "orderly departure programme" in 1979, under which individuals could apply for refugee status and arrange resettlement before leaving the country by air to agreed destinations. This programme worked well for several years. It was slowed down in 1986, but resumed in 1987–88. By the end of the latter year about 150,000 Vietnamese had left in this way. (*See also* **Hong Kong: Vietnamese Boat People**)

RBS

BOLKIAH, SULTAN SIR HASSANAL. Sir Muda Hassanal Bolkiah Mu'izuddin Waddaulah, the 29th Sultan of Brunei, was born in 1946 and graduated from the Royal Military Academy, Sandhurst. He was appointed Crown Prince and Heir Apparent in 1961. In October 1967, his father, Sir Omar Ali Saifuddin III, who had been Sultan since 1950, abdicated and the following year Sir Hassanal officially replaced him as Sultan. When Brunei became independent on Jan. 1, 1984, Sir Hassanal assumed the office of Prime Minister at the head of a new Cabinet. He currently holds additional responsibility for Defence.

DS

BOXER UPRISING. Known in Chinese as the Yi He Tuan or "Harmony Movement", this was a protest against Manchu misrule and creeping foreign penetration of Chinese society, especially by missionaries. It emerged in the Eastern province of Shandong in the late 1890s, and its followers practised martial exercises known as "Harmony Fists", hence the name "Boxer". They believed they were immune to bullets. The movement spread to nearby Beijing in 1899, and the imperial authorities deflected their fanaticism towards the foreign legations in the capital, which they besieged. An expedition of Western troops lifted the siege in August 1900, and foreign powers imposed crippling indemnities upon China, as well as foreign control of the Chinese customs service to ensure repayment. Russia seized Manchuria.

CIPF

BRITISH NATIONALITY FOR HONG KONG. Between 1843 and 1962, all persons born in Hong Kong were British subjects with unrestricted right to enter, live and work in the United Kingdom. They effectively lost this right under the Commonwealth Immigrants Act (1962). Their status as Citizen of the United Kingdom and Colonies (CUKC) was changed into British Dependant Territories Citizen (BDTC), without the right of abode in the United Kingdom, under the British Nationality Act (1981). The British Nationality (Hong Kong) Order 1986, creates a new status for them, British National (Overseas) (BN(O)), which is not transmissible to the holder's children, as their BDTC status will lapse in 1997. There are at present 550,000 CUKC, 890,000 BDTC and 60,000 BN(O) passport holders in Hong Kong, though 3,280,000 are eligible.

ST

BROADCASTING. Radio and television have become the major sources of hard news and entertainment throughout the Pacific region. Household ownership of both appliances is almost complete in the more affluent countries such as the United States and Japan and is growing fast in poorer countries. The governments of more authoritarian states recognize the high propaganda value of the two media, while in free market economies, television in particular has become a favoured means of commercial advertising. In most cases, governments in free market economies do not allow a "free-for-all" in broadcasting, instead supervising a system of controlled franchises.

Nonetheless, there is a bewildering degree of choice in the United States, augmented by the wide availability of Cable TV. Many of the stations and channels cater to a local audience. There is a fierce battle for ratings between the major TV networks. Advertising is far more intensive than in most Western European countries. Much of the programme output is entertainment-oriented, though public broadcasting services with a more educational or cultural content function alongside the overtly commercial channels. Well-funded special-interest groups, especially religious sects, have their own channels or broadcasts in some areas, though the reputation of Christian stations has suffered badly from a series of scandals involving TV evangelists and their financial or sexual activities.

US broadcasting output has a considerable influence in the Pacific region. US television programmes are sold worldwide. Satellite channels such as Worldnet and CNN bring global news coverage (from an American perspective) to growing numbers of more affluent viewers overseas, who have receiver dishes or who are on local cable systems. Satellite dishes are particularly noticeable in middle-class surburbs of US-influenced countries like Guatemala.

Australia has a much smaller number of commercial radio and TV stations than North America – about 130, compared with 20,000 in the USA and Canada – and these are more tightly controlled through licensing. Japanese TV audiences are considerable, including a notably large number of female viewers during the daytime.

In stark contrast to the situation in western industrialized nations and Japan, broadcasting in the Soviet Union is bereft of overall entertainment value, though the artistic or educative content of individual programmes can be high. Though the nightly TV news programme *Vremya* commands a huge audience, many Soviet citizens are sceptical of the breadth and objectivity of domestic news output. This largely accounts for the large (and until recently clandestine) following of foreign radio stations, such as the BBC World Service and Voice of America. In the mid-1980s,

the Soviet Union was believed to be spending over 100 million US dollars a year jamming such broadcasts, but under President **Gorbachev**, much of that interference has stopped. Moreover, the content of broadcasts has become much more informative. For example, TV reports now show nationalist unrest in various Soviet republics and disasters, such as earthquakes or train crashes.

As in most developing countries, far more people in China have radios than television sets. However, TV ownership is rising rapidly. In 1975, there were said to be only 200,000 sets in China, but this had risen to 3,000,000 in 1981 and to 40,000,000 by 1985. Domestic TV production was scaled up considerably under the economic liberalization programme of **Deng Xiaoping** and imported TVs (mainly from Japan) became an important (though for most people prohibitively expensive) status symbol. Programming comes under the Ministry of Radio and Television, which operates two national TV networks and about 50 local ones. Since 1979, there have been some commercials on Chinese TV.

JF

BRUNEI. *Population*: 227,000 (est. 1988). *Area*: 5,765 sq km. *Gross Domestic Product*: US$2,978 million (1986). *Trade (1986)*: imports US$725 million; exports US$1,995 million. *Top five trading partners*: Japan, United States, Singapore, South Korea and Thailand. *Defence spending*: US$236 million (1988). *Education spending*: US$158 million (1988). *Urban population as percentage of total*: 64. *Birth rate*: 31 per thousand. *Life expectancy*: 71 years.

Geographical background. The Sultanate of Brunei (Negara Brunei Darussalam) is situated on the north-west part of the island of Borneo, some 450 km north of the equator. The country shares a common border with Sarawak, one of the 13 constituent states of Malaysia. Brunei is mainly jungle, with forests covering some 85 per cent of the total land area. It is divided into four districts: Brunei/Muara (570 sq km); Seria/Belait (2,725 sq km); Tutong (1,165 sq km); and Temburong (1,305 sq km). The capital is Bandar Seri Begawan. The country's population is projected to reach 400,000 by the year 2000.

Socio-political background. The indigenous people of Brunei are mainly Malay and that language is the official one of the state. In 1988, of the country's estimated population of 227,000, Malays constituted 155,000, Chinese 41,000 and other indigenous peoples 11,500. There were over 20,000 expatriates from Europe and elsewhere working in Brunei, including guest workers from other Southeast Asian countries, notably Malaysia and the Philippines. Islam is the country's official religion, although the 1959 Constitution permits religious freedom and other faiths are practised by a small minority.

The Sultanate of Brunei became a fully independent sovereign state on Jan. 1, 1984, when a ministerial system of government was established. The Sultan, in whom the 1959 written Constitution vests supreme executive authority, presides over and is advised and assisted by a Council of Cabinet Ministers, a Religious Council and a Privy Council. The Sultan has ruled by decree and a state of emergency has been in force since the **Brunei Rebellion** of December 1962 which resulted in the suspension of sections of the Constitution.

Pre-modern history. The early history of Brunei is not well chronicled, but there are indications that it was a vassal state of China before it came under the influence of the Hindu Javanese empire of Majapahit in the fourteenth century. An independent and Islamic Sultanate of Brunei rose to prominence in the fifteenth and sixteenth centuries. Under the rule of Sultan Bolkiah (1473–1521) and Sultan Hassan (1605–1619), the country developed into a formidable power and its influence extended over much of Borneo and some smaller islands of the Malay archipelago.

The thrust of European, and particularly British, influence within the region in the seventeenth and eighteenth centuries saw a marked decline in the power and territory of Brunei, a process which was hastened in the nineteenth century. In 1841, Sultan Omar Ali Saifuddein II (1829–1852) was forced to cede Sarawak to the English adventurer and so-called "white raja", James Brooke. In 1847 Sultan Omar entered into a formal treaty with Britain in which the latter helped to promote Brunei's commercial interest and suppress piracy. Thereafter, the sultanate came under increasing pressure from Brooke to the south and European and US speculators to the north to cede even more territory. In 1888, by which time Brunei had been reduced in size to little more than 5,500 sq km, Britain formally extended its protection over the sultanate. A further measure of British control was accepted in 1906, when a British Resident was appointed to advise the Sultan on all matters, except those concerning local customs and religion.

Early modern history. Brunei was occupied by Japanese forces from 1941 to 1945 after which it reverted to its former status as a British Residency. The British-appointed Governor of Sarawak (Sarawak having been ceded to the UK by the Brooke family at the end of World War II)

was appointed to the additional post of High Commissioner for Brunei in 1948. In September 1959 Brunei promulgated its first written Constitution and an agreement was concluded between Sultan Omar Ali Saifuddien III (the father of the current Sultan) and the British government, which afforded the sultanate a large measure of independence over domestic internal affairs. The UK retained responsibility for Brunei's defence and foreign relations.

A large-scale revolt broke out in Brunei in December 1962 led by elements opposed to Brunei's entry into the projected Malaysian Federation (*see* **Malaysia: political history**). In November, 1971, a new UK–Brunei treaty was signed under which Britain retained control of Brunei's external affairs, but assumed only an advisory role on defence matters, leaving the Sultan in control of all internal affairs. A separate agreement provided for the stationing of a battalion of British Gurkhas in Brunei. During the 1970s the Brunei government was reluctant to enter negotiations with the UK over a full independence agreement, despite British pressure to do so. Brunei's reluctance was generally held to be based on fears of possible Malaysian territorial ambitions and of possible guerrilla action by exiled opponents of the Sultan. Negotiations proceeded in late 1978 only after Malaysia and Indonesia had given assurances to the Sultan that they would recognize the independence of Brunei, would prevent the establishment of guerrilla bases on their territories and would support Brunei's accession to the **Association of South-East Asian Nations (ASEAN)**. The agreement that resulted was signed in 1979 and envisaged that the state would become fully independent from Britain at the end of 1983.

Political history. The Sultanate of Brunei became a fully independent sovereign state on Dec. 31, 1983–Jan. 1, 1984, when the Brunei government assumed full responsibility for the country's defence and foreign relations. It was announced on Jan. 1 that a cabinet system of government would be adopted in place of the Privy Council and Council of Ministers set up under the 1959 Constitution, and that the posts of Chief Minister and State Secretary would be abolished. The Sultan assumed the office of Prime Minister at the head of a new cabinet in which the key posts were all held by members of his family. The state of emergency imposed during the internal rebellion of 1962 (see separate entry) remained in force and the Sultan subsequently appeared to rule out the possibility of a relaxation on the ban on political activity; he allegedly expressed his intention to rule Brunei in a manner similar to some Arab hereditary leaders of Gulf states.

The question of citizenship for the Brunei Chinese community, members of which controlled much of the private commercial and non-oil sector of the economy, was not resolved on independence; those without citizenship were granted certificates of identity in place of Brunei passports. The Chinese community appeared threatened in 1985 when the Sultan indicated that Brunei might become an Islamic state in which the country's indigenous Malay inhabitants would receive preferential treatment (*see* **New Economic Policy – Malaysia** for strategy since the early 1970s in neighbouring Malaysia to increase Malay participation in ownership and management of commerce and industry).

In May 1985 a new political party, the **Brunei National Democratic Party** was formed; the following year it splintered and the pro-government **Brunei National United Party** came into existence. The death of the Sultan's father in September 1986 appeared to herald the commencement of a more progressive phase of government, one example of which was the appointment of a number of commoners to the cabinet in October 1986.

Recent developments. In 1988 attention was focused on a large financial corruption trial which resulted in the closure of the National Bank of Brunei (NBB). In February, the country's high court sentenced Khoo Ban Hock, the NBB chairman, and Azlan Robert Teoh, NBB's managing director, to prison terms of 52 and 20 months respectively, after finding them guilty of financial corruption. The NBB had been closed down by the government in November 1986 and Khoo Ban Hock and other officials had been arrested and charged. The central allegation was that some US$606 million, or more than 90 per cent of the NBB's total loans, had been advanced without documentation of the money or security of the loans to "Khoo-related companies" headed by Khoo Ban Hock's father, Khoo Teck Puat, who reportedly held a 70 per cent stake in the NBB. The Brunei government also issued writs in Brunei, Hong Kong and Singapore against Khoo Teck Puat (who was based in Singapore) and 14 of his companies, in an attempt to recover the loaned NBB funds, alleging that he and his companies had acted as guarantors for the loans.

In March 1988, the government officially confirmed that it had ordered the deregistration of the Brunei National Democratic Party and that two of the party's leaders had been detained. Earlier, in February, four political prisoners connected with the **People's Party of Brunei** had been

released to mark the country's national day; 34 other political prisoners were released in July to mark the Sultan's birthday. All the releases reportedly followed the swearing of an oath of allegiance to the Sultan by the prisoners.

Outline of economic development. Brunei's economy is dominated by the oil and liquified natural gas (LNG) industries. Petroleum prospectors arrived in Brunei in the early 1900s but it was not until 1929 that the Shell Company began the commercial production of oil from an onshore deposit at Seria. Offshore oil production began in 1963 and now accounts for the vast majority of the sultanate's exports. In 1972, what was then the world's largest LNG plant came on stream at Lumut. Sales of five million tonnes a year of LNG are sent to Japan under a 20-year contract due to expire in 1993.

The petroleum sector has been adversely affected by depressed prices in the world oil market in the 1980s. Output reached a peak of about 260,000 barrels per day (bpd) in 1979, but in subsequent years production has steadily decreased. Export earnings for crude petroleum fell from B$5,778 million in 1981 to B$1,620 in 1986, reflecting reductions in both production and prices. The fall in petroleum production has led to a reduction in GDP. Between 1975 and 1979 GDP grew, in real terms, at an average rate of just over 12 per cent; between 1980 and 1986 GDP contracted by 1.4 per cent annually. Nevertheless, in terms of average income, Brunei remains one of the world's richest countries.

The government has implemented a series of National Development Plans; the first covering the period 1953–58, the second for 1962–66, the third for 1975–79 and the fourth for 1980–84. The third and fourth plans placed considerable emphasis on building up the country's infrastructure and communications (for details of fifth Development Plan see following paragraph).

Current economic situation. As of 1988, Brunei had charge of six offshore and two onshore fields producing crude petroleum. However, reduced world demand in the 1980s meant that production in 1988 had decreased to 150,000 bpd (from a peak of 260,000 bpd in 1979). In 1986 the government introduced the country's fifth Development Plan covering the period 1986–90. The fifth plan was reportedly the first stage of a 20-year master-plan which a UK consultancy firm had started preparation work on in mid-1985. The fifth plan's primary aim was to reduce Brunei's economic dependence on income from petroleum and natural gas. Towards this end the government shifted the plan's emphasis away from the infrastructure and social matters towards the creation of new industries in the private sector. As part of its encouragement of the private sector, the government established an Economic Development Board and an Industrial Development Unit to promote the development of new industries. The fifth plan lists some 350 specific projects and allocates total expenditure of B$16,000 million (compared with B$11,900 million for the fourth plan), of which B$3,700 was for development.

During 1988 Brunei Finance Ministry officials indicated that the country intended to play a larger role in the financial affairs of the ASEAN region. The main instruments of such a policy would be the **Brunei Investment Agency (BIA)** and the newly created International Bank of Brunei.

Foreign relations. Brunei became a member of the **Association of South-East Asian Nations (ASEAN)** in January 1984, a matter of days after the country had achieved formal independence from the UK. Also in January, Brunei became the 49th member state of the Commonwealth and its request for admission to the Islamic Conference Organization (ICO) was approved.

In December 1987 the Sultan attended his first ASEAN heads of government meeting in Manila. Brunei assumed the ASEAN chairmanship in mid-1988, as a result of which the annual Foreign Ministers' meeting was held in Bandar Seri Begawan in July 1989. Brunei has maintained close links with Britain since the granting of full independence, and throughout early 1985 there were persistent rumours that the Sultan had transferred large amounts of money to Britain in an attempt to reverse a decline in sterling. In March 1988, Britain's Secretary of State for Defence, George Younger, revealed that Brunei had expressed interest in joining the five-power defence agreement concluded in 1971 by Britain, Malaysia, Singapore, Australia and New Zealand.

Prospects for development. As oil reserves are expected to be exhausted by the end of the century, the main problem facing the government is one of broadening the economy. However, the government has had little success in achieving any real diversification, despite heavy investment. Brunei still imports a high percentage of its food, while the only significant industrial development has been in the construction industry. In view of the prosperity of the hydrocarbon sector there is little incentive to establish enterprises in the private sector and any such attempts are inevitably hampered by a shortage of manpower and very high wage levels. Despite the apparent failure of the policy of diversification, it remains at the heart of the government's long-term economic strategy. The fifth Development Plan, and the 20-year master-plan of which it is a part, both recognize the urgent need to encourage the creation of new private-sector industries, to achieve self-sufficiency in food and to boost import substitution.

DS

BRUNEI INVESTMENT AGENCY (BIA).
The Brunei Investment Agency was established in July 1983 to invest the country's massive international reserves (estimated at US$20,000 million as at early 1987) abroad, mainly in the United States, Japan, Western Europe and the ASEAN countries. Fluctuations in the world oil price in recent years, and in particular the sharp fall in crude oil prices in 1986, has meant that the Ministry of Finance has become increasingly reliant upon revenue created by the BIA.

The BIA took over the funds originally managed by the UK Crown Agents on behalf of the Brunei government. The BIA's managing director is Yang Mulia Dato Seri Laila Jasa Hj. Abd. Rahman bin Hj. karim. The BIA itself handles approximately 35 per cent of the country's foreign reserves, the remainder being allocated to eight foreign banks.

DS

BRUNEI NATIONAL DEMOCRATIC PARTY (BNDP).
The moderate Islamic and liberal nationalist Brunei National Democratic Party (BNDP, *Partai Kebang-Saam Demokratik Brunei*) was formed in September 1985 and sought the establishment of a parliamentary democracy under a constitutional monarch. State employees (forming some 40 per cent of the country's workforce) were prohibited from joining the new party, as were members of the minority Chinese community (making up about a fifth of the country's population). The government officially confirmed in March 1988 that it had ordered the deregistration of the BNDP and that Abdul Latif Hamid and Haji Abdul Latif Chuchu, respectively party president and general secretary, had been detained under the Internal Security Act in order to "prevent them from acting in a manner prejudicial to the security of Brunei Darussalam". According to the announcement, the BNDP had been deregistered under the Societies Act (reportedly in late January 1988) for its connections with a foreign organization, named as the Pacific Democrat Union (a grouping of conservative and centre-right parties in Australasian and Pacific countries).

DS

BRUNEI NATIONAL UNITED PARTY (BNUP). The Brunei National United Party (BNUP, *Partai Perpaduan Kebang-Saan Brunei*) is the country's sole official political party. It was formed in February 1986 by a pro-Government faction of the **Brunei National Democratic Party** and was described by its general secretary, Awang Hatta Haji Zainal Abiddin, as being open to all Malay ethnic groups, whether Muslim or non-Muslim.

DS

BRUNEI REBELLION. A large-scale revolt broke out on Dec. 8, 1962, in Brunei and also in adjoining areas of the other two territories comprising British Borneo – Sarawak and North Borneo (Sabah). At the time of the revolt, Britain was planning to merge all three Borneo territories, together with Malaya and Singapore, into a Malaysian Federation. The rebellion was carried out by the so-called "North Borneo Liberation Army", an organization linked with the **People's Party of Brunei** headed by A.M. Azahari and strongly opposed to Brunei's entry into the Malaysian Federation. In August 1962 the People's Party of Brunei had won all 16 elective seats in Brunei's 33-member Legislative Assembly. Azahari himself was in Manila at the time of the rebellion and remained there until late January 1963, when he left for Indonesia. Describing himself as "Prime Minister" of the "revolutionary state of Kalimantan Utara" (the Indonesian term for Sabah) he declared on Dec. 9 that he was prepared to fight Britain for the independence of the Borneo territories "even if it takes 20 years"; in the meantime he had ordered his forces to engage in general sabotage, particularly against the Shell Company's oil installations at Seria.

Apart from mopping-up operations, the revolt was quelled after 10 days' fighting during which all rebel-held localities in Brunei and adjacent areas of Sarawak and North Borneo were retaken by British and Gurkha troops rushed from Singapore. The Sultan suspended Brunei's Constitution on Dec. 20, dissolved the Legislative Council, and appointed a 14-man Emergency Council to hold power until the state of emergency was lifted. From this date the Sultan has ruled by decree and the state of emergency has remained in force. In the event, the Sultan decided, in 1963, against joining the proposed Malaysian Federation. President **Sukarno** of Indonesia, a vehement opponent of the creation of the Malaysian Federation, had been accused by Malaya of organizing the Brunei rebellion. In early 1963 Sukarno announced that Indonesian "volunteers" would "liberate" northern Borneo from colonialism, thus beginning what was known as the "Confrontation".

DS

BRUNEI SHELL. Brunei's economy depends almost entirely on its petroleum and natural gas resources. Brunei Shell, the country's principal company, is concerned with the exploration and production of oil and natural gas, oil refining and crude oil trading. There are five companies within Brunei Shell:

Brunei Shell Petroleum (BSP) owns the Brunei Refinery and explores and produces crude oil and gas. The Brunei government and the Royal Dutch/Shell Group are equal shareholders in the company.

Brunei LNG liquefies natural gas purchased from BSP and in turn sells it to Brunei Coldgas (see below). The Brunei government increased its share to 50 per cent of the company's equity in 1986. The other two partners (Royal Dutch/Shell and the Mitsubishi Corporation of Japan) each own 25 per cent of the equity.

Brunei Coldgas buys liquefied natural gas from Brunei LNG and arranges its transport and sale to Japanese customers, mainly the Tokyo Electric Power Company, the Tokyo Gas Company and the Osaka Gas Company. The shareholding is similar to Brunei LNG.

Brunei Shell Tankers was established in 1986 and owns seven LNG tankers which it charters to Brunei Coldgas. The Brunei government and the Royal Dutch/Shell Group are joint owners.

Brunei Shell Marketing markets petroleum products and chemicals within Brunei. The company is owned jointly by the Brunei government and the Royal Dutch/Shell Group.

DS

BUDDHISM. Of the three great international and missionary religions, Buddhism, **Christianity** and **Islam**, the first is the oldest. Buddhism began in India in the sixth century BCE and rapidly spread through much of Asia, entering China in the first century CE, Japan in the sixth, and arriving in America and Europe in modern times. However, its monastic organization and general ignorance of modern scientific thought render Buddhism more open to attack today than some other religions.

The historical monk Siddhartha, known more often by the family name of Gautama or the clan name of Shakyamuni, "the sage of the Shakyas", lived from about 563 to 483 BCE in north-central

India and Nepal. He was a prince of the Indian warrior caste, married and had a child, but at the age of 29 Gautama renounced family life and wandered round northern India until he gained enlightenment and became a Buddha, an "enlightened one". With a few followers the new Buddha taught the Dharma (or Dhamma), the religion, truth or virtue, explained as the Middle Way between the extremes of sensuality and asceticism.

Three Jewels or Refuges summarize Buddhist aims: Buddha, Dharma and Sangha, the last being the order of monks. The Sangha provided the core organization, a trained elite, an educating centre which traditionally trained all young men in some countries, and a creative source for literary and artistic achievement. Although world-renouncing and dependent on charity, the Sangha came to wield great power and own large estates, like monasteries in the West. Today this former strength often proves weakness as monasteries are attacked and social and political organizations change. The future of Buddhism often depends more on the laity than on the monks.

There are two major divisions in Buddhism, and numerous minor ones. The Mahayana, "great vehicle" of salvation for everyone, has prevailed in Vietnam, China including Tibet, Japan, Korea, and in some recent developments in Hawaii and the USA. Mahayanists call Hinayana, "small vehicle", what its own followers term the Theravada, "tradition of the elders", because the latter consider their way to be closest to the traditional doctrines of the Buddha himself.

GP

BURYATS. An ethnic group found in the east of the Soviet Union. The Buryats, who number nearly 400,000 people, are a Mongol people and mainly inhabit the area immediately to the north of the Mongolian border, where they enjoy administrative-territorial autonomy in the Buryat Autonomous Soviet Socialist Republic (established in 1923), and in the Ust'Orda Buryat and Aga Buryat National Districts (established in 1937).

IG

C

CAIRNS GROUP. The Cairns Group brings together 14 mainly Pacific and South American nations which are major exporters of agricultural produce. Under the chairmanship of Australia's Minister for Trade Negotiations Michael Duffy, it has become a major player in world trade negotiations. In particular, the Cairns Group has campaigned within the Uruguay Round of talks of the General Agreement on Tariffs and Trade (GATT) for an end to agricultural subsidies. Major aims include the liberalization of agriculture and its integration into a stronger GATT. The members are: Argentina, Australia, Brazil, Canada, Chile, Colombia, Fiji, Hungary, Indonesia, Malaysia, New Zealand, the Philippines, Thailand and Uruguay.

JF

CAMBODIA. (Note: *see also* **Democratic Kampuchea; Democratic Kampuchea, Coalition Government of; Kampuchea, People's Republic of.**) *Population*: estimates vary (e.g. 7.2 million, 1984; 6.7 million, 1988) but probably of the order of 7 million. *Area*: 181,000 sq km. *Urban population as percentage of total*: 11. *Birth rate*: 40 per thousand (est. 1988). *Life expectancy*: 48.

History: Occupying much of the lower course of the Mekong River (but not its coastal delta) and embracing the whole basin of the Tonle Sap ("Great Lake"), the Cambodia of today is a smaller country than it used to be. Its modern history has seen continual losses of territory to the neighbouring states of Thailand (Siam) and Vietnam. Its people nevertheless retain a memory of an earlier greatness, still symbolized by the temples of Angkor. In the early centuries A.D. the lower Mekong was among the first areas to be influenced by Indian trade and religion. It was also regularly visited by Chinese traders, who first referred to this area as "Funan" (third to fifth centuries) and later (from the sixth century) called it "Chenla". Culturally it was Indian influence, and the Sanskrit tradition, which prevailed. By the seventh to eighth centuries a number of small "Indianized" states had emerged in what is now lower Cambodia, whose legacy is a rich archaeological heritage of small temples and inscriptions. During the ninth century a new and much grander political centre grew up in the vicinity of Angkor, whose larger temples reflect greater control of manpower and territory lasting until the early thirteenth century. Many of the temples were restored meticulously by French archaeologists, the finest and most famous being Angkor Wat (built by the emperor Suryavarman II, who reigned from 1113 to 1150). Also impressive is the Bayon temple of Jayavarman VII (1181–1200), whose territorial control extended from central Vietnam to central and north-east Thailand. However, during the thirteenth and fourteenth centuries this part-Hindu, part-Mahayana-Buddhist tradition of the great temple builders gave way to the more modest religion (and much smaller temples) of Theravada Buddhism. The strength of the rulers also declined during that period, and after 1350 Angkor itself was threatened by the growing power of the Thai kingdom of Ayuthya.

The fall of Angkor to the Thais in 1420 (possibly for the second time) marked the beginning of a period of instability which eventually ended – nearly a century later – with the establishment of a new capital at Lovek, on the lower Mekong. Lovek, too, fell victim to a Thai invasion in 1593–4, followed by another period of instability. At one point it seemed as if lower Cambodia might be taken over by a group of Spanish adventurers from Manila, but that episode ended in a massacre of Europeans at the port of Phnom Penh in 1599. In the early seventeenth century a new dynasty emerged at Oudong, which remained the capital until the mid-nineteenth century. Seventeenth-century Cambodia – whose territory still included the coastal Mekong area – was an important trading centre and producer of rice and various forest products. The Dutch attempted to dominate it in the 1640s but were driven out by a king who subsequently accepted conversion to Islam. His successors, however, reverted to the Theravada tradition.

The real threat to the kingdom came in fact from the neighbouring countries of Siam and Vietnam, both of which were eager to expand their territory at Cambodia's expense. Between the late seventeenth and the early nineteenth centuries, Battambang and Siem Reap (including Angkor) were lost to the Thais. The lower Mekong provinces, after receiving a number of Chinese and Vietnamese settlers, were annexed by Vietnam. In the 1830s a Thai army actually invaded as far as South Vietnam, only to be driven out by a Vietnamese force which then sought to annex Oudong. Cambodia was saved from dismemberment by the establishment of a French protectorate in 1863 – which Bangkok was obliged to recognize two years later. In 1907 the French even obliged Siam to restore to Cambodia the provinces of Battambang and Siem Reap. The French, although they left the monarchy in existence, tightened their administrative control after 1884 in order to bring Cambodia into the Indochinese Union. But they continued to govern through a series of French residents and a French-educated elite of Cambodian civil servants. The area under rice, and other export crops, was expanded; but much of the countryside was left undisturbed and unmodernized. Phnom Penh, although overshadowed by Saigon, became a thriving colonial city and attracted substantial communities of Chinese and Vietnamese settlers. French rule continued in this form until 1945.

From 1940, however, events in Europe weakened the power of the French overseas, and towards the end of that year Thailand saw an opportunity to try to recover some of the territory lost in 1907, particularly Battambang and Siem Reap. After starting a war against French Indochina, Bangkok secured Japanese mediation with the result that the two provinces were transferred to Thailand in May 1941. In the second half of 1941 Japanese troops occupied southern Indochina, including Cambodia; but they left the French administration in being. Only in March 1945, afraid of anti-Japanese subversion, did they seize direct control and instruct the young King **Sihanouk** to renounce the protectorate treaties with France. The situation changed again following the sudden defeat and surrender of Japan in August 1945. An attempt by the pro-Japanese politician Son Ngoc Thanh to seize genuine independence was quickly suppressed, and French rule was restored. (It took until November 1946, however, to recover Battambang and Siem Reap from Thailand.)

In January 1946 Cambodia became an "autonomous state" and in May 1947 the French promulgated a constitution. The election of a national assembly in late 1947 permitted a measure of Cambodian political activity, but it was dissolved the following year. In 1949 a new treaty established Cambodia as an Associated State within the French Union; but France continued to control all important matters. Meanwhile the late 1940s also saw the beginnings of a Cambodian Communist movement which by 1950, in collaboration with the Viet Minh, generated a "national united front" (see **Kampuchean People's Revolutionary Party**). In the early 1950s, the war in Vietnam began to spill over into Cambodia; but the scale of guerrilla and political activity remained small. Concerned about the growing

disorder, King Sihanouk decided in 1952 to assume direct control over the government. He then embarked on a campaign to secure full independence from France, which bore fruit in a formal declaration of independence on Nov. 9, 1953.

The Sihanouk period (1954-70). The Geneva Conference which ended the conflict in Vietnam in July 1954 produced a separate agreement on Cambodia, under which both French and Viet Minh forces were to withdraw – leaving a Cambodian government to be established through national elections. The agreement also guaranteed Cambodia's national unity and international neutrality. In order to take advantage of this situation Sihanouk abdicated the throne on March 2, 1955, created his own political organization (the Sangkum Ryastr Niyum, or "Popular Socialist Community"), and won outright the elections held six months later. In September 1955 he became prime minister of a completely independent and neutral Cambodia, of which he retained firm control for the next 12 years. His movement won further election victories in 1958, 1962 and 1966. Although Sihanouk from time to time handed the premiership to others and spent periods of each year abroad, there was never any doubt that he was the effective ruler. Both leftist and rightist opponents were kept at bay, although he regularly accused Thailand and South Vietnam of aiding and abetting the small Khmer Serai resistance group still led by Son Ngoc Thanh. (Relations with Bangkok were also soured by a dispute over possession of the Preah Vihear temple on the Thai-Cambodian border, which in 1962 was judged by the International Court of Justice to be in Cambodian territory.)

Cambodia accepted a small amount of American economic and military aid down to 1964, but Sihanouk was determined not to be drawn into a close alliance with the United States. He sought to defend the country through diplomacy, making friendly visits to Beijing and Moscow as well as to Western capitals. However, in May 1965 pressures arising from the escalation of the Vietnam War led him to break off relations with the United States (but not with other Western powers). He then entered into closer relations with Beijing and Hanoi, allowing Vietnamese Communist forces to establish what eventually became substantial base areas inside Cambodia. In return, China and North Vietnam dissuaded the **Kampuchean Communist Party** from launching an armed struggle against Sihanouk's own regime.

In keeping with this international strategy, Sihanouk's economic policy concentrated on development projects designed to improve the country's basic infrastructure or to increase production of consumer goods in order to save foreign exchange. Anxious to escape dependence on the good will of South Vietnam, which controlled Phnom Penh's access to the sea via the Mekong, Sihanouk attached special priority to the creation of new port facilities on Cambodia's own coastline. The port of Sihanoukville (later renamed Kompong Som) was completed, with French aid, in 1960. Tragically, however, most of this effort to develop the Cambodian economy was rendered futile by the devastation, in one form or another, which the country suffered during the 1970s.

The decision to end US aid in 1964, and simultaneously to nationalize banks and other enterprises, led to serious financial difficulties by the late 1960s. Economic problems may also have created the opportunity for radical elements to launch a peasant uprising at Samlaut (Battambang) in 1967. Although that was easily suppressed, the political situation began to change more fundamentally in January 1968 when the *Khmer Rouge* (ultimately controlled by **Pol Pot**) embarked on a nation-wide armed struggle coinciding with the Tet Offensive in Vietnam. Sihanouk was unable to prevent a political shift to the right, and in 1969 he had to appoint Gen. Lon Nol as prime minister. He also resumed relations with the United States, and turned a blind eye to American bombing of Vietnamese Communist bases inside Cambodia. Thus by the end of 1969, when he left for a routine visit to France (and then to Moscow and Beijing), Sihanouk's policies were already in ruins. On March 18, 1970, following anti-Vietnamese riots in Phnom Penh and other places, he learned that he had been deposed by the national assembly in what amounted to a coup d'etat by Lon Nol and the rightists. (See also **Sihanouk, Prince**)

The Lon Nol period (1970-75). Since Lon Nol was already prime minister, with Sirik Matak as deputy, there was a large measure of continuity in Phnom Penh itself. But the country at large was soon in a state of crisis. Sihanouk himself retreated to Beijing, where on March 23, 1970, he formed a united front with the *Khmer Rouge* (known as FUNK – "Front Unifié National de Kampuchea"), soon recognized by China, North Korea and North Vietnam as the only legitimate authority in Cambodia. In April he appealed for an armed uprising inside the country. A popular rising had already occurred in several places, and during April the Communist forces (North Vietnamese as well as *Khmer Rouge*) launched a major offensive. Lon Nol meanwhile appealed for American military support. After some hesitation

Washington was convinced that the only way to prevent an early Communist victory in Cambodia – which would jeopardize their current strategy in Vietnam – was to undertake a US-South Vietnamese military operation against the Vietnamese Communist bases inside Cambodia (May-June 1970). US forces then withdrew but active support continued to be given to Lon Nol's regime in the form of military aid and advice, and increasingly heavy US bombing of targets around Phnom Penh and elsewhere. The war continued for another five years.

In October 1970, Lon Nol proclaimed the Khmer Republic. No constitutional changes were made at first, but a political crisis in March 1972 (involving student demonstrations) led him to assume the position of president and to dissolve the national assembly. A rigged presidential election confirmed him in office in June, and a new national assembly elected in September was dominated by his brother's political party. Meanwhile he appointed Son Ngoc Thanh as prime minister (March-October 1972), followed by Hang Thun Hak (1972-73) and Long Boret (1973-75). As the war continued, political stability became increasingly difficult to maintain. American bombing in support of Lon Nol's operations on the ground proved sufficiently effective to prevent *Khmer Rouge* forces from reaching the capital during their offensive of 1973. But the US Congress declared such support illegal after Aug. 15, 1973. Nor was it possible to negotiate a formal ceasefire in Cambodia (of the kind achieved in Vietnam and Laos in January-February 1973). Phnom Penh continued to hold out during 1973-74 but was coming under increasing pressure; it finally succumbed on April 17, 1975. Lon Nol fled to the United States, where he died 10 years later.

The Pol Pot period (1975-79). The sudden fall of Phnom Penh to *Khmer Rouge* forces, with only very limited assistance from the People's Army of Vietnam which was still advancing on Saigon, led immediately to the implementation of a plan to evacuate most of the urban population of Phnom Penh and other centres into the Communist-dominated countryside. One consequence of this move was to make it impossible for the Vietnamese to exercise indirect influence on the new regime. What emerged was a highly decentralized framework of revolutionary mobilization, in which each of eight or nine zones had its own leadership. Ultimate control was exercised by the Kampuchean Communist Party of Pol Pot, which for the first two years and more concealed its own existence behind the vague but sinister appellation *Angkar*: "the organization". Most foreigners were expelled, including the staff of the Soviet embassy – which had remained open until the end. The national bank was sacked and currency was completely abolished.

For the benefit of the outside world the new regime claimed continuity with the united front and government-in-exile formed by Sihanouk in Beijing in 1970. (In practice, substantive power over internal affairs had been transferred to ministries in the "liberated areas" during 1974.) As head of state, Sihanouk returned briefly to Phnom Penh in September 1975, then went to New York to address the United Nations. Back in Cambodia, he presided over the adoption of a new Constitution on Jan. 5, 1976, under which the country was renamed "**Democratic Kampuchea**". But the following April he resigned to allow Khieu Samphan to become president, while the still mysterious Pol Pot was appointed prime minister. Ieng Sary played the most visible role, as foreign minister. The first eight months of 1976 were a period of relative stability. Economic and other assistance from China, under an agreement negotiated by Khieu Samphan in August 1975, allowed an effort to restore agricultural production on the basis of harsh discipline and complete control over labour and distribution. Relations with Vietnam remained tense, however, and an attempt to resolve their differences at meetings in April–May 1976 came to nought.

A more critical phase of internal conflict appears to have begun in September 1976, when Pol Pot temporarily handed over the premiership to Nuon Chea. Conceivably politics in Phnom Penh were directly affected by the crisis in China which followed the death of Mao Zedong. The Chinese security chief Wang Dongxing, who became very powerful during 1976–77, may have had particularly close ties to Pol Pot. Whatever the reason, in early 1977 the latter decided that the time was right to purge his opponents in one "zone" after another. Thus began the period of political terror and mass executions which were to earn Pol Pot's Cambodia the epithet of "killing fields". The purges continued throughout 1977 and 1978. But already by September 1977 Pol Pot felt strong enough to unveil the existence of the Kampuchean Communist Party (on its 17th Anniversary) and to undertake a well-publicized trip to China and North Korea. These moves brought his conflict with Vietnam to a head. Border incidents had become increasingly destructive since the breakdown of a second attempt at reconciliation (June 1977). At the end of the year the Vietnamese launched a major incursion into Cambodia; but if it was an attempt to advance as far as Phnom Penh it was a failure. On Dec. 31, 1977, formal statements by the two sides brought the conflict into the open and amounted almost to declarations of war. The Vietnamese decided to solve the problem of Cambodia, as they saw it, by using maximum military force. They invaded on Dec. 25 and by Jan. 7 were in control of Phnom Penh. Pol Pot was forced to abandon the capital and other major centres and to continue the struggle in the maquis. The Vietnamese installed a group of Cambodian Communists more friendly to their own aspirations regarding Vietnamese–Cambodian cooperation. On Jan. 11, 1979, they proclaimed the People's Republic of Kampuchea (for which *see* **Kampuchea, People's Republic of**), with **Heng Samrin** as head of state.

The pro-Vietnamese regime justified its existence, at least in part, by emphasizing the "genocidal" destructiveness of the Pol Pot regime. There can be no doubt about the harshness of the years 1975–78. *Angkar* conducted many executions of those who had worked for previous governments, and probably eliminated many traders and rich peasants during the early phase of the revolution. Many other people were killed during the internecine conflicts that occurred within the Party itself during the years 1977–78. Many others would appear to have died of famine and disease, although we should be careful not to underestimate the effectiveness of the system, despite its harshness, in producing the minimum resources needed for survival. Finally, the border war with Vietnam probably took a heavy toll in casualties. The total number of deaths in Cambodia during this period will probably never be known for certain, and is inevitably a subject of controversy. The problem of calculation is made worse by the fact that we have no absolutely reliable estimates of the country's population for either the early 1970s or the early 1980s. Already by mid-1976 the more melodramatic accounts of the evacuation of Phnom Penh and the dislocation which supposedly followed were putting the number of deaths at over a million. In time the figure of "three million" came to grip the popular imagination and the Phnom Penh regime of the 1980s has tended to foster such exaggeration: in January 1987 it published an "official" figure of 3,314,718 deaths during the Pol Pot period. A more realistically calculated figure was offered in 1982 by the leading Western historian of Cambodia (Vickery) who put the total loss of population beyond the normal death rate at under 800,000, and estimated the number of political killings as no more than 300,000. Seen in proportion, even these lower figures would make the Pol Pot regime the equal of Stalin's Russia in the early 1930s or Hitler's Germany during World War II. (For further detail of period 1976–79 *see*

Democratic Kampuchea; for post-1979 development *see* **Kampuchea, People's Republic of**, and **Democratic Kampuchea, Coalition Government of**)

RBS

CANADA. *Population*: 25,612,000 (est. 1988 for this and following data). *Area*: 9,922,385 sq km. *Gross Domestic Product*: US$405,100 million. *Trade*: imports: $90,468 million; exports: $98,121 million; total: $188,589 million. *Top five trading partners*: United States (imports: $59,628 million; exports: $71,455 million; total: $131,083 million); Japan (imports: $5,740 million; exports: $5,335 million; total: $11,075 million); United Kingdom (imports: $3,273 million; exports: $2,285 million; total: $5,558 million); South Korea (imports: $1,391 million; exports: $889 million; total: $2,280 million); France (imports: $1,123 million; exports: $820 million; total: $1,943 million). *Total government spending*: $119,221 million. *Defence spending*: $9,607 million. *Education spending*: $4,187 million. *Urban population as percentage of total*: 76.8. *Birth rate*: 7.5 per thousand. *Life expectancy*: 78.9 years.

Political history. Canada's relatively small population of 26,000,000 people spread over such a vast area, divided further into English and French speaking regions, presents special problems of governance. The question of how best to govern Canada has frequently troubled the French, British, and more recently, the Canadian rulers themselves. Regional conflicts go back to the late eighteenth century, when 40,000 residents of the newly independent United States emigrated to Nova Scotia, New Foundland, and Ontario in order to remain British citizens. Canada's English speaking population was only slightly less than the 60,000 existing French speaking Canadians largely settled in the province of Quebec. Conflict between the French and English speaking regions has shaped politics to this day, exacerbated by the varying economic interests of the provinces. These problems of economic and ethnic regionalism have been alleviated through a Federal system whereby the ten provincial and two territorial governments share power with the national parliament.

Despite these difficulties, Canada's political history has been surprisingly free of violence. It took over a century, however, for the original French colony to become firmly established. The French explorer, Jacques Cartier, took possession of Canada for the King of France in 1534, but although different expeditions subsequently arrived to exploit the vast fur trade, the first French colony was not established until 1604.

However, few French emigrated to the Canadian wilderness during the early seventeenth century so in 1629 the King granted the Company of New France a monopoly over the fur trade in return for a promise to send several hundred settlers a year.

The transfer of Canada from French to British rule after the Treaty of Paris (1763) accelerated its development. Immigrants from Britain and later from the United States streamed into Canada to push back the frontiers. As Canada's population swelled in numbers and economic vitality grew, pressures rose for more local participation in government. London passed the Constitutional Act (1791) which added an elected legislative assembly with taxation and budget powers to the government, and divided the colony into French speaking Lower and English speaking Upper Canada.

Throughout the early nineteenth century French Canadians became more frustrated with the arrangement and pressures correspondingly grew for an elective Council. Economic depression in the mid-1830s and the fiery leadership of Louis Papineau sparked the 1837 Canadian Rebellion. Although the revolt was quickly put down, it stimulated a report by newly appointed governor, Lord Durham, calling for Canada's reunification with self-government in local issues. In 1840 Canada was unified, and in 1848 local autonomy was recognized. However, riots broke out the following year among the English Canadians over a government bill which compensated all victims of the 1837 revolt – loyalists and rebels alike. Governor Eligin's attempts to veto the London bill on grounds of local autonomy failed, and mobs ended up burning down parliament. More reforms followed.

On July 1, 1867, the North America Act united the four colonies; Nova Scotia and New Brunswick were joined with Quebec and Ontario to form the federal Dominion of Canada. Although Newfoundland refused to join until 1949, other provinces including Manitoba (1870), British Columbia (1871), Prince Edward Island (1873), and Alberta and Saskatchewan (1905) followed. Manitoba was created in response to the First Riel Rebellion (1869) in the Red River valley. Like other Canadian revolts the Riel Rebellion was fuelled from a combination of economic depression, political underrepresentation, and inspiring leadership under Louis Riel. A Second Riel Rebellion, this time in Saskatchewan, broke out in 1885 for similar reasons. The government quickly crushed the rebellion, executed Riel, yet refused to create a separate province. The government's refusal to compromise led to the emergence of a French separatist party in Quebec.

Despite some local discontent, Canadian politics became dominated by a two-party system shortly after receiving dominion status. Both the Liberal and Conservative parties were founded in 1867, modelled after their British counterparts. The Liberal Party favoured more Canadian autonomy, free trade, welcomed foreign investment for industrial development, and pushed for closer relations with the United States. In contrast, the Conservative Party which governed Canada for most of the late nineteenth century strongly supported allegiance to the British Empire, favoured high trade barriers to stimulate local industry, and was anti-American. In 1933, the two-party system became a multi-party system when the New Democratic Party (NDP) was formed out of an alliance of the United Farmers Party, Socialist Party, and smaller groups. Like its inspiration, the British Labour Party, the NDP favours democratic socialism and is more anti-American. In 1968 the *Parti Québécois* (PQ) was founded by former Liberal Party leader René Levesque who rallied mass support for an independent Quebec. Although his party won the province of Quebec from the Liberal Party in 1976, a 1980 referendum on independence was voted down by 59 per cent to 41 per cent.

Since 1869, Canada has been governed under a Westminster-style parliamentary system. The Queen is the head of state, represented by the London-appointed Governor-General in Ottawa and Lieutenant-Governors heading the provincial governments. Real power lies in the prime minister and cabinet whose ranks are filled by representatives of the largest party or coalition of parties in parliament. Although the prime minister does not need to be a current member of parliament, he must win in a by-election before he can take office. Policy is made in three arenas: 11 cabinet committees covering key issue areas include relevant ministers, party MPs, and senior civil service officials; the Prime Minister's Office and Privy Council then co-ordinate policy from the party and civil service perspectives.

Parliament has two chambers. The House of Commons has 282 single member district seats. Although its main duty is law-making and individual MPs can introduce legislature, most laws originate in the ministries. All citizens 18 years old and over can vote and election turnouts vary between 65 per cent to 80 per cent depending on the province and issues. Under the Election Campaign Act (1974) the state subsidizes candidates by allowing tax credits for gifts up to $500 if the party either has one MP already in parliament or fields candidates in at least 50 electoral districts. Campaign expenditures are limited to no more than 80 cents per voter. Candidates do not have to be from the district in which they are elected. The Senate has 104 seats, all of which are appointed by the Prime Minister as replacements occur when senators either resign or reach the mandatory retirement age of 75. The Senate has no power to block legislature and simply reviews lower house laws while serving chiefly as a retirement ground for older politicians rewarded for their long service.

Canada's Supreme Court includes eight Justices and one Chief Justice who are appointed by the prime minister with parliament's approval. The Supreme Court combines judicial review of court cases with the power of attorney general to review any law at the request of government. Each province has its own assembly with considerable powers. The provinces are often more effective than the opposition parties in parliament in blocking government initiatives.

Economic history. Until the mid-nineteenth century, Canada's economy was dominated by the fur trade, with farming and fishing playing supporting roles. The drive for new fur grounds lead the Hudson Bay Company, Northwest Company, and other ventures to spread west and north across the Canadian wilderness. Alexander Mackenzie led expeditions which reached the Arctic Ocean in 1789 and the Pacific Ocean in 1793. As in America the fur trappers led the way for subsequent settlement by mapping the wilderness and creating trade posts for farmers, miners, and merchants.

Canada first began to industrialize in the 1850s when the first railroads were built, stimulating a need for large-scale steel, mining, and related industries. Industrialization was further boosted by government tariff policies which protected infant industries. The settlement of the great plains during this time boosted large scale agriculture while the discovery of gold in British Columbia stimulated settlement in that province. In 1885 the transcontinental railroad was finally completed which united Canada in a tenuous economic union. Canada's economy has developed steadily throughout the twentieth century based on its rich spectrum of natural resources, vast farmlands, and expanding industrial base.

Foreign policy. Much of Canada's foreign policy since receiving Dominion status in 1867 has revolved around distancing itself from British foreign policy. The lockstep was first questioned in 1899 during the Boer War when many protested the use of Canadian troops in that distant struggle. Although few questioned Canadian participation in World War I, Canadian nationalism was given a boost when in 1916 four Canadian divisions were united into one corps under a Canadian commander, the prime minister was allowed a seat on the Imperial War Cabinet, and Canada received a separate seat at the Versailles Peace Conference in 1919.

Canada's ability to follow an independent foreign policy accelerated during the 1920s. In 1920, Canada's first official embassy was set up in Washington D.C. In 1922, Prime Minister King refused a British request for troops while the following year demonstrated Canada's treaty-making power by negotiating and signing the Hailibut treaty with the United States. At the 1926 Imperial Conference, Canada declared that its dominions were equal partners with Britain, bound together by a common crown. The Statute of Westminster (1931) legalized this policy. During the 1930s Canada broke again with Britain and refused to agree to sanctions against either Japan (1932) or Italy (1936), and in 1940 delayed a declaration of war against Germany one week after Britain.

While clearly independent, Ottawa's post-1945 foreign policy has centred on making Canada a firm and prosperous member of the Western military and economic alliance. Despite its relatively small population, Canada has been a member of the Group of Seven industrial nations throughout the 1980s. As its dominant trade and investment partner, the United States will remain the centre-piece of Canadian foreign policy. Relations remain good; a free trade treaty was signed in 1988 designed to remove all trade barriers between the two countries within a decade and negotiations continue over the acid rain issue.

Recent political and economic trends. The Liberal government under Pierre Trudeau gave Canadian sovereignty two major boosts in 1981. The Foreign Investments Review Act attempted to control American and other foreign investments in Canada to prevent "neocolonization". In November the Constitutional Reform Act was approved which at once strengthened the central government over the provinces, presented Canadians with a Charter of Rights, and asserted Canada's ability to amend the Constitution without London's approval provided that seven of 10 provinces with 50 per cent or more of the population agree.

These policies failed to address a faltering economy and the Progressive Conservative Party under Brian Mulroney swept into power in 1984 with 211 of the 282 seats in the House of Commons. Mulroney's government addressed popular concerns by introducing a simplified tax code and lower taxes, and regional concerns through an amendment allowing any province to opt out of an amendment for renewable five-year periods. In 1988 it signed a free-trade agreement with the United States designed to remove almost all trade and investment barriers within 10 years. Although the treaty was greatly criticized by the opposition parties, a December election resulted in another Conservative Party victory.

WN

CAPITAL PUNISHMENT. A large number of countries in the Pacific region retain the death penalty and have been the target of campaigning by the human rights organization Amnesty International. They include the United States, although the death penalty is employed only in the minority of the states, mostly in the south.

Some countries, like Tonga, have not employed the death penalty in recent years, though it remains on the statute books. Others retain it for a very restricted number of crimes, particularly treason and murder (e.g. Japan). Amnesty has been especially concerned about executions of people charged with drug trafficking in Southeast Asia, notably Malaysia and Singapore (where the death sentence is mandatory for that crime).

In China, the death penalty is available for a very wide range of offences and executions often take place very quickly after sentencing. In 1986, for example, 257 death sentences were documented in China. Some of the condemned prisoners were publicly paraded before being shot. A frequent method of execution in China is a single shot in the back of the head.

JF

CENSORSHIP. In theory, the whole gamut of censorship and the media is represented around the Pacific, from a rigidly controlled system such as China's, to a theoretically free press in the United States. In practice, the situation is far more blurred. Censorship of one kind or another is to be found in every nation. It is most obvious in hightly centralized, bureaucratic states such as North Korea, but most Marxist and Third World governments impose some sort of political control on the media. Violations can lead to enterprises being closed down (as happened for a while to the newspaper *La Prensa* in Nicaragua) or to the harassment, imprisonment or murder of offending journalists and publishers. Nor is it just governments which exert such control. Vested interests of one kind or another can be ruthless in trying to suppress exposes of their activities.

A classic case is the intimidation and assassination of journalists in Colombia by the big drugs cartels.

Self-censorship is even more widespread, though sometimes more difficult to identify. On occasions, this may be a voluntary editorial decision after an approach from government – such as the restraint of the US media in not reporting developments which might jeopardize the fate of US hostages in the Middle East. At other times, there is an underlying will not to offend those in power, in case this should lead to the cutting-off of sources of news – a phenomenon notable until recently in Japan. Newspapers and radio and TV stations in capitalist societies will also tend to try to avoid offending major advertisers. Direct or indirect interference in editorial control by big business is a sensitive area in countries such as the United States, Canada and Australia.

The 1980s saw a considerable liberalization of censorship in much of Latin America, including a relaxation of controls on sexually titillating material or pornography. Both the Catholic Church and Islam have championed a backlash against such liberalism in different parts of the Pacific region, as has the Communist Party in China. The situation does vary enormously from country to country, as well as within countries which have federal systems that give provincial or even city authorities considerable powers over what can be publicly shown or put on sale. The boom in videos has, however, undermined some of this censorship of visual material.

JF

CHAOVALIT YONGCHAIYUT, GEN.

Following rumours of an impending coup in Thailand in May 1986, Gen. Prem (the Prime Minister) dismissed his Army C.-in-C., Gen. Arthit Kamlang-Ek, and appointed in his place Gen. Chaovalit, hitherto Deputy Army Chief of Staff. Chaovalit, a class one graduate of Chulachomklo Royal Military Academy, immediately pledged to detach the military from politics and to retire from his post after two years. However, in public addresses and press interviews during early 1987 Gen. Chaovalit made numerous overtly political comments and, on a number of occasions, was harshly critical of politicians. In particular, he repeatedly advocated a "peaceful revolution" (*patiwat*) in Thailand, involving structural changes within the political, economic and social sphere. Chaovalit's self-proclaimed role as a "soldier for democracy" led to accusations (from, amongst others, Kukrit Pramoj) that he had been influenced by communism. However, his position

was strengthened in October 1987 when several of his former Chulachomklo classmates were promoted to some of the highest Army posts. Chaovalit took on, in an acting capacity, the largely ceremonial role of Supreme Commander of the Armed Forces. In April 1988 Chaovalit announced that he would soon retire as Army C.-in-C., thereby keeping the promise he had made at the time of his appointment. Gen. Prem refused to accept his resignation in an attempt, according to some reports, to stop him becoming a potential political rival. A staunch supporter of Prem, he was conspicuous by his absence of involvement in the July 1988 elections and was clearly aware of Prem's desire to step down from political life. His support for Prem's successor, **Maj.-Gen. Chatichai Choonhaven** appears to be firm and he has asserted that no military coup would be allowed to occur while he commanded the Army. According to some sources Chaovalit has already formulated plans for the formation of a new "mass" political party to ease his inevitable entry into politics.

DS

CHART THAI (THAILAND).

The right-wing *Chart Thai* (Thai Nation Party) gained the largest number of seats in the July 1988 House of Representative elections and subsequently became the dominant force in a six-member ruling coalition. The party's leader, **Maj.-Gen. Chatichai Choonhaven**, was appointed Prime Minister in August 1988. Defections from the **Prachachon** Party in April 1989 increased the number of *Chart Thai* MPs from 87 to 96.

The party was founded in 1974 by three generals who had played a prominent role in military regimes of the 1950s. It joined coalition governments headed by Kukrik and Seni Pramoj in the mid-1970s and following the October 1976 military coup, elements associated with the party tried and failed to stage their own coup in March 1977 (the leader of the attempt, Gen. Chalard Hiranyasiri, being executed). Having won 47 seats (the third largest number) in 1979, the party joined Gen. Prem's coalition government in March 1980. It gained the second largest number of seats in the 1983 elections, but was not included in Gen. Prem's new coalition. In the July 1986 elections it again achieved second place, and subsequently joined a further coalition headed by Gen. Prem.

DS

CHATICHAI CHOONHAVEN, MAJ.-GEN.

Maj. Gen. Chatichai was appointed Thailand's

Prime Minister and Minister of Defence in August 1988, succeeding Gen. Prem Tinsulanonda. He was the first Prime Minister to sit in the House of Representatives as an MP since the overthrow of Seni Pramoj by a right-wing military junta in October 1976.

Chatichai was born in 1922 and was a graduate of the Chulachomklao Royal Military Academy. He served in the First Royal Cavalry Guards until 1958 (when the Pibul regime, of which his father, Pin Choonhaven, had been a deputy Prime Minister, fell) before switching to a diplomatic career. He was elected as MP for Nakhon Ratchasima province in 1975 and that year was appointed Foreign Minister in the Kukrit Pramoj government. He became leader of the *Chart Thai* Party in 1986 and was appointed Deputy Prime Minister in the second Prem government the same year.

DS

CHIANG CHING-KUO. Chiang Ching-kuo, the eldest son of **Chiang Kai-shek**, was born in 1909 in Fenghua, Chekiang province. After attending middle school he went to the USSR in 1925 to study at Sun Yat-sen University in Moscow and the Tolmatzhev Military and Political Institute in Leningrad. During these years he entered the Communist Youth Corps and was accepted as a member of the Communist Party of the Soviet Union (CPSU). After finishing his studies in 1930 he engaged in political work among Chinese students in Moscow. Due to a conflict with the party leadership he was soon transferred and worked as a manager in the manufacturing industry.

After nearly 12 years in the USSR he was finally allowed to return to China, several previous requests having been declined by the Soviet authorities. In April 1937 he arrived in Shanghai, accompanied by his Russian wife and two children. Under the personal oversight of his father he spent several months studying the Chinese classics. Proving himself as a competent official in his first appointment late in 1937, he was soon promoted to a supervisory position in Southern Jiangsi. In 1938 he began to organize a youth league and also undertook a modest reform and rehabilitation programme for the society and the economy. The programme, combining elements of Marxism-Leninism and **Confucianism**, was carried out efficiently and sometimes ruthlessly, traits that came to characterize much of his later political career.

Having demonstrated his efficiency and reliability his father entrusted him with a number of important tasks from 1944. As Dean of the Youth Cadres Training School in Chungking he headed the belated efforts by the **Kuomintang** (KMT) to regain influence among China's youths. The following year he participated in two important missions to Moscow and was appointed special foreign affairs commissioner for Manchuria, responsible for the negotiations with the Soviet Army on the transfer of power to the Nationalist government. Although his appointment as deputy economic supervisor for Shanghai in 1948 proved to be unsuccessful, the methods he used to fight inflation reinforced his reputation as a ruthless administrator.

In the final year of KMT rule on the mainland, Chiang worked as a trusted aide of his father in a number of difficult missions. He established the KMT provincial party headquarters on Taiwan in preparation for the Nationalist retreat to the island and was also involved in the KMT's last efforts to defend the Mainland against the advancing Communists.

On Taiwan Chiang was instrumental in the efforts to secure the island for KMT rule. In the 1950s he was involved in the establishment of a number of organizations, with tasks as different as security, mobilization and social welfare. His influence in the KMT grew. He was called to serve on the KMT reform committee, and during the 7th National Congress (NC) in 1952 he was elected on to the Central and Central Standing Committees.

Chiang's close affiliation with military and security affairs lasted until 1969, when he was appointed Vice-Premier. During these years he held the positions of Deputy Secretary-General of the National Security Council (1954), Deputy Minister (1963) and Minister of Defence (1964). As Vice-Premier he became intimately involved in the planning of Taiwan's economic development and the transformation of its economy.

Promoted to the position of Premier in 1972 Chiang initiated a policy of rejuvenation and Taiwanizatioin in both government and party. His final ascent to the apex of Taiwan's power structure was accomplished with his election as president in 1978, having already succeeded his father as chairman of the KMT in 1975. His rule was marred by growing health problems and political crises, however, which inhibited further reforms. It was only after his re-election to a second term in office that Chiang began to promote political reform again, by initiating the six-point reform programme at the KMT's 3rd Plenum of 12th NC. He died, however, before the aims of the programme had been accomplished, in 1988.

HH

CHIANG KAI-SHEK. Chiang Kai-shek (Chiang Chieh-shih) was born in 1887 into a family of salt merchants in Fenghua, Zhejiang province. After finishing his middle school education Chiang entered a military academy continuing his studies at a military school for Chinese in Tokyo during the years 1908–10. In Japan Chiang came into contact with Sun Yat-sen's "Revolutionary Alliance" (*T'ung-meng-hui*) and became a member in 1908. During the republican revolution of 1911 and again in the 1913 revolution against Yuan Shih-k'ai, he fought in the Sunist forces. After Sun had re-established a base in Southern China, Chiang became one of his main military aides, entrusted with numerous difficult tasks.

As Sun's chief of staff he was sent on a study tour to the USSR in 1923. On his return he was elected into the **Kuomintang's** (KMT) Military Council and became head of the party's newly established Whampoa Military Academy. The Whampoa graduates were to form one of the important factions within the KMT and, deeply loyal to him, became one of the main pillars of his rule.

After Sun's death in 1925 Chiang was only an outsider in the ensuing struggle for succession. His position improved, however, due to his successful leadership in the Northern Campaign and his adroit handling of the Chinese Communists, whose influence in the KMT he reduced considerably. As commander of the party's armed forces, moreover, he was in control of one of the major power bases.

In the Nationalist government, established in Nanking in 1927 after the victory in the Northern Expedition, Chiang headed the National Military Council and, later on, also became chairman of the Central Political Council and the National Government.

Confronted with the Japanese invasion in Manchuria in 1931, Chiang as commander-in-chief of the armed forces, adopted a delaying strategy, to gain time to create armed forces that could match the technically superior Japanese Army. Convinced that success in repelling the Japanese invasion was predicated on a united home front Chiang decided first to eliminate the Communist rebellion before attacking Japan. This highly unpopular policy was changed in the aftermath of the Xian Incident in 1936, when disgruntled troops had imprisoned Chiang, demanding the termination of warfare against the Communists and a vigorous campaign against Japan. When war against Japan was formally declared in 1937, however, Chiang became the symbol of Chinese resistance against Japanese aggression.

Although forced by the advancing Japanese forces to retreat inland, Chiang's reputation grew during the war years. In 1943 he participated in the Cairo Conference and was elected chairman of the National Government, a position equivalent to head of state.

Within the KMT, Chiang strove to emulate Sun as politician and philosopher. In 1928, he was finally recognized as the party's paramount leader and elected *tsung-ts'ai*, giving him veto powers against all party decisions. As a political philosopher he tried to fuse traditional Chinese concepts with modern Western ideas. His ideas found their practical expression in the "New Life Movement", a programme of moral reform started in the area of the former Jiangsi Soviet, and in numerous speeches and publications.

With the Chinese victory over Japan in 1945 Chiang's popularity had reached its apex, but it soon began to wane. Returning to the liberated areas both the government and the KMT turned out to be incompetent and corrupt. Enmity between the KMT and the Chinese Communists had not ceased, negotiations between both parties soon ended in failure and the civil war flared up again.

In 1948 Chiang was elected as the Republic of China's first president under the new constitution, an office he held only until early 1949, when he retired due to the worsening situation in the civil war. He continued to serve as *tsung-ts'ai* of the KMT, however, and to exert strong influence on Chinese politics. His efforts to organize the defence of South-west China against the advancing Communist forces were unsuccessful, and in December 1949 Chiang retreated to Taiwan.

Chiang returned from political retirement in early 1950 and retook the presidency, an office to which he was re-elected several times until his death in 1975. Under his leadership the KMT underwent an extensive organizational and programmatical reform. With American aid Chiang reorganized his administration and the armed forces, and Taiwan was developed as a "model province" for a future re-unified China under Nationalist rule. Unimpressed by worsening international circumstances Chiang held fast to his hope of regaining the Chinese mainland and to the claim that his government represented the sole legal government of China.

HH

CHILE, REPUBLIC OF. *Population*: 12,500,000 (1981). *Area*: 765,945 sq km. *Gross Domestic Product*: US$9,810 million. *Trade*: US$7,357.1 million. *Main trading partners*: USA, Japan, West Germany, Brazil, UK. *Defence* *spending*: US$817 million. *Education spending as percentage of Gross National Product*: 5.8. *Urban population as percentage of total*: 68. *Birth rate*: 23 per thousand. *Life expectancy*: males 52; females 56.

Geographical background. Chile is a long strip of land 4,270 km north to south, only 64 km wide at its narrowest point. It is divided into three main regions: the desert north, the cold south with its fjords and island archipelagos terminating in Tierra del Fuego, and the temperate central area. The latter is divided laterally into the High Andes in the east along the border with Argentina, the low coastal mountains in the west and the fertile, alluvial plain of the Central Valley between the two. The country has an enormous range from subtropical desert in the north to tundra in the south. There is a mediterranean climate in the populous middle third, including the capital, Santiago, which is cooled by the Humboldt Current from the Antarctic. Around 1.2 million hectares of land are cultivated. There are 6,236 km (1983) of railways running on a variety of gauges used for both passenger and mineral transport. There are about 79,010 km (1983) of roads, 89 per cent completely unpaved. Coastal shipping is very important for transport within the country; inland navigation is very limited owing to waterfalls and rapids. Domestic and international air travel is provided by the national airline (LAN) as well as by foreign carriers. Ninety per cent of the population live in the central third of the country. Major cities are Santiago (with a population of four million) followed by Valparaíso (population 500,000) and Concepción (population 170,000).

Socio-political background. Aboout two-thirds of Chileans are *mestizo* (mixed Spanish and Amerindian), the remainder mainly European with a small number of pure Amerindian descent. Spanish is the national language. A small number of Indians speak Mapuche and some German is spoken in the area around the coastal city of Valdivia. The vast majority of the population is nominally Roman Catholic. Fundamentalist Protestant sects are becoming more influential. Jewish and Indian religions exist among small groups. Primary education is free and compulsory but non-attendance is high and illiteracy is 11 per cent. The two national universities, the University of Chile and the State Technical University, are located in Santiago, but both have subsidiary campuses in provincial cities. There are also several Catholic universities. Chilean universities were heavily purged in 1973.

Crude death rate is 6.7 per thousand, and the infant mortality rate per thousand is 23.5. The annual population increase is 1.6 per cent. There is an average of one doctor per 1,935 of the population. Relative health expenditure declined after 1973 and malnutrition remains a serious problem. Much of the extensive welfare system established before the 1973 coup has been suspended and/or transferred to the Private Corporation for Social Development (CPDS). Good housing is in short supply (only 13 per cent of rural homes have a water supply and 9 per cent sewerage) and both government and Church agencies are involved in low-cost provision.

Political history. Chile became effectively independent with the defeat of the Spanish forces by the troops of General José de San Martín at the Battle of Maipú in 1818, and after a short period of unrest power was consolidated by a conservative oligarchy which gave Chile stable government for most of the nineteenth century and led the country to victory in the **Pacific War**. Unparalleled prosperity followed the acquisition of the coastal nitrate fields and a brief civil war in 1891 led to the establishment of a parliamentary republic. After the Great War the demand for nitrates collapsed. A period of political instability ensued (1924–32) but democratic institutions survived until 1970 when the election of Dr Salvador Allende to the presidency at the head of a freely elected Marxist government led to increasing unrest and ultimately to the intervention of the armed forces in September 1973.

Following the coup, the commander of the Army, Gen. Augusto Pinochet (designated Supreme Chief of State in 1974) emerged as leader of a government dedicated to stamping out Marxism by force, and thousands of real or suspected opponents of the military regime died or "disappeared". In 1981 the Junta imposed a new Constitution and General Pinochet assumed the title of President he had been granted in 1975. A referendum held in 1988 unexpectedly failed to confirm him in power following which commanders of the armed forces insisted on a return to democratic rule and scheduled elections for the presidency in which the long-banned political parties would be permitted to take part.

Outline of economic development. With the decline of nitrate, copper from the northern mines became Chile's major export resource, making up 46.1 per cent of exports in 1985. Iron ore accounts for 2.5 per cent. Oil from Tierra del Fuego and hydro-electric power met much of domestic energy needs, fuelling industrial development in the central region. The Pinochet regime has carried out the most far reaching experiment in free market economics in the hemisphere under the guidance of adherents of the monetarist Chicago school. Growth in the late 1970s was spectacular, but a sharp recession starting in 1981 led to the failure of thousands of businesses, including some of Chile's largest corporations. Social inequality has increased markedly under the Pinochet regime and the middle classes have benefited while many now live in slum conditions excluded from social security.

Growth has been resumed in the late 1980s and inflation is low by Latin American standards, but Chile's debt stood at US$20.7 billion at the end of 1986, making up over a quarter of the value of exports. With the mineral markets depressed, revenues from copper are down. Over 18 per cent of the population work in agriculture, the prime growth area. Chile has to compete with other low-cost industrial producers, but has been successful with agricultural exports from the fertile central valley.

P&SC

CHINA. *Population*: 1,087 million. *Area*: 9,561,000 sq km. *Gross Domestic Product*: US$295,000 million. *Trade volume*: US$39,638 million. *Top five trading partners*: Hong Kong, Japan, United States, West Germany, USSR. *Defence spending*: US$5,600 million. *Education spending*: US$7,200 million. *Urban population as percentage of total*: 41. *Birth rate*: 21 per thousand. *Life expectancy*: 66 years.

China is by area the third largest state in the world, after the USSR and Canada. It has a land boundary of over 20,000 km and a coast of over 18,000 km. The general relief of the country slopes downwards in stages from the Himalayas in the west to the coastal plains in the east. Roughly 65 per cent of the land is mountainous or high plateau. Only 10 per cent is under cultivation, and most of that is in the east. The climate ranges from sub-tropical Hainan Island in the south east to the hot deserts of Xinjiang in the north west and the cold deserts of Tibet in the west. North-south variations in temperature are small in summer but large in winter. In the dry north and north-east summers are baking and winters very cold. All parts of China experience a winter that is colder than other countries at comparable latitudes.

Water is a particular problem. Rainfall is abundant along the central and southern coasts, but sporadic, or even inadequate, over much of the rest. In ancient China civilization spread along the valleys of the three giant rivers which flow from west to east: the Yellow River, the Yangze and the Pearl. Now largely tamed, those rivers are important sources of irrigation and major channels of communication.

The railway network is relatively small, although it is used intensively. Only 19 per cent of the lines are double-tracked. Road transport is only important locally. Transport bottlenecks are a major constraint upon economic growth. Large deposits of minerals are to be found in the west, and enormous reserves of coal in the central province of Shanxi, but moving them to factories and power stations is still difficult.

Overall population density in 1986 was 110 people per square kilometre, but 94 per cent of the population live on the eastern 40 per cent of the land. In Jiangsu, the most populous province, the density was 611 people per sq km. By contrast the western 60 per cent of Chinese territory contains only 6 per cent of the population. The combination of huge population and slender agricultural land is one of the biggest problems confronting the government. In the early 1980s it set a population target of a maximum of 1,200 million people by the year 2000, but it is already clear that that figure will be exceeded. Meanwhile the area of land under cultivation has been dwindling at the rate of 0.7 per cent per year.

Socio-political background. Roughly 94 per cent of the total population are ethnic Han Chinese. They share the same first language, at least in its written form. In 1956 the People's Republic published simplified versions of 2,200 characters, and these form the basis of written Chinese in China today, although their use has not spread to overseas Chinese communities, except Singapore. The modern standard pronunciation (Mandarin, or *putonghua*) stems from the north around Beijing, but there are major regional variations, with Cantonese (spoken in Guangdong province, in Hongkong, and in most overseas Chinese communities) the most extreme example. Many of these differences are as great as between European languages, and they have supported distinct regional cultural identities. This has complicated the integration of modern China.

Though the frontiers of the Chinese state have fluctuated, the heartland of the Han Chinese has commonly been regarded as the territory bounded in the north and the north west by the Great Wall. The 6 per cent of the population comprising the ethnic minorities chiefly inhabit areas close to China's borders. Some chiefly speak Chinese now (e.g. the Islamic Hui people in the north-west and the Manchus from the north-east). Other large ethnic minorities still speak their own languages, e.g. the Tibetans and the Yi in the west, the Uighurs in the north-west, the Mongols in the north, and the Zhuang and the Miao in the south.

Socially China is still predominantly a rural society. In 1949, 89.4 per cent of the population were officially estimated as living in rural areas, and in 1986 the figure was 58.6 per cent. The urban population has been growing rapidly in the 1980s, however.

Pre-modern history. The traditional Chinese state was based upon the principles of rule by the Emperor and **Confucianism**. It aimed at establishing and preserving a harmony between the human and the divine world, as well as between men. There was a widely held belief that Chinese civilization, which had discovered many of the secrets of such harmony, should be spread to enlighten other peoples. This underpinned the expansion of the Chinese empire.

The first dynasty (the Shang) was founded around 1500 BCE, but the state fell into confusion and civil war, before being reunified by the Qin dynasty (founded 221 BCE). The last dynasty (the Qing, founded 1644 CE) began with a period of unparalleled prosperity and population growth. In the nineteenth century, however, it sank into growing turmoil. Firstly there was renewed pressure and hostilities from across China's north-western border. Then came the Opium Wars in 1840 and 1856 when Britain and France attempted to impose upon China the legalization of the import of opium so as to stimulate trade with the outside world. Between 1850 and 1865 China was also in a state of civil war, with the Taiping and other rebellions in the south only being suppressed with foreign help. Millions of people died.

The imperial system was now fatally weakened and divided. In addition Western powers scrambled to impose increasing "concessions" upon China in the shape of trading centres on Chinese soil which were ruled according to foreign laws under the principle of **extra-territoriality** and where foreigners enjoyed privileged status. Worse, in 1895 China was defeated in a war with the now more rapidly modernizing Japan and was forced to surrender Korea and Taiwan. Following the abortive **Boxer Uprising** in 1900–01, the Chinese state was forced to concede foreign control over one of its chief sources of revenue, customs duties. This inhibited the state from protecting Chinese industrialists from foreign competition. In the end the system collapsed in an almost bloodless revolution in 1911.

Early modern history. There followed a period of great economic and cultural ferment. Industrialists and entrepreneurs took advantage of their new freedom to launch large new projects – this has been described as their "golden age". In culture a whole new movement appeared, inspired by the events of May 4, 1919 (*see* **May 4th Movement**).

Politically, however, the period saw even greater turmoil. The new state was declared a republic, but there was no consensus on the institutions of government. Into the vacuum stepped various regional warlords who vied for power. None proved strong enough to win outright, but together they stymied strong central government. China seemed to be disintegrating. There were, however, two political parties which were trying to restore national unity: the Nationalists (*Guomindang*) and the **Chinese Communist Party (CCP)**. At first they collaborated in fighting the warlords, but in 1927 the Nationalist leader, **Chiang Kai-shek**, arranged a massacre of communist leaders in Shanghai. He drove the CCP out of the cities and into the countryside for nearly twenty years. Between 1928 and 1937 Chiang patched together a fragile national unity. He established the national capital at Nanjing in the south and sought agreements with various warlords, whilst pursuing the communists implacably. In the end the communists were forced to abandon their bases in the south of the country and they embarked upon their epic **Long March** which ended at Yanan in the north.

Meanwhile Japan had been expanding her sphere of influence in China. In 1931 she took over Manchuria, creating the puppet regime of Manchukuo. In 1937 small groups of Chinese and Japanese soldiers clashed outside Beijing and in the aftermath Japan launched a full-scale invasion. Within one year Japan had occupied the cities and railways of eastern China, whilst the Nationalist government had been forced to retreat to the city of Chongqing in the south west. The Nationalist armies, despite their bravery and losses, could not drive back the Japanese, but nor would the government accept defeat. After 1936 it accepted a patriotic alliance with the Communists and this, combined with the Japanese crushing of warlords who had persecuted the Communists, allowed the latter to revive. They infiltrated occupied areas and began a series of guerilla activities to wear down the Japanese. In so doing, they enhanced their image as the most resolute enemies of the Japanese and they showed themselves ready to form alliances with patriotic non-Communist groupings under the principles of **New Democracy**. They also learnt to live and fight among the people, whilst spreading their ideas of revolution. The Nationalist commanders persisted with a strategy of positional warfare and large massed armies, without ever being able to defeat the Japanese.

With the Japanese surrender, the Nationalists were restored to power and they became one of the five great powers with a permanent seat on the newly created UN Security Council. In spring 1946 the civil war broke out again. The Nationalists sought to crush the Communists by massed military force, especially in Manchuria. During the first year they won many victories, even capturing the Communist capital Yanan. They overextended themselves, however, and from mid-1947 onwards the Communists began to roll them back. As the war began to go badly, corruption and incompetence of Nationalist officials alienated increasing numbers of civilians, whilst economic difficulties intensified. During 1948 inflation reached astronomic levels and was regarded as one of the prime causes of the Nationalists' defeat. The Communists won increasing support among the peasantry with moderate land reform. Finally in 1949 the Nationalists retreated to Taiwan, and on October 1 **Mao Zedong** proclaimed the People's Republic of China (PRC).

Political history. During its first three years the leaders of the new regime persisted with the policies of New Democracy. The main domestic consideration was to consolidate political power, re-estabilsh national unity, achieve as far as possible national reconciliation, and revive a mixed economy. In 1953, however, the regime launched its First Five-Year Plan to industrialize China, to create a centralized command economy on the Soviet model, and to carry out a socialist transformation of society. Private enterprise was abolished in urban areas and then, in 1955-56, in the countryside with collectivization of agriculture. Yet despite many successes, Mao became increasingly critical of the Soviet model. China seemed no nearer to catching up advanced industrialized nations, whilst new socio-economic inequalities had appeared. And younger generations seemed to be losing their revolutionary zeal. The intelligentsia expressed such vehement criticism of the regime in the **Hundred Flowers Campaign** of 1957 that the official response was a severe "anti-rightist" campaign, with some punishments lasting over 20 years.

Mao sought to revive mass revolutionary enthusiasm, as well as close the gap with more developed countries, with a new Chinese road to socialism – the Great Leap Forward (GLF). He sought to base it upon the one asset where China was already rich – its population, and to return to the spirit and methods of Yanan. By mobilizing the masses, the Communist leadership hoped to leap into prosperity and socialism. The starting point was decentralization of the command economy. Regional and even more local control was to be preferred. Large numbers of officials were transferred downwards. The new basic unit of life in the countryside, and even briefly in the cities, was to be the commune (*See* **Communes: China**). For the first time in over 20 years, however, Mao disastrously miscalculated. The state and people over-exerted themselves. Mountains of useless pig iron were accumulated in backyard furnaces in the countryside. Normal agricultural work was sacrificed for the sake of large earth-moving projects to build dams and irrigation channels as well as to terrace hills. Because communism now seemed so close, rationing of basic foodstuffs was abandoned. Thus when the weather proved unusually bad in 1959-60, the regime was caught out. In the ensuing famine the overall population declined in 1960 for the only time in the history of the PRC as the death rate almost doubled and over 17 million people died. The hopes of a rapid dash for prosperity died with them. The next few years were ones of reconstruction. The task was complicated by the emerging Sino-Soviet dispute and the decision of Khrushchev in 1960 to withdraw all Soviet aid almost without notice. It was not until 1965 that the Chinese economy regained its 1960 level of output. In the new situation Mao was under a cloud since he was blamed for the excesses of the GLF. Day-to-day management of the nation's affairs passed to the head of state, **Liu Shaoqi**, the Prime Minister, **Zhou Enlai**, and the party General Secretary, **Deng Xiaoping**.

Mao retreated to the second line of decision-making, except in the field of foreign affairs. He played a leading role in the embittering of Sino-Soviet relations in the first half of the 1960s and came to see the degeneration of the Soviet regime as a warning for the PRC. In the end he launched the Cultural Revolution in 1966. This swept away his rivals in the party. Liu Shaoqi was condemned as "China's Khrushchev" and hounded to death. Deng Xiaoping and others were driven from power. In their place emerged the Cultural Revolution Group led by Mao's former political secretary, Chen Boda, and Mao's wife, **Jiang Qing**. Beyond them, Mao exalted the Red Guards, whom he urged to "bombard the headquarters" and reviewed in mass parades on Tiananmen Square. The image of Mao, the "Great Helmsman", whose thoughts were encapsulated in the little Red Book and said to be higher than Mount Everest and deeper than the Pacific, soared over everything.

In 1967 the country sank into anarchy. Government was paralysed. The party ceased to play its leading role. The **People's Liberation Army (PLA)** was divided. Groups of Red Guards fought in the streets and stole weapons. Thousands of people were massacred. In the end regional army commanders felt impelled to restore order.

In April 1969, at the Ninth Party Congress, following border fighting with the Soviet Union the previous month, Defence Minister Lin Biao was hailed as Mao's new successor. Three-quarters of the old Central Committee had been removed, and now the PLA provided nearly half of all the members. The party organization and civilian administration were to be reconstructed under military tutelage. The regime was beginning to appear, certainly to the Soviet leadership, as a militarized dictatorship.

In 1971, however, Lin Biao was killed in a plane crash in Mongolia, allegedly while attempting to flee to the Soviet Union after an abortive plot to kill Mao. The role of the PLA was downgraded, and the national leadership was beset by factionalism and mutual suspicion. Mao was becoming more feeble, so that he found it increasingly difficult to impose his will or even know what he wanted. Prime Minister Zhou Enlai contracted cancer and increasingly conducted national business from his bed. Deng Xiaoping returned from the political wilderness in 1973 to act as Zhou's deputy, but was swept aside again in April 1976 after the **Tiananmen Incident**. Finally Mao died in September 1976. **Hua Guofeng** emerged as his successor, and within one month the rival "Maoist" **Gang of Four** had been arrested. Nevertheless there was still a lot of confusion over the future path of development, as well as over the legacy of the Cultural Revolution. There were still many of the Long March generation of party leaders alive who had suffered during the Cultural Revolution and to whom younger party members, including Hua Guofeng, had to defer now that Mao was dead. Amongst this older generation Deng was a symbol for their pent-up resentment about their treatment in the Cultural Revolution.

Deng's rehabilitation was agreed in 1977, and in December 1978 he was re-admitted to the Central Committee at its Third Plenum, which inaugurated the reforms of the 1980s. After that Deng pushed very hard for the rehabilitation of cadres disgraced during the Cultural Revolution. When the process was officially ended in 1983, unjust verdicts against three million cadres had been reversed, many posthumously.

Initially Hua Guofeng launched his version of the **Four Modernizations** programme, but this proved hopelessly over-ambitious. This undermined Hua Guofeng's credibility as a new Mao, and he was fairly swiftly pushed aside as General Secretary by **Hu Yaobang**, and as Prime Minister by **Zhao Ziyang**, both of whom were Deng's clients. The next few years saw a rapid expansion of the reform programme, as older generations of

political leaders were now retired and younger generations of cadres brought forward rapidly. According to Deng, the chief goal was to build "socialism with Chinese characteristics", and in 1987 it was officially declared that China was still in the "initial stage of socialism", a phase which might last until 2049.

In agriculture peasants acquired new freedoms. The communes were abolished in 1983, and with them the old forms of state interference in agriculture, although peasants were still expected to deliver quotas of staple crops to the state until 1985. In industry measures were taken to expand the use of market mechanisms for determining the performance of enterprises, e.g. through the vastly increased use of bank loans and credit as a source of new funds for enterprises, while the latter were also permitted to retain greater shares of their profits. Although prices were liberalized, however, they still remained subject to important state guidelines. The most dramatic element in the reform programme, however, was the decision to open the economy to the outside world, and to permit the establishment of **Special Economic Zones** on the south-east coast, where foreigners could invest and operate with much greater freedom from Beijing's control. The 1980s have seen an unprecedented opening of the country to the outside world, with mushrooming numbers of businessmen and tourists, as well as an increasing influx of foreign culture, not to mention pornography and crime.

Economically the 1980s saw a spurt in Chinese performance. Overall growth in output rose by an average annual rate of 10.1 per cent between 1979 and 1986. Once again regions were allowed to specialize in products for which they had been traditionally famous, rather than strive for local self-sufficiency in basic crops. The 30 provincial-level units of government acquired greater autonomy to run their own affairs than at any time since 1949. A greater variety of products appeared in the shops and the newly re-opened markets. On the other hand, the socialist purity of the regime seemed to be declining in the eyes of the old guard, and they were especially worried about corrupting foreign influences. In 1983 there was a campaign against "spiritual pollution" and in 1987 one against "bourgeois liberalization".

The issue of thorough-going political reform was less seriously addressed, and the apparent indifference of the party leadership to this issue, coupled with increasing evidence of individual corruption among cadres, provoked protests, especially among students. The end of 1986 saw student demonstrations demanding more extensive political reform, and Hu Yaobang was deposed as party General Secretary for failing to deal decisively with them, being replaced by Zhao Ziyang. In 1988 **Li Peng** replaced Zhao Ziyang as Prime Minister.

The first half of 1988 saw a more decisive push towards radical price reform. This also, however, pushed up the inflation rate, so that already by the late summer disagreements between leaders over the speed of economic reform had broken out. Social unrest intensified, and protests by dissidents such as Professor **Fang Lizhi** mounted. Finally on April 15, 1989 former General Secretary Hu Yaobang died, and in a spontaneous outburst to mark his death Beijing students mounted a demonstration on Tiananmen Square demanding political reform. This escalated as it merged with the commemoration of the 70th anniversary of the May 4 movement. The demonstration greatly disrupted the official arrangement for the official state visit to China of President Gorbachev. Even a declaration of martial law by Premier Li Peng merely strengthened resistance, and led to speculation about disagreements between PLA commanders. Zhao Ziyang and Li Peng attempted to negotiate with the students, but clearly could not agree among themselves how far to go. Finally in the early hours of June 4 new contingents of heavily armed troops loyal to Deng Xiaoping, President **Yang Shangkun**, and Li Peng, stormed into the square, supported by tanks and armoured personnel carriers, to crush the protests. NATO estimates have put the death toll in the region of 7,000, either in the square itself, or in the surrounding streets. The mayor of Beijing has claimed 200 civilians were killed, and 6,000 security personnel either killed or wounded.

In the aftermath Zhao Ziyang was removed as party General Secretary and was replaced by the party boss in Shanghai, Jiang Zemin. This was followed by a purge of the party, with liberal reformers being dismissed and many arrested. Some action was also taken against corrupt officials. It seemed to inaugurate the most draconian clampdown on foreign ideas in the 1980s, a slowing of economic reform, and an austerity drive.

Foreign relations. When Mao announced the establishment of the PRC, he declared that China had "stood up" in the world. The main preoccupation of the PRC leadership since then has been to ensure that China plays a full part in world affairs despite her economic backwardness. In addition, at least until the early 1980s, the line of the Chinese leadership was that world war between capitalism and socialism was inevitable.

Basically China's foreign relations can be divided into three periods: (i) between 1949 and 1957; (ii) between 1958 and 1971; and (iii) since 1971. Initially the PRC leaders opted for a full part in the socialist camp, and this led to China's isolation from the non-communist world. Despite past differences with Stalin, Mao visited Moscow in 1950 and signed a 30-year Treaty of Friendship with the USSR. This committed China to full economic and military co-operation. Its first Five-Year Plan was approved in Moscow before Beijing. When the Korean War broke out, China played a full part in providing first logistical support, and later large numbers of troops, to aid North Korea. Later China supported Soviet suppression of the rebellion in Hungary. During the 1950s the PRC saw itself as a source and model for revolution in Asia, with the United States as the principal opponent. The PRC actively aided guerrilla movements in South East Asia. At the same time, however, China was a founder member of the Non-Aligned Movement, and helped to formulate the **Five Principles of Peaceful Coexistence** which were supposed to serve as the basis for the new international order.

However, differences within the bloc rapidly escalated after 1957. In Mao's eyes, no sooner had the USSR achieved a superiority over the US by putting the first sputnik into space, than Khrushchev started to explore the possibilities for strategic arms treaties with the West. Also Mao was concerned by the USSR's apparent reluctance to come to its support during the Second Taiwan Straits crisis of 1958, although he had failed to warn Moscow before launching a bombardment of Nationalist positions. The Great Leap Forward was intended to demonstrate the viability of China's own road to socialism for other socialist states to follow, but only Albania responded. Its failure, coupled with the withdrawal of Soviet aid, made China's position much more difficult. In 1962 she fought a border war with India over disputed territory in Ladakh, and the USSR inclined towards India. She attempted to foment revolution in Southeast Asia, but this prevented a rapprochement with the United States, and it went disastrously wrong with a failed communist coup in Indonesia in 1965. Basically the 1960s saw China gradually retreat into herself, with occasional unpredictable outbursts, as during the Cultural Revolution. At the same time she built her own nuclear bomb as a guarantee of independence. She needed however to break out of isolation.

Two events between 1969 and 1971 transformed the situation. Firstly, there was the border conflict with the Soviet Union in 1969. Although the actual conflict remained localized, for a while Moscow considered a pre-emptive nuclear strike against the PRC's nuclear testing facilities in Xinjiang. This apparently split the PRC leadership. Some, such as Lin Biao, wanted an accommodation with Moscow. The other group, including Mao and Zhou Enlai, prevailed. They were prepared to seek a rapprochement with the USA, once it had become clear that it was scaling down its involvement in Vietnam, so as to counterbalance the threat from Moscow. Indeed they now came to see the Soviet Union, the source of "social imperialism", as a greater threat to world peace than the USA. Secret meetings between Zhou Enlai and US Secretary of State Kissinger laid the basis for the visit of President Nixon to China in February 1972. This, and the **Shanghai Communiqué** which was signed, opened a new era in Sino-Western co-operation. The US now officially accepted the view of both the PRC and also the Nationalists on Taiwan that the latter island was part of China, whoever happened to be ruling it. At least at the level of rhetoric, however, the PRC attached great store to what it now termed the "second world", i.e. the countries of Western and Eastern Europe, hoping that these countries together might prevent the two superpowers from launching a nuclear war.

The second event came in 1971, when the PRC finally won recognition of great power status when she gained enough votes to replace Taiwan as the sole representative of China at the United Nations. This opened a new arena for Chinese foreign policy, where she could use her position as the only Third World state with permanent representation on the Security Council to act as a leader of developing nations. It was only after Mao's death that this political opening was accompanied by economic and cultural changes. Increasing trade and cultural agreements have been signed between China and the rest of the world, and the PRC has sought to play a larger part in international economic organizations such as the World Bank. She also envisages joining GATT. Her foreign relations in the 1980s have become more omni-directional and more complex. Her relations with the USA, although warm, have lost some of their cordiality, whilst those with the USSR have become more sympathetic. She is also looking for closer co-operation with Western Europe and Latin America.

The integration of foreign policy has become looser. Relations with individual countries are handled on the basis of mutual interest with few ideological hindrances. During the Iran–Iraq war her Ministry of Defence allowed missiles to be sold to both sides, as well as selling Intermediate Range Ballistic Missiles to Saudi Arabia. This has, however, weakened her claim to moral leadership of the Third World. Although the PRC has

reduced the size of her armed forces by 25 per cent in the 1980s, she has been able to make a bigger impact on world affairs, as her leaders have become more skilled in international diplomacy, and as her neighbours have been reassured about her long-term intentions. Indonesia and Singapore have put the issue of normalizing relations with the PRC back on the agenda. Saudi Arabia, which still recognizes Taiwan as the legitimate government of China, plans to establish a government trade office in Beijing. There are, however, a number of territorial disputes. Though those with the USSR and India appear on the way to resolution, there is still the problem of the **Spratly Islands** in the South China Seas, which is disputed with Vietnam, Taiwan, Malaysia and the Philippines. The PRC navy sank some Vietnamese boats in a confrontation in 1988. There is the issue of Kampuchea, which led to a border war with Vietnam in 1979. More generally there is the possibility of increasing friction with Japan as both build up their economic strength and seek to play the roles of regional powers. (*See also* **China–North Korea Security Relations**; **China–Taiwan Conflict**; **China–Vietnam Conflict**)

Outline of economic development. In 1949 China was still an overwhelmingly agricultural country. The main direction of economic development since then has been to industrialize, whilst at the same time growing enough food to feed the population. Given China's economic backwardness, the construction of basic heavy industries, as well as of economic infrastructure, has obviously been the top priority. The first Five-Year Plan sought to lay the foundation for China's industrialization, using Soviet-type methods of centralized planning, the squeezing of newly collectivized agriculture to finance industry, the imposition of the Soviet principle of **one-man-management** to bring discipline to factories, and the readiness to use high piece-rates as an incentive for individual workers to produce more. Its achievements, however, fell short of Mao's expectations. In addition it also introduced principles of organization which seemed out of key with the Yanan tradition. It seemed to encourage individualism instead of collectivism, exploitation (especially of the peasantry) rather than equality. So Mao's thoughts turned towards a rush for growth, but with equity. He based his hopes on the size of China's population and its people's revolutionary fervour. Beautiful pictures could be painted upon them as on "blank sheets of paper", he wrote. It was essentially a political response to economic problems, as it relied upon mass political mobilization. The consequences for the structure of the economy were to unbalance it. Where the accumulation rate during the first Five-Year Plan had been 24 per cent, during the Great Leap Forward this figure rose to 44 per cent. Industrial output was directed towards accumulation rather than consumption – and much of that was useless.

In practice Maoist economic policies in the 1960s and 1970s gave priority to heavy industry, basic foodstuffs, and basic consumer goods. They stressed austerity and uniformity rather than consumer goods and variety. They led to over-investment. Meanwhile during the period 1957-77 the standard of living on average remained constant.

Current economic situation. After the failure of Hua Guofeng's Four Modernizations programme, the reformers under Deng Xiaoping made the level of consumption a top priority and they determined to make more use of economic methods in economic management. In practice this meant accepting the beneficial role of markets and material incentives. The peasants were the first to benefit with the introduction of the **production responsibility system** and the gradual abolition of collectivized farming. Between 1981 and 1986 agricultural output rose at an annual average rate of 11.7 per cent. This was the only time in the history of the PRC when agriculture grew faster than industry. It was only towards the end of the 1980s that industrial growth began to catch up, with monthly output gains of 13-20 per cent between October 1986 and September 1988. Particular growth in urban areas has been enjoyed by co-operative and individual enterprises, and there are now opportunities (albeit very limited) for individuals to invest in enterprises on a stock exchange in the cities of Shanghai and Shenyang. Growth has proceeded by fits and starts, as the leadership has experimented with market methods to manage the economy. In 1984, for example, RY 26.2 billion of newly issued currency went into circulation, which was RY 5 billion more than the total issued between 1950 and 1978, and 83.5 per cent of the total issue from 1979-83. The ensuing inflation has not yet been mastered.

Prospects for development. The main priorities of the PRC government remain the greater integration of the Chinese into the world economy, and the spreading of advanced technological and managerial know-how in industry. The long-term goal is to achieve the standard of living of medium-developed countries (though not the USA) by the middle of the next century. Further development of the economy, however, will necessarily be constrained by bottlenecks in transport and energy supply. Investment here, and in energy conservation, will take considerable time

to pay off. Also the growth spurt of agriculture is tailing off. Future growth here will become increasingly difficult, since fertilizer inputs are by the standards of the Third World already very high. A continuing problem is that of price reform, which will inevitably exacerbate inflation. Many prices are too low, and the state still spends about 25 per cent of its budget upon various subsidies. The nearer the economy moves towards market-determined prices, the greater the rises will have to be. In autumn 1988 the leadership decided that it would take at least five years to complete price reform, and the austerity measures of 1989 will prolong that. Then there are the potential dangers of popular reaction against increasing inequality, regional as well as between urban and rural areas.

There is also the potential obstruction from cadres who, either out of conviction or self-interest, try to slow down the process of reform, while others pursue local interests in the name of reform. In addition, there are the demographic and social implications of continued population growth and urbanization as agricultural land shrinks. Lastly there is the continuing uncertainty over Deng's successor, and the circumstances in which that succession will take place. All of these raise question marks over the prospects for smooth and rapid development in the 1990s, even before the massacre on Tiananmen Square. Nevertheless it should also be remembered that the economic changes and achievements in the PRC have been greater than expected in the 1980s. The same could be true for the next decade.

CIPF

CHINA–NORTH KOREA SECURITY RELATIONS. The Chinese relationship with North Korea has been extremely close since China intervened in the **Korean War** in 1950 and effectively saved North Korea from being defeated by US-led United Nations forces. Since this time the relationship between the two states has generally remained warm and although influenced at times by the Sino-Soviet dispute and by internal developments in China, it has displayed considerable stability. This is not entirely surprising. North Korea is of vital strategic importance to China and it is essential that the Korean peninsula should not be under the control of a hostile power or powers. After the Korean War, therefore, Chinese forces were not immediately withdrawn, staying in North Korea until 1958. During this period there was also a subtle competition between the Soviet Union and China for influence in North Korea. Indeed, Beijing became engaged in what was effectively a competitive programme of aid and military assistance. For their part, the North Koreans preferred to avoid any irrevocable choices and in 1961 **Kim Il Sung** signed treaties of friendship and co-operation with both Moscow and Beijing.

During the period of the Cultural Revolution in China, however, the relationship between North Korea and China cooled somewhat. In 1967-69 there were minor border clashes between the two states, after China had claimed 100 miles of territory near Mt Paektu. North Korea was anxious, however, that it should not become exclusively allied to Moscow which was also engaged in a territorial dispute with China. Even more important, China realized that it should not drive North Korea into the arms of the Soviets as this might allow Moscow to obtain bases in North Korea. In the autumn of 1969, therefore, tensions eased and in 1970 Beijing dropped its claim to the disputed territory on the border with North Korea. There was subsequently some attempt by China to compete with the Soviet Union for influence in North Korea. From 1965 to 1973 the Soviet Union dominated arms supplies to North Korea, but as the Soviet flow diminished, China moved to enhance its own position. There were periods when supplies from China exceeded those from Moscow. In 1982 after Kim Il Sung had made a very successful visit to China, Beijing provided Pyongyang with between 20 and 40 of the most advanced Chinese military aircraft, the A-5 fighter. China has also made clear that it wants to see stability on the Korean Peninsular maintained and has frequently provided reassurances to both the United States and Japan that Kim Il Sung has no intention of initiating another war with the South. Certainly this is something that China would be reluctant to be drawn into, yet find it very difficult to stay aloof from. It is also significant that, in accord with Deng Xiaoping's open door policy, China increased its contacts with South Korea. Initially this caused problems and North Korea protested at the growing trade. The links were subsequently reduced as China remained anxious not to offend its North Korean ally. By the mid-1980s, however, there was a significant expansion of trade between China and South Korea.

All this suggests that China has a strong interest in the maintenance of stability on the Korean Peninsula. The security commitment to North Korea that was evident in its involvement in the Korean War and is a product of geopolitical considerations, remains strong. Nevertheless, there is a reluctance to contemplate anything other than the maintenance of the *status quo*. This ensures that North Korea remains friendly while also avoiding any developments that might drag Beijing into a confrontation with Washington.

PW

CHINA-TAIWAN CONFLICT. The conflict between China and Taiwan is a legacy of the Chinese civil war and the Cold War of the early 1950s. It is a conflict between a massive land power and a smaller island power. Taiwan (formerly known as Formosa, and termed by its government the Republic of China) has a population of only 19 million and a total land area of 36,000 sq km. Located 130-200 km from the south-eastern border of mainland China, the island of Taiwan has historically been controlled by China, Holland and Japan. After World War II control reverted back to China and its nationalist government. When this government was defeated by the Chinese communists, the ruling **Kuomintang**, headed by **Chiang Kai-shek**, fled to Taiwan in December 1949, establishing a new capital at Taipei. The exodus from the mainland amounted to about one and a half million people including three-quarters of a million military personnel. The government in Taipei disputed the claim of the People's Republic of China, established on Oct. 1, 1949, to be the legitimate government of the mainland. The Nationalists retained control of the Pescadores, Quemoy, Matsu, the Nanchi Islands, and the Tachen Islands. In addition, they had a small garrison on one of the **Spratly Islands** in the South China Sea.

After fleeing to Taiwan the nationalist government announced a blockade of mainland China. What had been for the most part a local civil war became a major international issue, however, as a result of the Korean War. On June 27, 1950, a few days after the North Korean attack on the South, the United States interposed the Seventh Fleet between the combatants. President Eisenhower, however, announced in February 1953 that the Seventh Fleet would no longer shield Communist China. Although this was popularly described as "the unleashing of Chiang Kai-shek", the real concern was protecting the Nationalists. As a result of the Cold War, and as part of its global strategy of containing Communism, the United States gradually committed itself to the security and independence of Taiwan. This took on added urgency in late 1954. In September the Chinese People's Republic began bombarding the island of Quemoy, and in December, the United States and Taiwan signed a mutual security treaty in which the United States agreed to defend Taiwan, the Pescadores, and "such other territories as may be determined by mutual agreement". For its part, the Taiwan government agreed not to attack the mainland without prior consultation with the United States.

A small island, Yikiangshan, was captured by Communist forces on Jan. 18, 1955. Amidst growing tension, the US congress passed the "Formosa Resolution", authorising President Eisenhower to use force to protect Taiwan and the Pescadores, as well as other territories he judged appropriate. The following month the Tachen and Nanchi Islands were evacuated by Kuomintang forces. The crisis, however, was defused soon afterwards. A second crisis over Quemoy began on Aug. 23, 1958 when China resumed shelling of the island. On Sept. 4, Beijing extended the limits of China's territorial waters from three to 12 miles, and made clear that foreign warships or aircraft were prohibited unless given explicit permission to enter. Quemoy and Matsu fell within these new limits, but the United States on October 6 began to escort supplies to the Nationalist forces on the islands. Care was taken, however, to avoid a direct Sino-American clash and from Oct. 25 shelling was confined to alternate days to allow supplies to be brought in. It was clear that neither the People's Republic nor the United States was anxious to provoke another conflict. The conflict became almost ritualized and tensions in the area gradually relaxed.

Although the basic lines of conflict remain, and both governments threaten an attempt at "liberation", the likelihood of major confrontation diminished considerably after 1958. There have been occasional clashes between Nationalist and Communist forces, including a naval engagement in the Taiwan Strait in 1965. There have also been attacks by Kuomintang commandos against the mainland. For the most part, however, the conflict has become rather less salient. This was especially the case after 1971 when there was a dramatic breakthrough in Sino-American relations. The United States supported the admission of the People's Republic of China to the United Nations, although much to its chagrin, Taiwan was expelled. The Taiwan issue remained the major obstacle in the way of the normalization of Sino-American relations. In 1972 at the end of President Nixon's visit to China, Beijing reiterated that it was unwilling to accept the idea of "one China, two governments", "two Chinas" or "independent Taiwan". For its part, the United States acknowledged that all Chinese, on either side of the strait, maintain that there is one China and that the Taiwan issue should be settled by the Chinese themselves. It also affirmed that its ultimate objective was the withdrawal of all military forces and military installations from Taiwan and that it would progressively reduce its presence. The process of normalization continued

throughout the 1970s and it was announced on Dec. 15, 1978 that the United States had agreed to recognize the People's Republic of China as the sole legal government and that full diplomatic relations were to be established on Jan. 1 1979. Unofficial links were to be maintained with the people of Taiwan. Although the United States agreed to withdraw its remaining forces from Taiwan within four months it reiterated that it expected the peaceful resolution of the Taiwan issue. In the event little progress was made in this direction. Nevertheless, in 1979 China stopped its shelling of Quemoy. Statements made by Beijing in 1980 were also quite conciliatory. Furthermore, the less tense relationship was reflected in a very substantial expansion of trade between Taiwan and China, even if most of this trade was channelled through Hong Kong, Singapore and Japan.

In 1981 Marshall Ye Jianying proposed a nine-point plan for peaceful reunification, which would not only allow Taiwan considerable autonomy but also to retain its armed forces. The Kuomintang, however, rejected the plan as an attempt at annexation and continued to insist that unification could only take place in accordance with the "Three Principles of the People" – nationals, democracy and "the people's livelihood". After the 1984 agreement with Britain over Hong Kong, Beijing suggested that a similar arrangement could be made with Taiwan on the basis of "one country two systems". This was rejected by Taipei, however, which in 1987 went on to reiterate its claim, as the legitimate government of China, to sovereignty over the People's Republic of Mongolia. In effect, the China-Taiwan conflict had reached the stage of ritualization. Although neither side formally accepted the *status quo*, the practicalities of the situation made war unlikely. The early hopes of the Nationalists to retake the mainland had effectively been abandoned, while Beijing had recognized the costs and risks inherent in any attempt to recapture Taiwan. This is not to deny the significant imbalance in the military power of the two states. Indeed, in many areas of armament the Chinese People's Republic has a 10 to one numerical superiority over Taiwan.

Although the prospects of this superiority being used and of large-scale conflict breaking out between Taiwan and China have receded since the mid-1950s Taiwan, not surprisingly, remains anxious to deter any military adventurism by Beijing. It does this by ensuring that its armed forces are sufficiently modern and effective to inflict enormous costs upon China in the event that it attempted to retake Taiwan by force. Other contingencies for which Taiwan prepares are a naval blockade or economic embargo and a blockade or invasion of the Matsu islands. This has made Taiwan highly dependent on the United States for its arms supplies – a dependence that has become increasingly uncomfortable as the United States becomes reluctant to take steps which might complicate its relationship with Beijing. Indeed, the United States has been assisting the modernization of the armed forces of China, while also continuing with its military assistance to Taiwan. The Taiwanese navy, for example, has been granted permission to build 13 guided missile frigates based on American designs, while Taiwanese air defences, based on the US Patriot missiles, are to be augmented with the United States Chaparral Surface to Air Missiles. With the United States assisting China in upgrading its air capability, however, Taiwan has decided to develop a new fighter of its own with a higher performance specification than the F-5E which is currently its main fighter.

The internal unrest and the resurgence of a hard line government in China in mid-1989 has added a new element of uncertainty to the relationship between Beijing and Taipei. One of its consequences has been to make the Taiwanese even more determined to retain their independence. Yet there would be many advantages for Beijing if it could somehow re-establish its control over Taiwan. Among these are the economic benefits that would accrue from the incorporation of he dynamic Taiwanese economy, the prestige that would come from eliminating the symbol of a divided nation, and the strategic benefits that would come from control over the Taiwan Straits and the Bashi Channel, key choke points for the Soviet navy in the Pacific. The costs of a forcible re-integration of Taiwan into China, however, are very considerable. As well the direct costs resulting from formidable Taiwanese resistance are the diplomatic costs and the adverse impact on the relationship with the United States and other members of the international community. Although lesser military actions against the islands could appear more attractive, there does appear to have been an acceptance of the *status quo* by both sides. Certainly the population of Taiwan would be happy to exchange the dream of a claim to the mainland for a recognition of its right to exist as an independent state. Perhaps more likely, however, is a continuation of the current situation in which the division is tacitly accepted, and the use of force, although not inconceivable, is very unlikely.

PW

CHINA-VIETNAM CONFLICT. One of the most intense conflicts in the Pacific region in the last 20 years has been that between Vietnam and China. The nadir of this relationship came in February 1979 when 85,000 Chinese troops crossed into Vietnam. Claiming that this was an act of self-defence against aggression, China's intent was clearly punitive. Vietnam was to be put in its place. In the event, the 27-day war ended with China withdrawing its forces without having achieved its aim. Although the two states have avoided further clashes of this magnitude, relations between them have remained tense. They have been engaged in a struggle for regional influence which may ease but is unlikely to disappear. The irony is that during the war against the United States North Vietnam was heavily reliant on China as well as the Soviet Union. Although there were some complaints that China was less forthcoming with its aid than it might have been, as well as a feeling that the visit of US President Richard Nixon to Beijing in 1972 was a betrayal of North Vietnam, the alliance seemed to be reasonably close, if subject to periodic strain. The reunification of Vietnam in 1975 seems to have changed this and in the latter half of the 1970s there was a marked deterioration in the relationship. Some of the issues which led to this deterioration, however, had earlier roots. This was certainly true of the border conflict. The 1,200 km frontier was defined by France (as the colonial power in Vietnam) and China in agreements in 1887 and 1895, although some areas where there was population movement were deliberately left imprecise. The issue had arisen in the 1950s and there were Vietnamese allegations that China had encroached on Vietnamese territory. Most of the areas in dispute, however, were very small. Nevertheless, clashes on the border began in 1974. In 1975 there was some harassment of border residents and in 1976 Chinese railway workers were attacked. By the end of 1977 the border clashes had become more frequent and more intense. Although there were proposals by China for discussion of the border in 1975 negotiations did not open until 1977. These talks were soon deadlocked and ceased in the summer of 1978 without reaching any agreement.

The border issue was, in part, a barometer of Sino-Vietnamese relations. but it added to the deterioration of the relationship. Much the same could be said about the disputes in the South China Sea, although the substantive issues involved were perhaps more significant in this case. In 1973 and 1974 there were clashes between South Vietnamese and Chinese troops in the Paracel Islands. Although China took control of the Paracels, Hanoi subsequently secured control over the **Spratly Islands**. Both buttressed their case with claims that historically the islands had been in their control. Yet the dispute was less over past possession than future control as both Beijing and Hanoi were increasingly aware of the strategic and economic importance of the South China Sea. Indeed, as Charles McGregor wrote, "claims to the islands are linked inextricably with the claims to maritime boundaries in the South China Sea. China's claims in this region extend all the way southward to just off the coast of Borneo. China and Vietnam both support the concept of a 200-mile exclusive economic zone for coastal countries which, in the context of their claims to the Paracels and the Spratlys, gives both countries claims to an exclusive economic zone which encompasses most of the South China Sea". As increased significance is given to the exploitation of the resources of the sea-bed, and if optimistic estimates of offshore oil reserves prove correct, then this dispute will loom larger in Sino-Vietnamese relations.

Both the border and the maritime disputes were irritants in Sino-Vietnamese relations in the latter half of the 1970s. The relationship was also worsened by Vietnamese treatment of the 1,200,000 ethnic Chinese, the Hoa, who lived in Vietnam. In 1977, partly as a response to the increased tension on the border, the Hoa began an exodus from Vietnam. The presence of the refugees in turn contributed to further incidents on the border. None of these issues was sufficient in itself to lead China and Vietnam to war in 1979. The bilateral disputes, however, became bound up with the Sino-Soviet conflict and with regional issues in Indochina. The Sino-Soviet rivalry took on an added dimension in the late 1970s as Hanoi increasingly sided with the Soviet Union rather than China. This development led to fears of encirclement in Beijing. Indeed, the Sino-Soviet and the Sino-Vietnam conflicts fed into each other in ways which exacerbated tensions. Because Vietnam was a close ally of the Soviet Union, China was more suspicious of its policies in Indochina. Yet Chinese policies themselves contributed to Vietnamese dependence on Moscow. In June 1978 Vietnam joined the Council for Mutual Economic Assistance (CMEA or Comecon) and in November Hanoi signed a Treaty of Friendship and Co-operation with the Soviet Union.

At this juncture, the triangular relationship of Moscow, Hanoi and Beijing became inextricably entangled with regional issues in Indochina. At the regional level China has been traditionally anxious to deny pre-eminence to others, especially in Indochina. This is particularly the case in Cambodia which China saw as an important buffer state. During the 1950s and 1960s China worked very hard to maintain an indepen-dent neutral Cambodia and provided consider-able aid to **Prince Sihanouk**. China also gave some support to the **Kampuchean People's Revo-lutionary Party** under **Pol Pot**. After the fall of Sihanouk China increased its support for the *Khmer Rouge* and Pol Pot but found itself unable to control his escalating border clashes with Vietnam. In December 1978 Vietnam, partly out of concern over a two-front threat, partly out of ambition to be the dominant power in Indochina, and partly because of the nature of the provo-cations, invaded Cambodia, overthrew the *Khmer Rouge* and established the **People's Republic of Kampuchea** under **Heng Samrin**. This raised questions about the credibility of Chinese support for its allies and intensified Chinese con-cerns over Vietnamese ambitions. It was not entirely surprising, therefore, when on Feb. 17, 1979, China invaded Vietnam.

The war between China and Vietnam was inconclusive. On March 5 Beijing announced that its forces were withdrawing and on March 16 announced that this process was complete. The problem was that the war settled nothing. The Vietnamese were not taught the lesson that China intended and were not driven out of Cambodia. Furthermore, the position of Beijing in the early 1980s was increasingly uncomfortable. Its efforts to prevent Vietnamese dominance of Indochina had not only failed, but Vietnam had drawn much closer to the Soviet Union. During the period after the Sino-Vietnamese War the Soviet Union acquired and developed important military facili-ties in Vietnam. Soviet ships are regularly deployed at Cam Ranh Bay, Da Nang and Hai-phong while Soviet aircraft make extensive use of Vietnamese air bases. In addition, Vietnam hosts a network of radar and monitoring facilities. Although these are designed partly to gather intel-ligence on US activities in the Pacific, they are also directed against China. Indeed, in the event of Sino-Soviet military hostilities, they would give the Soviet Union considerable advantages.

Despite this increased Soviet presence – or perhaps because of it – Beijing from 1982 onwards adopted a much more conciliatory policy towards the Soviet Union. The relationship with Vietnam, however, has remained difficult. China has escalated border fighting in an effort to disrupt Vietnamese offensives in Cambodia in the dry season. Although the fighting has been limited, Vietnam has increased the number of forces on the border and by 1985 may have had as many as 600,000 troops in the northern region. Against this China had somewhere in the region of 250,000–300,000 men in the Kunming and Guangdong regions. Indeed, the continued pressure on the border is part of what McGregor has described as a three-pronged strategy by China. The second strand has been aid for the resistance in Cambodia, while the third objective has been to disrupt Vietnamese economic growth and to "bleed Vietnam white". The escalation of hostilities on the border has not only contributed to these objectives but has demonstrated Beijing's unwillingness to allow Vietnam to threaten Thailand. This strategy, however, had only limited success, and in its 1984–85 dry season offensive, Vietnam made considerable gains in its attempt to suppress the resistance in Kampuchea. After this the *Khmer* rebels ceased to pose a major threat to the Vietnamese occupation. Furthermore, continued Soviet support for Vietnam has made it easier for Vietnam to sustain its position in the light of continued Chinese pressure. Even so as China encouraged Moscow to put pressure on Hanoi, and Vietnam gradually became more conciliatory, China also maintained the pressure on the border and in early January 1987 there were once again serious clashes on the border. These were reported to be the largest clashes since the war in 1979, with both sides claiming success. At the same time, Hanoi made clear that it wanted normalization of relations "at any time, at any level, and at any place". Some progress seemed to have been made towards this by early 1988 and with Vietnam making a commitment to withdraw its forces from Kampuchea.

The effort to obtain a settlement of the Kampuchean conflict and an improvement in Sino-Vietnamese relations has been facilitated by the gradual improvement in Sino-Soviet relations since 1982. Yet while this development has helped to defuse slightly the tension between China and Vietnam, it is also clear that the conflict in Kampuchea made the detente in Sino-Soviet relations somewhat more difficult than it would otherwise have been. It was also clear that the military rivalry between China and Vietnam remains strong. Although the issue of the ethnic Chinese in Vietnam has more or less disappeared as a source of friction, other issues have increased in importance. The Sino-Vietnamese conflict over the South China Sea displays considerable potential to precipitate a further crisis in the relationship. During 1987–88 China was particularly assertive in naval power projection and in pressing its claims to the Spratly Islands (which are also claimed by Taiwan, the Philippines and Malaysia). In January 1988 a force of 10 Chinese warships moved to the Spratly Islands, and in March there was a serious clash between Chinese and Vietnamese forces, as a result of which two or three Vietnamese freighters were sunk. The following month each side accused the other of building up its military forces in preparation for

an invasion of the islands. In mid-May, however, Beijing adopted a more conciliatory approach and accepted an offer from Hanoi to negotiate over the future of the islands. A statement by the Chinese Foreign Ministry insisted that the Spratly Islands had long been Chinese territory but that China proposed "to settle the issue through consultation at a later date, while leaving it aside for the time being". This desire to prevent further escalation led to a degree of disengagement from naval conflict in May 1988. In June 1988, however, it was announced that the Chinese marine corps was strengthening its training and equipment in order to defend its claim to the Spratlys and that China would recover the islands "at an appropriate time". It is clear, therefore, that the potential for conflict over the Spratlys remains. If mineral and energy reserves are found in the seas around the islands the issue could once more emerge into prominence.

By mid-1989, it appeared that the China–Vietnam conflict had abated very considerably. Progress on Kampuchea had improved the situation as had the Sino-Soviet detente. Both developments helped to ease Chinese fears of encirclement and although several potential sources of conflict remain, it does appear that the prospects for stability in the area were particularly good. The events of May and June 1989 in China, however, must cast some doubts on this optimism.

PW

CHINESE COMMUNIST PARTY (CCP).
Founded in 1921 in Shanghai, it now has nearly 48 million members. It was organized on the Leninist principle of democratic centralism. In theory this means that there is the widest possible consultation of members before decisions are taken, but in practice lower levels of the party are required to implement decisions of the higher levels in a disciplined fashion.

Again in theory, it is the Party Congress which lays down the party line, but this only meets every five years. In the interim it is the Central Committee (CC) elected by the Congress which lays down policy, but with 175 full and 110 candidate (non-voting) members, it normally meets only every three to six months in plenary sessions (plenums). In practice it is the executive bodies elected by the CC and by lower level local party congresses which run party life. At the highest level there is the Political Bureau (Politburo) with 14 full members and one candidate member. Within the Political Bureau there is the institution unique among ruling communist parties of the Standing Committee. This is in day-to-day charge of party affairs, and the new one formed in June 1989 has six members: **Jiang Zemin**, **Li Peng**, Qiao Shi, Yao Yilin, Song Ping and Li Ruihuan. In practice, as the former General Secretary, **Zhao Ziyang**, admitted to President Gorbachev, all the most important decisions still have to be approved by **Deng Xiaoping**.

Assisting the Central Committee is its Secretariat, which is the administrative centre of the party. Below the centre there are party committees at the province, county and township levels. Each party committee elects its executive officers, or secretaries, and the first secretary is in practice the most important official at that level of administration. At the bottom are the primary party organizations in workplaces and residential units.

Internally the party has attempted since 1976 to institutionalize its workings so as to prevent a return to the personal dictatorship of the later **Mao** years, but the handling of the April–June 1989 crisis showed how far this still has to go. Even though most of them have now formally retired, the oldest generation of leaders still cling to power, exercising it through the specially created Central Advisory Commission. In this respect the internal workings of the CCP differ markedly from other ruling communist parties, where retirement leads to political oblivion. Most of that generation defer to Deng Xiaoping.

The party is reserved a special place in the country. Party members cannot be prosecuted for criminal offences unless the party agrees. In its control of society, the party relies upon personnel manipulation, especially as the leading role of ideology has shrunk considerably since Mao's death. Party bodies are responsible for either directly selecting or supervising the selection of the 27 million leading cadres (party and state officials) at all levels of responsibility throughout society. This principle will, however, come increasingly into conflict with the appointment of market-oriented managers of enterprises.

CIPF

CHOYBALSAN, MARSHAL HORLOOGIYN. Former Mongolian statesman, born in 1895, died in 1952. A leading figure in Mongolia's revolutionary movement in 1919–21 and the only founding member of the **Mongolian People's Revolutionary Party** to survive a series of purges between 1922 and 1939, he became Prime Minister of Mongolia in 1936. From then until his death he concentrated power in his own hands, developing a cult of personality not unlike that of Stalin in the Soviet Union. Choybalsan was responsible for establishing Mongolia's party and

government institutions largely in their present forms.

IG

CHRISTIANITY. There have been three waves of Christian infiltration into eastern Asia. In the seventh century Nestorian Christian missionaries from Syria arrived in the capital of T'ang China, and some Nestorian monuments remain. Roman Catholic orders entered in the sixteenth century, had considerable success, but declined in China and were expelled from Japan. Somewhat earlier Catholic missions began to spread in the Americas. In the nineteenth century there was a surge of missionary activity throughout the Pacific, primarily of Protestant inspiration but also of revived Roman Catholic work. Christian missions from the sixteenth century preceded or accompanied European exploration, trade and colonialism, sometimes checking exploitation, sometimes suffering from identification with Westernism. Emphasis placed upon education, from the Nestorians onwards who built schools with churches, helped to raise the standard of life and also sowed the dragon's teeth of later revolution. Christian conviction of a mission, and association with Westernism, often implied condemnation of Asian, Pacific and American native religions and cultures, but also produced scholars, Catholic and Protestant, who were among those who revealed something of the wisdom of the East to the West. Christian emphasis upon church organization gave the major churches international communities of their own, but on the fringes of Protestantism fissiparous tendencies produced multitudes of sects to divide countries and communities. Under pressure from hostile governments the larger churches were most able to survive and at times they linked up with nationalist aspirations in Pacific lands.

The only predominantly Christian country in Asia is the Philippines, with 84 per cent of the population. Church and state were separated by the constitution of 1973, freedom of religion was guaranteed "without discrimination", but the preamble implored "the aid of the Divine Providence". The first priest arrived in the Philippines in 1521 and a Dominican university was opened in 1611. After long foreign domination a Philippine Independent Church was founded in 1890 and it has experienced division, decline and revival. A Protestant Independent Church of Christ has more members than any mission-founded Protestant church. For long supporting the establishment, the churches were divided under the Marcos regime. In 1986 Cardinal Jaime

Sin warned of a "very sinister plot" to frustrate the elections, popular demonstrations included priests and nuns, and the churches threw their weight behind change to the Aquino government.

In the early years of this century there were thousands of Catholic and Protestant missionaries in China, and hundreds of schools and hospitals. In 1951 a Three-Self Reform Movement was founded to rid the churches of imperialism, feudalism and bourgeois thinking, and it became a Patriotic Church in which the various Protestant churches were made into one, with smaller churches being shut. Eventually all were closed, until some relaxation after 1972. At the same time Catholic missionaries were expelled or imprisoned, and a National Patriotic Catholic Association was created and Chinese bishops were consecrated independently of Rome, which considers their election valid but illicit. The last foreign bishop was released in 1970, but efforts at reconciliation of Rome with the national church have not succeeded, though some churches have been re-opened in towns and cities. Estimates of the numbers of Christians in China give between three and six million Catholics and three million Protestants. There are about one million each in Hong Kong and Taiwan.

After being closed to foreign missions for over 200 years Japan allowed the entry of Catholic and Protestant missions in 1859. Returning Catholics were surprised to discover crypto-Christians, the Hidden Christians (Sempuku or Kakure Kirishitan) who existed in secret from 1638–1859, and had kept the faith with some mixture of native customs, especially in the western islands. Some of them rejoined the Catholic Church and form its backbone in Nagasaki, but about 33,000 prefer to remain with their traditional ways, not appearing in census figures but known to exist. There are numerous indigenous Japanese denominations, notably the Non-church Movement (Mukyokai), founded by Uchimura Kanzo in 1900, which has no organization, special buildings or priests, but is strongly biblical. In 1940 the Japanese government ordered the unification of all Protestant churches in a United Church (Kyodan), and those which refused to join – Anglican, Salvation Army and Adventists – officially ceased to exist, though they have survived, but the Kyodan continues to unite the other Protestants. Numbers of all Christians in Japan are between three and four million.

The Christian population in Korea is second only in Asia to the Philippines. After frequent persecutions and martyrdoms freedom of evangelization was agreed in Korea in 1882, Catholic and Protestant missions entered in force, and the latter were especially active in education, social and rural projects, and in opposition to the Japanese occupation from 1910. Churches were closed in North Korea after communist rule, no organized religion remained, and some two million Christians fled to the South. Numbers of conversions in South Korea have risen dramatically since 1960, especially among Protestants, and mass baptisms have taken place. In the army numbers of Christians rose from 12 per cent in 1970 to 47 per cent in 1977. There are some 12 million Christians in Korea, 30 per cent of the population.

There are over three million Christians in Vietnam and half a million in Thailand. In the Pacific islands the predominant religion is now Christian, and for the most part Protestant. In Hawaii 68 per cent are Christians, in Papua New Guinea 96 per cent. Western Samoa is a Christian state, but in American Samoa church and state are separated. In Fiji 83 per cent of ethnic Fijians claim to be Methodists, but 80 per cent of Fijian Indians are Hindus, and this brought both political and religious clashes, leading to the military coup by native Fijians in 1987. Schisms among Methodists gave rise to indigenous churches in Fiji, and in Tonga Methodists are divided into four denominations, the monarch being head of the Free Wesleyan Church, the original mission organization. In French Polynesia the Evangelical Church is stronger than the Roman Catholic, but the reverse appears in New Caledonia with a large French population.

Chaplains accompanied the first convicts to Australia in 1788 and Roman Catholic priests arrived in 1803. Eighty-four per cent of Australians are reckoned as Christian, Protestants most numerous but numbers of Roman Catholics have increased with Irish, Italian and Spanish immigration. The state is secular, though the constitution invokes "the blessing of Almighty God". Aboriginal religion is still significant but most now claim to be Christian.

In New Zealand Maori traditional religion persists among a small number; most Maoris are formally Christian though some decline to state their religion in censuses. The Ratana church is one of several founded by Maoris, called after Takapotiki Ratana in 1918, whose followers have often held all four Maori seats in the national legislature. Of the total population 91 per cent is counted Christian.

The Americas are predominantly Christian, though with varying attitudes towards church-state relations. In Chile the 1925 constitution ended church dominance and declared freedom of conscience. In 1970 the Catholic bishops maintained neutrality towards the Allende regime, supported nationalization of copper mines, opposed violent revolution, and criticized educational changes. The Pinochet coup in 1973 purported to "remove the Marxist cancer", and was approved by some bishops. Priests who opposed it were expelled or fled the country. Growing concern by Catholics and Protestants brought protests against repression and assertion of human rights. But some conservative evangelicals gave the government full support. Numbers attending church in Latin America vary considerably, from 20 per cent weekly at Mass in Peru to 65 per cent in Colombia. The church hierarchy has often been conservative and traditionally enjoyed great power and material possessions. Some bishops now speak out against injustice, and notable is Dom Helder Camara of Brazil, once known as "the red bishop of the north-east" and greeted by the Pope as "brother of the poor". In 1980 Archbishop Oscar Romero of San Salvador, a moderate advocate of reform, was assassinated at the altar of his cathedral by unidentified gunmen as he officiated at the funeral of a victim of military shooting.

Pope John Paul II has visited Central and South America several times to regulate the involvement of the church in politics and urge non-violent solutions to social problems. In Nicaragua in 1984 five Jesuit priests took office in the Sandinista government, but were ordered by the Vatican to resign since canon law forbade priests to take civil public office. Fr Fernando Cardenal, Minister of Education, refused and maintained that the Pope could not take his priesthood away, though he was later forbidden to exercise it. However Cardinal Obando y Bravo accused the Nicaraguan government of being "a tool of Soviet interest" that had "gagged and bound" the Church. A Catholic newspaper *La Prensa* was banned in 1986 but allowed to publish again in 1987 and Cardinal Obando was asked to mediate between the government and the Contra rebels.

Throughout Latin America and beyond there is debate about "liberation theology", with its "option for the poor" and support for radical social change. Professor Gustavo Gutiérrez of Peru, in *A Theology of Liberation* traced its inspiration back to the reforming Pope John XXIII who indicated the need for the Church to concentrate on poverty. Gutiérrez asserts that poverty means unjust and early death because of disease, and cultural death when people are despised for their class, colour or sex. Latin American bishops meeting at Puebla in 1979 added "preferential" to the "option for the poor". However the Vatican attacked Liberation Theology for error "in the identification of scientific analysis with marxist analysis without critical study". Another leading exponent, Fr Leonardo Boff, a Franciscan from

Brazil, was summoned to Rome in 1984 to answer charges. He justified "the work of Marx and others in understanding political and economic structures", and he compared the centralized Roman Catholic Church with the Soviet Politburo which represented in each case "an elite group dominated by one nationality". The following year Fr Boff's writings were condemned for endangering the faith and a one-year silence was imposed on him.

How the church had taken root among the people is demonstrated at the basilica of the Virgin of Guadalupe north of Mexico City. In 1531 an Indian, Juan Diego, claimed to have had visions there of the Virgin Mary whose black image was imprinted on his serape cloth. A church was built for veneration of Madre Nueva, near an old shrine to an Aztec earth goddess, Madre Antigua. In 1976 a huge new basilica was opened and attracted two million pilgrims. Pictures of the Black Virgin are found all over Latin America, and every year pilgrims from many countries visit Guadalupe. It was the one shrine untouched during the persecutions of the twenties. Anti-clerical laws remain in Mexico, but they are rarely applied.

Numbers of Protestants vary in Latin America, from 1.5 per cent in Chile to four and five per cent in Nicaragua and Guatemala. Fundamentalist missions from the USA make great efforts for converts and tend to be more conservative politically than Catholics. Visiting Guatemala in 1983 the Pope was received by the "born again" Protestant General Ríos Montt, later overthrown, who asked the pontiff to call on Catholic clergy to refrain from political action, but the Pope replied that the Church would continue to "condemn injustice and denounce abuses".

In the USA 42 per cent are Protestant and 30 per cent Roman Catholic, and immigration during this century gave 2.2 per cent of Eastern Orthodox. There are black members of all major denominations, the largest numbers in Roman Catholic and Methodist churches, but most US blacks belong to 140 separate black denominations. Nine million Spanish speakers in the USA are Catholics. There are 19 groups of America Indian churches, the largest being the Native American Church of North America, begun in 1870 and found among most Indian tribes. The USA is a secular state, though the Pledge of Allegiance uses the words "under God". Freedom of religion is guaranteed, but issues such as school prayers, theories of creation or evolution, birth control and abortion, are constantly debated.

In Canada French influence reverses the proportions of religions, with 46 per cent Roman

Catholic and 38 per cent Protestant; Eastern Orthodox have 2.8 per cent. In 1925 a United Church of Canada brought together Presbyterian, Congregationalist and Methodist. Church and state were separated in 1852, with freedom of worship; privileges have been given to Roman Catholics in Quebec but secularization has accelerated.

Religion in Pacific Siberia has suffered repression as in the rest of the USSR, with churches closed and monasteries detroyed, Islamic mosques and Buddhist temples secularized. In the worst times clandestine religious sects continued and native shamanism persisted when official religions were crushed. Recent relaxations have given new life to all religions, and in 1988 650 new congregations were recognized in the whole of the USSR.

GP

CHUKCHIS. An ethinc group inhabiting the far eastern tip of the Soviet Union. Numbering fewer than 15,000 people, the Chukchis nevertheless enjoy administrative-territorial autonomy in the Chukchi National District.

IG

CLIPPERTON ISLAND (La Pasión). Volcanic atoll 6 by 4 km situated in the Pacific southwest of Mexico. Claimed by both France and Mexico, it was awarded to France by arbitration of King Vittorio Emmanuele III of Italy in 1931.

P&SC

COAL. One of the world's most important sources of energy, coal consists chiefly of carbon and was formed from the remains of vegetation, particularly wood, dating largely from the Carboniferous period, some 200 million years ago. There are three principal grades of coal: anthracite, bituminous and lignite. Anthracite is the hardest with a high carbon content. It gives off great heat and is smokeless. Bituminous and sub-bituminous coal, some of which is converted into coke, is widely used for industrial power. A wide range of products can be derived from bituminous coal including tar, drugs, perfumes, disinfectants, dyes, and creosote. Lignite, or brown coal, is the poorest grade of coal and geologically the nearest to the peat stage. The USA, China, South Korea, Colombia and Australia are the main coal producing nations of the Pacific.

According to the United Nations the People's Republic of China became the world's leading producer of hard coal in 1983 with its production of 687,600,000 tonnes. China is also known to have reserves of 770,000 million tonnes mainly to be found in the northern and central regions. However only about 100,000 million tonnes are recoverable using current mining technology. Only about half of China's mines are fully mechanized and even these are often using outdated Soviet technology from the 1950s. Chinese production of coal grew to an estimated 920,000,000 tonnes in 1987 and China has ambitious plans to increase annual output to between 1,200 million tonnes and 1,400 million tonnes by the year 2000. However, because of freight difficulties and increasing domestic demand China is not a big exporter of coal, less than one per cent of total production going abroad.

Australia is the Pacific's, and indeed the world's, largest exporter of coal, exporting 102,000,000 tonnes of coal in 1987. It is also an important producer: in 1987 it produced 139,000,000 tonnes of hard coal as well as some 40,000,000 tonnes of brown coal. Over 50 per cent of Australia's coal production is exported. Its biggest single buyer is the Japanese steel industry. Australia itself has only 5 per cent of the world's reserves of coal but it is the world's leading exporter because its coal is inexpensive to mine and domestic demand is low. Yet it is acutely conscious that before the end of the century it is likely to face tough competition from China for the position of leading coal exporter in the Pacific. In order to improve the Australian coal industry's competitiveness a modernization of the mining companies' operations is underway but this is causing serious labour difficulties, particularly in Queensland and New South Wales.

Indonesia has important coal mining operations sited on South Sumatra and Kalimantan. Since the oil crisis of 1973 South Korea has given priority to the production of coal. It yields 13,930 million tonnes per year. Its known reserves are estimated at 500,000,000 tonnes. The chief coal deposits are located near the east coast in Kangwon Province and on the south-western coast in South Cholla Province. North Korea produces coal but the mining sector's performance has been erratic.

On the American littoral the United States is the main producer and large deposits of coal have been identified in South America. Mexico's reserves of hard coal are put at 5,448 million tonnes and Colombia's reserves are between 12,000–Colombia produces about 25,000 million tonnes of coal a year, but not of high quality. Its richest field is at El Cerreion where Exxon started a US$3,200 million development contract in 1980. Production began four years later and it is hoped to yield 15,000,000 tonnes per year by

1999. Chile is another important producer with reserves of 1,177 million tonnes of low grade bituminous coal. In Peru 3,000 million tonnes of coal were found near Huanco in 1975.

An important factor in the production of coal in the Pacific region is Japan's need for coal. Japan's own coal seams are narrow, deep and difficult to exploit. Domestic production of coal cannot compete with much cheaper imported coal. Indeed the country's largest mine, Takashima, was closed in 1986. More generally Japanese mines have been cut back from 622 in 1960 to only 31 in 1986. By the 1990s Japan is expected to be producing less than 10,000,000 tonnes annually compared with a consumption of some 1,300 million tonnes. Japan has therefore become the Pacific's largest importer of coal.

The world demand for coal is likely to increase massively before the end of the century as the world's growing demand for energy is likely to outstrip petroleum supplies by a significant margin. The *annual production of coal*, in thousands of tonnes, is as follows: China, 810.0; USA, 741.3; Australia, 124.5; North Korea, 37.1; Canada, 32.1; South Korea, 20.6; Japan, 16.6; Mexico, 5.8; Colombia, 5.6; Vietnam, 5.3; Taiwan, 4.2; New Zealand, 1.8; Chile, 1.2; Indonesia, 1.1; Philippines, 0.4.

RS

COLOMBIA, REPUBLIC OF. *Population*: 27,000,000 (1981). *Area*: 1,138,914 sq km. *Gross Domestic Product*: US$21,417 million. *Trade*: US$9,251 million. *Top five trading partners*: USA, West Germany, Japan, France, UK. *Defence spending*: US$574 million. *Education spending (as percentage of GNP)*: 3.0. *Urban population as percentage of total*: 55. *Birth rate*: 31 per thousand. *Life expectancy*: males 49; females 53.

Geographical background. Colombia has three "coasts", a Pacific, a Caribbean and access to the Atlantic via the deep water port of Leticia on the upper Amazon. Inland the Andes Mountains split into three separate cordilleras, between which flow the two main rivers, the Cauca and the Magdalena, to join in the Northern coastal marshes of the Caribbean. The south-east region comprises plains and jungle, drained by the Orinoco and Amazon river systems. Lowland areas are tropical with temperatures elsewhere varying according to altitude. Just under four million hectares are cultivated.

Despite government programmes of rail (total 3,400 km) and road construction, the difficult topographic conditions have precluded fully effective development of land transport. River transportation of freight remains important and air passenger transport has developed greatly in recent years. The national airline, Avianca, is the oldest in Latin America, second oldest in the world.

The vast majority of the population live in the mountainous western part of the country. Colombia is heavily urbanized. The capital, Bogotá, has a population of seven million, followed by Medellín and Cali.

Socio-political background. The population is two-thirds *mestizo*. The remaining third includes, in order of magnitude, Europeans, mulattos, blacks and Indians. Spanish is the national language. A few Indian tribes use indigenous languages. The vast majority of people are Roman Catholic and more actively so than in many other countries of Latin America. Primary education is free and compulsory, and though non-attendance especially in rural areas is high (30 per cent nationally) the illiteracy rate is only 15 per cent and urban Colombians are keen readers. Colombia has many universities, the oldest and most important being the National University in Bogotá (founded 1572). Colombian law requires that at least 10 per cent of the budget be spent on education.

Public health is poor in much of Colombia. In the lowlands malaria is endemic. Public water supplies are inadequate (80 per cent of urban and 29 per cent of rural homes have a piped water supply) and malnutrition is a serious problem. Death rate is 7.7 per thousand and the infant mortality rate 59.5. There is one doctor to every 1,969 people. However all Colombians are covered by some public social security measures. Population growth and migration into urban areas are putting heavy pressures on the housing stock and despite US aid the main agencies involved in providing low-cost housing are unable to keep pace with demand.

Political history. Colombia is a centralist republic with a long tradition of stable rule by an educated oligarchy. In 1948 the assassination of the charismatic Liberal leader, Jorge Eliecer Gaitán, touched off *La Violencia*, six years of murderous feuding between adherents of the Liberal and Conservative Parties, during which power fell into the hands of a military dictator (1953–57) Since 1957 power has been held firstly by a coalition government and latterly by the Liberals, during which time guerrilla movements have reappeared in many areas. The Liberal presidential succession was broken in 1982–86 by a radical Conservative, Dr Belisario Betancur Cuartas. Betancur successfully negotiated peace agreements with the major guerrilla movements, but his efforts were frustrated both by some hotheads and by the armed forces, who when guerrillas seized the Supreme Court building in November 1985 razed it to the ground resulting in the deaths of several of the Judges.

Outline of economic development. The economy has traditionally been dominated by the growing of coffee whose consistent high quality acts as a price marker for the trade. Coffee accounts for 50 per cent of exports, with petroleum in second place at 11.5 per cent. Colombia has a conservative fiscal policy and has never had to renegotiate its debt, though it stood at US$13,400 million at the end of 1986, equivalent to 30 per cent of exports.

Current economic situation. The economy is stable and well diversified. Unfortunately in the 1980s the economy has been distorted by the rise of the "Medellín cartel" of drug-dealers running heroin to the USA, as a result of which much of the country has become ungovernable.

P&SC

COMMITTEE FOR CO-ORDINATION OF JOINT PROSPECTING FOR MINERAL RESOURCES IN ASIAN OFFSHORE AREAS (CCOP/EAST ASIA).

The CCOP/East Asia was founded in 1966 by most of the countries of east Asia with the objectives of reducing the cost of advanced mineral surveying and prospecting and of working in partnership with developed nations providing technical advisers. Its offices are located in Bangkok, Thailand. Membership includes China, Indonesia, Japan, Kampuchea, South Korea, Malaysia, Papua New Guinea, the Philippines, Singapore, Thailand and Vietnam.

RS

COMMITTEE FOR CO-ORDINATION OF JOINT PROSPECTING FOR MINERAL RESOURCES IN THE SOUTH PACIFIC AREA (CCOP/SOPAC).

The CCOP/SOPAC was set up in 1974 by the smaller south Pacific islands and New Zealand to co-operate in the prospecting for petroleum, **manganese**, and other minerals. Its membership consists of the Cook Islands, Fiji, Kiribati, New Zealand, Papua New Guinea, the Soloman Islands, Tonga, the US Trust Territory of the Pacific Islands, Tuvalu, Vanuatu and Western Samoa. It is based in Suva, Fiji.

RS

COMMONWEATH.

Fourteen sovereign independent states of the Pacific region are members of the Commonwealth, which groups most of the former British Empire and dominions (Australia, Brunei, Canada, Kiribati, Malaysia, Nauru, New Zealand, Papua New Guinea, Singapore, Solomon Islands, Tonga, Tuvalu, Vanuatu and Western Samoa). The two smallest members, Nauru and Tuvalu, have the right to participate in all functional Commonwealth meetings and activities, but not to attend the biennial meetings of Commonweath Heads of Government. The Cook Islands and Niue are associated states, through New Zealand.

The Commonweath Heads of Government meetings have become an increasingly important forum for North–South dialogue between the industrialized and developing worlds. In the 1980s, they also spent a considerable amount of time and energy discussing an appropriate response to the situation in a former member state, South Africa. Despite the dissent of Britain, many Commonwealth nations instituted wide-ranging economic and financial sanctions against South Africa. A meeting of the Commonwealth Committee of Foreign Ministers in Canberra in August 1989, adopted further measures recommended by Australia.

The Commonweath Secretariat in London has prepared a number of studies of special interest to the Pacific region, including an assessment of the vulnerability of small states.

JF

COMMUNES: CHINA.

First established as experiments in 1957, these institutions were one of the key elements of the Maoist "model" of socialism. They were inspired by Marx's praise for the Paris Commune of 1871, and they attempted to integrate administration, industrial and agricultural organization, militia training, and (at least during the Great Leap Forward) all social life on a communal, "self-reliant" basis. They were intended to increase the self-sufficiency of rural communes in basic industrial products, and of urban communes in food. They also provided social services for members – pensions, health-care, help in times of illness and injury – out of their own income. Above all they were supposed to reduce the demands upon state bodies for resources. In the 1960s and 1970s the Dazhai commune in Shanxi province became a national model for agriculture, since it had constructed large areas of terraced fields on stony hillsides through its own efforts and greatly increased output. Similarly the oil-producing

Daqing commune in Heilongjiang province became a model for industry.

During the Great Leap Forward there were approximately 25,000 communes, with populations of up to 100,000. After its collapse their size was reduced by about two-thirds, and the extravagant hopes of communal living and eating were abandoned. They remained the basic units of local social organization until 1984, when they were dissolved because, it was alleged, they allowed political cadres too much scope for interference in agricultural decisions. The state administrative functions remained concentrated in the townships which had been at the centre of the communes, but the peasants regained the freedom to manage their own fields under the production responsibility system. Land was redivided between families. Many of the old collective welfare schemes which had been organized by the commune disintegrated, however, whilst the peasants' readiness to engage in large-scale collective earth-moving works evaporated.

CIPF

COMMUNIST PARTY OF INDONESIA.
The Indies Social Democratic Organization, founded in 1914, was renamed the Communist Party of the Indies in 1920, becoming the first communist party in Asia, and assumed its present name, the Communist Party of Indonesia (*Partai Komunis Indonesia* – PKI) in 1924. It organized unsuccessful armed uprisings in West Java and Central Sumatra in the mid–1920s, and was subsequently banned, some of its members being executed and over 10,000 others imprisoned or deported. After the Japanese occupation, during which it took part in the resistance movement, it emerged from underground in 1945 and joined the nationalist revolt against Dutch rule. In 1948, however, it staged an abortive coup against the nationalist government in East Java, with the result that most of its leaders were killed or executed.

Under the leadership of Dwipa Nusantara Aidit, M.H. Lukman and Njoto, who took control in 1951, the PKI adopted a strongly nationalist policy, supporting the demand for the annexation of Irian Jaya (West New Guinea) and the government's opposition to the formation of the Malaysian Federation. Popular support grew rapidly; in the 1955 elections the PKI obtained 6,176,914 votes, emerging as the fourth strongest party, and its membership increased from 7,900 in 1952 to an estimated 1,750,000 in 1962. It also won the support of President **Sukarno**, who appointed Aidit and Lukman ministers without portfolio in 1962 and Njoto a minister in 1964. In May 1965

Aidit claimed that the PKI had three million members, making it the largest Communist Party in the world outside China and the Soviet Union, in addition to three million members of its youth movement and 20 million sympathizers. In the Sino-Soviet controversy the majority wing of the PKI strongly supported China.

On Oct. 1, 1965, a group of Communist officers, believing a right-wing coup to be imminent, themselves carried out a coup in Jakarta in which six generals were murdered. The revolt, for which the PKI had declared its support, was almost immediately crushed, and a massacre followed in which at least 500,000 known or suspected Communists, including Aidit and most of the other party leaders, were murdered by Moslem mobs or by the army. About 700,000 people were arrested, and in 1966 the PKI was banned, although it maintained a guerrilla resistance in central and east Java and west Kalimantan until 1968. Whereas the government claimed in December 1979 to have released all but the hard-core elements detained since the 1965 coup attempt, arrests of communists continued thereafter and the PKI remained banned. Antara, the Indonesian national news agency, confirmed in October 1986 that nine former PKI members had "recently" been executed after being sentenced to death at least 18 years earlier (except for two who were sentenced in 1972 and 1973) for their involvement in the 1965 coup attempt. Three of those executed (Supono Marsudiyono, Subono – alias Waluyo and Mulyono – and Syam Kamaruzzaman) had reportedly been leading figures in the PKI's "special bureau" and had played a key role in the 1965 coup attempt. Two former PKI members were reportedly executed in November 1987 after serving long prison terms. Both the government and the media issued a series of virulently anti-communist statements in June 1988, calling on Indonesian citizens to guard against a nascent revival by the PKI.

DS

COMMUNIST PARTY OF THAILAND. The
Communist Party of Thailand (CPT), founded in 1942 by ethnic Chinese, was represented in Parliament in 1946-47 by its general secretary, Prasad Sabsunthorn, but was banned in 1952. Its third congress, held in 1961, at which Charoen Wan-Ngam was elected general secretary, adopted a strongly pro-Chinese attitude towards the Sino-Soviet controversy, and decided to adopt Maoist guerrilla war tactics. Guerrilla operations were begun in 1965 in the north-eastern provinces bordering on Laos, where the CPT had won the support of the Hmong tribespeople, and sub-

sequently spread to the northern provinces and to the extreme south, where Malayan Communist guerrillas were already active. Outside aid was greatly increased after the communists took control of Indo-China in 1975. The coup of October 1976 forced thousands of Socialists and students to flee to the "liberated zones", and in the following year the Socialist Party and the United Socialist Front, which had been driven underground, formed an alliance with the CPT, the Coordinating Committee for Patriotic and Democratic Forces (CCPDF), to conduct a revolutionary struggle against the government. By 1978 it was estimated that about 12,000 guerrillas and 10,000–15,000 members of village militia groups were operating in 46 of the 72 provinces.

The split in 1978 between China and Vietnam and the Vietnamese occupation of Kampuchea in the following year greatly weakened the CPT. It at first attempted to maintain a neutral position, but in 1979 it adopted a pro-Chinese attitude. However, sections of the CPT and many of the Socialists in the CCPDF were pro-Vietnamese in their sympathies, and fighting was reported to have taken place between the two factions. Both China and Vietnam, which were anxious to improve their relations with Thailand, ended their aid to the guerrillas in 1979. Thousands of the guerrillas, including most of the non-communists who had joined them in 1976, defected from 1979 onwards, taking advantage of the government's offer of an amnesty. The CPT's fourth congress, held in 1982, led to a split on ideological and tactical questions between the Maoist leadership and the younger members, and a number of the latter defected. Fearing that the CPT would switch from guerrilla warfare to urban terrorism, the police arrested a number of leading Communists in Bangkok in mid-1984. Raids were also carried out in Bangkok in April 1987, when police arrested 18 suspected CPT members, including four politburo members who had met to prepare for a fifth party congress in October 1987. Of the 18 arrested, five were released in November 1987. In mid-June 1987, Bangkok First Army Division radio had reported that a "pro-Soviet" CPT splinter group called the Thai People's Revolutionary Movement had been formed.

DS

CONFUCIANISM

CONFUCIANISM. Kong-fu-zi, or Master Kong, whose name was Latinized as Confucius, lived from 551–478 BCE, mostly in the state of Lu in northern China. A teacher of personal and social moral maxims, he did not found a religion or have great success. He taught the duties of rulers as well as subjects, and urged filial piety and due performance of ancestral rituals. Some of the followers of Confucius were more successful than the one who came to be called "Teacher of Ten Thousand Generations", and his ideas were developed by other scholars, notably Meng-zi (Mencius) and Hsün-zi.

A collection of "Confucian" writings, including secular documents and traditions, formed a classical canon on which civil service examinations were based for two thousand years. Confucianism triumphed over other philosophical schools, and with its prescriptions for state rituals it became the official religion of the rulers of China and neighbouring countries. Especially important was the concept of the "Mandate of Heaven" (*t'ien-ming*), from which the ruling dynasty claimed authority. This concept went back to the Chou dynasty, before the first millenium BCE and it was elaborated by Han thinkers around the turn of the eras. The Book of Rites (*Li chi*) claimed to represent Confucius's ideals of an age of Grand Unity in which the world was shared by all the people under sage-kings. With the Mandate of Heaven the emperor not only exercised temporal powers but performed cosmic functions in state and religious rituals and had an aura of divinity as a Son of Heaven.

In modern times much has changed yet attitudes persist. Examination in Confucian classics ceased after the declaration of the Chinese republic in 1911, yet the motto of unity from the Book of Rites was inscribed on the tomb of Sun Yat-sen. **Mao Zedong** said that he hated Confucius, yet the tomb of the sage has been alternately preserved, desecrated and preserved. The dominance of a new bureaucracy continues the older rule of scholars, ordering the whole of society, shrouded in secrecy, jealous of power, and revering Chairman Mao like another Confucius. Outside China the ruling classes in countries under its influence often followed Confucian directions. In Vietnam Confucianism was introduced in the eleventh century and co-existed with popular Buddhism. In Korea the state religion was Confucian until this century, encouraging ancestral veneration. The ethical behaviour of the Japanese Samurai class had roots in Confucianism. Reverence for the emperor as divine, which still persists, has roots both in Confucianism and Shinto.

GP

CONSCIENTIOUS OBJECTION

CONSCIENTIOUS OBJECTION. As military service is considered in most of the Pacific region to be a national duty, official attitudes to conscientious objection are generally hostile. Provisions for alternative service do however exist in the liberal democracies, including the United States, at times when conscription is in force, particularly for people belonging to historic peace churches, such as the Quakers or Mennonites. Not all countries in the region operate compulsory military service and indeed Costa Rica has no proper regular army.

JF

CONVENTION OF THE LAW OF THE SEA.

The Convention of the Law of the Sea (1982) was an attempt, not wholly successful, to secure international agreement to define national waters and the extent of national sovereignty, over marine and mineral resources. The exploitation and control of species in national and international waters has been a recurring subject of controversy in the twentieth century. For most of the century most coastal countries accepted the traditional three-mile territorial limit. However, historically this was a military concept, three miles being just beyond the maximum range of ship-fired shells. The advent of air power and an increase in fishing disputes rendered the three-mile limit obsolete. This in turn led to the gradual acceptance of a 12-mile (22-km) limit to the sea boundaries of national states. Yet even this proved unacceptable to countries with short coastlines. Many Latin-American countries in particular increased their national jurisdiction over waters to a distance of up to 370 km from their shores. A growing desire to develop further the marine and mineral resources of the seas and ocean beds led to the holding of the first United Nations Law of the Sea Conference in 1958 aimed at reaching agreement on the partitioning of the seas and their resources. A second conference was held in 1960 but neither reached an agreement. A third Law of the Sea Conference convened in 1973 and met several times during the 1970s and early 1980s. Finally the Convention of the Law of the Sea was promulgated by a UN conference in 1982. Although the agreement was quickly signed by 117 countries, the USA and some 20 other largely developed nations felt unable to do so. However even the non-adopting countries did agree to recognize certain terms. These included that each coastal state has sovereign rights over a 12-mile territorial area of sea and sovereign rights over natural resources and economic activities within a 200-mile **exclusive economic zone** (EEZ). Ships and aircraft, however, are permitted innocent passage through territorial waters. Moreover coastal states are also deemed to have sovereign rights over exploration and exploitation of the continental shelf (sometimes further than 200 miles). Some provision is also made for the delimitation of boundaries for archipelagic states and for the provision of access to the sea for landlocked countries.

RS

COOK ISLANDS.

Population: 21,500 (est. 1988), mainly Polynesians. *Total land area*: 236 sq km. An internally self-governing territory of New Zealand, lying some 2,000 miles to the north-east, comprising 15 islands stretching over 900 miles. *Administrative capital*: Avarua, on the island of Raratonga. *Languages*: Polynesian Maori and English.

The islands were originally settled by Polynesians from Tonga and Samoa. European contacts date from 1595 (Alvara de Mendana de Neira). Captain James Cook, after whom they are named, explored many of the islands during his three voyages. A London Missionary Society mission arrived in 1821. A British protectorate was established progressively after 1888. New Zealand annexed the islands in 1901. They were given limited self-government in 1946 and a Legislative Assembly in 1957. In 1965, a UN-supervised election created the first fully elected Assembly (with a Prime Minister and Cabinet), which then voted for self-government as part of New Zealand. The economy is based on agriculture, fishing, light industry and tourism. There has been a significant migration from the outer islands to Raratonga and generally to New Zealand.

TBM

COPPER.

Copper is a metallic element widely distributed among surface rocks and occurs naturally as a pure metal, a sulphide, an oxide or in other compounds. About half of the world's copper is used for the production of generators, electric motors, radios, televisions, cables, telephone wires and transformers. It is also used in making ornamental ware and sometimes in plumbing. There are many copper alloys including brass and bronze. Copper is widely distributed in the Pacific region and is produced in Australia, Chile, Colombia, Ecuador, Indonesia, Japan, Malaysia, Papua New Guinea, Peru, the Philippines and the USA. Chile is the world's largest producer of copper, with 23 per cent of the world's copper reserves and 15 per cent of the annual output. Its principal mines are sited at El Teniente and Chuquicamata. Production is virtually a state monopoly but foreign participation resumed in the mid-1980s with a $240 million Canadian investment in the Andacolla deposits. In Colombia copper deposits estimated at 625 million tonnes have been located in Pantanos. Peru, another significant producer, is estimated to have copper reserves totalling 1,300 million tonnes. Its richest mine is located at Toquepala.

Papua New Guinea has plans for the expansion of its copper industry currently based on the Bougainville mine, considered to be one of the richest in the world. Exploration of three other major copper deposits has already begun. They are at Ok Tedi in the Star Mountains and at Yandera and Freida River near Madang on the northern coast. Through negotiation the government has obtained a greater share of the profits from Bougainville Copper Ltd. The Indonesian part of the island, Irian Jaya, is also producing copper from the Ertsberg mountains. The annual production of copper, in thousands of tonnes, is as follows: Chile, 1,290; USA, 1,091; Canada, 712; Peru, 364; Australia, 240; Philippines, 233; Mexico, 189; China, 180; Indonesia, 86; Japan, 43; Malaysia, 28; North Korea, 10.

RS

CORAL SEA ISLANDS TERRITORY. A territory of Australia comprising several islands and reefs east of Queensland, mostly uninhabited, including Cato Island, Chilcott Island, and the Willis Group where there is a meteorological station.

TBM

COSTA RICA, REPUBLIC OF. Population: 2,000,000 (1981). *Area*: 50,700 sq km. *Gross Domestic Product*: US$1,972 million. *Trade*: US$2,349.5 million. *Top five trading partners*: USA, West Germany, Japan, Guatemala, El Salvador. *Defence spending*: US$33,000,000. *Education spending (as a percentage of GNP)*: 6.0. *Urban population as percentage of total*: 30. *Birth rate*: 30.5 per thousand. *Life expectancy*: males 56; females 59.

Geographical background. Costa Rica can be divided into three areas: the central mountainous region with its valleys and plateaux, and the coastal lowlands of the Atlantic and Pacific. Temperature depends on altitude. The lowlands are hot and wet, the mountain valleys and plateaux temperate, the highlands cool. Rainfall is high. Some 358,000 hectares are cultivated.

Costa Rica has three railway lines but most people travel by road although only one tenth of the 29,094 km of roads are paved. Rivers are short and not much used for transport. There are ports on both the Atlantic and the Pacific, where Japanese investment has promoted the development of the port of Caldera.

The majority of the population live in rural areas, and a little over a third (35.1 per cent) of the working population work in agriculture. About half live in the central region where the main urban centres are also located. Annual increase is 2.2 per cent. The capital, San José (population: 395,000) is by far the largest city.

Socio-political background. The majority are European with a sizeable *mestizo* minority. There are small numbers of blacks and Indians. Spanish is the national language. Some English is spoken. Roman Catholicism is the main religion. Costa Ricans are very proud of their high standard of education. Primary education is free and compulsory. Almost all attend primary school and illiteracy is low (11.5 per cent). The University of Costa Rica is government-funded.

Relatively high government expenditure on public health is paying off and Costa Rica has one of the most impressive life expectancy figures in Latin America. Around 95 per cent of the urban and 60 per cent of the rural population have piped water. There is one doctor to every 1,441 people, though rural provision is still considered inadequate. Death rate is 4.2 per thousand, infant mortality rate 19. Most citizens are covered to some extent by the social security and pension provisions of the government's social insurance scheme. The government is investing in low-cost housing construction.

Political history. Part of independent Central America from 1821 and fully independent since 1839, Costa Rica has for the past century been an exceptionally stable democratic republic, with a brief interruption between 1917 and 1919. Following a democratic revolution led by José Figueres Ferrer in 1948 the armed forces were abolished and a new constitution instituted providing for an executive president and a 57-seat unicameral Legislative Assembly, since which time power has changed hands peacefully by free elections. In 1982 the National Liberation Party (*Partido de Liberación Nacional – PLN*) returned to power under Luis Alberto Monge. He was succeeded in 1986 by Oscar Arias Sánchez, author of the peace plan for the region that bears his name and which won him the Nobel Peace Prize.

Outline of economic development. Major exports are coffee and bananas. Coffee was introduced in the 1880s and is grown largely by small farmers. Banana growing was introduced by Minor Keith, who built Central America's railways. The soil is unusually rich owing to volcanic activity. The rise in world oil prices has however left the country with a huge debt for its size, US$4,000 million at end 1986, representing 36 per cent of export earnings.

P&SC

D

DALINTORG. Soviet trade organization responsible for border and coastal trade with China, Japan, North Korea and Vietnam.

IG

DAOISM (TAOISM). Popular religiosity thrived in China long before **Confucianism** and Daoism emerged as recognizable entities, and it was the latter which absorbed many magical and superstitious practices. After the introduction of Indian **Buddhism** to China there were reformulations of indigenous thought systems in Neo-Daoism and Neo-Confucianism.

The Dao (*Tao*) was the "Way", the way of heaven and the way of earth, the virtue which brought harmony in nature and society. The classical scripture was The Way and its Power, attributed to a legendary sage Lao-zi (*Lao-tsu*) but generally held to have been composed by a philosophical quietist about the third century BCE. While Confucians were activists and this-worldly, Daoists were other-worldly or sought self-cultivation through meditation and practices resembling Indian yoga. But abstract ideas and self-discipline became mingled with magic and idolatry in popular religion, and in modern times countless Daoist temples have been destroyed. Yet Daoist attitudes towards harmony with nature and a peaceful way of life remain, and Daoist classics have been translated into many languages. Daoist rituals continue among Chinese communities in Hong Kong, Taiwan, Malaysia and Singapore.

Daoist societies developed early and missionaries were sent to central and east China, where they persevered despite persecution. Daoist organizations have been spoken of as "churches" and their chief official as a "pope", but there was no central authority. Taoist societies split into sects and developed like secret societies, of which a well known example was the League of Righteous Energy, known to the West as the **Boxer Rebellion** in 1900. Daoist societies continued to trouble governments and only in the 1950s was a Pervading-unity Dao Society crushed by the government. Official recognition of Daoism was given later than that accorded to other religions, and a Chinese Daoist Association was only permitted in 1957, under strict government control and not in any sense as a state religion.

GP

DAYA BAY CONTROVERSY. Daya Bay, about 50 km north-east from the centre of Hong Kong, in Guangdong province, is the site for a nuclear power plant to be completed in 1992. It is a joint venture between Hong Kong's China Light and Power Limited and the Chinese authorities, which began in January 1985. In the wake of the Chernobyl disaster in 1986, a million Hong Kong residents petitioned the Chinese government to stop the project, but were ignored.

ST

DECOLONIZATION. Post-war decolonization proved to be a painful business in much of Southeast Asia. In some cases, the Japanese had encouraged nationalist sentiments during their own wartime occupation, urging people to resist the reimposition of white colonial rule. Attempts by the Dutch to reassert their control in Indonesia at the end of the war led to sporadic fighting and the independence of all but western New Guinea (West Irian) in 1949. The latter was incorporated into Indonesia, as Irian Jaya, in 1963.

Anti-French resistance in Indo-China led to the military defeat of the French in Vietnam, with the climax of the battle of Dien Bien Phu in 1954. Communists then took control of the North of that country. Largely because of the American intervention in the South, subsequent to partition, it was another 21 years before Vietnam was re-united. Outside Indo-China, Marxist movements proved unable to wrest power from the old European colonial authorities, resorting instead to prolonged guerrilla action both before and after independence. In Malaya, later incorporated into Malaysia, the British successfully stifled an insurgency. Independence came there in 1957. Brunei followed only in 1984.

The transfer of power in the South Pacific went relatively smoothly in most cases, though independence meant the splitting up of some former administrative units. The Gilbert and Ellice Islands separated, to become Kiribati (1979) and Tuvalu (1978), though the British drew the line at allowing full autonomy for Banaba (Ocean Island). More acrimonious has been the still uncompleted independence process for the French possession of New Caledonia, where the situation is complicated by the wishes of European settlers.

Hong Kong is due to be handed back by Britain

56

DEMOCRAT PARTY (THAILAND)

to China in 1997, which is being viewed more with trepidation than joy by the vast majority of the territory's Chinese population. The British are meanwhile being urged to use the last few years of colonial control to introduce as much democracy as possible in Hong Kong. The smaller nearby Portuguese enclave of Macau will similarly pass to China in 1999, though in fact the degree of outright control of Macau by Lisbon has been much reduced since the Portuguese revolution of 1974. Under the terms of the agreements made with China, both Hong Kong and Macau will in principle be able to maintain their capitalist way of life for 50 years following their incorporation as "special administrative regions" of China.

JF

DEMOCRACY. Several of the most firmly established democracies in the world are to be found in the Pacific region, notably the United States, Canada, Japan, Australia and New Zealand. The United States, particularly under President Reagan, saw as one of its major foreign policy goals the promotion of democracy around the world, though it is debatable how directly that resulted in the extraordinary democratic awakening in the region during the 1980s.

The most consistent pattern of democratic resurgence was in Latin America, where military regimes of one kind or another gave way to elective systems in countries such as Argentina, Brazil and Uruguay. The region's longest-serving dictator, General Alfredo Stroessner of Paraguay, was ousted in 1989 and General Augusto Pinochet of Chile unwittingly engineered his own probable downfall. Other dictatorial leaders pushed out without much bloodshed included President Chun Doo Hwan of South Korea and President **Ferdinand Marcos** of the Philippines. However, problems faced by Marcos's successor, President **Corazon Aquino**, both from Marxist insurgents and from anti-democratic forces within the military, illustrated the fragility of some fledgling democracies.

Democratic developments were not all positive. In Panama, for example, General Manuel Antonio Noriega strengthened his personal grip on power behind the facade of democracy and despite the determined efforts of Washington to remove him. Two coups in Fiji in 1987 brought an end to what had been a relative stable democracy and led to Fiji's leaving the Commonweath.

Limited democratic initiatives were taken in both Taiwan and Hong Kong. But a student-led effort to democratize the People's Republic of China in 1989 ended in bloody suppression by the armed forces in Beijing (*see* **Tiananmen Incidents**). Hardliners in China denounced democratic aspirations as a form of "bourgeois liberalization" that was said to be inappropriate to China's needs and unacceptably in contradiction to the guiding role of the Chinese Communist Party.

The reputation of democratic politics and politicians took a severe knocking in Japan, in the wake of a series of financial and sexual scandals affecting leaders of the ruling **Liberal Democratic Party**. These led to a series of resignations in 1988–1989 and a surge in support for the opposition socialists under the leadership of **Doi Takako.** Her rise to prominence, together with the presidency of Corazon Aquino in the Philippines, gave some hope to women in the region that a breakthrough had been made into what still remains an essentially male democratic preserve.

JF

DEMOCRAT PARTY (THAILAND). The Democrat Party (DP) is widely regarded as Thailand's principal "civilian" party, although like other formations it has military connections. It is the oldest of the present-day legal parties, having been founded in 1946 by liberal, pro-Western elements of the post-1932 ruling hierarchy. Under the leadership of Seni Pramoj and Khuang Aphaiwong, the DP headed governments in the postwar phase of parliamentary rule. Thereafter the party was banned under the military regimes which ruled for much of the period from 1951 to 1973, although in brief parliamentary interludes it obtained substantial electoral support. Following the 1973 student revolt against military rule and the promulgation of a democratic constitution, the DP emerged as the strongest party from both the 1975 and the 1976 elections. However, Seni Pramoj's DP-led coalition government was overthrown in October 1976 and in the 1979 elections, held under a partial restoration of parliamentary rule, the party retained only 32 of its 114 seats; nevertheless, it joined Gen. Prem's government formed in March 1980. The DP emerged as significantly the strongest party from the July 1986 elections, with 100 seats (out of 347), having not only consolidated its traditional support in the south, but also made gains in Bangkok and the north-east. It was thus the principal component of a further Prem-led coalition, with the party's leader, Bichai Rattakul, continuing as a Deputy Premier.

The DP general secretary, Veera Musikapong, resigned as Deputy Interior Minister in September 1986 after being charged with *lèse majesté* (Veera was subsequently sentenced to six years' imprisonment in late 1987, but was released in July 1988 having spent a month in prison after being pardoned by the King). In DP leadership elections held on Jan. 10, 1987, Bichai defeated a nominee of a faction led by Veera. Members of this anti-Bichai faction (the so-called "January 10" group) subsequently voted against the government in November 1987 and April 1988 over proposed legislation on copyright. The latter act of dissent prompted all DP government ministers to resign their posts, after which Gen. Prem called an early general election. After the dissolution, at least 31 DP dissidents resigned their membership of the DP and formed the *Prachachon* Party. In the July 1988 elections the DP managed to maintain its southern support and retained 48 seats, the third largest number. It joined the six-member **Chatichai**-coalition in August and gained five Cabinet seats.

DS

DEMOCRATIC ACTION PARTY (MALAYSIA).

The democratic socialist Democratic Action Party (DAP) is strongly but not exclusively based in the Malaysian Chinese community. Since the 1986 federal elections, when the DAP gained 24 seats and over 20 per cent of votes cast, it has constituted the main opposition to the ruling National Front coalition. It originated as the Malaysian wing of the ruling **People's Action Party** of Singapore, and was established as an independent party following Singapore's withdrawal from the Malaysian federation in August 1965. Contesting its first general elections in May 1969 in alliance with Gerakan, the DAP achieved a significant success, gaining 13 parliamentary seats. Seen as a political breakthrough for non-Malays, this result precipitated a wave of serious intercommunal violence. Thereafter the DAP's activities as an opposition party were circumscribed by various internal security and other measures enacted by successive National Front governments. The DAP described the August 1986 elections as "by far the most unfair and undemocratic in Malaysia's history" and intensified its opposition to the Mahathir government. The government responded in October–November 1987 by instituting a major security clampdown in which Lim Kit Siang, the DAP general secretary, and 15 other DAP leaders were among over 100 persons arrested for allegedly stimulating inter-racial tensions. Lim was eventually released from detention in April 1989.

DS

DEMOCRATIC JUSTICE PARTY (KOREA – DJP, Minju chŏngŭi-dang).

Founded in January 1981 as personal political vehicle for **Gen. Chun Doo Hwan** who seized effective power in the military coup of Dec. 12, 1979. It is sponsored by former members of the **Democratic Republican Party**. In the 1987 presidential election, candidate **Roh Tae Woo** polled 36 per cent of the vote and won the election. The party, however, failed to gain a majority of seats in the elections for the National Asembly of April 26, 1988.

JHG

DEMOCRATIC KAMPUCHEA (DK).

Name taken by Cambodia under the constitution adopted in January 1976, following the victory of the *Khmer Rouge* in April 1975. It was effectively dominated by Pol Pot's **Kampuchean Communist Party**, although the latter did not reveal its own existence until September 1977. The name continued to be used by Pol Pot's regime after the fall of Phnom Penh to Vietnamese forces in January 1979 and the emergence of the People's Republic of Cambodia under **Heng Samrin**. Following the "retirement" of **Pol Pot**, the DK president **Khieu Samphan** participated in negotiations with other anti-Vietnamese factions to establish the **Coalition Government of Democratic Kampuchea** in 1982. Democratic Kampuchea has continued to be recognized by the governments of the **Association of South-East Asian Nations (ASEAN)** and to occupy Cambodia's seat at the United Nations.

RBS

DEMOCRATIC KAMPUCHEA, COALITION GOVERNMENT OF (CGDK).

Established in June 1982, to supersede the government of Democratic Kampuchea which had been driven out of Phnom Penh by the Vietnamese in January 1979, and which had been under the premiership of **Khieu Samphan** since early 1980. The coalition grew out of negotiations encouraged by several of the governments of the **Association of South-East Asian Nations (ASEAN)**, which bore fruit in a conference in Singapore on Sept. 4, 1981, attended by Khieu Samphan, **Prince Sihanouk** and **Son Sann**. Under an agreement finalized in Kuala Lumpur on June 22, 1982, Sihanouk became president of the new government, Khieu Samphan vice-president, and Son Sann prime minister. It received international recognition from the ASEAN governments, from China and from several Western countries; and on that basis successfully laid claim to the Cambodian seat at the United Nations, where

Sihanouk made annual speeches to the General Assembly between 1982 and 1986.

Tensions within the coalition, together with the complicated nature of any possible negotiations on the Cambodian issue, led Sihanouk to seek one year's leave from the presidency in May 1987. That allowed him to meet **Hun Sen**, the prime minister of the People's Republic of Kampuchea as a private individual on two occasions in December 1987 and January 1988. Following the second meeting he threatened to resign completely from the coalition, but on Feb. 29, 1988 he agreed to resume the presidency in due course. In subsequent negotiations, all three component "factions" of the coalition participated directly, notably at the Jakarta Informal Meetings of July 25-28, 1988 and Feb. 16-21, 1989. By the latter date, tensions between Sihanouk and the **Khmer Rouge** within the coalition were extremely acute, with Sihanouk refusing to co-operate in any way with their former leader **Pol Pot**. However, on March 12, 1989 the coalition was reinvigorated at a meeting in Beijing, when Sihanouk, Khieu Samphan and Son Sann formed a "High Council for National Defence" from which the Pol Pot group was explicitly excluded. It remained to be seen what would become of the coalition in the event of a political settlement with Phnom Penh and the Vietnamese. It should be noted that while the CGDK operated as a single entity in the diplomatic sphere, each of its three components retained separate control of their respective armed forces inside Cambodia and had its own following among the *Khmer* refugees in camps along the Thai-Cambodian border. (*See also* **Democratic Kampuchea, National Army of; Khmer People's National Liberation Front**; and **Sihanoukist National Army**).

RBS

DEMOCRATIC KAMPUCHEA, NATIONAL ARMY OF (NADK).

Armed forces of the **Khmer Rouge** element within the **Coalition Government of Democratic Kampuchea** formed in 1982. Until September 1985 they were still under the command of **Pol Pot**, although he had resigned as prime minister of **Democratic Kampuchea** at the end of 1979 and the **Kampuchean Communist Party** (which he had led as secretary-general) had formally dissolved itself in December 1981. Pol Pot's successor as commander of the NADK was **Son Sen**, former defence minister in the period 1975-78. It is possible that a power struggle then developed between Son Sen and **Ta Mok**, thought to have been a much closer associate of Pol Pot during the 1970s. In the absence of detailed information about the command structure of the NADK it is difficult to assess which of the three enjoyed greatest actual military control by 1985.

RBS

DEMOCRATIC PROGRESS PARTY (TAIWAN – Min-chu chin-pu-tang).

Taiwan's first opposition party, the Democratic Progress Party (DPP), was founded on Sept. 28, 1986 by members of the *Tangwai*. An earlier attempt by a group of mainland intellectuals and Taiwanese politicans to organize a new political party, the China Democratic Party, had failed in 1961.

Prohibited by martial law to form new political parties, independent politicians and political activists in 1978 formed a loose alliance called *Tangwai*, literally meaning "outside the party", i.e. the **Kuomintang**, in order to co-ordinate their political activities and to develop a common political platform for the supplementary elections in December 1978. These elections were postponed by the government in response to American de-recognition. The *Tangwai* sought to stress their demands for political reforms by organizing a series of demonstrations. The magazine *Formosa* became the centre of *Tangwai* activities. Its leadership built up an organizational infrastructure for political activities. Through a number of local branches, it sought to affiliate all independent politicians on the island. These activities were suppressed after the **Kaohsiung Incident**. The government arrested numerous *Tangwai* members belonging to the Formosa faction on charges of sedition.

During the 1980s differences among the *Tangwai* over central political issues and opposition strategy became more pronounced. A mainstream group, including the majority of *Tangwai* parliamentarians, stressed political reforms within the existing political structures, while a radical tendency, dominated by young political activists, advocated confrontational tactics. The political programme of the DPP calls for the termination of the temporary provisions and the return to constitutional rule, a complete renewal of the membership of the national parliaments through elections and the establishment of a modern welfare state. It also advocates the re-establishment of international relations and the right of the inhabitants of Taiwan to decide their own fate. Party leadership consists of the chairman and a central executive commission with 31 members, daily business is conducted by an 11-member standing committee. In order to develop intra-party democracy and to avoid a concentration of power in the party leadership, the terms of office for both chairman and secretary-general have been limited to one year, with possible re-election to one additional term. Since the party's foundation, no chairman has been re-elected. The DPP's organizational structure is divided into three levels, national, county and municipality, although no party branches below the county level have been established until now. Its membership of 15,000 is recruited primarily from the lower middle classes and dominated by native Taiwanese.

In the supplementary elections held in December 1986, the DPP won 12 seats in the Legislative Yüan and 11 seats in the National Assembly. Although campaigning as a political party the party's share of votes (22 per cent for the Legislative Yüan and 19 per cent for the National Assembly) did not increase substantially compared with that of the *Tangwai* in preceding elections. Conflicts between the party's mainstream and radical tendencies have intensified. The "New Movement faction" favours mass action over electoral politics and calls for an alliance with the working classes. The reconstituted "Formosa Faction", consisting primarily of elected politicans and several former political prisoners affiliated with the magazine *Formosa*, advocates concentration on elections and looks for support among the middle classes.

A member of the DPP's parliamentary party in the Legislative Yüan, Wang Yi-hsiung, announced the formation of a new party in late 1987. The new Labour Party (*Kungtang*) intends to become the main political movement for Taiwan's industrial workforce.

HH

DEMOCRATIC REPUBLICAN PARTY (KOREA – DRP, Minju konghwa-dang). Founded on Jan. 1, 1963 as a political vehicle for Gen. **Park Chung-hee**, and the ruling party throughout the 1960s and 1970s. It was dissolved along with other parties in 1980 at the time of the advent of Chun Doo Hwan to power.

JHG

DEMOCRATIC SOCIALIST PARTY (JAPAN). The **Japan Socialist Party** (JSP) split in October 1951 over the question of acceptance of the San Francisco Peace Treaty and the US–Japan Security Treaty. Re-unification of the JSP was effected in 1955 without any final resolution of underlying ideological differences brought into focus by the Treaties. The divide was exacerbated by a rising standard of living which reduced the interest of labour in the **Sohyo** trade union federation although its militant rhetoric continued to have appeal to public sector

unions. Increasingly, private-sector unions affiliated to the moderate **Domei** federation. In the event, the Party split in October 1959 into the DSP, "right-wing and revisionist" and supported by Domei, and the JSP, left-wing, militant and buttressed by Sohyo and its adherents. Today, 30 years later, the parliamentary strength of the DSP is much as it was then. It has its place but has proved incapable of exploiting this or of creating a significant centrist niche. The DSP response in 1989 to the leadership ambitions of the JSP leader **Doi Takako** suggest that now, as then, hostility to the JSP remains a key characteristic of the party.

RAB

DEMOCRATIC STRUGGLE FOR THE PHILIPPINES. The pro-Aquino Democratic Struggle for the Philippines (*Lakas ng Demokratikong Pilipinas* – LDP) was established in late June 1988 and quicky became the principal political grouping in the House of Representatives as well as gaining substantial Senate membership. The LDP was based around the Philippine Democratic Party–People's Power (*Partido Demokratiko Pilipino–Lakas ng Bayan* – PDP–Laban) alliance and the *Lakas ng Bansa* (Power of the Nation), both of which were part of the ruling, pro-Aquino *Lakas ng Bayan* (People's Power) coalition. The formation of the LDP had been largely motivated by Jose "Peping" Cojuangco, the PDP–Laban president and President Aquino's younger brother. At the LDP's inaugural conference held in mid-September 1988, Ramon Mitra, the Speaker of the House of Representatives, was elected as the party's president, and congressman Emigdio Tanjuatco (another relative of the president) as the secretary-general.

DS

DENG XIAOPING. Born in Sichuan province in 1904, the chaos of China in the 1920s were a vital part of his formative influences. Deng became a student and worker in France between 1920 and 1926, where he met **Zhou Enlai** and joined the **Chinese Communist Party (CCP)**. He participated in the **Long March**, and in 1945 was elected to the party Central Committee. From 1929 he was an increasingly prominent political commissar with the Red Army, and after 1945 he became commissar for the Second Field Army. He established a reputation for energy, impatience, and an independent mind.

After consolidating communist power in the south west of China, Deng became party General Secretary from 1954 until the Cultural Revolution. He was one of the group of leaders forced to repair the damage caused by the Great Leap Forward, but the more pragmatic measures adopted increasingly set him at odds with **Mao Zedong**. He was credited with the remark that "It does not matter whether the cat is white or black, so long as it catches mice". Finally during the Cultural Revolution he was publicly criticized as "the No. 2 person taking the capitalist road" (after **Liu Shaoqi**). One of his sons was crippled by defenestration by Red Guards. He re-emerged in 1973 as a vice-Premier, and as Zhou Enlai became increasingly incapacitated by cancer, Deng took over the role of head of the government. He attempted to introduce a programme of Four Modernizations in 1975, which would have involved a greater opening of China to the outside world.

However, following the demonstrations in Tiananmen Square in 1976 (*See* **Tiananmen Incidents**), he was once again driven out of politics by the radicals. He made his second return in July 1977, and was reappointed to the Standing Committee of the Political Bureau. He rapidly and determinedly pushed aside **Hua Guofeng**, drove the party into opening China to the outside world, and launched the current programme of **Four Modernizations**. He used Maoist phrases against the later Mao to undermine the legacy of the Cultural Revolution. He skilfully appropriated Mao's injunction from Yanan to "seek truth from facts" and directed it against blind belief in Mao's ideas. He insisted (like Mao) upon the need for a "socialism with Chinese characteristics", whilst leaving open what that might mean. Unlike Mao, he has given economics a higher priority than politics, although he laid down that reformers should hold fast to four political principles: the socialist road, the dictatorship of the proletariat, leadership by the CCP, and Marxism-Leninism and Mao Thought.

Since the early 1980s he has been China's paramount leader, although formally he has not held the most senior position in either the party or state hierarchies. Since 1987 his only formal leading position has been Chairman of the party's Military Affairs Commission, which effectively made him commander of the armed forces. He attempted to restore the confidence of the intelligentsia after the traumas of the Cultural Revolution with the reform programme in the 1980s, but it was his description of the student movement of spring 1989 as counter-revolutionary which ensured that it would be crushed. Like Mao, he has now repudiated his two first choices as successors, **Hu Yaobang** and **Zhao Ziyang**. This will ensure that his succession will be unpredictable.

CIPF

DIAMOND. Most diamond production is in South Africa but Australia is a significant supplier producing some 5,700 carats annually. Indonesia also produces some 2,700 carats.

RS

DIOMEDE ISLANDS. Two small islands in the Bering Strait between the Chukchi peninsula in the Soviet Union and the Seward Peninsula in Alaska. Here the Soviet Union and the United States are geographically at their closest point, with only three miles separating Big Diomede, which is Soviet territory, from Little Diomede, which belongs to the United States.

IG

DO MUOI. Prime minister of the Socialist Republic of Vietnam since June 1988. A native of the Hanoi area, he joined the Indochinese Communist Party in 1939 and was imprisoned by the French authorities two years later. He escaped in time to participate in the "August Revolution" of 1945 and held a series of party positions in what is now Ha Nam Ninh province during the late 1940s and early 1950s. Following the Viet Minh takeover in the North, he was in charge of the port city of Haiphong in 1955-56; a position from which he graduated to become deputy, then minister, of internal trade (1956-60). In the 1960s he disappeared completely from view for seven years, to re-emerge in 1967 as minister in charge of state pricing policy. From 1969 to 1986 he was deputy prime minister with responsibilities in the state construction sector of the economy. He became an alternate member of the Politburo of the **Vietnamese Communist Party** in 1976; a full member in 1982. During 1978 he spent some time in the South, supervising the "socialist transformation" of industry and trade. He moved from the government to the Party secretariat in 1986 but returned to the government, as its head, two years later. He has the reputation of being strongly opposed to corruption, but with regard to economic reforms is thought to be more cautious than some of his colleagues.

RBS

DOI TAKAKO. In July 1986, the Japan Socialist Party experienced its worst general election defeat in the nearly 40 years since 1949. The JSP representation was reduced from 112 to 85 seats in the all important 512-seat lower house. Party Chairman Ishibashi resigned and was replaced by

Doi Takako, a seven-time Diet member and the first woman to be made head of the Socialist Party, or any other party, in Japan.

RAB

DOLGANS. A Turkic-speaking ethnic group found in the north of the East Siberian Region of the Soviet Union. Numbering fewer than 6,000 people, the Dolgans inhabit the Taymyr (formerly Dolgan-Nenets) National District, where they share administrative-territorial autonomy with the eastern Nenets (an ethnic group found in the far north of the Soviet Union from European Russia to the Taymyr peninsula).

IG

DOMEI (JAPANESE CONFEDERATION OF LABOUR). Founded in 1962 in opposition to **Sohyo**, when Sohyo unions decided not to affiliate to the ICFTU, Domei has been the principal social foundation of the **Democratic Socialist Party** (DSP). Domei was dissolved in 1987 on the formation of **Rengo**.

RAB

DRUGS. Two of the world's major drug-producing areas are on the Pacific rim: the "Golden Triangle" of Burma, Laos and northern Thailand and Andean countries, notably Peru and Bolivia.

The Golden Triangle is a major source of opium and derivatives such as heroin, though its predominant position in the global market has diminished in recent years. This is partly because of the expansion of drug production and export from other areas, in particular Afghanistan, but it also reflects an attempt by the authorities in Southeast Asia to limit the trade. Malaysia has particularly tough narcotics legislation. Minority tribes in mountainous areas of Southeast Asia have tended to be the major growers of opium poppies, though much of the refining and trafficking has been in the hands of armed rebel groups and drugs barons. After the Chinese Revolution, some units of **Chiang Kai-shek**'s defeated nationalist forces allegedly became involved. During the Vietnam War, the region's drug business boomed, both because of the difficulty of policing it at a time of regional conflict and because of the expanding market of US servicemen and other expatriates, both in the area and subsequently back home. More recently, the Thai authorities, in particular, have stepped up campaigns to curb drug production and drug use, receiving some US help for this.

The Andean countries are a principal source of coca, from which cocaine and other substances such as "crack" are derived. There has been a traditional use of coca by indigenous people in the Andes, mainly as a way of dulling the effects of cold and hunger, but much of the production is now geared to export, in refined form, to North America and beyond. About half of the cocaine consumed in the United States is thought to originate in the Upper Huallaga Valley of Peru, where anti-narcotics action by government security forces is considerably hampered by the local strength of the *Sendero Luminoso* ("Shining Path") guerrilla forces. Much of the region's cocaine trade is handled by Colombian middlemen, including the so-called Medellin Cartel and its smaller counterpart based at Cali.

The power, wealth and ruthlessness of the drugs barons in Latin America has destabilized several countries in the region, especially Colombia itself. In 1989, the Colombian government of President Virgilio Barco and the drug-traffickers declared outright war on each other, following a wave of assassinations and intimidation by the drug dealers' men. Nonetheless, the attitude of ordinary people in parts of Latin America towards the drugs trade is ambivalent. Some peasant farmers find they can earn more from growing coca than from anything else. Moreover, some of the drugs barons have built up popular support by funding the provision of housing and other amenities which would otherwise not be available.

US President Bush announced a new campaign against drugs in September 1989, attacking the problem both at home and in the producing countries. Washington recognizes that the high demand for drugs in the United States has been a major stimulant to the drugs trade and related crime. This has led to both loss of income and increased violence in the United States itself, as well as heightened instability and corruption in Latin America. Accordingly, President Bush authorized increased spending in drugs-control programmes abroad. That includes not only crop-substitution, but also material and technical assistance to the Colombian government and others to strengthen the security forces and protect the judiciary. A limited number of US military personnel have worked in Bolivia and Colombia, advising the authorities, but there was strong resistance among Latin Americans to the idea of US combat troops being sent to the region to take a more active role in the anti-drugs war. The contradiction between Latin American nations wishing to reduce the drugs problem while keeping their sovereignty and national pride intact was highlighted by widespread opposition in the region to US attempts to oust Panama's military strongman General Manuel Antonio Noriega, who was charged in absentia by a US federal court with drug-profiteering. A limited number of drug dealers have been extradited to the USA.

JF

E

EAST TIMOR. The island of Timor lies at the eastern end of the Lesser Sunda island chain in the Indonesian archipelago. For several centuries it was divided between Dutch and Portuguese colonial rule in the western and eastern halves of the island respectively. After West Timor had joined with other parts of the Dutch East Indies to become the Republic of Indonesia in 1949, East Timor continued under Portuguese rule until the mid-1970s but was then incorporated into Indonesia in August 1976 following Indonesian military intervention. Whereas the territory is now regarded by Indonesia as its 27th province (called Loro Sae), the Portuguese government and a majority of UN member states have refused to recognize Indonesia's claim to sovereignty over East Timor and have asserted that its people have the right to self-determination of their status.

DS

EASTER ISLAND (Isla de Pascus/Rapa Nui). The most isolated inhabited island in the world, 3,790 km west of the Chilean coast just south of the Tropic of Capricorn, measuring some 24 km long and 12 km wide, and in area 166 sq km. Its 2,000 inhabitants (1985) are of predominantly Polynesian origin and live by the cultivation of taro, yams and similar crops. Politically part of Valparaíso Province, Chile, the local administrative centre is Hanga Hoa. The mystery of the huge monolithic stone heads for which the island is celebrated has now been solved. They were raised by its inhabitants, and abandoned after the destruction of all trees on the island deprived them of the means to maintain them.

P&SC

ECONOMIC AND SOCIAL COMMISSION FOR ASIA AND THE PACIFIC (ESCAP). ESCAP is one of the United Nations' regional commissions. It was set up in 1947 to promote social and economic development in Asia and the Far East, and was known as the Economic Commission for Asia and the Far East (ECAFE) until 1974. It has 38 member countries. They are as follows:

Afghanistan
Australia
Bangladesh
Bhutan
Brunei
Burma
China (People's Republic)
Fiji
France
India
Indonesia
Iran
Japan
Kampuchea
South Korea
Laos
Malaysia
Maldives
Mongolia
Nauru
Nepal
Netherlands
New Zealand
Pakistan
Papua New Guinea
The Philippines
Singapore
Solomon Islands
Sri Lanka
Thailand
Tonga
Tuvalu
United Kingdom
United States
USSR
Vanuatu
Vietnam
Western Samoa

It also has a number of associated members. They are as follows:

Cook Islands
Guam
Hong Kong
Kiribati
Marshall Islands
Federated States of Micronesia
Niue
Northern Mariana Islands
Palau

The Commission meets annually at ministerial level to monitor progress in the region and construct programmes for future action, whilst committees of officials who deal with specific areas of the Commission's work meet annually or every two years. The Commission has a permanent secretariat.

ESCAP has a regular budget which is appropriated from the central UN budget. For the two-year period 1988–89 it was US$33.5 million. Its regular budget is supplemented from elsewhere to enable it to carry out its commitments to give technical assistance to its poorer members.

As a regional centre of the United Nations, the main functions of ESCAP are to act as an inter-governmental forum for the whole of Asia and the Pacific, and to implement a wide range of development programmes involving advisory services to governments, technical assistance, training and research. For example, as well as helping farmers to improve their methods by giving them advice and assistance and by introducing credit schemes and co-operative producing units, the commission provides assistance with industrial technology, demographic problems, transport, the exploitation of natural resources and in a number of other areas. It also helps the countries of the region with the task of the accurate collection of statistical data, as well as publishing valuable data of its own for the region.

DA

ECUADOR, REPUBLIC OF. *Population*: 8,000,000 (1981). *Area*: 283,561 sq km. *Gross Domestic Product*: US$5,877 million. *Trade*: US$5,014 million. *Top five trading partners*: USA, Japan, Korea, West Germany, Brazil. *Defence spending*: US$204 million (1984). *Education spending as percentage of GNP*: 5.6. *Urban population as percentage of total*: 40. *Birth rate*: 40 per thousand. *Life expectancy*: males 46; females 48.

Geographical background. Ecuador may be divided into three regions: the Pacific coastal lowlands, the mountainous highlands which comprise two ranges of the Andes with a plateau between, and the jungles of the Amazon Basin in the eastern interior of the country. The coastal region is mainly humid tropical forest. The climate of the central highlands varies with altitude but Quito, the capital, is temperate. The Amazon jungles are hot and wet. Some 1.6 million hectares are cultivated. Railways (only 966 km) are government owned but now in decline owing to financial neglect and competition from road transport. More than four-fifths (84 per cent) of the roads (35,718 km) are unpaved and routes are limited by the difficulties of crossing the Andes. Guayaquil is by far the most important port and the Guayas River enables transportation

of goods to the lowlands provinces. Air travel, both domestic and international, is well developed. The port city of Guayaquil (population 1,279,000) is the largest city. The population is growing at a high 3.1 per cent *per annum*.

Socio-political background. Nearly two-thirds of Ecuadorians are of Amerindian descent, nearly a third *mestizo*. A small remainder are European, black or mulatto. Spanish is the national language but Quechua is widely spoken, and is the sole language of a small proportion. The main religion is Roman Catholicism though there is some animism in the interior. Primary education is free and compulsory – 80 per cent of primary school age are enrolled. Literacy campaigns in the late 1960s and 1970s have reduced the illiteracy among adults over 15 to 26 per cent. Both Quito and Guayaquil have Catholic Universities. Malnutrition is still a serious problem. Although 1,622 persons per doctor is not a bad average and the death rate is 8.1 per thousand, facilities are concentrated in towns and the highland Indians have scant provision. Around 73 per cent of urban dwellers have piped water; only 6 per cent of those in the country do. The infant mortality rate is a high 86 per thousand. A sizeable minority of workers is covered by social security. The majority of housing both urban and rural is overcrowded and inadequate.

Political history. Ecuador seceded from Colombia in 1830. In the early part of the twentieth century its politics were dominated by the coastal oligarchy ruling through the Radical Liberal party, but since the 1930s politics have been turbulent and subject to frequent if relatively mild periods of military rule, the most recent between 1972 and 1979. Dominance of the army has been restrained by inter-service rivalry and the importance of the navy in protecting Ecuador's valuable tuna fisheries. In 1979 the present Constitution was established, providing for an executive president and a 71-member unicameral congress. The latter is an active and rebellious partner in government in Ecuador and coalitions change frequently. In 1984 a conservative businessman president, Sr León Febres Cordero Rivadeneira, who espoused free-market solutions, was elected. After accusations of corruption and mismanagement he received only 13 per cent of the votes at the polls in 1988, when Dr Rodrigo Borja Cevallos of the Democratic Left (ID) was elected.

Outline of economic development. The discovery of oil in the 1970s changed economic prospects, and in 1985 crude oil accounted for over 60 per cent of exports. Otherwise Ecuador depended principally on fishing and agriculture. Bananas were developed by the United Fruit Company in 1950s, and are now the second/largest export (7.6 per cent). Both military mismanagement and free-market experiment have left the country with a huge US$10,000 million debt, and no payments have been made since January 1988.

P&SC

EKKAPARB (THAILAND). *Ekkaparb* (solidarity) was created in Thailand in mid-April 1989 after the Supreme Court approved the merger of four opposition parties. *Prachachon* (People), the Progressive Party and the Community Action Party were dissolved and their members were permitted to merge with the main opposition grouping, *Ruam Thai* (United Thai), whose name was changed to *Ekkaparb*. The four opposition parties together commanded 71 MPs, making it the second-largest party. However, three days after the Supreme Court approved the merger, at least nine of the 71 MPs (all *Prachachon* members) defected to the leading party in the ruling coalition, *Chart Thai*, raising the number of *Chart Thai* MPs to 96 and the total number of government MPs to 229.

DS

EL SALVADOR, REPUBLIC OF. *Population*: 5,000,000 (1981). *Area*: 21,041 sq km. *Gross Domestic Product*: US$1,698 million. *Trade*: US$1,974.4 million. *Top five trading partners*: USA, Guatemala, West Germany, Costa Rica, Japan. *Defence spending*: US$251 million. *Education spending as percentage of GNP*: 3.7. *Urban population as percentage of total*: 25. *Birth rate*: 40 per thousand. *Life expectancy* males 44; females 46.5.

Geographical background. The Pacific coast of El Salvador is a strip of land often little more than 10 miles wide. Behind it the central plateau on which the capital San Salvador is sited is virtually ringed with volcanoes. The northern region comprises the valley formed by the River Lempa and a range of mountains separating El Salvador from neighbouring Honduras. Minor frontier disputes on this border were submitted to the International Court of Justice in 1986. Temperatures are generally warm but vary with altitude. May to November are the wettest months. Some 689,000 hectares are cultivated. Railways (602 km) are narrow gauge and single track. Most (86 per cent) of the 12,149 km of roads remain unpaved. The Pacific coastal ports of Acajutla, La Libertad and Cutuco are important. Domestic air travel is very limited but there is an international airport near San Salvador. El Salvador is the most densely populated country in Latin America and population increase is a high 3.1 per cent *per annum*. San Salvador (population 326,000) is the largest city, followed by Santa Ana and San Miguel.

Socio-political background. The vast majority of the population is *mestizo* with a few Indians and an even smaller number of Europeans. The national language is Spanish though a few Indians still use Nahuatl. Roman Catholicism is the main religion but is heavily penetrated by Protestant sects. Primary education is free and compulsory though attendance is limited, especially in rural areas, and only 70 per cent nationally are enrolled. Adult illiteracy has been brought down to 38 per cent following government literacy campaigns. The National University of El Salvador, founded in 1841, is located in San Salvador. Infant mortality remains relatively high at 42 per thousand despite public health initiatives, many of them funded by international agencies such as UNICEF. Diseases associated with malnutrition and poor sanitation remain the main causes of death. Only 54 per cent of town dwellers have piped water; in the country only 3 per cent. There are some 3,179 persons per physician. Like medical aid, social security provision is concentrated in urban areas. Inadequate housing characterizes urban and rural areas alike.

Political history. Dominance of the traditional oligarchy ("the fourteen families") broke up in the 1960s and was replaced by conservative military government. The Nicaraguan Revolutin of 1979 was imitated by the Left in El Salvador but lacked its wide social support, and after the assassination in 1980 of Archbishop Romero by right-wingers close to the Arena party violent repression brought general civil war which remains at stalemate. Heavy US military aid continues but direct US involvement has been avoided. At the 1989 elections the weak Christian Democratic government which had held office with US backing since 1984 was replaced by a hard right one. Guerrillas have indicated their willingness to talk peace since 1983 but exploratory talks have been halted by military and hard-line civilian resistance.

Outline of economic development. Traditionally dominated by coffee, which in 1985 still accounted for 66.9 per cent of exports, some modest industrialization in the 1960s has been negated by the civil war which has occasioned great loss of life and damage to the infrastructure. Cotton is the second largest export (4.5 per cent).

Current economic situation. North-south communication has been repeatedly interrupted by armed action and disruption is widespread. The national debt was US$2,100 million at end-1986, some 16 per cent of export earnings.

P&SC

ENRILE, JUAN PONCE. Enrile, aged 65 and a lawyer by profession, is perhaps the principal figure of opposition to the Aquino government in the Philippines and must be considered a credible contender for the presidency in 1992. One of only two opposition Senators, Enrile was elected Secretary-General of the right-wing **Nacionalista Party** (NP) in May 1989, prior to which he had been a joint leader of the opposition Grand Alliance for Democracy.

Enrile served under **Marcos** as Justice Secretary (1968-70) and Defence Secretary (1970-71 and 1972-86). As Defence Secretary he was largely responsible for bringing **Corazon Aquino** to power in February 1986, by rejecting President Marcos's continuing authority and, along with Gen. **Fidel Ramos**, initiating a decisive army mutiny. Aquino re-appointed Enrile as Defence Secretary in her new government, but following allegations that he had colluded with his supporters in the Army (many of whom were pro-Marcos officers) to overthrow Aquino in November 1986, he was dismissed from the Cabinet. Enrile opposed the adoption of the new 1987 Constitution and, in May 1987, he was elected to the Senate. Despite his dismissal as Defence Secretary, he had retained very close links with the Army, particularly with young officers associated with the Reform of the Armed Forces of the Philippines Movement (RAM).

DS

ENVIRONMENT. Environmental awareness has become a major political factor throughout most of the Pacific region, though standards of pollution control and environmental protection vary considerably. The transnational nature of many "green" issues has led to considerable co-operation between neighbouring states, as well as to international efforts to help save major global natural assets such as the Amazon rain forests, Antarctica and the Pacific Ocean. However, there has also been some tension as a result of environmental concerns, even between close allies such as Canada and the United States. The Canadians were particularly annoyed at what they saw to be the partial responsibility of US industry for the creation of acid rain, with consequent damage to forests, as well as the poisoning of Canadian lakes.

The Japanese government has been increasingly embarrassed by accusations that Japan is the "dirty man" of the Pacific. Tougher pollution controls in Japan itself in the 1960s and 1970s led to the migration of certain chemical and other high-polluting industries abroad, notably to the Philippines, where controls were weaker. Japanese fishing practices in the South Pacific during the 1980s were also singled out for international criticism, for allegedly depleting stocks to an unacceptable level. Non-governmental agencies working in environmental protection, such as Greenpeace, ran long campaigns attacking Japan's reluctance to halt commercial whaling.

Greenpeace was also active in the campaign to denuclearize the Pacific. This led to a major diplomatic row between New Zealand and France, when French security agents blew up a boat belonging to Greenpeace, the "Rainbow Warrior", in 1985, in the New Zealand port of Auckland. Nuclear concerns of a different kind led to a sudden growth of environmental awareness in the Soviet Union, following a major accident at an atomic power plant at Chernobyl in 1986. As *glasnost* spread inside the Soviet Union, so publicity was given in the Soviet media to the unsatisfactory nature and high pollution of much of Soviet industry. Similar problems could be found in China and in some of the newly-industrialized countries of East Asia, where the goal of economic development had been targeted without due concern for environmental effects. Some of the countries concerned argued that environmental controls were a luxury they could not afford at this stage of the development, given their low GDP. China insisted, for example, that it could not be expected to phase out ozone-damaging chlorofluorocarbons (CFCs) at a time when its population was demanding more refrigerators.

Such problems led to a growing recognition of the need for the international community to assist poorer countries in programmes to limit environmental damage, both through bilateral aid and through institutions such as the World Bank. The World Bank President, Barber Conable, set out specific priorities for World Bank schemes in this field at a conference on "Global environment and the Human Response towards Sustainable Development" in Tokyo in September 1989. These included assistance to developing countries to mitigate the emissions of greenhouse gases and support for the eventual total elimination of the use of CFCs.

However, international concern for the environment has not proved universally popular, especially when it has been seen to infringe on national sovereignty. Probably the most acute case of this is the resentment of several Andean states and Brazil about foreign "interference" in the way those countries are managing their forests and other natural resources. Leading local politicians in the Amazon states, for example, have argued that it was not up to the outside world to lecture Brazil on how it should use God-given natural wealth.

Local environmental groups have grown up in several Latin American and Pacific states, complementing the work of international organizations. This has sometimes prompted intimidation and even murder by vested interests or the authorities, when environmentalists have been seen to be hindering profitable schemes. However, there have been some successes. A campaign in 1988 by Catholic activists in the Philippines led to the withdrawal of a government licence from some logging concerns in the rain forest. On the other hand, countries such as Indonesia and Malaysia have tried to limit access to and publicity about forest schemes, in order to thwart "green" campaigns. Nonetheless, Malaysia is the home for one of the region's most active coalitions on environmental issues and consumer affairs, based in Penang, as well as a regional environmental news agency, APPEN.

JF

EVENKS. An ethnic group scattered throughout the east of the Soviet Union and parts of northern China. In the Soviet Union they number around 30,000 people and enjoy administrative-territorial autonomy in the Evenk National District.

IG

EXCLUSIVE ECONOMIC ZONE (EEZ). The area of sea within which the coastal state has sovereign rights to explore and exploit the natural resources of the sea. It extends up to 200 miles from the coast but is modified for certain archipelagic states according to the terms of the **Convention of the Law of the Sea**, 1982.

RS

EXTRA-TERRITORIALITY. This was the principle by which foreign powers in the nineteenth and early twentieth centuries claimed the right to run part of China according to their own laws, with their own police and their own courts.

CIPF

F

FANG LIZHI. Sometimes called China's Sakharov, Prof. Fang has been a leading critic of communism's achievements in China. By training an astro-physicist, he achieved national prominence as the Deputy Dean of the Chinese University of Science and Technology in Hefei, Anhui province in the mid-1980s, when he urged students openly to demand greater democracy from the government. Dismissed from his post, he was still allowed to engage in full-time scientific research in Beijing and to travel abroad, telling a scientific conference in Rome that communism's only achievements in China were in table tennis and volleyball. A letter which he jointly wrote to the authorities in January 1989 demanding greater intellectual freedom helped generate the momentum which later led to the student protests in spring. He became the subject of an international incident in March 1989 when President Bush, on a visit to Beijing, invited him to a banquet in Beijing, but the Chinese authorities turned him away. After the Tiananmen Square massacre (*see* **Tiananmen Incidents**), he and his wife sought asylum in the US Embassy.

CIPF

FEBRUARY 28 INCIDENT. Taiwan's return to Chinese control was envisaged in the Cairo Declaration on Dec. 1, 1943. Following the Japanese surrender, the Chinese government proclaimed sovereignty over Taiwan on Aug. 30, 1945. The population of Taiwan welcomed the island's return to China. The administration of Governor Ch'en I, however, quickly dissipated this goodwill, disregarding Taiwanese hopes for greater participation in the island's administration. His administration failed to cope with economic decline, high inflation rates, and rural and industrial production suffering from wartime destruction.

During 1946 the economic situation in Taiwan worsened and popular indignation was aroused by growing unemployment, shortages of food and official corruption. Numerous arrests of prominent Taiwanese and rumours about the transportation of scarce goods to the mainland increased popular discontent with the administration. The social tensions finally erupted into a violent uprising on Feb. 28, 1947, after government agents had mistreated a cigarette pedlar.

After two days of looting and burning, with attacks by Taiwanese mobs on mainlanders, police stations and government installations, resolution committees were formed and started negotiating with the administration. Their demands became more millitant during the following days. On March 7, the 42 demands of the Taipei Resolution Committee called for the following: the disarming of all central government troops; the abolition of the garrison command; only Taiwanese to serve in the judiciary and the police; and two-thirds of all commissioners to be Taiwanese.

On March 10, government troops arrived from the mainland and quickly put down the uprising. Immediately afterwards a wave of arrests began, the administration making every attempt to track down individuals it believed to have been involved in the urban violence. Many people were arrested or simply disappeared, among them many members of the educated elite. Widely differing accounts of the number of casualties have been given. The official casualty list mentions 1,860 civilians, other estimates put the number at about 6,000, with up to 2,000 killed.

Ch'en I's successor as governor of Taiwan, Wei Tao-ming, initiated a number of reforms and met several Taiwanese demands, ensuring greater Taiwanese participation in the provincial administration. The events left a legacy of hatred and suspicion between mainlanders and Taiwanese. Responding to the incident, a group of Taiwanese intellectuals formed the "Taiwan Independence Movement" in Hong Kong, calling for the secession of Taiwan from China and the establishment of an independent state.

HH

FIJI. *Population* 742,000 (est. 1988). (At the August 1986 census, the population was 715,375, of which 48.7 per cent were of Indian origin and 46.1 per cent were Fijians.) *Area*: 18,274 sq km. *Top five trading partners*: Australia, Canada, West Germany, United States, Japan.

Geographical and historical background. Fiji, an independent republic, comprises four main islands – Viti Levu, Vanua Levu, Tavenui and Kadavu – with around 300 other smaller islands, and 540 islets, atolls and reefs, and the island of Rotuma 700 km to the north. The capital is Suva, on Viti Levu.

Fiji was settled by Austronesian-speaking

peoples over 3,000 years ago. European contact began with Abel Tasman in 1643, and later with British and American explorers, missionaries, and traders, especially in sandalwood. A British consul was appointed in 1857, and 17 years later, partly as a result of internecine warfare, the Fijian king Cakabau signed a deed of cession to the British Crown and Fiji became a crown colony. In the 1880s, a sugar cane industry developed with labourers imported from India, who subsequently multiplied and outnumbered the Fijian population. Most of the land is owned by Fijians, but Indians work almost all the major sugar plantations.

Political history. Fiji became independent in October 1970, with an elected House of Representatives of 52 members (22 Fijian, 22 Indian, and eight general) serving five-year terms, an appointed Senate of 22 members serving six-year terms, and a Governor-General representing the British monarch. A Fijian Great Council of Chiefs advised on Fijian matters. Ratu Sir Kamisese Mara, leader of the Alliance party, was appointed Prime Minister.

At the 1977 general election Indians won a majority of seats in the lower house but were unable to form the government. In July 1985, sponsored by the Fijian Trades Union Congress (FTUC), the Fijian Labour Party (FLP) was formed, with Dr Timoci Bavadra as president. At a general election in April 1987, a coalition of the FLP and the National Federation Party (NFP) won a majority of seats in the House of Representatives, Bavadra became Prime Minister with a cabinet of five Fijians (including himself) and seven ethnic Indians, the first occasion when Indians were in a majority in government.

On May 14 there was a military coup, led by Lt Col. Sitiveni Rabuka, which abducted and imprisoned members of the government, including Bavadra. Rabuka formed an interim ruling council, including the former Prime Minister, Ratu Mara. The Governor-General, Ratu Sir Penaia Ganilau, refused to recognize Rabuka's administration, but appointed a 19-member advisory council that included Rabuka and swore him in as chief minister. Widespread civil violence, civil disobedience and racial conflict occurred, Indians demanding their democratic rights and Melanesians demanding a permanent majority in government. Various negotiations designed to produce political reconciliation and stability led to an agreement between Bavadra and Ratu Maru and their supporters for an interim bipartisan government and the restoration of democracy. But on Sept. 25 Rabuka (now a Brigadier) mounted a second coup, then revoked the constitution and announced (Oct. 7) that the Queen was no longer head of state and that Fiji was a republic, and installed an executive council of ministers with a majority drawn from the radical Fijian Taukei movement. On Oct. 14 Ratu Ganilau sent in his resignation as Governor-General, and two days later Commonwealth heads of government announced that Fiji's membership of the Commonwealth had lapsed. New Zealand and Australia applied temporary economic sanctions against Fiji. On Dec. 8 Ratu Ganilau, the former Governor-General, was appointed first President of the Republic of Fiji, and he in turn invited Ratu Mara to be Prime Minister, with Brig. Rabuka as Minister for Home Affairs. There is little doubt that power still resides with the army which is well-trained and has seen service in several wars as part of British forces.

Outline of economic development. Fiji has a market economy heavily dependent on sugar production. There are also cash crops, timber production, some minerals, and a well-devloped tourist industry. Its main trading partners are Australia, Japan, New Zealand, Singapore, Britain and the USA. The aftermath of the military coup disrupted sugar production and tourism, and led to an exodus of professionally trained people.

The headquarters of the **South Pacific Forum** – the consultative organization of independent South Pacific states -- is in Suva, as is the university of the South Pacific which serves the region.

TBM

FISHING. The Pacific Fisheries of North America and Japan are among the most important in the world. Commercial fish in the Pacific number some 350 to 400 different species. About 85 per cent of the total marine catch is made up of bony fish. Approximately 50 per cent of the catch is consumed fresh; the rest is frozen, tinned, cured or converted into meal, fertilizer or oil. The abdominal linings and scales of some types are used in the processing of paints and other products.

Fishing techniques vary with the kind of fish and the area of fishing. Generally, however, ocean fishing is carried out from large ships using drift nets, trawl nets and long lines. Traps, nets and weirs set close to the coast also produce significant fish harvests.

Among the most important types of fish harvested in the Pacific are barracudas, bonitos, butterfish, cod, croakers, cusks, drums, eels, flounders, haddocks, hakes, halibuts, herrings, mackerels, marlins, mullet, Pacific yellowtails, pompanos, rock, sable, sailfish, salmon, sardines, sea bass, trouts, sharks, soles, swordfish and tunas.

In the Latin American coastal states of Chile, Ecuador and Peru marlins and sailfish are particularly popular. The Japanese too have some specialized tastes, harvesting enormous numbers of marlins and giant bluefin tunas. Fish harvests (1983), in thousands of tonnes, are as follows: Japan, 11,250; China, 5,213; *USA, 4,143; Chile, 3,978; South Korea, 2,400; Indonesia, 2,112; Philippines, 1,837; North Korea, 1,600; Peru, 1,487; *Canada, 1,337; *Mexico, 1,070; Taiwan, 1,033; Malaysia, 741; Vietnam, 710; Ecuador, 307; Australia, 169; *Panama, 166; New Zealand, 142; Colombia, 56; Singapore, 20.

*The USA, Canada, Mexico and Panama figures include non-Pacific catches. Conversely the fishing catches of the USSR and other countries not principally concerned with the Pacific, but partially fishing there, are not included.

RS

FIVE PRINCIPLES OF PEACEFUL COEXISTENCE. First formulated by **Zhou Enlai** in 1954, these principles have been the theoretical cornerstone of Chinese foreign policy. They are: mutual respect for territorial integrity and sovereignty, non-aggression, non-interference in internal affairs, equality and mutual benefit, and peaceful coexistence.

CIPF

FOUR MODERNIZATIONS. In 1964 and 1975 **Zhou Enlai** proposed a programme to the National People's Congress aimed at all-round modernization of China's agriculture, industry, science and technology, and defence by the year 2000. These proposals were rejected, but in 1978 **Hua Guofeng** proposed a 10-year plan for economic development using the phrase. This proved over-ambitious, but the term Four Modernizations continued to be used by his successors, the only proviso being that defence had the lowest priority of the four.

CIPF

FRENCH NUCLEAR TESTING. For many states in the Pacific, one of the major security problems has been French nuclear testing. In August 1985 the members of the South Pacific Forum agreed on the **Rarotonga Declaration** establishing a nuclear-free zone in the region. One of the main targets of the treaty – which entered into force in December 1985 – was the French nuclear testing programme. Indeed, Protocol 3 attached to the Treaty prohibits the testing of any nuclear device in the zone. Not surprisingly, France has refused to sign this protocol.

Between 1960 and 1966 French nuclear testing was done in the Sahara. French Polynesia was then chosen, with the main testing site on Mururoa Atoll, located in the Turamoto archipelago in the eastern part of Polynesia, 1,000 km south-east of Tahiti and 6,000 km east of Australia. Starting in July 1966 France conducted 41 atmospheric tests in the period 1966-74. The programme generated much criticism and Greenpeace succeeded in delaying some of the tests. Atmospheric testing was condemned by the United Nations General Assembly and in 1973 Australia and New Zealand took the issue to the International Court of Justice. Although France contended that the Court had no jurisdiction as nuclear testing was a matter of national security, it announced in 1974 that it had reached a stage where it could rely on underground testing and no longer required atmospheric tests.

The underground tests were carried out on the Mururoa Atoll and a subsidiary site, the Fangataufa Atoll about 40 km south. Mururoa Atoll itself is about 30 km long by 10 km wide. The tests there have been very controversial and there have been allegations that they pose a major threat to the environment. There have been reports that the explosions have seriously damaged the Atoll itself and in 1981 it was disclosed that there was an underwater crack in the atoll, 50 cm wide and 800 m long. In 1982 a French government team investigated the site and concluded that there was little risk of nuclear contamination. In 1983 a team of scientists from Australia and New Zealand was invited to the site. The report of the team was published in July 1984 and appeared very reassuring. Critics, however, contended that the team had not been able to inspect all areas of the atoll and had not been able to monitor an actual test.

Throughout the controversy France continued with its testing programme of approximately eight explosions a year. On at least one occasion in 1985 it tested a 150 kilotonne device. Because of the concern over Mururoa Atoll the larger explosions are now being carried out on Fangataufa Atoll. In July 1985 the issue took a new turn, when French agents sank the Greenpeace ship, the Rainbow Warrior in Auckland, New Zealand, killing one man. Although this created an international outcry, France has continued its programme. In May 1987 Australia and New Zealand signed an agreement on seismic monitoring. While this enables them to assess French activities, it does nothing to ease the basic concerns of the governments and peoples of the region.

PW

FRENCH POLYNESIA (Territoire de la Polynésie Française). *Population*: 188,000 (est. 1988), about two-thirds Polynesian. *Area* (including inland water): 4,000 sq km. A French overseas territory in the south central Pacific comprising 130 islands divided into five archipelagos: the Society Islands, the Tuamotu Archipelago, the Gambier Islands, the Marquesas Islands, and the Tubuai Islands. Largest island is Tahiti in the Society group. *Capital*: Papeete.

The Marquesas were probably settled from Tonga and Samoa early in the Christian era. Captain James Cook named the Society Islands after his sponsor, the Royal Society. Tahiti became a French protectorate in 1842, and a colony in 1880; the Gambier group in 1844 and 1881 respectively. The Marquesas acknowledged French sovereignty in 1842. The islands were administered as part of the French colony of Oceania until after World War II, then becoming an overseas territory in 1958. Movements towards local autonomy developed in the 1950s and 1960s. In 1966 France began nuclear testing on Mururoa Atoll, which with its neighbour Fangataufa had been ceded to France two years earlier. In 1975, following widespread international protests, testing was moved to underground sites on Fangataufa. Partial autonomy was granted to the territory in 1977. There is a Territorial Assembly of 30 members elected for five-year terms, and two deputies and a senator represent the territory in the French National Assembly.

The economy is based on smallholdings, with copra and coconut oil exported, mostly to France. Living standards are generally low. The nuclear testing organization, *Centre d'Expérimentation du Pacifique*, gives substantial support to the economy. (*Also see* **French Nuclear Testing**)

TBM

G

GALAPAGOS ISLANDS (Archipiélago de Colón). These are a group of islands totalling 6,912 sq km in area, situated in the Pacific 970 km west of the mainland, which have belonged to Ecuador since 1832 (by agreement with Britain, which had formerly claimed and named the islands) and were constituted as a National Park in 1934. The four largest islands, San Cristóare inhabited; three smaller islands and 11 islets are not. The administrative centre is Baquerizo Moreno, San CristóPuerto Ayora, Santa Cruz. The islands are celebrated for the wildlife which inspired Darwin's theory of natural selection, and in particular for the giant turtles (galátheir popular name.

P&SC

GANG OF FOUR. These are the four leading radicals arrested one month after Mao's death: **Jiang Qing** (his widow), Zhang Chunqiao, Yao Wenyuan and Wang Hongwen. They were put on trial in 1980 and given death sentences, later commuted to life imprisonment.

CIPF

GOH CHOK TONG. Goh is the leading figure in the so-called "second generation" of Singaporean politicians along with **Lee Hsien Loong**, Ahmed Mattar and Suppiah Dhanabalan. Goh is expected to replace **Lee Kuan Yew** as Prime Minister in the early 1990s. He was appointed Minister of Defence in May 1982, and in early 1985 he became First Deputy Prime Minister.

DS

GOLD. Although rare and found only in relatively small deposits, gold is to be found in many of the countries of the Pacific. Alaska in the United States and Canada have some better-known deposits but significant quantities exist in Chile, Colombia, China, Australia, the Philippines and Mexico. The annual production of gold, in tonnes, is as follows: Canada, 81.3; USA, 71.5; China, 65; Australia, 39; Philippines, 34.1; Colombia, 21.3; Chile, 18; Mexico, 6.9; Ecuador, 5.4; Peru, 5.4; North Korea, 5; Japan, 3; South Korea, 2.2; Taiwan, 1.6; Nicaragua, 1.5; New Zealand, 0.3; Malaysia, O.185.

RS

GOLKAR (INDONESIA). The Joint Secretariat of Functional Groups (*Sekber Golongan Karya* or Golkar) was formed by Indonesian Army officers in 1964 as a loose federation of various groups representing sectional interests (including farmers, workers, professionals, civil servants, veterans, women and youth) and was designed to counter-balance the influence of the **Communist Party of Indonesia**, then the country's largest political grouping. Golkar was brought under government control in 1968 in order to provide a civilian base for Gen. Suharto's "New Order" military regime, **Suharto** being elected chairman of Golkar's advisory board in 1977. After the 1971 elections to the House of Representatives (in which Golkar obtained an absolute majority of seats), Golkar was reorganized in order to make it more responsive to a unified and centralized leadership. It was further strengthened in 1975 when legislation was approved which included Golkar among only three political organizations given a legal entitlement to participate in the political process. Golkar obtained absolute majorities in successive elections to the House of Representatives in 1977, 1982 and April 1987. In the latter 1987 contest Golkar for the first time gained an overall majority of seats in all 27 provinces, including the traditional Moslem stronghold of Aceh.

At a congress in 1983 various steps were taken to invigorate Golkar as an active political formation, including the appointment of a leading government minister, Lt.-Gen. (retd) Sudharmono, as Chairman of the national leadership council and of Sarwono Kusumaatmadja as Secretary-General. The latter (and over half of the newly appointed council) were members of the so-called "generation of 1966", i.e. mainly civilian figures being groomed for leadership in succession to Suharto's military "generation of 1945". At the same conference Golkar introduced a new system of individual membership based on village cadres (membership having hitherto been through constituent organizations). At its fourth congress held in October 1988, Sudharmono and Kusumaatmadja (who had been appointed Vice-President and Minister of Utilization of the State Departments, respectively, in March 1988) were replaced as Golkar Chairman and Secretary-General by Lt.-Gen. Wahono, and Rachmat Witoelar.

DS

GORBACHEV, MIKHAIL. Soviet statesman, born in 1931. He served as Chairman of the Presidium of the USSR Supreme Soviet (*de facto* Soviet head of state) between October 1988 and May 1989, when he was elected to the newly created office of Chairman of the USSR Supreme Soviet (i.e. Executive President of the Soviet Union). He has been General Secretary of the Communist Party of the Soviet Union since March 1985.

IG

GUAM. *Population* (est. 1988): 126,000, of mixed race. *Area*: 549 sq km. An unincorporated territory of the United States, the southernmost island of the Mariana chain, 5,000 km west of Hawaii. *Capital*: Agana.

Guam was formally claimed by Spain in 1565, and ceded to the United States after the Spanish-American war of 1898. Occupied by the Japanese in 1941, it was retaken by American forces in 1944 and became a major naval and air base, which it still is, with a nuclear submarine base and large repair docks. After several stages of internal self-government since 1950, Guam is virtually self-governing, with a Governor elected every four years, a 21-member legislative elected for two-year terms, and an elected commissioner in each village. Guam sends a non-voting member to the US House of Representatives. In 1987 the islanders voted to ask the federal (US) government for more autonomy, and to become a commonwealth like Puerto Rico. This will require an Act of Congress.

Guam has a basic subsistence economy, plus a few light industries and a sizeable tourist industry especially from Japan. The territorial and US governments employ nearly half of the workforce.

TBM

GUATEMALA, REPUBLIC OF. *Population*: 7,000,000 (1981). *Area*: 108,889 sq km. *Gross Domestic Product*: US$3,567 million. *Trade*: US$2,577.3 million. *Top five trading partners*: USA, El Salvador, West Germany, Japan, Honduras. *Defence spending*: US$179 million. *Education spending as percentage of GNP*: 1.8. *Urban population as percentage of total*: 19. *Birth rate*: 42.5 per thousand. *Life expectancy*: males 42; females 43.5.

Geographical background. A tropical coastal plain on the Pacific coast of Guatemala gives way to foothills and then high mountains which comprise the bulk of the country. Major rivers flow east to valleys on the Atlantic. The very sparsely populated northern third, El Petén, is a flat limestone plateau covered with tropical vegetation. Temperature varies with altitude from tropical to alpine, but the location of the principal settlements in the temperate southern highlands is the origin of the romantic description of the country as the Land of Eternal Spring. Nearly two million hectares are cultivated. Guatemala has a public service narrow gauge railway connecting both coasts and linking with both Mexico and El Salvador, and a considerable freight network in the eastern plantations (total 927 km). Most roads are unpaved. The main ports are on the narrow Caribbean coast though the Pacific port of Sipacate on the Pacific is being expanded. Domestic and international air links are fairly well developed. Most Guatemalans live in rural areas and over half the economically active population work in agriculture. The capital, Guatemala City (population 793,000) is by far the largest urban concentration. It lies in an earthquake zone and was last seriously damaged in 1976.

Socio-political background. About half the population is Indian, with most of the remainder mestizo. Small numbers of Europeans, blacks and mulattoes are also present. Spanish is the sole official language but many of the Indian population speak one of the Mayan family of languages. Roman Catholicism is the main religion, but there is heavy penetration by Protestant sects. Primary education is free and compulsory but non-attendance is high especially in rural areas and enrolment is only 53.3 per cent. Illiteracy is very high – 54 per cent of those over 15. The oldest and most prestigious institution of higher education is the University of San Carlos founded 1676, but educated Guatemalans have been particular targets of the endemic violence. The death rate is 10.5 per thousand. The main causes of death are conditions associated with poverty, malnutrition and poor sanitation. Only 58 per cent of urban and 6 per cent of rural homes have piped water and infant mortality remains at 64 per thousand. The ratio of physicians to population (1: 8,608) must rank among the worst in the world. Most rural and urban housing is inadequate, and water supplies are poor.

Political history. Dominated by a series of dictators since independence, Guatemala's social revolution of 1944 was cut short by a US-sponsored coup in 1954, and thinly disguised military dictatorship has been the norm since. Insurgency broke out in 1960 following the Cuban Revolution and has become endemic, despite periodic counter-insurgency campaigns by the government. The most recent, between 1978 and 1983, was accompanied by great violence and deliberate efforts to destroy traditional Indian settlements and ways of life. "Death squads" have targeted political and civic leaders, further reducing the prospects for democracy. In 1985 the Armed Forces gave way to an elected Christian Democrat president and Congress, but violence continues and there have been several abortive military coups.

Outline of economic development. Cultivation of cochineal and indigo gave way to coffee in the 1880s, many plantations being German owned. Banana cultivation shifted to the Pacific coast in the 1930s, and has declined steeply in the last decade or so. Cotton spread under government encouragement in the 1970s. In 1985 coffee accounted for 42.5 per cent of exports, cotton for 6.8 per cent. The discovery of oil in 1981 in the north-west gives promise of energy self-sufficiency, but has accentuated social strains. Debt is US$2,500 million, some 20 per cent of export earnings.

P&SC

GUERRILLA MOVEMENTS. Guerrilla movements have been a notable facet of Latin American politics since World War II, particularly with the growth of revolutionary ideology. The Nicaraguan revolution of 1979 drew both its name and its alleged inspiration from the nationalist fervour of Augusto Cesar Sandino half a century earlier. Left-wing guerrillas still operate in El Salvador and have been plaguing the government of Peru. For most of the 1980s, the right-wing Contra guerrillas from Nicaragua (dubbed "freedom-fighters" by President Reagan) undermined the Sandinista revolution, before most official US support was withdrawn and efforts were made to disband them.

In the South Pacific, activists in underground independence or secessionist movements have indulged in guerrilla tactics, for example in New Caledonia and on the island of Bougainville in Papua New Guinea. Probably the most serious contemporary insurgency in the area, however, is in the Philippines. Hopes that reconciliation with the Marxist-oriented New People's Army there would prove possible following the overthrow of President **Ferdinand Marcos** proved false. The civilian government of **Corazon Aquino** is under constant pressure from the military to use forceful measures to try to control the guerrillas, who enjoy a certain amount of support from peasants because of their campaigning for meaningful land reform. The Philippines is also home to some Muslim guerrilla groups, notably on the island of Mindanao.

Guerrilla armies have come to power in Indochina and China itself, fulfilling the goal of "people's liberation". Once in control, though, such regimes have shown themselves to be as intolerant of insurgency as their predecessors, as witnessed by the suppression by the Chinese of Tibetan independence movements. (*See also* **Terrorism**).

JF

GULF OF CALIFORNIA. ("The Sea of Cortez"). The shallow gulf enclosed by the peninsula of Baja California. (Baja California Sur was, with Quintana Roo, the last of Mexico's territories to gain statehood in 1974.) The area was the scene of US fears of Japanese settlement and possible naval penetration in 1907, giving rise to the so-called "Lodge Doctrine".

P&SC

H

HAWKE PLAN. During a visit to the South Korean capital Seoul early in 1989, Bob **Hawke**, The Australian Prime Minister, put forward an idea for closer co-operation amongst the nations of the Asia-Pacific region. The background to Hawke's initiative is the absolute magnitude and relative importance in total world trade of the trade that takes place amongst the countries on the Asian-Pacific rim (*see* **Trade**). Despite the large and growing importance of this trade, allied to massive additional flows of resources within the region in the form of aid, direct and indirect investment, Hawke pointed out that the region has no formal organization instituted at government level which can investigate this movement of resources, and attempt to quantify its benefits and drawbacks for the region as a whole and for its individual economies. In general terms, he wanted "some sort of mechanism which would enable us better to understand what was happening in each economy. We would then be able to best take advantage of the possible economic complementarities of the different countries in the region through closer economic co-operation". He loosely described this organization as a sort of Pacific OECD, and pronounced it as being "eminently sensible, non-threatening and possibly very useful".

In concrete terms, what Hawke proposed was that the economics ministers of the countries of the region should meet in Canberra in November, 1989 on their way to the next meeting of the **Pacific Economic Co-operation Conference (PECC)** in New Zealand. The purpose of the meeting would be to launch the process of inter-government consultation by discussing the setting-up of a permanent secretariat for the proposed organization. To the meeting have been invited the representatives of 10 "core" nations. They are: Australia, New Zealand, Japan, South Korea and the six nations of the **Association of South-East Asian Nations – ASEAN** (Thailand, Indonesia, Malaysia, Singapore, the Philippines and Brunei). In addition, Canada and the United States have been invited. The original Australian plan was to invite the "three Chinas" – Hong Kong, Taiwan and The Peoples' Republic – to attend, but in the aftermath of the events in Tiananmen Square in June (*see* **Tiananmen Incidents**) this does not seem a practicable possibility.

The attendance of United States' representatives seems assured, since the US Secretary of State, James Baker, has publicly voiced his support for the initiative. Indeed, he appears to favour the idea that the new organization considers cultural and environmental matters as well as the economic issues upon which Australia wishes to focus. The President of South Korea, **Roh Tae Woo**, was enthusiastic in his reception of Hawke's idea, and it is unlikely that either Canada or New Zealand will refuse some measure of support. The Japanese Ministry of International Trade and Industry (MITI) has already outlined some of the ideas it would like discussed in Canberra, and has taken a more positive stance towards the initiative than the Ministry of Foreign Affairs, in whose mind political and strategic considerations are uppermost. The ideas for discussion favoured by MITI include the expansion of trade through concerted regional action in the Uruguay Round of GATT negotiations; and matters of common concern in the fields of education, energy communications and statistical monitoring and reporting.

More problematical is the backing of the ASEAN countries. Essentially political issues are what have united the ASEAN countries in the past – notably opposition to the Vietnamese occupation of Kampuchea – and economic co-operation within ASEAN has been of minor concern. Indonesia in particular is anxious to guard against any diminution in the importance of ASEAN and its concerns should its members decide to participate in the new organization, and the same basic fears exist elsewhere in the governments of ASEAN members. Hence the Australian anxiety to stress the primacy of economic concerns as the focus for the new organization, almost to the exclusion of all else. However, there are also important economic barriers to enhanced economic co-operation in the Pacific region of the type Hawke desires. Notable among them is trade friction between the United States and Japan and between the Unites States and other Asian countries invited to Canberra with whom it has balance of payments deficits, such as Singapore, Thailand, Malaysia and South Korea. The problem is exacerbated by US anger over what it regards as wholesale infringement of intellectural property rights taking place in parts of the region.

Overshadowing the whole initiative is the question of whether the Hawke plan is no more than the first step in the formation of a Pacific trade bloc in retaliation to the formation of such blocs elsewhere – notably in Europe? Reactions to the question differ. Some politicians in the region believe that early regional preparation for the inevitable drift into protectionism is realistic. Some of Hawke's own utterances can be interpreted in this manner. He has referred to his brain child as forming the building blocks for a future trading bloc, should the need ever arise. Others believe protectionism is not inevitable and that every effort must be made to ensure that any new Pacific organization for economic co-operation must be seen by its members and the rest of the world as a vehicle for ironing out problems of trade friction. Thus countries like Japan, Singapore and Hong Kong who are especially dependent on their exports for their continuing prosperity, will probably press for the creation of the widest and loosest possible kind of forum. Talk of a Pacific OECD is proably premature.

DA

HAWKE, ROBERT JAMES LEE. Prime Minister of Australia since March 1983. Born Bordertown, South Australia, Dec 9, 1929. Rhodes Scholar for Western Australia 1953 and B. Litt (Oxon). Research officer and advocate for Australian Council of Trade Unions, 1958; President 1970. President of **Australian Labor Party** 1973-1978. Companion of the Order of Australia (AC) 1979. In 1980 Hawke won the Victorian seat of Wills in the House of Representatives, was elected leader of the Parliamentary Labor Party in February 1983. His government was again returned after elections in late 1984 and July 1987. Hawke is considered to be on the right of his party. He has put considerable effort into government by consensus.

TBM

HAYDEN, WILLIAM GEORGE. Governor-General of Australia since 1989. Member (Labor) of the House of Representatives for Oxley, Queensland, 1961-1988. Leader of the Opposition 1977-1983. Minister for Foreign Affairs 1983-1988.

TBM

HENG SAMRIN. Head of State of the People's Republic of Kampuchea since January 1979 and General Secretary of the **Kampuchean People's Revolutionary Party** since December 1981. Previously a divisional commander in the Armed Forces of Pol Pot's Democratic Kampuchea, he fled to Vietnam after a revolt in Eastern Cam-

bodia in spring 1978 and collaborated with the Vietnamese in forming a "national salvation front" that autumn. He returned to Phnom Penh immediately following its capture by Vietnamese forces, and is generally assumed to have pursued policies dictated by Hanoi. The true extent of his power, and his relations with Prime Minister **Hun Sen** are impossible to assess.

RBS

HIROHITO, EMPEROR. The death in September 1988 of the Japanese Emperor, referred to habitually in the West as "Hirohito", a name little used in Japan since it assumes an offensive intimacy with the monarch and where the more respectful Tenno Heika (August Majesty) is the normal form of address, triggered abroad an excited and often excitable debate about the precise role of the Emperor in the conduct of World War II and in Japan a justifiable sense that an age was ending. The debate revealed little. The questions asked assumed a political universe, a mode of leadership and command and not least a decision-making style unknown in Japan.

In Japan the death signalled the rupture of the principal linkage between pre-war and post-war Japan. Tenno Heika was one with his people in a war in which identities (and not least that of emperor and people), understandings and oppositions were fired and hardened; that these persisted long after the war had ended should be no surprise. It is also worth recalling, if the place of the Emperor in the Japanese psyche is to be understood, that whereas the Pacific War and Japan's role in it has been condemned abroad and with justice, as an imperialistic adventure of appalling cost to other Asiatic peoples, Japanese judgments have sometimes been more nuanced and ambiguous. The Emperor survived the war as he survived a crushing and climactic reckoning with the USA and its allies. He survived to be reconstituted for reasons of *real politik* as a symbol of a new Japan, as a post-war constitutional monarch no longer divine, who ceded also his sovereignty and conceded that of his people.

RAB

HMONG (MEO) PEOPLE. An important minority tribal group in northern and central Laos, numbering several hundred thousands and originally living in scattered upland areas to which they are believed to have moved (southwards from China) in the seventeenth or eighteenth century. Some of them also live in upland areas of northern Central Vietnam. Calling themselves "Hmong", they are known to the Lao and the Vietnamese – and appear in Western accounts before the 1970s – as "Meo". Under French rule the Hmong of Xieng Khouang province had a monopoly on the legal production of opium, and have always had an interest in that crop. After a serious rebellion in 1919–21 they were given their own autonomous district (Nong Het), in which two rival leading families emerged by the 1940s; the Lo, who sided with the anti-French movement in 1945 and whose leader in the 1950s (Faydang) joined the Pathet Lao, although he took relatively few followers with him; and the Ly, whose leader Touby Lyfoung worked with the French. One of Touby's associates, Vang Pao, began to collaborate with the Laotian rightists and with the American CIA from about 1960. In 1961 he led many of the Hmong of the Plain of Jars (Xieng Khouang) to evacuate their villages in order to avoid occupation by neutralist and Pathet Lao forces. They moved to positions where they were dependent on regular airlifts of USAID supplies. Vang Pao began to recruit a guerrilla force to be trained by the CIA and Thai mercenaries, which reached a peak of 30,000 men by the late 1960s. By then, too, substantial numbers of Hmong moved to the area protected by his base at Long Tieng. But his troops suffered heavy casualties, especially in fighting in 1966–67 and 1969–70 and they became badly demoralized. Vang Pao continued to fight the Pathet Lao until spring 1975, when he was obliged to leave for Thailand – taking several hundred of his men with him.

The Hmong leaders who remained behind launched a resistance movement against the Communist regime of **Kaysone Phomvihan** and established a base in the Phou Bia mountains. By 1977 this was sufficiently serious to oblige Vietnamese and Lao forces to engage in a major campaign to destroy the resistance, which led to a further influx of Hmong refugees into northern Thailand by 1978–79. Some refugees accused Vietnamese forces of having killed many people in their villages by using poison gas ("yellow rain") and American officials who investigated their accounts in the autumn of 1979 took the medical evidence seriously. The revolt was nevertheless suppressed, and many Hmong accepted resettlement in the Plain of Jars. Xieng Khouang province is now relatively peaceful, but the longer term loyalty of the Hmong remains in doubt.

RBS

HO CHI MINH. Founder of the Indochinese Communist Party and leader of Vietnam's "August Revolution" of 1945; President of the Democratic Republic of Vietnam (DRV) from 1945 until his death. Born in Nghe An province (probably in 1894, although his birthdate has been given officially as 1890) he ran away to sea in about 1911 and spent almost 30 years in exile. Having visited various countries he was in France by 1919–20, when he attempted to submit a petition to the Versailles Peace Conference and later became a founder member of the French Communist Party. He took the political name Nguyen Ai Quoc at that time. He was trained in Moscow (1923–25) before returning to Asia as a member of the Comintern mission to China (1925–27). In Guangzhou he founded the Vietnamese Revolutionary Youth Association. He also worked in Shanghai, and then in Siam (1928–29), before moving to Hong Kong where he played a key role in unifying the Vietnamese Communist movement into a single party in 1930. Imprisoned by the British (1931–32) he subsequently escaped and spent much of the 1930s in Moscow. After returning to China again (1938) he went to the Chinese-Vietnamese border and began to create an anti-imperialist base area. In 1945 (having taken the name Ho Chi Minh, partly to conceal his Communist past) he led the Viet Minh into Hanoi and proclaimed the independence of the DRV on Sept. 2. After leading the Viet Minh to victory over the French in 1954, he and his government took over the whole of North Vietnam and pursued a dual policy of socialist revolution in the north, and continuing the "national liberation" struggle in the south. During the Vietnam War of the 1960s, Ho became an international cult hero of the radical left – even though, after 1965, his control over day-to-day decisions was probably in decline. After his death (Sept. 3, 1969) his successors used his memory as a means to sustain national unity and to continue the struggle until the country was reunified in 1975. His remains are preserved in an impressive mausoleum in Hanoi, while the city of Saigon has been renamed after him.

RBS

HOANG VAN HOAN. Veteran leader of the Indochinese Communist Party and the Vietnamese Workers' Party who worked closely with **Ho Chi Minh** in the 1940s and 1950s and was a Politburo member from 1957 to 1976. A native of Nghe An province, he joined the revolutionary movement and spent some time in Guangzhou (Canton) in 1926. In the 1930s and 1940s he was involved for much of the time in liaison work with the Vietnamese communities in China and Siam and developed close relations with the **Chinese Communist Party (CCP).** On that basis he was chosen to be Viet Minh representative (later ambassador) in Beijing from 1950 to 1957. He entered the Politburo on his return home, and might have been promoted further; but as a rival of **Le Duan** he lost ground, and from 1958 to 1979 served as deputy chairman of the National Assembly. As Le Duan became more powerful and the Party moved closer to the Soviet line, Hoang Van Hoan lost his place in the Politburo at the **Vietnamese Communist Party** (VCP) Fourth Congress (December 1976). Following the Sino-Vietnamese War of 1979 he was the one VCP leader whose "pro-Chinese" views led him to defect to Beijing, where he was well-received by CCP leaders. In the early 1980s he made a number of broadcasts actively encouraging the Vietnamese Party and people to turn against Le Duan.

RBS

HONDURAS, REPUBLIC OF. *Population*:
4,000,000. *Area*: 112,088 sq km. *Gross Domestic Product*: US$1,213 million. *Trade*: US$1,816 million (1986). *Top five trading partners*: USA, Japan, Guatemala, West Germany, Italy. *Defence spending*: US$124 million. *Education spending as percentage of GNP*: 4.3. *Urban populations percentage of total*: 24. *Birth rate*: 44 per thousand. *Life expectancy*: males 41; females 43.5.

Geographical background. Honduras is a mountainous country with lowland plains on both her northern (Caribbean) coastline and on her narrow outlet to the Pacific via the Gulf of Fonseca between Nicaragua and El Salvador. The lowland areas are hot and wet, the mountains are drier and temperature varies with altitude. The Caribbean coast lies in the hurricane belt. Some 682,000 hectares are cultivated. A rail network (205 km) exists only in the northern coastal banana belt around the Caribbean ports of Tela and San Pedro Sula. Roads (12,058 km) are poor and there is little river transport. Air travel is important for both passengers and freight. Population increase is high at 3.1 per cent *per annum*. The largest city is the capital Tegucigalpa with a population of 485,000.

Socio-political background. The vast majority of Hondurans are *mestizo* with small proportions of Indians and Europeans. Some blacks live in the Caribbean lowlands. Spanish is the national language, though English is widely spoken, especially in the Caribbean region. A variety of Indian languages are still in daily use. The religion is Roman Catholicism. Primary education is free and compulsory but non-attendance is a problem and only 70 per cent are enrolled. Adult illiteracy (over 15) is 43 per cent. The National University is located in Tegucigalpa but it also has campuses in La Ceiba and San Pedro Sula. Major causes of death are the diseases associated with malnutrition and poor hygiene. Around 75 per cent of urban and 13 per cent of rural dwellings have piped water. Crude death rate is 10.1 per thousand, infant mortality 23. There is one doctor for every 3,120 people. Social security provision is limited. There is insufficient housing and most lacks basic facilities in both urban and rural areas.

Political history. Nominally a presidential republic with a unicameral Congress, Honduras has been dominated by military leaders for much of its history, and was often a battleground for the ambitions of would-be leaders of Central America. In 1969 anger at immigration from overpopulated El Salvador sparked a brief 13-day war (the so-called "Football War") with El Salvador, which killed 5,000 and disrupted the nascent Central American Common Market (formed in 1961) for 11 years. Since 1981 Honduras has been the base for the US-backed armed force, the so-called "contras", attempting to overthrow the government of Sandinista Nicaragua, and since 1983 US troops have been continuously stationed in the country.

Outline of economic development. The only true "banana republic", Honduras was dominated for many years by the United Fruit Company (now United Brands) of Boston. Bananas still account for 30 per cent of exports. Coffee comes second (22.7 per cent) and wood and wood products make up the bulk of exports. Influx of US military aid has improved imfrastructure in the border region but at the cost of new social problems. Debt at US$2,600 million represents some 18 per cent of exports.

P&SC

HONG KONG. *Population*: 5,740,000. *Area*:
1,061 sq km. *Gross Domestic Products*: US$54,567 million. *Trade*: US$127,162 million. *Top five trading partners*: China, USA, Japan, Taiwan, South Korea. *Defence spending*: US$215 million. *Education spending*: US$1,224 million. *Urban population as percentage of total*: 94. *Birth rate*: 13 per thousand. *Life expectancy*: 77.

Geographical background. Hong Kong lies just south of the Tropic of Cancer, at the mouth of the Pearl River, and 90 miles south-east of the Chinese city of Guangzhou (Canton). It has a monsoon type of climate, the north-east winds blow steadily from October to May, bringing generally dry and cool conditions; occasionally, in winter, when the prevailing wind is from the north, the temperature drops suddenly, though

79

seldom falls below freezing. From May to October the south-west monsoon brings great heat and humidity and 80 per cent of the annual rainfall, which averages 2,225 mm. Hong Kong is within the typhoon zone. The major population centres are: the Hong Kong island, Kowloon peninsula, and the new cites of Shatin, Tsuen Wan, Kwai Chung, and Tuen Mun, in the New Territories. Population density per sq km is 5,330, one of the highest in the world. Hong Kong is located along the modern trade route between Asia and Europe. The bulk of trade is handled at Kwai Chung container port, Kai Tak international airport, and Hung Hom railway terminal. The importance of road links with China is increasing as a result of expanding trade and the easing of border controls.

Political history. Prior to its occupation by the British under Captain Charles Elliot on Jan. 26 1841, Hong Kong was largely inhabited by fishermen and farmers, and was part of China's Guangdong province. It witnessed few major political dramas in the long history of China, except the final defeat of the Song (Sung) emperor by the invading Mongols in 1278.

As a result of China's defeat in the first Anglo-Chinese War (1840–43), which was about trade, including the British export of opium to China, and about diplomatic equality between the two countries, China ceded the island of Hong Kong to Britain in perpetuity in the Treaty of Nanking (1842). Hong Kong formally became a British colony on June 26, 1843. Between 1856 and 1860 China and Britain fought the Second Anglo-Chinese War (in which the French also took part, as Britain's ally) over the issues which the first war had failed to settle. This ended in the first convention of Peking (1860): Britain acquired the peninsula of Kowloon and the Stonecutters Island, and annexed them to Hong Kong. Following China's defeat by the Japanese (1894–95), major Western Powers scrambled for concessions from the crumbling Chinese Empire. In the second Convention of Peking (1898), Britain secured a lease of 99 years for the land adjacent to Hong Kong (including 235 islands), an area about nine times the size of the then Colony; this land has since been called the New Territories. The lease is due to expire on June 30, 1997.

The watershed in Hong Kong's modern history is the Japanese occupation from 1941 to 1945 during the Pacific War. Before the war, the Chinese and expatriate communities coexisted in a generally peaceful fashion but had little interaction. The input of the Chinese community into government was minimal, though a Chinese person was first admitted to the Legislative Council in 1884, and one appointed to the Executive Council in 1926. The main focuses of the Hong Kong government's work were governing the expatriate community and looking after municipal affairs of the urban areas. The primarily rural and Chinese-populated New Territories were governed by District Officers, who represented the government and were also responsible for administering justice, including the enforcement of Chinese laws and customs. In Hong Kong proper, political rivalries, including calls for the introduction of elections to the local legislature, were largely a matter for the expatriate community. The major exceptions were the seamen's strike of 1922 and, more importantly, the disturbance of 1925–26. In 1925, when the **Kuomintang** and the **Chinese Communist Party** (then based in Guangzhou) were mobilizing the Chinese masses in an anti-imperialist attempt to win public support for their causes, they organized a general strike in Hong Kong. Many Chinese workers responded voluntarily to this nationalistic appeal, some were persuaded by a variety of promises, and others were intimidated into joining. Hong Kong was virtually paralyzed for about a year until the British reached a settlement with the Guangzhou authorities.

After 1945 the pre-war snobbery of expatriates waned; local government increasingly handled the welfare of the Chinese and expatriate communities without prejudice, and interactions between the two communities grew. Finding itself in a world hostile to old-style imperialism, the colonial government of Hong Kong worked hard to provide good government, stability, prosperity and order. The activities and the rivalries of the Kuomintang and the Chinese Communist Party became the major sources of disorder, sometimes resulting in serious disturbances, as in 1956 and 1967. The Hong Kong Government has enjoyed overwhelming public support for its policy in this area, which is to remain neutral in Chinese politics but to respond with determination and swiftness if public order is disturbed. By the 1980s, most residents readily identified themselves with and supported the Hong Kong Government, although its specific policies are sometimes severely criticized.

Socio-political background. At present a British Crown Colony, Hong Kong is due to revert in its entirety to the People's Republic of China on July 1, 1997, as a special administrative region, under the terms of the 1984 Sino-British Joint Declaration. Meanwhile Hong Kong continues to be administered by a Governor and an Executive Council of four *ex-officio* and eight nominated members. The Governor (Sir David Wilson), an appointee from London, is the representative of the Queen, titular Commander-in-Chief, and Head of the Hong Kong Government. He presides over the Executive Council, the principal policy-making body, and the Legislative Council, which makes laws and authorizes public expenditure. His principal official adviser is the Chief Secretary (Sir David Ford), who heads the Civil Service. The formal constitutional arrangements are set out in the Letters Patent 1917–88 and Royal Instructions 1917–88.

The Governor enjoys extensive powers. He appoints all members of the Executive Council and 30 out of 56 members of the Legislative Council. He can refuse assent to Bills passed by the Legislative Council, appoint judges and senior public officials and may dissolve the Legislative Council. He is required to consult, but is not bound to accept, the advice of the Executive Council on all major issues. In practice, the Governor generally acts on the advice of the Executive Council, and seldom "steamrollers" legislation through in the Legislative Council. Although not a democracy, Hong Kong is not an authoritarian state either. The hallmark of its politics is self-restraint exercised by the Government, which lays heavy emphasis on consulting public opinion in policy-making.

The Governor is responsible not to the people of Hong Kong but to the British monarch and parliament. The Queen-in-Council still holds reserve powers to legislate for Hong Kong and can disallow local legislation on the advice of the Secretary of State, even though such prerogatives have seldom been exercised. This will change with the advent of Chinese rule, when Hong Kong legislation originating from the United Kingdom will either be replaced by locally enacted laws, or be allowed to lapse. The British Government is currently responsible for defence and foreign relations. The Chinese government will take over these responsibilities in 1997.

Local political culture has changed rapidly in post-war years. Until the early 1970s, political apathy was the order of the day. Now the degree of political awareness is high. There is as yet no political party, but there are indications that such organizations are being formed. The principal channels of political participation are: pressure group activities, periodic direct elections at district and municipal levels, indirect elections to the Legislative Council, and peaceful demonstrations and petitions to the Governor. Direct elections to approximately 18 per cent of Legislative Council seats on universal franchise will be introduced in 1992. Political violence is an anathema to the people of Hong Kong.

The Hong Kong way of life reflects a mixture of traditional Chinese and Western cultures, with influence from Japan growing rapidly. It is primarily an urban life which places great value on achievements, usually calculated in monetary terms. There is a well-defined Hong Kong identity. "Hong Kong Man", as Hugh Baker puts it, "is go-getting and highly competitive, tough for survival, quick-thinking and flexible. He wears western clothes, speaks English or expects his children to do so, drinks western alcohol, has sophisticated tastes in cars and household gadgetry, and expects life to provide a constant stream of excitement and new openings. But he is not British or Western (merely Westernized). At the same time he is not Chinese in the same way that the citizens of the People's Republic of China are Chinese."

Hong Kong is not a welfare state, but it has a well developed welfare system. This work is shared between government and numerous voluntary organizations. Social security schemes are non-contributory and are designed to meet the basic and special needs of vulnerable groups, the old and the disabled. Public assistance to able-bodied persons of working age is means-tested and conditional upon the applicant's actively seeking employment. The Government's biggest contributions to the community lie in the large scale provision of low-cost housing, education, medical and health services. The underlying principles are to provide the basic facilities for modern life and to help the fallen get back on their feet.

Recent developments. The Hong Kong Government still enjoys overwhelming public support, but public confidence in its efficacy in defending Hong Kong's interest against outside pressure is declining. This is the result of the Government's *volte face* in democratization under Chinese pressure; China's building of a nuclear power plant across the border against Hong Kong's wishes; and British refusal to restore the right of abode in the United Kingdom to Hong Kong British subjects.

In recent years, the Xinhau (New China) News Agency has greatly expanded its size and activities. It is the *de facto* Chinese mission in Hong Kong, and is headed by Xu Jiatun. It actively pursues united front work, and serves as the headquarters for members of the Chinese Communist party in Hong Kong. It does not challenge the authority of the Hong Kong government but is seen locally as a "shadow government". The presence of mainland Chinese personnel in Hong Kong has been increasing since 1984.

Outline of economic development From 1843 to 1941, Hong Kong functioned primarily as an *entrepôt*, a free port, to facilitate trade between

China and the outside world. Related services such as shipping, insurance and banking developed, and there were also some industries. A major change came after World War II. As a result of the civil war in China (1945-49) and the subsequent Communist victory there, there was an influx of capital, entrepreneurs, and skilled labour from Shanghai into Hong Kong, greatly benefiting the local economy. In 1950, the United Nations embargo on trade with China drastically disrupted Hong Kong's *entrepôt* trade. The local economy readjusted by developing light industries. Raw materials were imported and the manufactured products were mostly exported, notably to the USA, the British Commonwealth and Europe. Trade recovered and expanded, with domestically manufactured consumer products replacing goods imported from China as the major component of Hong Kong's export trade. By 1965 Hong Kong had become a thriving industrial and commercial centre. In the following decade, trade and industry continued to grow and diversify despite a banking crisis (1965), a year of political disturbances instigated by the Chinese Communists (1967), and a collapse of the stock market following the world energy crisis (1973). From 1976 to 1982, Hong Kong emerged as an international financial centre, and the economy grew faster than ever, culminating in an inflationary boom. Towards the end of this period, Hong Kong gradually regained its traditional role as an *entrepôt* for the China trade. Between 1982 and 1985, the economy slowed down, or suffered a mild recession by local standards, due to political uncertainty regarding Hong Kong's future status and the impact of the world recession. The economy recovered in 1985 and soon developed another boom.

Current economic situation. Owing to its open and small nature, as well as its heavy reliance on external trade, Hong Kong's economy is susceptible to external pressures. Government actions designed to offset unfavourable external influences are of limited effectiveness. Post-war economic growth and transformation are largely attributable to the resourcefulness and adaptability of local capitalists and workers. The most distinctive feature of the economy is its increasingly close links with China. China is now Hong Kong's largest trading partner, accounting for 29 per cent of its trade, and is a major investor. Hong Kong also invests heavily in China; it is the source of about two-thirds of China's external investments and provides one and a half to two million jobs in Guangdong province. As labour and other production costs in Hong Kong soar, its economy is readjusting by relying more heavily on the service and financial sectors rather than on manufacture. The current trend is for older, low-technology, and labour-intensive manufacturing establishments to move their factories to China, but to continue trading and operating in Hong Kong. Hong Kong's economy is, therefore, vulnerable to any major change in China's economic policy.

Since the late 1970s, local capitalists of the post-war generation, such as Li Ka-shing and Sir Y. K. Pao, have challenged the pre-eminence of the old established British *hongs* (merchant houses), and have recently surpassed the latter. For their part, some old *hongs*, such as Jardine and Matheson and Hong Kong Land, have moved their domicile overseas, while others, such as the Hong Kong and Shanghai Banking Corporation, have transformed themselves into multinational conglomerates, in anticipation of the Chinese takeover in 1997. Major local Chinese-controlled companies, such as the Cheung Kong Group, have also expanded overseas. In the meantime, American and Japanese investments have been multiplying, as Hong Kong continues to offer a good rate of return in the short term. Whether foreign investment in Hong Kong will taper off closer to 1997 remains to be seen.

The current boom is fuelled by growing trade and rising property prices and rental. A shortage of labour in all sectors, pressure of demand on resources within the economy, the surge in world commodity prices and higher prices of goods imported from China have all contributed to inflation, which reached 7.5 per cent in 1988, as compared to an average of 5.4 per cent in the preceding five years. The shortage of labour is aggravated by the serious problem of a "brain drain", with large numbers of middle managers, professionals, secretaries and other skilled workers emigrating to Canada, the United States and Australia, often for reasons related to the 1997 issue. Thus, the medium-term outlook for Hong Kong's economy is not entirely optimistic, though the short-term prospect remains good. In the long term, the central question is whether the political changes in 1997 will have a major impact on Hong Kong's economy.

Hong Kong believes that the most efficient way to allocate resources is to follow market forces, and its Government has long adopted a "positive non-intervention" policy. Government's role in promoting trade and industry is largely restricted to providing the infrastructure, negotiating trade agreements, advising businessmen on regulations and matters regarding international trade agreements, and giving support to Hong Kong businessmen overseas through its missions abroad. The Government has avoided intervention in the private sector, except where social considerations are regarded as overriding, or where regulations are vital for economic well-being, as in the case of the setting up of the Securities and Futures Commission after the October 1987 stock market crash. However, in the 1980s, the government has also intervened, albeit sparingly, for political considerations, usually in the form of selling land to mainland Chinese companies at concessionary prices by private treaty.

Prospects for development. Long term development in Hong Kong will depend on what changes the Chinese takeover in July 1997 brings. Despite the **Joint Declaration**, it is inconceivable that the Chinese Government's promise that Hong Kong will remain basically unchanged for 50 years after 1997 will be kept. The transformation of the last four decades testifies that unless Hong Kong is allowed to adapt to the changing world, it will cease to remain the Hong Kong we know. The crucial question is: after 1997, to what extent will the Chinese permit Hong Kong to evolve on its own? The **Basic Law** of the Hong Kong Special Administrative Region should in principle provide the answer. However, until China has learnt to understand and respect the rule of law, the value of this piece of Chinese legislation remains doubtful.

Barring major changes in China, there is likely to be a gradual introduction of the Chinese brand of politics into Hong Kong. Chinese cadres and the offspring of Chinese leaders will play an increasingly important role in Hong Kong's political, economic and social life. How long Hong Kong's legal and judicial services and the Independent Commission Against Corruption manage to resist encroachments on their independence depends on whether corruption and nepotism in China continues. The system will be tested when the offspring of a senior Chinese leader blatantly breaks the law but refuses to be subject to the due process, as has already happened in China. Trade and industry are likely to survive, though unlikely to grow at a rate comparable to today's pace. Closer collaboration between the state and the private sector will develop, giving rise to a system of government supervision and merchant/industrialist management. In the long term, Hong Kong will probably become a more advanced and efficient Shanghai, but not necessarily any less corrupt.

The speed and extent of Hong Kong's absorption into China also depends on the degree of international attention to, and involvement in, Hong Kong affairs. The lesser the international input, the bolder will Chinese cadres be in squeezing Hong Kong to their (not necessarily China's) advantage, and the faster will Hong Kong cease to be what it is today. (*See also* **Basic Law (Hong Kong); British Nationality for Hong Kong; Daya Bay Controversy; Hong Kong: Vietnamese Boat People; Joint Declaration on Hong Kong; Joint Liaison Group on Hong Kong; Kowloon Walled City**)

ST

HONG KONG: VIETNAMESE BOAT PEOPLE. The first Vietnamese refugees arrived in Hong Kong in May 1975, after the fall of Saigon. What began as a trickle became a flood in 1979. As a port of first asylum, Hong Kong provided temporary shelter to the refugees until they were resettled abroad. The burden gradually lightened after the Geneva Conference (1979). But a new influx began in 1987 and the resettlement rate remained low, resulting in a net increase. By February 1989, a total of 135,038 Vietnamese had arrived, and 116,225 were resettled overseas. Since June 1988, new arrivals have been screened: those classified as illegal immigrants are detained pending repatriation to Vietnam. (*See also* **"Boat People", Vietnamese**)

ST

HU YAOBANG. This former general-secretary of the **Chinese Communist Party** (born in 1915) first became involved in politics at the age of 12 in the 1927 Autumn Harvest Uprising. This followed with youth work for the party, and he participated in the **Long March**. He served as a political commissar with various **People's Liberation Army** units, latterly in the same Field Army as **Deng Xiaoping**, whose protégé he became. From 1954 to 1964 he was head of the New Democratic (later Communist) Youth League. Disgraced in the Cultural Revolution, he only re-emerged to prominence after Mao's death. In 1977 he became head of the Organization Department in the newly reconstituted Central Committee (CC) Secretariat, and pressed energetically for the rehabilitation of cadres unjustly condemned during the Cultural Revolution. He moved on to head other CC departments, and in 1980 he became the party's General Secretary, where he presided over large-scale generational change in its apparatus. He took the lead in urging reforms in the party's ideology and a liberalization of its leading role. He was forced to resign in January 1987 following student protests and complaints by conservatives that he had failed to deal with them effectively. He still retained his seat on the Political Bureau, however, and he remained a symbol of party liberalization. Student demonstrations to mourn his death in April 1989 were the first stage in mounting public protests which led to the Tiananmen massacre (*see* **Tiananmen Incidents**).

CIPF

HUA GUOFENG. Born into a peasant family in Shanxi province in 1920, he joined the Red Army at the end of the **Long March**. Between 1949 and 1971 he made his party career in Mao's native province of Hunan, where he came to Mao's attention. In 1971 he headed a party group investigating the **Lin Biao** affair. In 1975 he became Minister of Public Security and in 1976 he replaced **Deng Xiaoping** as Prime Minister. Taking advantage of Mao's apparent endorsement of him with the phrase "With you in charge, I am at ease", he became Chairman of the party after Mao's death. He arranged for the arrest of the **Gang of Four**, and a mini-cult grew up around him. However, he was out-manoeuvred by the resentful Deng Xiaoping, and his economic policies proved hopelessly over-ambitious. He was forced to resign as both party Chairman and as Prime Minister in 1980. He still retains his seat on the party Central Committe.

CIPF

HUKBALAHAP UPRISING. The Communist Party of the Philippines (*Partido Komunista ng Pilipinas* – PKP), founded in 1930, organized a People's Anti-Japanese Army (*Hukbalahap* or Huks) during World War II, which played a prominent part in the resistance movement. After the War the PKP resumed legal political activities, but the Huks, who commanded a broad peasant following in Central Luzon, refused to disband or surrender their weapons. In 1948 the Roxas administration proscribed the Huks (and the PKP) and launched a fierce counter-insurgency campaign against them. In 1950 the Huks renamed their organization the *Hukbong Mapagpalaya ng Bayan* (People's Liberation Army) and they continued with growing success their campaign of insurgency. In mid-1950 they controlled major areas of central Luzon and also temporarily captured two provincial capitals.

The success of the Huk rebellion forced President Quirino to reassess the government's counter-insurgency strategy. A new Defence Minister, Ramon Magsaysay, was appointed and he proceeded to virtually neutralize the rebellion within three years, through a combination of military successes (including the capture of the movement's leadership) and the initiation of a resettlement programme for landless peasants. Following

Magsaysay's success, the Huks failed to mount another significant offensive; however, in the early 1970s Huk remnants operating in the remote area of Luzon joined forces with the newly-emerging **New People's Army**.

DS

HUMAN RIGHTS. Few Pacific nations have a clean record on human rights, as documented by Amnesty International. Canada, New Zealand and some of the Pacific Islands have the lowest incidence of abuses; Australia has been criticized because of alleged discrimination against aborigines, a number of whom have committed suicide while in police custody. Some civil liberties in Fiji have been curtailed following the military coups.

Amnesty has noted a marked improvement in many Latin American countries with the end of military rule in places such as Argentina, Brazil and Uruguay and a relative softening of the regime in Chile. Even so, disappearances are still a feature of life in much of Latin America and torture and other forms of inhuman treatment are said to be widespread. Extrajudicial executions are also common, especially in El Salvador, Colombia and Peru. Assassination and intimidation are tools used by guerrilla armies, as well as some national security forces and criminal elements, including drug traffickers and thugs hired to protect the interests of landowners and developers. The Contra guerrillas in Nicaragua acquired a particularly bad human rights record.

Large numbers of political prisoners are held in the Communist-controlled countries of the Pacific region, as well as Indonesia. Since **Mikhail Gorbachev** came to power in the Soviet Union, there have been many releases of prisoners of conscience including some religious believers. Conditions are believed to have improved in some of the Siberian prison camps and Soviet mental institutions in which some political prisoners had been incarcerated. In China, though, the situation has deteriorated, particularly since the crackdown on Tibetan nationalism and the crushing in 1989 of the pro-democracy movement. (*See also* **Capital Punishment**).

JF

HUN SEN. Born 1951, Prime Minister of the People's Republic of Kampuchea since January 1985 and Foreign Minister since 1979, except for a period in 1986–under the Democratic Kampuchea regime of **Pol Pot**, he fled to Vietnam in 1977 and returned to Phnom Penh with the Vietnamese Armed Forces in January 1979. He has thus far pursued policies closely integrated with those of Vietnam and probably worked out in Hanoi. Nevertheless, as of 1989, he has aspirations to remain effective leader of a unified and more independent Cambodia following the anticipated withdrawal of Vietnamese troops. To that end, during 1988–he has engaged in dialogue both with **Prince Sihanouk** and with the Thai prime minister **Chatichai Choonhaven**.

RBS

HUNDRED FLOWERS CAMPAIGN. This was a movement launched by **Mao Zedong** in spring 1957 to encourage greater freedom of public discussion and criticism, especially among the intelligentsia. Its slogan was the ancient adage "Let a hundred flowers bloom, let a hundred schools contend". The **Chinese Communist Party**, however, could not tolerate the tide of criticism which it unleashed, and in June 1957 it responded with an anti-rightist campaign. After the Cultural Revolution and the return of **Deng Xiaoping** in the late 1970s, the party revived the slogan to build bridges to the intelligentsia.

CIPF

I

IMMIGRATION. Immigration regulations vary considerably in the Pacific region but in almost all cases, have been tightened in recent years. The four predominantly white, English-speaking nations of Australia, New Zealand, the United States and Canada only prospered because of intensive immigration during the nineteenth and twentieth centuries, though this was partly at the cost of the indigenous population. The USA is in fact an immigrant's country par excellence, in which a myth was built up that anyone seeking freedom and opportunity was welcome, no matter where that person came from or his or her station in life. Most of the immigrants until about 30 years ago were European, but more recently they have tended to be from elsewhere, including large numbers of Latin Americans, legally or clandestinely. This has led to an important shift in the balance of the US population (exacerbated by differential birthrates) and the emergence of a growing and vociferous Hispanic–American minority (as opposed to the shrinking but still vociferous French-speaking minority in Canada). Indeed, in contrast to the earlier situation in the United States, where the integration and homogenization of immigrants was seen as a priority, pluralism is now more favoured. That also means an enhanced black consciousness among the descendants of forced immigrants of yore: the slaves.

Australia (and to a lesser extent Canada) has also broadened its attitude towards immigrants' origins, having earlier been accused of favouring white Anglo-Saxons. Accordingly, substantial communities of Greeks and Vietnamese, to name but two, can now be found in Australia's cities. Indeed, many prospective emigrants from such places as Indo-China and Hong Kong now opt for Australia and Canada in preference to European countries, as they see those newer nations as offering greater opportunities.

Japan, in stark contrast, limits immigration severely, and has accepted relatively few refugees. Most of the immigrants into China have been ethnic Chinese, most fleeing the problems of Indochina. (*See also* **Refugees**)

JF

INDOCHINESE CO-OPERATION. The three Communist countries of Indochina are bound together by treaties of friendship: that between Vietnam and Laos was signed on July 18, 1977, during a visit to Vientiane by **Le Duan** and Pham Van Dong; that between Vietnam and the People's Republic of Kampuchea (PRK) was signed in Phnom Penh by Pham Van Dong and **Heng Samrin** on Feb. 18, 1979. Both specified a wide range of areas of co-operation and were to last for 25 years. In addition, an "agreement" on cultural, scientific and economic co-operation between Laos and the PRK was signed when **Souphanouvong** visited Phnom Penh in March 1979 a visit which Heng Samrin returned the following August.

Alignment of the foreign policies of the three countries was strengthened in January 1980, when their foreign ministers met in Phnom Penh to issue a statement endorsing the Vietnamese position on the Cambodian issue and denouncing the policies of Beijing. Thirteen such meetings were held between then and August 1986, and a fourteenth in July 1988. Further co-ordination was achieved after the first "summit" meeting of the Indochinese leaders held in Vientiane on Feb. 22-23, 1983. At an official level, practical co-ordination was strengthened by the creation of an office of "economic and cultural co-operation" in each of the three capitals, whose heads met annually between 1981 and 1986 and by meetings of planning ministers to discuss the details of the five-year plans for 1981–85 and 1986–90. Underlying these various levels of relationship between the three governments was the (probably even closer) collaboration between the **Vietnamese Communist Party**, the **Kampuchean People's Revolutionary Party** and the **Lao People's Revolutionary Party**.

RBS

INDONESIA. *Population*: 177 million. *Area*: 1,919,443 sq km. *Gross Domestic Product*: US$57,000 million (1986). *Trade (1987)*: imports US$17,237 million; exports US$12,328 million. *Top five trading partners*: (imports) Japan, United States, Singapore, West Germany and Saudi Arabia; (exports) Japan, United States, Singapore, South Korea and Netherlands. *Defence spending*: US$507,875 million (1989-90 est.). *Education spending*: US$1,052,000 million (1989-90 est.). *Urban population as percentage of total*: 22. *Birth rate*: 27 per thousand. *Life expectancy*: 58.

Geographical background. The Republic of Indonesia is the largest archipelagic nation in the world and the third largest country in Asia. Encompassing 13,667 islands, of which approximately 1,000 are inhabited, it lies on both sides of the equator stretching some 5,120 km from east to west. As of 1988, some 31 per cent of the country's total land area was under cultivation, whereas just over 30 per cent remained as forest and almost 6 per cent was identified as pasture.

The Indonesian islands are commonly divided into four groups; (i) the larger islands, formerly known as the great Sunda complex, consisting of Sumatra, Java, Kalimantan and Sulawesi; (ii) the smaller islands east of Java from Bali to Timor, formerly known as the lesser Sunda islands; (iii) the Molucca islands between Sulawesi and the lesser Sundas; and (iv) Irian Jaya, the western part of the island of New Guinea. Land boundaries are shared with the Malaysian states of Sarawak and Sabah (which occupy the north of the island of Borneo) and Papua New Guinea, to the east of Irian Jaya. Together, the islands of Java, Sumatra, Sulawesi and the territories of Kalimantan and Irian Jaya constitute 90 per cent of land area.

Indonesia has the fifth highest population in the world, increasing annually at a rate of about 2 per cent and estimated to reach 213,700,000 by the year 2000. Population is unevenly distributed, with a density rate of under 50 persons per sq km for the majority of the islands compared with a rate of over 700 persons per sq km for Java. Over 60 per cent of the population live on Java and Bali, which together constitute only 7 per cent of the total land area. The capital of Indonesia is Jakarta, situated on the north-western coast of Java, and other major urban centres include Surabaya, Bandung and Semarang (Java), Medan and Palembang (Sumatra) and Ujung Pandang (Sulawesi).

Socio-political background. Indonesian society is composed of a mixture of races and peoples belonging to over 300 different ethnic groups, speaking over 250 languages and dialects. Javanese is spoken by a majority of Indonesians, but the country's official language is Bahasa Indonesia, derived from "trade Malay" which had been used historically as a *lingua franca* throughout the islands.

The principal ethnic groups are the Javanese and Sundanese on Java, the Acehnese, Batak and Minangkabau on Sumatra, the Dayaks of the Kalimantan interior, the Irianese of Irian Jaya, the Makasarese, Buginese, Toraja and Menadonese of Sulawesi, the Ambonese of the Maluku islands, and the Balinese of Bali. The main ethnic minority are the Chinese who number approximately 3,500,000. The main ethnic type in the western two-thirds of the archipelago is Deutero-Malay, whereas in the remaining eastern third, with the exception of the coastal fringes, the Proto-Malay and Melanesoid types predominate. The main cultural divisions tend to run parallel to the ethnic divisions, with most of western Indonesia professing the Sunni Muslim faith as opposed to the majority animist and Christian beliefs of the people of the eastern interior. There are considerable exceptions, most notably the Balinese who have maintained their adherence to the Hindu religion. All Indonesian citizens are required by law to state their religion and in 1984 an estimated 78 per cent of the population were Muslims, 11 per cent were Christians, 5 per cent were animists and 2 per cent were Hindus. Indonesia has the largest Muslim population in the world. Muslims in Java are stratified according to the degree of participation in Islam, with a deep division between nominal (*abangan*) and devout (*santri*) Muslims.

The Republic of Indonesia is a unitary state with an executive president (a position held since 1968 by Gen. **Suharto**), supported by a Vice-President, who governs with the assistance of a cabinet appointed by him and who is elected for a five-year term (and is re-eligible) by a 1,000-member People's Consultative Assembly (*Majelis Permusyawaratan Rakyat*), the highest authority of the state. Of the Assembly's members, 500 are from the House of Representatives (*Dewan Perwakilan Rakyat*), the country's legislature, to which 400 members are elected for a five-year term by direct universal adult suffrage and 100 are appointed by the President. The Assembly's other 500 members are government appointees, delegates of the regional assemblies, and representatives of parties and groups (appointed in proportion to their elective seats in the House of Representatives).

All adults above the age of 17 years, or younger if married, are entitled to vote, except members of the armed forces and persons deprived of their civic rights, i.e. principally former members of the banned Communist Party of Indonesia detained in the wake of the abortive coup attempt of 1965. Candidates are elected in multi-member provinces under a system of simple proportional representation. Indonesia has a limited or "guided" party system under which the various political currents (with the exclusion of communism) are channelled into three officially recognized formations. By far the most dominant is the pro-government and state financed **Golkar** which secured a large majority in the April 1987 general elections, thereby providing a continued civilian basis for President Suharto's military regime.

Pre-modern history. Situated on the sea route between China and India and possessing abundant natural resources, the islands of the Indonesian archipelago have long attracted the attention of outside influences. The great Indian sanskrit poems Ramayana and Mahabharata as well as the second century CE Greek cartographer Ptolemy refer to islands of great wealth to the east of India. Early Chinese annals of the Han dynasty refer to an emissary sent by a Javanese king Devavarman to the Emperor of China in the year 132 CE. By the seventh century, Indianized kingdoms were the dominant powers in southern Sumatra and western and central Java. During the following centuries, two large empires emerged; Sri-Vijaya, covering large areas of Java, Sumatra and the Malay peninsula (c. 700–1200) and Majapahit, the greatest of all Javanese territorial empires which controlled much of the archipelago from 1300–1450. The first real evidence that Islam had emerged as an active force in the islands came from Marco Polo who landed in Sumatra on his way back to Venice from China in the late thirteenth century. Muslim traders from Gujarat in western India and, before them, Arab Merchants, played an important part in the propagation of the Islamic faith. The Islamic Kingdom of Aceh was founded in northern Sumatra in the mid-fifteenth century and with the expansion of Achinese power, Islam spread to other areas and islands. The process of Islamization lasted until the early twentieth century.

The first European intrusion came in the early sixteenth century, when the Portuguese gained control of the Moluccan clove trade. By the end of the sixteenth century, Dutch traders had replaced their Portuguese counterparts as the principal European power in the islands. In 1602, Dutch traders formed the United East India Company (VOC), under a Charter issued by the Dutch parliament, two years after the British had established a similar company in India. This charter was allowed to expire in 1799 and VOC territories, principally the Moluccas and parts of Java, became the property of the Dutch government. During the French occupation of the Netherlands in the early nineteenth century, Britain took temporary control of the East Indies, in the process liberalizing many of the harsher policies introduced by the Dutch. In their post-Napoleonic era the Dutch returned to the East Indies only to be confronted by a major Java-based rebellion which lasted from 1825–30. The end of the Java War marked the start of a period during which the Dutch intensified their exploitation of the archi-

pelago's many resources. In 1830 the *Culturstelsel* or Culture System (under which Javanese peasants were obliged to devote part of their land and labour to the cultivation of export crops prescribed by the government) was introduced on Java, a system so profitable that it was described as "the lifebelt on which the Netherlands kept afloat". Criticism of the *Culturstelsel* on humanitarian grounds led to its abandonment in 1870, but this, along with the government's fear of British imperialistic designs, encouraged the "Forward Movement" and Dutch expansion to the Outer islands; by 1910 all of current-day Indonesia was under Dutch control.

In 1901, the Dutch introduced a new "Ethical Policy" which aimed at providing limited educational and administrative opportunities for the indigenous population. A by-product of the "Ethical Policy" was the emergence in the early twentieth century of a class of western-educated, urban Indonesian intellectuals, whose nationalist aspirations were given impetus by events outside the archipelago, most notably Japan's defeat of the Soviet Union in 1905. During the first two decades of the twentieth century, the nationalist movement was fractured, with varying degrees of competition evident amongst the Islamic and secular groups. The late 1920s saw the emergence of Sukarno and Hatta to positions of prominence in the nationalist movement, but it was only as a result of Japanese occupation that the movement became a genuinely popular one.

Early modern history. During World War II, Indonesia was occupied by Japanese forces from March 1942. **Sukarno** and Hatta, the foremost nationalist leaders, agreed at an early stage of the occupation that co-operation with the Japanese forces would provide the best opportunity to secure independence. Therefore, in March 1943, they formed a united front with the Japanese occupying forces, organizing a Centre for People's Power (Putera) with Sukarno as its chairman and Hatta as his deputy. Later that year an independent military force (Peta) was created by the nationalists to assist the Japanese in repelling an Allied invasion of the Indonesian archipelago. The decline of the Axis Powers motivated the Japanese prime Minister, Koiso Kuniaki, to announce in September 1944 details of a plan to make the whole of the Indonesian archipelago independent. The plan was curtailed by Japanese defeat in mid-August 1945 and the nationalist leadership, pressured by radical youth groups, declared independence on Aug 17. Sukarno was named as provisional president of Indonesia and Hatta vice-president. The declaration of independence was not recognized by the Netherlands and in late 1945 Allied troops (including Dutch forces) arrived in Indonesia; fighting between the Europeans and the Indonesians soon erupted.

Sukarno was distrusted by both the Allied forces and also by radical nationalist elements and by late 1945 his position had been undermined to the extent that he was obliged to delegate most of his powers to Sutan Sjahrir. The leftist Sjahrir negotiated the Linggadjati Agreement with the Dutch in November 1946. The Agreement provided for Dutch recognition of republican rule in Java and Sumatra and the creation of a Netherlands-Indonesia Union under the Dutch Crown, consisting of the Netherlands, the republic and the states of the eastern archipelago (the latter two forming the United States of Indonesia). However, misunderstandings over the interpretation of the Agreement resulted in increased tension and in July 1947 the Dutch initiated a "police action" ostensibly against communist forces operating in republican territories. Republican forces were eventually driven out of Sumatra and eastern and western Java, congregating, after a UN imposed ceasefire had been effected in early 1948, around Yogyakarta in central Java. New peace negotiations were unsuccessful and in December 1948 Dutch forces launched their second "police action", this time capturing Yogyakarta and with it the entire republican government. However, the Dutch military action met with stiff international disapproval (notably from the United States and the UN Security Council), and the very real threat of the withdrawal of Marshall Plan aid by the US obliged the Dutch to enter into negotiations to facilitate a formal transfer of power. On Dec. 27, 1949, Indonesia became fully independent, with Sukarno continuing as President. A provisional Constitution promulgated in February 1950 provided for a federation of 16 equal states (excluding West New Guinea – Irian Jaya – which remained under Dutch control until 1962).

Political history. The concept of federalism was not welcomed by militant nationalists who denounced the February 1950 provisional Constitution as a Dutch scheme to retain influence in their former colony. Hence, the consolidation process commenced immediately after the formal transfer of sovereignty, with legitimacy initially being accorded to Jakarta's expansion of control throughout the provinces by an abortive coup attempt in West Java in January 1950. In the following months, successive provinces relinquished their federal status and in August 1950 the federation (the Republic of the United States of Indonesia – RSI) was dissolved and Indonesia was proclaimed a unitary republic (Republic of Indonesia). A provisional constitution was ratified by the legislature, and remained in force until July 1959 when the Constitution of 1945 (proclaimed after the declaration of independence that year) was re-enacted by presidential decree (see below). The country's first post-independence general election for 257 legislative seats was held in September 1955, and was contested by a total of 168 parties and groups, of which 28 parties returned one or more seats. Four parties emerged as the leading contenders; (i) *Partai Nasional Indonesia* (PNI – Indonesian Nationalist Party) (57 seats), a predominantly Javanese Sukarnoist front; (ii) *Majelis Syoro Muslimin Indonesia* (Masyumi – Council of Indonesian Muslim Associations) (57 seats), a Modernist Islamic party with heavy support in the Outer Islands; (iii) *Nahdatul Ulama* (NU – Muslim Scholars League) (45 seats), a traditionalist Muslim grouping with its principal support base in Java; and (iv) *Partai Kommunis Indonesia* (PKI – **Communist Party of Indonesia**) (39 seats) which enjoyed grass-roots support amongst a large number of urban Javanese. Despite the predominance of the four parties, no single group commanded an absolute majority, thereby necessitating the continuation of government by an unstable coalition cabinet. During the 1950–57 period, six cabinets were formed, none of which possessed the necessary authority to address the country's mounting problems (i.e. the economy, the role of Islam in the state and of the Armed Forces – ABRI – in the government and the pressing problem of Javanese domination of the regions).

In the mid-1950s attempts by Sukarno and the Army Chief of Staff, Maj.-Gen. Abdul Haris Nasution, to curb the powers of the military officers stationed in the Outer Islands precipitated a crisis that threatened the existence of the nation. The unrest convinced Sukarno that Indonesia was not ready for full-blown parliamentary democracy, and in late 1956, he initiated a more authoritarian, anti-parliamentary system of government, described by him as "Guided Democracy". Mohammed Hatta resigned that year as Vice-President in protest at Sukarno's initiation of Guided Democracy. Martial Law was proclaimed in March 1957 and in July 1959 Sukarno issued a presidential decree reinstating the 1945 Constitution, with its emphasis on broad presidential authority, and dissolving the legislature. In March 1960, a new legislature, the House of People's Representatives-Mutual Assistance (*Dewan Perwakilan Rakyat-Gotong Royong* – DPR-GR) was established. All 283 representatives were government appointees, and over half the seats were reserved for various socio-political or functional groups, including the military.

Sukarno's role during the Guided Democracy period was pivotal. His power was to a large extent based upon his populist appeal. His constant and charismatic articulation of a variety of concepts that together formed the basis of a national (and nationalist) ideology, helped him maintain his position at the apex of the country's complex power structure. Two of his most famous concepts were: (i) "Manipol – USDEK", Manipol referring to a political manifesto set forth by him in mid-1969, and USDEK being an acronym for the 1945 Constitution, Indonesian Socialism, Guided Democracy, Guided Economy and Indonesian Identity; and (ii) "Nasakom", the synthesis of nationalism, religion and communism.

Sukarno's exceptional political adeptness during the period of Guided Democracy was demonstrated through his ability to balance and play off the two great contending power factions, the PKI and ABRI. Sukarno had initially proposed that all political parties would be united in a National Front but this never came about, and most parties continued to operate clandestinely. The PKI alone flourished, its credibility boosted dramatically during the late 1950s as a result of its aggressive implementation of land reform policies in rural Java, Sumatra and Bali, and also, less directly, as a result of Sukarno's increasing economic dependence on the Soviet Union and China. The party announced support for both "Manipol – USDEK" and, at a later date, Guided Democracy, in an attempt to retain favour with Sukarno. During the Guided Democracy period ABRI's political position became effectively institutionalized, with officers gaining representation in cabinet, parliament and the civil service. In addition leading officers were given prominent positions in the country's economic enterprises, thereby securing vital economic power bases.

ABRI's position was further enhanced by Sukarno's activist foreign policy. During the parliamentary period, Indonesia had pursued a foreign policy with the emphasis placed firmly on neutrality and non-alignment. However, during Guided Democracy this stance shifted, until Sukarno's declaratory aim became the formation of a "Jakarta-Phnom Penh-Beijing-Hanoi-Pyongyang axis" to combat neo-colonialism, colonialism and imperialism (Nekolim). The pro-Chinese and anti-Western course of Sukarno's foreign policy became evident in his actions against the Netherlands over Irian Jaya (which developed into open hostilities in early 1962 and was settled by an agreement signed in August 1962 under which the territory became part of Indonesia in 1963), as well as in his opposition to neo-colonialism in the form of the creation of the Malaysian Federation (which developed into the "Confrontation" – "Konfrontasi" – with Malaysia, 1963–66).

Sukarno's increasing support for the PKI, and the party's growing influence within sections of the Armed Forces, meant that by 1965 the ABRI-PKI equilibrium, without which the Guided Democracy experiment could not have gone ahead, was moving inexorably towards disintegration. Konfrontasi and chronic economic mismanagement all added to the atmosphere of dangerous instability and the impression that Sukarno had lost control. On Sept. 30, 1965, a group of army officers (known as the September 30 Movement or Gestapu – Gerakan September Tiga Puluh) launched a coup attempt, assassinating six generals but failing in their attempt to kill Maj.-Gen. Nasution. The rebels justified their action by insisting that the generals had been plotting a coup of their own. The next day the rebels announced the formation of a revolutionary council and Cabinet before being crushed in a successful counter-coup led by Nasution and Commander of the Army's Strategic Reserve, Gen. Suharto (who had not been targeted by Gestapu). Sukarno was perceived as having been sympathetic to the Gestapu coup and was discredited, paving the way for the military's assumption of power. The military used the event as an excuse to take action against their rival, the PKI, which was quickly proscribed, and by December 1965 as many as 500,000 communists, leftists and supporters of the "old order" (orla) had been killed during violent protests in Java, Bali and Sumatra. The extermination of the PKI and the purge of Pro-Sukarno elements from within ABRI, left Sukarno with no power-base and he was gradually manoeuvred into a position of political impotence. In March 1966, military commanders led by Suharto assumed emergency powers and in February 1967 President Sukarno transferred full power to Suharto. The next month a provisional People's Consultative Assembly (a replacement for the DPR-GR) stripped Sukarno of all his powers and made Suharto acting president, a position he was formally elected to by the Assembly's members in March 1968.

Under President Suharto's "New Order" regime, ABRI, and in particular the Army, emerged as the nation's dominant political institution, constituting the power base for Suharto's continuing rule. The military's often brutal suppression of political dissent has provided the stability necessary for the implementation of liberal economic strategies and pro-Western foreign policies.

In 1970 the government called on all political

parties to contest the forthcoming legislative election on the basis of a three-way re-alignment. The first grouping would be associated with the supposedly neutral and non-political **Golkar**, which was in reality pro-Government and military/civil service-dominated. The second grouping, described as "spiritual", would comprise Muslim parties, and the third grouping, identified as "nationalist", would represent the remaining parties. The elections were held in July 1971 and Golkar won 236 out of 360 directly elected seats in the House of Representatives. In early 1973 Suharto was re-elected by the People's Consultative Assembly for a further five-year term as president. In January 1973 legislation was passed obliging the Islamic parties and the non-Islamic parties to officially amalgamate as the Development Unity Party (PPP) and the **Indonesian Democratic Party** (PDI) respectively. In general elections held in May 1977, Golkar's share of the vote fell slightly, but it still gained 232 seats. In March 1978 Suharto was elected unanimously, as the sole candidate, for a third presidential term.

Dissatisfaction with the Suharto regime, and in particular with the alleged widespread corruption within it, led to student riots and increasingly vocal criticism from respected elder statesmen during the late 1970s. In May 1980, a group of 50 prominent Indonesians (including Maj.-Gen. (retd) Nasution, Mohammad Natsir and Berhanuddin Harahap – the latter two both former Prime Ministers in the 1950s) presented a petition to the government asserting that President Suharto was dividing the nation and that he was encouraging ABRI to take sides in the forthcoming (i.e. May 1982) elections. Although ABRI described the "statement of concern" by the so-called "Petition of 50" group as "a constitutional coup d'etat", no arrests were made. Further student unrest and anti-Chinese riots were reported in 1980 and in September Adml. Sudomo (the then commander of the Command for Security and Restoration of Order – Kopkamtib) announced details of a new security programme for the coming decade, with increased powers of arrest and search for the armed forces, and new restrictions on those under political surveillance. Nevertheless, in September 1981, some 500 people signed a petition demanding a more democratic electoral law, but the army forbade the media to publicize details.

Elections to the House of Representatives were held in May 1982, with Golkar increasing its majority, winning 246 out of 364 contested seats. Campaigning was conducted during a fixed 45-day period, during which time separate days were allotted to each of the three groups (Golkar, the PPP and the PDI) for holding their campaign meetings. Various violent incidents occurred during the election period resulting in some 50 deaths, most notably in mid-March when serious rioting took place at a Golkar rally in Banteng Square in Jakarta. Following the election, allegations were made by the PDI and the PPP that electoral irregularities had occurred.

In October 1982 President Suharto signed into law four bills giving the so-called "dual (i.e. military and socio-economic) function" (*dwi fungsi*) of ABRI a firm legal basis. The military's dual function creed had legitimized its intervention in politics since the introduction of Suharto's New Order in the mid-1960s. The legislation stated specifically that ABRI were 'a component of the defence force and at the same time a component of the social force". Legislation passed in February 1988 amongst other things effectively codified the *dwi fungsi* doctrine. Although the legislation was for the most part uncontroversial, its passage through the House of Representatives had been preceded by several months of stormy debate. At the root of the controversy was the belief in some quarters that the military were attempting through the legislation to redefine to their advantage the relationship between ABRI and the state.

In March 1983, Suharto was re-elected by the People's Consultative Assembly for a fourth consecutive five-year term as President. The Assembly also conferred upon him the title "Father of Development" (Sukarno having been posthumously designated "Father of Independence" in 1978). Prior to his re-election, Suharto had informed the Assembly that the coming period from 1983 to 1988 would be "the last phase of the rounding up and completion of the historic task" of the so-called "generation of 1945" to which he himself belonged.

Attempts by the government during 1984 to introduce legislation requiring all political, social and religious organizations to adopt **Pancasila** as their sole ideology met with stiff opposition. In August, the Petition of 50 openly accused Suharto of attempting to establish a one-party system. Serious rioting in the port area of Tanjung Priok, Near Jakarta, in September and a subsequent spate of bombings were allegedly instigated by Muslim opponents of the proposed legislation. Among those arrested and imprisoned in connection with the unrest was Gen. Hartono Resko Dharsono, a prominent supporter of the Petition of 50 group and a former secretary-general of the **Association of South-East Asian Nations (ASEAN)**. The law concerning mass organizations was finally enacted in late May 1985, although Golkar, the PPP and the PDI had already adopted Pancasila ss their sole principle in 1984.

Recent developments. Elections were held in April 1987 to the 400 elective seats in the enlarged House of Representatives. After the election, President Suharto appointed 100 ABRI members (four more than in 1982) to the House. Legislation had been introduced in 1984 enlarging the People's Consultative Assembly, of which the House, as the legislative body proper, was a constituent part, to a total of 1,000 members. The remaining 500 Assembly members were subsequently appointed as representatives of the political parties and functional groups and from delegates of regional assemblies. In the elections, Golkar won 299 seats, the PPP 61 and the PDI 40. For the first time Golkar gained an overall majority of seats in all 27 provinces, including the traditional Muslim stronghold of Aceh in northern Sumatra. Compared with the previous elections in 1982, the PPP's strength declined in 19 of Indonesia's 27 provinces, whereas the PDI improved its performance in 20 provinces.

President Suharto was elected, unopposed, for a fifth five-year term by the People's Consultative Assembly in March 1988. In a significant development, the PPP forced two votes on government policy proposals during the Assembly session. Although the PPP's amendments were overwhelmingly rejected, they nonetheless undermined the traditional *musyawarah* process, by which members argued until a consensus was reached.

Suharto's re-election as President had never been in doubt, and therefore the proceedings were overshadowed by the unprecedented manner in which the usually routine election of a Vice-President was conducted. In previous presidential elections Suharto had made known his preferred candidate for the post and the Assembly had subsequently endorsed his choice. However, prior to the March 1988 elections Suharto let it be known that the Assembly should choose its own candidate. However, Dr Jailani Naro, the PPP president, and Lt.-Gen. (retd) Sudharmono, Secretary of State and Golkar general chairman, were both nominated for the post and Suharto was obliged to indicate his preference for Sudharmono before Naro withdrew. Many observers commented that Naro's candidacy had in fact been initiated by ABRI, possibly reflecting the military's distrust of Sudharmono and also even deeper divisions between Golkar and the armed forces (under Sudharmono's Chairmanship of Golkar, there had been a shift away from military dominance in the grouping). Sudharmono was not thought to command much loyalty within

ABRI, having had little active service experience and having been associated in the past with leftist organizations. In October 1988, Sudharmono was replaced as Golkar general chair by Gen. (retd) Wahono, a figure with credentials acceptable to ABRI and to the developing bureaucratic elite. Despite Sudharmono's replacement as Golkar chairman, ABRI were accused in some quarters of employing tactics to discredit Sudharmono during 1988/early 1989, with the launch of a new and vigorous campaign calling on Indonesian citizens to guard against a nascent PKI revival.

The dissolution of the powerful Kopkamtib (the Operational Command for the Restoration of Security and Order) in September 1988 was regarded by some commentators as a dilution of ABRI's independence and power. Kopkamtib had been the first creation of Gen. Suharto as he rose to power in late 1965, and over the years it had served the "New Order" regime as its key instrument to undermine political opponents. From March 1983 until its dissolution it was commanded by Gen. L.B. (Benny) Murdani (currently Minister of Defence and Security), who was replaced in February 1988 as ABRI C.-in-C. by Gen. **Try Sutrisno**. Kopkamtib was replaced by Bakorstanas (the Co-ordination Board to Help Solidify National Stability), chaired by Gen. Sutrisno, but under Suharto's overall command. Unlike its predecessor, members of Bakorstanas included representatives from the Cabinet and non-military government departments, and its main task was, allegedly, the exposure of corruption.

The issue of political succession in Indonesia dominated political debate during the first half of 1989. Between January and April several senior ministers, including Gen. Rudini (Internal Affairs) and Adml. (retd) Sudomo (Political Affairs and Security), aired freely their views on the succession process. In early June Suharto issued an 18-page statement calling for an end to speculation on the presidential succession; "conflicting statements", he said, could "disrupt society".

Outline of economic development. Upon the achievement of independence Sukarno inherited a stagnant economy that deteriorated through subsequent years of economic mismanagement by members of the armed forces, the administrators of the majority of the country's large-scale economic enterprises. At the end of the Sukarno era, the economy was distinguished by rapidly spiralling inflation and massive foreign debts. From 1960 to 1967, the real rate of GDP growth averaged less than 2 per cent, and on five occasions during this seven-year period the rate of economic expansion failed to keep pace with population growth. In 1966, debt service obligations exceeded export earnings by some US$100 million, and total foreign debt was estimated at US$2,300 million, a large element of which was owed to Eastern European nations for arms purchases.

The assumption of power by Suharto in 1966 resulted in a fundamental restructuring of economic methods and goals. Radical Sukarnoist priorities such as land reform and the nationalization of foreign enterprises were replaced by an emphasis on pragmatic approaches to increased production and income. A team of US-trained technocrats (the so-called "Berkeley Mafia") were appointed to senior positions in and around the National Development Planning Council (Bappenas), and they quickly formulated a comprehensive programme for economic recovery which included the utilization of substantial amounts of Western and Japanese assistance and investment.

In 1967 debt rescheduling and aid negotiations were initiated with Western and Japanese creditors and with multilateral aid agencies such as the World Bank and the International Monetary Fund, who had combined to establish the Inter-Governmental Group on Indonesia (IGGI). This group gained major influence over the formulation of national economic policies, and large volumes of foreign assistance have since been channelled through it, primarily in the form of programme aid and food aid. The stabilization measures introduced by the Suharto government during its first years included: (i) the imposition of fiscal and monetary discipline to curb inflation; (ii) the adoption of measures (e.g. devaluation of rupiah, introduction of relatively liberal foreign investment law) to restore the economy's external balance; and (iii) the shifting of national expenditure away from consumption towards productive investment. The successful application of these measures meant that by 1969 the economy had achieved a measure of stability and was well positioned to benefit from the favourable international situation of the 1970s.

The first of a series of five-year development plans, known by the acronym Repelita, was initiated by Bappenas in 1969. Its main emphasis was on agricultural and infrastructural development (with both public and private investment encouraged), and with a few important exceptions (such as rice production), most of Repelita I's targets were met. During the Repelita I period, the country's petroleum-producing capacity increased markedly as **Pertamina** (the national petroleum company) signed an increasing number of production sharing contracts with foreign companies. As a member of the Organization of Petroleum Exporting Countries (OPEC), Indonesia benefited greatly from the large increase in oil prices in the aftermath of the 1973 Arab-Israeli War. During the Repelita I period, an average annual real GDP growth rate of 7.3 per cent was achieved and this increased to 7.7 per cent during the term of the following plan (Repelita II – 1974–79), during which emphasis was placed on increasing employment and promoting income equity.

The decline of world production and consumption of petroleum in the early 1980s had serious repercussions for the Indonesian economy. At the start of the decade Indonesia was heavily reliant on the income from hydrocarbons, with the oil sector accounting for some 25 per cent of GDP, over 65 per cent of government revenue and 80 per cent of merchandise exports. A series of measures introduced to tackle the country's growing economic problems in the early 1980s included a domestic oil price increase of 50 per cent in May 1980, a reduction of subsidies in early 1982 leading to a further 60 per cent domestic oil price increase, reductions in rice and sugar subsidies in April 1982 (with consequent increases in prices by about 40 per cent), the introduction of strict import controls in December 1982 and the presentation of an austerity budget in January 1983. Despite the introduction of these measures, GDP growth turned negative in 1982/83, whilst oil and commodity prices fell further. The government responded in March 1983 by devaluing the rupiah by 27.5 per cent against the US dollar, to a new parity of 970 rupiahs=US$1.00. In addition, Bappenas decreased development expenditure and subsidies, liberalized internal distribution and external trade and brought about comprehensive tax and financial reforms. By 1985, the economy appeared to have adjusted to the oil price decline, as evidenced by a substantial decline in budget and current account deficit, the restoration of positive GDP growth and the containment of the debt-service burden to a manageable level.

However, in 1986 the economy suffered a major setback, resulting from a series of external factors, including: (i) a massive slump in oil prices (the most drastic upheaval in the world oil market since the early 1970s); (ii) weakening commodity prices; and (iii) a depreciating dollar. Consequently, in 1986/87 major fiscal and external imbalances re-emerged and the country's debt-to-export and debt service ratios worsened rapidly. The government responded with the introduction of a series of wide-ranging measures designed to contain the immediate economic difficulties in the short term, whilst, at the same time, strengthening the non-oil and non-gas sectors to ensure a long-term restructuring of the country's economic base. These measures included; (i) the adoption of austerity budgets in 1986/87 and 1987/88, aimed at reducing expenditure and improving tax administration; (ii) the introduction in 1986 of a "May 6 Package" of major fiscal and monetary reforms aimed at increasing non-oil exports by augmenting Indonesia's competitiveness in the world market, removing protectionist measures, improving the climate for foreign investment and increasing production from small businesses and co-operatives; and (iii) a further devaluation of the rupiah against the dollar by 31 per cent in September 1986, with a view to protecting external competitiveness, promoting growth of non-oil exports and reducing import demand. Further economic reforms were announced in December 1987. The package comprised 58 separate decrees and emphasised reforms in the areas of exports, tourism and the private capital market.

Current economic situation. Largely in response to the adjustment measures imposed by the government in 1986/87 (see section on Outline of Economic Development), the overall performance of the Indonesian economy improved significantly in 1987/88. Real GDP growth increased to 4.2 per cent (compared with 2.4 per cent in 1985/86) and inflation declined, moderately, to 8.5 per cent. Non-oil exports – in particular manufactured goods – performed especially strongly and imports remained stable. Export revenue from manufactured products totalled US$6,730 million in 1987/88, an increase of over 45 per cent compared with 1986/87.

In January 1988 President Suharto presented a draft budget for the 1988–89 fiscal year (the final year of Repelita IV), beginning April 1, 1988. The budget included further austerity measures, with the country's rapidly increasing foreign debt absorbing much of the projected increase in export revenues and tax receipts. Debt service payments were by far the largest single expenditure, accounting for about 36 per cent of all spending (a 56 per cent increase over the previous year, due largely to appreciation of the Japanese yen against the US dollar). Indonesia's foreign debt stood at some US$42,100 million and was the largest in south-east Asia. The budget offered no major new projects and, for the third year in a row, civil servants and the military were denied a pay increase.

In May 1988 Japan agreed to provide Indonesia with new grants and soft loans worth US$2,300 million. The package represented a significant easing of terms by Japan in its economic aid to developing countries. The Japanese government would provide US$1,400 million repayable over 30 years, with a 10-year deferment, at an annual interest rate of 2.7 per cent. The remainder would be in untied loans from the Japan Export-Import Bank.

Further economic reforms were announced by the government in November 1988, including the elimination of non-tariff barriers, the deregulation of the shipping industry and the elimination of the ban on the wholesale distribution of their products by foreign investors. The next month reforms were announced in the financial sector to allow foreign entrance into fields that had been previously limited.

After three years of strict austerity, President Suharto presented an expansionary 1989/90 state budget in January 1989, which provided for a 26 per cent increase in government spending to 36,574,900 million rupiahs. The budget included significant increases in government spending for development projects and health needs, as well as a 15 per cent pay rise for civil servants and the armed forces. It was estimated that non-oil revenues would contribute almost 70 per cent of national revenue (compared to as little as 22 per cent in 1983). Though projected to decline, oil revenues would remain the single largest source of government funds. Non-oil tax revenues were estimated to increase by almost 28 per cent over 1988/89 receipts. The budget anticipated that some US$6,590 million would be raised from foreign sources – chiefly the 14-member IGGI group – in the form of grants and concessionary loans, up from US$4,340 million provided during 1988/89. Debt-servicing costs again constituted the largest expenditure item, accounting for some 52 per cent of total routine expenditures. However, Sumarlin estimated that Indonesia's 1989/90 debt service ratio (the ratio of aggregate debt service payments to total gross exports) would be 35 per cent, down from 38 per cent in 1988–89, and dropping to 25 per cent by the end of Repelita V in 1994.

Foreign relations. Under President Suharto, Indonesia has pursued a non-aligned foreign policy, whilst maintaining strong contacts with the West. This contrasts sharply with the last years of Sukarno's rule, when Indonesia embarked on a policy of extreme nationalism and anti-western and anti-colonial confrontation. Suharto's refashioning of Indonesia's foreign policy made possible the formation of ASEAN in 1967, which has since acted as a cornerstone of Indonesia's external relations.

Indonesia is a key-player in ASEAN's principal foreign policy concern – Kampuchea. Of the six ASEAN countries, Indonesia has the closest relations with Vietnam (the two having shared similarly violent routes to independency and, subsequently, a comparable threat perception with regard to China) and Jakarta has hosted the two major gatherings of all Kampuchean factions (JIM I in July 1988, and JIM II in February 1989).

China and Portugal remain sources of friction with regard to Indonesia's foreign policy. Relations with the latter were broken off in December 1975 when Indonesian forces took control of Portuguese **East Timor**. Relations with China were suspended in 1967 over the issue of alleged Chinese involvement in the attempted coup of 1965. However, in July 1985, the two countries signed a memorandum of understanding on the resumption of direct trade links. A breakthrough occurred at the funeral of Japanese Emperor **Hirohito**, when Suharto held talks with the Chinese Foreign Minister, Qian Qichen, and it was agreed that the two country's respective UN missions begin normalization talks.

Relations with neighbouring Australia improved greatly in August 1985, when the **Hawke** government recognized Indonesia's *de facto* sovereignty in East Timor. Progress was impeded in 1986, when an article in an Australian newspaper detailed the business connections of Suharto and his family and studied possible analogy with the corrupt system of patronage that had operated in the Philippines under **Marcos**. Relations with Papua New Guinea (PNG) remain sensitive as a result of the activities of Irianese rebels of the Free Papua Movement (*Organaisai Papua Merdeka* – OPM), who aim to incorporate (Indonesian) Irian Jaya with PNG. In October 1986, Indonesia and PNG signed a treaty of mutual respect, friendship and co-operation.

Prospects for development. Indonesia's development prospects for the period up until the mid-1990s is largely dependent upon the successful continued application of the reform process initiated in the mid-1980s in order to reduce the economy's dependence on the depressed petroleum and gas sectors. In general, most recent surveys of the Indonesian economy have been optimistic about the government's ability to sustain the reform programme and lessen the economy's vulnerability to external events. The annual IMF review of the country's economy released in mid-1988 predicted accelerated growth into the 1990s with GDP increasing by at least 5 per cent annually until the early 1990s. This healthy performance would be "sufficient to absorb the growing labour force, while keeping domestic inflation low and gradually easing the

debt burden" the report said. In addition to predicting faster rates of growth in the future, the report also provided optimistic forecasts across the full range of other leading economic indicators: (i) inflation to slow to around 5 per cent by the late 1980s and remain at that level into the mid-1990s; (ii) the current account deficit to decline to US$40 million by fiscal 1992-93; (iii) steady continuous gains in export revenues into the 1990s; (iv) external debt to peak during 1992-93 at US$53,500 million, thereafter beginning to decline; and (v) the debt service ratio to decline to 28.9 per cent of export revenues by 1992-93.

In January 1989 the government released details of the annual budget for 1989-90 (beginning April 1, 1989) and of the fifth five-year national development plan (Repelita V – 1989-1993), both of which emphasized the importance of expansion in the non-oil sectors as well as the increased participation of the private sector in the country's economic development. The government's apparent acceptance of the need for the private sector to play a greater role in the economy, has led to some predictions that Indonesia's capital market might well be the region's next bull market.

Total expenditure for Repelita V was forecast at rph 239 billion, of which the government would contribute rph 107.5 billion, significantly less than the rph 131.5 billion to be invested by the foreign and domestic private sector. The plan projected an annual domestic growth rate of 5 per cent, compared with a rate of 4 per cent in 1988 and 3.6 per cent in 1987. Non-oil exports and domestic revenues were projected to grow by 15 and 16 per cent respectively, during the life of the plan. The plan also aimed to reduce the country's debt-service ratio from a 1988 level of over 35 per cent to around 25 per cent by 1993. Two key areas were selected for large-scale investment, namely infrastructure development and employment creation. Figures released in early 1989 showed that almost half the country's present workforce of 75,000,000 was employed for less than 35 hours a week, or had no job at all.

DS

INDONESIAN DEMOCRATIC PARTY. The Indonesian Democratic Party (*Partai Demokrasi Indonesia* – PDI) was formed in 1973 as a merger of three nationalist and two Christian parties, namely the Indonesian Nationalist Party (*Partai Nasional Indonesia* – PNI – established by **Sukarno** in 1927), the People's Party (*Partai Murba* – PM), the Movement for the Defence of Indonesian Independence (IPKI), the Catholic

Party (*Partai Katolik* – PK) and the Protestant Christian Party (*Partai Keristen Indonesia* – Parkindo). These formations had all been active under the late President Sukarno prior to the latter's displacement by Gen. **Suharto** in the mid-1960s. The PDI seeks a full restoration of civilian rule and contains elements loyal to Sukarno. The party is led by Dr Suryadi (chair) and Nico Daryanto (Secretary-General).

Having obtained 8.6 per cent of the vote and 29 elective seats (out of 360) in the 1977 House of Representatives elections, the PDI slipped to 8 per cent and 24 seats (out of 364) in 1982. In the April 1987 elections it increased its share of the valid vote to 10.9 per cent and its share of the elective seats to 40 (out of 400), improving its performance in 20 provinces. The PDI candidates in April 1987 included Negawati Sukarnoputri, a daughter of Sukarno, and pro-Sukarno sympathies were strongly evident in the PDI's campaign.

DS

"INITIAL STAGE OF SOCIALISM" (CHINA).

This term was officially launched in 1987 by the **Chinese Communist Party** General Secretary, **Zhao Ziyang**, to characterize the current historical period in China. He said that China, because of its backwardness, would need at least one hundred years before socialist modernization was "in the main" completed. By then China would have caught up with medium-developed countries in terms of per capital GNP, and its people would enjoy a relatively affluent life.

CIPF

INTERNATIONAL WHALING CONVENTION.

This was signed in 1946 following widespread concern at the depletion of the whale population. Hunted for whale oil, whalebone and other products the whale populations were being brought to the point of extinction. The International Whaling Convention sought to prevent this by establishing the International Whaling Commission (IWC) which would conduct studies of whale populations and recommend the limits on whale harvests necessary to preserve both the whale population and the whaling industry.

Unfortunately as the Commission lacked any enforcement authority it soon became easy for any signatory country to dispute the recommendation of the Commission and to insist on higher whaling quotas. The convention was also dependent on the honesty of signatory nations in reporting the number of each species of whale taken. While there is no evidence of the nations concerned disobeying the recommendations finally agreed upon or failing to provide the commission with absolutely correct figures it is certain that the number of whales continued to fall sharply.

Constant pressure from the conservation groups finally resulted in positive results. After 1967 the most endangered whales – the blue, grey and humpback were finally given complete protection. The blue whale, the world's largest mammal, estimated to have numbered about 200,000 when whaling began had been cut perilously low to about 2,000 by the mid-1960s. By 1989 it was believed to have climbed back to about 10,000. The grey whale, on the point of extinction in the mid-1960s, may be numbering as many as 15,000 in 1989. The humpback, reduced to an estimated 1,000 in 1962, is thought to be back to about 5,000 in 1989.

Beginning in the 1970s quotas for other species of whales were cut to points intended to ensure their survival. Meeting in 1983, the commission overruling the objections of Japan, Norway and the Soviet Union ordered the end of commercial whaling by 1986. Nonetheless some whaling continued after this date. By 1989 no commercial whaling officially existed but whaling for scientific purposes continued. Many conservationists thought the programme of scientific research into whale numbers and behaviour a cover for commercial purposes as the meat was still sold to Japan as a delicacy. Japan, Norway and Iceland were the remaining whaling nations with a strong prospect that Japan could be isolated as the only remaining whaling nation. Conservationists hoped that the final demise of whaling in Iceland and Norway would put irresistible pressure on Japan.

In the Pacific Japan continues a sizeable programme of scientific whaling taking about 825 minke whales and 50–200 sperm whales in a season. Soviet whaling in the Pacific, once a large programme, came to an end in May 1987 and the country's whaling vessels converted to other uses. The IWC tolerates the small amount of whaling carried out in the Pacific by aboriginal peoples as part of their traditional way of life. In 1988, for example, Inuit communities in Alaska were allowed to kill up to 35 bowhead whales.

The record of the International Whaling Convention is then a varied picture. It did not accomplish its original goals in the manner intended but without it the record of whale conservation would have been much worse: indeed it is doubtful whether some of the main species would have survived.

RS

IRON. In the Pacific region the major iron ore producers are the USA, Australia, Canada and China. However South Korea's iron ore reserves are estimated at 40 million tonnes and Peru's at 360 million. In Colombia small quantities of iron ore are mined near Bogotá and Medellín. The annual production of iron ore, in millions of tonnes, is as follows: Australia, 57.6; China, 37; USA, 32.8; Canada, 32.1; Mexico, 5.3; North Korea, 4.8; Chile, 3.4; Philippines, 2.6; Peru, 2.5; South Korea, 0.7; Japan, 0.3; Colombia, 0.2; Malaysia, 0.1.

RS

ISLAM. The religion of Islam, "surrender" to God and his laws, proclaimed by the Prophet Muhammad (570–632 CE) in Arabia, has been one of the world's most active missionary and international forces. With its scripture the Quran (Koran) as a revelation in the Arabic language, and still recited in Arabic ritually throughout the Islamic world, the faith has nevertheless spread among and united many diverse peoples.

The strong emphasis in Islam upon the community (*umma*) was first to unite all Arab peoples, and then it developed into a movement for the unity of all Muslims or believers. There should be no colour or racial bar in Islam, though the status of women is debated. Strictly there is no priesthood in Islam, but teachers and doctors of the law may be chosen by local communities to conduct worship and regulate conduct. As a layman's religion Islam has flourished especially in towns and among traders. It is most confident when it is a state religion, but its popular basis provides Islam with resilience in face of attacks from westernism or communism. Great cultures have flourished under Islam, and it has absorbed older civilizations and produced its own.

The chief Islamic area in the Pacific is Indonesia, claiming 78 per cent of the population, about 130 million, but the Department of Religion considers as "statistical Muslims" all those who do not follow another faith. Percentages of votes given to various Islamic political parties show smaller figures of "Quranic" or active orthodox Muslims. Islam was introduced to Sumatra from India in the thirteenth century and is strongest in western Indonesia, while in the east it is confined largely to coastal regions. Indonesian Muslims follow the Sunni "tradition" of the majority of Islam. They are in two principal groups, one of which favours reform, purging the practice of pre-Islamic customs and bringing Islam into line with Arab Islam, but also seeking to assimilate Western ideas. The other group is more conservative, opposing secular education and favouring retention of a customary mixture of Islam with native Indonesian customs.

In Malaysia Islam is the state religion, followed by practically all the Malays who form 50 per cent of the population of West Malaysia, while in East Malaysia about one third are Muslims. Brought by Arab traders it was Sunni in form, though there are now some elements of the Shia sect ("followers" of Ali) which gives sympathy with the major Shia country, Iran. Other educated Malays follow the orthodox Sunni of Cairo or seek Western education. In Singapore Islam dominates among Malays, Indians and Pakistanis, some 17 per cent of the population, making Islam the second largest religion after Chinese religions. In Brunei also Islam is the state religion, with the sultan at its head and 65 per cent of the population, mostly Malays, professing Sunni Islam.

After Indonesia the largest community of Muslims in eastern Asia is in China. The religion arrived by southern trade routes and ports during the T'ang dynasty, and eventually became strongest in the west and north. Estimates of the numbers of Chinese Muslims vary from 10 million in some official figures to 48 million from Muslim sources, though there are no mosque registers, and the true number may be between the two. Islam dominates among some ethnic minorities, who are mostly Sunni, but Tadzhiks are Shia. The fortunes of Islam have varied under communist rule, in China as in the USSR, but the lay basis of the religion has enabled it to weather difficulties better than other religions. Mosques were closed and leaders (*imams*) imprisoned, but a Chinese Islamic Association was founded in 1953 and revived in 1969.

Under the Cultural Revolution many mosques and Islamic schools were destroyed, and there was a Revolutionary Group for the Abolition of Islam. But desire for better relations with Islamic countries led to limited toleration. Mosques were reopened, first in Beijing for foreigners and then for general Islamic use in other cities. Islamic festivals have been allowed, and the Quran has been reprinted in Arabic and circulated.

There are Islamic minorities in other Pacific areas, two million each in the Philippines and the USA, and small numbers of traders and immigrants in Japan, Korea and Australasia. The Black Muslims of the USA, officially called the World Community of Al-Islam in the West, began in 1913. They claim a community of over half a million, mostly former Christian blacks, with over 235 mosques. Quranic verses are recited and broadcast, and there are moves for closer alignment with orthodox Sunni Islam.

GP

ISLAMIC PARTY OF MALAYSIA. The Islamic Party of Malaysia (*Parti Islam Se Malaysia* – PAS) is a fundamentalist organization which advocates the establishment of an Islamic state. In 1977 PAS was expelled from the National Front coalition, of which it had been a founder member in 1974, after its increasing radicalization had brought it into conflict with the dominant **United Malays National Organization**. In 1983 the PAS adopted an outright "fundamentalist and revolutionary" stance, in opposition to which its then president, Datuk Haji Mohammed Asri bin Haji Muda, left the party with four of the five PAS MPs to form the more moderate Muslim Front. In the 1986 federal elections PAS retained only one seat, although its share of the overall vote was over 15 per cent. In the simultaneous state elections it won 10 of the 39 Kelantan seats and also secured representation in Kedah and Trengganu.

DS

J

JAPAN. *Population*: 121,047,196. *Area*: 377,800 sq km. *Gross Domestic Product*: US$1,983,000 million (1986). *Trade*: (1986): US$335,561 million (imports US$126,408 million; exports US$209,153 million). *Top five trading partners*: USA, South Korea, West Germany, Taiwan, China. *Defence spending*: 3,508 billion yen (1987). *Education spending*: 5,064 billion yen (1987). *Percentage of population that is urban*: 85. *Birth rate*: 11.2 per thousand. *Life expectancy*: males 75.23; females 80.93.

Geographical background. The most striking features of the geography of Japan are that it is small and insular. Japan is an archipelago which lies to the east of the Asian mainland. Its total area is 377,800 sq km. This is a fraction of the size of its neighbour China (9,561,000 sq km) and much smaller than either its principal rival the USA (9,363,130 sq km) or the Soviet Union (22,272,200 sq km). It is not small, however, when compared with the European nations, West Germany, (248,534 sq km), France (543,998 sq km) or the United Kingdom (244,004 sq km). To exacerbate matters, only a small percentage (15 or 16%) of the land is level, generally useful or arable. Japan had the seventh largest population in the world in 1980 and so there is enormous pressure upon the land which is extremely scarce. Defeat in war substantially reduced the national territory (by 46% of its pre-war size). Japan lost Formosa, Korea, the Kwantung Leased Territory, the South Seas Mandated Islands, the Pescadores Islands and Manchukuo (which was technically independent even in the days of empire). Japan continues to press the Soviet Union for the return of the southern **Kuril Islands**, which were taken in war. There is scant prospect of their return.

Japan is a country of islands and mountains. The bulk of the territory is made up of four large, closely grouped islands, Hokkaido, Honshu, Shikoku and Kyushu. These account for 98% of the territory of Japan. There are more than 3,300 other islands within the national territory. The coastline is long and intricate. Features of the Pacific coast are three bay head alluvial plains (Kanto, Nobi and Kansai) which are home to more than one third of the population and one half of industrial production. That production depends upon imports from abroad of raw materials and above all of oil (43% of total import costs in 1985) since Japan is resource-poor to the point of impoverishment. The exceptions are **coal**

(poor to medium quality in seams thin and faulted), timber (67% of the total area of Japan is forested, but not all of the forest is commercially viable) and **iron** ore (production is less than 400,000 tonnes).

The population of Japan at the census of Oct. 1, 1985 was 121,047,196, which represents an average density of more than 320 per sq km. "Real" density is both more and less since the population is concentrated in that 15% of the land area which is level, cultivable and useful. In such areas population density ranks with the highest in the world. Conversely, mountainous, wooded areas are sparsely populated. Tokyo, Osaka and Nagoya are the hubs of great wheels of population and industry. One third of the Japanese live there. There are 11 cities with one million or more inhabitants and 66 with a quarter of a million or rather more. The greatest of these is Tokyo, one of the world's great cities, capital of Japan and home to 8,353,674 people.

Socio-political background. A factor of some importance in understanding Japan is the remarkably high degree of ethnic homogeneity which characterizes the population. It has been said and it remains true that no other major nation has so small an admixture of identifiable minority elements. The origins of the Japanese are not perfectly understood, although both Mongol and southern Pacific strains are evident in the population of today. As for the minority peoples who make up rather less than one per cent of the total population, these include the Ainu, a native people who exhibit some Caucasian features and who are numerically insignificant. More important is a Korean population, the largest minority group (in excess of 80% of the minority total), the absolute size of which is substantially underestimated since many ethnic Koreans have assumed Japanese citizenship. The Koreans' lot is often not a happy one. They are regarded as racially inferior, sometimes subject to abuse and worse and condemned to economic marginality.

It is usual to think of the "urban-dwelling", "rural-dwelling" distinction as a critical fact in explaining the behaviour of a people. In pre-industrial society the majority of the population is rural-dwelling and almost all of life (at work, at play and at prayer) is spent in one group, within which all participants are known one to the other. The group (which is often the village community, and within that the extended household or "*ie*") commands the loyalty of all and is the principal focus for individual identification. Industrialization draws in its wake the eclipse of the village and creates an urban world in which the primacy of face-to-face contact is lost. The single group is resolved into its individual parts which come together in a variety of different groups for different purposes. The urban world is one in which functions, indentities and loyalties are multiple and diverse.

In Japan too, industrialization has been associated with a massive rural-to-urban shift. In 1920 more than 80% of all Japanese lived in rural areas and just under 20% lived in the towns and cities. Today the proportions are more than reversed. In Japan, however, that demographic shift has not been associated with the kind of change referred to above. Instead, the conditions and values of village Japan have been carried over into urban Japan where they are projected and reproduced by different groups. The modern firm is perhaps, the archetypical "village", the new *ie*.

At the heart of the values carried over and sustained by new institutional vehicles are collectivity and hierarchy. To speak of collectivity is to argue that the role, importance and rights of the individual are much less than that of the group in social historical economic and philosophical terms. If there is a conflict between the interest of the group and the individual the group will take precedence. For that matter the individual will understand himself, shape his nature and ambitions and delineate his identity in accordance with and in view of the group. The combination of this basic socio-cultural propensity and of geographical isolation, a common language, a long history and racial homogeneity promotes a robust sense of identity, of "us" and "them" in the face of the outside world.

As fundamental and salient as collectivity is hierarchy. If the group is to persist, it must be organized. The range of organizational modes available is considerable; it runs from democracy to dictatorship. In Japan, the organizational preference is for hierarchy; this means that there is a widespread sense that groups should contain superiors and subordinates and that the former should exercise authority and control over the latter. And indeed there is, in Japan, a very easy and willing acceptance of hierarchical difference. People know, accept and are largely untroubled by their position in any particular hierarchy. There are limits to this. For example the constitution of 1947 enjoins upon Japan a higher degree of democracy than the indigenous organizational preference might anticipate. That constitution has worked well and is unchanged since that time. So also in personal relations, a new civil code

introduced in the aftermath of war and defeat substantially modified in principle the hierarchic basis of marriage in Japan. A pervasive sense of hierarchy colours Japan's understanding of and participation in international relations and diplomacy.

Japan is one of the most literate nations in the world. Since 1947 nine years of combined elementary and junior secondary education have been compulsory. Universal literacy (which is of the order of 97-98%) is an achievement of long standing. Enrolment levels are exemplary, some 99.9% of six- to fifteen-year-olds attending school. The proportion of students who proceed to some non-compulsory education is high, more than 82%. Performance with respect to higher education is no different and nearly one in two young Japanese aged 18 to 21 attends college or university. There is criticism of the mode and manner of the education system (it is said to stifle individual creativity). However, its standards and comprehensiveness are of some significance in explaining not only the level of skills of the workforce, but also the social cohesiveness of the society itself.

Pre-modern history. An elaborate and popular mythology has it that Japan is the creation of the gods, and that the first emperor, Jimmu (c. 660 BCE) was a direct descendant of the sun goddess. More prosaically, it is thought likely that Japan was first peopled by migrants from the Asian mainland and perhaps from Southeast Asia too. There is little doubt that the Ainu, reduced now to tiny and fragile communities in Hokkaido, once occupied the whole country.

Yamato Period. The route taken by the original immigrants passed through the Korean corridor and so to Kyushu and eastward to the Inland Sea. Beyond that was the Kansai plain and conditions which promoted the growth of a new civilization. Yamato society was dominated by priest kings and the cult of the Sun. It was enriched and transformed by cultural imports, notably the Chinese system of writing, **Buddhism** and **Confucianism**, which it in turn modified, made "Japanese" and absorbed.

Japanese civilization drew sustenance from the Kansai plain, and for much more than a millenium the capital was located there, first in Nara and later in Kyoto. It is appropriate that the imperial family, which has been rather more than titular head and symbol of Japan for more than a thousand years, should have had its home there right until 1868. Kyoto and Nara were built on the model of the Chinese capital – testimony to the persistence of influences from the mainland which coloured the theory and practice of religion, morality, aesthetics, government and economy. The date of the establishment of Kyoto is used to mark the opening of the Heian age (794–1185), a period remarkable to the present for its literary and artistic achievement.

Theories of imperial rule allowed and maybe even encouraged untrammeled competition for effective power among warrior households. First among their number were the Taira (dominant in Kyoto by the middle of the twelfth century) and their great rivals the Minamoto. Successful exercise of force in arms secured for these warriors a position of practical pre-eminence in government probably sanctioned by imperial authority which remained above and outside the struggle for power. For his efforts, the Emperor awarded Yoritomo the title of *sei-i tai shogun* (the "Shogun"), or "barbarian-subduing generalissimo".

Kamakura Period. The seat of Yoritomo's power was Kamakura, a town in the east of Japan and the hub of a system of government known as the *bakufu* which was to command the country until the mid-fourteenth century. The *bakufu* was predicated upon and sought to control and administer a warrior class which now came to prominence. This new elite force in Japanese society was to rule without serious interruption until modern times. It is noteworthy that successive occupants of the effective arm of government sought neither to replace nor to remove the emperor, whose right to rule was ritually and ceremonially celebrated at frequent intervals and remained unchallenged through the ages. The Kamakura *bakufu* survived the death of Yoritomo in 1199 and a century later the Mongol invasions of 1274 and 1281. Formal responsibility for repulsing the enemy lay with the Hojo family who had taken over from the Minamoto; informally credit rested with the gods who sent a wind (a divine wind or *kami kaze*) which scattered and rendered impotent the enemy fleets. The end of the regime came in civil war and the last act of the Hojo family was *seppuku* (the informal term is *hara kiri*) or ritual self-disembowelling.

Muromachi Period. The fall of Kamakura in the middle of the fourteenth century opened a troubled period of some 250 years of the Ashikaga civil wars. The office of shogun held by the Ashikaga (of the Minamoto line) was much diminished as new men and new houses rode to power and conquest. The miracle was that this desperately troubled time should witness an extraordinary outburst of cultural and artistic activity which affected landscape gardening, ceramics, the tea cermony, flower arrangement, drama, painting and architecture.

Early modern history. Tokugawa Period. The period of civil wars was to be ended by superior force. Oda Nobunaga (1534–and his work was completed by Toyotomi Hideyoshi (1536–rivals, secured domestic peace and forged the unity of Japan through force of arms. Hideyoshi's ambition was great; it reached but could not hold Korea. It was left to Hideyoshi's ally, Tokugawa Ieyasu, to consolidate the achievement of domestic unity. He removed the immediate threat of a return to civil war by defeating his rivals in the battle of Sekigahara and was appointed shogun in 1603. He established the Tokugawa *bakufu* in Edo (the modern Tokyo) and perfected a system of rule which kept his rivals weak and dependent upon the house of Tokugawa – a system of alternative residence which kept rival lords, and in their absence their wives and children, in Edo for part of every year. In order to insulate the system from threatening changes from outside, the country was closed, (the policy of *sakoku*); Japanese were not allowed to travel abroad and only Chinese and Dutch traders were allowed in and then only as far as the port of Nagasaki.

These arrangements secured the peace of the land and imposed upon Japan a more or less benign stasis which persisted for more than two centuries. It ended not through any domestic dislocation, but at the insistence of the USA. Cdr. Matthew Perry's squadron of US warships arrived in Edo (Tokyo bay) in 1853 and 1854. The opening of two ports was effected and the bakufu agreed to the presence on their soil of a resident US consul. Other Western powers soon followed. The arrival of the "barbarians" was welcomed by no-one, although opinion was split between those who would expel them out of hand and others who argued that Japan was weak, that expulsion was not a realistic option and that only by coming to terms with the West and acquiring its modern ways and techniques could Japan overcome its present weakness and prosper.

Modern political history. The coming of the West exposed the weaknesses of the Tokugawa shogunate which was able neither to repel the foreigner nor to decide a course to be taken by the nation. Matters were taken out of its hands and in 1868 the *bakufu* was overthrown by a coalition of lords from the provinces of the south-west. The "rebels" acted in the name of the emperor and aimed to restore him to a position of real authority said to have been usurped by the shogunate. The decision of the young emperor Meiji to move his court from Kyoto to Edo (which was now renamed Tokyo) helped substantiate this fiction and to legitimate the new regime. In fact the position of the emperor continued to be one of authority and symbol rather than power – this was the preserve of the provincial lords who constituted themselves as an oligarchy charged with the task of modernization and of making theirs a rich country of great military might.

These exceptional and single-minded men took Japan on a forced march which led away from feudalism to a world they discovered in the West, a world of industry, technology, banking and commerce and modern communications. To inculcate the values, knowledge and skills which underpin and inform the operation of these modern institutions primary education was made compulsory and the process was continued in schools, colleges and universities. The transformation of Japan was undertaken by the state and in the name of the nation. No opportunity was missed to remind pupils, students, soldiers and citizens of this. Theirs was a national mission which demanded their wholehearted efforts and unswerving loyalty. So successful were their efforts that by 1905 Japan was able to defeat in war Russia, one of the Great Powers that Japan had sought to emulate since 1868.

Forty years later, on Aug. 6 and Aug. 9 when atomic bombs devastated Hiroshima and then Nagasaki, the success and even the good sense of the forced march to modernity were in question. The endeavour had been aggressive and expansionist from the first; historical instincts underscored by more modern concerns with raw materials and markets had seen the new Japan at war with China in 1894, Russia in 1904–05, Germany in 1914–18 and China in 1931. In a later stage there was a seeming inevitability in Japan's drift to war with the Western powers which erupted in Pearl Harbour in 1941. The war was an unmitigated disaster. Not only hindsight but the balance of resources (economic and military) available to the two sides at the onset of war argue that it was never winnable. And so it proved.

If the war was a disaster the Occupation was a considerable success. Initially punitive in intent, (the aim was demilitarization – a project which envisaged the destruction of Japan's war potential and so of much of its economy), punishment yielded in a second and more constructive stage to a concern with democratization and the promotion of Japan as a stable and prosperous ally of the capitalist and liberal democratic West. A new constitution rejected war and the capacity to wage war, insisted that civilians and not military personnel should form the cabinet, declared the sovereignty of the people, and reduced the emperor to a symbolic statement of that sovereignty.

Formal constitutional arrangements are those of a liberal democracy much as any other which might be found in the West. The principal features are familiar; a binding constitution, universal suffrage, an elected house of two chambers, an elected chief executive, an executive constitutionally subordinate to the elected house, an independent judiciary and a supreme court with extensive rights of review of executive and legislative action.

The democratic movement was buttressed by reform which addressed the socio-economic foundations of democracy. Land reform, the dissolution of the economic conglomerates called *zaibatsu*, education reform, labour law reform, and the reworking of the civil code were features of this process. Certainly there were revisionists and fear of constitutional revision, particularly from 1956 when a Cabinet Commission to investigate the Constitution was established, until 1964 when the commission reported (the mood has now passed and the constitution appears secure). Similarly, there were great swathes of the population which distrusted the post-war Conservative political leadership and opposed the alliance with the USA.

About one third of the voters in the 1950s and nearer one half since 1967 support the parties of the opposition. These include the **Japan Socialist Party**, the **Komeito** or Clean Government Party, the **Democratic Socialist Party** (DSP) and the **Japan Communist Party** (JCP). The influence upon politics of the opposition parties is weak because they are fragmented and ideologically opposed.

Prior to 1955 the conservatives were also divided. The merger of the Democrat and Liberal Parties in November 1955 ended these divisions and created an electoral juggernaut which has won every general election since that time. The advantages enjoyed by the **Liberal Democratic party** (LDP) are considerable; as the incumbent governing party it derives the political benefits of the "economic miracle", while the opposition parties remain confined as permanent outsiders to a negative and critical role, which accords ill with the values of a society which has long favoured harmony and consensus. Electoral arrangements are another factor. Major demographic change which has seen a once predominantly rural-dwelling society become predominantly urban-dwelling (in 1945 the population was about 75 million of which 25 million were urban and 50 million were rural; in 1985, the population was about 120 million of whom 82 million were urban and 32 million were rural) was not matched by any fundamental redrawing of electoral boundaries. The result is that the rural areas where support for the LDP is strong are substantially over-represented at the expense of the towns. The unequal distribution of seats has been said to deny equal rights to urban voters (as guaranteed by the Japanese constitution); in consequence in April 1976 the supreme court ruled that the allocation of seats was unconstitutional. In December 1980 a high court in Tokyo ruled that the elections of the previous June had been unconstitutional. Such decisions have prompted a limited redrawing of boundaries and redistribution of seats.

Finance is no less a factor in the electoral success of the LDP. Elections are a spectacularly expensive business in Japan and without massive financial backing victory at the polls is likely to prove elusive. The LDP, which has held the highest offices for more than 30 years, has developed close ties with the business community which still regards it as a matter of good sense to fund the party.

The most recent general election (in fact a double election which involved both the house of representatives and the house of councillors) took place in July 1986 and produced decisive victories for the LDP. In the election for the house of representatives, the LDP polled 49.4% of the votes and its best performance since 1963, and won a massive and record 304 of the 512 seats. Three years later a series of scandals which centred on the Recruit Company (*see* **Recruit Scandal**) took their toll of the "new leaders" of the LDP (Takeshita, Abe Shintaro and Miyazawa Keiichi) thought likely to lead the LDP and Japan into the 1990s and triggered a leadership crisis which occasioned the downfall of Prime Ministers Takeshita and Uno, eroded the electoral support of the LDP and produced a quite unexpected and unprecedented success for the Socialist Party in the house of councillors elections of July 1989. The LDP now has a new leader and Japan has a new Prime Minister in **Kaifu Toshiki**. A general election is to be held in 1990. The outcome may well prove critical not only for Kaifu but also for the LDP and Japan itself in the 1990s.

Foreign policy. Japanese understanding of foreign relations is fundamentally informed by its experience of World War II. This touched both the content of foreign policy – henceforth a primary objective was peace and a non-violent resolution of foreign policy issues – and Japan's orientation to other major players in international diplomacy. America became both the lodestone and the dominant concern of Japanese foreign policy. Links of personal friendship established between Washington and politicians in Tokyo were underpinned by financial assistance for Japan's economic recovery and the provision of armed forces for the defence of Japan, and the whole was bonded by a strong sense of a shared commitment to a single ideology.

Outside official circles there was considerable resentment of what was perceived to be a dangerous and excessive dependence upon the USA. The dependence was real enough: the US–Japan defence pact signed in San Francisco on Sept. 8, 1951, agreed continued American administration of the strategic Bonin and Ryukyu islands and allowed the USA the right to suppress internal disorder in Japan. The danger (articulated loudest by the Japan Socialist Party for whom anti-Americanism was an article of faith) was said to be that the USA would encourage rearmament (something which did indeed happen by degrees from as early as 1950) and that Japan would be drawn into wars waged by the USA in pursuit of its global ambitions (this did not happen). The development of a paramilitary force which led in 1954 to the creation of the Ground, Maritime, and Air Self-Defence Forces with a strength of 214,000 men tested the limits of Article 9 of the constitution to the full; this renounced war "as a sovereign right of the nation" and declared that "land, sea and air forces ... will never be maintained". Resentment peaked and boiled over in popular reaction to, but was unable to prevent the negotiation of a treaty of mutual co-operation and security between the USA and Japan which was signed in Washington on Jan. 19, 1960. The conclusion of this treaty cemented the USA–Japan relationship which was placed now on a more equal footing. With the passage of time those fears expressed by the Japan Socialist Party have come to sound hollow and have been dropped.

Throughout this period the Soviet Union did much to guarantee the integrity of the Japan–USA relationship. Stalin's declaration of war upon Japan in August 1945 was seen as opportunistic; the act of a scavenger eager to profit from another's kill. Even after the surrender Soviet forces occupied South **Sakhalin** and the Kuril islands, a matter of dispute and symbol of a predatory Soviet Union to the present day.

The USA–Japan relationship has been called the world's most important bilateral relation. There is something in the claim and not least because their combined GNP is 40% of the world total. The relationship is important, longstanding but prickly. The USA is reluctant to accept the waning of its powers or concede the waxing of its partner's – particularly economic, and Japan is seemingly happy to accept the unchanged form of the relation but unwilling to accept any brake on a burgeoning growth which willy nilly transforms the formal relation. Of particular controversy has been the scale of the US trade deficit with Japan and specific issues of contention have included US participation in Japan's financial markets, access to the construction work on a major airport complex near Osaka, access and participation in the telecommunications industry in Japan, semi-conductors, beef and citrus, super computers, automobiles and so on. It remains the case that Japan tends to dig in its heels on economic matters but concedes the leading role of the USA in the definition of political goals in foreign policy.

In 1951 the Soviet Union refused to sign the San Francisco peace treaty, ostensibly because of objections to the scope it afforded Japan to rearm. In the event, it was not until 1956 that bilateral negotiations took place. Negotiations foundered on the rocks of fishing policy (Moscow has habitually refused Japan access to her traditional fishing grounds), and the occupied territories. In 1988, the Soviet Union made repeated efforts to improve its relations with Japan. These efforts were rebuffed by Japan which argued that no peace treaty could be signed (which remains the case so that technically the two countries remain at war). The grounds for the rebuttal had not changed in some 40 years; "there could be no treaty until the islands issue had been resolved". There is little prospect of any resolution of this problem given the strategic sensitivity (to the USSR) of the occupied areas and the equally earnest desire of Japan for their return. The Sino-Soviet split has made it easier for Japan to tolerate this unresolved relation.

Japan's relations with China have been complex to the point of impenetrability. Japanese feelings are ambiguous, their perceptions an uneasy mix of cultural inferiority and of racial superiority. These feelings and perceptions are further complicated by the fact of Japan's overwhelming economic superiority and China's need for financial and technological aid from a neighbour remembered as a cruel and brutal invader. For 20 years the problem was sidestepped. Japan took the American lead, signed a peace treaty with Chang Kai-shek's Nationalist regime on Formosa and refused the recognize Communist China. In the early 1970s, following the example of the USA, Japan began to explore a more flexible and nuanced policy towards the two Chinas. In the course of that exploration much was made of the seeming economic complementarity of China and Japan. Hopes have so far been disappointed. Certainly relations have improved (even here there are border disputes, this time over the **Senkaku Islands**) but it would seem that there has been some quite considerable underestimate of the yawning divide which continues to separate these two Asian economies.

Outline of economic development. In the 1850s Japan was a quasi-feudal country with an agricultural economy. In the 1980s Japan is one of the most advanced of the advanced industrial nations with a Gross National Product second only to that of the USA in the Western world. In accounting for this remarkable development it is useful to distinguish six key stages in the history of the Japanese economy as follows:

(i) The "seeds of growth" in the late Edo period to the Meiji Restoration. The modern Japanese economy did not emerge "out of the blue", but benefited from a significant economic inheritance from the Edo period (1603-1867). In particular, a developing commercialism and urbanization had the effect of transforming the feudal system of tenure and of promoting a diversification of relationships in the rural areas. Subsistence agriculture yielded to production for the market as the agricultural population was drawn into a money economy.

Perhaps the single greatest contribution of the Meiji Restoration (1868) was the unleashing of the energies of a literate population and the harnessing of those energies to a single national pursuit of strength through economic growth. The Meiji government created the framework for a modern economic system: a national monetary system with the Bank of Japan as the sole issuer of banknotes; a fiscal system based on the land tax, the expansion of infrastructure, including roads, railroads and shipping; a nationwide post and telegraph system; the adoption of the joint stock company form as the basic model for corporate organization; the import of machinery and foreign engineers and the establishment of government operated factories.

(ii) The early development of the modern economy to World War I (1868-1914). By the time of World War I, the institutional and infrastructural framework was largely in place and within this there had emerged a significant cotton spinning and an electric power industry. Development was state-led but private capital formation was on the rise. Even so agriculture remained the economic mainstay both as a supplier of food for a growing population and through the land tax as a revenue source for further industrial development. The balance in favour of industry shifted in the war years which stimulated a five-fold increase in industrial production and booming exports.

(iii) The inter-war period (1914-1939). Such was the war boom that by 1920 Japan was a creditor nation. However, that very same year the war boom ended and by the end of the decade the world knew global depression. The Great Depression took its toll in Japan as elsewhere, although here the effects were rather less and Japan was to emerge from depression rather sooner than other industrial nations. Food imports from Japan's colonies in Formosa and Korea reduced the significance of agriculture (which by 1936 accounted for less than 20% of national income). At the same time exports of light industrial goods (cotton and silk fabric) increased and the spread of heavy and chemical industries developed. Heavy industrialization was associated with a concentration of economic activity in the hands of family-controlled groups of monopolistic companies operating in key sectors. The most famous of these "*zaibatsu*" groups were Mitsui and Mitsubishi, conglomerates which have their counterparts in the post-war world.

(iv) World War II and post-war reform and reconstruction (1939-1951). The *zaibatsu* were viewed, in the West at least, as architects of the Pacific War and were prime targets of the Occupation authorities' policies of "demilitarization" and "democratization" in the aftermath of a war which left the Japanese economy in ruins, and its people facing starvation. The attitude of the United States shifted from retribution to reconstruction; a shift, hugely fortuitous for Japan, which was motivated by something rather more than the *realpolitik* calculation of a power newly engaged in a Cold War. The reconstruction of Japan as a stable and economically powerful ally of the liberal democratic countries of the West was furthered by the outbreak of the Korean War. The resultant boom led to substantial plant and equipment investment, and foreign reserves (critical if resource-poor Japan was to import the requisite raw materials) were boosted by the expenditure of the US military in Japan.

(v) The age of rapid growth (1951/52-1973). For nearly 20 years from 1952 when Japan regained her independence the Japanese economy experienced growth rates which bordered on the fabulous, no less than an average of 10%. International conditions were an important factor beginning with the millions of dollars poured by the USA into special procurements for the Korean War and the establishment of fixed exchange rates via the IMF in place of the gold standard which created a stable environment conducive to freer international trade. Domestically, government fiscal and monetary policy was geared to growth adumbrated in a series of five-year plans. The purge of a generation of business leaders cleared the way for younger men committed to aggressive growth strategies and eager to support these by the import of foreign technologies which increased productivity and cut costs. They were supported in this by the government's industrial policies which nurtured young industries and pro-

tected them from foreign competition, providing assistance for industries in recession through cartels, tax exemptions and such like. Confident of government support, business could look beyond equity capital and so to loans and the issue of debentures to fund great programmes of plant and equipment investment. Investment grew tenfold from 1952-1970. A hard-earned stability of labour management relations also played a part in the economic equation whose sum was high growth.

(vi) The end of rapid growth (1970s). The drive for GNP was heavily dependent upon oil which accounted for 75% of total energy consumption. Inevitably, the oil crisis of 1973 increased the import bill dramatically, sent shock waves throughout the economy and brought the period of high growth to a close. Great efforts were made to save energy and to increase energy efficiency. New technologies were introduced in order to reduce energy costs further. So successful were these efforts that Japan moved out of recession more quickly than any of her Western rivals. However a second oil shock, that consequent upon the Iranian Revolution in 1978, signalled that there would be no return to the cheap fuel of the 'fifties and 'sixties. Henceforth growth was to be pursued at more modest levels.

Current economic situation. There is little doubt that Japan is currently enjoying the strongest economic boom since the oil crisis of 1973. In 1988, real GNP grew by 5.7%, the best figure recorded since 1973. Fixed capital investment increased by more than 17%, industrial production rose by 8% and private final consumption increased by over 5%. The trade and current account surpluses stood at US$80,000 million and US$95,000 million respectively. A feature of recent economic activity is the rapid acceleration since 1986 of direct investment overseas (not least so as to take account of lower labour costs, as a hedge against exchange rate risks, and to expand capacity within the overseas market and so insure against protectionism). The thrust of the national economic strategy can be characterized in terms of domestic demand led growth. Here injections of public works spending and the lowering of interest rates have been important instruments of government policy.

Six major corporate groups exist in Japan and play a leading role in the economy. Their total sales accounted for 14.35% of Japan's corporate economy (excluding banks and insurance companies) in the financial year 1987. Their total assets were 12.96% and the number of their employees was 4.14% of the total. Mitsubishi is the largest of these groupings and has at its core

Mitsubishi Bank, Mitsubishi Corp., and Mitsubishi Heavy Industries Ltd. The bank, trading company, manufacturing company triad is typical of these corporate giants. The principal linkages are functional (banks to procure funds which were once in short supply, the trading company to secure the import of essential raw materials and a manufacturing company dependent on both of these and itself a vehicle for capital investment to expand its production). Functional ties are reinforced by stock cross holding and the exchange of directors.

Prospects for development. Can growth of this order be sustained? Will the current boom continue? The answer has two aspects, the one economic and the other political. With respect to the former of these, the short-term prospects for Japan look good indeed. It is true that in April 1989 the government introduced a tax on consumption (a move designed to redress the balance of direct and indirect revenue and so to anticipate the likely consequences for the economy of the rapid ageing of the population). But what dampening effect this may have on growth is likely to be offset by reductions in income and corporate tax which will stimulate domestic demand and encourage strong corporate investment. Any resultant inflationary pressure is containable as is an expected upturn in the cost of labour in consequence of shortages in that market, although even here rising labour productivity argues that unit labour costs are unlikely to rise – indeed they may well continue to fall, although not as much or as rapidly as they have in recent years.

The political dimension of continuing economic growth will pose problems which are less tractable. Here the problem is, and not for the first time, the consequence for others and principally the USA, of Japan's quite remarkable success in adjusting to and even profiting from life with a sharply more expensive yen. It is not so very long since Japanese manufacturers claimed despairingly that they could not survive with the yen at Y130 to the dollar. But now, and since summer 1988, dynamic growth of exports and profit-taking has proved compatible with even the "100-yen dollar". The explanation is often simple enough. In some sectors (memory chips, optical fibres and new materials) Japan has few significant competitors and has a dominant position in world markets. Cost-cutting and rationalization exercises are one factor and overseas investment is another; indeed it has been calculated that every US$1,000,000-worth of Japanese direct investment raises machinery exports (to equip the new factories) by US$436,000.

The bulk of the trade surplus is with the USA,

far and away Japan's most important trading partner and the principal market for Japanese exports. American resentment of Japan's economic success, whether justified or not, is a potent political force that Japan cannot afford to ignore. It is not lessened by a widespread recognition that the US federal budgetary deficit is heavily financed by Japanese funds. In the longer term Japanese deficits on invisibles (tourism and shipping services) and the correction, through the ageing of the population, of the savings/investment "imbalance" may well diminish trade surpluses. Whether or not American patience will endure beyond the short term is another matter.

RAB

JAPAN COMMUNIST PARTY. Its current political significance is real, but limited. Some 10 or 10.5% of the electorate will turn out and vote for it or merely against the administration of the day at every election. That one in ten seems to be a threshold the JCP is unlikely to cross. The parliamentary representation of the JCP depends less on any shift in the party's popularity; rather more upon the party's command of the electoral calculus, and so upon its ability and willingness to translate votes into seats. One factor in that equation is the value attached by the party to the democratic importance of being able to vote against the government wherever one may live, something which has led the party to run candidates in districts in which it has next to no chance of winning the seat. This guarantees the party a national presence and an enhanced possibility of reaching and politicizing groups which were hitherto inaccessible, and means simultaneously that the JCP vote is something more than the actual political clout of the party.

RAB

JAPAN LOBBY. Arguably the most powerful foreign lobby group in the United States. In 1985, 85 law and public relations firms employing over 100 former senior US officials worked as registered lobbyists for Japanese interests and spent over $120 million to shape American policy and opinion. Unofficially the Japan lobby is considered twice as large in terms of firms, influential American spokesmen, and spending power.

WN

JAPAN SOCIALIST PARTY. A feature of political life in Japan since 1955 has been the persistent and seemingly ineluctable decline of the JSP from a peak in 1958 of 13 million votes

(32.8%) and 166 seats (to the **Liberal Democratic Party**'s 287) to 10.4 million votes (17.2%) and only 85 seats (to the LDP's 300 and **Komeito**'s 56) in 1986. Decline has been associated with an increasing dependence upon the **Sohyo** federation of public workers' unions for finance, organization and candidates. The politically ambitious no longer join the JSP.

The party's appeal in the 1950s hinged upon defence of the constitution and opposition to the military alliance with the USA on the grounds that this was likely to draw Japan into wars of American making. With the passage of time, the absence of any threat to the constitution and a general public perception of the relationship with America as a good thing, the popularity of the JSP waned. This was not the only area in which the Socialists have failed to make essential adjustments: there is evidence that the electorate were not persuaded by an analysis of Japanese society couched in Marxist rhetoric – the reality of increasing standards of living and a general sense of a new prosperity proved to be rather more persuasive and so the decline continued.

There have been moments when it has seemed that the necessary adjustments might be made and might produce fruit in elections. These hopes have been disappointed. The light of Chairman Asukata (1977–1983) shone briefly and went out. He failed to do for the party what he had done as Mayor for Yokohama. Ishibashi Masashi took over as Chairman of a "New JSP" – a post-Marxist JSP – in 1983, and fared no better. He resigned in the wake of a calamitous election performance in 1986.

The new hope for the party is **Doi Takako**, an able enough politician, who seemed to get the chair almost by default. She and the JSP benefited from a spectacular and unanticipated gift from the LDP on the eve of the Upper House elections in July 1989. The **Recruit Scandal** has disgusted sections of the electorate and in that election at least they turned to the JSP in large numbers. Whether this was to vote for the JSP rather than against the LDP remains to be seen and will determine the capital that can be made out of an unprecedented victory.

RAB

JAPAN–SOVIET UNION CONFLICT. The outstanding issue between Japan and the Soviet Union concerns the ownership of several islands off the north-east coast of Japan. These islands were occupied by the Soviet Union towards the end of World War II and have been the focus of periodic negotiations ever since. Little has been

achieved, however, and the issue remains intractable.

The disputed islands are the Habomai group (Suisho, Shibotsu, Yuri Akiyiri and Taraku) together with Shikotan, Kunashiri and Etorofu. Kunashiri and Etorofu are the two most southerly islands in the chain which runs from the Kamchatka Peninsula to Hokkaido. Although there is no dispute over the 18 **Kuril Islands** stretching from Uruppu northwards, the islands south of this are occupied by the Soviet Union but are regarded by Japan as part of its national territory. The issue is partly one of sovereignty, and partly a reflection of traditional historical rivalry in the region, but also has important geo-political and resource aspects. The seas around the islands provide the Soviet Union with deep water access from the Sea of Okhotsk to the Pacific and the islands themselves contain natural harbours and areas suitable for military installations. In addition, the surrounding waters are rich in fish and traditionally have been exploited by Japan.

The rival claims to the islands are based on opposing historical interpretations as well as divergent views on the relevance and importance of treaties signed between Japan and Tsarist Russia in the nineteenth and early twentieth century. Japan claims in particular that the Shimoda Treaty of 1855 as well as a treaty 20 years later gave it sovereignty over the islands; the Soviet Union claims that the concessions were made under duress and were subsequently nullified by the Japanese aggression against Russia in 1904.

If the dispute has deep historical roots it emerged more directly from the Soviet occupation of the islands in August and the first few days of September 1945. The Soviet Union declared war on Japan on June 8, 1945, and justified its seizure of the islands by reference to the Potsdam Declaration. This was based partly on the Cairo Declaration of November 1943 which stated that Japan should be expelled from all the territory taken by violence or greed. A secret agreement at the Yalta Conference – in which the Soviet Union agreed to enter the war against Japan – also acknowledged that the rights of Russia violated by the 1904 Japanese attack would be restored. The Japanese counter to these arguments is that none of the wartime declarations mentioned the occupied islands by name and therefore was not intended to establish Soviet sovereignty over them.

The issue became bound up with the San Francisco Peace Treaty of September 1951. Although this was not signed by the Soviet Union, Japan impressed upon the United States that the northern islands were an integral part of Japan. In 1955 the Soviet Union and Japan began negotiations on a peace treaty but the islands issue dominated the negotiations and ultimately led to their breakdown in August 1956. In October 1956, however, a joint Japanese-Soviet declaration terminated the state of war and resumed diplomatic relations between the two states. In the Declaration the Soviet Union agreed to hand over to Japan the Habomais and Shikotan after the conclusion of a peace treaty. The fact that there was nothing in the declaration about continued negotiations over Etorofu and Kunashiri was politically controversial in Japan.

With the consolidation of US-Japanese links in the Treaty of mutual co-operation and security, the Soviet Union became more intractable, linking territorial concessions not only to a formal peace treaty but also to the withdrawal of all foreign troops from Japanese territory. This condition was rejected by Japan. Although there were few significant diplomatic developments through the 1960s economic relations between Japan and the Soviet Union expanded considerably. Furthermore, Andrei Gromyko visited Japan in both 1966 and 1972 with the latter visit leading to further talks about a possible peace treaty. Held in October 1972, these negotiations foundered on the territorial issue. The Japanese Prime Minister, **Tanaka**, visited Moscow in 1973 and in the Japanese view secured Brezhnev's agreement that there were unresolved territorial issues to be removed in a peace treaty.

Negotiations resumed in 1975, with the Soviet Union now placing the emphasis on the signing of a treaty of good neighbourliness and co-operation rather than a peace settlement. In 1976 Gromyko visited Tokyo and suggested that the Soviet Union would return the Habomais and Shikotan to Japan in return for such a treaty. The increased signs of flexibility on the part of the Soviet Union resulted from the improvement in Sino-Japanese relations, which Moscow felt was directed against it.

The latter half of the 1970s saw little progress on the issue and a general, if not dramatic, deterioration in Soviet-Japanese relations. In September 1976 a Soviet pilot landed a MIG-25 in Hokkaido and the plane was not returned until it had been examined by both Japanese and United States military experts. In December the island issue became entangled with fishery rights as the Soviet Union extended a 200-mile fishing zone and Japan responded by extending its territorial waters from three to 12 nautical miles. In 1979-80 Japan increasingly pointed to the militarization of the northern isles and in May 1980 estimated that there were 13,000 Soviet troops there – a 13-fold increase since 1976. In response to this build-up Japan announced that

it would begin aerial reconnaissance over Shikotan, a step which was condemned by Moscow.

The change in the international climate precipitated by the Soviet invasion of Afghanistan did nothing to alleviate the diplomatic tensions. These were further increased when a Japanese salvage company retrieved the contents of a tsarist naval vessel. Partly in response to its increasing frustration, Japan in January 1981 designated February 7 as an annual "Day of the Northern Territories" – a move which provoked further Soviet denials that there were any outstanding territorial issues. In September members of the Japanese government went on a "tour of inspection" of the northern islands, an initiative which Moscow described as "provocative". During the period 1980–84 Japan went from first to sixth among the Soviet Union's trading partners outside the Communist bloc, and there were frequent protests about violations of Japanese air space by Soviet planes.

In 1984 there were signs of improvement in Soviet-Japanese relations. These became more apparent in 1985 with **Gorbachev**'s accession to power and in January 1986 the new Soviet Foreign Minister, **Shevardnadze**, visited Tokyo. It was agreed that regular consultative meetings of foreign ministers would be held once a year and that negotiations on a peace treaty would continue at these. There was also an agreement that Japanese citizens would be allowed to visit family graves on the northern islands without visas (but with identification papers). Although this presaged an improvement in the relationship, in January 1987 *Pravda* noted that Gorbachev would not be visiting Japan, although an agreement had been reached in principle in 1986, because of persisting Japanese claims over the islands.

Other events also led to cooling of Japanese-Soviet relations. In May 1987 the Toshiba affair, in which Toshiba was accused by the US of selling computers to the Soviets, resulted in stricter control of Japanese exports and worsening of Soviet-Japanese relations. In August espionage charges and expulsions further cooled relations. Although there was still a mutual desire for dialogue, 1987 was a year in which Soviet-Japanese relations worsened rather than improved.

In February 1988 there were rallies protesting at the continued Soviet occupation of the islands. In April, Japan made clear that the islands were the key issue in Soviet-Japanese relations. A Japanese Foreign Ministry official stated: "There is no compromise. We consider this question one of the most fundamental for the Japanese nation." In May, however, Gorbachev met with the head of the Japanese Socialist party and said that a new page was opening in Soviet–Japanese relations. In July, Gorbachev met with former Prime Minister *Nakasone* and noted that Moscow was seeking better relations with Japan. He also referred to the formal offer of 1956 to return the two southernmost islands to Japan. It was clearly difficult for Gorbachev to improve the Soviet position as a Pacific power while there was diplomatic stalemate with Japan. Consequently, the Soviets initiated a two-track policy to settle the dispute. Officially they did not change their view on the islands, but they initiated unofficial contacts through the Soviet Academy of Sciences and the CPSU–Japanese Socialist party meetings, searching for a solution to the islands dispute.

In September 1988, Gorbachev called for better relations with Japan. While this was welcomed by the Japanese they did not soften their position on the islands and reiterated that a major improvement in the relationship could only come through a settlement of the dispute. A Japanese Foreign Ministry official stated that the Soviet Union had informally suggested a lease-back option for the islands, a suggestion which was unacceptable to the Japanese. The offer was subsequently denied by Moscow. In October, it was reported that because the Soviets had been talking about the islands Japan had begun scheduling high-level visits and that Japanese trade was on the rise. A month later, however, Japan once again insisted that relations could not improve significantly without a settlement of the territorial dispute.

In December Shevardnadze visited Japan, amidst hopes among Japanese that there would be a new Soviet initiative, and made statements indicating that a resolution should be possible to the islands dispute. After their first meeting, Shevardnadze and his Japanese counterpart **Uno** announced that they had agreed to refer the issue to a group of senior working officials and that the two ministers would continue talking about the issue. After the talks were completed, however, little had been accomplished on the islands dispute and there was once again a period of mutual recrimination.

In February 1989 the Soviet deputy foreign minister Rogachev acknowledged that a report in *Pravda* accusing the Japanese of issuing an ultimatum on the islands dispute was the official position of the government. The *Pravda* article said that the Tokyo visit by Shevardnadze "had been fruitful" but that the Japanese had eliminated all momentum towards a solution during a meeting in Paris in January. During late March, however, the two sides held three days of talks. Once again though there was little movement.

The Japanese refused to conclude six bilateral disagreements because of the continuing impasse over the islands.

In May 1989 the Japanese Foreign Minister Uno visited the Soviet Union. During his visit both sides again indicated their desire for improved relations, for a Gorbachev visit to Japan as well as improved economic ties. The meetings, however, were not successful and Gorbachev announced that he would not be visiting Tokyo in 1989. Both sides again disputed each other's claims to the islands. Two days after the meetings ended, however, Shevardnadze was quoted as saying that Japan and the Soviet Union would be able to resolve the dispute and normalize relations.

The significance of the islands dispute is that it inhibits a much more positive relationship between Japan and the Soviet Union. It is essentially a diplomatic dispute rather than one that will be settled by military means. It is conceivable that the Soviet desire to improve its position in Asia and to woo Japan will lead to greater flexibility by Moscow. In late 1988 and early 1989 the issue seemed to be back on the agenda in a way that suggested there was slightly more opportunity for agreement than at any time since the 1950s. It must be possible, for example, to solve the Japanese–Soviet dispute by backroom negotiations that would lead to a formal Soviet proposal only when the Soviets could be sure that it would be accepted. In the meantime, however, the issue has made Japan very resistant to the blandishments of Gorbachev. (*See also* **Northern Territories Dispute**)

PW

JEWISH AUTONOMOUS REGION. An administrative region (area: 36,000 sq km) in the far east of the Soviet Union, beside the border with China. Although established in 1934 as an autonomous "homeland" for Soviet Jews, very few of them migrated to the region from European Russia: the estimated 10,000 Jews currently living there constitute less than one per cent of the Soviet Union's Jewish population, and are outnumbered nearly 20 to one by Russians and Ukrainians.

IG

JIANG QING. A former Shanghai film starlet, born in 1913, she went to Yanan in 1937 and became Mao's third wife. Kept out of political life by consensus of the party leadership for 20 years, she became prominent during the Cultural Revolution, when she took her revenge. She became a leading member of the Cultural Revolution Small Group, and she was elected to the party Political Bureau in 1969. She was also the author of a few revolutionary operas which were supposed to replace the banned Peking opera. She was one of the **Gang of Four** arrested in October 1976. Put on trial in 1980, she remained defiant.

CIPF

JIANG ZEMIN. Jiang (born in 1926) joined the **Chinese Communist party** in 1946 and graduated from the Electrical Machinery Department of Jiatong University in Shanghai in 1947. After 1949 he worked in industry in Shanghai, and then spent 1955 as a trainee at the Stalin Car Plant in Moscow. Over the next 25 years he worked in heavy industrial plants in Shanghai and the Yangze region, and then in the First Ministry of Machine-Building. He was seemingly untouched by the Cultural Revolution. Between 1980 and 1982 he served as Vice-Chairman of the State Administration Commission on Import and Export Affairs and the State Administration Commission on Foreign Investment. From 1982 he was Minister of the Electronics Industry, and from 1985 Mayor of Shanghai. He was elected to the Central Committee in 1982, to the Political Bureau in 1987, and he replaced **Zhao Ziyang** as General Secretary in June 1989, despite his lack of experience in the party apparatus.

CIPF

JOINT DECLARATION ON HONG KONG. The Sino-British Joint Declaration – to maintain the prosperity and stability of Hong Kong and to further relations between the two countries – was the result of negotiations between Britain and China, which began in September 1982 and ended in September 1984. It was signed by the British and Chinese Prime Ministers in Beijing on Dec. 19, 1984, and came into force upon ratification on May 27, 1985.

The British undertook to transfer Hong Kong's sovereignty to China on July 1, 1997. The Chinese promised to set up a Special Administrative Region in Hong Kong with a "high degree of autonomy", and to allow the existing capitalist system and lifestyle there to remain basically unchanged for 50 years after the takeover. Until June 30, 1997, the British Government is "responsible for the administration of Hong Kong with the object of maintaining and preserving its economic prosperity and social stability", and the Chinese Government "will give its co-operation".

ST

JOINT LIAISON GROUP ON HONG KONG. In accordance with the **Joint Declaration**, a Sino-British Joint Liaison Group (JLG) was established in July 1985 to monitor its effective implementation and to ensure a smooth transition. It meets regularly, has had its principal base in Hong Kong since July 1988, and will continue until Jan. 1, 2000. The JLG is headed by diplomats of Ambassadorial rank, Ke Zaishuo for the Chinese, and Robin MacLaren (successor to Sir David Wilson) for the British.

ST

JUAN FERNANDEZ ISLANDS (Islas de Juan Fernández). Group of three islands, Más a Tierra, Más Afuera and Santa Clara, administratively part of Valparaíso Province, Chile, 640 km west of the mainland. Total area of the group is 181 sq km. Alexander Selkirk, shipwrecked on Más a Tierra in 1704, was the model for Swift's Robinson Crusoe.

P&SC

JUCHE (Chuch'e). Korean word meaning independence, autonomy, or individual sovereignty. Name of concept developed by north Korean leader **Kim Il Sung** which stresses political independence, economic self-sufficiency, and national self-defence. First developed in speech of Dec. 28, 1955 entitled "on eradicating dogmatism and formalism from ideological work and firmly establishing the Juche". Concept further refined in 1960s, and stressed as major political theme since 1970s. Initially formulated to strengthen Kim's political position in Korea, and to assert independence from communist superpowers.

JHG

K

KAIFU TOSHIKI. Prime Minister of Japan with effect from Aug. 10, 1989. Kaifu is a former minister of Education who came to prominence largely because his relative youth (58). His modern and common touch image distanced him from a discredited senior leadership and seemed likely to arrest a precipitous and potentially disastrous decline in the popularity of the LDP.

He was not the unanimous choice of the LDP. Other factions supported Ishihara Shintaro and Hayashi Yoshiro. Neither was he the unanimous choice of the Japanese parliament, the Diet. Kaifu garnered 294 votes in the 512-seat lower house, while **Doi Takako**, leader of the **Japan Socialist Party**, obtained the backing of 127 members of the 252-seat upper house. It was the first time in 48 years that the two houses chose different people to lead the nation. Kaifu survived, thanks to a ruling invoked by the Speaker.

RAB

KAMPUCHEA, PEOPLE'S REPUBLIC OF. (Note: *see also* **Cambodia; Democratic Kampuchea; Democratic Kampuchea, Coalition Government of.**)

Political History. The People's Republic of Kampuchea (PRK) was proclaimed on Jan. 11, 1979, following the successful invasion of Cambodia by Vietnamese forces and the expulsion from Phnom Penh of the government headed by **Pol Pot**. In the first instance the new regime embraced three groups of Cambodian political and military leaders who were willing to collaborate with Hanoi. The first consisted of defectors from the **Kampuchean Communist Party** of Pol Pot who had fled to Vietnam in 1977-78 and had established, with Vietnamese help, a "United Front for National Salvation" in December 1978. Among them may be mentioned **Heng Samrin**, who became (and remains) President of the PRK; **Hun Sen**, who became Foreign Minister and later (1985) Prime Minister; and Chea Sim, who served first as Interior Minister and later as Chairman of the National Assembly. A second group comprised leading cadres of the old **Kampuchean People's Revolutionary Party** (KPRP), who had gone to Hanoi in 1954 and were only now returning home with the Vietnamese army. Prominent in this group was Pen Sovan, who became Defence Minister of the PRK and later (1981) Prime Minister, as well as General Secretary of the revived KPRP. Chan Sy, his successor as Defence Minister and later as Prime Minister was also a member of the "Hanoi" group. Thirdly, there were some Cambodians who had been in Hanoi after 1954 and had returned home much earlier, but who had never accepted the leadership of Pol Pot in the 1970s. These included Bou Thang, who emerged as defence minister in 1982, and Say Phouthang, an important member of the KPRP secretariat.

During the first two years, which saw a slow and painful return to a kind of "normality" in Cambodia after the ravages of the Pol Pot regime and the violence of its overthrow, the PRK had difficulty in establishing itself as an effective political entity or getting itself taken seriously outside the country. The year 1981, however, saw a number of developments which marked a new stage in its evolution. Elections for a national assembly (May 1) were followed by the adoption of a new constitution on June 27. Also in May, the KPRP held its fourth national congress and emerged as an effective and expanding ruling Party in the Marxist-Leninist tradition. Pen Sovan, already Secretary-General of the Party, was appointed Prime Minister in June and seemed to be emerging – within the limits possible in a country occupied by a foreign army – as the new strongman. But in December 1981 he was suddenly removed from his party and government posts and disappeared: a fate which has never been adequately explained, but which may have been the consequence of a premature desire for independence from the Vietnamese. His formal successor within the party secretariat was Heng Samrin, who is thought to have been no more than a figurehead. More substantial power may have passed to his colleagues on that body, Chea Sim and Say Phouthang. Chan Sy, having succeeded Pen Sovan as Defence Minister in mid-1981, now took over the premiership, while Bou Thang became (in early 1982) Defence Minister and deputy Prime Minister.

This division of responsibilities lasted until the end of 1984, when Chan Sy suddenly died. He was succeeded as Prime Minister by Hun Sen, who retained his position as Foreign Minister except for an interlude in 1986–87. Meanwhile the KPRP, working closely with the **Vietnamese Communist Party**, also established a significant role in Cambodia's political life. It held its fifth congress in October 1985, at which a number of party veterans retired (none of them top leaders) and some new faces were promoted.

Further changes were made in 1988–89 as the PRK, anxious to achieve a political settlement with opposition groups in conjunction with the plan for a withdrawal of Vietnamese troops, also sought to present an image of greater respectability to the non-Communist world. Economic reforms in 1988 (see below) were designed partly to draw overseas Cambodians to invest in the country, and perhaps eventually to return home. In April 1989 the constitution was amended to restore **Theravada Buddhism** to its status as the national religion. At the same time the death penalty was abolished: a move probably intended to reassure former ***Khmer Rouge*** supporters who chose to "rally" to Phnom Penh in the event of a political compromise.

Outline of economic development. The new regime in Phnom Penh inherited a country already "transformed" by the Pol Pot regime, and the Vietnamese invasion itself produced still further dislocation during 1979. (It may never be possible to determine how much of the death and destruction normally attributed to Pol Pot actually occurred in the months after his departure from Phnom Penh). Heng Samrin and his Vietnamese advisers thus had to give highest priority to restoring economic life on whatever basis was practicable. In agriculture, for example, it was necessary to retreat from the extremes of communal living imposed under Democratic Kampuchea. A system of "solidarity teams" was maintained, involving redistribution of land to family units each year and restoring a measure of private property. But although state ownership of all land was reaffirmed, there was no immediate attempt to bring Cambodia's "socialist transformation" into line with the Vietnamese model. A PRK circular on agriculture in August 1980, recognizing the need for more incentives to encourage greater production, was nevertheless very much in line with Vietnamese decisions of September 1979 (which had been copied in Laos in December 1979). Private traders were also allowed to function, initially on the basis of barter arrangements. In 1979 Cambodia had no currency and no system of taxation. It took until March 1980 to re-establish the national bank and to introduce a new currency, which then made it possible to fix wages of state employees in *riel* and to establish a system of subsidized prices for them. Even so, officials remained much worse off than private traders operating in the free market. Given the scarcity of goods of all kinds, it seems likely that the government (probably with Soviet

help) had to work extremely hard to prevent rampant inflation.

The most urgent task in 1979–80 was to restore food production. The shortfall of that year, in the aftermath of the war and the change of regimes, was extreme – leading to appeals for international famine relief which brought a number of aid agencies to work in Phnom Penh (notably OXFAM). Fighting and famine combined to produce a stream of *Khmer* refugees across the borders of Thailand in the autumn of 1979, which also required a major international relief effort. From 1980 onwards, however, the area under cultivation was steadily restored. Even so, the roughly one and a half million tonnes of food produced in the next few years were inadequate to meet the needs of the population, let alone to build up reserves to meet the kind of shortfall that again occurred in 1984 as a result of heavy floods. Infrastructure was still poor, the use of water pumps and tractors extremely limited, and fertilizer in very short supply. That made it impossible to introduce high-yield varieties of rice which might have solved the immediate problem. Again in 1986–87, this time after serious droughts, Phnom Penh was again appealing for international food aid. During 1988 a United Nations team visited the country to make a systematic study of food needs and capabilities, but the problem was far from solved. Meanwhile an attempt was made in November 1984 to define the next stage of agricultural organization. The new programme imposed restrictions on private use of land and insisted on state purchase of rice and certain other crops, but still fell a long way short of co-operativization on the Vietnamese model. By the late 1980s, therefore, Cambodia had proceeded much less further than southern Vietnam (or even Laos) down the road towards full collectivization of agriculture. It had therefore less to dismantle when, in 1988, the Vietnamese reversed the trend and introduced a more liberal contract system.

Both for food aid and in other sectors of the economy, the role of Vietnam and of the Soviet Union has been vital since 1979; the more so in view of the success of the CGDK (backed by the **Association of South-East Asian Nations –** ASEAN) in blocking the PRK's membership of international financial organizations and even of the United Nations. Close relations with Vietnam and Laos have included economic co-operation, with periodic trade agreements and meetings of trade and planning ministers from the three countries. By 1985 Cambodia was able to think in terms of a five-year plan for 1986–90 which would be fully integrated into those of its Indochinese neighbours.

The Vietnamese have provided considerable aid and advice, involving the presence of substantial numbers of technical personnel in Cambodia. Soviet aid has also been vital in restoring the social and economic infrastructure, notably in building (and staffing) hospitals and educational institutions, developing electricity, (still on a small scale), repairing roads, and restoring the port of Kompong Som. Apart from seeking to restore a small number of plants in production before 1970, little attention has been paid to industrialization. Other sectors must take priority, at least until shortages of electricity and raw materials have been overcome. Cambodia's contribution to the "international division of labour" has therefore been in the field of primary products, particularly rubber. Some plantations were restored with Soviet aid, and by 1985 as many as 25,000 hectares had been brought back into production (employing around 15,000 people). But this compared with 64,000 hectares in 1967, and the plan for 1986–90 included the task of trying to restore production to its full pre-war level. By the late 1980s, some timber was also being produced for export. Apart from Vietnam and Laos, Cambodia's principal trading partner remains the Soviet Union.

Thus by 1989 a good deal of progress had been made towards revitalizing the economy, despite the conflict with the resistance movements and Cambodia's continuing international isolation. Phonm Penh was again a flourishing city of 800,000 people. But there was still much to be done before the country returned to even the modest targets of economic development cherished by the **Sihanouk** government in the 1960s.

Foreign Relations. Throughout the decade following the Vietnamese invasion at the beginning of 1979, the presence of the Vietnamese armed forces made the PRK completely dependent on Hanoi – even though dependence took the form of close co-operation within the framework of relations between the three Indochinese countries, involving Laos as well as Vietnam. Regular interministerial meetings have guaranteed a co-ordination of policies in the spheres of diplomacy, military affairs, economic planning; while co-operation between the three parties has ensured uniformity in the idealogical sphere. A formal treaty of friendship was signed between Vietnam and the PRK on 18 February 1979.

The first priority of the occupying forces was to prevent the Armed Forces of Democratic Kampuchea, and later those of other resistance groups, from recovering the initiative on the battlefield. By 1982, when the resistance groups combined to form the Coalition Government of Democratic Kampuchea, the situation had begun to stabilize. But the Vietnamese were far from satisfied with the degree of control they exercised in more outlying areas of the country. In the next few years they conducted a series of offensives in the border regions. The most ambitious of these, between November 1984 and March 1985, succeeded in eliminating the bases of the **Khmer People's National Liberation Front** at Nong Chan and Ampil; that of the *Khmer Rouge* at Phnom Malai; and finally that of the **Sihanoukist National Army** at Tatum. That did not end the fighting. The *Khmer Rouge*, in particular, continued to claim successes in the pursuit of a more mobile form of guerrilla warfare – on the basis of a continuing flow of weapons from China. But from 1985–86 it was possible for Vietnam to think of reducing its military forces and handing over some responsibility for defence to the Armed Forces of the PRK.

By 1986, Hanoi was publicly committed to withdrawing all its forces by the end of 1990. By then, too, international pressures were beginning to operate. China had identified the Vietnamese military presence in Cambodia as the principal "obstacle" to a normalization of its own relations with the Soviet Union; whilst the Soviet Union was anxious for Vietnam to develop economic relations with the non-Communist world. The latter could take place only if the United States and other Western powers lifted the embargo on trade and investment relations with Vietnam and Cambodia which had been imposed as a consequence of the invasion in 1979. In July 1987 both Hanoi and Phnom Penh expressed willingness to participate in informal talks, involving in the first instance a meeting between the "four factions" in Cambodia itself which the Indonesian government offered to arrange. There followed two "personal" meetings with Hun Sen in France (December 1987 and January 1988), then two "Jakarta Informal Meetings" in July 1988 and February 1989. Although only limited progress was made towards a final agreement, these moves provided the diplomatic context for a Vietnamese–Cambodian announcement in May 1988 that 50,000 Vietnamese troops would leave during the second half of that year. That withdrawal, completed on time, meant that fewer than 100,000 troops remained to be pulled out during 1989–90. In January 1989 the Vietnamese announced that they would be willing to accelerate that final withdrawal, to complete it by September 1989, if a satisfactory political agreement could be reached in the meantime. Nevertheless, it seemed unlikely that they would accept any agreement which did not contain a high degree of probability that in the longer term a pro-Vietnamese government would continue to rule in Phnom Penh.

Beyond the limits of Indochina, the PRK has been able to establish direct relations only with the Soviet Union and its close allies, which have been its principal trading partners and suppliers of aid. The fact that the United Nations has continued to recognize Democratic Kampuchea and to allow the CGDK to occupy Cambodia's seat in the General Assembly has contributed further to the isolation of the PRK and has tended to confirm its dependence on Vietnam. A political settlement, even on Vietnamese terms, might eventually allow Phnom Penh to develop relations with Thailand and the other countries of ASEAN, as well as with Japan and the Western powers, thus increasing its practical independence.

RBS

KAMPUCHEA-THAILAND CONFLICT.

One of the most recent conflicts to occur has been that on the border between Thailand and Kampuchea. This has been an escalation of the struggle in Kampuchea between the Vietnamese forces and the rebels. Some of the guerrilla forces have taken refuge in Thailand. Vietnamese forces, however, have not been willing to accept Thai territory as a sanctuary and in 1985 crossed the border in pursuit of the *Khmer Rouge*. In 1986 border violations continued and in January 1987 Thailand lodged a complaint at the United Nations that there had been 129 border infringements during November and December. The situation worsened in early 1987 when an estimated 800 Vietnamese troops crossed into Thailand in pursuit of the *Khmer Rouge* guerrillas. At the end of March the Thai army launched a counter-attack at the Chong Bok pass. They found Vietnamese troops well entrenched and difficult to dislodge. Thai military casualties were high and although officially it was acknowledged that 50–60 soldiers had been killed and 500 wounded, there were suggestions that the casualties were, in fact, much higher.

In June 1988 Thailand and Vietnam reached an accord over the Kampuchean issue, although the shelling of rebel forces inside Thailand did not cease immediately. This conflict has been essentially a spillover and as the Vietnamese forces leave Kampuchea so the tension along the border between Kampuchea and Thailand is likely to diminish.

PW

KAMPUCHEAN COMMUNIST PARTY (KCP).

According to **Pol Pot** this Party was founded in September 1960 and thus commemorated its 17th anniversary in 1977: the occasion on which its existence was first publicly revealed. But according to the (pro-Vietnamese) leaders of the **Kampuchean People's Revolutionary Party** the KCP never had any legitimate existence. They insist that their own Party was founded in June 1951, and that Pol Pot had usurped the leadership after being elected Secretary-General in 1963. Nevertheless, it was Pol Pot who led the *Khmer Rouge* forces which embarked on an armed struggle inside Cambodia in 1968–69 and which eventually won control of Phnom Penh in April 1975. From then until January 1979, the KCP was effectively the ruling party of Democratic Kampuchea – hiding its identity behind the vague term *Angkar* ("the Organization") from 1975 until 1977. The KCP continued to exist until its formal dissolution in December 1981.

RBS

KAMPUCHEAN PEOPLE'S REVOLUTIONARY PARTY (KPRP).

The party which emerged publicly under this name in Phnom Penh in 1981, at its fourth congress, traced its origins to the establishment of a People's Party in June 1951 by a group of Cambodian communists who had previously operated within the Indochinese Communist Party. They included Son Ngoc Minh, who headed the national united front from 1950 to 1954, but then withdrew to Hanoi and died in 1972 without returning home; and Tou Samouth, Secretary-General of the party from the mid-1950s until his death in 1962. Differences of opinion developed at the second congress of the party, held secretly in Phnom Penh in 1960, when Saloth Sar (or **Pol Pot**) increased his standing in the leadership. At the third congress (February 1963) Pol Pot was appointed Secretary-General; but this appointment was subsequently not recognized by the Hanoi group, nor by a pro-Vietnamese element which had returned to the Cambodian *maquis* in the late 1950s. The history of the party during the 1960s and early 1970s is obscure; there were probably several competing factions under a leadership which was not yet irrevocably split. Subsequently, however, Pol Pot would present himself as leader of a distinct **Kampuchean Communist Party** (KCP) which he claimed had been founded in September 1960. Its legitimacy was never recognized by pro-Vietnamese elements. The latter, returning to Phnom-Penh in January 1979 in the wake of the Vietnamese army, appear to have held their own third congress soon afterwards. Pen Sovan became Secretary-General of a reconstituted Central Committee which also included several members of Pol Pot's KCP who had defected to Vietnam in 1977–78: notably **Hun Sen** and **Heng Samrin**. Although Pen Sovan was confirmed in office at the fourth congress (May 1981) he suffered an eclipse not long afterwards, being removed from all his posts in party and government in December 1981. He was succeeded as Secretary-General by Heng Samrin (already head of state) but observers believed that real power was exercised by the Vietnamese – with other members of the secretariat playing important roles, notably Chea Sim, Say Phouthong, and Hun Sen. This collective leadership was confirmed, and a number of new men promoted, at the Party's fifth congress in October 1985.

RBS

KANG, YOUNG-HOON (Kang Yong-hun. Prime Minister of the Republic of Korea. Born May 30, 1922. Graduated Chienkuo University (Manchuria), 1943; US Army Command and General Staff College, 1958; Superintendent, Korea Military Academy, 1960; retired Lt.-Gen., 1961; Ph.D. (Political Science), University of Southern California, 1973; dean, Graduate School, Hankuk University of Foreign Languages, 1977; ambassador to UK, 1981–ambassador to the Holy See, 1984–Minister, 1988.

JHG

KAOHSIUNG INCIDENT. When the 1978 national supplementary elections in Taiwan were postponed by the government in response to American derecognition of the Republic of China, the *Tangwai* tried to maintain momentum in its drive for political reforms by organizing a series of mass rallies in various parts of the island.

An application by a group of *Tangwai* politicians from the "Formosa Faction" to hold a mass rally in Kaohsiung on Dec. 10, 1979, the 30th anniversary of the Declaration of Human Rights, was refused by the authorities. The rally was nevertheless held and led to riots in which 182 civil and military police were injured. The incident led to the arrest of 152 people connected with the opposition, 65 of whom were indicted.

The authorities considered the events in Kaohsiung as rebellion. Therefore the eight main defendants, all affiliated with the "Formosa Faction", were brought to trial before a Taipei military tribunal in March 1980. The state prosecutor demanded the death sentence for all of them. They were sentenced to prison terms, ranging from 12 years to life imprisonment, in spite of the defendants' protestations that their purported confessions had been extracted under duress and

that they had not attempted to overthrow the government.

A total of 31 alleged participants in the riots were given prison sentences ranging from 10 months to six years. In a related event, several people were sentenced for sheltering one of the main culprits of the Kaohsiung incident, Shih Ming-teh. Among them was the executive secretary of the Taiwan Presbyterian Church who was sentenced to seven years in prison, while 10 other church members were given prison sentences ranging from two to seven years. The suppression of the magazine *Formosa* and other opposition magazines and the imprisonment of many leading political activists severely weakened the *Tangwai* movement.

HH

KAYSONE PHOMVIHAN. Prime Minister of the Lao People's Democratic Republic since 1975, and General Secretary of the **Lao People's Revolutionary Party** since its founding in 1955. Born 1920 in the Savannakhet area, he is partly of Vietnamese descent and has worked closely with the Vietnamese Communist movement since his student days in Hanoi in the early 1940s. Returning home to participate in the independence movement of 1945–46, he was admitted to membership of the (then clandestine) Indochinese Communist Party in 1949. He was appointed General Secretary of the Lao People's (Revolutionary) Party at its first Congress in March 1955, and Vice-President of the Lao Patriotic Front in January 1956. But his leadership role was not publicized at that stage, and he appears to have remained in the *maquis* (or possibly sometimes in Hanoi) until his "return" to Vientiane as Prime Minister in December 1975. Since then he has remained a somewhat remote figure, mentioned mainly in connection with occasional speeches on public occasions, or when he makes visits abroad, which he has frequently done to Hanoi and Moscow.

RBS

KAZAKHS. A turkic-speaking ethnic group found predominantly in Soviet Central Asia, but also in Mongolia, where they numbered more than 80,000 people (over 5 per cent of the total population) at the last (1979) census and are the dominant group in the far western province of Bayan-Ölgiy, and in the Sinkiang-Uighur Autonomous Region of north-west China.

IG

KEATING, PAUL JOHN. Treasurer in the **Hawke** Australian Labor government since 1983. Member for Blaxland in the House of Representatives since 1969. He is considered Hawke's most likely successor.

TBM

KEIDANREN (JAPANESE FEDERATION OF ECONOMIC ORGANIZATIONS). Keidanren is the peak organization of business. In the view of the labour unions Keidanren is quite simply the power centre of Japanese society. It has a membership of more than 100 industry-wide associations, delimited by trade, finance, transportation, manufacturing, mining etc., and a further 88 or so of the largest corporations. Keidanren makes only modest claims about its function, which is to adjust and mediate differences of opinion among its various member industries and businesses, and to submit proposals to government regarding policies to stimulate the economy. The claim is perhaps too modest. Keidanren has a bureau with a remit to consider how best to improve government, and has on occasion made spectacular interventions to change the terms of the policy process in toto – an example is its orchestration of the merger of the Japan Democratic Party and the Liberal Party to form the **Liberal Democratic Party** (LDP) in 1955. The continuing power, influence and authority of Keidanren derives in part from its massive financial contributions to the LDP and from its ability to mediate conflicts and to secure agreements about the broad limits of the business interest.

RAB

KHAKASS. A group of turkic-speaking peoples found in the East Siberian region of the Soviet Union. Numbering more than 70,000, they enjoy administrative–territorial autonomy in the Khakass Autonomous Region.

IG

KHIEU SAMPHAN. Formerly President of Democratic Kampuchea (1976–79) and (since 1982) Vice-President of the Coalition Government of Democratic Kampuchea. The son of an official under the French protectorate, he was educated in Paris where he became active in leftist Cambodian politics in the 1950s. He completed a thesis in 1959 on the nature of Cambodian society and its possibilities for development. On returning home he lived in Phnom Penh until 1967, and for a short time (1962–63) held a junior government post under **Sihanouk**. He disappeared to the *maquis* in 1967, at the time of a rural uprising in Battambang, and reappeared in the early 1970s as a leader of the *Khmer Rouge* inside Cambodia, as well as a member of the united front "government" headed by Sihanouk in Beijing. In April 1976 he became president of Democratic Kampuchea but his actual power was small compared with that of **Pol Pot**. When the latter "retired" at the end of 1979, after the regime had been driven from Phnom Penh by the Vietnamese, Khieu Samphan became Prime Minister. In that capacity he joined with Sihanouk and **Son Sann** in the negotiations of 1981–82 which led to the formation of the Coalition Government of Democratic Kampuchea; and later participated in various meetings as leader of one of the four Cambodian "factions".

RBS

KHMER PEOPLE'S NATIONAL LIBERATION FRONT (KPNLF). Established in March 1979, initially in Paris, under the leadership of the non-Communist Cambodian politician **Son Sann**. Its aim was to oppose the pro-Vietnamese regime in Phnom Penh by launching its own armed struggle inside the country. By 1981–82 it claimed to have a force of 9,000 guerrillas, receiving military assistance from several ASEAN governments. In June 1982, Son Sann became Prime Minister of the Coalition Government of Democratic Kampuchea (CGDK) but the Armed Forces of the KPNLF remained under separate command. In addition to its following among the *Khmer* refugees in camps along the Thai-Cambodian border, it was able to establish bases inside the country, notably at Ampil. But these were eliminated by a Vietnamese military campaign early in 1985, and the KPNLF forces proved less effective than the National Army of Democratic Kampuchea in sustaining a guerrilla struggle without fixed bases. Serious divisions within the front had arisen by the end of 1985, weakening Son Sann's position within the CGDK. Unity was restored at the beginning of 1987; but Son Sann was no longer in a position to play as influential a role as he would have liked in the affairs of the coalition or in its negotiations with the Phnom Penh regime.

RBS

KHMER ROUGE. Name used, originally by **Prince Sihanouk**, to refer to the guerrilla forces led by **Khieu Samphan** – and ultimately controlled by the **Kampuchean Communist Party** of **Pol Pot** – engaged in armed struggle against his government in the late 1960s. With considerable support from North Vietnam, they built up their strength after 1970 during the period of the *Khmer* Republic of Lon Nol, which they finally overthrew in April 1975. The term has again been used since 1979, following the collapse of the Pol Pot regime of Democratic Kampuchea, to refer to the forces of the National Army of Democratic Kampuchea commanded by Pol Pot (until 1985) and subsequently by **Son Sann**.

RBS

KIM DAE JUNG (Kim Tae-Jung). Politician, Republic of Korea. Born Dec. 3, 1935. Graduated Kŏn'guk University, 1955; Member of the fifth (1960–63), sixth (1963–67), seventh (1967–71) and eighth (1971–73) National Assemblies; New Democratic Party candidate for President (1971); Chairman of Council for Promotion of Democracy, 1985–87; Party for Peace and Democracy candidate for President, 1987.

JHG

KIM IL SUNG (Kim Il-song). President, Democratic people's Republic of Korea (North Korea). Born April 15, 1912 (original name, Kim Sŏngju). Went with father to Manchuria at early age. Attended Yungmun Middle School (Chilin, Manchuria), 1926–29; member of Communist Youth League, 1926; Secretary of Eastern Manchuria Regional Communist Youth League, 1929; member of **Chinese Communist Party**, 1931; Commander of Korean People's Army Corps, Chinese Communist Party, 1932; changed name to Kim Il-song, 1935; fled to Soviet Union, 1942; member of Soviet Army, 1945; returned to Korea with Soviet forces, August, 1945; Secretary General of **Korean Workers Party**; President, 1948. Styled the "Great Leader".

JHG

KIM JONG IL (Kim Chong-il). Politician, Democratic People's Republic of Korea. Born Feb. 19, 1941, Samarkand, USSR. Graduated Kim Il-Song University, 1963. Member, Central Committee of the **Korean Workers Party**, 1964; elected member of party Politburo and the Presidium, and to the Military Committee of the Korean Workers Party at Sixth Party Congress, 1980; Designated heir to father **Kim Il Sung** at the same congress. Effective ruler of North Korea. Styled as the "Dear Leader".

JHG

KIM YOUNG-SAM (Kim Yong-sam). Politician, Republic of Korea. Born Dec. 20, 1927. Graduated Seoul National University, 1951; Member of third (1954–57), fifth (1960–63), sixth (1963–67), seventh (1967–71), eighth (1971–73), ninth (1973–79) and 10th (1980–) National Assemblies; President of the New Democratic Party (1973–, 1979–), President of Reunification Democratic Party (1987–), party candidate for President, 1987.

JHG

KIRIBATI (formerly Gilbert Islands). *Population* 68,200 (est. 1988), mainly Micronesians. *Area*: 746 sq km. Since 1979 an independent republic within the Commonwealth, lying on the equator north of New Zealand, and comprising 33 islands in three groups – the Gilbert Islands, the Phoenix Islands, Banaba (Ocean Island) and eight of the Live Islands. *Capital*: Tarawa.

The islands were settled by Austronesian-speaking peoples more than 2,000 years ago. European contact dates from 1765. A Christian mission was established in 1857. In 1892 Britain established a protectorate over the Gilbert and Ellis Islands, adding Banaba (Ocean Island) in 1900, Kiritimati (Christmas Island) in 1919 and the Phoenix Islands in 1917, to what since 1916 was a crown colony. Japan invaded the islands in World War II. In 1976 the Ellis Islands separated to form the independent state of Tuvalu. Self-government was achieved in 1977, and independence two years later.

There is a House of Assembly with 39 elected members and one nominated member from Banaba, serving four-year terms. The languages spoken are Gilbertise (Kiribati) and English.

Since the end of the phosphate deposits on Banaba (1979), the economy has declined, being subsidized by Britain and by international aid programmes. Copra and fish are exported to Australia, New Zealand, the UK, Japan, the USA and to Papua New Guinea and Fiji. In 1985, the government negotiated a one-year agreement allowing Soviet fishing vessels to operate within Kiribati's 200-mile exclusive fisheries area, for a fee of over US$ 1,500,000. The vessels were denied landing rights and were prohibited from the country's 12-mile territorial limit. Expressing disappointment with the catch obtained, the Soviet government sought unsuccessfully to renegotiate the treaty, which then lapsed.

Kiribati relies heavily on foreign aid, especially from Japan, the UK, Australia and New Zealand.

TBM

KOMEITO (JAPAN). Once regarded as a maverick in the party political scene, Komeito has established itself as a fixture in the Diet with which other parties, including the ruling **Liberal Democratic Party**, must reckon and whose co-operation is sought by both the LDP and the **Japan Socialist Party** (JSP). Its stable support and position as the second largest opposition party, with a representation in excess of 50 lower house seats, guarantees it – alone of all the opposition parties other than the JSP since 1955 – the right to submit budget-related legislation and motions of no confidence.

It was not always so. Komeito emerged in 1964 as the political arm of a religion, the *Soka Gakkai*, which drew its recruits from the economically and socially marginal, the shifting dispensable and replaceable elements in the urban mosaic, bar girls, sweat-shop workers and owners, clerks and such like, who had escaped the broad sweep of the principal means of social incorporation and advancement. The zeal and rapid advance of first *Soka Gakkai* and then of Komeito itself excited the opposition of established political forces unsympathetic to the emergence of vigorous rivals, particularly when they sought to cultivate large and hitherto neglected fields of support. This pragmatic, churlish and entirely understandable antagonism was reinforced by a genuine fear that Komeito and its parent (disavowed in 1972) was a new right-wing movement with aspirations incompatible with the Constitution of 1947. These fears were not realized.

RAB

KOREA. (Note: *see also* **Korea, Democratic People's Republic of; Korea, Republic of.**)

Geographical background. The Korean peninsula extends from north-east China (Manchuria) towards the Japanese archipelago for approximately 1,000 km between the 33rd and 43rd north parallels, and is never more than 216 km wide at any one point. The total landmass of the peninsula and outlying islands encompasses 221,325 sq km. Approximately 55 per cent of the landmass of the peninsula is in North Korea and 45 per cent is in South Korea. The Korean peninsula is separated from the north-east Asian mainland by two river systems, the Yalu River, which flows 790 km in a south-westerly direction towards Korea bay, and the Tumen River, which flows north-east for 521 km towards the East Sea (Sea of Japan). These rivers rise in the Paektu-san range (Ch'angpai Shan in Chinese, highest point 2,744 metres) from which also flows the Sungari River of Manchuria.

The peninsula is over 70 per cent mountains, hills and uplands. Aside from Paektu-san on the Chinese border, the principal mountain ranges are the Hamgyöng Range (highest point 2,184 metres) stretching from the north-east towards the north-west, the Taebaek Range (highest point 1,708 metres) stretching along the east coast from the north-east towards the south-east, and the Sobaek Range (highest point 1,420 metres) which branches off from the Taebaek Range to divide the south-eastern part of the peninsula from the other quarters. Other important mountains include Halla-san (1,950 metres) an extinct volcano on the island of Cheju, and Chiri-san (1,915 metres) in the south-west.

Excluding the Yalu and Tumen Rivers, there are four major river systems, three of which are in the southern part of the peninsula. These are the Taedong River (439 km) which flows via P'yöngyang into Korea Bay, the Han River (514 km) which flows past Seoul into the Yellow Sea, the Naktong River (525 km) in the south-east, and the Kŭm River (401 km) in the south-west. The Korean peninsula is geologically tilted north-east to south-west so that there is a smooth coastline and very little continental shelf on the east coast, whereas the west coast has over 3,400 islands. The daily tidal fall on the west coast is one of the greatest in the world measuring between six to 10 m.

The principal mineral resources are **coal**, magnesite, **zinc**, graphite, **tungsten** and **iron** in the north, in addition to which the south has reserves of **lead**, and **copper**. South Korean kaolin is of particularly high quality and the south's reserves of tungsten are said to be among the richest in the world.

The population of the peninsula is over 61.7 million with 19.6 million (1985) in the Democratic People's Republic of Korea (North Korea) and 42.1 million (1988) in the Republic of Korea (South Korea). In 1986, there were five cities with a population over a million persons: Seoul, (9,646,000) the capital of the Republic of Korea; Pusan, (3,517,00) the major port of the south-east; Taegu (2,030,000), the great inland city of the south-east; P'yöngyang (1,500,000), the capital of the Democratic People's Republic of Korea; and Inch'on (1,387,000), the port for Seoul.

Early historic period. From the fourth century BCE, Iron Age culture and technology began to spread throughout southern Manchuria and the Korean peninsula. The small tribal groups in those areas slowly began to form themselves into larger tribal leagues and confederations. By the end of the third century, there were several confederations which had begun to develop into formal states. Two great states emerged in the fourth century, Koguryo in southern Manchuria and northern Korea and Paekche in the central area of the peninsula, which entered into several centuries of conflict for dominance of the peninsula. The state of Silla, which arose during the late fifth century in the south-eastern part of the peninsula, also entered into the conflict. By the seventh century, the new T'ang Empire (618–907) became aware of the dangers which a strong state like Koguryo posed for the north-eastern border of the empire. Consequently, T'ang entered into an alliance with Silla to go to war first against Paekche and then against Koguryo. Paekche was conquered in 663 and Koguryo in 668. T'ang then tried unsuccessfully to absorb these territories and Silla into its empire. Silla was able to resist this and gain control of the peninsula as far north as modern P'yongyang. The subsequent period of history is known as the Unified Silla period (670–935).

The modern Korean people and their language are the direct descendants of the people of Silla, and the modern Korean state and its government is the direct descendant of the Unified Silla kingdom. During this period, **Buddhism** and the arts flourished with Silla becoming one of the major Buddhist centres of the East. From the eighth century on, Korean commerce became an important force in the East Asian economy with Korean shipping dominating the sea lanes of north-east Asia. By the ninth century, Silla – like the other states of East Asia – became enfeebled politically and economically, with the result that there were numerous local rebellions. Certain great provincial figures began to set up their own "alternative governments" which drew power away from the central authority. In 935, Silla was conquered by one of these warlords who established the Kingdom of Koryo.

The Koryo dynasty (935–1392) was a brilliant era of Buddhist culture and thought. The boundaries of the state were extended further north than in the Silla period. Nonetheless, it was from this period that Korean governments came to recognize that they could no longer enforce their claim to Koguryo's territory in Manchuria. By the middle of the thirteenth century, the country was militarily unprepared for the rise of the Mongols who ruled northern China from 1234. Korea became part of the Yuan empire (1234–1367) in the middle of the thirteenth century.

During the more than 500 years of the Confucian Choson dynasty, Korea was the most thoroughly Confucian culture and society of East Asia. At the time of the reign of the fourth king, Sejong (r. 1418–50), a government research body

was set up which was responsible for – among other inventions – the creation of the Korean alphabet. Because of the dissimilarity of the Chinese and Korean languages, the king wished there to be a simple system of transcription. The Korean alphabet is considered to be the most scientifically conceived writing system known.

The sixteenth century was the great era of **Confucian** philosophy in Korea and was also typified by rabid political strife. This strife left Korea unprepared for the Japanese invasions of the peninsula led by Toyotomi Hideyoshi (1536–98). These wars and the subsequent invasions of Korea by the Manchus in the seventeenth century left the country prostrate. The effect of these series of invasions led to a government policy which virtually severed Korea's ties with the outside world creating the "Hermit Kingdom" known to latter-day foreigners. The severe economic and commercial problems of that time led scholars to create a uniquely Korean form of Confucianism which focused on practical matters of agriculture, commerce and trade.

The first British and French warships appeared off the Korean coast in the 1790s and made increasingly frequent apperances from the middle of the nineteenth century. These incursions and a French invasion in 1866 and an American invasion in 1871 convinced the traditionally-minded state council that isolation from the outside was the safest policy for national survival. This isolation, however, proved impossible to maintain. The nation which opened Korea to the outside world was not a Western power, but Japan. In 1876, through a contrived incident with one of their warships, the Japanese forced the Koreans to conclude with them the Treaty of Kanghwa. This treaty was the first Western-style treaty which Korea signed. Modern Korean history may be dated from this year.

Modern history (1876–1945). The history of Korea from the 1880s to 1910 centres on the rivalry between China, Japan and Russia. Each of these powers saw Korea as an important part of its plans for geo-political dominance in the Far East. When the Chinese drove out the Japanese in 1884, Korea drew closer to China. The Chinese leader Li Hung-jang (1823–1901) convinced the Korean government to appoint the German Paul G. von Möllendorff (1847–1901) to the Home office and to oversee the Customs Service. He also had his protégé Yuan Shih-k'ai (1859–1916) appointed as Chinese Resident, thus bringing Korea more effectively into the Chinese orbit.

Chinese control and influence in Korea was eliminated a decade later following the Tonghak Rebellion in 1894–95. The Chinese troops brought in at the request of the Korean government to suppress the rebellion became an excuse for the Japanese to bring in their own troops. The ensuing Sino-Japanese War resulted in the military and political expulsion of China from Korea. Japan's pre-eminent position in Korean affairs was again displaced, this time by Russia. The Japanese murder of his queen in 1895 had led King Kojong to seek refuge in the Russian legation. Russian influence in Korean affairs remained a problem for Japan for another decade. To increase his authority within world politics, King Kojong established Korea as the Empire of Tae-Han in 1896 so that he could be seen as the equal of the emperors of China and Japan.

The outcome of the Russo-Japanese War of 1904-05 was to remove Russia from the Korean stage, leaving Japan to do as she wished in southern Manchuria and Korea. In 1905, Korea was made a Protectorate of the Japanese Empire with a Resident General, Ito Hirobumi (1841-1909), who had authority over Korean foreign affairs. In 1910, following the assassination of Ito and various civil disturbances, the Japanese formally annexed Korea into the empire and appointed a Governor General to oversee the colony.

With the annexation of Korea, the Japanese proceeded immediately to remake the country into a nation which would serve Japanese economic interests. The injustices of Japanese rule, and the harshness with which they governed led to a pan-national movement to re-establish the independence of Korea.

World opinion on Japanese activites in Korea forced Japan to replace the Governor General and to establish a more conciliatory policy towards governing the Koreans. Throughout the 1920s, the Japanese took a more cultural approach to the Koreans and encouraged various aspects of Korean modern culture to develop. This more enlightened policy was curtailed with the emergence of patriotic, military governments in Japan itself in the late 1920s and the 1930s. During this latter period of colonial rule, a policy of assimilation was pursued.

The Provisional Government of the Republic of Korea was founded by exiles in Shanghai in April, 1919. This became the major independence organization which kept the question of Korean independence before the world. Throughout the Japanese period, this group lobbied world governments and organizations on behalf of an independent Korea. There were various groups of guerrillas fighting against the Japanese from Manchuria which became linked to the Provisional Government. The Provisional Government also published a paper, *Independent News*, for Koreans inside and outside the country. There were other groups as well, on the right and the left. After the formation of the Korean Communist Party in the late 1920s, bands of Korean communist guerrillas operated from Manchuria and the Soviet Union.

In preparation for the eventual defeat of the Japanese in World War II, the great powers agreed at the Cairo Conference of December 1943 that Korea should become independent again, but only after a period of great power trusteeship. Later, in 1945 Moscow and Washington agreed to take the surrender of Japanese forces in Korea respectively north and south of the 38th parallel. The resultant Soviet and American zones became firmed into nations which effectively sundered in two a country which had been a single entity since 670.

JHG

KOREA, DEMOCRATIC PEOPLE'S REPUBLIC OF (NORTH KOREA).

(Note: *see also* **Korea**.) *Population*: 21,390,000 (1987). *Area*: 122,370 sq km. *Gross Domestic Product*: US$ 12,600 million (1982). *Trade*: imports US$ 1,480 million; exports US$ 1,430 million (1984). *Top five trading partners*: Soviet Union, China, Japan, West Germany, "Eastern Bloc" (1986). *Defence spending*: US$ 3,030 million. *Urban population as percentage of total*: 62 (1985). *Birth rate*: 30 per thousand (1984). *Life expectancy*: males 65; females 72 (1984).

Outline of political history. In accordance with the agreement reached by the Soviet Union with the United States, Soviet forces entered the northern part of Korea on Aug. 15, 1945 to take the surrender of the Japanese forces there. The forces were commanded by Lt Gen. T. F. Shtikov. He immediately recognized the People's Committees which had grown up in the wake of the collapse of the Japanese administration of Korea. The Soviets also introduced to the Korean people a figure called **Kim Il Sung** (1912-) whom the populace was told had been a great revolutionary fighter and hero in Manchuria. He was 33 years old. Shortly afterwards, a Central People's Committee was established which was soon dominated by the North Korean Communist party. On Feb. 9, 1946, a Provisional People's Committee was created at which meeting Kim Il Sung was elected chairman. Kim then made a proposal for a future Korean government which was sent on to the US–USSR Joint Commission.

On Nov. 3, 1946 elections were held for a Congress of People's Committees at which time the Democratic Front (dominated by the **Korean Workers Party**, the renamed Communist Party) won 97 per cent of the vote. This Committee created a People's Assembly which was to meet every two years. When the UN suggested that general elections should be held under UN auspices, the Soviet Union forbade the holding of the elections in their zone. Instead, in November 1947, a constitutional committee was formed which produced a basic law which was promulgated in May 1948. Elections were held under this constitution on Aug. 25, 1948. These elections effectively created the Democratic People's Republic of Korea. The first meeting of the Supreme People's Assembly was on Sept. 3, 1948 at which time Kim Il Sung was elected premier. The Soviet Union recognized this government in October and withdrew its troops in December of the same year.

During the period before the **Korean War**, the North Korean government and the party made numerous attempts to control and limit the degree of political discussion within the new state. Religious groups were strictly controlled and effectively eliminated as independent bodies of opinion. Political parties were similarly muzzled or eliminated. With these challenges to his rule gone, Kim Il Sung had only to face opposition from within the communist ranks itself. The possible sources of opposition were the four communist factions other than Kim's own Manchurian group: i) communists from northern Korea; ii) communists from southern Korea; iii) communists who had been in the Soviet Union; and iv) communists who had been in China with the Chinese communists (the Yenan faction). Kim purged the North Korean communists as early as 1946. The South Korean faction was purged in 1953 following the Korean War on the charge that they had acted as agents of American imperialism. The Yenan and Soviet factions were attacked by Kim's henchmen from 1953 until the First Conference of Party Representatives in March, 1958. The purge of those latter two factions meant that from then on Kim's power would be complete and supreme.

During the battle for political supremacy, Kim developed a theory of national development called **Juche (Chuch'e)** which emphasized independent development in the areas of party political thought, economic development and defence. While this idea has a great deal of appeal to nationalists as an independent line of development, it was clearly developed for the purpose of solidifying Kim's personal political power.

In terms of international politics, North Korea during the late 1950s moved closer to China, and became especially close in the early 1960s following the Sino-Soviet split. However, following the fall of Khruschev, relations with the

Soviet Union improved again. Since then, North Korea has played a cagey game of balancing its relationship with one of these powers against the other.

The question of the succession to Kim Il Sung became a major political problem once it was clear that Kim was tightly in control of the political scene. Throughout the 1960s it seemed that his younger brother Kim Yŏng-ju (1922–) would succeed him as leader. However, from the early 1970s, Kim Yŏng-ju's position was increasingly threatened by **Kim Jong Il** (1941–), the son of Kim Il Sung's first wife. When Kim Jong Il was made a member of the party secretariat, Kim Yŏng-ju left that body to become Deputy premier, and was then dropped altogether in 1977. Strangely, nothing further was heard of Kim Jong Il until 1979.

By 1980, at the sixth congress of the Korean Workers Party, Kim Jong Il was confirmed as his father's successor and was styled as the "Dear Leader". Since then, Kim Jong Il has become Secretary of the Party Central Committee, and a member of the Politburo, the Presidium and the party Military Committee. A personality cult of Kim Jong Il rivalling his father's cult was also inaugurated. In 1983, Japanese newspapers reported that more than 1,000 people had been purged because of their opposition to the dynastic succession of Kim Jong Il to his father's position, and there were rumours a few years ago of an unsuccessful coup.

From the late 1950s to the present day, a Stalinist type of personality cult adulating Kim Il Sung has been one of the most significant features of the North Korean political landscape. Everything which has happened – and some things which may not have happened – are attributed to the "Great Leader". The yearly calendar is filled with dates concerned with his life, and places alleged to have been associated with his exploits have become historic, pilgrimage sites. The economic development of the nation has been attributed solely to his wisdom and especially the Juche idea. In October 1988, the 40th anniversary of the founding of the Democratic People's Republic of Korea was celebrated as a victory of Kim's thought. In 1989 Kim is celebrating his 77th birthday, and the entire populace have been urged to make some contribution to the celebrations. Even foreign organizations were requested to send special congratulations in his honour.

Recent developments. Being a closed society, it is very difficult to say anything with certainty about internal developments in North Korea. However, it does seem that the question of the succession to Kim Il Sung and the relatively poor economic performance of the country are two matters of profound concern in the leading political circles of the country. Since Kim Jong Ils's elevation to the role of successor, there have been several indications of discontent including the flight of senior military officers to China in 1982, the alleged purge of a 1,000 or more party officials in 1983, and the subsequent radio report of the "death" of Kim Il Sung heard in the south at the Demilitarized Zone. It is clear that not all accept the verdict of the 1980 party conference. The succession question will remain a constant source for internal instability.

Increasing awareness of the outstanding economic performance of South Korea, and their own knowledge of the failure of the North Korean economy to meet designated goals, and to pay off their incurred debts will undoubtedly lead many in the leading circles of North Korea to be critical of the system as it presently exists. This economic dissatisfaction is another potential source of political instability.

Externally, the picture is not bright for the northern regime, either. South Korea's consistent foreign policy goal since the early 1970s has been to woo the Eastern bloc, especially the Soviet Union and China. North Korea's policy has been the reverse, to vilify their enemies, especially the United States. Very little thought is given to the effects on world opinion with regard to the acts of terrorism committed by North Korea against the South. Thus, the Rangoon bombing incident of 1983 when members of the South Korean cabinet were killed, and the planting of a bomb in November, 1987 aboard a Korean Air aeroplane which exploded over Thailand cost the North dearly in world opinion. Superficially, world condemnation of such acts seemed to go unnoticed by the North Korean authorities. Because of such terrorist involvement, the communist bloc refused to support a North Korean boycott of the Seoul Olympics in 1988. Moreover, as a result of these terrorist acts the south has drawn closer with virtually all the communist nations and will probably establish diplomatic relations with many of them. In the long term, North Korea cannot sustain continued diplomatic losses such as these.

Probably as a "consolation gift" to avoid a total North Korean loss of face over the hosting of the twenty-fourth Olympiad in Seoul by South Korea (ROK), the Soviet Union and its bloc gave the hosting in July, 1989 of the World Festival of Youth and Students to North Korea (the DPRK). Tremendous construction projects have been undertaken in P'yongyang with financial assistance from the Soviet Union and certain pro-North Korean figures in Japan.

The question of national re-unification is probably the matter of greatest political concern in contemporary South Korea. It is hard to meeasure North Korean public opinion on this matter, but it is undoubtedly the same. President Kim has on several occasions made various pronouncements with regard to national re-unification, largely revolving around the idea of the creation of a confederal union of states with a single army. He has also stated on several occasions his willingness to meet with the head of the ROK, and in a message at the beginning of this year announced a list of respected persons from the South whom he would like to invite to the North for consultations. However, in spite of these formal announcements, the North Korean government has produced little in the way of public documents which set out in detail the goals of re-unification talks and the methods by which these goals might be achieved. The south on the other hand has not only produced volumes of material on the subject of re-unification, but has an entire government ministry devoted to the task.

Outline of economic development. In discussing the North Korean economy, it is important to remember that significant amounts of quantifiable economic statistics have not been issued since the 1960s. The foundations of North Korean economic growth are the same as in South Korea with the additional observation that North Korea is richer in mineral resources than the South. Prior to the war, there was an extensive land reform programme which initially returned the land to the tiller. Immediately following the Korean War, a Three-Year Economic Plan (1953–56) was instituted to return industrial and agricultural production to pre-war levels. During this plan there was extensive Soviet and Chinese aid. Reconstruction of the national economy was based upon a rigid, centralized plan which expropriated any agricultural surplus and severely restricted domestic consumption. Under such measures, an annual growth rate of 41.8 per cent was said to have been achieved.

Following this plan, a Five-Year Plan (1957–61) was instituted. The goals of this plan were achieved a year ahead of schedule, and an annual economic growth rate of 36 per cent was said to have been achieved. At the Central Committee plenum which established this Five-Year Plan, a new movement, the Chollima (One Thousand Li Horse, or Flying Horse) Movement was started. Like the horse which could move a thousand *li*, the North Korean economy was supposed to fly into the future. Although this plan had been immensely successful, analysis of the results made it clear that there were also important economic problems which were attributable to over-centralization.

These same economic problems emerged again in the Seven-Year Plan (1960–67). The goals of this plan were not achieved and the date for the completion of the ambitious plan had to be postponed until 1970. Although a growth rate of 18 per cent per year had been intended, an actual growth rate of only 12 per cent was achieved. Analysis of the plan showed the failings to be the result of inefficient management and the labour force's general lack of necessary advanced skills. During the course of this plan, two new ideas were put forward, the Chongsan-ni method and the Taean method. Said to be the idea of the "Great Leader", it was suggested that agricultural and industrial leaders should consult with their workers in order to find ways to best achieve the designated economic targets.

The Six-Year Plan (1971–76) intended to advance through the importation of sophisticated technology as had been done in the South. This plan was clearly designed as a reaction to the growing economic power of the South with which the North was now in competition. In spite of extensive importation of technology and materials, exports dropped sharply, and North Korea failed to pay off its massive debts. The drought of 1976 also meant that many agricultural goals were not achieved. 1977 was declared a year of readjustment. In the same year, world banks and financial institutions rescheduled North Korea's debts for another five years.

Since debt restructuring, there have been two Seven-Year Plans. The Seven-Year Plan for 1978–84 was announced in 1978. Analysis of this plan revealed that all of the targets for development except for electricity output were lower than the goals which had been set for the year 1974. Special emphasis was laid on mining, the export of minerals being a major North Korean source of revenue. In 1985, the government announced that all economic goals had been exceeded and that an annual growth rate of 12.2 per cent had been achieved. There was a three-year hiatus before the announcement of another Seven-Year Plan. The goals for the Seven-Year Plan for 1987–93 call for a 90 per cent increase in industrial output, a 40 per cent increase in agricultural output, and an 80 per cent rise in the production of consumer goods. It is an indication of the stagnation of the North Korean economy that the goals set to be achieved by 1993 were in fact goals which were to have been achieved by 1989 according to predictions made in 1980.

Current economic situation and prospects for development. Although North Korea possesses a highly literate and educated population, and in spite of the fact that the nation is rich in mineral resources, the overall economic situation is not good. Not only is North Korea not able to meet its own long-range goals on target, it is falling further behind in the economic competition with the South – which started its economic development with far greater disadvantages than the North. The paralysis of the North Korean economy is attributable to over-centralization of planning, and an inability to produce workers and technicians with sophisticated technical knowledge. The North Korean economy, in a word, is stagnant and will remain so in all probability.

North Korea has poor investment potential not only because of its economic stagnation, but because of its poor debt repayment record, possibly the worst in the world. It is also unlikely that massive outside investment from the Western world would be accepted even if it were offered. To have significant numbers of Westerners in North Korea would undoubtedly bring about the demise of the political system itself, which could not be tolerated. It is for this reason that it was plain from the first that the offer by the head of the Hyundai Group, Chong Chuyong, to participate in the development of North Korea would be refused. Politically, knowledge of the superior economic position of the South could not be tolerated.

Unless there is a massive change in the political structure of the nation, there does not seem to be any significant prospect for economic reform.

JHG

KOREA, REPUBLIC OF (SOUTH KOREA).
Note: *see also* **Korea**.) *Population*: 42,110,895. *Area*: 99,143 sq km. *Gross Domestic Product*: US$ 158,200 million. *Trade*: US$ 112.3 billion (exports: US$ 60,600 million; imports: US$ 51,700 million). *Top five trading partners*: Japan, USA, Hong Kong, Canada, West Germany. *Defence spending*: US$ 8,330 million (1989). *Education spending*: US$ 4,540 million (1989). *Urban population as percentage of total*: 69. *Birth-rate*: 16.5 per thousand. *Life expectancy*: males, 65.2; females, 71.5.

Outline of political history. In conformity with the principles agreed upon at the Cairo conference of December 1943 and the Yalta conference of February 1945, the United States and the Soviet Union agreed to take the surrender of the

Japanese forces in Korea north and south of the 38th parallel. During the twilight period of Japanese rule in Korea in the summer of 1945, citizen committees arose in many communities to run the functions of government. In the southern half of Korea, these committees formed themselves into a "People's Republic of Korea" on Sept. 6, 1945. When the American forces under the command of Lt. Gen. John R. Hodge arrived in Korea on Sept. 8 they were under orders not to recognize any political party or group. Due to the inability of the Soviet and American commanders of the various surrender zones to agree upon various matters, a conference was held in December 1945 in Moscow which approved the principle of a limited term of trusteeship for Korea, the setting up of a provisional government, and the creation of US–USSR Joint Commission.

The USA made various attempts to implement this agreement. The meetings of the Joint Commission utterly failed to reach any common agreement on the future of Korea. Consequently, the American Military Government proceeded to pursue a policy of land reform, to hold legislative elections and to create a South Korean Interim government by February, 1947, while at the same time the US government brought the issue of Korea's future before the United Nations. A Temporary Commission on Korea was created which supervised elections in the southern half of Korea on May 9, 1948. Due to the refusal of the Soviet authorities, United Nations representatives were not allowed into the north. The elections led to the creation of an assembly, a national constitution and the former proclamation of the Republic of Korea (ROK) on Aug 15, 1945. **Syngman Rhee** was elected as the first president of the republic. The nation was immediately recognized by the UN.

The early years of the Republic were plagued by internal political strife, local insurrections and economic difficulties. The most notable uprising was the Yosu Incident of November, 1948, a rebellion of young ROK army officers. The political development of the Republic was abruptly halted by the invasion of North Korean forces on 25 June, 1950. By Sept. 15, the North Koreans had pushed the South Korean forces into a narrow area in the south-east with the city of Taegu at its northern point and bounded by the Naktong River on the west side. Pusan became the temporary capital of the country. the UN forces, which had been brought into the conflict as the result of an American request to aid the young Republic, under the command of Gen. Douglas MacArthur (1880–1964) struck back and pushed the North Koreans beyond their capital P'yon-gyang by Oct. 26, 1950. With the counter-attack led by the forces of the People's Republic of China, the UN forces were pushed back to a position south of the 38th parallel. Skirmishing continued back and forth over this parallel for a further two years – even during peace negotiations – until a formal armistice was signed July 27, 1953.

The remaining years of Syngman Rhee's presidency were characterized by political corruption and the manipulation of elections, which led to considerable political unrest. In the spring of 1960, following a manipulated national election, the discovery of a murdered boy's body in Masan sparked off demonstrations which culminated in the Student Revolution of April 14, 1960 in Seoul. This led directly to the overthrow of Rhee and his government. New elections under a new constitution were held on July 29 of that year, installing a cabinet form of government under Yun Poson as President, and Chang Myon as Prime Minister. During the year in which it was in existence, the Second Republic was characterized by extensive student activism and economic instability.

On May 16, 1961, a military coup overthrew the government, and established a military Revolutionary Committee (later, Supreme Council for National Reconstruction) to govern the country. The eventual leader of this group was Gen. **Park Chung-hee** (Pak Chong-hui, 1917–79). In July 1961, a Five-Year Economic Plan was inaugurated and a new constitution promulgated on Dec. 17, 1962. Political parties were formed in early 1963, and elections for the presidency were held on Oct. 15, 1963 and for the National Assembly on Nov. 26 of the same year. Park Chung-hee was inaugurated as president on Dec. 17.

The Third Republic (1963–72) was the period in which the foundations for south Korea's amazing economic growth were laid. The Five-Year Plan from 1962–66 saw an annual growth rate of 8.5 per cent. There was also considerable political turmoil, especially over the question of establishing diplomatic relations with Korea's former colonial master, Japan. In 1963 and again in 1965, there were massive student demonstrations. Although the constitution limited the president to two terms of office, Park had the National Assembly approve a waiver so that he could serve for a third term. This was approved by a referendum in October, 1969. Park was narrowly returned in the presidential elections of April 27, 1971. On July 4, 1972, Park startled the nation with the announcement that his regime had been in secret contact with the North over the question of national re-unification. Because of growing restiveness with Park's authoritarian rule and questions over dialogue with the North, on Oct. 17, 1972, Park dissolved the National Assembly and established martial law, thus bringing the Third Republic to an end.

On Oct. 27, 1972, a new constitution was announced which was approved by referendum on Nov. 21, 1972. This gave the president extraordinary powers, weakened the National Assembly and created a body, the National Conference for Unification which elected the president and one third of the members of the National Assembly. The years of the Fourth Republic under the Yusin (Revitalization) Constitution were politically turbulent and economically active and progressive. A Presidential Decree of Jan. 4, 1974 made any criticism of the constitution a severely punishable offence. This only led to further demonstrations and unrest. On Aug. 15, 1974, Park's wife died in an assassination attempt on his life. The decrees were relazed after this and a referendum held on the constitution in February, 1975. Confirmation of 73 per cent was obtained.

Continued suppression of political dissent throughout 1975 and 1976 led to a statement by leading dissidents demanding Park's resignation which was read out in the Roman Catholic cathedral in Seoul on March 1, 1976. The reaction to this declaration led to further suppression of dissent and to further political unrest. Park could probably have ridden out this political unrest, but was undone by economic problems. By the spring and summer of 1979, there was increasing labour unrest over low wages culminating in massive civil unrest in various southern cities. On Oct. 26, 1979, Park was assassinated by Kim Chae-gyu, the head of the Korean CIA, probably as a result of the criticism which Park had made of the way in which Kim had handled the civil unrest.

Following the death of Park Chung-hee, the Premier, Choi Kyu-hah (1919-) became Acting President, and was confirmed in office by the National Conference on Dec. 6, 1979 as President. President Choi promised a new and more democratic constitution would be written. Shortly after that, on Dec. 12, there was a military revolt against the existing structure which brought Gen. Chun Doo Hwan (1931-) to power. Throughout the early part of 1980, demonstrations against the current political situation continued. One of the most severe, and the most brutally suppressed, was the **Kwangju Incident** of May, 1980. Gen. Chun became effective ruler of the country after that and forced President Choi to resign on Aug. 16. Chun was made President on Aug. 27 by the National Conference. A new constitution was announced on Sept. 29 and

approved by referendum on Oct. 22. This constitution had a strong presidential system and a relatively weak National Assembly. In November 1980, all political parties and the national Assembly were dissolved and 500 "polluted" politicians were excluded from political life.

The presidential elections under the constitution of the Fifth Republic took place on Feb. 25 and for the Assembly on March 25, 1981. Like its predecessor republics, the Fifth Republic was characterized by continued economic growth, significant betterment in the standard of living and political unrest. There were external problems as well, such as the attempt by a North Korean assassination squad to kill Chun on Oct. 9, 1983 in Rangoon. In May 1984, the two leading political dissident figures who were banned from official political activity, **Kim Dae Jung** (Kim Tae-jung, 1935-) and **Kim Young-sam** (1927-) formed the Committee for the promotion of Democracy which became the basis of the New Korea Democratic party founded in January 1985. This suddenly emerged as the largest opposition party in the Assembly elections of February 1985.

During 1985 and 1986, there was continued political unrest, primarily over the authoritarian nature of the Chun regime and its corruption. It was increasingly clear that members of the family of the President and of the President's wife had benefited enormously from the position of their relations. The death of a student, Pak Chongch'ol, in police custody ignited a nationwide series of demonstrations. On 8 April, 1986, the followers of Kim Dae-Jung and Kim Young-sam left the New Korea Democratic Party over questions of how to deal with the Chun regime and formed the Reunification Democratic Party.

Chun, true to his promise not to serve another seven-year term, announced the name of his successor on June 2, 1986. This announcement led to the greatest civil unrest in modern Korean history. Unlike previous demonstrations which were largely confined to student dissidents, these demonstrations occurred in 57 cities and encompassed people of all ages and social classes. Chun's protégé, **Roh Tae Woo** (No T'ae-u, 1932-) acceded to the opposition leaders' demands, which included a change in the constitution permitting direct election of the president by popular vote.

This major victory of the opposition was spoiled by the opposition's inability to produce a single candidate for the elections. On Dec. 16, 1987, Roh faced a divided opposition, Kim Young-sam as head of the Reunification Democratic Party and Kim Dae Jung as head of the **Party for Peace and Democracy**. Roh obtained 35 per cent of the popular vote, Kim Young-sam,

27.5 per cent, and Kim Dae Jung 26.5 per cent. On Dec. 21, 1987, the two major opposition parties apologized to the nation for splitting the opposition. The position of the political opposition was greatly improved in the elections for the National Assembly on April 26, 1988. The three major opposition parties collectively for the first time in decades controlled the Assembly.

Under the new constitution which had been approved, the Sixth Republic was given an Assembly with considerable power and strength. This meant that the President and his cabinet could not automatically do as they wished.

Recent developments. Important events of 1988–89 included the close co-operation between the various opposition forces and consultation by the president with opposition leaders. The Three Kims (Kim Young-sam, Kim Dae Jung and Kim Jong Pil – a former associate and premier of Park Chung-hee) met frequently to discuss joint courses of action. One of Roh's first significant acts after the Assembly elections was a meeting with the Three Kims on May 28, 1988.

Now that the political situation has improved, Koreans have placed greater interest on the achievement of national re-unification. ROK government proposals for re-unification go back at least as far as the July 4, 1972 announcement by President Park that the North and South had been in secret consultation about prospects for re-unifying the nation. On July 7, 1988, President Roh proposed a six-point plan for national re-unification. Points covered included i) the exchange visits of selected groups of people; ii) the exchange of correspondence with and visits by members of families who were separated during the **Korean War**; iii) free and open trade between the two sections of the Korean nation; iv) the acceptance by the Republic of Korea to the North's trading with nations friendly to the South; v) the end to a confrontational diplomatic war to achieve recognition at the expense of the other side; and vi) a pledge by the government of the Republic of Korea to assist the North in gaining diplomatic and commercial recognition by the South's allies.

The focus of recent student demonstrations has been over the achievement of national re-unification. These recent demonstrations have taken an increasingly violent and anti-American turn. The United States is seen to be solely responsible for the division of Korea and for the support of successive authoritarian military regimes in the south.

From July 1988 the National Assembly has had a committee which has been investigating the financial misdeeds of the family members of the Chun regime. The effect of these investigations was to alienate Chun and Roh. Chun was forced to make a statement of apology to the nation on Nov. 23, 1988, and went into internal exile in a Buddhist temple on the east coast.

There remains the parliamentary investigation of the Kwangju Incident. This is potentially the most sensitive issue of all. Throughout the Chun years, it was impossible to discuss the brutal suppression of this popular uprising. It has lain as a festering sore for years. Because the USA is blamed for supporting the Korean military – including Chun and Roh – during this period, the Kwangju Incident has become the prime source of anti-Americanism. Continued investigation into this tragedy has in some measure helped to soothe feelings but not to resolve the essential problem.

Foreign relations. The Republic of Korea has made great strides in the international sphere. Among important events during 1988–89 were the successful holding of the Olympics in Seoul betwen Sept. 17 and Oct. 2, 1988. The 1988 Seoul Olympics (the twenty-fourth Olympiad) was the most successful in decades.

In recognition of the economic development of the Republic, many Eastern bloc nations, including the Soviet Union and China, have taken an interest in developing commercial ties with the ROK. On Feb. 1, 1989, Hungary established formal diplomatic relations with South Korea, being the first communist nation to do so.

Outline of economic development. The phenomenal growth of the economy of the Republic of Korea in the past 30 years was founded on at least three principal factors: i) the economic infrastructure of roads, railways, ports and harbours, etc. which was left behind by the Japanese; ii) the Confucian regard for the value and acquisition of education; and iii) the education system from elementary through university level which was created by Protestant missionaries and the Japanese government. During the 1940s, under the first years of the American Military Government and the Rhee regime, there was an initial land reform undertaken which sold farmland to the tiller. This land reform helped to form the basis of a land-holding class in the countryside. The Korean War effectively halted the feeble beginnings of economic development. Folowing the conclusion of hostilities in 1953, the nation was concerned with reconstruction rather than further development. Also, during the end of the Rhee years, corruption was rife and the government had no firm, long-range plans for the development of the national economy.

The real growth of the South Korean economy began during the early years of the 1960s following upon the military overthrow of parliamentary government and the establishment of the Third Republic. Even before the formal, constitutional establishment of the new republic, the Supreme Council for National Reconstruction created an economic framework and planning policy for the country which continues more or less to the present day. It was the Council which introduced the idea of strong government intervention in the growth of a capitalistic economy. The government would set the parameters for frowth and private capital and companies would set out to fulfill the goals laid down by the government economic planners.

South Korea has had six successive five-year economic plans. The overall long-term goal of these plans has been to create an export-led economy producing a range of goods from textiles to highly sophisticated technological machinery. Each phase has set a higher priority not only in terms of productive output but in terms of the quality and sophistication of the goods produced. It has also meant initially that there would have to be a dependence on foreign capital and the importation of sophisticated technology and techniques. The First Five-Year Plan (1962–66) emphasized textiles and other light industrial exports and achieved an annual growth rate of 8.5 per cent. The Second Five-Year Plan (1967–71) had the same export goals and achieved an annual growth rate of 10.5 per cent and even reached a peak of 15.9 per cent in 1969. The Third Five-Year Plan (1972–76) emphasized the growth of heavy industry especially shipbuilding, steel manufacture, and automobile and motor production. The Hyundai shipyards in Ulsan were enlarged in 1972 and produced 313,000 tonnes of ships by 1974. The P'ohang steelworks commenced operation in 1973 and by 1975 were producing 1.4 million tonnes of steel. Korean-designed cars were being produced by 1976. The annual growth during this period was 10.9 per cent, exceeding the projected figure of 8.6 per cent. The Fourth Five-Year Plan (1977–81) emphasized the growth of "high-tech" industries and the end of Korea's chronic balance of payments deficit. This latter goal was not achieved in this period. The Fifth Five-Year Plan (1982–86), the first of the Chun Fifth Republic, had the same goals as the previous plan. From 1982 onward, South Korean exports have exceeded imports in value. We are presently in the midst of the Sixth Plan (1987–91). Perhaps the most significant feature to date is that in 1988 the volume of trade by South Korea exceeded US$ 100,000, million.

Prospects for development. During the years 1988–89, the opening of commercial relations with the Eastern bloc is a milestone. On May 31, 1988, Hungary opened a trade office with South Korea, which subsequently became an embassy. Discussions and agreements have been reached with several other East European nations including the Soviet Union. In August 1988 commercial sea lanes between the ROK and the Soviet Union were opened. In October 1988 discussions were held with the People's Republic of China with regard to formal commerical ties. In December 1988 the Overseas Construction Association of Korea announced that it was considering plans to assist in the development of Siberian mineral resources.

It was reported in August 1988 that although the growth rate of the South Korean economy had slowed down, it was running around 11.8 per cent. In September 1988 it was reported that the economic position of South Korea was better than Japan in its Olympic year in 1964. It was announced in October that South Korean debt repayment was now running ahead of schedule. In November 1988, total trade volume exceeded US$ 100,000 million. In February 1989, analysis of the volume of trade on the Korean stock market showed it to be the 11th largest in the world.

Various indicators showed that the standard of living continued to increase. Economic reports released in January, 1989 showed that over one half of the Korean population were economically in the middle class. Although farm income lagged behind urban income, in 1988, farm income rose 24 per cent.

It seems likely that the South Korean economy will maintain a high-level of growth with a continued broader distribution of the economic benefits of an advanced economy. Although the country may seem politically to be in turmoil, national economic performance has not been hindered and probably will not be in the future. In fact, greater internal and external political stability may be expected from the ever-growing contacts which the ROK has with the communist Eastern bloc. If the Korean economy would become more open to foreign sales and if the Korean stock market would open to foreign investors, the country would make a most attractive place for investment. Korea itself will probably continue to seek greater commercial ties with the East and possibly to expand formal diplomatic relations with this bloc while at the same time looking to invest Korean money and industry overseas.

JHG

KOREAN WAR. Of all the conflicts in the Pacific, that between North and South Korea has been perhaps the most virulent and long lasting. It is also a conflict that has involved others, partly because of the strategic importance of the Korean peninsula, and partly because it became bound up with the Cold War between the West and the communist world.

Both China and Japan have long seen Korea as a dagger which can be pointed at the heart of either of them. Not surprisingly, therefore, both countries throughout much of their history have been anxious to control Korea. In 1910 Japan annexed Korea and controlled it until World War II. During the war the allies agreed that Korea should become an independent state, but also made provision for temporary division of the country at the 38th parallel with the Soviet Union in charge of the northern zone and the United States the southern zone. Although the two outside powers were expected to set up a provisional government for the whole of Korea this did not occur. Instead, a provisional communist government was established in the north in February 1946 and the Soviet Union subsequently refused to allow elections there. Elections were held in the southern zone and in August 1948 the independent Republic of Korea was established. In December 1948 the Soviet Union withdrew its forces from North Korea and the United States followed suit, leaving South Korea in mid-1949.

Neither North nor South Korea was happy with the division of the country and tension between the new governments escalated until on 25 June 1950, North Korean forces crossed the 38th parallel and advanced into the South. This was seen in Washington not as part of a civil war but as an aggression which presaged a change in Soviet tactics and which had to be contained if further aggression was to be deterred. Analogies between the North Korean attack and the actions of Hitler in the 1930s gave the issue considerable urgency in Washington as did the similarities between divided Korea and divided Germany. The result was that when American air power failed to halt the North Korean assault, the United States committed its ground forces under the auspices of the United Nations. General Douglas MacArthur was placed in command of the UN force.

The war itself initially went very badly for South Korean and United Nations forces, but with the landing of United States forces at Inchon, North Korean forces were forced to retreat. In spite of reassurances that the United States was only interested in restoring the *status quo ante*, the success in repelling the attack encouraged MacArthur to advance into North Korea. Assurances were given to Communist China that the United States was not interested in going beyond

the Yalu. MacArthur, however, made more threatening statements. In response, Beijing attempted to make clear to Washington how seriously it viewed the attempt to unify Korea under United Nations auspices. This concern was not fully appreciated in Washington and MacArthur was allowed to exploit his success. When this, in turn provoked Chinese intervention, the United States was taken by surprise both politically and operationally. The UN forces were compelled to retreat in the face of the North Korean offensive. Fighting eventually stabilized along the 38th parallel, and the war continued until 1953 when President Eisenhower let it be known that unless there was a cessation of hostilities the United States might be prepared to contemplate the use of nuclear weapons. An armistice was concluded and a provisional boundary was agreed along a demilitarized zone (DMZ) mainly to the north of the 38th parallel and to be supervised by UN forces. This has remained the effective boundary between the two Koreas. A joint military armistice commission consisting of representatives of UN and North Korean forces has met in Panmunjon since 1953. The war solidified the division of the country and revealed very clearly that attempts to change the *status quo* in either direction were likely to prove both risky and costly. It also helped to draw the battle lines of the Cold War more clearly in the Pacific, doing much to crystallize the American commitment not only to South Korea itself, but also the commitment to Taiwan and to the French in Indochina. The Chinese intervention also meant that US–Chinese relations were to be frozen into a pattern of hostility until the early 1970s.

In spite of the armistice in 1953, Korea has been a scene of considerable tension and occasional crises which have threatened to engulf the peninsula in war once again. North Korea was responsible for seizing the United States intelligence gathering ship, the *Pueblo*, in 1968. During 1974–75 several incidents occurred at sea, in which gunboats and fishing vessels of both sides were sunk. The discovery that North Korea had dug a series of tunnels beneath the demilitarized zone also served to increase tension. In an incident near Panmunjon in August 1976 two US officers were killed. There was also a sharp deterioration in the relationship in 1980. The infiltration of agents into the South and several naval clashes forces led both sides to place their forces on alert.

There have, of course, been negotiations aimed at overcoming the division of the country. Proposals for talks on possible re-unification were made by North Korea in April 1971 but were rejected by South Korea as unreasonable. On July 4, 1972, however, it was announced that North and South Korea had reached agreement that "peaceful unification of the fatherland" should be achieved as early as possible, that hostile propaganda and armed provocation should cease, and that a co-ordinating committee should be set up. This committee subsequently held its first meeting at the end of November 1972. Although negotiations continued sporadically throughout the 1970s, there were important differences of emphasis. South Korea proposed a non-aggression pact, while North Korea placed considerable emphasis on the withdrawal of foreign troops from Korea (a proposal aimed at the US contingent of over 40,000 men in South Korea) and on reduction of each side's armed forces. In effect, both sides were using the negotiating process to continue their competition rather than to search seriously for a settlement. Nevertheless, there were some important developments. In 1980, North Korea declared itself ready to sign a peace treaty with the United States prior to the removal of US forces from the South. It also proposed that the two Koreas be reunited as a confederal state, with each retaining its own social system. South Korea rejected these proposals and, in 1982, elucidated plans for re-unification through a conference of representatives which would draw up a draft constitution. This idea was rejected by North Korea.

These diplomatic exchanges were accompanied by continued incidents between North and South Korea. Infiltrators were shot in South Korea while North Korea seized South Korean fishing boats and "spy ships". While these incidents had become fairly commonplace, a more serious development took place on Oct. 9, 1983 when 21 people, including four members of the South Korean government, were killed by a bomb explosion in Rangoon (Burma). The President of South Korea arrived a few minutes later and it was widely believed that the intention had been to kill him. Burma announced the following month that the bomb had been planted by North Korean army captains, and in December two North Korean officers were sentenced to death in Rangoon for their part in the bombing.

Against this background, North Korea, in January 1984, presented new proposals for re-unification, which suggested that there be tripartite talks to include the USA. While this suggested a new flexibility on the part of North Korea, it was accompanied by statements warning of the danger of nuclear war on the Korean peninsula – a danger that, it was claimed, had been increased by American deployment of nuclear weapons in the South. North Korea was also very quick to condemn the announcement by South Korea that annual military exercises of South Korean and United States forces would begin on Feb. 1, 1985. This also became an issue in 1986 and in response to the announcement that the annual "Team Spirit" joint exercise involving 200,000 men would be held in February, North Korea suspended all negotiations with the South. On April 24, 1986, North Korea announced that it would only resume negotiations if there was a change in attitude in South Korea towards these joint exercises. On the same day a North Korean vessel was sunk by a South Korean warship. An additional source of tension in 1986 was the proposed construction of the Kumgangsang hydroelectric dam about 10 km north of the DMZ. There were fears in South Korea that if the water was ever released it would submerge much of central Korea including Seoul. Consequently, the South announced that it was to begin work on a dam of equal size as a precaution against flooding from the North.

Throughout much of 1987 the familiar pattern of proposal and mutual denunciation continued. There were signs of increased flexibility on the part of South Korea which, in September, announced that it would encourage wider contacts beween North and South. With the Olympic Games to be held in South Korea in 1988, however, there was a concerted effort by the United States and South Korea to deter aggressive actions by the North. In October 1987 the first military parade for three years was held in Seoul and displayed for the first time Korean-made tanks and missiles. Although there were some signs of flexibility on the part of the North, on Nov. 29, a Korean Air Line Boeing 707 crashed over Burma killing 115 people. There was considerable circumstantial evidence suggesting that it had been sabotaged and that North Korea was involved.

Because of this 1988 started very badly for the relationship between the two Koreas. North Korea found itself in a particularly difficult position as evidence mounted that it had been responsible for the destruction of the KAL flight. The admission by a North Korean woman that she had helped to plant the bomb led to a quick response. The United States placed North Korea on its list of terrorist nations while Japan imposed trade and diplomatic sanctions. Although South Korea responded in a fairly restrained fashion, the incident had dispelled the sense of progress that had begun to appear in 1987.

During 1988 the pattern continued much as before. Tensions increased in late March and early April as a result of the annual exercise "Team Spirit 88" involving 120,000 South

Koreans and 80,000 Americans. In response to this exercise North Korea placed its forces on full military alert. In the aftermath of this, however, both sides appeared somewhat more conciliatory. North Korea announced a cut of 17 per cent in defence spending while, in July, South Korea announced that it wanted to integrate the North into the international community and that it desired increased trade, family visits and student exchanges. In September Japan lifted its sanctions on North Korea and in October both South Korea and the United States eased their trade restrictions with the North. The fact that the Olympic Games passed without major incident or the systematic attempt at disruption by the North that some had predicted also encouraged further relaxation. Furthermore, partly because of the Olympic Games, South Korea was able to establish better links with the North Korea's major ideological allies – the Soviet Union, China and the East European countries.

There were also signs during the year that both Koreas were prepared to make slight modifications at the diplomatic level and were prepared, if somewhat hesitantly, to allow trading links to develop. What remains unclear is whether this will result in sufficient flexibility at the political level to move beyond the stalemate. In early 1989 it appeared that the traditional pattern of hostility and dialogue was continuing as North Korea insisted that progress in the relationship was impossible so long as South Korea and the United States continued to hold large-scale military exercises.

By this time, however, it was clear that the military conflict had become almost ritualized, and that tension could increase quickly but diminish equally rapidly. The military balance between the two Koreas remained reasonably stable, although both sides are heavily armed. North Korean armed forces number 842,000, although these can be augmented very quickly indeed, with over half a million reserves. The North has around 3,000 main battle tanks and 800 combat aircraft. South Korea has 629,000 members of the armed forces and also has a large reserve system which, in 1988, was undergoing some reorganization. It deploys 1500 main battle tanks and 437 combat aircraft. While there are certain indicators on which North Korea has superiority over the South, this is eroded somewhat by the qualitative edge of at least some South Korean equipment. The balance appears to be sufficiently robust that neither side could initiate hostilities in the expectation that they would result in a rapid or easy victory.

The other constraint on another outbreak of hostilities is, of course, the great powers. Neither Beijing nor Moscow could see much advantage in another war on the Korean peninsula while the United States commitment of forces to South Korea provides a powerful constraint on the North even while exacerbating the diplomatic obstacles to re-unification. Indeed, the annual South Korean–US exercises have an aggravating effect on the relationship between the two Koreas, although even this seems to have something of a ritualistic quality abut it. The implication is that while further hostilities on the Korean peninsula cannot be ruled out completely, especially if there is large-scale domestic instability in either the North or the South, in practice, there does seem to have been an acceptance of the *status quo* and a realization that the costs involved in any attempt to change it could well outweight the gains.

PW

KOREAN WORKERS PARTY (KWP). Established in 1945, the KWP became the ruling party of North Korea in 1948. Initially pro-Soviet in outlook, it became more Chinese in outlook after 1963. In 1966 the KWP asserted the right of independent thought and action of all fraternal communist parties. From 1975 the party stressed the thought of **Kim Il Sung** called **Juche**. In 1980, it designated **Kim Jong Il** as Kim Il Sung's successor. One thousand party members are said to have been purged over the succession question in 1983. The party claimed 1987 membership of three million.

JHG

KORYAKS. An ethnic group inhabiting the northern end of the Kamchatka peninsula in the Far Eastern Region of the Soviet Union. Numbering fewer than 10,000 people, they enjoy administrative–territorial autonomy in the Koryak National District (founded in 1930).

IG

KOWLOON WALLED CITY. In December 1899, a year after leasing the New Territories, the British, under the authority of a Royal Order-in-Council, took over a small Chinese garrison compound called the Walled City of Kowloon, within the leased territory. The British justified this by citing the 1898 Convention of Peking, but successive Chinese governments refused to recognize the legality of the British action. Consequently, the Hong Kong Government refrained from exercising full jurisdiction over this six and a half acres of land. When it has since attempted to do so, it has caused controversies and conflicts between China and Britain, notably in 1934, 1946, 1947-of the 1984 **Joint Declaration**, the two Powers agreed to clear the area for redevelopment.

ST

KUOMINTANG (KMT). The Kuomintang (Chung-kuo Kuo-min-tang) was established after the successful revolution of 1911, by merging the Revolutionary Alliance (Tung-meng-hui), led by Sun Yat-sen, and several smaller parties. With the help of Soviet advisors the party was reorganized along marxist-leninist lines in 1923-1924. Completing the unification of war-torn China in 1927, the KMT became the ruling party until its defeat by the **Chinese Communist Party** in 1949.

Following this defeat the party leadership moved to Taiwan. Under the chairmanship of **Chiang Kai-shek**, the KMT started a comprehensive reform effort in 1950. Replacing the established party institutions, a "Central Reform Committee" mapped out plans for restructuring the party and its membership. When the 7th Party Congress was convened in March 1952 to mark the end of the party reform, about 20,000 party members had been purged. A new party leadership was elected, among the 50 members of the Central Committee only 21 of the 222 members of its predecessor were re-elected.

The party's ideology is based on the "Three Principles of the People" by Sun Yat-sen in its conservative interpretation by Chiang Kai-shek. Aiming at the realization of Sun's teaching and making Taiwan a model province for the future development of China, the KMT is still striving for the destruction of Communist rule on the Chinese mainland and an eventual re-unification of China.

The chairman of the party, an office held by Chiang Kai-shek until his death in 1975, thereafter by his eldest son, **Chiang Ching-kuo**, stands at the apex of an elaborate party apparatus run by more than 3,200 professional cadres. Below the national party headquarters, comprising seven departments and four commissions, are 17 provincial-level party headquarters organized along geographical and sectoral lines. To finance its activities, the party can rely on the returns of a number of business enterprises, comprising publishing and insurance companies as well as several productive enterprises.

Although the party leadership has been dominated by mainland Chinese, the party membership of 2.4 million consists mostly of Taiwanese. More than 60 per cent are younger than 35 years of age. Considering itself an elite party membership recruitment has been directed primarily at persons with a better than average education. Workers, farmers and fishermen constitute only 28 per cent of the membership.

The KMT derives its legitimacy to rule Taiwan from the so-called "*fa-t'ung*", the constitution and the results of the elections of 1948. Since the early 1970s, the KMT has made great efforts to strengthen its legitimacy by obtaining electoral support on Taiwan. Its share of votes in national supplementary elections averaged 70 per cent in the last decade. The growing importance of elections has increased the influence of parliamentarians vis-à-vis the government bureaucracy and the party apparatus.

While the party leadership, consisting of the chairman and the 31 members of the central standing committee (CSC), meets regularly once a week, neither the party's national convention nor its central committee have been convened according to the prescriptions of the party charter in the last two decades, due to the often precarious health of the party chairmen.

After the death of Chiang Ching-kuo in January 1988 **Lee Teng-hui**, Chiang's successor as President, has been elected as Acting Chairman of the party. Preparing for increasing competition with other political parties after the termination of martial law the KMT took steps to enlarge the scope of intra-party democracy. Reforms in the organizational structure will strengthen the party's role in policy-making and its performance in electoral compaigns. In July 1988, the party's 13th National Convention confirmed Lee Teng-hui as party chairman. Sixteen of the newly elected 31 members of the CSC are of Taiwanese origin.

HH

KURIL ISLANDS. A chain of islands running south-west from the southern tip of the Kamchatka peninsula in the far east of the Soviet Union to the north-east of Hokkaido in Japan. They passed from Japanese to Soviet control in 1945 on the basis of the 1945 Yalta agreement, although Japan still claims sovereignty over the southernmost islands. (*See also* **Japan-Soviet Union Conflict; Northern Territories Dispute**)

IG

KWANGJU INCIDENT. The most significant public disturbance in South Korea since the 1940s. Continued student demonstrations throughout Korea in early 1980 led to the imposition of martial law on May 17, 1980. The violent suppression of student demonstrations in

Kwangju on May 18 led to a popular uprising beginning May 19 which drove army out of the city. By May 21, unrest had spread throughout South Chŏlla Province. Citizen groups began negotiations with the army on May 22, but the army moved into city in force on May 27 killing at least 170 people by government estimates. Locals claimed that as many as 2,000 people were brutally killed. Because of the command relation of the US Army to the Korean Army, radical student groups blame the United States for the incident.

JHG

L

LABOUR PARTY (NEW ZEALAND). The party represents working class interests, and is dedicated to guaranteeing an adequate standard of living to everyone able and willing to work, as well as to care for the disadvantaged. Since 1984, when the party regained power, it has been committed to an anti-nuclear policy.

TBM

LAND REFORM. Land reform has been an essential basis of social change and economic growth throughout much of the Pacific region. Post-war reform in Japan, Taiwan and South Korea undoubtedly was a contributory factor to those countries' economic lift-off. Revolutionary societies such as China and the Soviet Union similarly put great emphasis on the redistribution of land ownership, though in such cases public ownership and co-operatives took precedence over giving land titles to individual farmers or families. It became clear however that within socialist societies, the productivity of private plots was usually higher than that of co-operatives and collectives, especially when the financial incentive of a freer market was added, as happened in China during the 1980s as a result of the reforms of **Deng Xiaoping**.

The demand for land reform has long been a major campaigning issue of insurgents in the Philippines. Despite **Corazon Aquino's** own family's large landholdings, a prime expectation of her government has been the implementation of "land to the people". Accordingly, a land reform bill was passed in 1988, under which about a quarter of the country's agricultural land would be handed over to approximately 2,000,000 landless Filipinos over a period of 10 years. Large landowners would be obliged to sell most of their holding to the government, but since the passing of the bill, there have been successful attempts to increase the amount of land families could retain for themselves. Observers expect the whole process to be subject to legal and other delays.

Several Latin American countries instituted land reform during this century, notably Mexico, Bolivia and Peru. But the pattern of land ownership is still inequitable in many parts of the continent, especially in Brazil and Guatemala. The Sandinistas in Nicaragua appropriated land after the Revolution of 1979, much of which had under Anastasio Somoza been in the hands of just a few families. In El Salvador too, the Christian Democrat government of Jose Napoleon Duarte managed to bring in some significant land reform during the 1980s, despite the raging civil war.

Within free enterprise societies, there is always the danger that the benefits of land reform will be undone by the subsequent re-concentration of land under the control of wealthy families or companies. Moreover, in Malaysia and Thailand, for example, there has been acute concern about the threat of increased foreign ownership of land. Legislative steps have been taken to try to prevent that.

JF

LANGE, RT HON DAVID RUSSELL. Prime Minister and Minister of Education of New Zealand 1984–89. Born in Auckland August 1942. LlB and LlM (Auckland). Barrister and solicitor. Entered parliament (Labour Party) 1977 for the Auckland seat of Mangere. Deputy Leader of the Opposition 1979, Leader 1983. An active member of the Methodist church, Prime Minister Lange initiated the policy of denying entry of nuclear-armed or nuclear-powered ships to New Zealand ports, which led to the United States suspending the application to New Zealand of the terms of the **ANZUS Pact**.

TBM

LANGUAGE. The Pacific is an area of considerable linguistic diversity; there are several hundred vernacular groups in Papua New Guinea alone. In many cases, however, one linguistic group is predominant in individual countries, e.g. Thai, Vietnamese, Korean and Japanese. The vast majority of Chinese nationals speak one or other of the Chinese languages, which are written in the same way, even though the pronunciation may be completely different. China's national language, *putong hua* (Mandarin) is said to be the most widely spoken mother tongue in the world, though English has wider overall usage.

Colonial rulers have left their stamp in many places. Accordingly, Spanish is the official language of most of Latin America. But in Latin countries with large Indian communities, such as Guatemala and Peru, local languages are still vibrant. Among minority groups and cultures around the Pacific, indigenous languages are regarded as an important element of their identity. Attempts by other predominant groups to suppress that identity have sometimes met stiff resistance.

English is the first language of Australia, New Zealand and the United States, as well as the majority language in Canada. A pidgin form is the *lingua franca* of much of the South Pacific. English is also very widely spoken in the Philippines (as a result of the American colonial period) and former British-controlled territories such as Malaysia and Singapore, at least among more educated people. It has also become the major language of international exchange and commerce throughout the region. The spread of computer technology has served to accelerate that process.

JF

LAO PEOPLE'S DEMOCRATIC REPUBLIC (LPDR). *Population*: 3,800,000 (est. 1988). *Area*: 236,800 sq km. *Urban population as percentage of total*: 16. *Birth rate*: 41 per thousand. *Life expectancy*: 50.

Political history. The LPDR was proclaimed in Vientiane on Dec. 5, 1975, following a "national congress of people's representatives" (Dec. 1–2) which had abolished the monarchy. A supreme people's assembly was set up, with **Prince Souphanouvong** as President (and also Head of State). The Council of Ministers was headed by **Kaysone Phomvihan**, already leader of the **Lao People's Revolutionary Party (LPRP)** which had operated in secrecy for 20 years but now emerged as the ruling party: the real power behind the Lao Patriotic Front (which in 1979 was renamed the Lao Front for National Reconstruction). The Patriotic Front, together with the Lao People's Liberation Army, had been free to operate in much of the country during the period since the negotiation of a ceasefire in February 1973 and even more vigorously after May 1975 when they launched a national uprising against the old order.

Nevertheless the new government had to move cautiously and was faced with a number of opposition movements during the next few years, particularly following the right-wing coup in Bangkok in October 1976. In March 1977 the situation was sufficiently serious for the authorities to move King Savang Vatthana and his family out of Luang Prabang to a more remote area, where he is said to have died in 1980. Also in 1977, Laotian and Vietnamese forces began a campaign to suppress a resistance movement by the **Hmong People** who had previously been mobilized by the CIA against the Pathet Lao.

Other resistance groups were mentioned from time to time, led by former ministers in pre-1975 governments. From 1980 there were stories that China was encouraging dissident forces in northern Laos but it was always difficult to assess the reliability of reports or the strength of supposed guerrilla groups. What emerged by 1982, however, was that the ASEAN countries had no intention of giving the same kind of support to anti-government groups in Laos as they were giving to the Coalition Government of Democratic Kampuchea. When former defence minister Phoumi Nosavan claimed to have set up such a government in August that year he was rebuffed by the Thai authorities. The regime could feel fairly secure by the time the LPRP held its third congress in Vientiane in April 1982.

The leadership of the LPDR (and of the Party) was remarkably stable throughout the late 1970s and 1980s, with Kaysone apparently in firm control while his "no. 2", **Nouhak Phomsavan**, was in charge of economic affairs. In a government reorganization at the end of 1982 a number of new faces were promoted, and some veterans retired. It was more difficult to assess reports that at the middle and lower levels of the regime a significant number of cadres were purged after 1980 for being too closely associated with the **Chinese Communist Party**. The first major leadership change came in October 1986, when it became known that Souphanouvong was seriously ill. **Phoumi Vongvichit** took over his position, but shortly afterwards it was emphasized that he was only Acting President.

Foreign relations. The close relationship between the LPRP and the Vietnamese Communist movement ever since the 1950s, and the longstanding connections with Vietnam of both Kaysone Phomvihan and Souphanouvong, have guaranteed essential harmony between Vientiane and Hanoi since 1975. Although the final emergence of the LPDR did not depend on military operations and did not involve Vietnamese military support, the People's Army of Vietnam had played an active role inside Laos ever since 1961 and had provided the real muscle behind the operations of the Pathet Lao. Vietnamese troops stayed in Laos after 1975, and were estimated at various dates to number between 30,000 and 60,000. Their presence (although not such high figures) was acknowledged by the LPDR.

Relations between the two governments were formalized by a treaty of friendship and co-operation signed on July 18, 1977 when **Le Duan** and Pham Van Dong visited Vientiane. In foreign policy, Laos has been content to follow Hanoi's lead, within the context of periodic meetings of the three Indochinese foreign ministers. Kaysone has also followed the Vietnamese lead in developing warm relations with the Soviet Union and has himself paid a number of visits to Moscow. Even though Laos has not joined the CMEA (Comecon), it has received substantial amounts of Soviet and East European economic aid.

The Laotian Communists also maintained friendly relations with China down to the late 1970s. The Chinese had become especially influential in the Pathet Lao province of Phong Saly, in the far north, where as early as 1962 they began to build roads linking it more closely to Yunnan. Following the Sino-Vietnamese War of 1979 a total break occurred, and Chinese teams were withdrawn from northern Laos. In the improving climate of Sino-Soviet relations after 1985, however, Laos was ready to move ahead of its Vietnamese allies in restoring contacts with Beijing.

Another important difference between Laos and Vietnam is that the LPDR automatically inherited the international position of previous regimes, as a member of the United Nations and of various international agencies. It also still had relations with a number of Western countries, although some of these were gradually broken off. Relations with France, broken in 1978, were restored four years later.

Above all, any government in Laos had to establish some kind of working relationship with Bangkok. Laos was dependent on transport routes through Thailand for its most basic supplies while Bangkok was interested in continuing projects under the Mekong development scheme, including the Nam Ngum Dam in Laos, which would eventually supply electricity to north-east Thailand. Relations nevertheless became strained during the 1980s and open conflict erupted on a number of occasions. A dispute erupted in June 1984 over the control of three villages on the border of northern Laos and northern Thailand. An armed confrontation developed, but eventually subsided. There was further tension in the autumn of 1987, when Thailand suspended its purchase of electricity from Laos (now substantial following completion of the second phase of the Nam Ngum project in 1985). Vientiane was forced to sign a new agreement at lower prices than before, which reduced its foreign exchange income. By November, a new and more serious conflict had broken out in the northern border area, and on Dec. 15, 1987 Thai fighters bombed Lao positions in Sayaboury province. A small border war was fought during January – February 1988, with the Lao claiming to have shot down a number of Thai planes. Finally an exchange of visits between Bangkok and Vientiane brought about a ceasefire on Feb. 19 – opening the way to new efforts to improve relations. Relations did in fact improve in 1988–89 following the appointment of **Chatichai Choonhaven** as Thai Prime Minister.

Outline of economic development. The new government of 1975 set about introducing principles of "socialist transformation" and "socialist construction" (based on the Vietnamese model) into an economy which had remained extremely under-developed under colonial rule and was now shattered by the consequences of war. It suffered from a desperate shortage of skilled manpower, made worse by the exodus of the better educated people as refugees and the government's own policy of sending captured members of the former regime for "re-education". On the positive side, however, Laos was already a full member of international financial institutions and a participant in the Mekong Development project, and therefore in a position to continue with some existing programmes not tied to United States aid. It depended on maintaining economic relations with Thailand, in which the Thais themselves had a continuing interest.

"Socialist transformation" implied the gradual co-operativization of agriculture and the creation of state enterprises. By 1979 the government claimed to have created over 2,500 co-operatives (embracing 20–25 per cent of rural families) but much of this total was accounted for by the resettlement of several hundred thousand people displaced by the war, made possible by assistance from the UNHCR. From 1977 there was also a programme of mobilizing labour to clear new land and build irrigation systems and to force hill peoples to abandon "slash-and-burn" in favour of wet-rice agriculture, again involving co-operativization. Laos, unlike many Asian countries, was not short of land. But it was worried about the effects of "slash-and-burn" methods on the forest areas, which still covered about half the country. Timber production was the most important non-agricultural sector of the economy, and it was there that state enterprises were established. Laos had very little industry. The system established in both state enterprises and government departments involved fixed wages, and access to food and other necessities at subsidised prices.

By late 1979 it was recognized that the new economy was functioning badly. Partly owing to three years of unfavourable weather, output of food crops had fallen and forestry, previously an expanding source of export income, had suffered a collapse in 1976–77. Vietnam itself was facing its own crisis following the Sino-Vietnamese war and was in no position to help.

In December 1979 the LPRP's 7th plenum adopted a new economic policy similar to that approved in Vietnam a few months earlier. Agricultural co-operativization was to be slowed down, or even put into reverse in some cases. Restrictions on inter-province trade were reduced and a new wage and price policy represented a first step towards eliminating subsidized prices for state employees. In addition a new currency was introduced to replace the "liberation" *kip* which had become standard in 1976.

One factor in the 1979 changes was encouragement from the IMF, which had greater influence on Laos than on Vietnam. The year 1979 was also a critical one for the continuation of non-Communist aid projects in Laos. In particular the second phase of the Nam Ngum hydroelectricity and irrigation project (under the Mekong Development plan) had been completed in 1978. Other loans were made in 1979 by the International Development Association and the **Asian Development Bank**. This did not, however, alter the fact that by now the LPDR was becoming more closely tied to the socialist economies of Vietnam and of the CMEA countries. Vietnam was eager to strengthen the relationship – for example by modernizing Highway 9, linking Laos with Central Vietnam, and in the longer term by building an oil pipeline from the Vientiane area to Vinh. Of more immediate importance were the growing number of aid projects financed by Soviet and East European aid, including a restoration of tin production (for export to the Soviet Union). Transport was still a major problem. Laos has no railways but Soviet aid was used to improve road communications, particularly between Vientiane and Luang Prabang, and also to open new internal air routes.

The willingness of Laos to co-ordinate its own plans with those of Vietnam and Cambodia became evident during the early 1980s, particularly in the preparation of Five-Year Plans for 1981–85 and 1986–90. Vientiane also followed Hanoi's lead in the sphere of economic reforms. In 1984–85 the trend towards co-operativization was resumed: between January 1985 and February 1987 the number of co-operatives (mostly low-level) grew from around 2,500 to nearly 4,000. But the effect on output was less than the authorities hoped for, and in 1987–88 there were again shortfalls in food production. In 1988, again following Vietnam's lead, the party introduced a new contract system in agriculture which was so liberal as to amount to virtual de-co-operativization. Meanwhile in 1987 decrees were passed to reform both pricing and taxation, and controls on inter-provincial trade were again relaxed. During 1987–88 there was also a determined effort to convert enterprise management from the old system of bureaucratic planning to socialist business accounting: about half the country's 377 enterprises had changed over by March 1988. In July 1988 Laos passed another measure in imitation of the trend in Vietnam: a foreign investment law, allowing 15-year contracts and guaranteeing no nationalization. One area where foreign capital was needed was that of timber production, in which a number of Thai firms had an interest. (Logging was a factor in the border confrontation between Laos and Thailand in 1987–88). Vientiane announced plans to prohibit the export of logs and raw bark after 1988, and to allow only processed wood and rattan products to be exported. But given the poor quality of the Lao processing industry, that policy could only be effective with the injection of foreign capital.

RBS

LAO PEOPLE'S REVOLUTIONARY PARTY (LPRP).

Although it was founded in March 1955, at what was remembered as its first congress, the LPRP did not reveal its existence publicly until late in 1975. It nevertheless played a key role in organizing and commanding the Pathet Lao fighting forces (later the Lao People's Liberation Army, from 1965) and the Lao Patriotic Front during those 20 years. It emerged, fully fledged, as the ruling party of the Lao People's Democratic Republic. Its leading figures – **Kaysone Phomvihan**, **Nouhak Phomsavan** and **Prince Souphanouvong** – were all members of the Indochinese Communist Party by 1949; and the LPRP has continued to collaborate closely with the Vietnamese Communist movement throughout its existence. The second congress of the Party was held, secretly, in February 1972, when the word "Revolutionary" was added to its name. Its third (April 1982) and fourth congress (November 1986) were more public affairs. Kaysone was elected to the position of Secretary-General at all four congresses.

RBS

LAOS. (Note: *see also* **Lao People's Democratic Republic**.)

Geographical background. Present-day Laos occupies a large area of country stretching from the eastern bank of the Mekong River to the mountain areas bordering on Vietnam in the east and China in the north. It also includes some territory on the right bank of the river; but for the most part the Mekong itself constitutes the long border between Laos and Thailand. The ethnic term "Lao", however, includes a substantial number of people living outside Laos – mainly in northeast Thailand. Ironically, too, the presence of a large number of "minority" tribal groups in the upland areas of Laos itself – notably the Tai, the Kha and the **Hmong** – means that inside the country the Lao make up barely half of the total population. There is also a significant Vietnamese minority living in Vientiane and other towns. Culturally, the Laos have been strongly influenced by **Theravada Buddhism** and by the Thai language, to which Lao is closely related.

Pre-modern history. Historically the country was divided between a number of Lao states, the oldest of which (Luang Prabang) is said to have been founded in 1353 by King Fa Ngum who had ties with the *Khmer* capital at Angkor. His kingdom continued to flourish in the fifteenth and sixteenth centuries, despite a Vietnamese incursion in 1478, and developed close relations for a time with the then independent kingdom of Chiang Mai (now in northern Thailand). Around 1560, Vientiane emerged as another important centre. But shortly afterwards all three states came under pressure from the Burmese kingdom of Pegu, and a Burmese army actually captured Vientiane in 1575. The "golden age" came in the time of Souligna Vongsa (1637–94) who reigned in Vientiane and controlled most of what is now Laos as well as part of Thailand. But in the early eighteenth century, following further Vietnamese intrusions, four distinct principalities emerged: at Luang Prabang and at Vientiane (which were relatively independent but paid nominal tribute to either the Vietnamese or the Thai, or to both); at Xieng Khouang, which had close ties with Vietnam; and at Champassak, in the south, which was always a Thai dependency. In 1778 a Thai army actually occupied Vientiane but the balance of influence was restored with the revival of Vietnamese power after 1802. Pressure from the Thai and Vietnamese became even greater during the decade from 1826 to 1836, starting with an attack by Chao Anu of Vientiane on Siam – to which the Thais responded in 1828 by capturing and destroying Vientiane itself and deporting a large number of Lao families across the Mekong into north-east Thailand. The Vietnamese decided not to aid Chao Anu, but asserted stronger control over Xieng Khouang. Further fighting occurred in 1834–36 when, in the context of a wider conflict between Bangkok and Hue, Thai forces invaded the Vietnamese-dominated Plain of Jars. The Vietnamese eventually hit back and drove the Thais out of the area. In all this,

Luang Prabang retained a degree of independence; although it had to pay tribute at one time or another to both Bangkok and Hue it also sent tribute missions to China on a number of occasions between 1730 and the mid-nineteenth century.

The peace of northern Laos was more seriously disturbed from the early 1870s with the arrival in the area of Chinese bands (known as the Ho) who allied themselves with the upland Tai people and began to threaten Luang Prabang. In 1886 Bangkok sent a military expedition to occupy Luang Prabang; a move which in other circumstances might have culminated in Thai annexation of all of what is now Laos. But the French already controlled Vietnam and Cambodia. Further trouble in 1887 led the king to seek French assistance. During the next five years the official and explorer Auguste Pavie laid a basis for French claims to a protectorate over the "east bank" of the Mekong, which Thailand was obliged to accept after a Franco-Thai confrontation in 1893. Laos was thereupon incorporated into the Indochinese Union and remained under French rule until 1945. Vientiane was revived as the administrative capital while Luang Prabang remained the "royal capital"; the royal families of Xieng Khouang and Champassak became mere "governors". In 1907 the French acquired additional territory on the west bank of the Mekong. Following the fall of France in 1940 Thailand made an effort to recover the latter area, as well as part of Cambodia also lost in 1907. A short border war, followed by Japanese mediation, forced the surrender of the territory but it was returned to Laos in 1946. The precise border of Sayaboury was not clearly defined, however; an omission which led to renewed conflict in the area in the 1980s.

French rule was accepted by the lowland Lao people and by an elite which was content to acquire French education and serve the colonial regime. Many aspects of life were completely undisturbed; European investment in the region was limited to the development of a few tin mines. The "tribal" groups in the upland areas were less docile. The Kha people were in a state of simmering revolt from about 1907 to 1936, and rebellions occurred among the Tai and the Lu peoples in the North between 1910 and 1916. The Hmong (or Meo) in Xieng Khouang rebelled in 1919–21. None of this unrest seriously challenged French control of the country, but it reflected the limited extent to which the colonial regime was able to create a unified political entity in Laos.

Early modern history. In April 1945 Japanese troops arrived in Luang Prabang and persuaded

King Sisavang Vong to renounce his allegiance to France. An "independent" government under Prince Phetsarath survived until August, and was then allowed by the Japanese to take effective control in Vientiane. On Sept. 1 the prince issued a new declaration of independence in the hope of securing recognition from the United States and its allies (who had supported a small "free Lao" movement during the war). He was also in touch with the Viet Minh through his half-brother **Prince Souphanouvong**, and could take advantage of the fact that northern Laos fell within the sphere of responsibility of Chinese nationalist forces. But the new regime was unable to prevent French forces from recovering control of Vientiane and Luang Prabang in spring 1946 and Phetsarath's government had to flee to Bangkok. The French introduced a form of constitution in 1947, and a Franco-Laotian convention in July 1949 established the kingdom of Laos as an Associated State within the French Union, with limited autonomy over internal affairs.

By mid-1949 the Phetsarath government-in-exile was in disarray. Many of its supporters returned to Vientiane, including Prince Souvanna Phouma who emerged as Prime Minister of the Associated State. Souphanouvong left Bangkok in May 1949 to rejoin the Viet Minh. In August 1950, somewhere in the Vietnamese *maquis*, he launched his own "Lao Issara" front to fight for independence. With Viet Minh help he created the "Pathet Lao Fighting Forces", which became increasingly active as the anti-French war spilled over into northern Laos. A Viet Minh invasion of Laos in spring 1953 greatly alarmed the French (and the other Western powers). But the Vietnamese then chose to concentrate all their efforts on the battle of Dien Bien Phu and on securing control of the northern half of Vietnam. The Geneva Agreement on Laos (July 21, 1954) left the Pathet Lao in administrative control of the provinces of Sam Neua and Phong Saly but otherwise recognized the essential unity, independence and neutrality of Laos under the government already established in Vientiane. The war ended, but political polarization increased during 1955-56. The Pathet Lao refused to participate in elections held in December 1955, which were conducted by a Royal government now headed by the rightist Katay Don Sasorith. Instead Souphanouvong launched the Lao Patriotic Front in January 1956 to rally support for the Pathet Lao. (Only 20 years later was it revealed that real power behind the front lay with the **Lao People's Revolutionary Party** founded secretly by the Communist leader **Kaysone Phomvihane** in April 1955).

Negotiations between Souvanna Phouma (again Prime Minister by 1956) and Souphanouvong eventually succeeded in establishing a coalition government in November 1958. But opposition from the rightists (and some interference by the American embassy in Vientiane) ensured that it was short-lived. The rightist Phoui Sananikone took over as Prime Minister in mid-1958 and in May 1959 a major crisis erupted. A battalion of Pathet Lao troops refused to be integrated into the Royal Lao Army and went into open revolt. Souphanouvong was detained in Vientiane (until he escaped a year later) and the coalition broke up.

The year 1960 was one of conflict and crisis. A rightist coup in January (led by "strong man" Phoumi Nosavan) was followed by a neutralist coup in August (led by Kong Le) and then a confrontation between the two sides, in which the Phoumists received arms from the United States while Kong Le was supported by Hanoi and by the Soviet Union. In the inevitable fighting the rightists recovered Vientiane in December 1960 but were too weak to counter a Pathet Lao offensive in March-April 1961. The North Vietnamese in the meantime took the opportunity to occupy the whole eastern side of Laos, where the "Ho Chi Minh Trail" was becoming vital to the supply and reinforcement of Communist guerrillas in South Vietnam.

The United States considered direct military intervention but decided to accept a ceasefire negotiated in early May, which opened the way for a new international conference on Laos at Geneva (May 1961–July 1962). The outcome was a reaffirmation of Laotian neutrality – which was to inhibit the Americans from invading Laos throughout the Vietnam War – and the appointment of a new coalition government under Souvanna Phouma. The latter remained premier until 1975, but the coalition soon ran into difficulties and broke up completely following the murder of the neutralist (but pro-Hanoi) foreign minister in April 1963.

Laos was now unable to avoid the repercussions of the conflict in Vietnam, which began to escalate during 1964 and became a "big unit war" from 1965 to 1975. In northern Laos the main American objective was to hold the Communist forces at bay and so preserve Souvanna Phouma's government, which became increasingly pro-American despite its formal neutrality. To this end the Americans not only expanded their military assistance to the Royal army but also used the CIA to mobilize various minority groups, notably the Hmong under the leadership of Vang Pao. There were several periods of heavy fighting on the ground, especially in the much-contested "Plain of Jars"; and almost continuous heavy bombing of the Pathet Lao "liberated" areas. In the south the Americans began bombing the Ho Chi Minh trail in late 1964 and steadily intensified their attacks until the early 1970s. But even B-52s were unable to stop the relentless expansion of North Vietnamese infiltration. Having earlier decided against sending in ground troops to cut it, the Americans supported an ill-fated South Vietnamese incursion in early 1971 which had only limited success and ended in humiliating retreat.

The eventual outcome in Laos depended on the course of the war in Vietnam. In the aftermath of the Paris Agreement there, a parallel agreement was reached in Vientiane on Feb. 21, 1973 imposing a ceasefire in Laos and calling for negotiations to establish yet another coalition government. The negotiations were drawn out but at each stage the Patriotic Front and the Liberation Army (as it had been called since 1965) gradually strengthened their position. At the end of 1973 an agreement to "neutralize" Vientiane allowed them to enter the capital. But it was not until April 1974 that the king signed a decree setting up a government of national union (headed by Souvanna Phouma, with the Communist Phoumi Vongvichit as his deputy) and a "national political consultative council", headed by Souphanouvong who now returned to Vientiane.

The next climax came in May 1975 immediately after the collapse of South Vietnam, when the Party called for a national uprising. Souvanna Phouma was obliged to dismiss the right-wing ministers, and a student movement came into the open calling for an end to American aid operations. The USA was forced to close its AID and other offices in Vientiane on June 30, although it continued to maintain a small embassy there. The Royal army was disbanded and its officers sent for "re-education". On Aug. 23 Vientiane itself was declared "liberated" and most communications with the outside world were broken. Finally on Dec. 1-2, 1975 – although it was not publicly reported until Dec. 5 – a "national congress of people's representatives" abolished the monarchy and proclaimed the Lao People's Democratic Republic.

RBS

LAUREL, SALVADOR. Ex-senator Salvador Laurel of the Philippines, as president of the opposition coalition the United Nationalist Democratic Organization (UNIDO), was **Corazon Aquino**'s running mate during the February 1986 presidential elections; following Aquino's victory and the fall of the **Marcos** regime he was sworn in on Feb. 25, 1986, as Vice-President and appointed on the same day as Prime Minister and the next day as Foreign Minister.

During late 1986 and 1987 Laurel increasingly distanced himself from the Aquino administration, whilst forging links with the right-wing opposition. The largely opportunistic alliance between Aquino and Laurel (compacted with the specific aim of overthrowing Marcos) had begun to break down in the immediate aftermath of their 1986 victory. In September 1987 Laurel complained that Aquino had no clear-cut policies to combat communist insurrection and accused the government of containing communist sympathizers. He also asserted that the President had reneged on an agreement made when he agreed to be her running mate in the 1986 presidential elections, whereby she undertook to allow him to appoint one third of the government. Claiming to have been ignored in the decision making process, he announced on Sept. 16 that he no longer wished to remain as Foreign Secretary (he remained in the elective post of Vice-President). The relationship between Aquino and Laurel continued to worsen during 1988, and in August the Vice-President announced that he had established a new political party, the Union of National Action, with the avowed aim of uniting the right-wing anti-Aquino forces. This it failed to do, but in May 1989 he joined with **Juan Ponce Enrile** in reviving the old **Nacionalista Party**, thereby formalizing the process of political estrangement between himself and the President.

DS

LE DUAN. First Secretary (1960–76) of the Vietnamese Workers' Party (VWP) and then General Secretary of the **Vietnamese Communist Party** (VCP) from 1976 until his death; effectively party leader following the death of **Ho Chi Minh** in 1969. Born in Quang Tri province (Central Vietnam) in 1907, he joined the Indochinese Communist Party in 1930, and was imprisoned by the French from 1931 to 1936 and again in 1940–45. Returning briefly to Hanoi in 1946, he was assigned by Ho Chi Minh to lead the resistance movement in the South – where he remained until 1957 as secretary of the regional party organization; he was elected to the Politburo in 1951. He was recalled to Hanoi in 1957, following the removal of **Truong Chinh** as Secretary-General of the Party. Le Duan himself joined the secretariat, and became its head at the VWP's third congress in September 1960, a position in which he was confirmed at the fourth congress (1976) and fifth congress (1982). As "no 2" in the party, he emerged as Ho Chi Minh's effective successor in 1969–70; and by the mid-1970s was the most powerful figure in the country, even though he never held any government position. Ideologically a pragmatist, he was deeply committed to completing the revolution in the South and bringing about re-unification. He also emerged as strongly "pro-Soviet" and paid numerous visits to Moscow, where he appeared to have special rapport with Leonid Brezhnev. He led Vietnam into a close alliance with the Soviet Union, formalized in a treaty of friendship signed on Nov. 3, 1978. He contined this policy in the early 1980s, signing important aid agreements in Moscow – which he visited for the last time in 1985. He became ill in 1985-6 and had probably already lost most of his influence by the time he died on July 11, 1986.

RBS

LE DUC THO. Veteran leader of the **Vietnamese Communist Party** (VCP) who is said to enjoy continuing influence behind the scenes despite his formal retirement in December 1986. A native of Nam Dinh, in the North, he joined the Indochinese Communist Party in 1929-30 and was imprisoned on Con Son island for most of the 1930s. From 1945 he participated in the "August Revolution" in the Hanoi area, although his precise role is unclear. He was sent to the South in 1951-52 to impose a new party line, which may have brought him into conflict for a time with **Le Duan**. Promoted to the Politburo in 1955, back in Hanoi, he was appointed to the party secretariat by 1960 and had responsibilities in the fields of organization and ideology. He was to retain that role until 1968, when he was appointed "special adviser" – in effect leader – of the North Vietnamese delegation at talks with the United States in Paris. In that capacity he conducted secret negotiations with Henry Kissinger in 1970 and 1972-73, which led to the initialling of the Paris Agreement of January 1973 and a further joint communiqué in June that year. In 1973 Tho again went to the South, to join Pham Hung and Van Tien Dung in taking charge of the final campaign which led to the capture of Saigon. Confirmed in his positions at the fourth (1976) and fifth (1982) congresses of the VCP, he emerged as "no. 2" in the secretariat under Le Duan. In December 1986 he was obliged to retire from the Politburo and secretariat, at the Party's sixth congress, but continued as an "adviser" to the new leadership. His younger brother is Mai Chi Tho (born Phan Dinh Dinh) who was a clandestine party leader in the South during the 1960s and early 1970s, then took charge of security in Saigon after 1975; and who has been minister of the interior in Hanoi since 1987.

RBS

LEAD. Lead is a metallic element chiefly associated with other ores. The principal lead ore is galena. The main producers in the region are Australia, the USA, Mexico and Canada. Peru and Chile also have significant reserves. The annual production of lead, in thousands of tonnes, is as follows: Australia, 440; USA, 333; Canada, 307; Peru, 198; Mexico, 183; China, 165; North Korea, 110; Japan, 49; Chile, 1.

RS

LEE HSIEN LOONG. Brig.-Gen. (reserve) Lee, the Singapore Prime Minister's eldest son (born in 1953), entered the Cabinet in January 1985 as Minister of State for Defence and Trade and Industry. Prior to his entry into politics, he had served in the Armed Forces, most recently as Chief of Staff (General Staff) Singapore Army. He currently holds the post of Minister of Trade and Industry and Second Minister for Defence (Service). Lee and **Goh Chok Tong** are together widely regarded as the leading members of the so-called "second generation" of Singaporean politicans who are expected to take over the running of the country in the 1990s.

DS

LEE KUAN YEW. Lee was born in Singapore and was educated at Fitzwilliam College, Cambridge, before being called to the Bar at Middle Temple, London, in 1950. He became Singapore's first Prime Minister in 1959, and has held the post since, being re-elected in 1963, 1968, 1972, 1976, 1980, 1984 and most recently, in 1988. He has also held the post of Secretary-General of the **People's Action Party** since its formation in 1954. Lee is expected to resign the premiership in the early 1990s in favour of **Goh Chok Tong**, his deputy and leader of the so-called "second generation".

DS

LEE TENG-HUI. Born in 1923 to a family of Hakka farmers, Lee Teng-hui was among the few Chinese who received an advanced education under Japanese colonial rule. After graduating from High School he was admitted to Kyoto University and studied agricultural economics. Returning to Taiwan in 1946 he continued his studies at National Taiwan University (NTU), where he received an B.Sc. degree in 1949. Until his entry into the Joint Commission on Rural Reconstruction (JCRR) as head of the Rural Economy Division in 1970, Lee pursued a teaching career at NTU and worked as a consultant for JCRR. During these years he spent two extended periods of graduate study in the USA, receiving a M.A. from Iowa State in 1953 and a PH.D. from Cornell University in 1968.

Lee's career as a politician owes much to the support of **Chiang Ching-kuo**. Looking for a specialist in agricultural affairs to serve in his first cabinet, Chiang in 1972 appointed Lee as Minister without Portfolio. While serving in the Executive Yuan Lee maintained his ties with the scientific community, giving classes at NTU and working as a consultant for JCCR. In 1978 he was appointed mayor of Taipei City, and three years later was transferred to the governorship of Taiwan Province.

As head of these regional governments Lee showed himself to be an efficient administrator, with a distinct technocratic touch. Though his offices provided him with ample opportunity to establish an individual power base, Lee refrained from allying himself to one of the existing intra-party factions or organizing one of his own.

Commensurate with his advancement in the government Lee also rose in the **Kuomintang** (KMT). He was elected a member of the Central Committee during the 11th National Convention (NC) in 1976 and became a member of the Central Standing Committee (CSC) at the 12th NC in 1981.

Lee's nomination as candidate for the office of Vice-President and potential successor as head of state by Chiang Ching-kuo came as a surprise to many observers. After his election in 1984 Lee was systematically groomed for the succession, becoming involved in the design of national policies and gaining experience in foreign affairs through a number of state visits.

After the death of President Chiang, Lee was sworn in as President of the Republic of China on Jan. 18, 1988, the first Taiwanese to hold this office. He also succeeded Chiang as chairman of the KMT. His appointment as acting chairman in January 1988 by the CSC was followed by a formal election at the KMT's 13th NC in July 1988.

During his short term in office, President Lee has compensated for the lack of a power base through adroit handling of the prerogatives of office, establishing himself as *primus inter pares* among the KMT leadership. His political style shows few signs of the ideological bent shared by the elder generation of mainland politicians, though on several occasions he has expressed his commitment to an eventual re-unification of China. Until that happens, his particular attention is directed to the area of foreign policy where he has shown a readiness to sacrifice concern for

precedents in favour of concrete measures to consolidate Taiwan's international position.

HH

LI PENG. Li's father was executed by the **Kuomintang** on Hainan Island when Li (born in 1928) was three years old. Li was subsequently adopted by **Zhou Enlai**. He joined the **Chinese Communist Party** in 1945, and in 1948 was sent to study at the Moscow Power Institute. After returning in 1955 he worked in power plants and their administrative offices in the north east. He became Director of the Beijing Electric Power Administration in 1966, keeping the power plants working normally in Beijing and Tianjin throughout the "10 years of chaos" of the Cultural Revolution. Between 1979 and 1983 he became Minister of the Power Industry and then of Water Conservation and Power Resources. Between 1983 and 1988 he served as Deputy Prime Minister, and member of the party Central Committee Leadership Group in charge of Finance and the Economy. After 1985 he served concurrently as Minster in charge of the State Education Commission. In 1987 he was elected to the Standing Commission of the party's Political bureau, and in 1988 he replaced **Zhao Ziyang** as Prime Minister. In May 1989 he was a leading hardliner over the student demonstrations. He announced the introduction of martial law, and he took the leading role in justifying it.

CIPF

LIBERAL DEMOCRATIC PARTY (JAPAN). The LDP's unbroken monopoly of government dates from the creation of the party through the dissolution of the Liberal and the Democratic parties on Nov. 15, 1955. The merger of the two was a response to the re-unification of the **Japan Socialist Party** in the face of which the persistent fragmentation of the conservatives would have constituted a rejection of office.

Differences of ideology, of policy, of personality and even of faction (the intra-party syntax of power) are subordinate and dependent elements to the imperatives of sustaining power. In short, the LDP is not to be recognized in a history, a tradition, an ideology or what passes in politics for a "philosophy" (although it does, of course, have most or even all of these) so much as in the pursuit of power, in which considerable expertise and sophistication have been demonstrated and accumulated. It is not unfair to say that the LDP is more politically skilled than its rivals.

If the factions are the informal in that internal

syntax, the Executive Committee, the Policy Affairs Research Council and their chairmen, the Secretary General and the President of the Party are the formal moments. These are positions which bestow power and are sought by the rising powerful. The LDP's majority command of the Diet has enabled it to pick prime ministers in accordance with its private internal processes. In this respect the 1989 selection and election of **Kaifu Toshiki** is of interest since his seems to be a case in which the LDP has gone further than ever before to ensure that its internal processes produce conclusions which take account of public and popular understanding of who is and who is not fit to lead.

When attention turns to the present and the prospects of the LDP it can be noted that in a year of unprecedented crisis, repeated scandals and universal criticism the LDP remains the "Government-party" – numerically the strongest element in the Diet, to be threatened by no single party but at worst *in extremis* by a coalition of all the opposition elements in either the lower or the upper house.

RAB

LIBERAL PARTY (AUSTRALIA). Committed to private enterprise and individual liberty and initiative, the party is supported by employer and commercial organizations as well as by self-employed people. The federal parliamentary leader is Andrew Peacock. A state party forms the government currently only in New South Wales. The Liberal Party (by one name or another) has held office for some two-thirds of the time since federation, often with the direct or indirect support of breakaway elements of the **Australian Labor Party**.

TBM

LIBERAL PARTY (PHILIPPINES). The Liberal Party was founded in 1946 by centrist elements of the **Nacionalista Party** and was in power until 1952. In 1961 its then leader, Diosdado Macapagal, was elected President. It was in opposition to President **Marcos** after 1965 and its Secretary-General until his arrest under martial law in 1972 was Benigno Aquino, who was assassinated in 1983. In 1982 the party had become a member of the **United Nationalist Democratic Organization** (UNIDO).

The Liberal Party was revived by ex-senator Jovito Salonga, who returned to Manila after almost four years of voluntary exile abroad in January 1985. Salonga was instrumental in the formation of an alliance in late 1985 to organize

support for **Corazon Aquino**'s candidacy in the February 1986 presidential elections against the incumbent Marcos. The Liberal Party were a part of the *Lakas ng Bayan* (People's Power) coalition, which supported pro-Aquino government candidates in the May 1987 congressional elections. Salonga, who was appointed to the post of Senate President and Chairman of the Commission on Appointments following the elections, has since attempted to build the Liberal Party into an independent political force, although he has remained broadly supportive of the Aquino government. By late 1988 the party claimed to have 42 members in the House of Representatives and seven in the Senate, and Salonga, although in ill health, was widely viewed as a potentially strong presidential candidate in 1992.

DS

LIMA GROUP. The Lima Group is an informal grouping of Argentina, Brazil, Peru and Uruguay, established in July 1985 on the occasion of the Declaration of Lima, in Peru, which was itself a milestone in the integration of the continent. The Group's stated object is to help find "Latin American solutions to Latin American problems". Though originally intended to give assistance to the Contadora Group in its attempt to find a workable peace solution to the problems of Central America, the Lima Group's mandate broadened into areas such as reinforcing democracy in the wake of military dictatorship and seeking a common approach to the problem of debt. Together, the Lima and Contadora Groups form a potentially powerful octet which is taking tentative initiatives in co-ordinated action vis-à-vis international institutions and outside powers, notably the United States. The Lima Group has, however, been weakened by ideological differences and the internal problems experienced by Peru under President Alán García.

JF

LIN BIAO. Born in 1907, Lin joined the **Chinese Communist Party** in 1925 and became one of the **People's Liberation Army**'s (PLA) most outstanding marshals. He was commander of vanguard forces on the **Long March**, he won battles against the Japanese during World War II (suffering severe wounds and being forced to recuperate in the Soviet Union), and he commanded the troops which defeated the nationalist armies in Manchuria in the Civil War. He became Minister of Defence in 1959, and he turned the PLA into a "model" Maoist institution, whose work-style was supposed to be studied by all

Chinese in the early 1960s. He actively supported **Mao Zedong** during the Cultural Revolution, and in 1969 Mao declared him his future successor. Disagreements quickly emerged, however, and in 1971 he was killed, apparently in a still-mysterious plane crash in Mongolia whilst attempting to flee to the USSR after a failed attempt to assassinate Mao and stage a coup d'état.

CIPF

LIU SHAOQI. Born in 1898, Liu joined the **Chinese Communist Party (CCP)** in 1921, and was active in the socialist labour and trade union movement in the 1920s. Already in 1927 elected to the Central Committee, he took over leadership of the underground party organization in North China from the mid-1930s until 1949. This background, and his own organizational talents, made him a more natural "Leninist" than other CCP leaders. He believed in the vital importance of party organization.

Initially he complemented **Mao Zedong**, and he became head of state in 1959. Already Mao's deputy in 1949, he later became his officially designated successor. After the failure of the Great Leap Forward, however, Liu's remedies for the economy created an ever-widening wedge between himself and Mao. As the latter became obsessed by the danger of degeneration of the revoluton, he identified the party apparatus as the chief block upon the creativity of the masses, and Liu Shaoqi as the chief representative of the apparatus. In 1966 he was branded as a renegade, traitor and "China's Khrushchev". He was vilified by the Red Guards and imprisoned, where he died in humiliating circumstances in 1969. He was rehabilitated in 1980.

CIPF

LONG MARCH. Towards the end of 1934 in China the **Kuomintang**'s fifth encirclement campaign threatened to overrun the Jiangxi Soviet base area controlled by the communists. The latter broke out and headed for a small base area in northern Shaanxi province at Yanan by a roundabout route of nearly 6,000 miles. Along the way **Mao Zedong** supplanted rivals within the party leadership at the Zunyi conference in January 1935, where he became head of the party's Military Affairs Commission and effectively leader. Roughly 90–100,000 people set out, and one tenth struggled into Yanan a year or more later. The Long March was a feat of great heroism and enormous privations. It saved the party from destruction, although it was only the Japanese invasion, and the truce with the Nationalists, which enabled it to revive. The survivors of the Long March, even in retirement, still dominate key decision-making.

CIPF

M

MACAU. *Population*: 434,300. *Area*: 16.04 sq km. *Gross Domestic Product*: US$2,283 million. *Trade*: US$2,528 million. *Top five trading partners*: USA, Hong Kong, West Germany, France, UK. *Education spending*: US$17,000,000. *Urban population as percentage of total*: 100.

Macau lies just south of the Tropic of Cancer, on the west bank of the Pearl River estuary in south China, at about 70 miles south of Guangzhou (Canton) and 40 miles west of Hong Kong. The territory of Macau consists of a peninsula and two outlying islands. Macau lies in the typhoon zone, and has a monsoon type of climate with a hot wet summer and a generally cool and dry winter.

Macau came under Portuguese administration with the permission of the Chinese Emperor during the Ming dynasty in 1557 for the purpose of trade. The Portuguese presence continued to be tolerated by the Manchus who conquered China in the seventeenth century. Macau formally became a Portuguese colony in 1888, following the ratification of the Sino–Portuguese Treaty of Beijing (Peking) – a development encouraged by the British who did not wish to see Macau come under the control of the French. Following the revolution in Portugal, Macau's status was redefined in the Portuguese Constitution of 1976, which states that Macau is not part of Portuguese territory but is a territory under Portuguese administration. Since that time the Portuguese Government has made no claim over the sovereignty of Macau.

In June 1986, Portugal and the People's Republic of China entered into negotiations in regard to the future of Macau. In April 1987 the two governments signed a joint declaration – Declaração Conjunta do Governo da Republica Portuguesa e do Governo da Republica Popular da China Sobre a Questão de Macau – by which Macau will revert in its entirety to the People's Republic of China on Dec. 20 1999, as a special administrative region, roughly along the lines of the Sino-British agreement for Hong Kong. The main difference between the Hong Kong arrangement and the Macau agreement is that the Portuguese nationals of Macau will continue to enjoy full Portuguese citizenship after the territory reverts to China, whereas Hong Kong's British subjects will not be entitled to United Kingdom citizenship after 1997. In 1987 a Sino–Portuguese Joint Liaison Group was set up to monitor the implementation of the agreement and to ensure a smooth transition in Macau.

At present, the Portuguese continue to govern Macau in accordance with the Organic Statute (Estatuto Organico de Macau) of 1976. The territory is administered by the Governor, who is appointed by the President of Portugal, after consultation with the local Legislative Assembly and representatives of various local organizations. The Governor has both executive and legislative powers. As the head of the executive branch, he is responsible for formulating general policies, co-ordinating the public administration, executing the laws, administering the finances, defining the structures of the monetary and financial markets. In carrying out these duties, he is assisted by five Secretaries (Secretarios Adjuntos) and is advised by the Conselho Consultivo, a consultative council of five elected members, three ex-officio members and two appointed members, which the Governor himself chairs. The Legislative Assembly provides for the representation of local interests. Amongst its 17 members, five are appointed by the Governor, six are indirectly elected, and six are directly elected by universal franchise.

The mainstay of Macau's economy is tourism-related service industries, including gambling. Income from this source accounts for roughly 58 per cent of Macau's public revenue and 73 per cent of its public expenditure. The holder of the government gambling franchise since January 1962 has been Dr Stanley Ho's Sociedade de Turismo e Diversoes de Macau (STDM). Under the present franchise arrangement, STDM is obliged to support worthy public projects and pay a 26 per cent tax on the gross revenue of the casinos and the percentage will go up to 30 per cent in 1991. The other principal economic activity of the territory is manufacturing. Textiles and garments are the leading export earners but diversification efforts are apparent in electronics, toys, optical goods and artificial flowers. Macau has also continued to play its traditional role as a distributing centre for fish and Chinese products.

ST

MAHATHIR, MOHAMED SERI. Dr Mahathir replaced Datuk Hussein bin Onn as Prime Minister in July 1981, having replaced him as the **United Malays National Organization**

(UMNO) president the previous month. Mahathir, born in Kedah in 1925, was the first Prime Minister whose political career had been largely shaped since Malaysia's attainment of independence (whereas his predecessors had held various posts under British rule and had been significantly involved in the negotiation of independence). In addition, he was the first to be educated locally (rather than in the UK) and to be unconnected with any Malay royal house, and (as a medical graduate) the first Prime Minister not to be a lawyer by profession. During the earlier stages of his political career Dr Mahathir had tended to stand on the right wing of UMNO politics, and his party membership had been suspended for a period for expressing what were considered by the then UMNO leadership to be "extremist Malay views" during the racial tension surrounding the 1969 emergency.

He entered the Cabinet for the first time in 1974 as Minister of Education, and prior to his appointment as Prime Minister he also held the Trade and Industry portfolio and the deputy premiership. He is currently responsible for the additional posts of Home Affairs and Justice.

DS

MAHAYANA BUDDHISM. The Great Vehicle arose in the early centuries of **Buddhism** as a wider path to salvation than that of monks who sought nirvana for themselves. The ideal was presented of the Bodhisattva, "Buddha-to-be", who deferred his own salvation in the service of others. Beyond the single historical Buddha there were held to be countless Buddhas and Bodhisattvas, and by this means as the religion spread from India into eastern Asia it was able to come to terms with or embrace other faiths: **Confucianism**, **Daoism** or **Shinto**. Ethical and philosophical writings abounded, and Buddhism fashioned much of the culture of Asia.

Before the arrival of Islam in the fifteenth century both major forms of Buddhism flourished in Indonesia and they still claim 1,500,000 adherents. Mahayana Buddhism gained the ascendancy from the eighth century and under its inspiration great monuments were built of which the chief is Borobudur in Java, which is a mystic diagram in stone with temples and galleries richly adorned with reliefs illustrating the life of the Buddha.

Chinese influence in Vietnam led to the domination of Mahayana there, though with minority **Theravada Buddhism**. The ideology of the court in Vietnam was Confucian, but Buddhism and Daoism held popular allegiance and assimilated indigenous folk customs, with male and female mediums exercising powers of healing and influencing community affairs. In modern times a United Buddhist Church was inaugurated in 1963 with the aim of integrating the two Vehicles and renewing the religion. There were tensions with christianity which were stronger in Vietnam than anywhere else in Asia apart from the Philippines.

In recent political struggles in Vietnam two tendencies appeared among Buddhists. One was anti-communist, and in the south it was swollen by thousands of refugees from the north. The majority opposed outside intervention and, led by Thich Tri Quang of the An Quang pagoda, presented Buddhism as the conscience of the nation. Some Buddhist monks burnt themselves to death in protest against the government, an action condemned by some as un-Buddhist though it received popular support. After the end of the war Buddhist leaders sought reconciliation, and most people regard themselves as Buddhist even if they do not attend pagoda services and continue with Confucian ancestral rites.

Buddhism entered China in the first century CE, monasteries were founded and scriptures translated. There were conflicts with Confucian scholars who saw Buddhist beliefs in reincarnation and practices of recruiting youths as monks to be against their own ancestral cults and family bonds. Daoists more easily accepted the many Buddhas as akin to their own gods. Eventually Buddhism settled down as one of the three "ways", not separate religions, of China and many people followed all three ways on suitable occasions.

Chinese Buddhists developed their own theories and practices, with new schools. Two of these were the Meditation School, called in Chinese Ch'an (from Sanskrit *dhyana*, "meditation"), and known to the wider world as Japanese Zen. More popular was the Pure Land, Ch'ing-t'u, a movement of devotion which emphasized piety and faith in celestial beings in a Pure Land or Western Paradise, similar to those of Daoism. There were countless temples and monasteries and great works of art were produced.

Already attacked in this century for superstitious practices, Buddhism like all religions was repressed under communist rule, most fiercely during the Cultural Revolution. Many buildings were destroyed, or turned to secular uses, and their occupants sent to work on the land. Since then some monasteries have been restored and their artistic treasures preserved, though much has been lost.

Under **Mao Zedong** much of the educational system disintegrated and religion was banned. But his Little Red Book was used like a sacred scripture, carried at rallies, taken to bed, and serving as a guide to action. Mao himself was regarded with great reverence, and in ritual, doctrine and morality there were religious expressions which partly remain and partly return to former channels.

In Hong Kong and Taiwan traditional Chinese faiths and practices persist, with some syncretism into new expressions. It is in Tibet that there has been the greatest struggle of traditional Buddhism with Chinese communist domination. Tibet had its own forms of Mahayana Buddhism, often known as Lamaism from the names of superior abbots, and it mingled with a pre-Buddhist animistic religion. The Dalai Lama, head of Tibetan Buddhism, fled to India from the Chinese in 1959 and remains there. Another leading abbot, the Panchen Lama, was taken to Peking (Beijing) and presented as director of Tibetan Buddhists, but he died in 1989. Many Tibetan monasteries have been destroyed, and monks secularized or killed. A few temples have recently been reopened but some monks have led demonstrations against the government.

Mahayana Buddhism entered Korea from China in the fourth century and passed thence to Japan. The Chinese Ch'an school, called "Son" in Korea, gave rise to a distinctively Korean order, the Chogye school which emphasized harmony with nature and direct experience of the truth. Official circles followed Confucian rituals, but the mass of the people practised either Pure Land Devotion or Son meditation. Many temples and monasteries have been closed in North Korea, but in the south in 1987 there were over 8,000 temples and 12,800 monks.

Mahayana Buddhism came to Japan in the sixth or seventh century, like Christianity into Europe bringing an ancient culture and literacy, and even writing down the sacred legends of another religion, the native Shinto. After initial difficulties Buddhism took root in offical life in Japan with its adoption by Prince Shotoku Taishi (547–622) who commended the Three Jewels of Buddhism to be revered by all beings. Further accommodation with Shinto came when in 749 a colossal bronze image, the greatest metal figure in the world, was erected at Nara for the Buddha Roshana or Vairochana, said to be completed with the permission of the Shinto sun goddess Amaterasu. Most Japanese follow both Shinto and Buddhism, Shinto especially for childhood and life-giving rituals and Buddhism for funerals.

Japanese developments of Buddhism include traditional sects and their own schools. The monk Nichiren in the thirteenth century criticized both Zen and Pure Land Buddhism and urged a return to the major Mahayana scripture, the Lotus Sutra, and he formulated a confession, "Hail to the Lotus of the Perfect Law", whose repetition would harmonize present life. In this century the Nicheren tradition has been revived as Nichiren Shoshu in the Soka Gakkai, or Value-Creation Society, which claims 13 million members. As a lay organization with a political wing in the **Komeito** Party it has been a forceful right-wing influence. Another popular Nichiren sect is the Rissho-koseikai, "society for establishing righteous and friendly association", which has many lay workers, vast buildings for social help and counselling, and claims five million members. The Reiyukai, "Association of Friends of the Spirit", with five million members, is a more traditional lay Buddhist movement which emphasizes ancestral cults and patriarchal morals.

As a missionary religion Buddhism has spread in modern times through much of the Pacific area, in Malaysia among Chinese immigrants, and in Hawaii and the USA, especially California. Many Buddhist study groups include both Theravada and Mahayana, with the latter popular among Japanese immigrants. There are Pure Land temples and schools in Hawaii, and Zen groups for intellectuals. Of the Japanese new religious movements in the USA the largest is Nichiren Shoshu of America, begun in Los Angeles in 1960 and now claiming over 300,000 members. Many converts are non-Asians, and 60,000 young white Americans each year follow an "aggressive-conversion process" (*shakubuku*).

GP

MALAYSIA. *Population*. 17,000,000 est. 1988. *Area*: 330,434 sq km. *Gross Domestic Product*: US$33,050 million (est. 1988). *Trade volume*: (est. 1988): imports US$116,181,000; exports, US$20,331,000. *Top five trading partners*: Japan, USA, Singapore, UK, West Germany. *Defence spending*: US$860 million (1987). *Education spending*: US$1,620, million (1986). *Urban population as percentage of total*: 35. *Birth rate*: 31 per thousand. *Life expectancy*: 67.

Geographical background. The Federation of Malaysia comprises the 11 states of Peninsular Malaysia (Perlis, Kedah, Kelantan, Trengganu, Penang, Perak, Pahang, Selangor, Negri, Sembilan, Malacca and Johore) together with the two eastern states of Sarawak and Sabah in northern Borneo. Peninsular Malaysia covers an area of 131,587 sq km to the south of Thailand on the Kra Peninsula, extending southwards to the island of Singapore. Sabah and Sarawak, with areas respectively of 74,398 sq km and 124,449 sq km, are bordered to the south by the Indonesian territory of Kalimantan. North-eastern Sarawak is also bordered by the country of Brunei. As of 1988, at least 80 per cent of the country's total land area was covered with forest.

Peninsular Malaysia has at least 10 cities of over 100,000 people, including Kuala Lumpur, the country's capital, situated close to the western coastline of the peninsula. In contrast, eastern Malaysia has few urban areas, the exceptions being Kuching and Miri in Sarawak and Kota Kinabalu and Sandakan in Sabah. Malaysia's population is projected to increase to 20,900,000 by the year 2000.

Socio-political background. Malaysia's complex racial and religious composition, a product of British colonial policies, has been at the root of many of the country's most sensitive political and economic issues. According to the 1980 census, in Malaysia as a whole, Malays constituted 47 per cent of the population, Chinese 33 per cent, Indians (a term applying to people from the Indian sub-continent) 9 per cent, Borneo indigenes 9 per cent and others 2 per cent.

The country's principal and official language is a variation of Malay known as Bahasa Malaysia, although English is in widespread use. The introduction of Bahasa Malaysia was encouraged by the country's early independent leadership in an attempt to deal with the problem of national integration. Although the Chinese and Indian minorities have generally accepted the use of Bahasa Malaysia, Mandarin, Cantonese, Hokkien, Tamil, Punjabi and Iban, amongst others, are in widespread use.

Almost all Malays are Muslims, representing approximately 53 per cent of the total population in 1985. In Peninsular Malaysia 9 per cent are Buddhists, over 11 per cent follow Chinese faiths, including **Confucianism** and **Daoism**, and 7 per cent are Christians. A higher level of **Christianity** is recorded in Eastern Malaysia, where animist religions are also followed by many indigenous peoples. In 1988 Malaysia had a 75 per cent literacy rate, just over four million students and a total workforce of almost seven million.

Malaysia is an independent member of the Commonwealth and a parliamentary monarchy. A Supreme Head of State (*Yang di-Pertuan Agong*) is elected every five years from among their own number by the nine hereditary Malay rulers of Peninsular Malaysia. The *Yang di-Pertuan Agong* appoints a Cabinet headed by a Prime Minister. Malaysia has a federal form of government, with a bicameral legislature, residual legislative power resting with the states. Parliament consists of: (i) a 69-member Senate (*Dewan Negara*), serving a six-year term, two members of which are elected by the Legislative Assemblies of each of the states, the remaining 43 members being nominated by the *Yang di-Pertuan Agong*; and (ii) a 177-member House of Representatives (*Dewan Rakyat*) elected by universal adult suffrage for a five-year term and by simple majority in single-member constituencies.

Pre-modern history. In 1511 a Portuguese force led by Alberquerque took control of Malacca on the Malay Peninsular, thereby establishing the first European outpost in Southeast Asia. Prior to its capture, the sultanate of Malacca (established by Malays in the fifteenth century) had been the region's dominant trading centre. Aside from Malacca and Johore (which developed under an alliance with the Netherlands), the Malay states evolved up until the mid-eighteenth century outside the political influence of the European colonial nations.

However, in the late eighteenth century, Britain began to acquire Malay territory along the peninsula's western coast in order to protect and consolidate the trade route between India and China through the Straits of Malacca. Penang and Malacca were acquired in 1786 and 1795 respectively and in 1819 a trading settlement was established on the island of Singapore. In 1826, Penang, Malacca and Singapore were merged into a single administrative unit, the Straits Settlements, which remained under the control of Calcutta until 1867, when jurisdiction was passed to London. Following the formation of the Straits Settlement, Britain attempted to distance itself from the other Malay states, but economic development in the residual states (and particularly the discovery of tin deposits) made this impossible. Disputes over commercial interests, notably in Perak and Selangor, began to have an adverse effect on trading in the region. The lack of administrative control outside of the Settlements led European and Chinese merchants to petition Britain to restore order. Eventually in 1873 the British government accepted the need for intervention, possibly in an attempt to pre-empt what were perceived as German ambitions to exploit the disorder. In 1874 Britain accepted administrative responsibility for Perak and by 1888 this had been extended to include Selangor, Negri Sembilan and Pahang. These four states were brought together in 1896 as the Federated Malay States, with the federal capital at Kuala Lumpur. In 1914 British authority was extended to the whole peninsular when the five remaining Malay states, Kedah, Perlis, Trengganu, Kelantan and Johore, were united as the Unfederated Malay States.

Early modern history. The development and expansion of **tin** extraction and rubber production under British rule induced significant demographic changes in most of the Malay states. Both industries were heavily dependent upon immigrant labour, from the southern coastal province of China in the case of the tin industry, and from south India in the case of rubber. By 1931 the Chinese population of British Malaya constituted some 39 per cent of the total population. The indigenous Malays maintained their numerical superiority only in the four northern unfederated states while Chinese immigrants dominated the west coast and the urban centres. The Malays were predominantly subsistence rice farmers, whereas the Chinese and Indians came to control not only the lucrative tin and rubber industries, but much of the country's internal trade and finance.

The Communist Party of Malaya (CPM), founded in 1930 by members of the Chinese community, was the solitary radical challenge to the pre-World War II colonial order. British rule was supported by the Malay aristocracy and the wealthy Chinese merchant class, and was consolidated by a high degree of political indifference amongst the large immigrant community, most of whom were primarily concerned with the upheavals taking place in their countries of origin. However, the Japanese invasion and occupation of Malaya between 1942–45 swept aside the colonial order and made its full restoration untenable. For the most part the Malay aristocracy collaborated with the Japanese, who proceeded to undermine the authority of the individual Sultans by encouraging pan-Malayan aspirations amongst the Malay youth. The Chinese community suffered most under the occupation, and it was they, in turn, who offered the only serious resistance to Japanese rule, comprising by far the largest component of the CPM-dominated Malayan People's Anti-Japanese Army. As a result of this, when Japanese rule collapsed in August 1945, the CPM was left as the sole political-military organization in the peninsular in advance of the returning British.

Upon its return to Malaya in early 1946, Britain announced plans to remodel its administration of the peninsular. It was proposed that sovereignty be transferred from the Malay rulers to the British Crown, that all the Malay states (with the exception of Singapore) be unified into a Malayan Union, and that all Chinese and Indian immigrants be awarded citizenship and equal rights. The Malayan Union was formally introduced in April 1946, but it met with such resistance from the Malay community (brought together in a new political grouping, the **United Malays National Organization**—UMNO) that its provisions were never brought into full effect. Following negotiations between Britain, UMNO and the Malay rulers it was agreed to form a Federation of Malaya (eventually inaugurated in February 1948), which formalized the policy of unification, but allowed the Sultans to maintain sovereign control and introduced restrictive citizenship provisions for members of the Chinese and Indian communities.

In the immediate aftermath of Britain's return to the peninsula in early 1946, the CPM had concerned itself largely with the organization of a labour movement in Malaya. However, just prior to the formation of the Federation the British administration inroduced stringent trade union controls, which led the CPM to reject its policy of "open and legal" struggle and, instead, take up arms. The CPM campaign of guerrilla attacks began with some success, exploiting a lack of co-ordination between the army and the civil authorities in Malaya. On June 18, 1948, a state of emergency was declared which remained in force until 1960. The communist insurrection had, however, been effectively broken six years earlier, in 1954, following Britain's successful application of the "Briggs Plan" which had isolated the insurgents. Moreover, the CPM's strength had been undermined in the mid-1950s by a British announcement that Malaya would be moved quickly to political independence.

Political history. Malaya's independence from Britain was secured on Aug. 31, 1957, with Tunku Abdul Rahman, president of the UMNO, as the first Prime Minister. Independent Malaya's most pressing problem was the achievement of some sort of unification between the Malay, Chinese and Indian communities. It was clear that the Malay majority had to achieve some move towards economic parity with the two other communities, and likewise that the Indians and Chinese had to achieve similar political and administrative rights to those enjoyed by the Malays. In order to achieve an effective political leadership for independent Malaya, a political organization which, at least ostensibly, crossed the boundaries of race, had been formed. This alliance of the country's three main parties (UMNO, the **Malaysian Chinese Association – MCA** – and the **Malaysian Indian Congress – MIC**) had arisen out of municipal elections held in Kuala Lumpur in 1952, and had been confirmed in the national elections of 1955. The three parties retained a separate identity in terms of policy, but worked together in order to select the appropriate candidate for each constituency. As a result, the UMNO–MCA–MIC alliance secured 81 per cent of the vote and all but one of the 52 contested seats in the 1955 election.

Malaysia was established in September 1963, through the union of the independent Federation of Malaya, the internally self-governing state of Singapore, and the former British colonies of Sarawak and North Borneo (Sabah). The incorporation of Singapore into the new federation had been proposed by Tunku Abdul Rahman, who was apparently reluctant to allow the emergence of a (predominantly Chinese) rival power on Malaya's southern coastline. Sabah and Sarawak, neither of which had been prepared by the British for independence, were included in the federation partly in order to secure the numerical superiority of the Malay community.

The addition of Singapore, Sabah and Sarawak to the new Malaysian Federation immediately caused the government a number of serious problems. Indonesia and the Philippines (both of which had territorial claims to Sabah) broke off diplomatic relations with Malaysia in September 1963, and, that month, President **Sukarno** of Indonesia ordered the first regular troop raids into Sabah and Sarawak. The Malaysian and Commonwealth forces contained the Indonesian challenge and, in 1966, both the Philippines and Indonesia reconciled themselves to Malaysia. Problems also arose in Singapore, where **Lee Kuan Yew's People's Action Party** was threatening the Alliance by openly competing against the MCA for Chinese support. Against Lee's wishes, Singapore was removed from the Federation in August 1965, reducing the number of Malaysia's component states from 14 to 13.

In May 1969 hundreds of people were killed in serious inter-communal rioting which broke out in Kuala Lumpur after federal election results had hinted at an increasing radicalism amongst the Chinese community. To restore order, the Constitution was suspended and a national emergency declared. The unrest precipitated the resignation of Tunku Abdul Rahman who was replaced in September 1970 by Tun Abdul Razak. The new Prime Minister widened the UMNO-dominated government coalition, to create a **National Front** within which bargaining of communal interests could theoretically take place. Razak also introduced the **New Economic Policy** (NEP) in an attempt to secure for the Malay community economic parity with the Chinese community. Tun Abdul Razak died in early 1976 and he was replaced as Prime Minister by his deputy, Dato Hussein bin Onn. Federal and state elections held in July 1978 consolidated the position of the National Front coalition. Underlying the election campaign, but not widely debated because of a ban imposed on the public discussion of sensitive topics after the 1969 riots, was Chinese apprehension over the manner in which the government was implementing the NEP. In particular, Chinese concern was focused upon the use of a quota system for admissions to institutions of tertiary education which was designed to widen the career opportunities open to Malays. Racial tension was also heightened in 1978 by the activities of Islamic extremists.

Recent developments. Datuk Seri Dr **Mahathir Mohamed** succeeded Datuk Hussein bin Onn as UMNO president in June 1981 and as Prime Minister the following month. Mahathir called federal and state elections in April 1982, when the National Front recorded an overwhelming victory, winning 132 of the 154 seats in the House of Representatives and 281 of the 312 state seats at issue in the 11 peninsular legislatures being renewed. The main National Front slogan in the elections was "clean, efficient and trustworthy government", measures to this end having featured prominently in the programme of the so-called "double-M administration" (i.e., under the premiership of Mahathir and the deputy premiership of Datuk Musa bin Hitam) since its formation in mid-1981.

The government was embarrassed by a major banking scandal that came to light in October 1983 when it was revealed that Bumiputra Malaysia Finance, a subsidiary of Bank Bumiputra Malaysia (Malaysia's largest bank), had improperly loaned the Hong Kong-based Carrian group of companies (subsequently liquidated) US$589 million, which represented 80 per cent of the capital and reserves of Bank Bumiputra. Allegations that ministers had been involved in the scandal damaged the credibility of the government. A five-month constitutional crisis ended in January 1984, when the House of Representatives passed a series of amendments to proposed constitutional reforms, tabled in August 1983, restricting the power of hereditary state rulers. The controversy surrounding the crisis was a further blow to the Mahathir government, which had already been affected by the banking scandal. Nevertheless, at the annual UMNO congress in May 1984, Mahathir was re-elected unopposed as leader.

Dr Mahathir faced the first serious challenge to his leadership in February 1986, when Datuk Musa Hitam resigned as Deputy Prime Minister and Minister of Home Affairs, citing "irreconcilable differences" with the Prime Minister. Mahathir's problems were confounded by serious sectarian unrest in Sabah and an economic recession. In addition, Tan Koon Swan, leader of the MCA, was arrested in Singapore in January

1986 and was subsequently convicted and imprisoned on charges of commercial fraud. The Prime Minister called what promised to be a difficult election in August 1986. In the event, however, the elections resulted in a landslide victory for the National Front, which won 148 of the 177 seats in the enlarged House of Representatives. Of the opposition parties, the **Democratic Action Party** (DAP) won 24 seats (seven more than the MCA), having gained support from disillusioned ethnic Chinese voters. Shortly after the elections, perceived allies of Datuk Musa in the Cabinet were transferred to less influential positions or dropped.

Mahathir faced a renewed challenge to his leadership in April 1987, this time from within UMNO, when the Minister of Trade and Industry, Tengku Tan Sri Razaleigh Hamzah, ran against him for the party presidency. Mahathir defeated Razaleigh by a slender majority of 43 votes out of 1,479 cast. Razaleigh and his supporters were dismissed from the Cabinet, but 11 of his followers filed a lawsuit claiming that the UMNO leadership election had been invalid because of improper selection procedures. The legal battle which ensued resulted in UMNO being declared an "illegal society" under the country's Societies Act in early February 1988. Mahathir subsequently managed to revive the party, as UMNO – *Baru* and maintain control of it despite concerted opposition from Razaleigh and former Prime Minister and elder statesman Tunku Abdul Rahman amongst others. However, by the end of 1988 Mahathir had consolidated his position to such an extent that he felt able to offer Razaleigh and Musa ministerial posts. In January 1989, Musa was eventually reconciled with Mahathir, announcing his membership of UMNO – *Baru*. Razaleigh, however, continued his opposition to the Prime Minister, establishing an UMNO splinter group.

At the end of a month of rising racial tension between Malays and ethnic Chinese, the police, between Oct. 27 and mid-November 1987, detained at least 106 people under the Internal Security Act which allowed indefinite detention without trial. Those detained included Lim Kit Siang, the DAP secretary general, other politicans from all parties, lawyers, journalists and leaders of pressure groups. Three newspapers were closed by the government, and political rallies were prohibited. Mahathir told parliament that the arrrests had been made because the government could not wait until the outbreak of riots before taking action. Lim Kit Siang and his son Lim Guan Eng were the last of those arrested to be freed in mid-April 1989.

The House of Representatives approved Constitutional amendments in March 1988 limiting the power of the judiciary to interpret laws. The amendment provoked a strong degree of concern within the traditionally independent Malaysian courts and brought to a head a confrontation between the executive arm of government and the judiciary. The conflict resulted in the suspension and eventual dismissal in August 1988 of the Lord President of the Supreme Court, Tun Mohamed Salleh Abas.

Outline of economic development. Malaysia's economic development has been shaped by two main factors; (i) its location on the north-eastern edge of the Straits of Malacca which gave an opportunity for the western coast to develop through trade with the European colonizing powers; and (ii) an abundance of natural resources, principally tin, hydrocarbons, timber, rubber and oil palm.

The discovery of tin in the 1840s led to an influx of Chinese immigrants who proceeded to dominate the tin-mining industry until the late nineteenth century, at which time innovative Western technology and the exhaustion of the most accessible seams allowed British industry to command the sector. The Chinese community began to move into rubber production, thereby presenting a serious challenge to British control of the industry. In contrast to the entrepreneurial Chinese, the indigenous Malay population concentrated their labour on the agricultural sector, principally subsistence rice farming. The concentration of Malays in the traditional, agricultural sectors of the economy and the Chinese in the modern rural and urban sectors has been a basic feature of the country's economic development. In the aftermath of racial riots in 1969, the government introduced the New Economic Policy aimed, partly, at eliminating the identification of race with economic function.

Since independence, Malaysia has launched a series of five-year development plans, 1956-60 and 1961-65 (the first and second Malayan Plans) and 1966-70, 1971-75, 1976-80, 1981-85 and 1986-90 (the first to fifth Malaysian Plans). In the early 1980s the government launched an ambitious heavy industrialization policy designed to propel the country to the front ranks of industralized nations by the turn of the century. However, by the mid-1980s, the government had replaced its heavy-industry policy with a more realistic, UN-assisted "master plan", which emphasized, above all else, the production of light and intermediate goods.

Current economic situation. The year 1988 registered a dramatic economic recovery in Malaysia in which every major sector of the economy achieved growth. Real GDP growth of 8.1 per cent in 1988 (compared with 5.2 per cent in 1987 and 1.2 per cent in 1986) was the result not only of high commodity prices and a competitive *ringgit*, but also of strong foreign investment, major new infrastructure development projects and the introduction of a moderately expansionary budget. The improvement was tempered slightly by forecasts that the rate of growth in 1989 would slow down to an estimated 6.5 per cent due to a projected weakening in worldwide commodity prices and uncertainty over the price of oil (the revenue from oil accounting for an estimated 8 per cent of gross national product in nominal terms). The government has based its growth forecast on a conservative price of US$14 a barrel in 1989 and an output of 526,600 barrels a day (compared with 540,000 in 1988).

All of Malaysia's major export commodities – rubber, palm oil, timber, cocoa, tin and petroleum – recorded high price-levels during 1988, encouraging a large increase in private sector consumption. Investment in the private sector increased by nearly 18 per cent, three times higher than 1987. Foreign capital (particularly Japanese) accounted for the major proportion of this increase, and accordingly concern was expressed over the need to stimulate local private investors. Despite the upturn, unemployment rose from 9.1 per cent in 1987 to 9.6 per cent in 1988; this contributed to keeping labour costs low, thereby making Malaysia an attractive country for the relocation of labour-intensive industries from Japan, Singapore and Taiwan. Inflation doubled in 1988 to 2.7 per cent with an expected increase to 3.2 per cent in 1989. The continued depreciation of the *ringgit*, which at one stage in November 1988, reached its lowest point ever at US$1.00=2.70 *ringgits*, was given as the reason for this increase. However, the lower rate against the US dollar had the effect of assisting export sales which in turn helped the balance of payment figures. Export of manufactures earned more foreign exchange than exports of commodities for the first time during 1988. Also, for the first time the share of manufacturing in Malaysia's GDP was higher then the share of agriculture.

In October 1988, the Finance Minister Daim Zainuddin introduced an expansionary budget for 1989, proposing a 7 per cent increase in federal government expenditure to M$30,165 million. The rationale behind Daim's increased spending was the need to stimulate private investment and productivity so as to sustain growth in the face of an expected slowdown in world demand during 1989. In an attempt to make Malaysia tax-competitive with some of its neighbours, Daim reduced the corporate tax rate from 40 to 35 per cent and anounced the gradual removal of the 5 per cent development tax over a five-year period. He also announced that a value-added tax would be introduced in 1990.

Foreign relations. Malaysia was a founder member of the **Association of South-East Asian Nations (ASEAN)** in 1967 and its foreign policy objectives have since been set firmly within that organization's general framework. Along with the other five ASEAN members, Malaysia has consistently opposed the presence of Vietnamese forces in Kampuchea since their entry in late 1978.

During the 1960s and 1970s, Malaysia enjoyed a strong relationship with the Western powers, notably the UK. However, Malaysian–British relations deteriorated in the early 1980s, largely as a result of the British government's decision in late 1979 to stop subsidizing overseas students. The Mahathir government had responded with the introduction of a "look east" policy which aimed to lessen the economic links between Malaysia and the UK. Relations improved during the mid-1980s and in September 1988 the two countries signed a memorandum of understanding on the purchase by Malaysia of defence equipment estimated to be worth eventually between US$1,600 million and US$2,700 million.

After much concerted lobbying, Malaysia was elected by the UN General Assembly as one of the 100 non-permanent members of the UN Security Council in New York in October 1988. The following month Malaysia was one of the first countries to offer recognition to the recently proclaimed independent State of Palestine. In October 1989 Malaysia will, for the first time, host the annual Commonwealth Heads of Government Meeting.

Prospects for development. In late 1988 and early 1989 some commentators were predicting that Malaysia might be poised to join the ranks of the so-called "newly industrialized countries". Whether Malaysia can measure up to such an optimistic account of its future development is largely dependent upon a continuation of the manufacturing boom of 1987-89. Buoyed by strong external demand (an essential ingredient given the country's small domestic market), forecasts indicate that rubber-based industries and the electrical and electronic sectors are firmly on an upward trend. However, at present the performance of manufactured exports rest on a relatively narrow base (principally electronics and textiles) and diversification into areas such as food and agro-based industry will not only broaden this base, but also further reduce the economy's diminishing reliance on primary commodity exports.

The future of the New Economic Policy is of great relevance to the country's future development. Dr Mahathir, the Prime Minister, indicated on a number of occasions during 1988–89 that the government aims to promote the national wealth creation and not the equity restructuring aspect of the NEP. A relaxation of the NEP's wealth redistribution tenet is vital if Malaysia is to instill foreign investors with confidence.

DS

MALAYSIAN CHINESE ASSOCIATION (MCA).

Founded in 1949, the MCA is a purely Chinese-based party which represents the interests of the Chinese community (especially the business sector) within the ruling **National Front** coalition. The MCA was an original partner in the tripartite Alliance coalition – with the **United Malays National Organization** (UMNO) and the **Malaysian Indian Congress** – which came to power in 1955 and led the country to independence in 1957. The MCA was also a founder member of the succeeding broader UMNO-led National Front, which has been in power since 1974, with the MCA normally holding four full ministerial posts in the federal government. As of mid-1989, the MCA president, Datuk Dr Ling Liong Sik holds the Transport portfolio. In early 1986 the party's newly appointed president Dato Tan Koon Swan was arrested in Singapore on financial fraud charges. He was subsequently convicted and imprisoned, and the resultant loss of credibility led to the MCA being overtaken by the opposition **Democratic Action Party** (DAP) as the leading Chinese party in the August 1986 elections.

DS

MALAYSIAN INDIAN CONGRESS (MIC).

Founded in 1946 with the encouragement of Jawaharlal Nehru (the leader of the Indian National Congress), the MIC has represented the country's Indian community in the **United Malays National Organization** (UMNO)-dominated coalition governments since 1954. In the August 1986 elections, the party gained six seats and in December Dato S. Samy Vellu (Minister of Works) was re-elected party president in the first uncontested leadership election for 15 years.

DS

MANGANESE.

Manganese is a widely distributed metallic agent largely used in steel manufacture where it is important as a purifying agent. Between 1–12 per cent of manganese is added to steel to improve its strength and hardness. The metal is also used in small amounts in the chemical industry and the production of paints and varnishes. It is produced in Australia, China, Japan the USA, Mexico and Chile. The annual production of manganese, in thousands of tonnes, is as follows: Australia, 1,033; China, 480; Japan, 27.

RS

MAO ZEDONG.

Born in 1893 into a peasant family in Hunan province, Mao had a spasmodic education. Steeped in Chinese history, a poet as well as a political and military figure, he became the indispensable leader of the Chinese revolution. He was a revolutionary romantic, who believed in the power of the collective will of the masses, rather than Leninist party organization, to transform nature and history.

His political career began in earnest in the aftermath of the **May 4th Movement**, and in 1921 he was one of the delegates to the founding congress of the **Chinese Communist Party (CCP)**. In 1926 he made an inspection of the peasant movement in Hunan province, and his report argued the need for the party to help the peasants overthrow the landlord system. His pro-peasant orientation became much more important to the party after 1927 when the communists were driven out of the cities into the countryside. He still had Moscow-supported rivals within the party leadership, but he swept them aside during the **Long March**.

From then until 1949, and indeed until 1957, his career was one of almost unbroken success, and he established himself as a genuinely charismatic leader. He became a skilful guerrilla strategist, who wore down first Japanese, and then later Nationalist, opposition. To win peasant support, he insisted upon a disciplined **People's Liberation Army** (PLA) which could live and merge with the people, and he organized moderate land reform programmes to avoid antagonizing too many opponents. After 1937 he set out to win over anti-Japanese support with his theories of New Democracy, insisting that the CCP could work with all patriots, almost irrespective of class background. In addition he set himself up as the theoretician of the Chinese revolution, "sinifying" Marxism, ready to use ideas and aid from the Soviet Union, but only where this would further the revolution in China. He stressed practice as the measure and also the starting-point of theory, and he presented contradictions in society as the driving force of history.

Between 1949 and 1957 he was content to allow China to follow in the Soviet Union's footsteps. Towards the end of the First Five-Year Plan he became increasingly dissatisfied with the achievements of socialism in China, as well as in the rest of the communist bloc. He urged the Great Leap Forward upon a reluctant party leadership as the Chinese road to socialism with "Mao Zedong thought" as its theoretical basis. It embodied Mao's preference for mass movements and campaigns rather than bureaucratic organization. It was intended to create a society which felt socialist, and where the masses would be inspired to achieve socialism at an unparalleled rate. He also insisted that government policies should be completely adapted to Chinese conditions and not blindly copied from foreign, especially Soviet, advisers and models.

The failure of the Great Leap Forward led Mao to retire to the "second line of decision-making". But his embarrassment turned to resentment, as he saw his colleagues abandoning socialism and ignoring him. Parallels with the fate of socialism in the USSR after Stalin's death struck him more forcibly, as he sharpened the Sino-Soviet dispute.

In the end he lured his opponents into a trap and sprang the Cultural Revolution upon them. He declared that "to rebel is justified". He urged the Red Guards to "bombard the headquarters", and he presided over the dismantling of the party apparatus which he had built up. He took the side of the masses against the communist "establishment" and the intelligentsia. Both cadres and intellectuals were expected to learn "real" life and consciousness through physical labour among the peasants.

From then until his death he again dominated China, but as he developed Parkinson's disease and became more feeble, he was less capable of dynamic leadership, although he did preside over the political opening of China to the West in the early 1970s.

He left behind, however, a bitterly resentful core of senior political leaders who had been purged during the Cultural Revolution and who coalesced under the leadership of **Deng Xiaoping** to overturn the main features of the later Mao period. They produced a "Resolution on Party History" in 1981 which condemned virtually all of Mao's actions after 1957.

CIPF

MARCOS, FERDINAND. Marcos was elected as President in late 1965 and was re-elected on two occasions prior to his downfall in early 1986. Prior to his election as President he served as a special assistant to President Roxas in the 1940s and as a member of the House of Representatives and Senate in the 1950s and early 1960s.

During his 20-year rule, Marcos developed a corrupt system of patronage, under which relatives and friends of the "first family" grew fabulously rich through a mixture of blatant corruption and monopolistic control of key companies and state enterprises. Marcos and his wife Imelda (who had resided in Hawaii since fleeing the Philippines in the aftermath of the Aquino revolution) were indicted by a US grand jury in October 1988 on charges of illegally transferring into the USA over US$100 million in funds embezzled from the Philippines government or extorted through "bribes, kickbacks and gratuities" in the form of cash and corporate stock. They were indicted after failing to respond to grand jury subpoenas in connection with the case in August. Amongst others charged in connection with the Marcos' activities was Adnan Khashoggi, a rich Saudi businessman. Imelda travelled to New York in late October in order to be present at the trial, but her husband was excused attendance on the grounds of ill-health. Also in late 1988, the Philippine government filed a civil lawsuit in a Los Angeles court, which could lead in theory to the forfeiture of all the Marcos property. Marcos died in September 1989, and the Aquino government refused to allow his burial in the Philippines.

DS

MARSHALL ISLANDS, REPUBLIC OF. *Population* (est. 1988): 34,000, mostly Micronesians. *Area*: 181 sq km scattered over some 465,000 sq km of the central Pacific. The Marshalls comprise over 1,200 islands, the largest being Kwajalein. The capital is Darrit-Uliga-Dalap, on Majuro. From 1946 to 1958 the islands of Bikini and Enewetak provided testing grounds for US nuclear weapons.

Germany declared a protectorate over the islands in 1885. In 1914 they were seized by Japan, which was given a League of Nations mandate over them in 1919. After heavy fighting in World War II, they were occupied by American forces, and in 1947 were made part of the United Nations Trust Territory of the Pacific Islands, under US administration, along with Micronesia, the Northern Marianas, and Palau.

The Marshall Islands became internally self-governing in 1979, and in 1982 signed a Compact of Free Association with the USA, endorsed by referendum in 1983, the USA providing financial assistance and being responsible for internal security and defence. The Trust Territory was dissolved in 1986.

The economy is supported by subsistence farming, tourism, and the US civil and military administration.

TBM

MAY 4TH MOVEMENT. On May 4, 1919, news of the terms of the Versailles Peace Treaty reached Beijing and provoked an immediate public demonstration by students and intellectuals. The former German-controlled territories in Shandong province had been ceded to Japan rather than returned to China. This sparked off a series of protests throughout China. What began as protest then turned into a movement for national recovery and modernization. In language and literature it advocated popular rather than classical forms of expression. In politics, it led to renewed support for the nationalist party, although later some went on to join the newly formed **Chinese Communist Party**.

CIPF

MENZIES, SIR ROBERT GORDON. Prime Minister of Australia (United Australia Party) April 1938–August 1941, and (as leader of a coalition of the Liberal and Country parties) December 1949–January 1966. His government negotiated the Colombo Plan of economic assistance, the **ANZUS Pact**, and took the decisions for Australia to participate in the Malayan emergency, the **Korean War**, the war of confrontation with Indonesia, and the Vietnam War. Menzies was strongly attached to the British connection, including the Monarchy. He died in 1978.

TBM

MEXICO, UNITED STATES OF. *Population*: 82,000,000 (1988). *Area*: 1,972,547 sq km. *Gross Domestic Product*: US$97,302 million. *Trade*: US$28,897 million (1986). *Top five trading partners*: USA, Japan, West Germany, Spain, France. *Defence spending*: US$966 million. *Education spending as a percentage of GNP*: 2.7. *Urban population as percentage of total*: 43. *Birth rate*: 33.5 per thousand. *Life expectancy*: males 50.5; females 53.5.

Geographical background. Mexico has coastal lowlands along both its Pacific and Caribbean shorelines merging in the Isthmus of Tehuantepec and continuing eastward into the flat limestone plain of the Yucatán Peninsula. The northern interior consists of a highland plateau bounded by ranges of the Sierra Madre mountains to both the West and the East. Temperatures varies with

altitude. The North, in the rain shadow of the Sierra Madre Occidental, is desert. The coastal lowlands of the Yucatán Peninsula have subtropical and tropical climates. Mexico City, situated at 6,000 ft, is much cooler. Nearly 15 million hectares are cultivated.

Mexico has some of the best asphalted trunk roads in Latin America. Almost 50 per cent of the country's 214,403 km of road are paved. It also has a well-developed railway system (20,000 km) now much neglected. The Caribbean ports, especially Tampico, Tuxpam and Coatzacoalcos, are important serving a relatively large merchant marine and fleet of tankers; Pacific ports, though adequate, are less used, and Acapulco, the best known, is primarily a tourist resort. National and international Airlines service the capital and major centres.

A fifth of Latin America's population lives in Mexico, the largest Spanish-speaking country in the world, and its capital, Mexico City (properly México, D.F. – with a population of 14.5 million) is probably the largest city in the world. Population growth at 2.7 per cent *per annum* is rapid enough to strain existing educational and housing resources.

Socio-political background. Mexico's population is three-quarters *mestizo*. The majority of the rest is Indian with a small number of Europeans and blacks. Spanish is the national language, though over 200 Indian languages survive in use, the most important being Nahuatl, spoken by some four million inhabitants. There is no official religion. Most are nominally Roman Catholic but secularized with animist undertones. Primary education is free and compulsory and 94.2 per cent of school age are enrolled. Non-attendance is a problem in rural areas, as is the drop-out rate, and adult illiteracy is still at approximately 19 per cent. In addition to the National University (UNAM) in Mexico City, with over 200,000 students, Mexico has many good higher education institutions; each state has both public and private universities and government-supported technical education.

Campaigns by both the national government and international agencies have greatly reduced deaths from diseases such as cholera and typhoid, but the consequences of malnutrition, inadequate housing and poor sanitation remain. Around 70 per cent of urban and 30 per cent of rural homes have piped water, but only 40 per cent of urban homes have sewerage and in the countryside it is unknown. The infant mortality rate is a high 60 per thousand. Mexico's doctor to population ratio (1: 1251) is relatively good, but does not indicate the concentration of facilities in some wealthier areas. Social security provision is likewise concentrated in urban districts.

Political history. Independent in 1821, Mexico lost Central America in 1824. Texas seceded in 1836 and was annexed by the USA in 1848; in the war that followed Mexico lost over half its national territory to the USA. The dictatorship of Porfirio Díaz lasted for 35 years and in the great Revolution that began in 1910 over half a million people died before power was consolidated by the creation in 1929 of the Party of the National Revolution (PNR), known since 1946 as the Party of the Institutionalized Revolution (PRI). Major land reform was carried out under the presidency of Lázaro Cárdenas (1934–40) and under his successors Mexico underwent a major industrial transformation averaging 6 per cent growth from 1940 to 1975. Mexico is a federal republic of 32 states and a Federal District whose governor is appointed by the President. The Federal Government is headed by an elected civilian President with extensive powers over government and economy. The bicameral Congress of two houses, the 64-member Senate and the 500-member Chamber of Deputies, has historically been subordinate. Each state has an elected governor and legislature, but there is only one unified judiciary. The law of *amparo* is an important safeguard of individual rights, and both individual and social rights are spelt out in detail in the 1917 Constitution.

Recent developments. Domination by the ruling party has been increasingly questioned by intellectuals. When the earthquake of 1986 revealed the extent of corruption a major opposition force emerged which posed a threat to the election of Carlos Salinas de Gortari in 1988 and overnight achieved substantial representation in Congress. Power nationally and at state level remains for the present, however, effectively in the hands of the PRI.

Outline of economic development. An important oil producer since 1914. Mexico's oil wealth helped fuel her industrialization, based on the coal and steel complex of the area around Monterrey, Nuevo León. Petroleum accounts for two-thirds of all exports; coffee for 2.4 per cent. Other minerals exported include **gold**, silver, copper, **lead** and sulphur. A major producer of sugar and cotton, Mexico lacks good agricultural land and feeding its growing population is becoming a serious problem.

Current economic situation. Mexico found huge new oil reserves in the Isthmus in the 1970s but after the first "oil shock" of 1973 unwisely borrowed and spent in anticipation of the revenues. In 1982 her default gave the world the term "the debt crisis". At the end of 1988 total indebtedness was still over US$102,000 million, equivalent to some 37 per cent of exports. The rising price of crude is critical. Mexico has a sophisticated economy, but it fluctuates both with the oil market and with the health of the US economy. Closeness to the USA is crucial in two burgeoning areas: export of fruit and vegetables and manufacturing "white goods".

P&SC

MICRONESIA, FEDERAL STATE OF. *Population* (est. 1988): 101,000, Micronesian. *Total land area:* 702 sq km. The country comprises over 600 islands scattered over an area 965 km north to south and 2,800 km east to west, and divided into two groups. The eastern group includes the "states" of Truck, Pohnpei, and Kosrae; the western group includes Yap. The capital is Kolonia, on Pohnpei.

The islands were probably settled from eastern Melanesia about 3,500 years ago. They were colonized by Spain in the seventeenth century, and came under Japanese control after World War I. During World War II they were taken by American forces and in 1947 became part of the United Nations Trust Territory of the Pacific Islands including also the Marshall Islands, the Northern Marianas, and Palau, administered by the USA. The Federated States of Micronesia became internally self-governing in 1979 and in 1982 signed a Compact of Free Association with the United States, endorsed by referendum in 1983 and by US law in 1985. The Trust Territory was dissolved in 1986. The terms of the "free association" require the USA to be responsible for internal and external security, and to provide financial subventions. The federation could become fully independent at any time by plebiscite.

There is a single chamber National Congress, electing a president and vice-president. Congress comprises one senator at large from each of the four states, elected for four-year terms, and single district senators with two-year terms elected on a population basis. Each state has an elected legislative and governor.

The economy is based on subsistence farming and fishing, with exports of copra and black pepper, but about 70 per cent of revenue is from US grants.

TBM

MIDWAY ISLANDS. *Population* (1980): 453. *Area:* 5 sq km. An unincorporated territory of the

United States comprising a coral atoll enclosing two islands, Eastern and Sand, located some 1850 km north-west of Hawaii. Claimed by the USA in 1859 and formally annexed in 1867, Midway Islands have been administered by the US Navy, providing a submarine cable station and a naval and air base. In World War II the battle of Midway (June 3-6, 1942) was the turning point of the Pacific War as US aircraft destroyed a major part of the Japanese carrier fleet. There is a national wildlife reserve on the islands.

TBM

MIGRATION. Migration towards the Pacific coast and its hinterland has been a notable phenomenon in recent decades in both the Soviet Union and the United States. This has been through a mixture of financial or other incentives and perceived new opportunities. In the USA, the movement accelerated as a result of public concern from the 1960s on for a better quality of life, which was seen to be available either in sunny California or in the physically beautiful states of Oregon and Washington. The attractions of the Soviet Far East were less obvious and indeed, living conditions are still quite harsh in eastern Siberia, Kamchatka and the north-west Pacific coast. The scientifically or militarily sensitive nature of some of the activities carried out in the Soviet Far East has also made it more attractive to well paid specialists than to general settlers.

In many of the developing countries in the region, there has been rapid urbanization during the 1980s, especially in Latin America. Demographic projections indicate that this trend will continue at least up to the end of the century. Mexico City is predicted to be the largest city on earth by the year 2000, with a population of over 30,000,000. Other Pacific mega-cities already include Shanghai, Beijing and Tokyo-Yokohama, emphasizing the shift of urban dynamism away from the northern Atlantic rim, where in pre-war times London, Paris and New York were supreme (though São Paulo, Rio de Janeiro and Buenos Aires illustrate the continued urban growth in the south-west Atlantic). Continued urbanization in the Pacific region has important social and economic implications, and is likely to stimulate the region's growing supremacy in several sectors of manufacturing industries and communications.

The **Pol Pot** regime in Cambodia reversed the urbanization trend by sending people out of the capital Phnom Penh, though that situation is now being changed. Moreover, conflicts in Southeast Asia and Central America have provoked considerable migrations, both within countries and over national borders. In Indonesia, though, large migrations have taken place as part of government policy, to try to reduce population pressure in overcrowded islands, notably Java. This "transmigration" scheme has been the subject of considerable controversy, not only because of the often basic facilities awaiting migrants, but also because of their impact on the local environment and indigenous population of the host communities. (*See also* **Refugees**)

JF

MONGOLIA. (Note: *see also* **Mongolian People's Republic**)

Geographical background. Mongolia is a landlocked country situated on the Central Asiatic Plateau. Almost all of the country lies more than 1,000 metres above sea level, rising to over 4,300 metres in the Altai mountains in the west and to between 2,500 and 3,900 metres in the Hentai and Hangai mountain ranges in the north-central part of the country. Between these mountain ranges lie relatively fertile basins dotted with lakes and crossed by numerous rivers. The east of the country is a vast hilly plain. The Gobi region, covering most of the south, is semi-desert. Mongolia's climate is harsh, with a long, cold, dry winter, and a short mild summer during which most of the annual rainfall occurs.

Socio-political background. The Mongol peoples were originally pastoral nomads or semi-nomads, and were organized until the first half of the twentieth century along feudal lines. Until the arrival of atheistic Communist regimes in the lands inhabited by Mongols (not only the Mongolian People's Republic and the Inner Mongolian Autonomous Region of China, but also parts of western China and the Buryat, Kalmyk and Tuva republics in the Soviet Union), Buddhist Lamaism was the predominant religion.

Pre-modern history. The first indentifiably Mongol state was formed by the consolidation of nomadic tribal groupings in 1206 under Chingis (Genghis) Khan. In the ensuing 60 years the armies of Chingis and his successors conquered much of Eurasia, from China and Korea in the east to the borders of Hungary and Poland in the west, and south into Iran. Within a century of its creation, however, the Mongol empire began to disintegrate as a result of dissentions between its various khanates, and later because of foreign military pressures. It finally collapsed in the seventeenth century in the face of the rising power of the Manchus, who were expanding south-westwards out of Manchuria and eventually conquered China in 1644-62. The last Mongol emperor died in 1636, and after half a century as tributaries to the Manchus, the Mongol princes finally surrendered their independence and accepted Manchu Chinese overlordship in 1691.

Early modern history. Chinese control of Mongolia lasted until 1911, when the collapse of the Qing dynasty prompted the aristocracy and church hierarchy in the province of Outer Mongolia to enter into a struggle culminating in full independence in 1921, to become the Mongolian People's Republic. Inner Mongolia has remained part of China.

IG

MONGOLIAN PEOPLE'S REPUBLIC.
Population: 2,000,000 (official est. end-1987). *Area*: 1,564,000 sq km. *Gross National Product*: (1986) US$3,620 million. *Trade*: US$1,315 million (1986). *Principal trading partners*: Soviet Union (80%, 1986); other Comecon members (18%, 1986). *Defence spending*: (est. 1988) US$266 million. *Education spending*: (est. 1988) US$354,600,000. *Urban population as percentage of total*: 52 (1988). *Birth rate*: 37 per thousand (1988). *Life expectancy*: 64 (1987).

General background. The Mongolian People's Republic, according to the Constitution of 1960, is "a sovereign democratic state of working people" in which "supreme state power" is vested in the unicameral People's Great *Hural* (Assembly), whose members (currently numbering 370) are elected unopposed at five-yearly intervals by universal adult suffrage from a single list of officially nominated candidates; the most recent elections were held in June 1986. The members of the People's Great *Hural* in turn elect a Presidium, whose Chairman is the head of state, and the Council of Ministers, but these elections are a formality, the People's Great *Hural* having no real power and normally meeting only for a few days each year to endorse policies formulated by the leadership of the **Mongolian People's Revolutionary Party**, the only legal political grouping.

The capital of Mongolia is Ulan Bator (literally "Red Hero"), formerly Urga. For local administration, the country is divided into 18 provinces (*aymags*), which elect their own provincial *hurals*. The predominant population group are the Khalkha (Halh) Mongols, comprising 77.5 per cent at the last census (1979); other Mongol groups make up a further 10 per cent of the population. Khalkha Mongol is the official language; in 1946 the traditional alphabet was replaced by a form of Cyrillic script. The largest minority groups are the turkic-speaking **Kazakhs** (Hasags), who comprise over 5 per cent of the total population and are concentrated in the far western province of Bayan-Ölgiy.

Political history. In 1911, in the aftermath of the collapse of the imperial regime in China, the aristocracy and church hierarchy in the province of Outer Mongolia, supported by Tsarist Russia, declared it an independent monarchy, with the Living Buddha of Urga, the head of the lamaist church, as the Bogdo Gegen (head of state). In 1915, after an inconclusive war with China, it was agreed by Mongolian, Russian and Chinese negotiators that Mongolia should become an autonomous state under Chinese suzerainty, although it enjoyed the *de facto* status of a Russian protectorate. With the fall of the Russian Tsarist regime in 1917 and Russia's ensuing revolutionary turmoil, the Chinese seized the opportunity to abrogate Mongolia's autonomy and reassert their control, and in 1919–20 Mongolia was occupied by Chinese troops. These were expelled at the beginning of 1921 by White Russian forces, who were in turn expelled in July 1921 by Mongolian partisans organized by the Mongolian People's Party, with significant Soviet military support. Mongolia's independence was proclaimed and the Bogdo Gegen's government nominally restored to power, although in fact the country was firmly under Soviet direction. Upon the death of the Bogdo Gegen in 1924 the renamed Mongolian People's Revolutionary Party (MPRP) took power, and a constitution on the Soviet model was introduced under which the People's Republic was declared.

Although the MPRP congress of 1925 adopted a resolution declaring that Mongolia would be transformed into a socialist country without passing through a capitalist stage, no radical changes were made until 1928, when campaigns were initiated to collectivize the economy and to dispossess the nobility and the Buddhist priesthood; these campaigns aroused such strong resistance, however, that they were modified in 1932. A series of political purges took place between 1922 and 1939, in which not only the former nobility and clergy but most of the revolutionary old guard, the military leadership and leftist intellectuals were liquidated. Marshal **Horloogiyn Choybalsan**, who was the only member of the original MPRP leadership to survive the purges, became Prime Minister in 1936, and thereafter power was largely concentrated in his hands.

In the summer of 1939 Mongolian and Soviet forces repulsed a Japanese invasion from Manchuria, and thereafter a truce reigned until August 1945, when Mongolia joined the Soviet Union in declaring war on Japan four days before the

Japanese surrender. There followed a brief Mongolian military incursion into northern China.

Choybalsan died in 1952, whereupon he was succeeded as Prime Minister by **Yumjaagiyn Tsedenbal**, the first secretary of the MPRP. Tsedenbal relinquished this latter post in 1954 to Dashiyn Damba, but resumed it in 1958. Tsedenbal was elected President in 1974, relinquishing the premiership to **Jambyn Batmönh**, but in 1984 he retired unexpectedly from the presidency and the party leadership, ostensibly on health grounds, and Batmönh succeeded him in both these posts.

Recent developments. The strong and all-pervasive Soviet influence has meant that the currents of reform emanating from the Soviet political leadership are being emulated, albeit cautiously, in Mongolia. Since the ouster of Tsedenbal in 1984 he has been blamed (albeit so far not explicitly), in much the same way as the late Leonid Brezhnev in the Soviet Union, for "stagnation" which afflicted Mongolia's socioeconomic development throughout the 1960s and 1970s, and a campaign against "negative phenomena", including corruption amongst officials, was stepped up at the beginning of 1986. A measure of Soviet-style *glasnost* ("openness") has also been in evidence since 1988 with the limited rerappraisal of both pre- and post-revolutionary Mongolian history.

Outline of economic development. At the time of the declaration of the People's Republic in 1924, Mongolia's economy was almost wholly dependent on animal herding. The first national currency and a state bank were created in 1925, but otherwise the MPRP regime did not embark on a programme of economic development until 1928, when a collectivization drive, which included the expropriation by the state of foreign (i.e. mostly Chinese) businesses and church properties, was begun. However, in the course of the next three years this generally ill-prepared programme had a devastating effect on Mongolia's economic mainstay, with cattle stocks dropping by at least a third, and in 1932 it was partially reversed under the "New Turn Policy", which again encouraged private ownership of cattle and private trade.

There was very little industrial development until 1948, when a concerted programme to modernize the economy was initiated. Since then economic development has been co-ordinated by a series of five-year plans, and has been greatly assisted by the Soviet Union and the communist states of Eastern Europe. Mongolia's state-owned industry, centred on Ulan Bator and Darhan (mid-way between the capital and the Soviet

border), has so far been oriented largely towards the exploitation of the country's wealth of raw materials (notably coal, lime, copper, molybdenum, gold and fluorspar), and the processing of products derived from animal husbandry. In agriculture, large-scale crop growing, which had been a feature of the Mongolian economy only since the creation of state farms by the MPRP regime, increased drastically after 1959 by the ploughing of large tracts of virgin land. Collectivization of herding was again encouraged after 1947, and was virtually completed by the late 1950s.

Current economic situation. In early 1988 a senior MPRP official publicly observed that Mongolia still lacked the material and technical base to realize the objectives of a report from the 15th MPRP congress in 1966, which had said that about 15 years would be required for Mongolia to complete the transition from an agrarian-industrial economy to one where industrial production was the main feature. Agriculture, particularly animal herding, remains the dominant economic activity, employing an estimated 34 per cent of the workforce in 1986 but contributing somewhat less than 20 per cent of net material product. Since the late 1970s the growth of the animal husbandry sector has been disrupted by devastating livestock losses due to a series of severe winters.

The eighth Five-Year Plan (1986–90) places great emphasis on industrial development, but this continues to be retarded by the chronic inefficiency, waste and poor technical develoment inherited from the "period of stagnation" in the 1960s and 1970s. Furthermore, Mongolia's foreign trade balance is adversely affected by high prices for technology and low prices for raw materials.

Mongolia's population growth (nearly 3 per cent a year) is currently running ahead of infrastructural development. This has led to growing youth unemployment, which the government is trying to alleviate by sending surplus manpower to the Soviet Union.

Foreign relations. Mongolia has been heavily dependent on Soviet political, military and economic support since the foundation of the People's Republic. It is a member of the Council for Mutual Economic Assistance (CMEA, or Comecon), the Soviet-dominated trading bloc which also incorporates the Soviet allies in Eastern Europe, along with Cuba and Vietnam. Until the 1950s Mongolia was recognized as a sovereign state only by the Soviet Union and its communist allies, but it now has diplomatic relations with over 100 countries, including (since

1987) the United States. China formally recognized Mongolia's independence in 1946, but relations between the two countries were severely strained after Mongolia sided with the Soviet Union in the Sino-Soviet split at the beginning of the 1960s. Major improvements have taken place since the mid-1980s, however, espcially in the context of the Sino-Soviet rapprochement and the planned 75 per cent reduction, announced in March 1989, of the estimated 50,000 Soviet troops stationed on Mongolian soil.

Prospects for development. The Mongolian authorities have begun to emulate aspects of Soviet *perestroika* (restructuring) in economic management in an effort to overcome the country's current economic woes. A law granting considerable organizational and financial autonomy to individual enterprises entered into force at the beginning of 1989, and in 1988 wages in the light and food industries, internal trade and supply were linked to enterprise revenue. Also in 1988 the number of private co-operatives supplying goods and services rose to nearly 500, and there was an increase in family and collective contracting in herdsmen's collectives. Furthermore, certain enterprises were leased by the state to the labour collective.

The eighth Five-Year Plan (1986–90) calls for the modernization of production processes and more efficient use of existing production capacity and material resources. New projects are limited to energy development, expansion of the copper and molybdenum mining and concentrating combine at Erdenet near the Soviet border, and studies for the development, with Comecon assistance, of coking-coal and phosphate mining.

IG

MONGOLIAN PEOPLE'S REVOLUTIONARY PARTY (MPRP). Founded in March 1921 as the Mongolian People's Party and renamed in 1924, the (communist) MPRP is the sole legal political party in the Mongolian People's Republic. The MPRP originally constituted a broad front of forces opposed to the restoration of Chinese sovereignty over Outer Mongolia in 1919-20, these forces succeeding, with Soviet assistance, in establishing the country's independence in 1921. The MPRP formally took power and declared the People's Republic in 1924. A series of purges took place between 1922 and 1939, out of which **Horloogiyn Choybalsan**, Prime Minister after 1936 and the only surviving founder member of the party, emerged as paramount leader. For most of the period of Choybalsan's dictatorship, the MPRP was led

by **Yumjaagiyn Tsedenbal**, who took over the premiership upon Choybalsan's death in 1952; Tsedenbal relinquished the office of MPRP first secretary in 1954 to Dashiyn Damba, only to resume it in 1958 (the title was changed to general secretary in 1981). However, in 1984 Tsedenbal was ousted and replaced by **Jambyn Batmönh**.

The MPRP has nearly 90,000 members, and is led by an 85-member central committee. Its congress meets at five-yearly intervals, most recently in May 1986.

IG

MORO NATIONAL LIBERATION FRONT (MNLF). The MNLF was established in the Philippines in 1968 about the same time as the **New People's Army** – NPA — as the vehicle for achieving independence or autonomy for the Muslim population of the Philippines. According to the 1970 census returns, Muslims represented over 5 per cent of the country's population. They were mostly concentrated in the southern provinces of Mindanao where they represented a culturally homogeneous and distinctive group which suffered levels of social and economic deprivation greater than that of their Christian neighbours. By 1971 it was estimated that some 800,000 Muslims were refugees having been evicted from their lands by Christians, and almost 2,000 people had been killed over an 18-month period in the regular fighting which had occurred between armed groups from the two communities. In 1973 the Islamic Conference Organization (ICO) demanded of the **Marcos** government revisions in its policy towards the Muslim community. Cosmetic changes were introduced, but nevertheless the MNLF pursued their policy of armed struggle. In early 1975 talks between representatives of the Marcos regime and the MNLF held under ICO auspices in Saudi Arabia broke down over the government's refusal to countenance any significant autonomy for the southern provinces.

Renewed ICO-sponsored talks between the rebels and the government, which were held in Libya in late 1976, resulted in agreement on a ceasefire in return for the granting of autonomy to the 13 provinces comprising Mindanao, the Sulu archipelago and Palawan island. The agreement foundered upon the later insistence by the government that referenda should be held in the affected provinces. Nevertheless, in March 1977 the government declared the 13 provinces as an autonomous region and began creating the basis of a regional administrative structure. A referendum was held in April, despite the MNLF's refusal to participate. According to the government's figures, 75 per cent of the electorate participated in the poll, the overwhelming majority of whom voted against the autonomy proposals. Despite the result, the regional government remained in place (under the terms of a law of February 1977 which had theoretically divided the country into 12 autonomous regions) but the MNLF refused to participate within it and was reported to have reverted to its original demand for complete independence. The war continued on a sporadic basis, and during the latter years of the Marcos regime the Muslim threat, which had been weakened as a result of severe internal divisions, was secondary to that posed by the communist NPA. Nevertheless, when martial law was lifted elsewhere in the country in 1981, it was retained in the Muslim provinces.

During her election campaign in early 1986, **Corazon Aquino** pledged to "respect and substantiate" the Muslim aspirations for autonomy and following her election she urged insurgents of all persuasions to cease fighting and begin negotiations with the new government.

However, the optimism which surrounded the Aquino government's early talks with Muslim rebels quickly gave way to recrimination and deadlock during her second year in office, with neither side able to agree on a formula for autonomy to end the rebellion in the southern provinces. Muslim guerrilla activities appeared to subside during 1988, largely as a result of internal divisions within the MNLF and the other organizations (most notably the Moro Islamic Liberation Front). In February of that year the MNLF had rejected participation in the newly formed Regional Consultative Commission, the establishment of which had been announced during a tour of Mindanao by President Aquino earlier in the month.

DS

MOULINAKA (KAMPUCHEA). Moulinaka (Mouvement pour la Libération Nationale de Kampuchea) was established in August 1979 by supporters of **Prince Sihanouk** under the leadership of Kong Silea (until his death, in August 1980). Its aim was to launch a guerrilla struggle against the pro-Vietnamese regime in Phnom Penh, but it was much weaker than other such groups and its base inside Cambodia was captured by the Vietnamese in 1983. The survivors were subsequently absorbed into the **Sihanoukist National Army**.

RBS

MULDOON, RT HON SIR ROBERT. Born in Auckland in 1921, he served in the Pacific and in Italy during World War II. He was elected as Member for Tamaki in 1960. In 1967 he became Minister of Finance, in 1972 Deputy Prime Minister, and was Prime Minister of New Zealand from 1975 to 1984. He was knighted in 1983, and was leader of the Opposition from July to November 1984.

TBM

MURDOCH, RUPERT. Australian-born publisher and media tycoon, now a US citizen (born in 1931). Group Chief Executive, The News Corporation Ltd., Australia; Chief Executive and Managing Director, News International plc, UK; Chairman and President, News America Publishing Inc.; Chairman, Times Newspaper Holdings plc, UK. Rupert Murdoch inherited his interest in the media and publishing from his father, Sir Keith Murdoch, who was Managing Director of the Melbourne Herald. He decided that, unlike his father, he would have full control of all his enterprises rather than working for others. His controversial career, not only in Australia but also on both sides of the Atlantic, involved a number of well-publicized takeovers and buy-outs, leading to the acquisition of many well-known newspapers and broadcasting institutions. Rupert Murdoch has been a pioneer in the use of new technology, sometimes in the face of considerable union opposition, both in the field of newspaper production and in satellite TV.

JF

N

NACIONALISTA PARTY (PHILIPPINES).
The Nacionalista Party (NP) represents the right wing of the former *Partido Nacionalista*, which was formed in 1907 and divided into two factions in 1946. The NP held power between 1952 and 1961 and was in 1965 joined by **Ferdinand Marcos** who was, as that party's candidate, elected President in November of that year. After the establishment of the **New Society Movement** by Marcos in 1978, the party went into opposition and in 1982 it joined the **United Nationalist Democratic Organization**.

In mid-May 1989 the oppositon NP held a revival convention at which Vice-President **Salvador Laurel** was elected as the party's president, and President Aquino's erstwhile ally and former Defence Secretary, **Juan Ponce Enrile**, was chosen as the party's general secretary. Present at the NPs revival convention were most of the constituent elements of the Grand Alliance for Democracy, a loose coalition of mainly conservative politicans which had opposed **Aquino** in the 1987 congressional elections. The relaunched NP also incorporated the members of the Union for National Action, the political grouping established by Laurel in 1988, which had failed in its avowed aim of uniting the right-wing opponents of Aquino.

DS

NAKASONE YASUHIRO. The first Japanese Prime Minister since 1972 to remain in office for more than one two-year term, Nakasone became president of the **Liberal Democratic Party** and so Prime Minister in 1982. He was re-elected unopposed in 1984, and was given an exceptional one-year extension in 1986. Unusually popular at home and abroad, Nakasone generated a sense that he was at ease with foreigners and foreign leaders felt that here was a Japanese they could understand, a sentiment captured in the "Ron-Yasu" relation (Ronald Reagan and Nakasone Yasuhiro).

RAB

NATIONAL FRONT (MALAYSIA). The ruling National Front (*Barisan Nasional*) of Malaysia (NF) was created in 1974 as a broader-based successor to the Alliance coalition headed by the three main communal parties (Malay,

Chinese and Indian) which had come to power in 1955 and had led the country to independence in 1957. The NF is an essentially conservative grouping and its dominant component is the **United Malays National Organization** (UMNO), which has provided all of Malaysia's Prime Ministers. As of mid-1989 the NF was chaired by the Prime Minister, Dr **Mahathir**, and its general secretary was the Deputy Prime Minister, Abdul Ghafer Baba.

The composition of the NF has varied over the years, as parties have been expelled or have withdrawn and others have been admitted to membership. At the time of the August 1986 general elections it embraced 13 formations, namely (federal seat distribution in parenthesis): (i) *national parties*: UMNO (83), **Malaysian Chinese Association** (17), **Malaysian Indian Congress** (6), Gerakan (5), the Muslim Front (1) and Berjasa (0); *regional parties*: United Sabah Party (10), United Sabah National Organization (5), United Traditional Bumiputra Party of Sarawak (8), Sarawak National Party (5), Sarawak Dayak People's Party (4), Sarawak United People's Party (4) and the People's Progressive Party of Perak (0). At state level, NF parties were confirmed in power in all 11 Peninsular Malaysia states in August 1986 and also formed the governments of Sabah and Sarawak as a result of state elections in May 1986 and April 1987 respectively.

Following a High court ruling in February 1988 effectively declaring UMNO to be an "illegal society" Dr Mahathir launched a successor party called New Umno. The new formation was immediately admitted to membership of the NF.

DS

NATIONAL PARTY OF AUSTRALIA. Until 1982 known as the Country Party, formed during World War I to represent the interests and needs of people living outside the main metropolitan areas. It is a free enterprise party dedicated to national development. It has held office in coalition with the **Liberal Party**.

TBM

NATIONAL REVOLUTIONARY COUNCIL. The National Revolutionary Council (*sapa patiwat*), of Thailand led by former communist Prasert Sapsunthorn, claimed at its inaugural meeting in April 1987 that it supported Gen. Chaovalit's concept of a "peaceful revolution". The Council has connections with the Democratic Labour Party and the so-called Democratic Soldiers group. Members of both groups were thought to have played a role in the formulation of Prime Ministerial Guideline 66/2523 in 1980 and had past associations with **Chaovalit**. In mid-May the Council extended an invitation to Prime Minister Prem (which he refused) to become its chairman and proposed that it be allowed to temporarily assume the duties of the House of Representatives until after the July general election had been held. The next month Prasert announced that the Council had changed its name to the National Democratic Council. He said that the Thai people had misinterpreted the word "revolution" (*patiwat*) in the Council's title. In late May 1989 Gen. Chaovalit ordered the arrest of 14 Council leaders (including Prasert and Rainan Arunrangsi) after leaflets had been distributed demanding the dissolution of the House of Representatives and called for the appointment of Chaovalit as Prime Minister.

DS

NATURAL GAS. Natural gas usually occurs in association with oil borings and is largely composed of methane. Large regional producers are the USA and Indonesia. Brunei too is a major producer: through the Lumut plant set up in 1973 Brunei has agreed to sell five million tonnes of liquid natural gas yearly to Japan until 1993. The annual production of natural gas, in terajoules, is as follows: USA, 15,879; Canada, 2,740; Mexico, 1,048; Indonesia, 690; China, 475; Australia, 463; Colombia, 181; Japan, 90; New Zealand, 85; Chile, 37.

RS

NAURU. *Population* (est. 1986): 8,000. *Area*: 21 sq km. A republic within the Commonwealth (associate member). Nauru was settled from other Pacific islands at different periods, indicated by the two physical sub-types and the existence of 12 clans with individual dialects. European contact dates from 1798. The island was annexed by Germany in 1888. Phosphate deposits were discovered in 1899 and have been the basis of the economy ever since. Australia occupied Nauru in 1914, and after the war administered the territory as a League of Nations mandate on behalf of Britain, New Zealand and itself. Japan occupied the island in World War II, and in 1947 the United Nations made it a trust territory administered by Australia. A local Government Council

was set up in 1951, a legislative Council in 1966, and complete independence came in 1968. There is a parliament of 18 members, which elects the president.

The phosphate deposits, currently exported to Australia, New Zealand, Japan and the Republic of Korea, are expected to be exhausted by 1995. Revenue from their sales is shared between the government, land owners, a trust fund and the Nauru local government council. The country has invested in real estate, commercial and industrial projects, in Australia, Hawaii, and New Zealand, as well as in phosphate plants in India and the Philippines. Some rehabilitation of the land is in progress, and fishing and tourist industries are being developed, as well as tax haven facilities.

Nauruans have by far the highest per capita standard of living among the Pacific Islands territories and among the highest worldwide. There is no taxation.

TBM

NEW CALEDONIA. *Population* (est. 1988): 154,000 (Melanesians 43%, Europeans 37%, Wallisians and Tahitians 8%). *Area*: 19,103 sq km. The French overseas territory of New Caledonia (Territoire de la Nouvelle-Calédonie et Dépendances) comprises the islands of New Caledonia (16,750 sq km) and Walpole, the Isle of Pines (Ile des Pins) and the Loyalty, Belep, Huon, Surprise and Chesterfield island groups plus numerous uninhabited atolls. The capital is Nouméa, on New Caledonia.

There has been an Austronesian presence in the islands for 3,000–4,000 years. Captain James Cook landed in 1774, British and French missionaries in the early nineteenth century. France annexed the group in 1853, as part of the territory of Tahiti, and New Caledonia was a French penal colony from 1864 to 1897. **Nickel** was discovered in 1863.

With Australian assistance, New Caledonia joined the Free French movement in 1940, the USA subsequently building a military base, airfields and roads. In 1946 the islands became a French Overseas Territory, and in 1958 there was an election for a Council of Government, which increased in size as demands for self-government grew. In 1979 France dismissed the Council of Government and the territory was placed under the direct authority of the French high commissioner. In the late 1970s and early 1980s, pro-independence groups, largely Melanesian, pressed for independence, but they were effectively excluded from the July 1979 election, two parties loyal to France winning 22 of the 36 assembly seats.

In September 1981, Pierre Declercq, leader of the *Union Calédonienne*, a pro-independence party, was assassinated, causing increased tension. The French government of President Mitterrand introduced a number of social reforms during a one-year period of government by decree. Proposals for a five-year programme leading to an act of self-determination in 1989 (with the possibility of independence) were opposed in New Caledonia as giving too much or too little, and were rejected by the assembly in April 1984.

In April 1985 the French Prime Minister, M. Laurent Fabius, introduced a plan for regional council elections, each sending representatives to a new territory-wide congress, with a referendum on independence not later than December 1987. The main opposition group, the *Front de Libération Nationale Kanake Socialiste* (FLNKS), whose adherents had boycotted earlier elections, agreed to take part, despite reservations by more extreme factions, especially the *Front Uni de Libération Kanak* (FULK). FLNKS boycotted the 1986 French legislative elections which led to a conservative, Jacques Chirac, becoming prime minister. Chirac offered a referendum with a choice between independence and an extension of regional autonomy, believing the latter would succeed. In December 1986, at the recommendation of the South Pacific Forum, the United Nations General Assembly reinscribed New Caledonia on the list of non-self-governing territories. In May 1987 the FLNKS decided to boycott a referendum, to be held in September, and did so, with the result that a large majority of those voting supported remaining as part of the French republic. Kanak-supported public demonstrations, some accompanied by violence, continued throughout this period. In protest against alleged Australian support of the independence movement, its diplomatic representative in Nouméa was declared *persona non grata* and France suspended for several months ministerial visits between the two countries. The FLNKS boycotted the regional elections in April 1988.

The re-election in May of M. Mitterrand as President of France, and the replacement of the Gaullist Chirac government by a socialist administration, meant greater official sympathy for Kanak independence aspirations. On June 26, 1988, an accord was signed in Paris (at the Prime Minister's official residence, Matignon) between representatives of the Kanak and the white communities, providing for one year of direct administration from Paris, then 10 years with powers divided between the three provinces, with an act of self-determination in 1998. This was approved by the Territorial Congress in September, and a national referendum was held on Nov. 6, resulting in a favourable majority both nationwide (of a low turnout) and in New Caledonia, especially in Kanak areas.

On May 4, 1989, a Kanak extremist shot dead two moderate FLNKS leaders – Jean-Marie Tjibaou, chairman of the Front, and Yeiwéné Yeiwéné. This has raised the prospect of further turbulence but most parties appear determined to try to carry through the new arrangements.

Current economic situation. New Caledonia has the world's largest known deposits of nickel (about 30 per cent of the world total), and the free-enterprise economy has for many years been based on mining and metallurgical enterprises especially with nickel, and with cobalt and chromium. These provide 97 per cent of export income but the economy is thus especially vulnerable to international price fluctuations, as well as to internal unrest, and the budget is subsidized up to a third by France, including help to the tourist industry. Attempts have been made, with some success, to diversify the agricultural sector. France accounts for some 40 per cent of exports and nearly 60 per cent of imports.

TBM

NEW DEMOCRACY. In 1940 in China **Mao Zedong** outlined the programme for a "new" democracy under proletarian dictatorship, as opposed to the "old" democracy under bourgeois dictatorship. This was to unite all patriotic forces opposed to the Japanese occupation, and was intended to be the equivalent of the bourgeois revolution which Marx had specified for Western societies.

The main features were joint dictatorship of all revolutionary classes, democratic centralism in government, a mixed economy with large state-owned enterprises and banks coexisting with private enterprise, a "land to the tiller" campaign, and an anti-feudal and anti-imperialist culture. In 1949 the **Chinese Communist Party** established the Chinese People's Political Consultative Conference to implement this programme, with representation from a wide variety of groups. This phase came to an end in 1953–55 with the nationalization of industry and commerce, the introduction of state planning, and the collectivization of agriculture.

CIPF

NEW DEMOCRATIC PARTY (NDP – S. KOREA). Former political party of the Republic of Korea. Founded 1967, dissolved by Chun Doo

Hwan in 1980. Major opposition party during the presidency of **Park Chung-hee**. Presidential candidate Yun Po-son polled 40.9 per cent of votes in 1967 elections and candidate **Kim Dae Jung** polled just under half of the electorate in the 1971 elections.

JHG

NEW DEMOCRATIC REPUBLICAN PARTY (NDRP – S. KOREA). Founded in the Republic of Korea in 1987 to support the presidential aspirations of Kim Jong Pil, who received 7.9 per cent of votes cast in the presidential election of November 1987. The party received 15.6 per cent of the votes cast in the April 1988 National Assembly elections.

JHG

NEW ECONOMIC POLICY. The New Economic Policy (NEP) in Malaysia was inaugurated by the government in 1970 in the aftermath of serious inter-communal rioting which had broken out the previous year. The rioting had been engendered in part by resentment amongst Malays of the Chinese community's economic dominance. The NEP had as its central aims the reduction and eradication of poverty for all Malaysians by 1990, and the reduction and elimination of the identification of race with economic function by the same date. One element of the latter objective proposed that 30 per cent of commercial and industrial share capital would be in *bumiputra* ownership by 1990 (*bumiputra* literally meaning "sons of the soil", i.e. the Malays and other indigenous peoples).

The fourth national economic development plan (Fourth Malaysia Plan – FMP) for the period 1981–85 allocated some $M4,500 million for expenditure on various forms of "*bumiputra* advancement". It was proposed that a third of the money would be spent by the National Equity Corporation on the acquisition of corporate wealth for redistribution to *bumiputras*. Furthermore, the allocation of regional development funds between the states was strongly weighted in favour of the less developed states (which were populated predominantly by *bumiputras*). Nevertheless, at the time of the launching of the FMP, *bumiputras* owned and controlled less than 13 per cent of corporate stock (compared with 4.3 per cent in 1971). By 1986, ownership had risen to 18 per cent, but economic problems had forced the government to liberalize foreign equity participation the previous year in order to prevent the NEP from discouraging foreign investors. Despite an economic recovery in the late 1980s,

developments in the domestic economy and in the international economic environment, and the need to stimulate private investment, indicate that the NEP's central tenets might be altered after 1990. In December 1988 the government announced the formation of a non-partisan and multi-racial National Economic Consultative Committee to draft a replacement for the NEP upon its expiry.

DS

NEW PEOPLE'S ARMY. The Maoist Communist Party of the Philippines – Marxist–Leninist (CPP-ML), formed in late 1968 as a breakaway of the (pro-Soviet) Communist Party of the Philippines (PKP), quickly established an armed wing, the New People's Army (NPA), which by the early 1970s had succeeded in constructing an effective guerrilla organization upon the foundations of the Huk movement. Like the Huks (many of whose fighters joined the new force), the NPA advocated wholesale land reform and a programme of social justice as the solution to traditional peasant grievances. The NPA pursued the classic Maoist strategy of gradually expanding its control of the countryside in preparation for taking over the cities and by 1972 it was acknowledged to be the *de facto* administration in numerous remote areas of the country including parts of Luzon and on several outlying islands, where it undertook land redistribution and raised revenue through the collection of rents and taxes.

In 1981, the government forces resorted to the "strategic hamlets" concept, which involved the uprooting of families from their homes and lands and the relocation of about 250,000 people (mainly in Mindanao). Exploiting the government's unpopularity in the aftermath of the Aquino assassination, the NPA increased both the sphere and the scale of its operations throughout 1983 and 1984. The government gradually abandoned its "strategic hamlets" concept and returned to a policy of local military offensives in NPA-controlled territory, although the increasing demoralization of the Armed Forces meant that few successes were achieved. The movement also increased its urban activities, through a concerted campaign of political assassinations carried out by so-called "sparrow squads". In early 1985, the Defence Minister, **Juan Ponce Enrile**, stated that the NPA constituted the "most formidable threat" to the country's national security; he estimated that the movement had grown by over 20 per cent *per annum* since 1981, and had been active during 1984 in over 80 per cent of the country's 73 provinces resulting in the death of over 900 soldiers and 1,000 civilians. He claimed that the NPA's front-line strength stood at upwards of 20,000 fighters.

The NPA remained aloof from **Corazon Aquino**'s populist campaign in 1985–86 to remove **Marcos** from office, characterizing it as "a conflict within the ruling class". In March 1986, the CCP-ML rejected a government amnesty offer, but in June of that year, secret ceasefire talks between the NPA and the government started. The negotiations were impeded by procedural disagreements and also by actions attributed to the army, including the arrest of Rodolfo Salas, the NPA's overall commander in September. However, in November the two sides agreed to observe a truce, which only lasted until early February 1987 when fighting resumed. The Secretary of Local Government, Jaime Ferrer, was assassinated by one of a number of active NPA "sparrow squads" in Manila in August 1987. Upon the appointment of Gen. **Ramos** as Defence Secretary in January 1988, the government launched an intensified military campaign against the NPA. The movement's military commander, Romulo Kintanar, and the secretary-general of the CCP-ML, Rafael Baylosis, were arrested in Manila in March; Kintanar subsequently escaped from custody in November. Throughout 1988, sporadic clashes between the NPA and the army were reported, as were reciprocal killings by NPA and right-wing vigilante group members.

In February 1989 the NPA indicated that it would be willing to enter into peace talks with the government on condition that President Aquino promised not to renew the leases on US military bases due to expire in 1991. She refused to make such a commitment, and in late April Col. James Rowe, an officer of the Joint US Military Assistance Group, which co-ordinated US military assistance to the Philippines, was assassinated by a NPA "sparrow cell". Rowe was the highest ranking US officer to be killed by the NPA.

DS

NEW SOCIETY MOVEMENT (PHILIPPINES).
The New Society Movement (*Kilusan Bagong Lipunan* – KBL) was established in 1978 with the object of supporting the policies of President **Marcos**. After his fall from power in 1986 the KBL still existed as a political organization (especially in the Marcos home base of Ilocos Norte), but nationally it is politically irrelevant.

DS

NEW WORLD INFORMATION AND COMMUNICATION ORDER (NWICO).

NWICO is a cherished goal of many non-aligned countries in the region which wish to promote what has been described as the "decolonization of the media". Proponents maintain that about 90 per cent of news output in the developing world is controlled by western concerns, particularly through the major news agency wire services, such as Reuters, AFP and UPI. The basic argument is that such western sources inevitably reflect occidental viewpoints and prejudices and tend to concentrate on disasters, corruption and other negative stories which correspond to their stereotyped image of the Third World. In the words of President **Suharto** of Indonesia (hosting a conference of Information Ministers from Non-Aligned countries in 1984): "We are being flooded with news which, on the one hand, benefits only the interests of the advanced industrial countries and, on the other, harms the image of our countries which we are developing".

The principles of a New Order were extensively debated within the United Nations Educational, Scientific and Cultural Organisation (UNESCO), winning the keen support of its then Director-General Mahtar M'Bow. The Soviet Union and several of its allies backed a campaign to get NWICO formally adopted. This met strong resistance from the United States and some other western countries, which saw NWICO as an attempt by many Third World and socialist governments to get an even tighter stranglehold over the media of their countries than they had already. Thus NWICO was characterized by the Reagan administration in Washington as a means of increasing censorship and information control. The arguments became very bitter and were a contributing factor to the decision by the United States to leave UNESCO in 1985.

Subsequently, the impetus behind the NWICO campaign faltered, with most developing countries instead concentrating on building up their own national media, including domestic news agencies and broadcasting. In many cases, they were able to attract foreign funding for such initiatives.

JF

NEW ZEALAND. *Population* (1986 census): 3,307,084, of which 295,659 Maori. *Area*: 267,844 sq km. *Gross Domestic Product* (1988): $NZ59,257 million. *Trade* (1987–88): imports $NZ11,606 million; exports $NZ12,451 million. *Main trading partners*: European Communities, Japan, USA, Australia. *Defence spending* (est. 1988/89): $NZ1,390 million. *Education spending* (est. 1988/89): $NZ3,481 million. *Urban population as percentage of total*: 74. *Birth rate*: 16.1

per thousand (including Maori 21.9). *Life expectancy*: males 66; females 73.

New Zealand, known to Polynesian (Maori) inhabitants as Aotearoa ("the land of the long white cloud"), is thought to have been settled from Polynesia about 1,200 years ago, and by the twelfth century the Maori were scattered over most of the country. By the late eighteenth century, the Maori probably numbered over 100,000, organized into tribal groups often with warlike propensities.

The first European contact was made by Abel Tasman in 1642. James Cook came 127 years later and circumnavigated the islands. After the British penal colony was established in New South Wales (1788), New Zealand became in economic terms an offshoot of that colony, being developed for sealing, whaling, the growing of flax, timber milling, agriculture, sheep and cattle. A Church Missionary Society mission was established in 1814. The European or *pakeha* (non-Maori) impact varied, but included the introduction of diseases, alcoholism, prostitution and firearms. British jurisdiction and colonization was imposed by degrees. Governor Gipps of New South Wales proclaimed sovereignty over New Zealand on Jan. 14, 1840. On Feb. 6 his Lieutenant-Governor, Captain William Hobson, with a small group of officials, obtained signatures from Maori chiefs at Waitangi to a "treaty" whose significance is still debated. In its English-language original, the chiefs ceded all rights and powers of sovereignty to Queen Victoria, while in return the chiefs were assured possession of land, forests and fisheries, the Crown alone having right to purchase land. Not all chiefs signed the document, whose Maori language versions were more vaguely and not identically drafted. In 1841 New Zealand became formally a British colony and the capital was established at Auckland, subsequently moving to Wellington.

Under the (British) New Zealand Constitution Act of 1852, there was a central government consisting of a governor and a two-chamber elected General Assembly, and the country was divided into six provinces each with a superintendent and a provincial council. The powers of provincial councils, and of the governor-general, were steadily reduced and New Zealand developed a strong central government which from 1950 had a single chamber, the House of Representatives, currently with 97 seats. It is a member of the Commonwealth and the British Monarch is head of state. For the first time the Governor-General (Sir Paul Reeves) is of Maori descent.

During the 1850s, race relations deteriorated, mainly over the question of land as the settler population increased, Maori procedures and promises made under the Treaty of Waitangi were short-cut or ignored. This led to a decade of open conflict in the 1860s, the Maori often showing remarkable military capacity from an inferior position; but during the rest of the century the Maori lost most of their best land, while maintaining spiritual values and becoming increasingly skilled advocates of Maori rights within the *pakeha*-dominated social system and economy.

The Liberal government that took office in 1891 accelerated the processes of change, by extensive land purchases, offering perpetual leaseholds, building roads and railways, giving credit for land purchase and improvement. Refrigeration of meat exports had been introduced in 1882, and gradually expanded, to include butter. There thus developed great dairying and meat producing areas, especially in the North Island, New Zealand, becoming, as it remains, one of the most efficient producers of wool, lamb and dairy products in the world. The government also introduced a range of social legislation. From 1893, women were entitled to vote. Trade unions were encouraged, and in 1894 a compulsory conciliation and arbitration system gave protection to union members. Old Age pensions were introduced in 1898.

New Zealanders took part on the British side in the war in South Africa (1899-1902), establishing a high combat reputation, and again in World War I. The war stimulated the economy and nationalist sentiment, but at great cost in men killed and wounded (one in every three men aged 20-40). New Zealand signed the Versailles peace treaty in its own right and became a founding member of the League of Nations. Between the wars, New Zealand demonstrated an independence in foreign policy out of keeping with its reluctance until 1947 to adopt the Statute of Westminster.

In 1914 it had captured Western Samoa from Germany, and in 1920 it was granted a League of Nations Mandate over the territory, translated into a United Nations trust territory after World War II. Western Samoa became independent in 1962.

As elsewhere, New Zealand was seriously affected by the depression of the early thirties, with primary product prices slow to recover. The Labour party, formed in 1916 from socialist and radical groups, was elected to government in 1935, to what turned out to be a 14-year period in office, and introduced social reforms at a time when the economy was on the mend and could afford them: a public works and housing programme, medical benefits, improved pensions, and wider education opportunities.

In World War II, New Zealand was again quick to demonstrate its strong ties with Britain, sending forces to the Middle East from where they saw action in North Africa, Greece, Crete and Italy. They were also engaged, under American command, against Japan in the Pacific theatre. New Zealand, with Australia, unsuccessfully sought a part in determining the post-war settlement, but in January 1944 it negotiated an agreement with Australia (the Canberra, or ANZAC, Pact) asserting a role in the post-war security of the Southwest Pacific and in the welfare of its peoples. New Zealand helped shape the trusteeship provisions of the United Nations Charter drawn up at the San Francisco conference in early 1945, and the creation of the **South Pacific Commission**.

World War II, especially the activities of Japan and the inability of Britain to protect its remote Commonwealth partners when engaged in war in Europe, brought home to New Zealanders the problems of their security. For the next 30 years they were involved in Southeast and East Asia – supporting the British in Malaya and later Malaysia, taking part in the defence of South Korea, and in the war in Vietnam. New Zealand had helped negotiate the 1951 security agreement with Australia and the US (the **ANZUS Pact**), and the South East Asia Collective Defence Treaty (*see* **SEATO**). Prolonged participation in Vietnam led to growing debate on foreign and defence policy, and a turning away from overseas involvements.

The Maori population had risen from 45,500 in 1901 to 57,000 in 1921, but they remained a largely disadvantaged element of society in terms of health, standards of education, economic opportunity and life expectancy. In 1933, three out of every four adult Maori were registered as unemployed. In 1938, the Maori death rate was 24 per 1000 compared with 10 for *pakeha*, and infant mortality was more than four times as great. Government housing and health programmes gradually took effect, and Maori life expectancy rose from 46 years in 1925 to 58 in 1956. These factors, and a continuing high birth rate, saw the Maori population reach 116,000 in 1951. It was still less than 10 per cent of the population, the *pakehas* having increased by large-scale immigration which more than compensated for a declining birth rate. During and after World War II many Maori moved from the country to cities. Some 11 per cent of Maoris lived in urban areas in 1936; in 1976, the figure was 75 per cent, but often in sub-standard housing. Although helped by free secondary education, Maori on average had a lower educational achievement and thus frequently a lower occupational status.

Political power in the period since World War II has alternated between the **New Zealand National Party** (1949-57, 1960-72, 1975-84) and the **Labour Party** (1957-60, 1972-75, and since 1984), roughly matching the situation in Australia. For a time a Social Credit Party was successful in winning votes (up to 20 per cent) but only two seats. The government of **Sir Robert Muldoon** (1975-84) was a strong supporter of the Western Alliance, and of Britain during the Falklands War. In July 1984, the Labour Party, led by **David Lange**, won the election, and in the context of a divided opposition it set about radical changes in social, economic and foreign policies. It started a process of addressing Maori land grievances. Contrary to its traditional more socialist stance, it sought to correct a high level of inflation and balance of payments problems by a series of free-market measures, reducing government expenditure, establishing value-added (goods and services) tax, and reducing agricultural price supports. These were initially successful. In foreign affairs, Lange adopted a policy of refusing to allow aircraft or vessels carrying nuclear weapons, or nuclear-propelled vessels, to enter New Zealand airports or ports. The United States, with a long held policy of refusing to say whether nuclear weapons were being carried on its ships or aircraft, objected strongly to this policy, and when Lange remained firm, and indeed introduced implementing legislation despite representations from Australia and Britain, the USA suspended the application of the ANZUS Pact to New Zealand. At an election in August 1987, the Labour government was returned to office. The country faced severe debt problems (debt-servicing costs absorbing some 20 per cent of government income) and from October 1987 to March 1988 the government sold off New Zealand Steel, Petrocorp (the national oil and gas producer and distributor) and the Development Finance Corporation, for $NZ1,200 million. The July 1988 budget announced a series of further privatizations, with sales of assets expected ultimately to realize $NZ9,000 million.

On other foreign policy issues, New Zealand has sought to foster unity among the Pacific island states. It supported the creation of the University of the South Pacific in Fiji, has been a strong member of the **South Pacific Forum**, opposed French nuclear testing in the Pacific and helped negotiate the **Raratonga Declaration** for a nuclear-free zone. New Zealand strongly condemned the military coups in Fiji in May and September 1987.

In July 1985 the Greenpeace environmental protection group's trawler *Rainbow Warrior*, part of a group protesting against French nuclear testing, was blown up and sunk in Auckland harbour, killing the vessel's photographer. Two agents of the French secret service, the Direction Générale de la Sécurité Extérieure, were subsequently arrested, convicted of manslaughter and imprisoned. After some equivocation, France formally apologized for the incident, paid compensation and the two agents were released into custody in French Polynesia before being repatriated to France.

New Zealand has always had strong political, defence and economic links with Australia. The economic links were strengthened by the Closer Economic Relations (CER) agreement of December 1982, by which tariffs were to be phased out over five years and import licensing and tariff quotas were to be eliminated over a period – initially by 1995, and later by 1990. An accord signed with Australia in August 1988 agreed to the creation of a single market between the two countries within two years. New Zealand was badly affected by the oil crisis of 1973, more recently by protectionist lobbies in some major markets, and by dumping of primary products by competitors. For some years there has been a chronic imbalance in overseas services. The country has scaled back its already modest defence expenditure as an economy measure, and engaged in the sale of state-owned enterprises. It is still heavily dependent on agriculture, which provides around 70 per cent of all merchandise export income. If New Zealand is to reverse the decline in its standard of living, it will need to increase significantly its exports of manufactured goods.

David Lange, Prime Minister since 1984, resigned in August 1989 and was replaced by former Deputy Prime Minister Geoffrey Palmer. Lange's action came within a few days of the Labour party caucus voting his chief opponent in the party, Roger Douglas, into the Cabinet.

TBM

NEW ZEALAND NATIONAL PARTY. Currently the main opposition party. It supports free and competitive private enterprise, and maximum individual liberty. The parliamentary leader is James Bolger.

TBM

NEWS AGENCIES. For many years, the two big US-based international news agencies, Associated Press (AP), and United Press International (UPI), dominated news dissemination in the Pacific region, alongside their European counterparts Agence France Presse (AFP) and Reuters. This was a major reason for the determination of newly independent countries to establish their own national news agencies, which would give fuller, less western-oriented and more easily-controllable reports of local events. A lack of resources prevents most developing countries from making any serious attempt to replace the international agencies as sources of foreign news. That has not, however, stopped the so-far fruitless search for a new international organization, the **New World Information and Communications Order (NWICO)**, which would help break the virtual monopoly of the western agencies. In Latin America, there is slightly more diversity, in that the Spanish agency, EFE, is widely represented.

The Soviet Union and China have restricted the amount of dependency on western agencies by setting up costly national agencies which have a network of correspondents overseas. The TASS news agency was established in 1925 as the central organ for information for the Soviet Union. It is the source of a very high percentage of both domestic and foreign news, as printed in Soviet newspapers. TASS acts as an invaluable filter for the state, selecting what information should be disseminated and in what form. The Chinese equivalent is Xinhua. Some Xinhua correspondents abroad play an almost diplomatic role, and in Hong Kong the Xinhua office is a sort of Chinese legation to the colony.

The Japanese media rely heavily on western news agencies, although major newspapers have their own correspondents in important overseas capitals. The Kyodo news agency was established by a group of Japanese newspapers to supplement incoming material, keeping a particular lookout for stories of interest to Japan. Kyodo is a non-profit-making, non-governmental organization.

Australia, because of its size and sparse population, has developed domestic news agencies which transmit internal news around the country. The Australian Associated Press (AAP), which was formed by major newspapers, is a news agency which concentrates exclusively on international news.

JF

NEWSPAPERS. Three major tendencies can be discerned in the Pacific media, reflecting both the nature of power in the countries concerned and the perceived role of information dissemination: authoritarian, libertarian and socially responsible. Most Marxist states and some other authoritarian regimes produce highly controlled newspapers, either directly in the hands of the state or the ruling party or else effectively forbidden to divert too far from the official line. "News" as such is not given the high profile that it is in the capitalist world. The information communicated is very selective and politically correct interpretation is given considerable importance. To western tastes, this makes most "authoritarian" newspapers boring.

In libertarian societies, however, newspapers have a rather different function. The balance between information and entertainment is more flexible, depending on the paper concerned. Moreover, newspapers themselves frequently act as a bridge between consumers (the readers) and commerce (the advertisers). Advertising revenue and circulation are in many cases as important to newspaper proprietors as intellectual content, if not more so. A great strength of the sector in libertarian societies, is diversity, and therefore breadth of choice – even if sometimes readers tend to reinforce their own views by buying like-minded publications.

The newspapers of many developing countries do not really fall into either of the preceding stark categories, as the demands of commercial success are often not as strong (partly because of comparatively small readership) and at least a degree of plurality may be tolerated. A common feature of many papers in the Third World – including countries of the Pacific region – is their acceptance of a civic duty to enlighten the population on development issues, such as primary health or agriculture, particularly as a high proportion of their readers will be officials, teachers or other professionals directly involved in the implementation of schemes or the heightening of public awareness about them.

Newspaper readership is falling in most of the developed countries of the Pacific. It peaked in Australia in 1956, in the United States in 1971 and in Japan in 1981. This is largely because of the wider availability of alternative media (radio, TV, videos, cable and satellite technology etc.). In some developing countries, in contrast, readership is rising, as literacy and prosperity have spread. While the price of newspapers in the industrialized world is minimal in relation to people's earnings (and is subsidized by hefty advertising revenues), for the residents of most developing countries, a newspaper subscription represents a substantial claim upon their disposable income.

The United States has by far the biggest number of newspapers of any country in the world; 1,688 dailies alone in 1986. The majority of these are only available in a restricted geographical area and largely reflect rather parochial interests. The sheer size of the country precluded successful nationwide newspapers until advances in satellite technology made something like *USA Today* possible. In comparison to circulations in the Soviet Union, China, Japan (or even Britain), US newspapers sell rather small numbers of copies. The biggest is the Wall Street Journal, at just under two million. The daily sales of prestigious titles such as the *New York Times* and the *Los Angeles Times* is under one million each.

Japan has the highest newspaper consumption per head in the world, as well as the biggest circulations of individual titles in the "free" world. The "Big Three" (*Yomiuri Shimbun, Asahi Shimbun* and *Mainichi Shimbun*, in that order) sell over 21 million copies daily. Japanese newspapers have in the past tended to be more respectful of the government (in other words, the ruling Liberal Democrat Party) than their western counterparts would be, thus being seen as part of the establishment. With the exposure of scandals about the LDP in 1988–1989, however, that may be beginning to change.

Australia and Canada have lively, free presses and have both produced newspaper "barons" with international interests (e.g. **Rupert Murdoch** and Roy Thomson). The Canadians have helped preserve a certain independence from their huge southern neighbours by insisting on Canadian ownership of their newspapers.

Until **Mikhail Gorbachev** in the Soviet Union introduced the concept of *glasnost* or openness, the Soviet Press was notoriously fettered and stodgy, which meant that people who wished to be well informed about world events tended to look to other sources (such as foreign radio broadcasts). Nonetheless the three big dailies *Pravda*, *Trud* and *Komsomolskaya Pravda* all claimed circulations of about 10 million each. Since *glasnost*, newspapers have diversified in their coverage, embracing formerly taboo subjects, such as disasters or corruption.

For a brief period up to June 1989, the Chinese Press also saw an unfamiliar liberalization, though that is no longer the case. The *People's Daily* (official circulation about seven million) has reverted to pushing the party line. Access to more specialized Chinese newspapers, such as *Reference News*, which has wide coverage of events and opinions abroad, is severely restricted. Moreover, most newspapers are available only by postal subscription – which gives the authorities a tighter control of who reads what. The contrast presented by Hong Kong is startling, with about 60 Chinese-language dailies functioning openly and reflecting a wide range of views. Among other Southeast Asian countries, the Philippines has one of the most diverse and liberal newspaper industries.

Though several Latin American countries have lively newspapers (including Chile, even in the last years of the Pinochet dictatorship), the written press has tended to be overshadowed by the broadcasting media. This has meant that newspapers have tended to appeal to an urbanized elite. (*See also* **Censorship**)

JF

NGUYEN VAN LINH. General secretary of the **Vietnamese Communist Party** (VCP) since December 1986; having previously played a leading role in the southern struggle down to 1975, and in the administration of Ho Chi Minh City from then until 1985. Born in 1915, and native of the Hanoi area, he was arrested for political activities at the age of 15 and spent the years 1931–36 on the prison island of Con Son. He joined the Indochinese Communist Party in 1936 and was active in Haiphong for the next three years. He then moved to Saigon and later to Central Vietnam, but was again imprisoned from 1941 to 1945. He participated in the revolution of 1945 in Saigon, and remained in the South throughout the wars against the French (1945–54) and the United States (1955–75). By 1960 he was a secretary of the regional Party committee and is thought to have been "number 2" in the southern organization from then until 1975; he used the pseudonym "Muoi Cuc". From 1975 to 1985 he was Party secretary in Saigon, and by the end of that period had the reputation of an economic pragmatist and reformer. He was promoted to the VCP Politburo at its 4th Congress (1976), but then removed from it at the 5th Congress (1982) when his policies in Saigon came in for disapproval. Reappointed to the Politburo in 1985, he moved to the central secretariat of the Party the following year and became increasingly pro-government following the death of **Le Duan**. He became general secretary at the Party's 6th Congress (December 1986); and although he still faced opposition to many of the reforming policies he advocated, he seemed to be gaining the upper hand by the spring of 1989. He has attempted to set an example of frugality in his own life-style and has been a merciless critic of bureaucratic corruption.

RBS

NICARAGUA, REPUBLIC OF. *Population*: 3 million. *Area*: 133,000 sq km. *Gross Domestic Product*: US$896 million. *Trade*: US$859 million. *Main trading partners*: Guatemala, France, West Germany, USSR, Japan. *Defence spending*: US$473 million. *Education spending as percentage of Gross National Product*: 4.0. *Urban population as percentage of total (centres over 20,000)*: 37. *Birth rate*: 44 per thousand. *Life expectancy*: males 41.5; females 45.

Geographical background. The jungle lowlands of the Mosquito (Miskito) Coast dominate the eastern side of Nicaragua. The central part of the country comprises mountains and a high plateau with a range of volcanoes on its north-western side. The Pacific coast is lowland plain with two great lakes, Managua and Nicaragua, joined by the San Juan River to each other and to the Caribbean. Most of Nicaragua is warm and wet, with a cooler, drier region in the central highlands. 715,00 hectares are cultivated. The majority of roads remain unpaved and the railway system is very limited (331 km). Air transport has historically been very important as a result of these limitations. The main port is Bluefields on the Caribbean coast. Nicaragua's great potential is as an alternative route to Panama for an inter-oceanic canal (*see* **Nicaraguan Canal, Proposals for**). Despite a decade of revolution and civil war, the population is increasing at a very high 3.2 per cent *per annum*. The administrative capital, Managua (population 608,000), is by far the largest city, and was last severely damaged by earthquake in 1973.

Socio-political background. Three-quarters of the population is *mestizo*; of the remainder half is European and the rest Indian (mostly Miskito), black or mulatto. Spanish is the national language. English is spoken amongst the Miskito and on the Caribbean coast. The principal religion is Roman Catholic with a sizeable Protestant minority. A massive government educational campaign has reduced illiteracy to 13 per cent since 1979. Since the 1979 Revolution public health campaigns and the efforts of volunteer workers have greatly reduced the incidence of many major diseases, and poliomyelitis has been virtually eradicated. New clinics and medical facilities have been established, bringing the ratio of doctors to population down to 1:2228. Despite these achievements problems of poverty remain and have been exacerbated by US-backed "contra" attacks on "economic" (i.e. civilian) targets such as clinics, plantations and schools. Diseases associated with malnutrition, poor hygiene and inadequate housing keep the infant mortality rate at a high 72 per thousand. Sixty-five per cent of urban homes and 9 per cent of rural homes have piped water.

Political history. Political turbulence in the early years of the century led to US intervention and the establishment of a virtual protectorate. US marines were withdrawn in 1933, following a long guerrilla struggle led by Gen. Augusto Sandino, but Sandino was murdered and power seized by Anastasio Somoza. It later passed in turn to two of his sons. Anastasio Somoza Debayle was overthrown by a massive popular revolution in 1979, aided by Costa Rica, Panama and Cuba.

The provisional government installed by the Sandinista Liberation Front was replaced by a constitutional government headed by Daniel Ortega Saavedra in free elections in 1985. Since 1981 the US government has sponsored the so-called Nicaraguan Democratic Force (FDN), commonly nicknamed the "contras".

Outline of economic development. Of the working population 42.8 per cent work in agriculture. Since the nineteenth century coffee has dominated exports and still accounted for 36.8 per cent of exports in 1980. Ranching was established in colonial times and meat was still the second largest export product (13.8 per cent). Cut off from their traditional market in the USA, the Nicaraguans were forced to diversify and in 1985 cotton came to account for a third of exports with coffee just behind in second place.

The US boycott of Nicaragua has not only hit production and trade, but also finance. The national debt was US$5,200 million in 1986.

P&SC

NICARAGUAN CANAL, PROPOSALS FOR. The waters of Lake Nicaragua and the San Juan river have been used to cross the isthmus since Spanish times and a route for an interoceanic canal was surveyed by US engineers in the early 1870s. Following its acquisition of the **Panama Canal Zone** the US government acquired sole rights to the rival route by the Bryan-Chamorro Treaty of 1914. A proposal to construct a sea-level canal using nuclear explosives was mooted by Anastasio Somoza Debayle but strongly opposed by Costa Rica on environmental grounds.

P&SC

NICKEL. Nickel's most important application is in the production of stainless steel; it is also important in military equipment, high temperature applications and in coinage. The chief nickel-producing countries in the region are Canada, Australia and New Caledonia. Japan too is an important producer of refined nickel derived from raw imports. Demand for nickel in recent decades has fluctuated considerably with substan-

tial affects on producers. During the 1960s world consumption of nickel exceeded production but the world recession of the early 1970s led to a massive fall in consumption. This in turn led to large surpluses and a build-up of world stocks of nickel which by 1977 reached approximately 227,000 tonnes. Yet with increased production of stainless steel the following year nickel production was again short of demand. The renewed world recession of 1980 hit the steel industries particularly hard; consumption of nickel falling from the 1979's high of 620,000 tons to 521,000. Production of nickel too fell to 535,000 tons. As a result all the major producers have been adversely affected and obliged to cut production or to close mines at least temporarily. It was not until April/May 1987 that the prices began to improve partly due to strikes at large plants operated by Falconbridge in Canada. A revival in the stainless steel market rapidly increased demand for nickel. As consumption rose and stocks fell the price of nickel rose to a record high. This cycle of fall and rise in production has been reflected in the state of the region's nickel industry. In Australia, for example, the production of nickel from Australian mines varied from around 64,000 tonnes to 87,000 tonnes a year over the period 1975–85.

New Caledonia has the world's largest known nickel deposits containing roughly one-third of the world's known reserves. It is the world's fourth largest producer and nickel provides one third of the island's GNP and 90 per cent of its export earnings. In recent years production has been seriously disrupted by political unrest. In January 1985 three mines accounting for half of the island's production were forced to close because of sabotage. Although the main operating company Société Le Nickel (SLN) has attempted to counter these problems by raising production at Kouaua and increasing purchases of ore from independent miners, political unrest has continued to dog production.

One of the region's comparative newcomers to nickel production is Indonesia. International Nickel (Inco) began work in Sulawesi in 1979 and production was nearing 30,000 tonnes by the mid-1980's. Reserves are estimated at 40 million tonnes. The Philippines has four nickel plants although production at the Nonoc processing plant has fluctuated because of equipment and labour difficulties. The Bogota region of New Zealand and the Cerromatoso area of Colombia are also important reserves. The latter is estimated to have 70 million tonnes of nickel reserves.

The studies have proven the existence of large deposits of ferromanganese nodules on the

Pacific's ocean bed which contain nickel, **copper** and cobalt. However the extraction of metals from the nodules is not commercially practicable this century.

The annual production of nickel, in thousands of tonnes, is as follows: China, 175; Canada, 174.2; Australia, 76.9; Indonesia, 47.8; Ecuador, 16.5; Philippines, 15.6; Chile, 12.7; USA, 8.7.

RS

NIUE. *Population* (est. 1986): 3,000, mainly Polynesians. *Area*: 259 sq km. Island state lying 1,340 miles east of New Zealand, with which it is in free association. *Capital*: Alofi. The island was visited by Cook in 1774, and the people were converted to **Christianity** in the mid-nineteenth century. Annexed by Britain in 1900 and by New Zealand in 1901, the island obtained internal self-government in 1974 in free association with New Zealand, from which it receives an annual subvention. There have been five general elections, the latest in March 1978, by universal suffrage. The Premier is Sir Robert Rex. The Head of State is the British Monarch. The economy is based on agriculture and fishing.

TBM

NON-ALIGNMENT. The theory of non-alignment really took shape at the Bandung Conference in Indonesia in 1955, although the Non-aligned Movement itself did not hold its first conference until six years later, at Belgrade in Yugoslavia. Behind the Bandung Conference was the idea of a commonality of interests between former colonies, most of which at the time were in Asia, as the independence process in Africa was largely a phenomenon of the 1960s. At Bandung, the then Chinese Foreign Minister, **Zhou Enlai**, made a great impression, particularly with regard to the possibility of a "third way" for developing countries, independent of both of the super-powers. However, most of the impetus for the development of a non-aligned ideology then came from outside the Pacific region – notably from Presidents Tito and Nasser of Yugoslavia and Egypt and Prime Minister Nehru of India.

By 1989, the Non-aligned Movement had one hundred member states, plus a couple of liberation movements, including a high proportion of the countries of the Pacific region. Their very diversity underlines the problem of finding a common voice, despite the fact that all decisions and declarations are made by consensus. Some of the more conservative or western-oriented members objected to the way that during the 1960s and 1970s, true non-alignment was compromised by preference being given to relations with the Soviet Union. This line – propagated by President Fidel Castro of Cuba, in particular – was based on the theory of the Socialist bloc's being the "natural ally" of the Non-aligned, in the latter's struggle against imperialism and neo-colonialism. As the United States was identified by many Pacific region states (both during and after the Vietnam War) as the prime "imperialist" power, this situation was accepted by a majority of the Movement's members. Some, like North Korea, were passionate advocates of it.

However, the Movement's ninth summit, in Belgrade in 1989, softened its approach to the western, industrialized world, despite opposition from Pyongyang, calling for concordance rather than confrontation. The Summit's final declaration spoke of the need to work with the industrialized world in order to overcome problems such as overseas debt and the continuing gap between the rich and poor worlds. Detente between the United States and the Soviet Union was greeted as offering a new "window of opportunity" to the global community.

At the Belgrade Summit, Indonesia seemingly failed in its attempts to become heir-apparent to the Movement's triennial presidency. The failure to find a workable peace settlement for Cambodia, despite Indonesia's best efforts during 1988–1989, possibly hindered its candidacy. Yet that failure was in many ways symbolic of the Non-aligned Movement's own failure to resolve conflicts between its own members. Hostility between Iran and Iraq, even after the ceasefire in the Gulf War, is a classic case. Moreover, the Movement could hardly claim credit for intervening usefully in regional conflicts, such as in Central America. It was notable at Belgrade that the main related concern was whether Nicaragua, under the Sandinistas, was a worthy possible president of the Movement in 1992.

JF

NORFOLK ISLAND. *Population* (1986): 2.367. *Area*: 34.5 sq km. An Australian territory 1,400 km east of Brisbane. *Capital*: Kingston. Discovered by James Cook, it was used as a British penal colony from 1788 to 1814 and from 1825 to 1855. In 1856 it was resettled by emigrants from Pitcairn Island. In 1897 Norfolk Island became a dependency of New South Wales and in 1913 of Australia. It is internally self-governing, with an elected nine-member legislative assembly and an executive council. The main industry is tourism, with some 30,000 visitors a year.

TBM

NORTHERN MARIANA ISLANDS, COM-MONWEALTH OF (Northern Marianas).

Population (est. 1986): 19,500, of Micronesian and mixed race. *Total land area*: 471 sq km. The islands comprise all the Marianas group (16 islands) except Guam. They include Saipan, Tinian and Rota. *Capital*: Chalan Kanoa, on Saipan.

The islands were discovered by Magellan in 1521, formally occupied by Spain in 1668, and sold to Germany in 1899 when Guam was ceded to the USA. They were occupied by Japan in 1914, became a Japanese mandate from the League of Nations, and were seized by the USA in World War II. They were in the United Nations Trust Territory of the Pacific Islands in 1947, administered by the United States. In 1975 the islands voted for commonwealth status, which was formally achieved in 1986. The constitution provides for a governor, a lieutenant-governor, a senate and house of representatives.

The economy is based on subsistence farming, copra, handicrafts, tourism, and employment in the US civil and military administrations.

TBM

NORTHERN TERRITORIES DISPUTE.

The "Northern Territories" is a term used by Japan to denote the islands of Kunashiri, Etorofu, Shikotan, and the Habomai group, all of which lie at the southern end of the **Kuril Islands** chain running between the Soviet Union's Kamchatka Peninsula and the Japanese island of Hokkaido. The whole island chain was annexed from Japan by the Soviet Union in 1945, but since then sovereignty of the "Northern Territories" has remained the subject of a Japanese claim.

This claim is based on the Treaty of Commerce, Navigation and Delimitation (also known as the Shimoda treaty) signed by Japan and the Russian Empire in 1855, which established the maritime boundary between the two countries as lying immediately to the north of the disputed islands, and also on the 1875 Russo-Japanese treaty under which Japan conceded Russian sovereignty over **Sakhalin** island in exchange for the Kuril Islands. The Soviet Union has contended that these treaties have no present-day significance, arguing that Russian territorial concessions to Japan during this period were exacted under duress and specifically that the Russo-Japanese war of 1904–05 nullified all agreements between the two sides. The Soviet Union occupied the islands in 1945 on the basis of the 1945 Yalta agreement, which provided for the return to the Soviet Union of the Kuril islands and the southern half of Sakhalin (which had been awarded to Japan by

the Treaty of Portsmouth in 1905). Japan has consistently maintained, however, that the "Northern Territories" are distinct from the Kuril islands and did not therefore fall within the purview of the Yalta agreement.

In 1956 the Soviet Union and Japan entered into discussions on the conclusion of a peace treaty (the Soviet Union having refused to sign the 1951 Allied-Japan peace treaty). The "Northern Territories" issue eventually caused the breakdown of talks, although agreement on the termination of the state of war and the resumption of diplomatic relations was set out in a joint declaration of Oct. 19, 1956, which included an agreement in principle for the return of Shikotan and the Habomais upon the conclusion of a peace treaty. There has been little progress on the issue since 1956. In the communiqué of a meeting between the then Soviet leader Leonid Brezhnev and the then Japanese Prime Minister **Kakuei Tanaka** on Oct. 10, 1973, the Soviet side accepted that there were "yet unresolved problems remaining since World War II". In recent years Japan has sought a reaffirmation of this position, and has rejected Soviet assertions that there is no outstanding territorial issue to resolve.

IG

NOUHAK PHOMSAVAN.

Deputy prime minister of the Lao People's Democratic Republic (LPDR) since 1975, and a leading member of the **Lao People's Revolutionary Party**. Born in southern Laos in 1914, he took part in the independence movement from 1946 and joined "the Party" (according to one account) in 1952. Three years later he was a founder member of the Lao People's (Revolutionary) Party, and was promoted to its standing committee in 1966. By the 1970s he was recognized as a specialist in economic affairs, and in addition to his deputy premiership of the LPDR he served as minister of finance from 1975 to 1982.

RBS

NUCLEAR FREE ZONE TREATY.

In 1971 Australia, the Cook Islands, Fiji, Kiribati, Nauru, New Zealand, Niue, Papua New Guinea, the Solomon Islands, Tonga, Tuvalu, Vanuatu and Western Samoa established the **South Pacific Forum** (SPF) to provide informal opportunities for discussion on matters of common interest. Although many of the issues discussed were economic, an SPF conference held Aug. 28-29, 1983, reaffirmed the total opposition of the member states to the French underground nuclear testing programme at Mururoa Atoll in French Polynesia. It was a natural development from this concern over the French testing programme to the **Raratonga Declaration** establishing a nuclear-free zone in the South Pacific.

The Treaty was concluded on Aug. 5, 1985 by Australia, Fiji, Kiribati, New Zealand, Niue, Papua New Guinea, Tuvalu, and Western Samoa. The signatories agreed not to manufacture, acquire or have control of nuclear explosive devices within their territories, and to prevent the dumping of nuclear waste. The one major loophole in the Treaty – and one that was made necessary on the insistence of Australia – was that no restrictions were imposed on access to the region by nuclear-powered or, even more significant, nuclear-armed ships and aircraft.

The Treaty also contained three protocols, which nuclear powers were called on to sign. The first allowed parties with dependent territories within the zone to comply with the relevant provisions; the second was designed to enable the five nuclear powers to undertake not to assist in violations of the Treaty and not to use or threaten the use of nuclear weapons against any of the signatories; the third was an undertaking not to test nuclear weapons within the zone.

The problem with the Treaty was that the protocols could not be imposed. China and the Soviet Union both signed them, although Moscow made clear that it might be compelled to target American facilities and forces in the treaty zone. The

United States, on the other hand, refused to sign on the grounds that it would undermine US "global security interests and commitments". Britain too refused to sign. In these circumstances, there was far less pressure on France to agree to the protocols than the Forum members had expected and hoped for. In effect, therefore, the Treaty did little more than underline the principle of horizontal non-proliferation among states who lacked the inclination, and in most cases also the ability to become nuclear weapons states. The overall impact of the Treaty was marginal. France continued testing, while Australia has not only been able to maintain its policy of allowing port visits by United States ships which may be nuclear-armed but has also permitted the continued use by the United States of the facilities at Pine Gap, Nurrungar and North West Cape, all of which have a nuclear dimension.

Other states, including Indonesia have given their support to the concept of the nuclear-free zone in the South Pacific. Perhaps the most significant aspect of it, however, is that Australia, in effect, has given notice that it does not intend to become a nuclear power. It has also highlighted the difficulties inherent in the very notion of nuclear-free zones and has at least made a start, if a very tentative one, in providing some kind of arms control framework in the Pacific.

PW

O

ONE-MAN MANAGEMENT. This was the principle of industrial management in China borrowed from Soviet practice in the 1950s. Under it, the enterprise director was responsible to higher authorities for all aspects of work of his enterprise. Associated with **Liu Shaoqi**, it was replaced during the Cultural Revolution by the factory revolutionary committee, but it has made a comeback in the 1980s.

CIPF

OVERSEAS AID. The Pacific region's two wealthiest nations, the United States and Japan, are also the world's two largest aid donors. That does not mean they are the most generous. Both fall well short of the United Nations target of 0.70 per cent of gross national product as development assistance. Canada far exceeds them in percentage terms. Japan became the biggest single donor, in cash terms, in 1988, though the figures were somewhat distorted by the phenomenal rise of the yen in relation to the US dollar.

Though recently desirous of proving its international credentials by sharply increasing its overseas aid programme, Japan has also been responding pragmatically to intense pressure from Washington and Brussels to recycle some of its enormous trade surplus. The government in Tokyo announced its intention of doubling aid funds over the period 1987–1992 and is well on course to reach that target. But Japan is still, in percentage terms, below the OECD average of 0.35 per cent of GNP. Japan has also come under some criticism for using aid as a means of trade promotion (a practice that is fairly widespread among donors). About two-thirds of Japanese aid (total: approx. nine billion US dollars) goes to other parts of Asia (including South Asia), of which the top two recipients recently have been China and the Philippines. One imaginative but controversial Japanese scheme for Latin America is a proposed new Atlantic–Pacific Canal, through Nicaragua.

A much smaller percentage of US aid goes to other Pacific nations. The United States – like the Soviet Union – has a policy of targeting a large percentage of its aid at close political allies which are considered to have strategic importance. Hence the massive allocations to Israel, Egypt and Pakistan. The four major Pacific beneficiaries accordingly are El Salvador, the Philippines, Honduras and Guatemala. This is mirrored on the Soviet side by support for Mongolia, Vietnam, Cambodia and Laos. Moscow has, however, resisted pressures to shore up Nicaragua in the way that it has done for Cuba.

Australia has concentrated most of its aid in Southeast Asia, notably Papua New Guinea, for which Australia previously had administrative responsibility. Under a Labour government, Australia has been examining the appropriateness of aid to Indochina. Canada, unburdened by any colonial legacies or recent direct military involvement overseas (outside UN auspices), has tended to target its overseas aid at the poorest countries in the world, especially fellow Commonwealth members in Africa and South Asia.

It is not only the richest countries which give aid. China has run projects in several parts of Africa, such as the railway linking Tanzania and Zambia. So too has Taiwan. As recipients, the poorer Pacific nations receive assistance from donors outside the region, both bilaterally (e.g. from Britain and France) and through multilateral agencies. Most of the Pacific island nations are members of the Lomé Convention, which links the European Communities with 66 African and Caribbean states.

JF

P

PACIFIC BASIN ECONOMIC COUNCIL (PBEC). This was founded in 1967 and first met in 1968. It is an unofficial, informal organization of senior businessmen from 400 companies in 20 countries. The countries with member committees are:

Australia	Papua New Guinea
Canada	Peru
Chile	Philippines
Fiji	Singapore
Hong Kong	South Korea
Indonesia	Sri Lanka
Japan	Taiwan
Malaysia	Thailand
Mexico	Tonga
New Zealand	USA

An annual meeting is held in one of the countries of the member committees. The task of acting as host rotates among the members. The first meeting was held in San Francisco, and the latest (1988) in Sydney. The richer countries represented on the Council tend, more often than not, to act as host. Each national committee has a chairman and one or more vice-chairmen, there is a steering committee and a secretariat. The PBEC's working languages are English and Japanese.

The PBEC exists to forge, consolidate and strengthen business and other economic relationships among its member countries. It is particularly concerned to foster more rapid economic and social progress in the less-developed countries of the region. Another of its stated aims is to promote the idea of a Pacific economic community.

To further these aims, the Council provides support for programmes of education, runs private training schemes for technicians and middle managers from the developing countries amongst its members, and promotes scientific and cultural exchanges. In addition, it acts as a forceful advocate for an international investment code to guide the activities of the countries undertaking direct investment in the region, and also to help the host countries with the problems that may arise therefrom.

DA

PACIFIC ECONOMIC CO-OPERATION CONFERENCE (PECC). This resulted from a meeting that took place in 1980 in Australia between the then Prime Ministers of Australia and Japan, Robert Fraser and Masayoshi Ohira. Ohira had gone to Japan armed with a copy of the report of the Pacific basin study group, a group of politicians, diplomats, scholars and others who had been meeting in Japan with the aim of spreading the idea of a "Pacific Community" to be promoted by a new, broadly-based organization. Ohira mooted the idea of such an organization, Fraser was receptive, and a seminar was subsequently held in Canberra hosted by Sir John Crawford, the President of the Australian National University. This proved to be the first meeting of the PECC.

The first meeting was small in scale, as were subsequent gatherings in Bangkok and Bali. However, the PECC got on a sounder footing in Seoul in 1985 when a larger number of countries were represented, whilst at the fifth meeting in Vancouver in November 1986 both Chinas sent representatives. The sixth meeting was held in Osaka in May 1988, and the seventh is to be in New Zealand in late 1989. Countries participate through their member committees, of which there are now 15, representing 13 fully independent Pacific nations, Taiwan and the Pacific Island States. In addition, PECC meetings include representatives from Latin American countries such as Chile, Mexico and Peru; from non-member countries like France and the Soviet Union; and from international organizations such as OECD and the **Asian Development Bank**, all of them in the capacity of observers. Representatives of the **Pacific Basin Economic Council (PBEC)** and the **Pacific Trade and Development Conference (PAFTAD)** participate on the executive council of PECC.

In structure the PECC is broadly-based, encompassing representatives from government, industry, commerce, academia and wider intellectual circles. It is consultative in nature, hoping to devise policies for the future that governments of the region may adopt through a process of discussion leading to a consensus. Besides the member committees and contact institutions of the countries belonging to PECC, there is a standing committee composed of representatives answerable to their member committees which is responsible for devising operating procedures. There are also task forces and fora which meet between the roughly one-and-a-half yearly meetings of the PECC and which were set up to to examine specific problems of co-operation, such as, for example, direct investment flows or energy provision. There is a co-ordinating group, consisting of task force leaders and various specialists, whose main function is the preparation of studies and material, as well as preparing for the General Meeting of the Conference. The PECC has no permanent secretariat, the national committee of the country hosting the next conference acting as an international secretariat in its turn.

The members of PECC believe in mobilizing the respective strengths of government, the intelligensia, industry and commerce to promote co-operation in achieving greater economic growth and social progress in the Pacific region. Thus it seeks to devise ways to promote trade, joint ventures, aid and technical assistance amongst its members, as well as attempting to raise the level of inter-member collaboration in the fields of science, technology and management. The co-operative development and exploitation of natural resources, and the provisions of training and research facilities to develop human resources also fall within the general aims of the organization.

Since delegates to the conference, even if they are in the service of governments, attend in their capacity as private individuals, the power of the conference to produce rapid tangible results is severely circumscribed. The influence the organization exerts is a longer-term one, and rests chiefly on its ability to draw together important poeple from different backgrounds and countries and allow them to exchange views, investigate new ideas and air their fears and hopes for the future of the region.

DA

PACIFIC TRADE AND DEVELOPMENT CONFERENCE (PAFTAD).

PAFTAD is in fact a series of private, informal academic conferences which began in 1968 with the support of the Japanese Ministry of Foreign Affairs. The original conference was held to consider a proposal for a Pacific free trade area. Since that time, regular conferences have been held in different countries of the Pacific, attended mainly by economists of widely differing persuasions but all with an orientation towards policy formation. Their discussions have centred on economic issues of concern both to the developed countries of the region, and also to the developing countries of the Asia–Pacific region. It is probably true to say that the conference has been the major intellectual resource and stimulus for those seriously interested in the question of economic co-oper-

ation and development in the region, and has sponsored much academic study.

PAFTAD's deliberations and proceedings are guided by a steering committee of members from Australia, Canada, Japan, the United States and the Southeast Asian sector of the region. Participants from Latin America, the Soviet Union and other parts of Oceania have been involved in the proceedings of the conference from time to time.

DA

PACIFIC, WAR OF THE.

Following complaints about the treatment of its nationals in the nitrate fields, Chile seized the then Bolivian port of Antofagasta and the surrounding coastline in 1879. In the war that followed, Peru, coming to the aid of Bolivia, lost its own southern provinces of Tacna, Arica and Tarapacá to Chile after its fleet had been destroyed and Chilean forces had occupied Lima. It retrieved Tacna in 1929 under the Treaty of Ancón, which provides that no Chilean territory formerly belonging to Peru could be alienated to a third country (i.e. Bolivia) without Peruvian consent. Bolivia thus remains landlocked and dependent on access to the Pacific by the railway to Arica in Chilean territory.

P&SC

PALAU, REPUBLIC OF (Belau, or Pelew).

Population (est. 1986): 13,873, of Micronesian and mixed races. *Total land area*: 488 sq km. Self-governing republic in the western Pacific, comprising about 350 islands especially the Palau islands in the north, forming the western end of the Caroline chain.

European contact dates from 1543 (Ruy Lopez de Villalobos), and the islands were under nominal Spanish ownership until the Palau group, the Caroline and Mariana islands were sold to Germany. Japan occupied the Palau islands in 1914, and they became a major Japanese base in World War II. In 1947 they were incorporated in the United Nations as Trust Territory of the Pacific Islands, administered by the United States, and comprising also the Federated States of Micronesia, the Marshall Islands, and the Marianas except Guam. With each of these the USA negotiated internal self-government, and "compacts of association". In the case of Palau, this compact exchanged assurances of extensive US economic aid for the right to maintain US military facilities in the islands, to include nuclear materials. The US government saw Palau as a possible alternative to the Philippines if American bases there were forced to close.

The Palau constitution of 1980 prohibited the

entry, storage or disposal of nuclear, chemical or biological weapons and waste. Amending the constitution required a 75 per cent vote in favour. In five successive referenda, this proportion was not obtained. A proposal that the compact was consistent with the constitution was then approved by a simple majority, but this procedure was ruled invalid by the Palau Supreme Court in April 1988. While the trusteeship over the other three parts of the Trust Territory has been terminated, the status of Palau is uncertain. The assassination of one president (Remilik) and the suicide of his successor (Salii) have compounded the problem. Palau has a popularly elected president and a two-chamber legislature.

The economy is based on subsistence farming, fishing and tourism.

TBM

PANAMA CANAL ZONE. Formerly a district of some 1,676 sq km (647 sq miles) on either side of the 82 km route of the proposed canal, which was opened to traffic in 1914 (population in 1970; 51,000). By the Panama Canal Treaties of 1977 the USA returned four-fifths of the Zone to Panama in 1979 and the remaining area and the Canal itself will revert in 2,000. A transisthmian pipeline (capacity 830,000 barrels per day) was opened in 1982 running from Puerto Armuelles on the Pacific to Chiriqui Grande on the Caribbean.

P&SC

PANAMA, REPUBLIC OF. *Population*: 2,000,000. *Area*: 73,650 sq km. *Gross Domestic Product*: US$2,416 million. *Trade*: US$5,261 million. *Main trading partners* (1985): USA, Japan, (Norway), Italy, Sweden, Mexico. *Defence spending*: US$98 million. *Education spending as percentage of Gross National Product*: 5.5. *Urban population as percentage of total (centres over 20,000)*: 41. *Birth rate*: 28 per thousand. *Life expectancy*: males 58; females 60.

Geographical background. Panama is a land of densely forested hills and mountains. The lowland temperature is high and the climate tropical, but temperature falls with altitude. A third of the population work in agriculture. A railway parallels the Canal and branches total 109 km. Road transport has been limited by the topography: the northern section of the Pan American Highway still ends at the "Darien Gap". Minimal charges and regulations make Panamanian registration of shipping one of the most popular "flags of convenience" – on paper, her

merchant marine is immense. International shipping concentrates on the ports in or near the Canal Zone but internal trade keeps other ports busy. Panama City (population 389,000) is by far the largest centre.

Socio-political background. Three-quarters of the population is *mestizo* or mulatto; the remainder (in descending order), blacks, Europeans, Indians and Orientals. Spanish is the national language, but English and Indian languages are also used. The principal religion is Roman Catholic with a substantial Protestant minority. Primary education is free and compulsory and 95 per cent are enrolled. Educational expenditure is relatively high and adult illiteracy has been reduced to 15.5 per cent. The most important higher education institution, the University of Panama, is located in Panama City. Support from international agencies for government programmes has reduced the crude death rate to 5.4 per thousand and infant mortality rate to 20 per thousand. Ninety-two per cent of urban homes have piped water. There are 1,129 people per doctor. Social security provision has been greatly extended over the last 20 years. The internal migration resulting from the attractions of US affluence in the Canal Zone produced problems of over-urbanization in the cities near the Canal. Government schemes for low-cost housing have tried to tackle some of the overcrowding and squalor this causes.

Political history. A US-sponsored revolution declared independence from Colombia in 1903 and within three days the new government had signed away Panama's rights in perpetuity to the **Panama Canal Zone**. Domestic politics was long controlled by a small unrepresentative minority until increasing nationalist awareness in the 1960s brought student riots. From 1968 until his death in an air crash in 1982 politics was dominated by Gen. Omar Torrijos, a left-leaning progressive who successfully negotiated the Canal Treaties of 1977 with the USA.

Since 1982 politics has been dominated by the commander of the Defence Forces, Gen. Noriega, who appoints or dismisses Presidents at will. President Reagan's attempt to squeeze Noriega in 1988 failed and following the abortive elections of 1989 Gen. Noriega remained in charge and the USA reinforced its garrison in the Canal Zone.

Outline of economic development. Panama's sole resource remains the Canal, though large recently-discovered copper reserves could be exploited if the world price rose. Bananas were the principal export in 1985 (23.3 per cent) followed by shrimp (17.8 per cent). A heavy deficit on visible balance of trade is made up by invisibles, principally offshore banking and financial services. Panama's position and lax economic regulation make it a natural haven for smuggling, especially of drugs. National debt was US$6,500 million at end-1986.

US pressure has harmed the economy extensively, and it is currently essentially bankrupt.

P&SC

PANCASILA. The Indonesian secularist state ideology, first propounded by **Sukarno** in 1945 as the philosophical foundation of the Indonesian revolution. *Pancasila*'s five principles include; (i) belief in the one supreme God; (ii) just and civilized humanity; (iii) the unity of Indonesia; (iv) democracy led by the wisdom of deliberations (*musyawarah*) among representatives; and (v) social justice for all the people of Indonesia. Legislation passed at the end of May 1985 required all mass social organizations to redraft their constitutions within two years, so as to accept *Pancasila* as their "sole ideological foundation". The new legislation also provided for the banning or "freezing" of social organizations if they were deemed to be violating the tenets of *Pancasila* in any way. Most organizations had adopted *Pancasila* as their sole principle in 1984 at the time the legislation was first proposed. However, the proposal had also met with some opposition, notably from the so-called "Petition of 50" opposition grouping which had been formed in 1980 and comprised generals, academics, former politicians and other prominent citizens dissatisfied with **Suharto**'s rule. In addition, serious rioting and a series of bombings in and around Jakarta in September–October 1984 were allegedly instigated by Muslims opposed to the proposed *Pancasila* legislation.

DS

PAPUA NEW GUINEA. *Population* (est. 1986): 3,422,300. *Area*: 462,840 sq km. *Main trading partners*: Australia, Japan, Singapore, USA, Britain. *Urban population as percentage of total*: about 14. *Birth rate*: 34.7 per thousand.

Papua New Guinea (PNG) comprises the eastern half of the island of New Guinea and numerous adjacent islands including the Bismarck Archipelago (main islands: New Britain, New Ireland, and Manus) and Bougainville in the Solomons group. The state is bounded on the West by Irian Jaya, part of Indonesia. The capital is Port Moresby.

The island of New Guinea was probably populated from Southeast Asia via the Indonesian archipelago about 50,000 years ago. The island was claimed for Spain in 1545, and there was a British settlement in 1793. In 1828, the Netherlands claimed the western half of the island as part of its East Indies. In April 1883, the British colony of Queensland (Australia) "took possession" of "all that portion of New Guinea and the adjacent islands not already in occupation by the Dutch". The act was disowned by the British government, but between October 1884 and early 1885 the latter declared and reaffirmed a protection over the southern portion and reached a *modus vivendi* with Germany which claimed the northern portion, dividing the eastern half of the island roughly along its backbone. The British area, known as Papua, became a colony in 1888, being transferred to the control of the new federated Commonwealth of Australia in 1906. On the outbreak of World War I, Australia seized German New Guinea, and in 1920 was given a League of Nations mandate over the territory.

During World War II, much of New Guinea and adjacent islands was occupied by the Japanese who were eventually contained and defeated by Australian and American forces. After the war, the mandated territory became a United Nations trust territory, administered by Australia jointly with Papua (as the Territory of Papua and New Guinea – TPNG), the trust territory retaining its separate identity. Self-governing institutions developed, the House of Assembly having an elected indigenous majority from 1964. It achieved internal self-government in December 1973 and full independence (as Papua New Guinea – PNG) on Sept. 16, 1975, retaining the British monarch as head of state. There is a single-chamber national parliament of 109 members elected by universal adult suffrage, normally for five years. Government has been exercised by coalitions among the political parties especially the Pangu (Papua New Guinea Unity) Pati, the People's Democratic Movement, the Papua Party and the People's Progress Party.

PNG's most important external relations are with Indonesia, with which it shares a common border, and with Australia which has been heavily involved in the private sector, has consistently subsidized the PNG budget, though by reducing amounts, and helped establish the PNG defence force. There is still a sizeable expatriate Australian community in the country. Indonesia's incorporation and colonialization of West New Guinea (Irian Jaya) after 1969 led to a flow of refugees across the border into PNG, some of whom engaged in irredentist political activities in the Free Papua Movement (OPM). With Australian logistical support, PNG provided troops to Vanuatu in July 1980 to help restore order during an attempted secessionist revolt on Espiritu Santo at the time of independence. PNG is a member of the **South Pacific Forum**, and has observer status in the **Association of South-East Asian Nations (ASEAN)**.

Papua New Guinea has a subsistence economy that meets basic domestic needs; exports of coffee, cocoa, copra, timber and fish; some modest secondary and tertiary industry; and one of the world's largest copper mines (on Bougainville), with gold and silver deposits. Copper is the principal export. Further copper and gold mining is being developed at Ok Tedi in the remote western district. Reserves of oil and natural gas, and other minerals, are being assessed, and look promising. PNG is a member of the **Asian Development Bank** and of the World Bank, and has received significant long-term loans from both organizations. In October 1986 PNG joined with other South Pacific states to sign a fishing agreement with the USA, whose tuna fleet was allowed, for a fee, to operate within the countries' exclusive fishing zones.

TBM

PARK, CHUNG-HEE (Pak Chŏng-hŭi). A
former President, Republic of Korea. Born Nov. 14, 1917; assassinated Oct. 26, 1979. Graduated Taegu Normal School, 1937; graduated Japanese Military Academy, 1944; graduated Korea Military Academy, 1946; attended Korean War College, 1957; retired Gen., 1963; Vice Commander Second Army, 1960; Vice-Chairman, Military Revolutionary Committee, 1961; Acting President, 1962–63; President, 1963–79. His policies laid the foundations for the social and economic development of modern South Korea. His authoritarian control of the political scene created internal political tensions which ultimately led to his assassination.

JHG

PARTY FOR PEACE AND DEMOCRACY (S. KOREA). Founded in November, 1987 as
party to support presidential candidacy of **Kim Dae Jung**. This party is a breakoff of the major opposition Reunification Democratic Party headed by **Kim Young-sam**. Kim Dae Jung received 26.5 per cent of the votes in the presidential contest of November, 1987. The party received 19.3 per cent of the votes in the elections for the National Assembly in April, 1988.

JHG

PEOPLE'S ACTION PARTY (SINGAPORE). The PAP was formed as a democratic
socialist party in late 1954 by a group of trade unionists and intellectuals around **Lee Kuan Yew**. Having won only three out of 30 seats in its first election in 1955, in elections held in May 1959 to the 51-member Legislative Assembly (under the 1957 Constitution conferring internal autonomy on Singapore) the PAP gained an absolute majority of 43 seats and thereupon formed a government. In 1961, however, the party's effective majority was reduced to 26 out of 51 members of the Assembly as a result of defections and the formation of the **Socialist Front**. In elections held to the Singapore Legislative Assembly shortly after the incorporation of Singapore in the newly-established Federation of Malaysia in September 1963, the PAP gained 37 seats and the Socialist Front 13.

In August 1965 Singapore seceded from the Federation of Malaysia, and since December 1965 the PAP has been in government as the country's ruling party. In September 1988, the PAP was returned for its eighth consecutive term of office, winning all but one of the 81 elected seats.

Although the PAP was formed as a democratic socialist party, in recent years it has shifted its ideological orientation, combining strong anti-communism with pragmatism, and promoting the country's economic development on the basis of a strongly free-market economy whilst at the same time continuing to place emphasis on social welfare. In a move to the so-called "second generation" of leaders, the PAP conference in September 1984 elected several new younger members to the central executive committee. Nevertheless, Lee Kuan Yew remained as PAP secretary general as of mid-1989, a post he had held since the party's foundation.

DS

PEOPLE'S LIBERATION ARMY (PLA). The
Chinese Army traces its history back to the forces thrown together for the attempted armed uprising in autumn 1927. It acquired its present title in 1947, and includes naval and air as well as ground forces. At the beginning of 1989 PLA manpower was estimated at 3.2 million, with a further 1.2 million in reserve. This represents a cut of one million since the early 1980s, and is set to go down further. Roughly 2.3 million are in the ground forces, and a further 12 million are in paramilitary militia forces. The country is now divided into seven Military Regions, and 30 Military Districts based upon provinces.

Between the late 1950s and the late 1970s PLA military doctrine was based upon the principles of People's War, which accorded relatively lower priority to technology in winning battles, just as the PLA had done in fighting the Japanese and the Civil War. The reverses suffered in the limited war with Vietnam in 1979, however, brought home the PLA's vulnerability to technologically more advanced opponents. Since then doctrine has been evolving, with more resources being devoted to technological development at the same time as the numbers of troops are reduced. Currently the ground forces are being reorganized into 22 Integrated Group Armies, with their own tanks, engineers, and artillery.

Between 1959 and the early 1980s the PLA, and especially its High Command, played a leading part in party politics. Old ties of comradeship linked party and military leaders. The PLA was viewed as a "model" Maoist institution in the early 1960s, and became embroiled in local administration in the turmoil following the Cultural Revolution. Half of the party Central Committee elected in 1969 consisted of serving PLA officers. Although the status of the PLA fell in the aftermath of the **Lin Biao** affair, senior military figures played a key role in Mao's succession, firstly supporting **Hua Guofeng**, and then organizing the arrest of the **Gang of Four**.

In the 1980s, with the retirement of the oldest military figures, **Deng Xiaoping** has made an attempt to confine the PLA to a more purely professional military role. The crushing of the demonstrations on Tiananmen Square in June 1989 (*see* **Tiananmen Incidents**) brought the military back into politics and suggests the possibility of renewed prominence for them to maintain order, as well as influence the post-Deng succession.

CIPF

PEOPLE'S PARTY OF BRUNEI. Established in 1959, the People's Party of Brunei (*Partai Ra'ayat Brunei* – *PRB*) was suppressed and banned and hundreds of its members arrested following a PRB-led rebellion in 1962. The PRB subsequently operated from exile in Malaysia, with the use of facilities in Sarawak. At the United Nations, the PRB has been one of several petitioners for the granting of "the inalienable right of the people of Brunei to self-determination and independence". A number of PRB members and supporters were released from prison in the first half of 1988, at least one of whom had been in detention without trial since 1962. According to the London-based human rights organization Amnesty International, four PRB members remained in prison as of May 1989.

DS

PERTAMINA. Pertamina (*Perusahaan Tambang dan Minyak Nasional* – National Oil and Natural Gas Mining Company), the state-owned Indonesian oil and gas company, is currently the country's largest industrial enterprise. It was established by the merger of two existing companies in 1968 after oil production had reached 500,000 barrels per day for the first time during the previous year. Its terms of reference were "to develop and to implement the oil and natural gas mining exploitation in the broadest sense for the prosperity of the People and State". Foreign oil companies are encouraged to operate in Indonesia, but under a system of production sharing they are forced to surrender a considerable percentage of their profits.

A major financial crisis was caused in Indonesia by the disclosure in March 1975 that Pertamina — which had developed a wide degree of autonomy from government control and had diversified into numerous non-oil fields — was unable to meet its short-term debt obligations. The Indonesian central bank assumed full responsibility for all Pertamina's debts, which were then estimated at US$2,500 million, and loans were negotiated with a consortium of international banks. In November 1975, however, it was discovered that the president-director of Pertamina, Lt.-Gen. Ibnu Sutowo, had entered into international contracts for the hire-purchase of a fleet of 31 oil tankers without the government's knowledge; as a result, Sutowo was relieved of his duties in March 1976, and replaced by Maj.-Gen. Piet Harjono. The House of Representatives was informed in May 1976 that Pertamina's debts had exceeded US$10,500 million. The failure of Pertamina produced repercussions throughout the Indonesian banking and business world, and led to widespread unemployment in the construction industry. It was reported in April 1977 that over 150 companies had defaulted on debts, and that two state-owned commercial banks had debts totalling US$500 million. One of the companies most seriously affected was the P.T. Astra Corporation, the country's largest single private employer, which had contracted to build a town near Jakarta for American technicians employed by Pertamina.

In mid-1988, Dr Faisal Abda'oe, finance director and board member of Pertamina since 1981, was appointed to succeed Abdul Rachman Ramly as the company's president-director. Abda'oe had been widely credited with introducing rigorous cost accounting procedures at Pertamina during his tenure as finance director. He was the company's first non-military chief executive.

DS

PERU, REPUBLIC OF. *Population*: 18,000,000. *Area*: 1,285,216 sq km. *Gross Domestic Product*: US$10,838 million. *Trade*: US$4,245.4 million. *Main trading partners*: USA, Japan, West Germany, Brazil, Argentina. *Defence spending*: US$1,450 million. *Education spending as percentage of Gross National Product*: 3.3. *Urban population as percentage of total (centres over 20,000)*: 47. *Birth rate*: 37 per thousand. *Life expectancy*: males 43; females 45.

Geographical background. The coastal plain is largely desert with a few oases. The central highlands comprises the mountains of the Andes rising to more than 22,000 ft, plateaux, intermontane basins and deep valleys. More than half of the country lies to the east of the mountains and mainly consists of rain-forest and dense jungle. The cold Humboldt Current cools the coastal area and altitude reduces temperatures in the mountains. The eastern area is hot and wet. 1.7 million hectares are cultivated. Peru had the first railway in Latin America and still has the highest standard-gauge railway in the world, the Peruvian Central. But apart from mineral lines to ports such as Callao, the 2,159 km of railways are now of little economic importance and most roads are unpaved. The tributaries of the Amazon provide water transport in the eastern region and deep sea vessels can reach Iquitos, its capital. Air transport has inevitably developed to overcome some of these deficiencies and the national airline, Aeroperú, and international companies serve the country. Nearly a third of the population live in the coastal region with a huge concentration in the Lima-Callao area. Lima, the capital, is by far the largest city (population 4,601,000). More than half of Peruvians live in the central highlands. The Amazon jungles are very sparsely populated.

Socio-political background. Nearly half the population is Indian and "*indigenismo*" (Indian-feeling) is very strong. Most of the rest are *mestizo* with a significant minority of Europeans. Both Spanish and Quechua are official languages. Other Indian languages are also used. The religion is Roman Catholic with strong traditional Indian elements. Education is free and officially compulsory where available from six to 15. Nationally primary enrolment is 84 per cent but non-attendance is a problem especially in the remoter areas where there are too few schools. Despite a major emphasis on literacy under the military governments of 1968–80 adult illiteracy is still 27.5 per cent. The national University, San Marcos, was founded in 1551; the central campus is at Lima. International agencies have played a key role in helping reduce some of the major diseases, but Peru still has a death rate of 10.7 per thousand and an infant mortality rate of 140.5 – one of the worst in the world. Although a ratio of one doctor to 1,480 people has been achieved, the problems of poor nutrition, lack of sanitation (only 1 per cent of rural dwellings have this), primitive rural housing and urban slums are all compounded by the cold and thin air. Fifty-five per cent of urban but only 3 per cent of rural homes have piped water supply.

Political history. The last of the major South American states to obtain independence, Peru has had a troubled history punctuated by frequent military intervention. The American Popular Revolutionary Alliance (APRA), a disciplined revolutionary movement of vaguely Marxist inspiration, struck roots in the 1930s but was viewed with suspicion by the armed forces who would not allow it to take power in 1962. Younger military officers who came to the fore at that time recognized the strength of social and nationalist feeling and deposed the popularly elected President Belaúnde in 1968 when his government failed to nationalize the holdings of the International Petroleum Corporation. They then sought to carry out a social revolution from the top down, breaking the power of the coastal landowners and taking control of major industries. In 1980 the military withdrew from power and Belaúnde was re-elected, becoming the first Peruvian President for 40 years to serve a full elected term. His term, however, was one of drift and inactivity, allowing a formidable (though geographically limited) indigenous guerrilla movement, the Sendero Luminoso, to take root in the Department of Ayacucho. His successor, Alan García Pérez, the first Aprista candidate to reach the presidency (1986), has taken a populist line with Peru's creditors but was soon in serious financial and political difficulties.

Outline of economic development. The principal export is copper (15.6 per cent) the price of which has been depressed in the 1980s. Petroleum was developed in the southern departments in the 1950s and crude petroleum ranks second at 14.1 per cent. Anchovy has been over-fished and the "Niño" current has caused the *anchoveta* to shift their habitual grounds.

Peru's debt at the end of 1986 totalled US$14,300 million, representing only 8 per cent of export earnings, and García in 1985 had announced a policy of limiting repayments to 10 per cent of the level of exports. The main problem is that the economy lacks sufficient export potential and in addition is top-heavy with bureaucracy.

P&SC

PERU–ECUADOR BOUNDARY DISPUTE. Since independence Ecuador has claimed a large area of the Amazon basin, but following armed conflict in 1941 in which Ecuador sought access to the Marañon River the entire area was awarded to Peru by the Protocol of Rio de Janeiro of January 1942. The Protocol was resented as an imposition and after agreement on demarcation had broken down it was unilaterally abrogated by Ecuador in 1960. In 1981 hostilites broke out in the Condor Mountains, but peace was restored after five days by the diplomatic interposition of the four guarantor Powers: Argentina, Brazil, Chile and the United States. A further clash occurred in January 1984 when an Ecuadorian soldier was killed.

P&SC

PETROLEUM. The hydrocarbon reserves of the Pacific are vast: Australia, Brunei, China, Indonesia, Malaysia, Mexico, Canada and the United States are all important producers. The continental shelves of Australia, Indonesia and Korea are particularly well endowed. Much of it lies in the **Association of South-East Asian Nations (ASEAN)** area. Recent discoveries in the South China Sea are particularly promising: two especially large deposits east of Hainan Island are thought to contain reserves around 1,700 million barrels.

Relaxation of governments' controls on exploration, the improvements in oil companies' profits and the reduction in drilling costs have made a larger capital investment programme possible since 1987. An additional consideration is that the rate of discovery of new deposits is still not keeping pace with the exhaustion of existing oil reserves. Consequently exploration activity is continuing to increase.

Of the Pacific oil producers Brunei, Indonesia and Malaysia export most of their produce. Indonesia, the region's sole OPEC member, has progressively cut its level of output to meet OPEC quotas. As a result it was overtaken by China as east Asia's largest oil exporter. Yet Indonesia still exports 70 per cent of its production, Malaysia about 80 per cent. Brunei is the third biggest oil producer in Southeast Asia exporting almost all its oil to Japan. There the rich onshore Seira field was first discovered in 1929. Offshore production began in 1964 and today there are over 200 offshore structures operated by **Brunei Shell**, jointly owned by the government and Shell. The vast Champion-7 complex, the largest of its type in Southeast Asia, was completed in 1984 at a cost of B$340 million. Like Indonesia, Brunei has cut back production dramatically since 1979 but its oil reserves are expected to last until well into the next century.

Although China is Asia's largest oil producer, after the USSR, less than 15 per cent of its output is exported. Total oil production increased in each of the four years 1984–87 but exports are unlikely to rise. Accelerating domestic demand is likely to squeeze oil exports in the 1990s. Fifty per cent of China's oil comes from the now declining Daqing Field and China is encouraging foreign investment in the hope of developing large new fields. In addition to off-shore development, oil companies are interested in the exploration of the Tarim Basin in the far west of China.

Among those producers with a large degree of self-sufficiency are Australia, Canada, the USA and Mexico. Australia has relaxed controls on foreign companies to facilitate the development of fields such as Saladin on the North-West Shelf. The country should become an exporter in the 1990s with Japan a likely recipient. New Zealand too has offered several exploration licences in the Taranakin Basin and has a reasonable expectation of becoming self-sufficient in oil, as does Vietnam, providing sufficient investment is forthcoming.

The annual crude petroleum production, in millions of tonnes, is as follows: USA 435.8; Mexico 136.6; China 112.5; Canada 71.2; Indonesia 66.3; Australia 23.9; Malaysia 23.0; Ecuador 12.6; Peru 10.0; Colombia 8.2; Chile 1.8; New Zealand 0.7; Japan 0.2.

RS

PETRONAS. Petronas is Malaysia's state-run oil company and the country's leading enterprise with sales of US$3,297 million for the 1987–88 fiscal year, a 27 per cent decline over 1986–87. The decline in Petronas's sales (reflecting the fall in oil prices) did not impede improved profits, up by 11 per cent to US$1,700 million. The company's assets were reported to be US$10,832 million in 1987–88 and it had 10,832 employees.

DS

PHILIPPINES. *Population*: 63,200,000 (est. 1988). *Area*: 300,000 sq km. *Gross Domestic Product*: US$33,940 million (1987). *Trade (1987)*: imports US$6,737 million; exports US$5,720 million. *Top five trading partners*: (imports) USA, Japan, Malaysia, China and Saudi Arabia; (exports) USA, Japan, Singapore, Hong Kong and Malaysia. *Defence spending*: US$504 million (1986). *Education spending*: US$1,033 million (1988). *Urban population as percentage of* *total*: 41. *Life expectancy*: 66 years. *Birth rate per thousand*: 35.

Geographical background. Like Indonesia and Japan, the Republic of the Philippines is an Asian archipelagic nation, consisting of some 7,100 islands, lying to the east of mainland Southeast Asia between the South China Sea and the Pacific Ocean. Of its islands, some 880 are inhabited and the two largest, Luzon in the north and Mindanao in the south, have a combined area of 199,318 sq km accounting for over 65 per cent of the country's territory. The next largest islands are Samar, Negros, Palawan, Panay, Mindoro, Leyte, Cebu, Bohol and Masbate which have a combined area of 77,580 sq km. As of 1988, 52 per cent of the country's total land area was estimated to be forest, 41 per cent was cultivated and 1.5 per cent was pasture.

In mid-1988 the country's population was estimated at 63,200,000 and it was projected to reach over 85,000,000 by the year 2000. Manila is the nation's capital, with a population in excess of 1,500,000 at the 1980 census. The boundaries of the administrative unit of Metropolitan Manila (Metro Manila) encompass a large number of former towns and districts including Quezon City, Caloocan and Pasay, and contain a total population of at least 6,000,000. Other principal population centres include Angeles, Olongapo, Batangas, Cabanatuan and San Pablo on Luzon, Davao, Zamboanga, Cagayan de Oro, Butuan and Iligan on Mindanao, Cebu City on Cebu, Bacolod on Negros and Iloilo on Panay.

Socio-political background. The bulk of the population are lowland Roman Catholics, and it is their shared religion that has tended to promote a common Filipino culture. Communities of animist hill peoples live in the uplands of Luzon and Mindanao and the Muslim Moros inhabit sizeable areas in the southern part of the archipelago. Of the many languages spoken in the Philippines, those most widely used are Tagalog, Cebuano, Iloco and Ifugao. Progress has been recorded in the government's attempt to promote Tagalog (the language of central Luzon) as a national language (Pilipino).

As of 1988, the Philippines had an 83 per cent literacy rate, a student population approaching 15.5 million (of which over two million were attending university) and a total workforce over 21 million strong.

Under the terms of its 1987 Constitution, the Republic of the Philippines is a liberal democracy with a directly elected executive and legislature. The President, who is also C.-in-C. of the Armed Forces, is eligible for a single six-year term and governs with the assistance of an appointed Cabinet; the legislature (elected most recently in May 1987) consists of a 200-member House of Representatives (with provision for a further 50 appointed members) and a 24-member Senate.

Pre-modern history. Prior to Spanish conquest in the sixteenth century, the multitude of islands which today constitute the Republic of the Philippines had no central government and little cultural homogeneity. Unlike many Southeast Asian territories, the country had enjoyed no previous period of imperial integrity, and possessed neither written history nor common language. The population lived in small isolated settlements (*barangays*) of up to 500 people founded upon subsistence agriculture. The social structure of the *barangays* maintained a considerable degree of fluidity, in marked contrast to the rigid, economically-defined class structure of their Spanish conquerors who gradually exerted control over the archipelago throughout the sixteenth century in the aftermath of Ferdinand Magellan's expedition to Cebu in 1521.

The port of Manila, situated on the main island of Luzon, became the main transshipment post on the trade route between the Far East and Spanish colonies in Latin America. Elsewhere within the territory, local administration was usually in the hands of the Catholic Church which became a substantial landowner upon profits derived from the galleon trade. Only in the remote northern area of Luzon and in the southern islands of Mindanao and the Sulu archipelago (where Islam had become well established a century before the arrival of the Spanish), was there any sustained resistance to the Spanish conquest.

During the eighteenth century the agricultural potential of the Philippines was developed through the growth of plantations or *haciendas*, and share-cropping became widespread. This served to develop economic divisions and encouraged the rise of a native gentry class (*ilustrados*), who were eager to exploit the labour of the less fortunate. The plantation system intensified as Spain's hold on the archipelago weakened and capital investment from Britain and the United States increased. The investors favoured high profit cash crops and the over-production of sugar meant that the colony as a whole lost its self-sufficiency in the production of food. The territory's economic development in conjunction with the decline of Spain led the *ilustrados* to demand a voice in government in the mid-to-late nineteenth century. The first to articulate fully the aspirations of the *ilustrados* were Jose Rizal, whose execution by the Spanish authorities in 1896 ensured that he became a martyr to, and enduring symbol of, Filipino nationalism. During the last five years of the nineteenth century a revolutionary nationalist movement was founded and grew rapidly under the leadership of Emilio Aguinaldo. The Spanish authorities bribed Aguinaldo to go into exile in Hong Kong, but with the outbreak of the Spanish–American war in April 1898, he returned with US support and proclaimed Philippine independence in June 1898.

Early modern history. Under the terms of the Treaty of Paris (which was signed in December 1898 following the defeat of Spain), the Philippines was ceded to the USA in return for US$20 million. Aguinaldo's relationship with the US forces of occupation rapidly deteriorated into open warfare as he pursued his demand for complete independence. Even after his capture and arrest in March 1901, sporadic resistance to the US occupation continued. Nevertheless, US rule was considerably more enlightened than its predecessor and an increasing degree of internal self-government was granted to the Philippines, with a gradual extension of the franchise from 1907 onwards. The political process remained under the control of the *ilustrados*, however, and the US agricultural policy strongly favoured the landed elite. Peasant unrest in the 1920s was accompanied by a growth in unionization and increasing militancy in the urban areas; the Communist Party of the Philippines was founded in 1930. The Great Depression and the attendant clamour for increased protection for the severely depressed US agricultural sector led to extensive lobbying in the US by farm interests in support of an (economically) independent Philippines. In November 1935, the Commonwealth of the Philippines was established under the Presidency of Manuel Quezon. The move, which resulted from an Act which had been ratified by President Roosevelt in March 1934, was designed as a transitory stage with full independence to follow within 10 years. The outbreak of the Pacific War in late 1941 disturbed this period of preparation.

Japanese troops invaded the Philippines in December 1941, shortly after the Japanese air attack on the US naval base at Pearl Harbour. By May 1942, the combined US and Filipino army of 50,000 men had surrendered. The brutally exploitative nature of the following years of Japanese occupation fostered the growth of pro-US sentiments amongst a large number of Filipinos, many of whom saw the USA as a potential liberator. However, sections of the political establishment co-operated with the Japanese. Jose Vargas led a collaborationist government, and Benigno Aquino headed an anti-American nationalist movement called *Kalibapi*. Active resistance to the Japanese was in general sporadic and ineffective, with the exception of the peasant-based, leftist *Hukbalahap* movement which operated in central and southern Luzon. From mid-1942 onwards the war began to run in favour of the Allies and Japan attempted to harness its faltering war effort by encouraging genuine popular support among Filipinos. The culmination of this process was the granting to full independence in October 1943, under President Jose Laurel, whereupon the Philippines became a "voluntary" member of the Greater East Asia Co-Prosperity Sphere.

US forces invaded the Philippines in October 1944, and, with the support of *Huk* guerrillas, Manila was liberated by February 1945. The Filipino government-in-exile under Sergio Osmena (who had become President following the death of Quezon in 1944) returned to resume Commonwealth rule. Osmena became increasingly unpopular with the US authorities as he made clear his opposition to the imposition of preferential trading rights to the US in return for reconstruction aid. In particular, Osmena opposed the proposed granting of American parity rights with Filipinos in the exploitation, disposition and utilization of natural resources and the operation of public utilities. At the Presidential election held in April 1946, Osmena was defeated by (the US supported) Manuel Roxas, who had left the Nationalist Party to contest the election as a Liberal. On July 4, 1946, the Philippine Republic was proclaimed as an independent state with Roxas as its first President.

Political history. The Roxas administration was strongly pro-USA and, using dubious political methods to disqualify some of its opponents, succeeded in gaining the 75 per cent Congressional majority necessary to amend the constitution and thereby assure parity rights for US citizens. In April 1948 Roxas died and was replaced by his Vice-President Elpidio Quirino. At the Presidential election of 1949 he defeated Jose Laurel amidst numerous accusations of fraud and corruption. In the 1953 presidential elections Quirino was defeated by his former Defence Minister, Ramon Magsaysay, who had left the Liberals to contest the Presidency as the representative of the Nationalist Party. As President he continued the pro-US policies of his predecessors. Shortly before the presidential election of 1957 he was killed in an aircrash and was succeeded by his Vice-President, Carlos Garcia, who was subsequently elected President. The Liberals recaptured the Presidency in 1961 when Garcia was defeated by Diosdado Macapagal.

In the presidential elections of November 1965, Macapagal was defeated by **Ferdinand Marcos** who had left the Liberals a year earlier and who contested the elections as the Nationalist candidate. Marcos, like his predecessors, proved a staunch ally of the USA. Despite a deterioration in the overall performance of the economy, Marcos broke the traditional pattern of one-term presidents by defeating the challenge of Sergio Osmena in the presidential elections of November 1969. The campaign, like that of 1965, was characterized by a high level of political violence. Rising prices and endemic corruption led to repeated demonstrations and strikes throughout the early 1970s. Opposition to the Marcos regime was co-ordinated by the Movement for a Democratic Philippines (MDP), which embraced workers' and students' organizations. Demonstrations were also held to demand the inclusion of independent figures in the Constitutional Convention (which was due to begin drafting a new constitution in 1971 to replace that drawn up in 1935) and to ensure that Marcos would not attempt to serve a third term as president.

The Marcos government also faced an increasing guerrilla challenge during the early 1970s by the **New People's Army** (NPA), the armed wing of the banned Maoist Communist Party of the Philippines (CPP-ML), in the north of the country, and by the **Moro National Liberation Front** (MNLF), a Muslim separatist movement, in the south.

The campaign for the legislative elections of November 1971, in which the Liberals achieved considerable gains, was marred by serious violence. Unrest continued during 1972, and in September of that year Marcos used his emergency powers to decree a state of full martial law throughout the country. Under the decree military commanders in the provinces were ordered to assume the powers of provincial governors and mayors. Benigno Aquino, the secretary general of the Liberal Party, was quickly arrested, as were many other prominent opposition figures. The government also took control of public services and prohibited strikes in the utilities and schools.

In November 1972, the Constitutional Convention approved a new constitution, with provisions for the replacement of the existing system of presidential government with a Cabinet system headed by a Prime Minister elected by and responsible to a unicameral legislature. Upon receipt of the draft constitution Marcos announced that the document would be offered for popular approval in a referendum in January 1973. However, the referendum was subsequently postponed indefinitely; Citizens' Assemblies

(*barangays*) were established throughout the country and Marcos claimed that they had endorsed the proposals within the draft constitution. These assemblies were also used to provide the membership of a 4,600 strong "Popular Congress", before which Marcos announced the ratification of the new constitution in mid-January 1973. He also stated that elections would be suspended for at least seven years and that martial law would remain in force for as long as was deemed necessary. Attempts to challenge the legality of Marcos' actions were dismissed by the Supreme Court, and in July 1973 a referendum was held which gave Marcos a mandate "to remain in office beyond 1973 and to complete the reforms which he has initiated under martial law". Referenda in February 1975 and in October 1976 approved the continuation of martial law and the adoption of constitutional amendments, including a provision for the formation of an interim constituent assembly (*Batasang Pambansa*). In late 1977 a fourth referendum approved the extension of Marcos's presidential term.

When elections for the interim assembly were held in April 1978, the recently created **New Society Movement** (*Kilusan Bagong Lipunan* – KBL), led by Marcos, won 152 of the 165 elected seats. Although the martial law prohibition on political parties had been lifted prior to the voting, the government was accused of intimidation and fraud. The opposition People's Power Movement (*Lakas Ng Bayan*, known by the acronym *Laban*, which means "fight"), led by Benigno Aquino, lost all of the seats which it contested. When the newly elected assembly convened in June 1978 Marcos accepted the post of Prime Minister in addition to that of President. Marcos extended his grip on the country in early 1980 when the KBL won most of the seats at stake in the first elections for local, regional and provincial offices since 1971. Both *Laban* and the Liberal Party boycotted the elections in protest over the continuation of martial law, although the **Nacionalista Party** did succeed in winning some of the posts.

In a nationwide broadcast in mid-January 1981 Marcos announced the lifting of martial law in all but the southernmost provinces of the country. Nevertheless, Marcos retained most of his former powers. Legislative power was formally transferred to the interim National assembly elected in April 1978, and it was confirmed that elections to a permanent Assembly would be held in 1984. Marcos also announced that the first presidential election since 1969 would be held during 1981. A referendum in April approved constitutional amendments which permitted the president to be popularly elected, rather than being chosen by the Assembly. In June, Marcos, standing as the official KBL candidate, was returned to office for a six-year term. Amid allegations of widespread malpractice and fraud concerning both the campaign and the count, Marcos was declared to have been elected with 88 per cent of the votes cast. The next month, the Finance Minister, Cesar Virata, was appointed Prime Minister.

The re-election of Marcos acted as an important catalyst in accelerating the movement towards opposition unity. In February 1982 the **United Nationalist Democratic Organization** (UNIDO) was established as an anti-Marcos alliance. Although the movement was led within the Philippines by **Salvador Laurel**, it was Benigno Aquino (who had remained in the USA since being permitted to travel there in 1980 for medical treatment) who was widely recognized as the most influential opposition figure. In August 1983, Aquino returned to the Philippines, but was shot dead as he stepped from the airliner at Manila airport. The official version of the assassination maintained that Aquino had been shot by Rolando Galman, a communist assassin, who in turn had been shot dead immediately by troops. From the start, however, there were inconsistencies in the official version of events and it was widely suspected that the crime had been committed with the connivance of members of the armed forces or the government. A commission of inquiry established by the government in late 1983 concluded, in October 1984, that Aquino's murder had resulted from a military conspiracy which had been sanctioned by the Chief of Staff of the Armed Forces, Gen. Fabian Ver. In early 1985, 26 people, including Ver, were charged with involvement in the crime. After a nine-month trial, the Supreme Court announced in December 1985 that all 26 were acquitted, ruling that the evidence given to the commission of inquiry was inadmissible and upholding the Government's assertion that Galman alone was responsible for the crime.

Despite widespread popular unrest and repeated opposition calls for Marcos' resignation after Aquino's assassination, elections to the National Assembly were still held in May 1984. The elections were again marred by violence and numerous allegations of malpractice and intimidation of the voters by the KBL. The final distribution of seats within the Assembly increased the opposition's representation from 13 to 55, out of a total of 200, 17 of whom were nominated by Marcos. By early 1985, the political opposition had formed itself into two distinctive groups; (i) the conservative-liberal Unido led by Laurel; and (ii) a more loosely organized liberal-left grouping

within which **Corazon Aquino**, the widow of Benigno, was playing an increasingly prominent role. Opposition demonstrations calling for the resignation of Marcos, often supported by leading members of the clergy, became a common feature within Manila. Under growing US pressure to re-establish the basis of some democratic legitimacy for his continued rule, Marcos announced in early November 1985 that a presidential election would be held in January 1986. UNIDO challenged Marcos's right to call a snap election, and after discussions between the KBL and opposition Assembly members, it was agreed to delay the election until Feb. 7, 1986. In mid-December 1985, Aquino and Laurel announced unexpectedly that they had agreed on a joint UNIDO ticket with the former as the presidential candidate and the latter as the vice-presidential candidate. Marcos announced that Arturo Tolentino, a former Foreign Minister, was to be his Vice-Presidential running mate.

Over 50 people were killed in election-related incidents during the period up to Feb. 6 and at least 26 people were killed on election day itself. The vote-counting was carried out by the official National committee on Elections (Comelec) and the independent National Citizens' Movement for Free Elections (Namfrel), and accusations by the latter organization of large-scale electoral fraud and irregularities were largely substantiated by international observer groups, including a US team. Under the electoral system both Comelec and Namfrel were to check the returns, which were then passed to the National Assembly where the result was to be confirmed and formally declared. According to Comelec, Marcos had gained the most votes, whereas Namfrel claimed Aquino had received the greater number. On Feb. 15 the (KBL-dominated) Assembly proclaimed the re-election of Marcos as President. That day, the US President Ronald Reagan announced that the election's credibility had been called into question because of "widespread fraud and violence". On Feb. 16, Aquino told a massive rally in Manila that she would launch a national strike and campaign of "active resistance by peaceful means" in protest at Marcos's "victory", and that the campaign would continue until the Marcos regime was brought down. A serious blow was struck against Marcos on Feb. 22 when **Juan Ponce Enrile** (the Defence Minister) and Gen. **Fidel Ramos** (the Deputy Chief of Staff of the Armed Forces) announced that they no longer considered Marcos to be the legitimate president, and that Aquino had been cheated of victory. To protect the rebel forces, Cardinal Sin called people onto the Manila streets to form a protective human shield around the rebel bases. Thus was born the concept of "people power" which was to become the enduring hallmark of the Aquino revolution. On Feb. 24, after rebel forces had taken control of the main government radio and TV network, Marcos declared a state of emergency. The next day, both Marcos and Aquino were formally sworn in as President in ceremonies held in separate parts of Manila. That evening, in the light of growing defections in the armed forces, mass popular demonstrations and the imminent US recognition of Aquino as President, Marcos, Ver and various family members left the Philippines aboard US military aircraft for Hawaii.

Recent developments. Upon her inauguration as President on Feb. 25, 1986, Corazon Aquino appointed her Vice-President, Salvador Laurel, as Prime Minister, with Juan Ponce Enrile as Defence Minister and Gen. Fidel Ramos as Chief of Staff of the Armed Forces. Three days later Aquino ordered the release of all the country's estimated 450 political prisoners, including leading members of the New People's Army. During March the President announced: (i) the full restoration of the right of *habeas corpus*; (ii) the replacement of all local and provincial officials; (iii) the resignation of all 13 justices of the Supreme Court; (iv) the abolition of media censorship; (v) an unofficial inquiry into the death of Benigno Aquino. The process of dismantling the coercive apparatus of the Marcos years continued on March 25 with the suspension of the 1973 Constitution and its replacement by an interim "Freedom Constitution", which empowered Aquino to appoint local and provincial officials and members of the judiciary, and to decree and revoke legislation. It also provided for the abolition of the National Assembly and for the inauguration of a provisional government, with Aquino herself being granted emergency powers. The post of Prime Minister was temporarily abolished, and on May 25, before a crowd of 100,000 people gathered to celebrate her first three months in office, the President announced the creation of a 50-member Constitutional Commission (Concom) to draft a new Constitution.

Although the country's senior military officers pledged loyalty to President Aquino (the Commander-in-Chief of the Armed Forces) in mid-March, it was widely accepted that Marcos-loyalists were well represented within the forces. Accordingly, in an attempt to reduce the incidence of military dissatisfaction and in line with earlier pledges to give consideration to the demands of the Reform the Armed Forces of the Philippines Movement (RAM) within the Army, the new government started to implement a far-reaching programme of military reform, including the forced retirement of "overstaying" officers and a structural reorganisation of the Defence Ministry and the security and intelligence wings. Meanwhile, in early July an abortive coup took place in Manila, when Arturo Tolentino (who in the February elections had been Marcos's running-mate), supported by some 300 pro-Marcos troops, proclaimed himself acting President and named a five-member "cabinet", including the current Defence Minister, Juan Ponce Enrile. The rebellion collapsed within 24-hours after Enrile refused to be associated with the coup and ordered troops to surround the Manila hotel where Tolentino was based. Amid growing fears concerning the loyalty of the army, on July 28 all members of the country's 250,000-strong armed forces (including the participants in the coup attempt, who had gone unpunished) were required to swear allegiance to the interim Constitution. In early September Tolentino took an oath recognizing the "existence" of the Aquino government, in return for the dropping of all charges against him and other civilians implicated in the coup attempt.

One of the principal reasons for dissatisfaction within the army was the alleged leniency of the Aquino government towards the communist insurgents of the New People's Army. Enrile, in particular, was a strident critic of the government's attempts to initiate meaningful negotiation with the rebels, and in mid-October he chose not to attend a Cabinet meeting. Amid increasing rumours of an impending military coup, there were public calls for Enrile's resignation from several Cabinet members. Following intervention by Salvador Laurel, a reconciliation between Enrile and Aquino was reported to have taken place in late October, with the latter promising to effect a less conciliatory attitude towards the NPA. However, on Nov. 23 Aquino accepted Enrile's resignation from the Cabinet after allegations that he had been involved in a coup plot. The previous day army units had taken up positions around key sites in the capital to prevent attempts by officers associated with RAM, who were loyal to Enrile, to reconvene the National Assembly. In the face of the continuing loyalty of Ramos, the coup attempt failed to materialize. The position of the government was further shaken by a third attempted coup in late January 1987 which was considerably more serious than the two which had preceded it. Rebellious troops led by Col. Oscar Canlas seized a television station and other installations in Manila and there followed a two-day siege of the television studio before the last of the troops surrendered on Jan. 29. The rebellion was believed to be linked to the planned return of Marcos, who had been purchasing military material in the USA during January and had chartered an airliner to take him to Manila.

In a referendum on Feb. 2, 1987, the electorate by 21,764,901 votes to 4,949,901 approved the country's new Constitution, which was accordingly promulgated on Feb. 11. All members of the Armed Forces were obliged to swear an oath of allegiance to the new Constitution. Three months after the formal adoption of the Constitution, the Aquino regime faced its next test with the congressional elections of May 1987. Support for the government was grouped in the People's Struggle – Laban (*Lakas ng Bayan*) and UNIDO. The main opposition grouping was the Grand Alliance for Democracy (GAD), a coalition of disparate (though largely conservative) elements, led by Enrile and Tolentino. When the results of the Senate elections were declared in early June, it emerged that candidates aligned with Aquino had won 22 seats and the GAD (including Enrile himself) the remaining two. Prior to the announcement of the results Enrile and other GAD members had accused the government of having engaged in electoral fraud on a massive scale, a charge that was widely rejected, the campaign generally being perceived as having been fairer than any which had been held under the Marcos regime. Counting for the House of Representatives continued into July, and, by the time of the official opening of Congress on July 27, 13 seats remained in dispute. At this stage, Aquino's supporters held 127 seats, and of the remainder, 25 had been won by independents (some of whom claimed presidential endorsement), 33 by the right-wing opposition and two by the left-wing People's Party. Prior to the inauguration of the Congress, when legislative authority would be formally transferred from the executive to the new legislature, Aquino took the opportunity to enact a series of presidential decrees, imposing a maximum penalty of life imprisonment for NPA membership and providing for the formation of a "citizen's army" to combat guerrilla insurgency.

Jaime Ferrer, the Minister of Local Government and an outspoken supporter of anti-communist vigilante groups, was shot dead in early August 1987, allegedly by an NPA "sparrow squad". Throughout August left-wing organizations and trade unions organized strikes and demonstrations in protest at price rises and other aspects of the government's economic policies. On August 27 the police made large-scale arrests of trade union leaders and left-wing activists in Manila. The next day an attempted right-wing coup led by Col. Gregorio "Gringo" Honasan (leader of the RAM group and an officer closely associated with Enrile) and dissident junior officers led to over 50 deaths before loyal troops recaptured the Aguinaldo military headquarters and other installations in Manila the following day. Col. Honasan and some of his supporters escaped by helicopter and declared the establishment of a "provisional government" on Aug. 31. Honasan was captured in December, but escaped from captivity the following April. In the week following the coup, there was widespread allegations in the press and Congress that US officials had been seen with rebel forces, giving rise to accusations that the USA was pursuing a "twin-track" policy of backing both the Aquino government and those attempting to overthrow it.

In early September, Aquino demanded the resignation of the entire Cabinet, to allow her complete freedom to make new appointments. The ensuing reshuffle included the replacement of Vice-President Laurel as Foreign Secretary by senator Raul Manglapus. The growing influence of Gen. Ramos in the government was confirmed in January 1988 when he took over the post of Defence Secretary from Rafael Ileto. Indicative of the strengthening of Ramos's position was the issuing of arrest orders for a number of prominent RAM members in late February on charges of complicity in the murder of the trade union leader, Rolando Olalia, in November 1986. Within days of Ramos's appointment the government announced an intensification of its campaign against the NPA.

Elections were held in January 1988 to more than 16,000 local government offices, including provincial governorships and mayoralties. Although voting was generally peaceful, over 100 people, including 39 candidates, died in election-related violence in the weeks leading up to the vote. In all 105 parties were registered as participating in the poll, with the majority of candidates expressing support for the government. Although the results showed that a number of close associates of President Aquino had failed to gain office, overall, she could be said to have won the election. However, some observers saw the elections as representing something of a return to the patronage politics of the Marcos years, with powerful local figures ensuring electoral success by a mixture of bribery and coercion. The local elections were the last scheduled nationwide polls, excluding the elections for *barangay* (local community) officials, until the presidential elections in May 1992. In late September 1988, President Aquino announced that the *barangay* elections, due to have taken place in November, had been postponed on account of the unstable security situation.

The relationship between Aquino and Laurel,

which had started to break down soon after their defeat of Marcos in February 1986, continued to deteriorate throughout 1988. In a letter addressed to Aquino in mid-August, Laurel called upon the President to resign and to hold immediate elections "to enable our people to choose another leader for these critical times", stating that if she was ready to make the "supreme sacrifice" of resigning he was ready to do so too. He completed his political estrangement from Aquino a few days later, announcing that he had established a new political party, the Union for National Action (UNA), with the avowed aim of uniting the (right-wing) anti-Aquino forces. The new party was based on the National Movement for Economic Reconstruction and Survival ("Nation Movers"), set up by Laurel and Enrile in March. In response, government supporters in mid-September formed the **Democratic Struggle for the Philippines** (*Laban A Demokratiko ng Pilipino*), which soon claimed to command the support of 158 members of the 200-member House of Representatives.

The UNA failed in its attempt to unite Aquino's opponents, and in May 1989 many of its members along with members of the Grand Alliance for Democracy (GAD) joined the opposition Nacionalista Party at its revival convention, at which Laurel was elected party president and Enrile secretary-general.

Outline of economic development. Post-World War II economic reconstruction in the Philippines was heavily dependent upon US aid, the availability of which was inextricably tied to the concession of preferential trading rights with the USA. Thus, necessity forced the Philippines to surrender a considerable measure of economic sovereignty to the USA upon the attainment of independence in 1946. By the late 1940s, the country faced a deepening economic crisis, with both the Roxas and Quirino administrations lacking the political will to raise the necessary taxes to fund reconstruction. In 1950, President Truman of the USA offered a fresh economic aid package conditional upon the imposition of exchange and import controls and the reform of the tax administration. Hence, in the 1950s a strategy of import-substituting industralization was pursued, based on a regime of exchange controls.

In the early 1960s, under the presidency of Diosdado Macapagal, exchange controls were dismantled in return for US stabilization loans, which were conditional on the devaluation of the peso and other concessions to bilateral trade. The continuing rise in the Philippines' balance of payments deficit with the USA, however, necessitated further loans. The effect of the devaluation upon the country's embryonic industrial sector was particularly damaging and caused widespread bankruptcies with many manufacturing enterprises being purchased cheaply by US entrepreneurs.

For much of the 20-year rule of Ferdinand Marcos, the Philippines appeared to enjoy a prospering economy. During the 1970s, for example, the country's gross national product (GNP) increased by an average of 7 per cent per annum. The high growth rate, however, disguised a number of structural weaknesses in the economy. The government's emphasis on high levels of investment aimed at rapid industrialization led to substantial trade deficits due to the level of imports of producer goods and increasingly expensive oil supplies. These undercut the overall aim of the strategy, which was to achieve sustained growth via import substitution. Industries were protected against foreign competition by high tariff barriers, which helped conceal inefficient manufacturing methods, and were heavily supported by foreign finance. However, by the early 1980s world recession reduced the amount of foreign finance available, and the inherent weaknesses of the country's economy became evident. Together with other factors, including the emergence of rival producers, the recession reduced demand for the Philippines' traditional commodity exports. Consequently, as its capacity to earn foreign exchange diminished, the Philippines' ability to service its rising debt bill was placed under increasing strain. In an effort to halt the decline, the government announced a number of austerity measures from 1982 onwards, including cutbacks in state expenditure and the introduction of a floating exchange rate.

The crisis intensified from 1983 onwards; the assassination of Benigno Aquino in August 1983 caused a slump in investor confidence, with a resultant high level of capital outflow and a steady slide in the value of the peso against the US dollar. Real GNP fell by almost 7 per cent in 1984, while inflation, fuelled by the growth in money supply, reached a high of 65 per cent per annum at the end of the year. In December 1984 the International Monetary Fund (IMF) agreed a major standby credit agreement. During 1985 the government reduced inflation to just over 20 per cent, but the austerity measures merely exacerbated the stagnation of the economy, reducing domestic demand and encouraging the flight of capital. The depression was exacerbated by the rising tide of "cronyism", in which Marcos distributed monopolistic control of key companies and state enterprises to his close friends and family.

After establishing itself in power, the Aquino administration announced a series of reforms aimed at restoring internal and international confidence in the economy, and at revitalizing it by eliminating the cronyism of the Marcos regime. Crony-dominated monopolies (e.g. sugar, coconut and grain) were dismantled and a "Presidential Commission on good Government" was established to oversee the recovery of assets accumulated illicitly by Marcos and his cohorts. In an effort to stimulate the domestic economy, the government cut interest rates and lowered fuel prices, resulting in a fall in the cost of basic foods and consumer goods. A number of tax reforms were introduced, reducing the burden on agricultural and industrial production. In an attempt to alleviate rural poverty and boost consumer demand, the new administration launched a "Community Employment Development Programme" (CEDP) to create jobs through labour-intensive projects to improve local infrastructure. By late 1987, the CEDP was planned to have created 1,000,000 jobs. Further revitalization measures included the progressive removal of import controls on some 1,200 products, and the establishment of an "Omnibus Investment Code" to attract foreign investment. The government also launched a "debt-to-equity swap" in which commercial creditors would be offered the opportunity of transforming debt into equity investment through the use of non-interest-bearing certificates, denominated in US dollars and available at discount rates.

The Aquino government's long-term objectives were enshrined in a development plan covering the period 1987–92, which predicted an annual growth in real GNP of 6.5 per cent. Investment was planned to grow at a rate of 10 per cent annually, with exports and imports both set to increase by about 7 per cent. The plan also aimed to reduce unemployment and poverty. The government's policies received a seal of approval from the IMF which agreed a new aid package in July 1986 equivalent to US$513,000,000. After protracted negotiations, the "Paris Club" of 14 Western creditor nations agreed to a major reorganization of loan repayments in January 1987. Two months later, an agreement was reached on rescheduling and restructuring of debt repayments to the country's 483 commercial bank creditors. At the end of 1986, the Philippines' total external debt was estimated at US$28,617 million, making it the tenth biggest debtor in the world.

The strongest economic growth for a decade was recorded in 1987 (6.4 per cent real GNP growth). Manufacturing output increased by almost 7 per cent and construction by 20 per cent.

The performance of agriculture, which accounted for some 50 per cent of total employment, was disappointing, registering only 0.5 per cent growth. Inflation for the year remained under 4 per cent, with an official unemployment rate of 11 per cent. The trade account deteriorated during 1987, recording a deficit of US$1,020 million; the value of exports advanced by 18 per cent, with imports expanding by almost double this figure.

Current economic situation. Economic growth, led to a large extent by domestic demand, continued at a fast pace during 1988, leading to an increase in private investment. In the first half of 1988, GNP rose by just under 7 per cent, fuelled by good performances in manufacturing, industry, services and agriculture. The strong economic performance of the 1986–88 period weakened during early 1989, with a GNP growth rate of just over 4 per cent being recorded during the first quarter (compared with 7.3 per cent for January–March 1988), leading some commentators to claim that the previous year's surge had largely involved industry taking up slack capacity.

In May 1989 the IMF approved a new credit package for the Philippines worth some US$1,170 million. In line with US debt reduction proposals presented in March 1989 by the US Treasury secretary Nicholas Brady, the IMF package included provisions for part of the loan to be "set aside" and used to settle foreign debts. A few weeks after the IMF had approved the loan, the Philippines reached agreement with the so-called "Paris Club" of Western government creditors to reschedule US$2,200 million of official debt over the next 10 years. The government had stopped servicing its debt obligations in September 1988 when a previous restructuring agreement ended. Under the new agreement, creditor governments extended from 18 months to three years the period during which repayments are to be made. In early June, legislation was approved effectively increasing the mandatory daily wage by close to 40 per cent. It was claimed that the new law would increase inflationary pressure, with some forecasts estimating an 11 per cent rate for 1989.

Foreign relations. Despite gaining formal independence in 1946, the fortunes of the Philippines remained inextricably bound up with those of its former colonial ruler, the United States. Achieving self-determination at the outset of the "Cold War", meant that the Philippines became tied to the USA's foreign policy priorities. In 1947 the USA and the Philippines signed an agreement which gave the USA a 99-year lease upon 23 US military facilities. In 1959 the agreement with the USA on military bases was revised, the length of lease being shortened from 99 to 25 years and the principle of Philippine sovereignty over the bases being reaffirmed.

During the period of US involvement in Indo-China, the Philippines was an important US base and President Marcos committed Filipino troops to fight alongside US forces. The US withdrawal from Indo-China in 1975 meant that their off-shore bases in the Philippines assumed a far greater strategic importance, particularly in the light of Vietnam's decision in 1979 to grant the Soviet Union deep-water harbour facilities (built by the Americans) at Cam Ranh Bay. A fresh agreement was signed between the US and the Philippines in 1983, providing for the continued use by US forces of Subic Bay and Clark Field until 1989. Although the existence of US bases in the Philippines had been strongly condemned by various opposition groups, the fall of Marcos in 1986 did not lead to a renunciation of the bases agreement and President Aquino confirmed that she intended to respect the arrangement. After protracted negotiation the US government agreed in mid-October 1988 to provide an annual package of US$481,000,000 in economic and military aid in return for the continued use of the military bases until 1991.

The Philippines was a founder member of the **Association of South-East Asian Nations (ASEAN)** in 1967 and in December 1987 the heads of state or government of the six member countries held their third summit meeting in Manila. Philippine relations with the other five ASEAN countries are good, the only real source of friction being a territorial claim by the Philippines to the Malaysian state of Sabah, first raised in 1962. In 1977 President Marcos had announced that as a contribution toward ASEAN unity, his government would cease actively prosecuting its claim to Sabah. The prospects of final negotiations taking place on a settlement were enhanced by news in August 1988 that the Philippines Foreign Secretary, Raul Manglapus, had agreed to a proposal whereby the Philippines would drop the claim.

Prospects for development. The likelihood of the country's post-Marcos economic recovery continuing into the 1990s is largely dependent on the ability of the Aquino regime to secure political stability, thereby encouraging investment growth. The execution of the land reform programme introduced in 1988 (see below) poses a fundamental dilemma for the government – on the one hand, vigorous application of land reform policies appear to be the only means of effectively undermining communist insurrection (barring a massive and expensive military campaign),

thereby reducing the possibility of full-scale civil war. On the other hand, early indications show that agrarian reform has motivated entrepreneurs and landowners to delay investment in the plantation industries. Particularly worrying for the government is the prospect of multinational companies such as Del Monte and Dole, both of whom invest heavily in Mindanao plantations, relocating to Thailand and Indonesia.

Other major problems threatening future growth and investment include deficiencies in the basic infrastructure (power shortages are forecast for the early 1990s) and the threat of a resurgence of the serious labour unrest which marked 1986-87. Some have predicted that the Philippines might benefit from the serious political upheavals taking place in China during mid-1989, the expectation being that investors in Hong Kong and Taiwan will shift money from China to the Philippines. According to the government's own figures (as set out in a "Memorandum on Economic Policy" delivered to the IMF in early 1989), the Philippines is set to achieve real GNP growth of 6.5 per cent per annum to 1992, with inflation averaging at about 8 per cent. The current-account deficit will rise to 2.5 per cent of GNP through 1990, declining to 2.2 per cent by 1992. The ratio of debt-to-GNP will decrease from over 70 per cent in 1989 to just over 50 per cent in 1992.

Land reform. A major plank of Corazon Aquino's election campaign had been a commitment to the implementation of a major redistribution of the country's agricultural land. It was widely believed that, aside from the humanitarian imperative, land reform would encourage agricultural diversification, stimulate domestic demand and undercut the level of support among rural communities for the communist New People's Army guerrillas. Some limited land reforms had been carried out by Marcos under a scheme established in 1973, and by 1986 some 300,000 hectares were officially said to have been distributed to about 200,000 beneficiaries. Although Aquino reiterated her desire to implement land reform policies when she came to power, during her first year little action was taken against the owners of the large plantations. Nevertheless, the February 1987 Constitution enshrined the state's commitment to "encourage and undertake the just distribution of all agricultural lands".

In late January 1987, troops opened fire upon a pro-land reform demonstration at Mendiola Bridge in Manila, killing at least 20 people and injuring over 100 others. The incident was the worst of its type since Aquino had taken power and prompted the government to outline a hastily prepared programme for Agrarian reform in February 1987. However, the government showed little enthusiasm during the rest of the year for pursuing its land reform goal. In January, 1988, Aquino repeated earlier assurances that her family's sugar plantation at Hacienda Luisita in Tarlac province (central Luzon) would be included in a forthcoming redistribution programme.

Eventually, in June 1988 Congress approved a land reform bill providing for the progressive redistribution of landholdings of over 50 hectares. The bill aimed to transfer a total of over 5,000,000 hectares to approximately 2,000,000 farm workers and tenants over the ensuing decade. This was to be accomplished in two stages; within four years, the maximum individual private holding would be 50 hectares; after a further six years, landowners would be restricted to five hectares each, although each of their children would be allowed a further three hectares. Under the bill, an amount equivalent to US$3,000 million was equivalent to US$5,000 million for farm credit, seed capital and infrastructural improvements to assist the new smallholdings. Large estates (including the Aquino family's Hacienda Luisita) would not be broken up but turned into "co-operatives" with estate workers receiving a share of the profits, while foreign companies would be permitted to lease plantations from the co-operatives. Farmers' unions criticized these two provisions, claiming that they would prevent any meaningful land redistribution. They also criticized a clause which allowed landowners three months to register their land titles, on the grounds that landowners would use this period to transfer the nominal ownership of portions of their land to relatives, thereby effectively keeping their estates intact.

DS

PHILIPPINES–MALAYSIA DISPUTE OVER SABAH.

Sabah, or North Borneo as it was known until 1963, has been a contentious issue since the early 1960s. When plans were being formulated for the creation of a Federation of Malaysia, the government of the Philippines protested against the inclusion of British North Borneo into the Federation, claiming that it originally belonged to the Philippines and had been sold illegally to Britain by the Sultans of Brunei and Sulu in the nineteenth century. Contending that the transaction was illegal since the Sultan of Sulu had no right to dispose of the territory, the Philippines also claimed that North Borneo was essential to its national security.

The British government along with the United Nations, was satisfied that the majority of the inhabitants approved the incorporation into the Federation. The Federation of Malaysia itself came into being on Sept. 16, 1963, and North Borneo was renamed Sabah. The Philippines, however, remained unhappy about this and downgraded its embassy in Kuala Lumpur to the status of a consulate, a move that led to the suspension of diplomatic relations until 1966. In 1968 the claim by the Philippines was revived and once again diplomatic relations were suspended. Both states, however, were members of the **Association of South-East Asian Nations (ASEAN)** which had been formed in 1967 and they announced at an ASEAN meeting in December 1969 that diplomatic relations were being resumed. The issue then became dormant and at another ASEAN meeting in August 1977 President **Marcos** of the Philippines declared that his government intended to renounce its claim to Sabah.

In the event, this did not occur and the dispute remained unresolved. Although Malaysia agreed to take measures to prevent extremist Malaysian Muslims smuggling weapons to Muslim separatists in the Southern Philippines, hostilities between the Philippine military and the **Moro National Liberation Front** continued. There were also allegations that Col. Gaddafi of Libya was providing aid to the Muslim guerrillas. On occasion the issue threatened to erupt into more serious conflict. Relations became particularly strained in 1985 following reports that Malaysian gunboats engaged in anti-piracy operations had killed or abducted over 50 Filipinos in an attack on the Philippine island of Maddanas.

In April 1986 both sides made clear that they wanted to resolve the Sabah issue, and established a panel of Foreign Ministry officials from the Philippines and Malaysia to consider the problem. The difficulty, however, was that the claim to Sabah was enshrined in the constitution of the Philippines, and although, in December 1987, the government of **Corazon Aquino** tried to push through legislation amending this, the legislation failed to pass.

Although the continued territorial dispute over Sabah retains some potential for making mischief between Malaysia and the Philippines, the issue does seem to have diminished in importance. Both sides have managed to co-operate within the framework of ASEAN, although it is clear that their bilateral relationship would also be improved if a solution were devised. Some kind of solution does seem possible in that the main concern of the Philippines is with ensuring that Sabah does not become a threat to its security. If this could be guaranteed by Malaysia, then Cory Aquino might manage to obtain domestic support for a more flexible approach. The history of the dispute since the early 1960s, however, suggests that it could well continue to rumble away with little likelihood of erupting into a serious military conflict.

PW

PHOUMI VONGVICHIT. Acting President of the Lao People's Democratic Republic (LPDR) since October 1986, and leading member of the **Lao People's Revolutionary Party** since 1955. A native of Xieng Khouang province, he entered government service in the 1930s and was "governor" of Sam Neua province when he began to work with **Prince Souphanouvong** in the independence movement of 1945. He joined the Indochinese Communist Party in 1949, and the Lao Issara Front the following year; in 1956 he became secretary of the Lao Patriotic Front. He served in the two coalition governments formed by Prince Souvanna Phouma in 1957-58 and in 1962-63, but left Vientiane for the Pathet Lao area in April 1963 and spent nearly 10 years in the maquis. In February 1973 he returned to the capital to represent the Lao Patriotic Front and its armed forces in negotiating a ceasefire, and later to work out the formation of a third coalition government. He was deputy prime minister, again under Souvanna Phouma, in the "provisional government of national union" formed in April 1974 then became deputy prime minister in the government of **Kaysone Phomvihan** when the LPDR was established in December 1975. In the latter he was also minister of education, health and culture. When Souphanouvong became ill in the autumn of 1986, Phoumi was appointed acting president.

RBS

PITCAIRN ISLAND. *Population* (est. 1986): 60. *Land area*: 27 sq km. British crown colony comprising Pitcairn Island and uninhabited dependent islands of Ducie, Henderson, and Oeno. Settlement: Adamstown. Discovered in 1767 by a British naval officer, Philip Carteret. The population is descended from the mutineers of the HMS *Bounty*, led by the first mate Fletcher Christian, and their Tahitian Polynesian consorts, who landed in 1790. In 1898 it came under the administrative control of the British High Commissioner for the Western Pacific, in 1952 under the governor of Fiji, and in 1970 (when Fiji became independent) under the British High Commissioner to New Zealand, exercising auth-

ority through a locally elected council. The subsistence economy is based on livestock, vegetables and fishing.

TBM

PLAZA ACCORD. An agreement drawn up on Sept. 28, 1985, by the "Group of Five" industrial nations (USA, Japan, West Germany, France, and UK) to intervene with their central banks to bring down the value of the dollar. The accord helped double the yen's value against the dollar from about 245 yen to 120 yen to the dollar by 1988.

DA

POL POT. Prime minister of Democratic Kampuchea from 1976 to 1979 and secretary-general of the **Kampuchean Communist Party** (KCP) from 1963 to 1981. Born in Kompong Thom province (Cambodia), Pol Pot (Saloth Sar) enjoyed elite patronage and was sent to study in France in the late 1940s. He joined a leftist student group and his interest in revolution led him to spend a period in Yugoslavia around 1950. After returning home in 1952 (without a degree) he joined the clandestine **Kampuchean People's Revolutionary Party** and by 1960 was the leader of a youthful radical faction within it. He lived in Phnom Penh until 1963. He then disappeared into the maquis, from which he did not re-emerge publicly until after 1975 (having taken the revolutionary name of Pol Pot). It subsequently became known that he had become secretary-general of the party at its third congress in February 1963, and had been responsible for re-naming it the Kampuchean Communist Party, supposedly "founded" in September 1960. He is also known to have made important visits to Hanoi and Beijing, as Party leader, in 1965 and 1969-70; and to have quarrelled with the **Vietnamese Communist Party** leader **Le Duan** on the latter occasion. He is presumed to have been responsible for the decision to launch an armed struggle in 1968, which was intensified the following year, but he played no public role in the united front which the Party formed with **Sihanouk** in March 1970. He was named prime minister of Democratic Kampuchea in April 1976 and (with a short break in the autumn of the same year) held that post until his "retirement" in December 1979, by which time he and his government had been driven from Phnom Penh by the Vietnamese. During the years 1977-78 he was responsible for massive purges, in which many thousands of people were killed and which led to his being convicted of the crime of "genocide". After handing over the premiership to **Khieu Samphan** at the end of 1979, then formally dissolving the KCP at the end of 1981, he remained commander of the National Army of Democratic Kampuchea until September 1985. Since then he is believed to have been living in Thailand, apart from a period of medical treatment in China in late 1986.

RBS

PRACHACHON (THAILAND). The *Prachachon* (People's) Party of Thailand was formed in mid-1988 by dissident members of the **Democrat Party**. The party won 19 seats in the July 1988 elections, the new MPs entering the House on the opposition benches. In April 1989 the party divided after merger negotiations with three other opposition parties. Of the 19 *Prachachon* MPs, 10 were pro-merger and joined the newly formed *Ekkaparb*, whilst the remaining nine MPs, led by Harn Leenanond, defected to Prime Minister **Chatichai**'s *Chart Thai* Party.

DS

PRACHAKORN THAI (THAILAND). The right-wing *Prachakorn Thai* (Thai Citizens') Party was founded in 1979 and won 36 seats in the 1983 elections, thus becoming the fourth largest party entering into Gen. Prem's coalition government. In the July 1986 elections, however, it fell back to 24 seats and pledged its support for a further Prem coalition without joining the government. The party reversed a trend of decreasing support in the July 1988 elections, winning 31 seats (the fourth highest), most of which were Bangkok constituencies gained at the expense of the Democrats, the Social Action party and *Palang Dharma*.

DS

PRODUCTION RESPONSIBILITY SYSTEM (CHINA). This system gradually emerged as the communes declined in the early 1980s. The primary responsibility for growing crops was transferred to the peasants. Peasant families, whether individually or in groups would contract to produce their share of the local quota of particular crops and sell it to the state at prices which the state set. Any additional produce grown could be sold on open markets at unrestricted prices. The peasants themselves would reap the profits or bear any losses. By the mid-1980s most land had been subcontracted to individual families, and the leasing arrangements could last for 15–30 years.

CIPF

R

RACE RELATIONS. Ethnic conflicts and jealousies have destabilized a number of Pacific states, including both the United States and the Soviet Union. Subjugation of the US black minority led to the flowering of the civil rights movement in the 1950s and 1960s. Great gains have been made since then, but racial tension has by no means disappeared. This is not only true in the less liberal South, but also in major northern cities with large black populations, including Detroit and New York. Far from there being a sense of solidarity between US blacks and other minorities, such as the Hispanics, Italians or the Jews, there have been open conflicts between the different groups. Nonetheless, representatives of most minority communities have made their mark in US politics, especially at mayoral level.

Most of the ethnic tensions in the Soviet Union have also been outside the Pacific zone as such, concentrated more in the south-western Muslim-dominated states and Georgia, as well as the European republics. Ethnic nationalism has been one of the most striking (and in some ways disturbing) consequences of President Gorbachev's reforms. This is rather ironic, considering long-standing Soviet propaganda about ethnic harmony with the USSR. Similarly, claims of Soviet solidarity with the peoples of the world have been undermined by numerous complaints by African students in the Soviet Union experiencing blatant racial discrimination.

Similar stories have come from Africans in China. The People's Republic has one of the most homogenous racial make-ups in the region, but the minorities which do exist have complained sometimes of being treated rather as curiosities. In the case of the Tibetans, the Han Chinese attitude has been denounced for being one of self-assumed superiority.

Chinese minorities elsewhere in the region have in turn experienced discrimination of various kinds, especially in Southeast Asia, where Malaysia, for example, has tried to protect and enchance the position of ethnic Malays. Similarly, Fiji took steps to try to curb the influence of South Asians (mainly the descendants of plantation workers brought in by the British) – which led directly to the 1987 coups. In other parts of the Pacific islands, notably New Caledonia, there have been tensions between the indigenous people and white settlers.

JF

RAMOS, GEN. FIDEL. Gen. Ramos was appointed as Defence Secretary of the Philippines in January 1988. His responsibilities as Chief of Staff of the Armed Forces (a post he had held since Aquino's inauguration in February 1986) were assumed by Gen. Renato de Villa.

Ramos, a graduate of the US Military Academy at West Point, saw active service in Korea and Vietnam. In 1981 he was appointed Deputy Chief of Staff, under Gen. Fabian Ver. Along with **Juan Ponce Enrile** Ramos had denounced **Marcos** and offered his support to **Aquino** three days before Marcos and his entourage fled the Philippines. He has remained intensely loyal to Aquino, and despite lacking a party political base, Ramos is widely regarded as a potential future president.

DS

RAROTONGA DECLARATION. The South Pacific Declaration on Natural Resources and the Environment (the Rarotonga Declaration) was adopted at a conference on the human environment in the South Pacific, held in March 1982. Related documents provided guidelines for the sustainable management of land, sea and air resources in the region. The declaration also called for the prevention of the storage and release of nuclear wastes in the Pacific regional environment and the testing of nuclear devices. (*See also* **Nuclear Free Zone Treaty**)

JF

RASSADORN (THAILAND). The *Rassadorn* (Citizen's) Party was formed in May 1986 and is a conservative grouping with strong military connections. The party's leader, Gen. Tienchai Sirisampan, is a former Deputy Army Commander who played a significant part in the counter-coup operation launched in September 1985. He was appointed a Deputy Premier in August 1986 after his party had gained 18 seats in elections held the previous month. He retained his post after the July 1988 elections when *Rassadorn* won 21 seats and joined the six-party **Chatichai** coalition. Apart from Gen. Tienchai, *Rassadorn* is represented in the Cabinet by Gen. Mana Rattanakoses, Minister of Education.

DS

RECRUIT SCANDAL. The Recruit scandal is the latest in a long series of scandals that has attended Japanese politics throughout the post-war period. It is nothing new. From the Showa Denko scandal in the 'forties, through the series of scandals known collectively as the Black Mist, and so to the Lockheed affair of the mid-1970s, which brought about the demise of then Prime Minister **Tanaka Kakuei** scandal has been part and parcel of political life in Japan.

Typically, these scandals are about political finance; that is the movement of money from big business into the coffers of the ruling **Liberal Democratic Party**, Japan's rulers since 1955.

In the case of Recruit, insider trading, the transfer to key figures in the world of Conservative politics, of large numbers of shares in the firm at preferential rates and prior to public trading, have provided the mechanism which has generated substantial windfall profits. Such factors have generated critical comment in the Japanese news media, led to the resignation of three government ministers and eventually to the collapse of the Takeshita government and the resignation of **Takeshitsa Noboru** himself. Subsequently the scandal was to lead to the first defeat of the Liberal Democratic Party in elections to the upper house in July 1989. That defeat led to the resignation of a second prime minister, **Uno Sosuke**. A forthcoming general election (due in summer 1990) will determine whether the Recruit affair will have a permanent effect upon the allegiance of conservative voters.

RAB

REFUGEES. Prolonged conflicts in Central America and Indo-China have led to hundreds of thousands of refugees seeking sanctuary in other parts of the Pacific region and beyond. Under the 1951 Geneva Convention, host nations and the international community at large have specific responsibilities for helping refugees. However, as the numbers have swollen and the years have gone by, there has been a growing reluctance both on the part of other Pacific states and among European nations to shoulder the burden of refugees. Increasingly, host governments have tried to distinguish between "genuine" refugees, escaping persecution, and "economic migrants", escaping poverty or merely looking for a better life. Tougher immigration rules, introduced in most industrialized countries during the 1980s, have in fact deterred both categories or have kept thousands of refugees trapped in transit camps awaiting visas. Increasingly, repatriation (voluntary or otherwise) is being considered as a means

of reducing the numbers of refugees in camps and as a disincentive to others to leave home.

The United States is the first preference as a country of settlement for most refugees from Central America. According to the US Committee for Refugees, in 1988 there were at least 152,000 official refugees from El Salvador in the region, plus an unknown figure of "unofficials" who had found their way into Mexico or the United States clandestinely. Most of the Salvadoreans have fled the country's civil war and the terror created by both right-wing death squads and left-wing guerrillas. Similarly, tens of thousands of Nicaraguans have streamed out of Sandinista-controlled Nicaragua since the 1979 Revolution. Some of these have been fleeing Nicaragua's own civil war and in particular the terror tactics of the US-backed Contra guerrillas. But others have a strong ideological objection to the Sandinistas' philosophy. Many, however, are simply weary of the continuing economic crisis in Nicaragua, with its rampant inflation and chronic shortages.

Large numbers of the better-off refugees or emigrants from El Salvador and Nicaragua have settled in the southern United States and especially in Florida. Central Americans have in fact stamped their own identity on parts of Miami, alongside Cubans and Haitians. A smaller number of Guatemalans have also made for the United States, but the main concentration of Guatemalan refugees is in southern Mexico. Mexico also played host to large numbers of Chileans who fled the military dictatorship of General Augusto Pinochet, following the 1973 overthrow of President Salvador Allende. The improved political climate in Chile has now enabled many of those to return.

Still unresolved in 1989 was the situation of hundreds of thousands of refugees from Indo-china. Well over 300,000 Cambodian refugees are to be found in other parts of Southeast Asia, the vast majority just over the border in Thailand. The Thai authorities have received considerable assistance from the United Nations High Commission for Refugees (UNHCR) and other agencies and foreign governments to help meet the needs of Cambodian refugees in their camps. However, the situation has been considerably complicated by the highly politicized nature of some of the camps, most of which have firm loyalties to one or other of the various factions of the armed Cambodian resistance, including the ***Khmer Rouge***. The failure of the Paris Peace Conference on Cambodia in August 1989 and continued uncertainty about the country's future set back any resolution of the Cambodian refugee problem.

The biggest single source of refugees in the

Pacific region is Vietnam. Over 1.6 million Vietnamese (including ethnic Chinese) have fled Vietnam since the fall of Saigon in 1975. Large numbers of these are "*Boat People*", who left the country in whatever craft was available, often after paying extortionate fees or bribes in money or gold. Unknown thousands perished at sea, by drowning, hunger, thirst, exposure or at the hands of pirates, most of whom have been operating off the Thai coast. The sheer numbers of people involved quickly led to what has been termed "compassion fatigue" by potential host countries. Boats reaching the shores of some neighbouring countries were sent back out to sea before refugees could disembark and visas for countries of final settlement became increasingly difficult to obtain. Conditions in some of the camps in which the Vietnamese have been housed have been far from satisfactory.

The situation has been most acute in Hong Kong, where about 45,000 Vietnamese refugees were being housed in camps in 1989. Although the overcrowding and prison-like nature of some of the Hong Kong accommodation was publicized worldwide, this did not stop the colony becoming the target destination of new boat people. The influx caused considerable resentment among large sections of the Chinese population in Hong Kong, many of whom are themselves first or second generation refugees from the People's Republic of China. The irony did not escape the western media that at a time when many Hong Kong Chinese were looking for a possible new home overseas, out of fear of what would happen to Hong Kong after the Communist Chinese takeover in 1997, they were keen to keep Vietnamese out of the densely-populated territory. In the summer of 1989, there were disturbances at some of the camps in Hong Kong, as Vietnamese protested at their conditions and also wished to draw international attention to their plight (*See also* **Hong Kong: Vietnamese Boat People**).

In per capita terms, Australia was the most welcoming developed country as far as refugees were concerned, accepting 120,000 from Indochina alone since 1975. On top of that, nearly 14,000 Vietnamese were settled in Australia under Canberra's bilateral Vietnam Migration Programme with Hanoi. Like Australia, Canada augmented its sparse population with refugees, though entry formalities were considerably tightened there in the wake of the highly-publicized arrival of Tamils from Sri Lanka in 1988 and the negative effect this had on domestic public opinion. In terms of numbers, however, the United States took in by far the largest number of refugees during the 1980s, not only from the Pacific region but also from Afghanistan, Ethiopia and other areas of conflict around the world. Nonetheless, while it may be the preferred destination of most refugees, the USA is increasingly choosy about who it accepts.

JF

REGIONAL CO-OPERATION. In common with many other parts of the world, the Pacific rim saw the growth of regional organizations during the 1980s. This was in the interest of security, peace-making and the promotion of economic and social development. For smaller states, regional co-operation has helped them overcome some of the problems of small-scale economies, dependent on a very limited number of commodities or activities, though in many cases, co-operative schemes between states remain theoretical rather than already being in practice. Some regional organizations have become useful fora for political and foreign policy initiatives; the **Association of South-East Asian Nations (ASEAN)** and the **South Pacific Forum** are good examples. However, the degree of integration of regional groupings varies widely. Attempts to forge greater unity in Central America, for example, have been thwarted by longstanding national rivalries and armed conflicts, though efforts to achieve a true Central American parliament (somewhat along the lines of the European Parliament in Strasbourg) continue. Probably the most integrated of all the groupings is that binding Vietnam, Cambodia and Laos, as a result of Vietnamese hegemony and Indochina's relative diplomatic isolation. The 1990s could however see the formation of a number of "common markets", along the lines currently being pursued on the Atlantic side of South America by Argentina, Brazil and Uruguay. (*See also* **Andean Pact**; **ANZUS Pact**; **Cairns Group**; **Commonwealth**; **Lima Group**)

JF

RELIGION. The two major religious influences in the countries in and bordering on the Pacific Ocean are **Buddhism** and **Christianity** and although these religions differ greatly in history and doctrine they are complementary. There is however another great historical and international religion in this area, for Indonesia has a larger number of Muslims than any other country in the Islamic world. There are also many varieties of religion, traditional forms and modern creations that flourish in other lands. There are ancient religious "ways", **Confucianism** and **Daoism** (Taoism) in China and beyond, the still potent national **Shinto** in Japan, and local or new developments. Atheistic communism has decimated religion, notably in China and the USSR, though there has been some relaxation of repression in recent years.

In the USA Protestants, Catholics and Jews are called the "triple melting pot". With over seven million Jews the USA has more than Israel and the USSR combined, and Jews are influential in religion, politics, education and general culture, with strength in 10 major cities. Three principal branches of American Judaism are: Orthodox, 28 per cent; Conservative, 42 per cent; and Reform, 30 per cent; each with its own religious organizations and many social activities. The strength of American Jewry has great influence in support for the state of Israel and tensions with the Arab and Islamic world. In Canada there are 340,000 Jews and in Mexico 48,000, with small minorities in many other Pacific countries: 75,000 in Australia and 1,000 in Japan.

The only predominantly Hindu area in the Pacific region is the island of Bali in Indonesia, but Hindu elements persist in the Javanese highlands and numbers of Hindus in Indonesia are reckoned at over three million. There is a university for Hindu teachers in the capital of Bali, and a Hindu Dharma Society in Java which runs schools and distributes literature. Hindus in Fiji came from India as plantation workers in the nineteenth century and their descendants form the largest ethnic group in the country. In the USA half a million counted as Hindus include immigrants but the majority belong to neo-Hindu sects (see below).

A modern missionary faith, present in many countries, is that of the Baha'is, founded by Baha'u'llah in 1863. Baha'is present a synthesis of religions, claimed also as evolutionary and scientific, and keep a close account of numbers. They count over 200,000 in the USA, 115,000 in the Philippines, 18,000 in Korea, and decreasing minorities elsewhere.

Non-scriptural religions. In many countries there are religious beliefs and practices whose history and sacred texts are largely or wholly oral and unwritten. In Siberia the term "Shamanism" has been used to describe practices of Tungus, Samoyed and kindred people. The word comes from Tungus *saman* which some scholars have derived from an Indian Buddhist term *samana* for a monk. The Siberian Shaman is a magician and medicine-man who goes into trances and is believed to cure all manner of ills. Siberian Shamans believe in ancestral and nature spirits and in a supreme sky deity. By extension, the term Shamanism is applied to similar practices in other countries. Shamanistic beliefs, while opposed by modern political and educational leaders, provide resistance to world views of the state or alternative theories to them. While opposed also by historical and scriptural religions there is often co-existence of apparently contradictory faiths. Further, with the destruction of churches and temples there were widespread revivals of traditional shamanistic religions.

In mountainous areas of China because of isolation, and despite extensive propaganda against superstition, primitive beliefs are widespread; "animistic" beliefs which see all nature animated by spiritual forces. The study is complicated by the manner in which in China historical Daoism has been interwoven with folk religion, and the elevated philosophy has been overlaid by magical notions.

Tungusic or Altaic practices spread throughout northern Asia and America, and in Japan they infiltrated Shinto and Buddhism. The charismatic leaders of Sect Shinto and neo-Buddhism continue an agelong tradition of mediums, often female, who give oracles and practice exorcism. The Ainu of Hokkaido have shamans whose origins are closely related to those of Korea and Siberia.

In Canada and the USA Eskimos and Indians had shamanistic type religion, and even where the majority of Indian tribes now claim to be Christian their use of traditional ideas and practices, including the peyote drug, makes other churches regard them as marginally Christian. In Mexico and other central and south American lands Indian tribes follow traditional non-scriptural religious ways or produce a syncretism, a mixture of religion which has been called christo-paganism.

In Laos beliefs in spirits and ancestral veneration are important among the 30 per cent non-Lao and non-Buddhist ethnic minorities. In Indonesia traditional animism mingled first with Hinduism and Buddhism and later with Islam. The religion of Java (Agama Jawa) is a syncretism found not only among peasants but also among upper classes in towns. Classed officially as Muslims, many followers of Agama Jawa react against campaigns for Islamization, or turn to Buddhism, Hinduism or Christianity. Similar retention of animistic beliefs is found in Malaysia, mingling with Islam among Malays and remaining in more purely traditional forms in Sarawak and Sabah. In Timor the traditional tribal religions continue among some 60 per cent of the population.

Most Australian aborigines now profess Christianity but traditional ideas are still significant. Much was made by early writers of Australian use of the "totem" (an American Indian word for a clan emblem), but recent studies of Australia have paid more attention to belief in supernatural beings, cultural heroes, the mythical geography of the "Dream Time", and medicine men or shamans.

The word and concept of "taboo" or "tapu" for a sacred or prohibited object or action came however from Polynesia, where it was first noticed by Captain Cook, and the notion of "mana" for a spiritual power comes from the same area. Papua and New Guinea provided romantic theories of religion for some writers, but more scientific anthropology has revealed similarities with animism and polytheism elsewhere.

In Papua and New Guinea there developed so-called Cargo Cults under the impact of the West, which mingled Christian, secular and ancestral hopes for vast cargoes of goods arriving supernaturally. In Papua there have been 30 such cults and 70 in New Guinea, led by charismatic prophets and stimulated especially by the sight of food and equipment brought by soldiers in two world wars. A Taro cult, begun by a prophet Buninia in 1914, developed agricultural rites and spirits were invoked to improve taro crops and bring foreign goods.

In New Zealand the Maori shared the concept of the sacred power of "mana" which resided especially in priests and chiefs. Belief in a supreme God, Io, has been attributed by some to Christian influence, but others claim it was not discovered by early research since the name was too sacred to mention. Although Maoris form only 8 per cent of the population of New Zealand, and most profess Christianity, yet their formation of indigenous churches such as Ratana, political activity, and revival of national consciousness, show the importance and power of traditional beliefs even when unwritten.

New Religions. If some of the old historical religions have declined under scientific, economic and political pressures, there are new religious movements in the Pacific area which are sometimes called Asiatic Twentieth Century New Religions. Some of these are like the Japanese neo-Shinto and neo-Buddhist sects, with highly developed organizations and newly composed scriptures. Others are syncretistic mass religious movements, which may use elements from Christian and other cultures. The Baha'is, who arose in Iran in the last century and are now widespread, have been mentioned earlier.

Notable among recent religious movements, for its syncretistic and international character, is the Unification Church, more fully entitled The Holy Spirit Association for the Unification of World Christianity. It was founded in 1954, significantly among the varieties of religion in Korea, by a Presbyterian minister, the Rev. Sun Myung Moon, and hence his followers are popularly called Moonies. Most of them believe Moon to be the Messiah of the Second Advent, although apparently he has not claimed this publicly. Unification theology is expressed in a scripture, *Divine Principle*, which discusses the dual characteristics of God (like the Chinese Yin and Yang), emphasizes the family in Confucian manner, and expounds the Bible in the hope of unifying the world's religions and destroying communism. The Unification Church owns several valuable businesses, commits members to work sacrificially for the leader and movement, and spends lavishly on international conferences. It claims followers in many countries, especially Korea, Japan, the USA and Europe, and its international headquarters are now in New York.

Another Korean new religion is Ch'ondogyo, the Religion of the Heavenly Way, founded by Ch'oe Suun in 1860 as an "Eastern Learning" in contrast to that of the West, though it is a blend of Shamanism, Buddhism, Confucianism and Christianity. Ch'ondogyo opposed the Japanese occupation of Korea but now plays little part in politics. There are many other such syncretistic new religions, said to be over 250 in Korea alone.

In Vietnam a powerful movement has been Cao Dai, "High Tower", a Daoist representation of the supreme being. This mingles popular Buddhism, Confucian ethics and ancestral cults, and Catholic-type organization. Reverence is given to the Buddha, Confucius, Jesus, Muhammad, and even figures of the former French rulers such as Joan of Arc and Victor Hugo. Cao Dai was founded in 1919 by Le Van Trung, but its nationalism brought alliance with the Japanese against the French and later opposition to the communists. Many of its followers fled to Cambodia where they were massacred by the Lon Nol regime. Seeking a middle path, Cao Dai claims 2.8 million members, mostly in the south of Vietnam.

Hinduism, for centuries not a missionary movement, developed modern propagandist organizations with travelling gurus, especially during the sixties and seventies. Transcendental Meditation (TM) is a system of yoga with an Indian monistic philosophy, and claims 1.3 million meditators, mostly in the USA and Europe. ISKCON (International Society for Krishna Consciousness), or Hare Krishna, is in the Indian tradition of popular devotion and has also spread internationally.

Older syncretistic movements, such as the Theosophical Society founded in New York in 1875, seek to combine eastern and western philosophy and religion, with branches in many countries especially among middle classes and intellectuals. Other religious groups may be local adaptations of Buddhist, Christian or Islamic teachings, with Confucian or Daoist elements according to the country or tradition. The general emphasis upon mutual understanding, mingling of ideas, international harmony, and world peace, makes these movements important factors in the world scene.

GP

RENGO. Japanese Private Sector Trade Union Confederation. Until 1987 there were four national trade union centres: **Sohyo** (General Council of Trade Unions of Japan), which was the largest, **Domei** (Japanese Confederation of Labour), the second largest, and two smaller organizations, Churitsuroren (Federation of Independent Unions of Japan) and Shinsanbetsu (National Federation of Industrial Organizations). Of these only one was affiliated to one of the three international trade union centres of the ICFTU, WFTU and WCL (that was Domei to the ICFTU). On Nov. 20, 1987, a new national centre, the Japanese Private Sector Trade Union Confederation (Rengo), was created. This was made up of the affiliated union federations of Domei and Chiritsuroren and a number of private sector federations from Sohyo. Domei and Chiritsuroren were merged into Rengo. They were followed in October 1988 by Shinsanbetsu. After protracted and difficult negotiations Sohyo has decided to join Rengo in the Autumn of 1989.

The political implications of this transformation of the organization of the Labour Movement are evident and important. Domei supports the **Democratic Socialist Party**. Sohyo supports the **Japan Socialist Party**; linkages the JCP is desperate to rupture. The reorganization is a response to the restructuring of the Japanese economy. In particular, the drive to privatize the National Corporations, particularly the Japan National Railways (JNR) has persuaded many public sector unions that the time has come to associate more closely with the more thriving private-sector federations. A membership crisis has also been a powerful stimulus to change. The rate of unionization has fallen every year for the last 13 years and stands now at 28.2 per cent. Membership of Rengo is 5,330,000, or 43.6 per cent of unionized labour; that of Sohyo is 3,980,000, or 32.5 per cent of organized labour.

RAB

RHEE, SYNGMAN (Yi Sŭng-man). First President, Republic of Korea. Born, 1875, died in exile, 1965. Educated, Paejae High School, 1895; Ph.D. Princeton University, 1910; leader in Korean independence movement, especially in Hawaii; President, Provisional Government of the Republic of Korea, 1919–21; first President of the Republic of Korea, 1948–60; deposed, 1960; in exile, 1960–65; buried in Korean National Cemetery. Although a fervent patriot, his authoritarian rule, the corruption of his government, and the stagnation of the post-**Korean War** economy led directly to his overthrow.

JHG

ROH TAE WOO (No T'ae-u). Current President of the Republic of Korea. Born Dec. 4, 1932. Graduated Korea Military Academy, 1955; retired as General, 1982; Minister of Sport, 1982; Minister of Home Affairs, 1982; Chairman of the **Democratic Justice Party**, 1985–87; inaugurated President Feb. 25, 1988.

JHG

RUAM THAI (THAILAND). The conservative *Ruam Thai* (United Thai) Party, led by Narong Wongwan, was the main opposition party after the July 1988 elections in which it won 35 seats (compared with 19 in 1986). In April 1989, the party was given legal approval to merge with three other opposition groupings to form *Ekkaparb*.

DS

S

SAIFUDDIN, SULTAN SIR OMAR ALI.
Sultan of Brunei from 1950 until his abdication
in 1967, when his son, Sir **Hassanal Bolkiah** (then
the Crown Prince) was appointed as his successor.
Sir Omar introduced Brunei's first written constitution in 1959, conferring upon himself supreme
executive authority. Following the 1962 revolt a
state of emergency was imposed and Sir Omar
ruled by decree. When the Sultanate of Brunei
became a fully independent sovereign state on
Jan. 1, 1984, Sir Omar was appointed Minister
of Defence, a post he held until his death in
September 1986, aged 71.

DS

SAKHALIN (SAGHALIEN). A large island
(76,000 sq km) in the Sea of Okhotsk off the east
coast of the Soviet Union and immediately to the
north of Japan. Sakhalin, together with the **Kuril
Islands**, was under joint Russian and Japanese
control from 1855 until 1875, when Sakhalin
passed to Russia and the Kurils to Japan. As part
of the settlement of the Russo-Japanese War of
1904–05 Japan gained control of the southern
half of Sakhalin. This was regained by the Soviet
Union, together with the Kuril Islands, in 1945,
on the basis of the 1945 Yalta agreement. (*See
also* **Northern Territories Dispute**)

IG

SEALING. During the nineteenth century the
fur seals of the Pacific were severely reduced by
excessive slaughtering stimulated by the large
market for fur coats and other sealskin products.
The first attempt to protect the Pacific fur seal
was made in 1911 when Canada, Japan, Russia
and the United States signed a treaty limiting the
permitted target of seal harvesting to a level
which would ensure an overall growth in the seal
population. In an imaginative move the profits
from sealing were divided proportionately among
the signatory countries thus helping to ensure the
treaty was honestly adhered to. Seals in the Pacific
have now grown in numbers and fully stock the
breeding grounds especially in the Pribilof
Islands, in the Bering Sea.

RS

**SEATO OR THE SOUTH-EAST ASIA COL-
LECTIVE DEFENCE TREATY.** This Treaty

was signed in Manila on Sep. 8, 1954, and came
into force on Feb. 9, 1955. The Treaty was concluded by the governments of Australia, France,
New Zealand, Pakistan, the Philippines, Thailand, the UK and the USA, which also agreed on
the establishment of a South-East Asia Treaty
Organization (SEATO) to be headed by the
Council provided for in Article 5 of the treaty.
Although it was hoped that SEATO would work
like NATO this never materialized. In comparison to NATO the members lacked a geographical focus, a common appreciation of the
threat, and a unified command structure. Pakistan did not really fit into the main geopolitical
thrust of the Organization and there was never
any serious effort to respond to crises in a concerted fashion. Furthermore, SEATO never really
matched the importance of the bilateral security
relationships that the United States developed
with key states in both Southeast and Northeast
Asia.

During the 1970s the irrelevance of SEATO
became increasingly apparent. Pakistan left in
1972. By then France had ceased to participate
in the Organization's military activities although
it continued to make a financial contribution
until 1974. In September 1975 the member states
agreed to dissolve the organization and this
became effective on June 30, 1977. By this time,
of course, the United States as well as the Philippines and Thailand had improved their relations
with the People's Republic of China. The Treaty
or Manila Pact, as it was often called, nevertheless
remained in force and the United States, along
with Australia and New Zealand, reiterated a
commitment to the security of the SEATO states,
especially Thailand and the Philippines.

PW

SENKAKU ISLANDS DISPUTE. The Senkaku Islands are a source of contention between
China, Japan and Taiwan. The islands themselves – which are known to the Chinese as Tiao
yu Tai – are located 200 miles west of Okinawa
in the Ryukyu islands and about 100 miles north-
east of Taiwan. The islands were ceded to Japan
by Imperial China in 1895. As a result of the
San Francisco Peace Treaty of 1951, they were
included in the Ryukyu islands and came under
the administration of the USA.

Although Beijing had denounced the 1951

Treaty as illegal, the issue became far more salient in the late 1960s when several research teams reported that the Senkakus were potentially rich in oil. In August 1970 Taiwan disclosed that it had granted Pacific Gulf the right to explore for oil in an area that included the islands. The Japanese government made a formal protest while the USA made clear that it regarded the Senkaku islands as part of the Ryukyu chain. In November 1969, the USA and Japan had agreed that the Ryukyus were to be returned to Japan in 1972 and Washington reaffirmed that this transfer was to include the Senkakus.

A compromise of sorts was reached through the formation by Taiwan, Japan and South Korea of a liaison committee to develop undersea resources in the area. This was an attempt to set aside the question of sovereignty. It did not entirely succeed, however, and the issue was further complicated in December 1970 when Communist China also asserted its sovereignty over the islands. In February 1972 the Nationalist Chinese announced that the islands had been incorporated into Taiwan while in March Beijing claimed that Taiwan province and all the islands pertaining to it were part of China's sacred territory. Nevertheless, the Senkaku Islands reverted to Japan in May 1972. The issue did not immediately abate however and in December Japan announced that 169 Taiwanese fishing boats had entered Japanese territorial waters around the Senkakus.

The issue then went into abeyance but arose again during negotiations between Japan and Communist China which led to the signing of a treaty of friendship on Aug. 12, 1978. In April 1978 a flotilla of Chinese fishing boats entered the waters around the islands and appeared to challenge the Japanese claim to sovereignty. Although there was some evidence that this was a deliberate move after protest by Japan it was announced by Beijing that the incident was an "accidental affair". The Chinese boats withdrew and Beijing made clear that it would try to avoid conflict over the islands. After this the issue once again went into abeyance although Beijing made clear that it retains a legal claim. Taiwan too has reiterated its claim for sole sovereignty over the islands. While the issue has the potential to re-emerge it seems unlikely that the challenge to Japanese sovereignty will intensify.

PW

SEVENTH FIVE-YEAR PLAN: CHINA. This covers the period 1986–90. The first two years were intended to stabilize the economy, whilst from 1988 onwards there was supposed to be more radical restructuring. The main features were 7.5 per cent a year average GNP growth, equivalent to 6.2 per cent per capital growth. Light and heavy industry were planned to grow at 7 per cent annually. The sectors given priority were refrigerators and beer, followed by soda ash and locomotives, whilst energy-intensive electrical goods were to be restrained. The annual agricultural growth rate was supposed to be 4 per cent. Particular emphasis was placed on the tertiary sector, especially tourism, post and telecommunications, which were supposed to grow overall at 11 per cent per year. Overall living standards were expected to rise at the rate of 5 per cent per year.

A new feature of this plan has been an explicit vertical division of the country into separate regions with differing economic roles and targets. The Eastern region is assigned the role of chief export base. This would involve the upgrading of existing enterprises, the creation of knowledge- and technology-intensive industries, and the development of tourism, financial and information services. The Central region is seen as the base for mining, power and materials industries, as well as commodity grain and other cash crops. The Western region will concentrate upon agriculture, including livestock and forestry, the development of transport links with the rest of China, and selective energy and mining projects. This region also has a major share of defence industries.

The targets of the Plan were challenging but feasible. However, the turmoil caused by the radical attempts at restructuring in 1988–89, the energy bottlenecks which emerged, the events of spring 1989, the ensuing crackdown, the slowdown in foreign trade and especially tourism, and the anti-inflationary austerity drive will no doubt mean that the final targets will be missed.

CIPF

SHAH, AZLAN MUHIBUDDIN. The Sultan of Perak, Azlan Muhibuddin Shah, was elected to replace the Sultan of Johore, Mahmood Iskander, as Malaysia's *Yang di-Pertuan Agong* (Supreme Head of State, or King) on March 2, 1989. He took office on April 26. Azlan Shah, 60, had been educated in the United Kingdom, at Nottingham University, and practised as a barrister at Lincoln's Inn. He became Malaysia's youngest High Court judge before he was 40 years old, and in 1977 he sentenced Mahmood Iskander (the outgoing King) to a prison term for culpable homicide. He was Lord President of the Supreme Court between 1982 and 1984 and was elected Deputy King in the latter year.

The election of a new King in 1989 attracted more attention than usual, partly because of a recent dispute between the government and the judiciary in which the outgoing King had supported Prime Minister **Mahathir**, by dismissing the Lord President of the Supreme Court, Mohammed Salleh Abas. According to some sources, Azlan Shah had privately condemned Salleh's dismissal. Other sources claimed that Mahathir's preferred candidate for King had been Ja'afar Abdul Rahamn, the *Yang di-Pertuan Besar* of Negri Sembilan, who was instead elected Deputy King.

DS

SHANGHAI COMMUNIQUE. Signed by President Nixon and Prime Minister **Zhou Enlai** in February 1972, this Communiqué regularized Sino-US relations and marked the acceptance of China as a great power in world affairs. It thus underlaid the later opening of China to the outside world. The two sides agreed in effect to base their relations upon the **Five Principles of Peaceful Coexistence**. The USA reassured China that it would not conspire with the USSR against it. Also the USA formally accepted that Taiwan was part of China, and it indicated that as tension was reduced in Southeast Asia, American forces would be withdrawn from Taiwan – which was completed in 1978.

CIPF

SHEVARDNADZE, EDUARD. Soviet politician, born in 1928. He has been Foreign Minister of the Soviet Union since 1985.

IG

SHINTO. This was the name given by Chinese Buddhist monks in Japan, to Shen-dao, the Way of the Gods, to distinguish it from the Way of the Buddha, Butsu-dao. In Japanese it is Kamino-Michi, the Way of the Kami, the countless gods and spirits of nature and tradition. Often disregarded as local or outdated, Shinto is a powerful force in Japanese life in two major forms. It has been estimated that there are 100,000 Shinto shrines in Japan, one in every district, and most shops and large companies have Shinto shrines. Shinto ceremonies are observed at beginning and completing buildings, and at launching communication satellites. A survey of 1986 found that 60 per cent of Japanese homes had a Shinto shelf for religious objects and rituals, and 61 per cent a Buddhist altar.

State Shinto provided the mythology and rituals of royal and noble families, with the emperor a descendant of the supreme sun-goddess, Amaterasu-O-mi-kami. The constitution of 1889 granted freedom to **Buddhism** and **Christianity**, but an Imperial Rescript on education declared that State Shinto, despite its ceremonial and mythology, was not religious and so was incumbent on all Japanese citizens. Reverence was to be paid to the emperor, in public buildings and schools, as son of the divine ancestress. Those who refused, like Uchimura Kanzo of the Non-Church movement, caused a furore.

After World War II in 1946 the emperor repudiated "the false conception that the Emperor is divine and that the Japanese people are superior to other races and are fated to rule the world". But the emperor remains the high priest of Shinto, performing 28 rituals each year in that office, going to the major Shinto shrine at Ise, and receiving the sacred Shinto symbols.

State Shinto was disestablished after the war and most shrines are incorporated in the Association of Shinto Shrines. But the status of certain shrines, notably the Yasukuni, "nation-protecting" shrine in Tokyo, to commemorate those who died in wars and revolutions, arouses debate among Buddhists, Christians and secularists as to whether state support should be given to shrines in a state that is formally secular.

In classifying Japanese religions distinction is made between Shrine (Jinja) Shinto and Sect (Kyoha) Shinto. The Shinto sects are of varied types: some are of Confucian inspiration and concerned with ancestral rituals, others continue animistic and mountain worship and organize popular pilgrimages, and yet others had charismatic founders and have well organized communal societies with voluntary labour in building shrines and halls. They parallel the Japanese Buddhist sects of Nichiren Shoshu.

Among the largest Shinto sects are Tenri-kyo, the Religion of Divine Wisdom, with headquarters at the new town of Tenri near Nara and with over two million adherents. Other sects had under two million members in 1970 but by 1975 claimed nearly three million; such as the syncretistic P.L. Kyodan or Perfect Liberty Association, and Seicho no Ie or House of Growth which propounds a form of mental training similar to Christian Science.

GP

SIDDHI SAVETSILA, AIR CHIEF MARSHAL. First appointed Minister of Foreign Affairs, Thailand, in February 1980 by Gen. Kriangsak, having previously held the post of Minister attached to the Prime Minister's Office. The

Kriangsak government encountered an economic crisis and fell in March 1980, but Siddhi was reappointed Minister of Foreign Affairs by Gen. Prem. He served as Foreign Minister throughout all of Prem's terms and has continued in the post under Maj.-Gen. **Chatichai**. In December 1985 Siddhi replaced Kukrit Pramoj as leader of the **Social Action Party**.

DS

SIHANOUK, PRINCE. Former ruler of Cambodia (1955-70) and, since 1982, president of the Coalition Government of Democratic Kampuchea. Born in 1922, as a great grandson of both King Norodom and King Sisowath, he was chosen by the French governor-general to succeed to the throne of Cambodia in 1941 and remained king until 1955. Then, having played a leading political role in securing independence from France, he abdicated in order to become the effective head of government and leader of his own mass movement, the *Sangkum Nyastr Niyum*. He played that role successfully until 1969, also maintaining the international neutrality required of Cambodia under the Geneva Agreement of 1954. However, under the impact of international pressures arising from the use of Cambodian territory by Vietnamese Communist forces and an internal revolt by the *Khmer Rouge*, he was deposed as national leader in March 1970 by his prime minister and minister of defence Lon Nol. He withdrew to Beijing, where with Chinese encouragement he entered a national united front with the leaders of the **Kampuchean Communist Party** which was steadily building up its own armed forces inside Cambodia. Having virtually lost real power to the Communist members of the front by 1974, the prince nonetheless agreed to return to Phnom Penh as a national figurehead in the spring of 1975. He stayed there (under house arrest from early 1976) until he was again smuggled out shortly before the fall of Phnom Penh at the beginning of 1979. Since that time he has lived either in Pyongyang or Beijing, when not making diplomatic trips on behalf of the "coalition" which he formed with the former leaders of Democratic Kampuchea in 1982. In the latter year he also appointed his son, Norodom Rannariddh, to command the **Sihanoukist National Army** operating along the Thai-Cambodian border. Although his supporters are militarily much less powerful than the National Army of Democratic Kampuchea, his reputation and diplomatic skills have made him a key figure in the negotiations of 1987-89 which he hopes will bring to an end the Vietnamese occupation of Cambodia and produce an eventual political settlement.

RBS

SIHANOUKIST NATIONAL ARMY. (Usually known as ANS, from the French "Armée Nationale Sihanoukiste".) Armed forces of the "National United Front for an Independent, National, Peaceful and Co-operative Cambodia" formed in March 1982 by **Prince Sihanouk**, which subsequently participated in the Coalition Government of Democratic Kampuchea. Sihanouk's son, Prince Ranariddh, was appointed commander of the ANS, which remained separate from the armed forces of the other two factions within the coalition. They continued to operate as a guerrilla force inside Cambodia, even after the Vietnamese captured their principal base at Tatum in March 1985. But they were considerably weaker and less well armed than the National Army of Democratic Kampuchea (NADK), led first by **Pol Pot** and then by **Son Sen**. In the spring of 1989, Ranariddh was attempting to secure military assistance from the United States in the hope of being able to compete more effectively with the NADK (the "*Khmer Rouge*") after the anticipated withdrawal of Vietnamese forces from Cambodia.

RBS

SINGAPORE. *Population*: 2,600,000 (est. 1988). *Area*: 621.7 sq km. *Gross Domestic Product*: US$19,040 million (1987). *Trade (1987)*: imports US$30,098 million; exports US$27,394 million. *Top five trading partners*: (imports) Japan, USA, Malaysia, China and Iran; (exports) USA, Malaysia, Japan, Hong Kong and Thailand. *Defence spending*; US$1,236 million (1987/88). *Education spending*: US$203 million (1987/88). *Urban population as percentage of total*; 100. *Life expectancy*: 73. *Birth rate*: 15 per thousand.

Geographical background. Located less than 125 km north of the equator, the Republic of Singapore comprises a group of small islands, the largest of which (Singapore Island containing the capital Singapore City) is joined by a 1.2 km causeway to the southernmost tip of the Malay Peninsula. Singapore Island occupies a focal position at the turning-point on the shortest sea-route from the Indian Ocean to the South China Sea. As of 1988, over 9 per cent of Singapore's total land area was cultivated and just under 5 per cent was forest. Singapore has one of the highest population densities in the world; the population was expected to reach 2,900,000 by the year 2,000.

Socio-political background. In mid-1986 Singapore's population density was 4,160 per sq km, one of the highest in the world. Of the total population, it was officially estimated in mid-1986 that approximately 76 per cent were Chinese, 14 per cent Malay and 6 per cent Indian. There are four official languages – Malay (the national language), Chinese (Mandarin), Tamil and English. The principal religions are **Buddhism**, practised as of 1988 by 28 per cent of the population, **Christianity** (19 per cent), **Islam** (16 per cent), **Daoism** (13 per cent) and Hinduism (5 per cent).

As of 1988, Singapore had a literacy rate of 86.8 per cent, a student population of 507,000 (44,700 of whom were university students), and a total workforce of 1,200,000.

The Republic of Singapore, a member of the Commonwealth, has a unicameral Parliament of 81 members elected by adult suffrage for five years. Parliament elects a President for a five-year term who appoints a Cabinet headed by a Prime Minister and responsible to Parliament.

Pre-modern history. The island of Singapore is mentioned in the *Malay Annals*, where it is called Temasek and is referred to as a busy fourteenth century trading centre. At about this time it became known as Singapura (Sanskrit for Lion City) and was claimed by the rival expanding empires of Javanese Majapahit and Thai Ayuthia. Attacked by armies from both empires, and further divided by internal dissension, Singapura was laid to waste at the end of the fourteenth century.

The island remained almost deserted for 400 years, with European, and particularly Dutch interests, centred primarily on Java and the Moluccas. However, the opening of trade routes between India and China by the British East India Company in the early nineteenth century meant that Singapore, situated at the southernmost tip of the Malay Peninsular and the Straits of Malacca, assumed a fresh commercial and strategic value as a base from which to protect the new trade routes and challenge the Dutch monopoly in the region. In 1819, Sir Stamford Raffles, an East India Company official, gained permission from the Malay sultan of Riau-Johor and the local chief to establish a trading post at the mouth of the Singapore river. In 1824, the Malays ceded the whole island to the Company in perpetuity.

Early modern history. In 1826 the British East India Company merged Singapore with its two other West Malay Peninsular territories, namely Malacca and Penang, to form the Straits Settlements. Free from all customs duties and immigration restrictions (as stipulated by Sir Stamford Raffles), Singapore developed rapidly as a commercial trading post. As the volume of trade between China and India increased, so Singapore prospered. However, in 1833 the Company lost its monopoly of the China trade and, correspondingly, its interest in the Settlements diminished. The resulting lack of administrative efficiency in the territories provoked a circle of European merchants to petition for direct British rule, and in 1867 the Settlements became a Crown Colony.

Thereafter Singapore's economic development was promoted by the opening of the Suez Canal in 1869, which effectively placed the island at the heart of the new trade route between Europe and East Asia. Britain's expanding colonial role along the west coast of the Malay Peninsula during the late nineteenth century also had a positive effect on Singapore's economic development, and the island became Britain's regional financial centre, port and smelting and processing centre for Malay tin and rubber.

As a Crown Colony, Singapore was ruled by a British-appointed Governor aided by legislative and executive councils, comprised almost exclusively of Europeans. The transient nature of the majority of Singapore's free trading inhabitants did little to encourage opposition to the order, and calls for an elected legislature in the 1920s received little support from the administration and the people.

After World War I and the emergence of Japan as a naval power, Singapore acquired a new strategic and military significance. In 1938 the British completed the construction of a large naval base, between the island and the State of Johore. The defences of Singapore were therefore designed for defence against sea-attack, and in February 1942 the island fell to a Japanese land attack down the Malay Peninsular. On the liberation of Singapore in 1945, the island was severed from the other Straits Settlements and established as a separate Crown Colony.

Political history. Upon the dissolution of the Straits Settlements and the establishment in April 1946 of Singapore as a separate Crown Colony, a Provisional Advisory Council was established pending the creation of representative Executive and Legislative Councils. A partly elected Legislative Council met for the first time in April 1948, with six members elected from territorial constituencies. Voting was confined to British subjects and the majority of the seats went to the pro-British Singapore Progressive Party; the radical Malayan Democratic Union (MDU), formed in 1945 to press for the island's incorporation in a democratic socialist Malayan Union, boycotted the election. The MDU was disbanded in 1948 at the outbreak of the Malayan Emergency, which led to the containment of all radical politics in Singapore. The number of elected members was increased to nine in Legislative Council elections held in 1951.

In 1953 a Commission under the chairmanship of Sir George Rendel was established to advise on the formation of a new Constitution, which came into force in February 1955, allowing Singapore a large measure of self-government. The Constitution provided for a Council of Ministers, responsible collectively to a 32-member Legislative Assembly, of whom 25 members were elected from single member constituencies. Two new left-wing parties were formed to fight the 1955 election, the **People's Action Party** (PAP) and the Labour Front, and it was the latter that formed a minority government with its leader, David Marshal, becoming Singapore's first Chief Minister. Marshall resigned in 1956 having failed to negotiate immediate self-government, and was succeeded by Lim Yew Hock.

An Agreement was signed in 1957 between the Lim government and London providing for the creation of a State of Singapore with full internal self-government. Elections were held in 1959 to implement the Agreement and the PAP won an outright majority. A fresh Constitution came into force in June 1959, with the establishment of a self-governing State of Singapore. The new Constitution provided for a fully elective 51-member Legislative Assembly and a Head of State (*Yang di-Pertuan Negara*). The British government retained control of defence and certain responsibilities with respect to external affairs and internal security. In elections held in 1959, the PAP swept to power (gaining 43 out of the 51 seats) and **Lee Kuan Yew**, the PAP leader, became Prime Minister. Under his leadership, the party has remained in power ever since.

The Federation of Malaysia came into being in 1963, with Singapore as a constituent state. Upon coming to power, Lee Kuan Yew had made it clear that he favoured entry into the Federation (principally on economic and security grounds) despite the obvious reluctance of the Malay leadership to allow entry into the Federation of what they perceived as a left-wing Chinese-dominated state. However, Lee overcame both internal and external opposition to his plan, and entry was secured in September 1963. The association was strained from the start, with a constant stream of disputes arising between Lee's government and the central Malaysian government. The crisis reached a head in 1964 during the general election, and the following year the central government forced Singapore to agree to a separation. On Aug. 9, 1965 the Malaysian parliament approved legislation providing for Singapore to become an independent state within the Commonwealth on that date. By legislation passed in December 1965, with retrospective effect to Aug. 9, Singapore became a Republic, the *Yang di-Pertuan Negara* was re-styled as a (non-executive) President and the Legislative Assembly re-named Parliament. In September 1972 the PAP won all 65 parliamentary seats in a general election contested by a number of opposition parties.

Recent developments. Following the gaining of full independence in 1965 the People's Action Party won all the seats in elections held in 1968, 1972, 1976 and 1980. The PAP's monopoly ended in October 1981 when a parliamentary by-election held to fill the vacancy created by C.V. Devan Nair's accession to the presidency was won by the secretary general of the opposition **Workers' Party** (WP), J.B. Jeyaretnam, who had stood for Parliament unsuccessfully on five previous occasions. In a speech given in December 1982, Lee Kuan Yew said that he had come to the conclusion that "we have to ensure that several better and more intelligent opposition members are in Parliament" because "without opposition members the younger team [of the PAP] has no sparring partners" to keep them "fit and agile". In July 1984 Parliament passed a constitutional amendment creating three "non-constituency" seats in the legislature for opposition candidates. The amendment stated that if the opposition won no seats in a general election, then the three opposition candidates who won the highest percentages of votes would be offered these seats. The holders of these special seats would not be eligible to vote on constitutional amendments, motions of no-confidence, the budget and important financial bills. In a general election held in December 1984, the PAP failed to win two out of 79 contested seats, and its share of the overall valid vote fell by almost 13 per cent compared with 1980. Observers regarded two of the main issues in the elections as (i) access to the compulsory Central Provident Fund (CPF) saving scheme; and (ii) Lee Kuan Yew's controversial ideas on social engineering which were reflected in many of the government's social policies. J.B. Jeyaratnam retained the Anson seat he had won in 1981, and Chiam See Tong, leader of the **Singapore Democratic Party** (SDP), won the Potong Pasir constituency. The WP rejected the offer of one "non-constituency" seat. Prior to the election, in September 1984, a biennial PAP conference had taken place at which many older members of the party had been voted off the party's central executive committee to be replaced by younger members of the so-called "second generation". At its next conference held in late 1986, **Lee Hsien Loong**, the Prime Minister's son and a Cabinet Minister, was one of four new central executive committee members.

In 1986 the government began to display increasingly authoritarian tendencies. A judicial inquiry was established in March to investigate claims made in Parliament by Jeyaretnam which brought into question the independence of the country's subordinate courts. In August Parliament passed a bill amending the Newspaper and Printing Press Act (1974) to enable the government to restrict the sale or distribution of foreign publications "engaging in domestic politics". In October, *Time* magazine became the first foreign publication to have its circulation reduced. In November, Jeyaretnam was fined US$5,000 and imprisoned for one month after Singapore's Supreme Court had upheld a conviction for perjury in connection with bankruptcy proceedings brought against the WP in 1982. The fine was sufficient, according to the Constitution, to deprive Jeyaretnam of his parliamentary seat and prevent him from standing for election for five years.

In May 1987, 16 people were arrested under the country's Internal Security Act (ISA) after the government claimed to have uncovered a Marxist conspiracy to "subvert the existing social and political system in Singapore through communist united front tactics and to establish a communist state". Those detained were described as "comfortably well-off English-educated graduates and professionals" and included Roman Catholic Church and local community workers, journalists and lawyers. In June, four of the detainees were released (after making televised confessions), but six more arrests occurred. By December 1987, all detainees except Vincent Cheng had been released. In connection with the so-called "Marxist conspiracy case", the government in late December limited the permitted circulation within Singapore of the Hong Kong-based weekly magazine, the *Far Eastern Economic Review*. In April 1988, nine of those arrested in 1987 issued a statement claiming that their televised confessions of guilt had been coerced with beatings. The next day eight of the nine in addition to their lawyer were re-arrested. All except Teo Soh Lung and Vincent Cheng had eventually been released by March 1989, the month in which Teo's British lawyer, Anthony Lester, was barred from representing her in Singapore.

A general election was held in September 1988, and the PAP, which campaigned under the slogan "More Good Years", won all but one of the 81 seats; Chiam See Tong retained his seat for the Poting Pasir constituency. The opposition parties, who had been expecting as many as 10 seats, attributed their lack of success partly to changes in electoral law, including the introduction in May 1988 of a system of group representation constituencies (GRCs). The GRC system merged 39 existing constituencies to create 13 three-constituency groups. Candidates could contest these 13 GRCs only as teams of three, with at least one member of the team being of non-Chinese minority ethnic origin, an arrangement which guaranteed that at least 13 MPs would be from the ethnic minorities, but which created problems for small parties without the resources to field a three-member team. Following the September election, the WP accepted the government's offer to allow Francis Seow, of the WP, and Lee Siew Choh, of the *Barisan Socialis*, to sit in parliament as "non-constituency MPs". Seow, a former Solicitor-General and president of the Singapore Law Society, had at one time been expected to lead a significant electoral challenge by the WP, but his candidacy had suffered from his being detained in May–July 1988.

In an address to the PAP youth wing in October 1988, the First Deputy Prime Minister, **Goh Chok Tong**, called for the formulation of a Singaporean national idealogy. He subsequently announced that a parliamentary committee was to be established to identify "core values" common to all Singaporeans for incorporation into a national ethics which would enhance the country's resilience and competitiveness.

Outline of economic development. Singapore's natural deep water wharves and its strategic geographical location allowed it to develop as a prosperous Asian trading centre as far back as the fourteenth century. When trade routes between Asia and Europe opened up in the sixteenth century, Singapore was situated too far north to be of great significance and it did not resurface as a commercial centre until the early nineteenth century, when the British East India Company required a base on the southern section of the Straits of Malacca to protect its trade with China. Freedom from custom duties and taxes, combined with unrestricted levels of immigration, meant that Singapore became an economic success based largely on the sale and distribution of raw materials from surrounding territories (initially tin and rubber from the Malay peninsula) and on entrepôt trade in finished goods, the latter eventually becoming the keystone of the economy.

Singapore's prosperity as an entrepôt continued

until Japanese occupation during World War II, following which Europe's control of Southeast Asia waned and the former colonies began to develop direct trade services and facilities, rendering Singapore's historical trading role partly redundant. Mounting post-war unemployment, the result of a rising birth rate and the country's unrestricted immigration policy, added to Singapore's economic uncertainty as also did burgeoning industrial unrest.

In 1961 the government, in recognition of the limits of growth based on entrepot trade, created an Economic Development Board (EDB) to formulate an industrialization programme in an attempt to broaden the base of the economy and provide for more rapid growth. For most of the 1960s (in the middle of which Singapore became an independent sovereign state) the EDB concentrated, with some success, on the development of import-substituting activities. In 1968 legislation was passed which effectively undermined the relatively strong position of the trade union movement, thereby almost completely eliminating industrial unrest. At the same time the government enhanced the investment climate by offering tax and other incentives and free repatriation of profits. The government's motivation to encourage increased industrialization was boosted by Britain's 1971 declaration of its intention to withdraw its forces from Singapore in 1976 (the forces at that time generating a fifth of the island's gross domestic product); in addition, the end of the Vietnam War in 1975 had the effect of further damaging the entrepôt trade sector, which had, nevertheless, already assumed a greatly diminished role.

During the 1970s Singapore's economic growth rate (of real gross domestic product) averaged 9.4 per cent per annum, compared with 8.7 per cent during the previous decade, and by 1979 its per capital income at current prices had reached US$3,800 (second only to Japan's among Asian countries). Whereas economic policy during the 1960s was based on labour-intensive industrialization, increasing emphasis was placed during the 1970s on diversification and in particular on the development of capital-intensive "high technology" industries and of Singapore's growing role as an international financial and communication centre. Foreign investment in Singapore's economy totalled about US$2,900 million at the end of 1979, and was a major stimulus to economic growth. During 1979 the government adopted a programme designed to accelerate Singapore's "second industrial revolution", involving the introduction of new incentives to stimulate investment in technologically-advanced manufacturing and service industries

and of certain disincentives to low-skilled labour-intensive industries (including a substantial increase in the level of wages). Priority sectors for development during the 1980s included equipment for the motor and aircraft industries, machine tools, medical and surgical instruments, computers, computer peripherals and other electronic equipment, optical products, precision instruments and hydraulic and pneumatic control systems. Other "target activities" included chemicals, pharmaceutical and capital equipment for oil production.

Singapore recorded a growth in GDP of 8.2 per cent in 1984, a slight increase on the figure for 1983. However in 1985 the economy underwent a sudden downturn, with GDP registering negative growth of 1.7 per cent, the first contraction in over 20 years. Unemployment had risen to over 4 per cent with the loss of over 90,000 jobs, the majority involving foreign workers. Exports had fallen by 1.5 per cent and zero growth was forecast for 1986. The recession was blamed on (i) adverse developments in the economies of Singapore's main trading partners, and in particular a slowdown in US economic growth; (ii) high domestic labour costs; and (iii) excess supply in the property market. An Economic Committee formed in April 1985 in response to the country's current economic difficulties, and chaired by Lee Hsien Loong, presented in mid-February 1986 a package of proposed reliefs and reforms. Among the committee's policy recommendations were reforms of the wages and tax systems, an upgrading of business efficiency and productivity and promotion of the service industries. Goh Chok Tong announced to parliament in late February the government's decision to implement a number of the committee's recommendations as of the new financial year beginning April 1, including a cut in the employers' contribution to the mandatory government pension shceme, the Central Provident Fund, from 25 per cent of an employee's salary to 10 per cent, wage restraint for two years and numerous tax concessions. The 1986–87 budget formalized Goh's measures.

In a New Year message delivered on Jan. 1, 1987, Lee Kuan Yew reported 1.9 per cent economic growth for 1986 and said that the economy was "on the mend". The modest economic upturn had been initiated by the manufacturing, transport and communications sectors, whereas commerce, financial and business services and construction remained depressed. The 1987–88 budget included special tax relief measures for married couples with three children. The measures were part of the government's new population policy which aimed to increase Singapore's falling birth rate because of concern about a future labour shortage. Previously, the government had endorsed small families and had adopted the campaign slogan "stop at two". In March 1987 a report compiled by the government-appointed public-sector divestment committee was released, recommending the introduction of a policy of "robust privatization". The report specifically recommended the sale of varying amounts of shares in 41 government-linked companies; it was estimated that this might release (for purchase by local and foreign investors) between US$180 million and US$250 million of company shares annually for a 10-year period.

The 1988–89 budget, introduced by Richard Hu in March 1988, retained nearly all of the cost-cutting and fiscal incentives introduced in 1986. Nevertheless, the economy had continued its upward trend, growing by 8.8 per cent in 1987 with good performances in all leading sectors, except construction, which showed a negative growth figure of 11 per cent. Unemployment fell from 4.6 per cent to 2.8 per cent during 1987.

Current economic situation. The Singapore economy grew by an estimated 10.9 per cent in 1988, its highest annual growth in the 1980s. Growth would have been even higher if not for a slow-down in the manufacturing sector in the last quarter. All other major sectors – commerce, transport and communications, as well as financial and business services – continued to register strong growth in the October–December period. The star performer was the electronics sector, which recorded a 32 per cent increase in output between January and September. For the first time in over four years, the construction sector rallied toward the year end and recorded positive growth in the last quarter. The 1988 boom was largely due to strong external demand, which accounted for almost 90 per cent of the overall economic expansion (compared to domestic demand which accounted for 7 per cent). Promotion efforts by the Economic Development Board (EDB) brought in a record level of commitments, with an estimated US$1,025 million invested during 1988 by local and foreign companies in all sectors except petro-chemicals. Although Singapore has no petroleum reserves of its own, it has the third largest refining complex in the world (after Houston and Rotterdam); petroleum refining accounts for some 40 per cent of manufacturing output.

In late 1988 the EDB outlined its priority areas for 1989, including: (i) encouragement of high quality investments; (ii) promotion of the services sector; (iii) creation of incentives for Singapore companies to venture abroad; (iv) introduction of greater automation in manufacturing; and (v) increased emphasis on biotechnology.

The budget for 1989-90, introduced in March 1989, proposed expenditure of some US$6,477 million (of which US$2,215 million would be for development purposes) and revenue of US$6,805 million. Although the budget proposed minor changes in corporate and property taxes, the focal point was clearly the introduction of substantial tax reliefs for those who have a fourth child, in support of the government's policy of "encouraging family formation and procreation". Tax rebates for the parents of three children had been in force since 1987 (see above).

Foreign relations. Singapore's principal foreign relations objective is the maintenance of good relations with its neighbouring fellow members of the **Association of South-East Asian Nations (ASEAN)**. On the whole Singapore's relations with the other five ASEAN states are good, although problems occasionally occur. For example, Thailand reacted angrily to the enforcement of a law in late March 1989 facilitating the removal from Singapore of some 10,000 illegal Thai workers. However, relations with Malaysia, which had been tense during 1987, largely as a result of Malaysia's annoyance at Israeli President Herzog's visit to Singapore in late 1986, improved greatly during 1989 with joint military exercises due to take place late in the year. Indonesia's apparent decision taken in early 1989 to restore diplomatic relations with China in 1990 has paved the way for Singapore to follow suit. The Singapore government has long stated that it would be the last of the ASEAN countries to restore relations with Beijing in order to dispel notions once prevalent in the region that the island-state was a potential "third China". In April 1989, the Taiwan President, **Lee Teng-hui**, made an unprecedented official visit to Singapore. During 1988, Singapore's relations with the United States (its principal trading partner) deteriorated as a result of disputes over trade and human rights; relations reached a low point in May when the two countries expelled each other's diplomats, one for one.

Prospects for development. Although geographically part of Southeast Asia, Singapore has, during the 1980s, been counted as one of the so-called "newly industrialized countries" (NICs), along with the Northeast Asian States of Taiwan, South Korea and Hong Kong. According to some commentators it is Singapore's anomalous position as a Northeast Asia-style economy situated in the heart of Southeast Asia that portends a continuation of the country's successful economic development during the 1990s and the fulfilment of the government's declared aim to join the ranks of the world's developed nations by the year 2000. It is predicted that Singapore will be ideally placed to prosper as a harbour, banker and investor for its expanding ASEAN neighbours. In this way, Singapore is expected to avoid the economic slowdown being predicted for the Northeast Asian economies in the early 1990s.

Malaysia, and Indonesia to a lesser extent, are expected to allow Singapore greater opportunities to invest its massive surpluses in their economies. It is expected that Singapore will attempt to facilitate a substantial increase in intra-ASEAN trade in the early 1990s, in an attempt to limit its sensitivity to alterations in international trading patterns. In particular, Singapore may be adversely affected by the creation of the single European market in 1992 and also by US attempts to rectify its trade deficit.

There are a number of potential problems that might hinder Singapore's development, none greater than a possible worsening of the country's labour shortage. Reports in early 1989 indicated that increasing emigration of professionals to countries such as Australia and Canada might seriously aggravate the problems caused by a small population increasing at a slow rate. Labour constraints will be eased through more capital-intensive industry, greater sophistication in services and investment in education and training. Major emphasis is to be placed on quality and excellence in manufacturing exports.

DS

SINGAPORE DEMOCRATIC PARTY (SDP). The SDP was formed in opposition to the ruling **People's Action Party** in 1981. In the December 1984 elections it contested four seats and returned Chiam See Tong, the party's secretary-general, in the Potong Pasir constituency as one of only two opposition candidates elected. Chiam retained his seat with a slightly increased majority in September 1988, but was the only opposition MP directly elected to the new parliament.

DS

SINO-SOVIET CONFLICT. This conflict has involved ideological competition, territorial disputes, and a general struggle for power and influence in the international Communist movement. In the late 1960s it resulted in significant military clashes along the border. In the mid and late 1980s, however, there has been a marked improvement in the relationship between the two major Communist states – an improvement which culminated in May 1988 in the visit of President **Gorbachev** to Beijing.

Russia and China share a long common frontier. This is divided into two sections by the buffer state of Outer Mongolia. The Far Eastern sector separates Manchuria from Eastern Siberia while the central Asian Sector separates Xinjiang from the Soviet Republics of Kazakhstan, Kirghizia and Tajikistan. The details of these boundaries were laid down in treaties signed in 1858, 1860, 1864 and 1881 during a period of Chinese weakness and Russian assertiveness. Although the Bolshevik government which seized power in 1917 renounced these unequal treaties, the Civil War in China effectively placed territorial issues in abeyance. Furthermore, after the victory of the Chinese Communists in 1949, the Soviet Union and China in 1950 signed a 30-year treaty of friendship alliance and mutual assistance. Territorial disputes appeared to be either non-existent or of only marginal significance. In April 1960, after relations between China and the Soviet Union had begun to deteriorate, the Chinese Prime Minister **Zhou Enlai** described differences on the broader questions between the Communist allies as "insignificant divergences on the maps" which could easily be "peacefully resolved". It is clear from this that the sources of the Sino-Soviet dispute were not territorial in origin – although the territorial issues exacerbated tensions and clashes over the disputed border regions became a major manifestation of the Sino-Soviet conflict.

The Sino-Soviet dispute which became increasingly discernible in the early 1960s reflected Chinese dissatisfaction with the post-Stalinist leadership of the Soviet Union. **Mao Zedong** was an original revolutionary leader and did not regard Khrushchev as having a legitimate claim to leadership of the International Communist movement. Furthermore, by emphasizing that there were separate roads to socialism and that China was further towards this goal than the Soviet Union, Beijing was initiating a frontal challenge for the leadership of an ideological movement. There were also difficulties over strategy especially towards the United States with the Chinese advocating a more assertive policy than the Soviet Union was willing to assume. Against this background the territorial disputes, which had hitherto appeared relatively trivial, took on greater significance, if only as a symptom of the underlying differences and tensions, and as a manifestation of the Chinese desire to be treated by the Soviet Union as an equal.

There were several border incidents in 1960 and by 1963 there was considerable tension on the Xinjiang border. In February 1964 an attempt was made to clarify certain sections of the border during negotiations, but these made little progress. In July 1964 Chairman Mao stated that "China has not yet asked the Soviet Union for an account about Vladivostok, Khabarovsk, Kamchatka and other towns and regions east of Lake Baikal, which became Russian territory about 100 years ago". Against this background of claim and counter-claim, it was not entirely surprising that the negotiations were suspended in May 1965. The issue of disputed territory on the border was brought up by Mao in 1964 and in 1965, and in early 1966 there seems to have been an escalation in the number of border incidents which occurred. The Cultural Revolution in China led to mass demonstrations on the frontier supporting Chinese claims, and in February 1967 the Soviet embassy in Beijing was besieged. By this time, it is estimated that there were 40 Soviet divisions and between 50 and 60 Chinese divisions on the frontier. During late 1967 and throughout 1968 fighting seems to have broken out on several occasions around what the Russians know as Damansky Island and what the Chinese term Zhenbao Island in the Ussuri River.

These clashes escalated significantly in March 1969 and there were indications that the Soviet Union felt it had been provoked too far. After Chinese troops had ambushed a Soviet patrol, the Soviet Union responded by killing hundreds of Chinese soldiers in what was a clear display of military superiority. Further incidents culminated in fighting on Aug. 13, 1969, and on Aug. 23 the **Chinese Communist Party** announced that war might break out at any time. Not surprisingly, each side blamed the other for this escalation. There have been some suggestions, however, that China was primarily responsible for the intensification of the conflict partly out of a desire to inhibit any additional Soviet moves in Eastern Europe after the invasion of Czechoslovakia in 1968. An additional concern might well have been to emphasize to Moscow that the Brezhnev doctrine, which had promulgated an attempt to justify the Soviet intervention in Czechoslovakia in 1968 and in which the Soviet Union proclaimed a right to intervene in the Socialist Commonwealth, did not apply to China.

It appears that the Soviet Union was extremely concerned about the possibility of a large-scale Chinese incursion. Accordingly, the Soviet response was three-fold. The first element was an attempt to increase Soviet room for manoeuvre in the event that military action became necessary. It was at this point that Sino-Soviet relations became bound up with the emerging triangular relationship. Kissinger and Nixon were trying to extricate the United States from Vietnam and thought this would be easier if they could persuade Moscow and Beijing to put pressure on Hanoi. Furthermore, they believed that a system of triangular diplomacy would allow them to exploit the Sino-Soviet split for their own purposes. Indeed, the announcement in July 1971 that President Nixon would be visiting Beijing placed considerable pressure on Moscow and prompted the Soviet leadership to accelerate its efforts to improve the relationship with the United States. There is considerable evidence that Moscow saw US–Soviet detente as inextricably related to its conflict with China. At the very least, it hoped to obtain American neutrality in the event of a Sino-Soviet war. At most, there was a desire to establish an anti-Chinese condominium.

The second and closely related strand in the Soviet response was to increase the coercive pressure on China. There is some evidence that during late 1969 the Soviet Union seriously considered launching a preventive strike against Chinese nuclear installations. Its bomber forces in Siberia and Mongolia were strengthened and exercises were conducted against targets which were made to resemble Chinese nuclear installations. Moscow made no secret of the fact that it was considering a "surgical strike" against Chinese military installations. Whether the military preparations were intended as coercive measures or as a preliminary to an attack remains uncertain. Whatever the case they encouraged China to discuss the issues in an attempt to defuse what was clearly the most dangerous crisis of the post-war period in the Pacific.

The Soviet Union was also careful to ensure that its coercive actions were accompanied by a third strand of policy which involved conciliatory gestures and a willingness to negotiate. This was facilitated by the death of **Ho Chi Minh** of North Vietnam in September 1969 and the release of his political testament appealing for a restoration of unity offered an opportunity for a resumption of negotiations. Following Ho Chi Minh's funeral the Soviet Prime Minister, Alexei Kosygin, flew to Beijing for talks. The two countries agreed to discussions on the border issue, and these negotiations began on Oct. 20 1969, and continued through to June 1978. Little progress was made, however, in dealing with the substantive territorial disputes. It appears that there were 20 areas of varying size and importance along the Xinjiang border which were in dispute. In this region, the problem had been compounded, at least according to Chinese sources, by the fact that Soviet forces had occupied 185 sq miles of Chinese territory during 1960–69 and another 1,080 sq miles between 1972 and July 1977. In the Far Eastern sector the border disputes centred on islands in the Ussuri and Amur rivers. Although the Soviet Union in 1977 made a concession in allowing Chinese shipping to use the water-course east of one of the islands, no agreement was reached on the more fundamental issues regarding ownership of the islands. The relationship between the two governments remained strained and little substantive progress was made in the negotiations.

It was not surprising, therefore, that through the 1970s the Soviet Union placed particular emphasis on upgrading its military capabilities in the Pacific. By the end of the 1970s the Soviet Union had deployed 52 divisions on the border while the Chinese had 78 divisions. In 1979 further negotiations were initiated in which the Chinese demanded the withdrawal of Soviet troops from the disputed areas. The Soviet intervention in Afghanistan led China to postpone the second round of negotiations. From September 1981 and in the early months of 1982 Moscow made several overtures on border negotiations. China, however, continued to emphasize the difficulties that were posed by the deployment of large numbers of Soviet troops on the Chinese border and in Mongolia, the Soviet occupation of Afghanistan and Soviet support for the Vietnamese occupation of Kampuchea. Some shift in Soviet policies in these three areas was made a precondition of improvement in the relationship.

In October 1982 talks took place at Deputy Foreign Minister level on normalization of relations. The following month, after Brezhnev's funeral, talks took place between the Chinese and Soviet Foreign Ministers on how progress might be made in the normalization talks. This was followed by further consultations on normalization in March and October 1983. While the Soviet Union emphasized the value of a non-aggression pact, however, China insisted that the three conditions had first to be met.

These moves towards detente in the early 1980s, although tentative, were given considerable impetus by the assertive policies of the Reagan administration. The hard-line policies towards Moscow combined with Sino-American disputes over Taiwan to give both communist states an incentive to improve their bilateral link in the triangular relationship. The major change, however, came with the emergence of Gorbachev as the new Soviet leader. On the day he was elected General Secretary Gorbachev stated that the Soviet Union would seek "a serious improvement in relations with China".

Although the formal obstacles to this improvement were not immediately overcome, there was a relaxation in the military confrontation along the Sino-Soviet border. The measures were tacit but there does seem to have been an element of reciprocity. China not only removed many troops from the frontier but between 1985 and 1987 cut its armed forces by a million men. For its part, the Soviet Union placed its border divisions on a lower level of readiness. In July 1986 there was a border incident in which a Chinese was killed but both sides played down this incident, which was the first admitted flare-up since 1980. The fact that it was dismissed as an isolated incident was itself symptomatic of the change in the climate of relations between the two states.

A far more significant development was Gorbachev's Vladivostok speech on July 28, 1986, in which he made a very obvious and determined effort to improve Sino-Soviet relations. Announcing the Soviet desire for discussions to create a good neighbourly atmosphere, Gorbachev also dealt with some specific Chinese concerns relating to SS-20s and to Soviet troops in Mongolia. He also announced that six regiments would be withdrawn from Afghanistan before the end of the year and that all Soviet troops would be withdrawn once a political settlement was achieved. In his speech Gorbachev also made an important concession on the Far Eastern border question. He acknowledged that the official border on the Amur and the Ussuri "might pass along the main ship channel". The implication was that several of the disputed islands would be transferred to China.

Although China remained unhappy about the lack of any commitment on the withdrawal of Vietnamese troops from Kampuchea, Beijing nevertheless welcomed the initiative. There was an increase in both the pace and intensity of the negotiations on normalization following the Vladivostok initiative. In September 1988 in Krasnoyarsk, Gorbachev reiterated his call for an improvement and emphasized the Soviet desire to reduce military activity and resolve regional conflicts in East Asia. In his speech at the United Nations in December 1988 he announced that the Soviet Union would withdraw a large portion of its forces in Mongolia and on the border. This dealt with one of the three obstacles that China saw as preventing normal relations while the Soviet withdrawal from Afghanistan dealt with the second.

The UN initiative was accompanied by accelerated diplomatic activity and in December 1988 the Chinese Foreign Minister visited Moscow and the Chinese agreed that Gorbachev should visit Beijing in May 1989. As part of the preparations for the Summit, Soviet Foreign Minister **Shevardnadze** visited Beijing in February 1989. During this visit progress was made in several areas, most notably on Kampuchea, where the two governments reached agreement on a nine-point plan regarding its future. Although there was disagreement on the form a future government should take after the withdrawal of Vietnamese troops, there was clearly a willingness on the part of the two governments to work together to solve the conflict. During the meeting Shevardnadze also reiterated that the Soviet Union would cut the number of troops along the Sino-Soviet border, and would remove 75 per cent of the 50,000 Soviet troops in Mongolia. There was also a proposal that working groups be established to determine the appropriate level of troops along the border in order to achieve greater trust.

Against this background, the visit of Gorbachev to Beijing held out considerable promise. It was the first Sino-Soviet Summit for 30 years and reflected the new detente that had been reached through the 1980s. In the months preceding the Summit, however, there were continuing differences over Kampuchea. The Summit itself, May 15–18 1989, was overshadowed by the student protests in Tiananmen Square (*see* **Tiananmen Incidents**). Even so it was a historic occasion which symbolized Sino-Soviet reconciliation and led to the announcement of further measures towards military detente. In the opening address President Gorbachev referred to the meeting as a watershed, while President **Yang Shangkun** stated that after a tortuous course the two nations were at a new starting point.

Gorbachev also unveiled his plans for military detente. He made clear that of the 200,000 troops to be cut in the Asian part of the Soviet Union 120,000 would come from the far east region, directly threatening China. In addition to these 12 divisions of ground troops and 11 air force regiments, he also announced that the Soviet Union would withdraw 16 battleships from the Pacific fleet. Equally if not more significantly, Gorbachev confirmed that Moscow wanted a full demilitarization of the 4,000 mile border, stating that, with joint efforts, the frontier could be turned into a "border of peace". A joint military commission was to be set up to promote this objective. The Chinese issued a communiqué stating that the two sides had "agreed to take measures to cut the military forces in the areas along the Sino-Soviet boundary to a minimum level commensurate with the normal, good neighbourly relations between the two countries" and to speed up discussions aimed at settling the border line.

PW

SOCIAL ACTION PARTY (THAILAND). The moderate conservative Social Action Party (SAP) was formed in 1974 as an offshoot of the **Democrat Party** (DP) and was originally led by Kukrit Pramoj (brother of the then Democrat leader), who became Prime Minister after the 1975 elections, in which the SAP won 28 seats. Although the party increased its representation to 45 seats in 1976, it did not join the subsequent DP-led coalition (which was deposed by the military in October 1976. The SAP was in opposition until March 1980 when, having won 82 seats in the 1979 elections, it became the strongest party in Gen. Prem's first coalition government. It left this coalition a year later, but rejoined in late 1981 amid some internal dissension about the terms of its participation. In the 1983 elections it retained its position as the largest parliamentary party, winning 92 of the 324 seats in the House of Representatives. It then entered a new coalition formed by Prem, whereafter its electoral support declined in by-elections, this contributing to Kukrit Pramoj's resignation from the leadership in December 1985. He was replaced by the Foreign Minister, ACM **Siddhi Savetsila**. Further internal divisions leading to defections then developed in the SAP, which in the July 1986 elections slipped to third place, retaining only 51 seats (out of 347). The party nevertheless joined a further coalition formed by Prem. In the July 1988 elections, the SAP lifted its performance slightly, gaining 54 seats (out of 357), second only to *Chart Thai*. The following month the SAP joined the new six-member coalition government led by Maj.-Gen. **Chatichai**, obtaining five posts in a 24-member Cabinet.

DS

SOCIALIST FRONT (SINGAPORE). The Socialist Front (*Barisan Socialis*) was formed by **People's Action Party** renegades in 1961 with the final objective of achieving a unified democratic Malaya, including Singapore. Most of the party's leaders were arrested in early 1963 and detained without trial and in elections held later that year the Front gained 13 out of 51 seats. However, 11 of the party's members subsequently resigned from the Legislative Assembly. The party refused to accept Singapore's secession from Malaysia in 1965, and it boycotted the sessions of the Singapore Parliament and also the 1968 elections. Front candidates competed unsuccessfully in elections held between 1972–84. In the September 1988 elections it failed to field any candidates, but Lee Siew Choh, the Front's secretary-general, accepted an invitation to sit in parliament as a "non-constituency MP".

DS

SODNOM, DUMAAGIYN. Mongolian politician, born in 1933. He has been Chairman of the Mongolian Council of Ministers (Prime Minister) since 1984.

IG

SOHYO (GENERAL COUNCIL OF TRADE UNIONS OF JAPAN). Until the formation of **Rengo**, Sohyo was the major labour centre in Japan. Much of its current character and posture was defined in the mid-'fifties when economic demands were for the first time given priority over political and foreign policy issues (such as conflict with the USA). There is evidence again in the 1980s that radical politics and class struggle ideology is a lesser imperative than organizational and attitudinal adjustment to the harsh realities (for labour) of industrial restructuring and the fact of the decline of employment in the public sector. Sohyo's major strength is in the public sector. The merger of Sohyo and Rengo, due in Autumn 1989, is a major step in the process of adjustment and will effect arguably the most dramatic transformation of the landscape of organized labour since the formation of Sohyo itself in 1950.

RAB

SOLOMON ISLANDS. *Population* (est. 1988): 302,000, mostly Melanesians. *Total land area*: 28,446 sq km. The state of the Solomon Islands comprises eight large volcanic islands and island groups in two parallel chains: Villa Lavella, Kolombangara, New Georgia and Guadalcanal, and Choiseul, Santa Isabel and Malaita, plus some outlying islands. Islands in the northern Solomons group are part of Papua New Guinea.

The islands have probably been occupied for at least 3,000 years. Sporadic European contact began in 1568, but became significant only in the late nineteenth century, when many inhabitants were used as labour on the plantations of Fiji and other islands. Germany declared a protectorate over the northern islands in 1886, but except for Buka and Bougainville these came under the British Solomon Islands Protectorate in return for recognition of the German claim to Western Samoa. Japan invaded the islands in 1942, and there was fierce fighting on Guadalcanal. After World War II an independence movement developed, with full self-government by stages culminating in 1978. The Solomon Islands are a constitutional monarchy under the British crown, with a single-chamber Legislative Assembly of 38 members elected for four-year terms. The Prime Minister (since January 1988) is Ezekiel Alebua.

The economy is based on small holdings at subsistence level, with exports of timber and processed fish. Communications are poor, making government difficult.

In May 1986 the Islands were extensively damaged by cyclone *Namu*, with over 100 dead and virtually all crops destroyed. An international aid programme brought relief food and clothing and is helping rebuild the economy. Main sources of imports are Australia, Singapore and Japan; main export markets are Japan, Britain and the Netherlands.

TBM

SON SANN. Veteran Cambodian politician, since 1982 prime minister of the Coalition Government of Democratic Kampuchea. Born in 1911 and educated in Paris in the 1920s and 1930s, he returned home to join the government service (under the French protectorate) in 1935. He served as minister of finance in the government of 1946–47, and deputy premier in the Associated State established in 1949. Under **Prince Sihanouk** he was governor of the national bank from 1955 to 1968 and held various ministerial posts, including that of prime minister (1967). He attempted to play a role under Lon Nol after 1970, but then went into exile in Paris. In 1979 he formed the **Khmer People's National Liberation Front**.

RBS

SON SEN. Succeeded **Pol Pot** as commander of the National Army of Democratic Kampuchea in September 1985. Originally from a Khmer Krom family in Tra-Vinh province (southern Vietnam) he studied in France during the 1950s and became involved in leftist politics. By 1963, back in Cambodia, he was a member of the central committee of the **Kampuchean Communist Party**. After 1975 he rose to be a deputy premier and defence minister of Democratic Kampuchea; but he retreated to the countryside in autumn 1978 following the failure of a visit to Beijing to secure a more direct Chinese military commitment to the defence of Phnom Penh. His precise movements since then have been obscure, but he is thought to be opposed to **Ta Mok** and to operate in a different region of the country.

RBS

SOUPHANOUVONG, PRINCE. Veteran leader of the Pathet Lao and president of the Lao People's Democratic Republic (LPDR) from its foundation in 1975 until his retirement in 1986.

A member of the royal family of Luang Prabang, born in 1909, he was educated in Hanoi and Paris and returned to work in Vietnam as a qualified engineer in 1938. Through his Vietnamese wife he became involved in the Vietnamese independence movement and was in touch with **Ho Chi Minh** in Hanoi in August–September 1945. He then returned to Laos and joined the Free Lao government which was attempting to resist the return of the French. Wounded in the battle of Thakhek, which failed to stop the French advance, he retreated to Thailand and became defence minister in a Laotian government-in-exile organized in Bangkok (1946–49).

In 1949 he rejoined the Viet Minh and began to organize resistance (with their help) in northern Laos. He became leader of the Lao Issara united front in August 1950; the movement which came to be known as the Pathet Lao. Its forces retained *de facto* control of two provinces after the Geneva ceasefire of 1954, under which a coalition was supposed to be formed. Souphanouvong became president of the Lao Patriotic Front at its foundation in early 1956, but his role as a member of the secret Lao People's Party was not revealed. In 1957–58 and in 1962–63 he participated in coalition governments formed in Vientiane by his half-brother Prince Souvanna Phouma, but neither was capable of achieving national unity. From 1964 until 1974 he was again in the *maquis*, as titular leader of the pro-Vietnamese (and ultimately Communist-organized) resistance movement which opposed Vientiane's collaboration with the United States.

Returning to Vientiane after a ceasefire agreement (reached in February 1973 but only slowly implemented) he was head of a National People's Consultative Committee and led the task of paving the way for an eventual Communist takeover. He became president of the LPDR on Dec. 5, 1975 and retired (owing to illness) on Oct. 29, 1986. Within the Party leadership he was always overshadowed by **Kaysone Phomvihan** but he appears nonetheless to have been much more than a figurehead for much of his career.

RBS

SOUTH PACIFIC COMMISSION. In January 1944, Australia and New Zealand proposed a South Seas Regional Commission to secure a common policy on the welfare of native peoples in the South Pacific; their social, economic and political development. This led in 1947 to the establishment of the South Pacific Commission, a consultative and advisory body comprised of metropolitan powers, and subsequently independent states, in the region. The Commission's headquarters is in Noumea, New Caledonia, and approximately a third of its budget is provided by Australia. It conducts research into economic, social, educational, biological and medical problems. Each member appoints two delegates to the South Pacific Conference which meets once a year.

TBM

SOUTH PACIFIC FORUM. An organization established in 1971 to enable governments of the South Pacific region to discuss common problems. Members are Australia, the Cook Islands, Federated States of Micronesia, Fiji, Kiribati, Marshall Islands, Nauru, New Zealand, Niue, Papua New Guinea, the Solomon Islands, Tonga, Tuvalu, Vanuatu and Western Samoa. Headquarters is in Suva, Fiji. The Forum has established the South Pacific Bureau for Economic Cooperation relating to trade, tourism, transportation and economic development. It has consistently opposed French nuclear testing, negotiated a treaty among members banning the testing or deployment of nuclear weapons or the disposal of nuclear waste, and negotiated a treaty with the United States by which the latter pays a fee to member states for fishing for highly migratory species in their exclusive fishing zones.

TBM

SOUTH PACIFIC REGIONAL TRADE AND ECONOMIC CO-OPERATION AGREEMENT (SPARTECA). The agreement was concluded in July, 1980 at a meeting held on Kiribati. The signatories to the agreement are the members of the **South Pacific Forum**, with the single exception of Fiji.

The agreement removes all duty on a wide range of goods traded amongst the signatories, with the aim of making the South Pacific Forum members less dependent on goods imported from Australia and New Zealand. Since this is the purpose of the agreement, exports to the Pacific Island countries from their two large neighbours and fellow members of the Forum are naturally excluded from it. Changes to the structure of aid from Australia and New Zealand in recent years also reflects this theme of decreasing dependence.

DA

SOVIET FAR EAST AND EAST SIBERIA. *Population*: 16,303,000; 6% of the total Soviet population (est. 1985). *Area*: 10,340,000 sq km; 46% of the Soviet Union's total area. *Trade*: US$212,000 million (1987 total Soviet foreign trade). *Top five Soviet trading partners in Pacific region*: Japan, China, Vietnam, Mongolia, North Korea. *Defence spending*: US$129,000 million (1989 Soviet official est.). *Education spending*: US$100,000 million (1988 Soviet budget allocation). *Urban population as percentage of total*: 75 (compared with 67% for total Soviet population). *Birth rate per thousand*: 19.9 (total Soviet population, 1986). *Life expectancy*: 66 (total Soviet population, 1987).

Geographical background. The territories of the Soviet Union stretching eastward from the Yenisey river valley (roughly separating east and west Siberia) to the Pacific seaboard begin with the vast Central Siberian plateau, which is mainly at heights of between 450 and 900 metres above sea level. Further east the basin of the Lena river, including the central Yakut plain, divides the plateau from the complex series of mountain ranges and intermontane basins which cover the Soviet Far East. South of the plateau, other mountain ranges extend along the Mongolian border.

Major vegetation zones extend almost uniformly east–west across the whole of Siberia, with tundra covering the extreme north beside the Arctic Ocean, and giving way to swampy coniferous forest or taiga further south. The climate over most of East Siberia and the Far East is sharply continental, with winters which are notorious for their length and severity, and very low precipitation. Permafrost covers almost the whole region, and ranges in depth from one metre in the south to over 360 metres in the far north. The climate and vegetation differ markedly, however, in the territories of the south-eastern corner beside the Sea of Japan, where Pacific summer monsoon conditions prevail.

General background. The Union of Soviet Socialist Republics (USSR), which was established in 1922, is formally a federal state comprising 15 Union (constituent) Republics of equal status, voluntarily linked and having the right to secede. Under amendments made in 1988 to the 1977 Constitution, the supreme representative body is the Congress of People's Deputies, comprising 1,500 deputies elected by popular vote from 750 constituencies organized to include roughly equal numbers of voters and 750 constituencies designed to give representation to the majority of the Soviet Union's recognized ethnic groups, together with a further 750 deputies elected by approved social organizations; the first Congress elections were held in March 1989. The Congress is elected for a five-year term and convenes once a year to decide on major constitutional, political and socio-economic questions. It elects from among its own members a standing

legislature, the bicameral Supreme Soviet, which meets twice a year for three- or four-month sessions and is responsible for all legislative and administrative matters. The Congress also elects an executive President, known as the Chairman of the Supreme Soviet, who is the country's head of state.

Political power is effectively in the hands of the Communist Party of the Soviet Union (CPSU, *Kommunisticheskaya Partiya Sovietskogo Soyuza*), the only legal political party.

Siberia, which in general Soviet usage is considered to comprise the territories of the Soviet Union between the Ural mountains and the Pacific Ocean, excluding the Central Asian republics, is subdivided for the purposes of economic planning into three regions: West Siberia, East Siberia and the Soviet Far East. These regions, which are not designated administrative-territorial entities, comprise three-quarters of the area of the Russian Soviet Federative Socialist Republic (RSFSR, or Russian Federation), the largest of the Union Republics, which has Moscow as its capital city. Like the other Union Republics, the Russian Federation has a constitution and state structure modelled on that of the central USSR administration, including a unicameral Supreme Soviet and a Council of Ministers to deal with internal affairs.

This study concentrates on East Siberia and the Soviet Far East; West Siberia, very little of which lies further east than longitude 85°, is excluded. The Soviet Far East comprises the Khabarovsk and Primorye (Maritime) territories (*kraya*), the administrative regions (*oblasti*) of Amur, Kamchatka, Magadan and Sakhalin, and the Yakut Autonomous Soviet Socialist Republic (ASSR); within these are also to be found the Chukchi and Koryak National Districts (NOs), and the Jewish Autonomous *Oblast* (AO). Eastern Siberia comprises Krasnoyarsk *kray*, Chita and Irkutsk *oblasti*, and the Buryat and Tuva ASSRs; within these are also to be found the Aga Buryat, Evenk, Taymyr and Ust'Orda Buryat NOs, and the Khakass AO.

Pre-modern history. The tribal peoples of southern Siberia became subject to the overlordship of the succession of Turkic-Mongol states centred on what is now Mongolia from the third century BCE. The Mongol empire created by Chingis (Genghis) Khan at the beginning of the thirteenth century incorporated virtually the whole of Siberia, although the relationship between the indigenous Siberian peoples and their Mongol masters was almost wholly tributary.

Early modern history. Siberia was opened to the Russians in 1581 when a Cossack expedition overthrew the small Tatar khanate of Sibir (literally "sleeping land"), which occupied the eastern flank of the Ural mountains and gave its name to the whole territory beyond. Thereafter, fur trappers, traders and explorers moved rapidly eastward with little hindrance from the indigenous peoples, reaching the Pacific coast near what is now Okhotsk in 1639. Government officials followed in their wake to claim the territories for the Russian Tsar; by the end of the seventeenth century over 3,000 km of Asia's Pacific coastline had been brought under Russian control, including the Kamchatka peninsula. When Russian explorers and trappers crossed into Eastern Siberia in the sixteenth and seventeenth centuries, they encountered a large number of indigenous groups, most of them very small in numbers and generally primitive and loosely organized. In the south the Siberian peoples were pastoral nomads; in the central band of forest they lived by fishing and reindeer herding. The Siberian peoples offered little resistance to Russian conquest, and following the annexation of their territories by the Russian empire their social organization and way of life were generally not interfered with aside from the collection by the Russians of tribute (usually in the form of furs). Their autonomy has nominally been preserved in the state structure of the Soviet Union, although all have now been assimilated in varying degrees to Russian–Soviet culture. In the first half of the eighteenth century the Chukchi Peninsula was annexed, and the impetus of this expansion in the far north carried Russians across the Bering Sea into Alaska and down the eastern Pacific coast. However, the North American territories were too remote for European Russia for effective control, and were finally given up in 1867 when Alaska was sold to the United States for US$7,200,000.

Annexation by the Russian Empire was followed by a modest influx into the region of state peasants and runaway serfs from European Russia (serfdom, the system of bonding peasants to a private landlord which existed in Russia until 1861, was not translated to Siberia). The region also became used as a place of exile for criminals and political prisoners. Settlement from Europe remained insignificant, however, until the turn of the twentieth century, when the building of the **Trans-Siberian Railway** facilitated economic exploitation, and large-scale migration developed. European peoples (mostly Russians and Ukrainians) now make up around 85 per cent of the population of East Siberia and the Soviet Far East.

In the south-east, Russian territorial ambitions intitialy were thwarted by China. Russian encroachment as far as the mouth of the Amur river began in 1644, but soon met with armed resistance from the Manchus, and after nearly 40 years of sporadic fighting the Treaty of Nerchinsk, signed in 1689, fixed the boundary between the Russian and Manchu Chinese empires far to the north of the Amur along the line of the Stanovoy mountains. However, Russian troops and colonists in the mid-nineteenth century took advantage of a China weakened by internal and foreign pressures again to occupy the territory immediately to the north of the Amur. The Chinese commander in the area was forced in 1858 to sign the Treaty of Aigun, which gave Russia sovereignty over 480,000 sq km of territory north of the Amur and placed 340,000 sq km between the Ussuri (the Amur's principal tributary) and the Pacific under joint Sino-Russian sovereignty. The latter territory passed wholly to Russian control in 1860 by the Treaty of Beijing (Peking), and in the following year the Russians founded there the port of Vladivostok.

From the mid-nineteenth century the main challenge to Russian expansion in the Far East came from Japan, with which it had first come into contact because of rival attempts to annex **Sakhalin** and the **Kuril Islands** to the north of Japan. After controlling these islands jointly for more than 20 years the two countries in 1875 agreed to Russian sovereignty over Sakhalin Island in exchange for Japanese sovereignty over the Kuril Islands. In 1904–05 Japan and Russia went to war largely over spheres of influence in Manchuria, and the decisive Japanese victory resulted in Russia being forced to cede to Japan Sakhalin's southern half.

Russian administration of Siberia from 1614 to 1763 was directed from the Siberian Office in the Russian capital (first Moscow, then from 1712 St Petersburg). Several provinces were formed in the latter part of the eighteenth century, and after 1822 the provinces of East Siberia were subordinated to the office of a governor-general based in the city of Irkutsk. In 1884 a viceroy was appointed for the territories newly annexed from China, together with the older Russian possessions on the Pacific seaboard.

Political history. Siberia and the Soviet Far East were the scene of some of the most dramatic events of the civil war which followed the November 1917 Bolshevik revolution in Russia. Early in 1918, Soviet power in Siberia was overthrown by anti-Bolshevik White Russian forces, who rapidly came under the control of Adml. Aleksandr Kolchak. The latter established his own extreme right-wing dictatorship in November 1918, with his headquarters at Omsk in western Siberia. Meanwhile, in April 1918 Japanese forces landed at Vladivostok on the Pacific coast, ostensibly with the aim of supporting the White Russian forces, and quickly established a military presence throughout Russia's Far Eastern provinces.

By mid-1919 the Bolshevik Red Army had forced the Whites into a retreat eastward through Siberia, and in January 1920 Kolchak fell into Bolshevik hands and was executed. The Bolsheviks were by now firmly in control of the territories to the west of Lake Baykal, but the Japanese still occupied the Pacific coast, and it was decided by the Bolsheviks to create a nominally independent buffer state between Soviet and Japanese holdings. This state, which was known as the Far Eastern or Chita Republic, survived until 1922, when Japanese forces were withdrawn and it was absorbed into the Soviet Union.

Under the Soviet regime, Siberia and the Far East retained their role as a destination for criminals and political prisoners. The drive to collectivize agriculture begun at the end of the 1920s saw the deportation to the north of Siberia and other remote areas of the *kulaks*, the richest class of peasant farmers, who were put to forced labour. Forced labour camps spread in the 1930s as the purges ordered by Stalin and his supporters led to the incarceration, often without trial and almost always for lengthy terms, of millions of people. These severe political repressions lasted until Stalin's death in 1953.

East Siberia and the Soviet Far East were not directly affected by the military campaigns of World War II. Following a brief skirmish on the Mongolia–Manchuria border in the summer of 1939 a truce reigned between Soviet and Japanese forces until August 1945, when the Soviet Union declared war on Japan only days before Japan's capitulation. However, with the evacuation eastward of a large part of the Soviet Union's industrial capacity away from the Nazi German armies advancing deep into the European part of the country, Siberia, together with the Urals and Central Asia, provided the industrial backbone of the Soviet war effort. At the end of the war, as part of the 1945 Yalta agreement, the Soviet Union annexed from Japan the southern half of Sakhalin and the Kurils.

In the post-war period the chief political significance of East Siberia and the Soviet Far East has been in the dispute between the Soviet and Chinese leaderships, and in the militarization of the Far East (see foreign relations, below).

Recent developments. Regional administrations across the Soviet Union are believed to be one of the main bastions of conservative resistance by bureaucrats and careerists to the reformist policies of *perestroika* ("restructuring") and *glasnost* ("openness") which were introduced after **Mikhail Gorbachev** was elected as CPSU general secretary in March 1985. There has been evidence of such resistance in certain regions of East Siberia and the Soviet Far East, notably Irkutsk, where local officials were among the first to be reprimanded or dismissed for incompetence or corruption following Gorbachev's election. The East Siberian city of Krasnoyarsk also provided the most dramatic evidence of popular dissatisfaction with the failure of *perestroika* to improve living standards and to eliminate food and consumer goods shortages, when in September 1988 Gorbachev was shown by the media around the world being heckled by local people during an official visit.

The East Siberian town of Sharypovo recently benefited from the reappraisal of Soviet history taking place under *glasnost*. In 1985 it had been renamed Chernenko in honour of the late Konstantin Chernenko, a native of the Sharypovo area who had been Gorbachev's predecessor as Soviet leader, but at the end of 1988 it reverted to its original name because of the discrediting of Chernenko as an associate of the late Leonid Brezhnev, the Soviet leader from 1964 to 1982 who was blamed for the "stagnation" which was afflicting Soviet socio-economic life when Gorbachev came to power.

Economic development. East Siberia and the Soviet Far East have an immense wealth of natural resources, including **coal**, most ferrous and non-ferrous metals, **diamonds**, asbestos, salt, timber and furs. However, the physical conditions in the regions, especially the climate and permafrost cover, create huge technical problems in the exploitation of most of these resources. These conditions also render the land almost wholly unsuited to agriculture; arable land is confined to the area along the Far Eastern border with China, parts of Irkutsk *oblast*, the Minusinsk area of southern Krasnoyarsk *kray*, central Yakutia and parts of Sakhalin; land favourable to livestock breeding is to be found only in Buryatia and Khakassia, and in Chita and Amur *oblasti*.

Before the 1917 Bolshevik revolution there was little economic development of East Siberia and the Soviet Far East apart from hunting, fishing and fur trapping, and small-scale mining and metallurgy. In the last years before the revolution the building of the Trans-Siberian railway brought from European Russia an influx of settlers who intensified the use of the available arable land, and serviced the railway, and the coal mining and engineering which were started along its route.

Following the consolidation of Soviet power by 1922, the Soviet authorities set the objective of comprehensive economic and social development of Siberia and the Soviet Far East. Much of the next 15 years was spent in exploration and planning, and the regions were largely exempted from the first Soviet Five-Year Plan (1928–32). Exploitation of the regions' raw material wealth to furnish industrialization in the European part of the country was the dominant feature of their economic development for most of the 1930s and 1940s, the labour force being provided largely from the vast penal colonies of the Stalinist era.

Interest in Siberia's economic potential was expressed by Nikita Khrushchev at the 20th and 21st CPSU congresses (1956 and 1961), and resolutions were adopted to exploit Siberian natural resources more intensively. Investment funds were allotted for energy extraction and engineering projects, and what little unused arable land was available in East Siberia and the Soviet Far East was ploughed up during the "virgin lands" campaign. In the late 1950s and 1960s major infrastructural projects were completed, including giant hydroelectric power stations such as at Bratsk and Ust-Ilim on the Angara river and Krasnoyarsk on the Yenisey. New industries included aluminium smelting and cellulose manufacture around Lake Baykal, and new mineral resources were discovered and exploited.

Current economic situation. East Siberia and the Soviet Far East remain primarily the source of raw materials for industrial capacity elsewhere in the Soviet Union, and to a much more modest extent for export markets. There has been until recently relatively little interest in developing integrated social–industrial complexes, primarily because of prohibitive development costs. Manpower is still the most scarce resource in the regions, even though since the 1960s considerably higher wages and other incentives have been offered to attract workers, and there have been patriotic appeals through the Communist Youth Union (Komsomol) and other social organizations to participate in major development projects such as the **Baykal-Amur Mainline (BAM)**.

Currently, around 80 per cent of exports from the Soviet Far East and East Siberia consist of mainly unprocessed timber, fuel and fish. Total exports from the regions currently account for well under 10 per cent of total Soviet exports.

Foreign relations. In line with the reforms introduced by Gorbachev in the economic, social and cultural spheres, and the explicit rejection of the practices of the 1970s, there has also been what observers have termed a "global diplomatic offensive" intended to revive a Soviet foreign policy which had been largely moribund since the mid-1970s. The Soviet withdrawal from Afghanistan by 1989, reductions in the military presence in the Soviet Far East and Mongolia, and Soviet pressure on Vietnam to withdraw its troops from Kampuchea, have been the key elements in efforts to improve Soviet diplomatic contacts in Asia, notably its relations with China and Japan.

The new Soviet initiative towards Asia was unveiled in a July 1986 speech by Gorbachev in Vladivostok. This featured the announcement that the Soviet Union was prepared "at any time and at any level to discuss with China questions of additional measures for creating a good-neighbourly atmosphere". Evidently with that end in view Gorbachev disclosed that the withdrawal of "a substantial portion" of Soviet troops from Mongolia was under consideration, and that the Soviet Union was willing to discuss the reduction of land forces elsewhere in the vicinity of the Sino-Soviet border, as well as the disputed demarcation of that border.

Sino-Soviet normalization talks aimed at healing the ideological rift of the early 1960s had been taking place since 1982. They were given considerable impetus by this new Soviet willingness to discuss the most contentious issues, and by a partial withdrawal of Soviet troops from Mongolia in mid-1987. This led to a considerable improvement in relations in the course of 1987 and 1988. Soviet Foreign Minister **Eduard Shevardnadze** visited China in February 1989, and in official talks it was agreed that Gorbachev should go to Beijing in May for a Sino-Soviet summit, the first since 1959. Furthermore, it was announced in March 1989 that 75 per cent of Soviet troops in Mongolia were to be withdrawn.

In November 1988 China and the Soviet Union reached agreement on the course of their Far Eastern border along the Amur and Ussuri rivers. Consequently, it appears that the claims revived by China in the 1960s to the territories lost to Tsarist Russia by the so-called "unequal treaties" of the nineteenth century are now in abeyance.

Relations with Japan have also benefited from the Soviet willingness to reduce its military presence in Asia, and as early as the beginning of 1986 the Soviet leadership signalled its intention to improve diplomatic contacts when Shevardnadze visited Japan, marking a resumption of high-level meetings after a lapse of nearly 10 years. However, the new Soviet leadership made little progress in resolving the main issue hindering a major improvement in Japanese–Soviet relations, namely Japanese insistence that the Soviet Union negotiate on the status of the "northern territories", a group of islands at the southern end of the Kuril chain over which Japan continues to claim sovereignty (*see* **Northern Territories Dispute**). Nevertheless, Soviet economic relations with Japan have been substantial for many years, and are planned to develop further with increased Japanese capital investment in the exploitation of Siberia through joint venture companies.

Elsewhere in the Pacific region, the Soviet Union since 1985 has established or upgraded diplomatic contacts with most nations.

In the Bering Strait at the northern end of the Pacific Ocean the territories of the Soviet Union and the United States are only three miles apart. A purely Pacific dimension in Soviet–US relations emerges only rarely, however, and usually in connection with issues of military balance.

The precise maritime boundary between the United States and the Soviet Union in the Bering Strait was never properly demarcated after Russia's sale of Alaska to the United States in 1867; boundary negotiations to that end have been going on intermittently since 1981. In April 1989 the governments of Alaska and of Magadan *oblast* (region) in the Soviet Far East signed an agreement calling on their respective national governments to remove restrictions on the free passage of people across the Bering Strait. This was aimed specifically at reuniting the Eskimos living on either side of the divide.

Prospects for development. The Soviet State Planning Committee (Gosplan) announced in late 1987 a long-term plan for economic development of the Soviet Far East, involving the investment of 232,000 million roubles (US$359,000 million). This development is to concentrate on making the Far East more autonomous in planning and in foreign economic relations, and to convert it from merely a source of raw materials to a processing zone through the reconstruction of the region's machine building industry and the refurbishment of its metallurgical plant.

The plan envisages that by the year 2000 electricity production will have increased by 260 per cent, oil extraction by 300 per cent, and natural gas extraction by between 700 and 900 per cent. By the end of the thirteenth Five-Year Plan in 1995 the Soviet Far East is intended to be self-sufficient in electricity and fuel. Timber exports are planned to grow by 11 per cent, but there is to be a greater emphasis on processing, including a 200 per cent increase in cellulose production. The fish processing industry is to be substantially relocated in the Far East, where the fishing industry provides around one third of the total Soviet catch of fish and other seafood (this in

turn is about 14 per cent of the world total) but is performing below its potential because exports are mostly of unprocessed goods.

These ambitious plans will depend on a substantial influx of workers. Along the route of the BAM planners reportedly hope to increase the population by 1.7 times by the year 2000, and 30 per cent of investment capital has been allocated to social infrastructure development in the region in an effort to curb the current high turnover of manpower.

Five years after it was officially declared completed, the BAM is finally due to become fully operational in the latter part of 1989. The BAM was designed to open access to rich reserves of natural gas, coal, iron ore, and other minerals, but recently doubts have been expressed by Soviet officials about its value, and it is not thought likely to recoup its construction costs of at least 15,000 million roubles (US$25,000 million) until well into the twenty-first century.

An important step was taken towards more rapid economic development of a key area of the Soviet Far East with the removal in September 1988 of the "closed border" status of the Primorye (Maritime) territory, closest to Japan and Korea, thereby allowing access to foreign investors and freer mobility of labour. Two parts of the territory, the twin ports of Nakhodka and Vostochny and the Posyet-Khasan area southwest of Vladivostok, are currently being considered for the status of "special economic zone", in which tax concessions, lower customs tariffs and subsidised wages and raw materials would be offered as an incentive to joint ventures with foreign investors.

The Soviet Union is interested in joint ventures in order to boost exports and gain access to new technology. In 1988 three Soviet-Japanese joint venture companies were established in the fishing and timber industries, and both Japanese and South Korean business partners are being sought for technological and infrastructural development projects in the Soviet Far East. It is planned that more efficient exploitation of Siberian and Far Eastern natural resources should underpin an upsurge of Soviet trade with the nations of the Pacific area, especially the raw materials-deficient nations of north-east Asia. In order to boost trade with the Pacific countries the Soviet Union is currently seeking admission to the **Pacific Economic Co-operation Conference (PECC).** A Soviet National Committee for Pacific Economic Co-operation was formed at the beginning of 1988.

IG

SOVIET–NORTH KOREAN SECURITY RELATIONS. The partition of Korea in the

221

closing stages of World War II grew out of the fact that the Allies established separate zones of occupation along the 38th parallel. During the war the principle of independence for Korea was confirmed on several occasions. Soviet forces moved into North Korea in the closing stages of the war as Japan collapsed. This prompted the United States to declare that the division between Soviet and American forces should be made along the 38th parallel. With the development of the Soviet-American Cold War the division was solidified and while the South became closely linked with the United States, North Korea became aligned to the Soviet Union. The Soviet occupying authorities supported **Kim Il Sung** – who had worked for Soviet intelligence during World War II – in a struggle against other factions. With this support Kim Il Sung gradually prevailed and in September 1948 the Democratic People's Republic of Korea was proclaimed. Neither the new People's Republic nor the Republic of Korea, which had been founded in the South on Aug. 15, 1948, was willing to accept the division or the other government as legitimate.

On June 25, 1950, after clashes had occurred along the parallel, the Korean War began with the forces of North Korea invading the South. Although this was essentially a civil war, the United States saw the hand of the Soviet Union behind the invasion and became involved under UN auspices on the side of South Korea. In some respects this was not surprising as the relationship between Kim Il Sung and Stalin was very close, while the invading North Korean forces were equipped with Soviet-made T-34 tanks.

During the Korean War the Soviet Union avoided direct involvement. Furthermore, the amount of military aid given to the North Koreans and to Communist China, after its entry to the war, was somewhat meagre. The heaviest and most effective Soviet howitzers, tanks and artillery were not supplied. Instead the communist forces had to rely on Soviet surplus stock from World War II, much of which was obsolescent. Nevertheless, after the war the Soviet Union played a part in North Korean reconstruction. The Soviet Union also provided North Korea with a steady flow of military equipment.

The gradual emergence of the Sino-Soviet split posed problems for North Korea, however, which would have much preferred to remain under dual protection and to avoid choosing between Moscow and Beijing. Initially Kim Il Sung adopted a strictly neutral stance, and in June 1961, in response to concerns that the United States was becoming increasingly aggressive in East Asia, North Korea signed Treaties of Friendship, Co-operation and Mutual Assistance with the Soviet Union, and five days later with China.

In the early 1960s there was a deterioration in the relationship between Pyongyang and Moscow. For a period in the first half of the 1960s Moscow ceased to provide economic aid and military assistance to North Korea. In 1965, however, Kosygin visited North Korea and efforts were made by both sides to improve the relationship. Finding that its military arsenal required modernizing, and sensitive to the inability of China to fulfil its needs, North Korea was increasingly receptive to Soviet overtures and shifted its alignment from China back towards the Soviet Union. Although Chinese-North Korean relations were to improve again in the late 1960s, by then the Soviet Union had consolidated its position as North Korea's major ally and arms supplier.

During the 1960s in fact North Korea placed considerable emphasis on military expenditure. Spending on defence rose to about 30 per cent of the government's budget from 1967 to 1971 and although it dropped in percentage terms thereafter, there was nonetheless a continuing increase in the size of North Korea's armed forces. In 1971 North Korea had 580 combat aircraft, 900 tanks, 300 surface-to-air missiles at 60 sites and 90 naval vessels. It has been estimated that between 1964 and 1973 about three-quarters of its imported armaments came from the Soviet Union and one quarter from China. After 1973 there was a slight move in favour of China, but North Korea's armed forces were clearly patterned on Soviet models, and it was still the Soviet Union which provided the most modern weaponry. In the early 1970s North Korea acquired SU-7 fighter bombers while in the mid-1970s Moscow provided the technology to enable North Korea to produce the T-62 tank, which had been the mainstay of the Soviet army during the 1960s. Soviet arms transfers to North Korea, however, demonstrated considerable caution, and Moscow did not make available the T-72 tank nor the advanced aircraft and missiles of the kind it sent to its allies in the Middle East. During 1984 and 1985 there was a further warming in the Soviet-North Korean relationship and Moscow made available military systems such as the MIG23s and SA-3s that it had earlier denied to its ally.

Soviet support for North Korea, however, has always been somewhat ambivalent. Moscow has been interested in ensuring that North Korean territory – which has a land border 12 miles long with the Soviet Union – remains in friendly hands. At the same time, the Soviet Union has been anxious not to encourage any actions on the part of North Korea which might drag Moscow into a confrontation with the United States. A variety of North Korean actions – the capture of the US spy ship, the Pueblo, the digging of tunnels under the demilitarized zone (DMZ) between North and South Korea, the shooting down of an EC-121 reconnaissance plane, commando raids, the assassination attempt on **Park Chung-hee** and the brutal killing of two US officers in the DMZ – has discomfited Moscow. Furthermore, Kim Il Sung has hardly been a model client and Moscow may well have concluded that Pyongyang would be even more resistant to Soviet influence if it controlled all Korea. Not surprisingly, therefore, Moscow has given little more than token support to North Korean policies aimed at re-unification.

PW

SOVIET–VIETNAMESE SECURITY RELATIONS. In the 1970s and 1980s one of the most important bilateral military relationships in the Pacific has been that between the Soviet Union and Vietnam. This alliance, however, did not have an auspicious start. During the 1930s the Vietnamese communists under **Ho Chi Minh**, although looking to the Soviet Union as a model, were disappointed at the lack of practical support from Moscow in the struggle for independence against the French. Even during the immediate post-war period under Stalin, Moscow was less forthcoming with assistance than Ho Chi Minh and the Viet Minh expected. At the Geneva conference in 1954 Hanoi was pressed by the Soviet Union to accept a settlement based on the partition of the country. This ended the war on less favourable terms than might have been expected given that the French in Indochina had been defeated. Although this subsequently caused some irritation to the relationship, in the late 1950s the Soviet Union was fairly generous in its aid to Hanoi.

In Krushchev's final years in power, however, he became extremely concerned that the growing conflict in Indochina might provoke a clash between the two superpowers. He was also anxious that North Vietnam should side with the Soviet Union against China in the growing Sino-Soviet dispute. Accordingly Khrushchev distanced the Soviet Union from Hanoi. After his downfall however, the relationship between the two governments improved markedly. The new leadership in Moscow was much more sympathetic to the cause of North Vietnam. This is explicable partly as a tactical move in the Sino-Soviet conflict. Furthermore, as the United States escalated the war in Vietnam, so Hanoi had little

alternative other than to turn to Moscow to provide the arms necessary for its war effort. In February 1965 Kosygin went to Hanoi for discussions with North Vietnam about Soviet aid and the Sino-Soviet dispute. A communiqué was issued at the end of the meeting in which the Soviet Union applauded the actions of the National Liberation Front in South Vietnam, and pledged itself to provide necessary assistance to strengthen the defence potential of North Vietnam and to hold regular consultations with Hanoi. This communiqué was treated by the Soviet Union as a formal agreement and provided the framework for Soviet–North Vietnamese relations well into the 1970s.

If the Soviet Union was unequivocal in supporting Hanoi, however, it was also concerned that it should not become entrapped or dragged into a direct military confrontation with the United States – a concern that encouraged the perception in North Vietnam that Moscow was less forthcoming with its assistance than it should have been. Hanoi was also concerned when in 1972 President Nixon visited Moscow as part of the evolving superpower detente. In spite of these developments, the Soviet Union provided far more military aid to North Vietnam than China, and Moscow, in spite of all the difficulties in the relationship, increasingly became the main supporter and patron of Hanoi. It has been estimated that Moscow supplied North Vietnam with 500,000 tons of war material during 1965. At this stage particular emphasis was placed on radar-controlled surface-to-air missiles, and by the end of 1965 there were 4,000 Soviet military advisers and technicians helping North Vietnam to operate its SAMs in the air war. In the following years the Soviet Union supplied a variety of MIG fighter planes and tanks. After the military setback encountered in the Tet offensive, the Soviet Union increased its aid to Hanoi by 20 per cent. In addition, the Soviet Union helped to maintain the infrastructure of North Vietnam and it has been estimated that during the period 1965–75 the Soviet Union provided North Vietnam with something like five billion dollars' worth of military assistance, i.e. about 20 per cent of Soviet military aid world-wide.

As the United States began to disengage from Vietnam the Soviet Union stepped up its activities in Asia. Not surprisingly, therefore, it played a key role in the post-war reconstruction in Vietnam. Although Vietnam was anxious to maintain a policy of equidistance between the two communist supporters, its relationship with China deteriorated, and it increasingly turned to Moscow for support. On Nov. 2, 1978 the Soviet Union and Vietnam signed a Treaty of Friendship and Co-operation, as well as a military assistance agreement. Article 6 of the Treaty pledges that, in the event of either party being threatened or attacked, the signatories "shall immediately consult each other with a view to eliminating the threat, and shall take appropriate and effective measures to safeguard the peace and security of the two countries". The guarantee is, in effect, a very weak one and there has been some speculation that there was a secret protocol which contained a stronger pledge and gave the Soviet Union permission to use Vietnamese naval and military facilities. Even in the absence of a stronger pledge of this kind, however, the alliance between Vietnam and the Soviet Union has clearly been of advantage to both parties.

One of the benefits for the Soviet Union, of course, has been its access to air and naval bases in Vietnam. Soviet naval forces make extensive use of the naval facilities at Cam Ranh Bay, Da Nang and Haiphong, while use is also made of four major air bases, at Da Nang, Cam Rahn, Bien Hoa and Tan Son Nhut. In addition an electronic intelligence complex at Da Nang enables the Soviet Union to monitor US activities at Clark Field and Subic Bay in the Philippines, as well as elsewhere in the Pacific. Soviet spy planes fly regularly from Da Nang and Cam Ranh while the Soviet Union has constructed radar and monitoring stations along the Chinese border as well as along the coast. In addition to these benefits, the bases in Vietnam also provide useful transit facilities for Soviet naval forces deployed in the Indian Ocean.

For its part, the Soviet Union has continued to provide Vietnam with considerable military aid. In terms of tonnage the military aid increased very considerably in the late 1970s as Vietnam not only invaded Cambodia but also had to resist the Chinese retaliatory invasion of February 1979. Although it has tapered off since then, according to reliable sources, during the first half of the 1980s Soviet military assistance totalled over six billion dollars. It has also covered ground, sea and air forces. The Soviet Union has provided Vietnam with over 23 combat vessels, 110 helicopters, and at least three squadrons of MIg 21s. This aid has a great advantage for the Soviet Union in that it helped contain Chinese power in the region. The Soviet Union also provided the military backing necessary for Hanoi to maintain its position in Kampuchea. According to some estimates the Soviet Union was, in one way or another, paying about 80 per cent of the 12 million dollars a day that it was reportedly costing to fund the war in Kampuchea during 1986.

In effect, the bilateral relationship between Vietnam and the Soviet Union has been one of the most relevant alliances in the Pacific region in operational terms. The Soviet Union has supported Hanoi through its struggle with the United States and subsequently in its military activities in Kampuchea and in its conflict with China. In return for this support, Moscow has made significant gains in terms of military facilities.

There have been signs recently, however, that there could be some downgrading of the Soviet-Vietnamese alliance by both Moscow and Hanoi. The Vietnamese withdrawal from Kampuchea will mean that Vietnam is slightly less dependent on Moscow's support, while the Soviet Union has seemed somewhat unhappy at the economic burden imposed by Vietnamese dependence. Indeed, the Soviet Union, under **Gorbachev**, has pressed Vietnam to reform its economy and to improve relations with its neighbours. This has reflected the shift in the Soviet approach to the Pacific and the new emphasis on co-operation that was emphasized by Gorbachev in his Vladivostok speech in July 1986. Although the Sino-Soviet detente means that Vietnam may not be quite as salient in Soviet calculations as it has been, there is unlikely to be a dramatic shift. The Soviet-Vietnamese military alliance will continue to be a prominent feature of the geopolitics of the region.

PW

SPECIAL ECONOMIC ZONES (SEZs). The four original SEZs in China (Shenzhen, Zhuhai, Shantou and Xiamen) were created in 1979 in Guangdong and Fujian provinces on the model of export-processing zones in Southeast Asia. A fifth Zone, Hainan Island, was established in 1988 after the island became a separate province. They were intended to attract foreign investment, especially if it produced exports, as well as advanced technology and managerial techniques, which could then be transferred to the Chinese hinterland. To that end they have offered various inducements and concessions to foreign investors, particualrly Overseas Chinese.

In practice they have achieved less than had been hoped, especially in terms of exports, and they have been blamed by conservative leaders for spreading speculation, corruption and harmful foreign ideas. They have, however, made a major contribution to the opening of the Chinese economy to the outside world, and they have encouraged a number of other provinces to try to emulate them by offering special arrangements to foreign investors in coastal cities.

CIPF

SPRATLY ISLANDS. One of the most complicated disputes in the Pacific is that over the Spratly Islands. The islands – which lie 300 miles west of the Philippine island of Palawan, 300 miles east of Vietnam and 650 miles south of the nearest Chinese territory – are little more than a widely dispersed group of islets, coral reefs and sandbars in the South China Seas. Partly because they occupy an important strategic position, commanding the sea passage from Japan to Singapore, and partly because of the belief that the seas around them are rich in oil and other mineral resources, they are claimed, in whole or in part, by the People's Republic of China, Taiwan, Vietnam, the Philippines and Malaysia.

Both China and Taiwan claim that the islands were traditionally under Chinese sovereignty. The fact that in 1933 they were annexed by France, which then ruled Vietnam, has provided Vietnam with a claim, while in 1956, the government of the Philippines also laid claim to the main group of islands.

During the 1970s seven of the islands were occupied by forces of the Philippines and President **Marcos** made clear that his government's claim was limited to these islands. Subsequently, the Philippines pledged that it would defend these islands against encroachment by any other power. Other parts of the Spratly Islands were under the control of South Vietnamese forces and, after the fall of Saigon, came under the control of Hanoi. Indeed, the most serious element in the multilateral dispute over the islands is that between Vietnam and the People's Republic of China – although in 1983 when a Malaysian naval unit landed on a southern atoll of the islands, both Hanoi and Beijing were quick to protest.

In 1987 the dispute between China and Vietnam over the islands intensified and China became more assertive in its claims. Its claims were backed up by naval exercises in June 1987 and in early 1988 there were skirmishes between Chinese and Vietnamese forces in the area as a result of which two or three Vietnamese ships were sunk, three Vietnamese were killed and 74 were missing. With both sides increasing their forces in the area, it appeared that the conflict might escalate and there was considerable concern among the members of the **Association of South-East Asian Nations (ASEAN)** that the Spratly Islands had become a new area of conflict in the Pacific.

In May 1988, however, tensions lessened as Hanoi offered to hold negotiations about the islands. Beijing responded by suggesting that the dispute be set aside until talks could be arranged.

PW

STUDENT MOVEMENTS. Students have often been at the forefront of nationalist movements and campaigns for reform. They were at the centre of the pro-democracy campaign in China, which was crushed in 1989. Students were among some of the more fanatical Red Guards at the time of the Cultural Revolution, though they were also among its victims, many of them being forced to spend long periods in remote rural areas, learning the realities of peasant life.

Most Marxist and developing countries have tried to make students conform and channel their energies either totally into their studies or else into officially sanctioned student organizations. These organizations promote ideals such as international co-operation and world peace. But governments in general take a dim view of student activism which indicates overt approval of the lifestyles or value systems of different cultures or else challenges the domestic political status quo. During the Vietnam War, many college campuses in the United States became centres for anti-war campaigns and draft-resisting, leading to some violent clashes with the security forces. A similar phenomenon, albeit on a smaller scale, occurred in Australia.

In Malaysia and Indonesia, some students have been active in promoting the global cause of Muslim fundamentalism. In Latin America, left-wing underground movements have often found some of their most committed members within universities.

JF

SUHARTO. Gen. Suharto was virtually unknown to the Indonesian people until Oct. 1, 1965, when as commander of the Army's Strategic Reserve he led the troops who retook control of vital points in Jakarta and began rounding up leaders of the abortive coup.

Born of a farming family in 1921 near Jogjakarta, he joined the Netherlands East Indies Army at the age of 19, held a guerrilla command in the war of independence against the Dutch after World War II, and became a career Army officer when Indonesia achieved independence in 1949. He was Deputy Chief of the Army when he was given command in 1962 of the campaign to wrest Irian Jaya (West New Guinea) from the Dutch; after the negotiated settlement which gave Indonesia control of that territory in 1963, he took control of the Strategic Reserve, a mobile striking force. He became Army Commander and Chief of Staff after his predecessor in those posts, Gen. Ahmad Jani, was murdered in the abortive 1965 coup. In March 1966, it was announced that President **Sukarno** had conferred upon Gen.

Suharto written authority to take in the President's name "all measures required for the safe-guarding and stability of government administration". Suharto immediately outlawed the **Communist Party** (PKI). In late March a new Cabinet was formed (ostensibly under Sukarno's Premiership) in which Gen. Suharto held the posts of Deputy Prime Minister for Defence and Security and Army Minister. In February 1967, President Sukarno transferred full powers to Gen. Suharto, and the next month Sukarno was removed from office and Suharto was appointed acting President. He became Prime Minister in October and, following his election by the People's Consultative Assembly, he was inaugurated in March 1968 as President. He was elected for a fifth five-year term as President in March 1988.

DS

SUKARNO. Dr Ahmed Sukarno, the first President of independent Indonesia and one of the leading personalities among Asian nationalist leaders after World War II, ended his life in relative obscurity, having been deprived of all governmental and executive powers in 1967. Before relinquishing his powers to Gen. Suharto in that year he had ruled as a virtual dictator for more than 20 years.

Born in Java in 1901, the son of a Muslim Javanese school teacher and a Balinese mother, Ahmed Sukarno studied engineering at a Dutch technical college in Bandung, took a doctor's degree in civil engineering, but refused several good offers from Dutch companies in order to devote himself to the Indonesian nationalist movement, of which he became a leader while still in his twenties. Arrested by the Dutch authorities in 1929 for nationalist activities, he was sentenced to four years' imprisonment, released after two years, but rearrested in 1932, and spent the next eight or nine years in exile from Java, being interned in remote areas of the archipelago. He was released by the Japanese in Sumatra in 1942, after the invasion of the Dutch East Indies, and invited in the following year to Tokyo, where he was decorated by Gen. Tojo, the wartime Japanese Prime Minister. On the Japanese surrender in 1945, Sukarno and Mohammed Hatta, his closest collaborator in the nationalist movement, proclaimed the independence of Indonesia from Dutch rule and its republican status.

When in 1949 the Netherlands transferred power to the Indonesian nationalists, after a four-year war, Sukarno became the first president of the United States of Indonesia – the country's name being changed in 1950 to the Republic of Indonesia. His convening of the first Afro-Asian conference at Bandung in 1955 brought him a leading position and much prestige among the developing and non-aligned nations. Bitterly opposed to the formation of the Malaysian Federation, Sukarno was responsible for the unsuccessful "confrontation" with Britain. He took Indonesia out of the United Nations when Malaysia was elected to the Security Council; Indonesia re-entered the UN, however, under his successor, Gen. **Suharto**. For many years after independence, the internal position of Indonesia was extremely unstable and in 1959, under the name of "guided democracy", Sukarno instituted what was in effect a personal dictatorship. In 1963 he was made Life Chief of State, combining that office with the Premiership, which he had held since 1959.

Sukarno's fall from power stemmed from the abortive coup attempt of 1965, in which the **Communist Party of Indonesia** (PKI) was believed to be primarily implicated, and which was followed by the mass slaughter of PKI members and sympathizers. In March 1966 Sukarno conferred special powers on Gen. Suharto, the Army Commander, who outlawed the PKI, and in the following year his personal rule ended when he was deprived of all governmental and executive powers, and also of the title of Life President. Allegations of large-scale financial corruption were made against him at the time by the Supreme Court of Indonesia, while there were subsequent demands that he should stand trial for alleged links with the unsuccessful Communist coup of 1965. No further action was taken against him, however, and from 1967 he lived in retirement and, according to some reports, under virtual house arrest. He died on June 21, 1970, and was buried with State honours the following day at Blitar, in eastern Java, his birthplace.

Sukarno's posthumous rehabilitation led to his being designated in 1978 as a national hero and accepted as the "Father of Independence" (the title "Father of Development" being used to distinguish President Suharto).

DS

SUPERPOWER RIVALRY IN THE PACIFIC. The Pacific has been one of the crucial arenas in which the United States and the Soviet Union have played out their rivalry during the post-war period. This rivalry has been characterized by direct American involvement in two ground wars in Asia, by Soviet support for allies in North Korea and North Vietnam, by efforts to ensure that the rivalry did not result in direct military confrontation between Washington and

Moscow, by a search for bases to support power projection and naval activities, and by the additional uncertainty that stemmed from the presence of China as a third major power in the region. The Pacific has also been an area where the United States, essentially a maritime power, could play to its strengths.

The Pacific is a crucial strategic area for the United States and its allies. The rapid economic growth of the states around the Pacific basin and the growth of trade between the USA and these states have underlined the economic importance of the Pacific. Similarly, the growth of the Soviet Pacific fleet has underlined the significance of the region as an arena of superpower competition. It is further suggested that as the military uses of outer space increase the Pacific will become even more important because it contains "gateways" for satellite interception. It is also a region where there are many opportunities for more terrestrial disputes. Around the Pacific there are many indigenous conflicts, numerous territorial disputes, and local rivalries that occasionally erupt into low-level violence. Some of these regional conflicts have the potential for generating considerable mischief between the superpowers.

The rivalry between the superpowers in the Pacific has had something of a strange quality in that there has never been the kind of demarcation line between East and West that there was in the European theatre of the Cold War. It was also influenced by the tendency of the United States to elevate what were essentially local or regional issues to matters of immense symbolic importance, requiring an American response. The Korean War, for example, could have been seen as a civil war on the Korean peninsula, with no wider relevance. Instead it was interpreted in Washington as part of the Soviet global strategy, an interpretation which led to the militarization of containment in both Asia and Europe. Furthermore, even though the Eisenhower administration had emphasized that the major lesson of Korea was that the USA should not get involved in future ground wars in Asia, this lesson was forgotten in the 1960s as the prevailing notion became that of a monolithic communist bloc extending its influence over one country after another – a concept that was embodied in the image of falling dominoes. The strategic visions of US policy-makers encouraged the involvement in Vietnam which led, in turn, to the disintegration of the Cold War consensus that had upheld containment since the early 1950s.

In the aftermath of the Vietnam War there was some concern that the United States was ceasing to be an Asian power. To some extent this can be understood in terms of the reappraisal that had been undertaken by Nixon and Kissinger and which recognized not only that there was no longer a monolithic adversary in Asia but that with skill it would be possible to play the two major communist powers against each other as part of a system of triangular diplomacy. In these circumstances some retrenchment was possible without undermining American security interests. The withdrawal from Vietnam and the very divisive debate over overseas commitments that occurred in the United States during the early 1970s also contributed to the belief that the USA was about to go beyond military retrenchment to political disengagement. President Carter's announcement in 1977 that the United States was to withdraw its ground forces from South Korea by the early 1990s increased these fears. In the event the withdrawal of troops from South Korea was shelved, and it became apparent in the early 1980s that US interests in the region remained substantial, as did the level of its involvement and its military presence. These interests though were primarily off-shore. The US containment strategy in Asia has always had a significant maritime and off-shore dimension – based on Japan, Taiwan and the Philippines – and it is when the United States has gone beyond this to military involvement on the mainland of Asia that it has encountered most difficulties in obtaining its objectives.

It was not entirely surprising, therefore, that the reassertion of American power that was evident in the early 1980s in Asia (as part of a global resurgence initiated by the Reagan administration) was centred primarily on sea power. In response to the decline of the Navy in both numbers and quality of ships that occurred during the 1970s the Reagan administration committed itself to the goal of a 600-ship navy. The US Navy itself formulated a new strategy for utilizing its capabilities. This strategy, known as the Maritime Strategy, was initially enunciated in global terms and challenged the predominance of the Atlantic region in American strategic planning that had been evident under President Carter. John Lehman, Secretary of the Navy for much of the Reagan era, emphasized that US "security interests in the Pacific . . . are of equal importance to our other global commitments. No longer is it feasible for us to plan to swing the entire Pacific fleet in support of NATO in a global war. That is why we must expand the fleet".

The renewed emphasis on military operations in the Pacific was partly a response to increased Soviet naval activity. The Soviet Pacific Fleet has increased significantly since the late 1960s and has expanded from 25 to 32 per cent of Soviet naval strength. The Pacific Fleet is the largest of the four Soviet fleets and includes 32 nuclear missile-firing submarines, half of which are capable of hitting targets in the United States from the Sea of Okhotsk, two aircraft carriers, 80 major surface warships, 76 missile and attack submarines, and 21 amphibious ships. The Pacific Fleet Air Force has 110 bombers and 170 anti-submarine aircraft. Although this is a formidable array of power, there are also significant weaknesses in the Soviet posture. While the Fleet has several bases around the Kamchatka Peninsula and the Sea of Okhotsk, these bases could prove to be highly vulnerable during hostilities. Furthermore, those ships in the Sea of Japan would have to move through straits that would be controlled by hostile forces in order to get into the Pacific.

The United States Maritime Strategy can be understood as a response both to the increase in the strength of the Soviet Pacific Fleet and to the continued vulnerabilities that are evident in the Soviet posture. The Maritime Strategy presupposes that the USA, in the event of a major conflict with the Soviet Union, could exploit these vulnerabilities. Accordingly the United States has adopted a forward offensive strategy that would include attacks against the Soviet nuclear submarine bastions and against the Soviet bases. Part of the rationale for this is that it would place Soviet forces on the defensive and this would prevent them from attacking US and allied shipping. The United States would maintain control of the sea lines of communication not through convoys and other measures associated with "defensive sea control" but through offensive sea control. By moving forward early in a crisis the US Navy would place Soviet forces on the defensive and contain it behind the key choke points. The forces deployed in and around Japan would be crucial in this role.

The forward strategy has been criticized not only as being overly provocative and liable to prove destabilizing in a crisis but also as unrealistic. By carrying the battle to the enemy the US carriers would go "in harm's way" and incur the risk of serious attrition. Although the impact of the Maritime Strategy on crisis stability remains a potential problem the vulnerability argument about US forces is less persuasive now that the USA has deployed Tomahawk cruise missiles on many of its ships. The sea-launched cruise missiles, which have a range of 1,350 miles and can carry either nuclear or conventional warheads, significantly augment the striking power of the US navy and give the Maritime Strategy a credibility that might otherwise be lacking. In this connection, it is significant that the United States has insisted on Japan taking on more of the burden for its own defence, thereby freeing US forces for the more offensive roles and missions.

The Maritime Strategy contributes to American credibility as a Pacific power and provides added confidence to US allies in the region that the United States would honour its commitments in the event of aggression. Yet the forward elements of the strategy, as well as the fact that it reflects a more assertive approach by the USA, has raised the level of competition in the Pacific during the 1980s. In 1982 the US Pacific Fleet held exercises in the Sea of Japan for the first time since the late 1960s, and over a three-month period had eight carrier battle groups moving to support contingencies in South Korea and elsewhere. This was intended to display to the Soviet Union that the United States was still a Pacific power to be reckoned with. As the Chief of Naval Operations, Admiral Watkins, put it: "we were back in the vicinity of the western reaches of the Aleutian islands, within 500 miles of Petropavlovsk". Although these exercises near Soviet waters were criticized by some commentators as provocative, they seem to have encouraged a reappraisal of Soviet force deployment patterns which has resulted in a more defensive posture based on the bastions.

This is not to deny that the Soviet Union would be a formidable enemy in the event of a maritime conflict in the Pacific. The bases in Vietnam, even though they would be vulnerable in hostilities, have given Soviet forces greater sustainability. And while it is clear that Soviet forces lack the command control and communications architecture that the United States has built up in the region, doubts over the future of the American bases in the Philippines as well as the cuts in the defence budget during Reagan's second term and under President Bush (which mean that the 600-ship navy is unlikely to be achieved) result in uncertainty over the long-term future of American maritime preponderance. Yet the extensiveness of the infrastructure which supports this preponderance is impressive and even if the United States is forced to leave the bases in the Philippines, it has contingency plans for relocating them elsewhere. Unless the Soviet Union obtained the use of the bases, therefore, the USA would not be unduly disadvantaged. Indeed, the bases in the Philippines form part of a Pacific network of forward bases that the Soviet Union can only envy. There are around 39,000 US military personnel based in Japan, over 40,000 in South Korea, and around 15,000 in the Philippines. These support the formidable array of maritime capabilities that was outlined above.

If American preponderance in the Pacific may be challenged during the 1990s it is unlikely to disappear. Yet it is a preponderance that may be more important for purposes of denial or deterrence than for advancement. Indeed, it is clear that mutual deterrence is fairly robust in the Pacific. Neither the Soviet Union nor the United States has embarked upon high-risk ventures and both have exerted restraint on allies who have the capability to drag them into direct confrontation. If the *status quo* seems likely to endure at the military level, however, there is considerable potential for political development. Much of the competition between the superpowers takes on a political form, and much of this has centred on the relationship with China. The biggest shift in the balance of power in the Pacific was not the result of introducing a particular weapons system or even the US disengagement from Vietnam. Rather it was the Sino-Soviet schism. Similarly the Sino-Soviet detente which evolved during the 1980s and was crystallized by Gorbachev's visit to Beijing in 1989, marks an important political if not strategic gain for the Soviet Union. It also suggests, however, that the political competition between Moscow and Washington for the allegiance of the Chinese People's Republic could become more intense in the future. Yet this has to be set against a background in which **Gorbachev** has changed the thrust of the Soviet approach to the Pacific. Rather than following the kind of assertive policy that has often proved counter-productive in the past, Gorbachev initiated a more co-operative approach. In a major speech on the Pacific at Vladivostok in July 1986 he outlined his vision for a new approach to the Pacific. His starting point was the danger of current trends. As he put it, "the Pacific region has not as yet been militarized to the extent that has taken place in Europe. But the potentialities for its militarization are truly immense, and the consequences are extremely dangerous". In order to avert these consequences Gorbachev proposed a "conference in the mould of the Helsinki Conference to be attended by all the countries gravitating towards the ocean". Although this has not yet led to concrete measures, it has changed the climate of the debate about the Pacific and raised the possibility that the military confrontation between the superpowers – which has something of a diffuse nature – might be scaled down. This competition is unlikely to disappear during the 1990s, but it may be regulated and controlled to a far greater degree than in the past. The Pacific is unlikely to cease being a zone of competition between the superpowers, but might at least become a zone of relatively safe competition based upon mutual acceptance of explicit rules of the game.

PW

SUTRISNO, GEN. TRY. Gen. Try Sutrisno was installed as Commander-in-Chief of the Indonesian Armed Forces on Feb. 27, 1988, succeeding Gen. L.B. (Benny) Murdani. His appointment marked the final accession of the so-called "academy" trained generation of officers to full control of the armed forces. He is a devout Muslim and is widely regarded as a major contender for the post-**Suharto** leadership.

Sutrisno was born in Surabaya in 1935, and after the revolution he was a member of the first graduating class (1959) of the Bandung Army Technical Academy. In 1974 he was appointed a Presidential aide-de-camp, a post he held until 1978. After a short period as Chief-of-Staff in the Udayana command in Bali, he became the first of the new generation to be appointed to a regional command in Java – the Jakarta command in 1982. In 1985 he became Deputy Chief-of-Staff of the Army and the following year he was appointed Chief-of-Staff. In September 1988 he was appointed chairman of the newly created security agency, Bakorstanas.

DS

T

TA MOK. Close associate of **Pol Pot** during the 1970s and 1980s; said to be in command (by 1987) of 10,000 *Khmer Rouge* guerrillas in northern Cambodia. A native of Takeo province, his career remains remarkably obscure. He was already involved in radical activity by 1950, and a member of the central committee of the **Kampuchean Communist Party** by 1963. He is said to have been one of the most brutal among the leaders of the Democratic Kampuchea regime of 1975-78.

RBS

TAIWAN (REPUBLIC OF CHINA). *Population*: 20,000,000 (est. 1989). *Area*: 36,000 sq km. *Gross National Product*: US$119,661 million (1988). *Trade Volume*: US$110,237 million (1988). *Top five trading partners*: USA, Japan, Hong Kong, Federal Republic of Germany, United Kingdom (1987). *Defence spending*: US$7,740 million. *Education spending*: US$3,820 million. (The ROC Statistical Data Book treats the expenses for defence and general administrative expenses and those for education, science and culture as one item without further differentiation.) *Urban population as percentage of total*: 66.3 (1978). *Birth rate*: 17.2 per thousand (1988). *Life expectancy*: 74 (1987).

Political history. Established in the wake of the Hsin-hai Revolution in October 1911 that brought an end to monarchical rule, the Republic of China (ROC) has been ruled by the **Kuomintang (KMT)** since 1927. After its defeat in the Civil War against the **Chinese Communist Party** the government moved to Taiwan in December 1949 and established its temporary capital in Taipei.

Since then, the territory under effective control of the government of the ROC is limited to the island of Taiwan, the Pescadores, and several island groups along the coast of mainland China, most notably Kinmen (Quemoy) and Matsu.

Taiwan had been restored to Chinese sovereignty after the defeat of Japan in 1945, after a 50-year period of Japanese colonial rule. This change was initially welcomed in Taiwan, but mismanagement by the new administration created tensions that led to a revolt in 1947, the **February 28 incident.** Its bloody suppression by Nationalist armed forces led to strained relations with the native Taiwanese and the approximately 1,500,000 mainland refugees that came to Taiwan in 1949 and 1950.

The Nationalist government considers itself to be the sole legitimate government of China, staking its claim on the constitution of 1947 and the representative bodies elected in 1948. According to the constitution the republic is founded on the Three Principles of the People, the main teachings of Sun Yat-sen, comprising Nationalism. Democracy and Welfare. The political institutions of the Republic consist of the president of the Republic, the National Assembly (NA) and five Yüan, also in accord with the teachings of Sun Yat-sen. The president is elected for a six-year term by the NA, which also has the power to amend the constitution. The Executive Yüan, the government of the ROC, is elected by the Legislative Yüan, the highest legislative organ. In addition to the Judicial Yüan, comprising a council of grand judges, who interpret the constitution, laws and decrees, the supreme court, an administrative court and the disciplinary commission, the Examination Yüan is responsible for the selection of public functionaries, while the Control Yüan as the highest supervisory organ has extensive powers of auditing, censure, consent and impeachment of government institution and personnel. The provincial level consists of only three units, Taiwan province and the special municipalities of Kaohsiung and Taipei, plus two counties of Fukien province.

Political development in Taiwan has been strongly influenced by the fact that its government is still engaged in a Civil War with the Chinese Communists. Since the end of 1948, the Constitution has been modified by several temporary provisions. The adoption of the "temporary provisions effective during the period of Communist rebellion" by the Legislative Yüan in 1948 changed the institutional structure of the ROC, considerably enlarging the scope of presidential powers, most notably through making the president the Commander-in-Chief of the armed forces and the establishment of the National Security Council. Under martial law, in force since 1949, the press and the media are controlled by the government. Public meetings, strikes, demonstrations, petitions and the "spreading of rumours" as well as the establishment of political parties are forbidden. Several hundred people were still detained for political reasons in the early 1980s, including alleged "communist agents" as well as "rebels" of the Formosan Independence Movement.

Although two small political parties, the Young China Party and the Democratic Socialist Party, also moved to Taiwan in 1949, they were unable to challenge the power of the KMT, which has established a *de facto* one-party system. Since his reinstatement as president of the republic in 1950, **Chiang Kai-shek** dominated the political scene on Taiwan, both as president and chairman of the KMT, till his death in 1975. His candidacy for a third term in office, running contrary to the stipulations of the Constitution, created considerable opposition. To enable further terms of office the NA voted in February 1960 to suspend the constitutional stipulation that limited the number of presidential terms. His role as pre-eminent leader was inherited by his son **Chiang Ching-kuo**, who took over the chairmanship of the KMT in 1975 and was elected president in 1978.

The 1970s saw a decline in the international position of the ROC. It was expelled from the United Nations, its most important allies (Japan and the USA) broke relations with the ROC in order to recognize the People's Republic of China (PRC). The endangering of Taiwan's international position had the unexpected effect of bringing the mainlanders and the Taiwanese closer together. As Peking considered both the Nationalist government and the Taiwan Independence Movement illegal, international isolation meant that they now faced the same fragile future. Under the premiership of Chiang Ching-kuo a policy of promoting Taiwanese citizens to offices in the government and party bureaucracies was introduced. The number of Taiwanese in all levels of government increased. Several prestigious positions like the vice-presidency or the governor of Taiwan province were henceforth occupied by Taiwanese.

Political participation by the inhabitants of Taiwan was initially limited to the provincial and local levels, while members of the national parliaments continued to hold their mandates until free elections could be held in their electoral districts on the Chinese mainland. Responding to changing conditions in Taiwan the government in 1968 conducted the first elections on the national level since 1948, thus giving the population a chance to elect replacements for vacated seats in the national parliaments. Since 1972 supplementary elections have been conducted regularly. The number of seats contested in these elections has increased to 73 in the Legislative Yüan and 84 in the NA in the 1986 supplementary elections.

The decline of the ROC's international position and the effects of socio-economic change on the island itself favoured the evolution of the political opposition. Taking advantage of election campaigns to propagate their views to a wider audience it grew organizationally as well as programmatically during the 1970s. In spite of several stirring electoral victories the political opposition has posed no serious challenge to the KMT, which consistently won around 70 per cent of the vote in national elections during the last decade.

Recent developments. The process of political liberalization gained momentum in March 1986. The KMT decided to end martial law in the near future and began a process of deliberation on policies leading to the establishment of new political parties, the rejuvenation of the national parliaments and the strengthening of local self-government vis-à-vis the central government.

Reacting to these developments members of the opposition founded the **Democratic Progress Party (Taiwan)** in September 1986. Although the formation of the party contravened Taiwan's martial law regulations it was allowed to contest the elections.

On July 14, 1987, martial law, which had been in force in Taiwan for 38 years, was lifted. It was replaced by a National Security Law. A Civic Organizations Law regulated the formation of new parties provided they fulfil a number of strict requirements. By June 1989 16 political parties were officially registered by the Ministry of the Interior, 13 of them having been newly established.

The government's attitude towards relations with the Chinese mainland also began to change. Visits to the mainland by Taiwan residents were permitted from October 1986, ostensibly to enable people to visit relatives. Although still opposed to intensified economic contacts with China the government ceased to take measures against Taiwanese businessmen investing in factories on the mainland, provided they operate via third countries.

Chiang Ching-kuo, president of the ROC and chairman of the KMT, died on Jan. 12, 1988. He was succeeded by **Lee Teng-hui**, hitherto vice-president. Lee is the first native Taiwanese to be appointed head of state, the previous incumbents having been born in mainland China. He also succeeded Chiang Ching-kuo as chairman of the KMT.

Foreign relations. The ROC's foreign policy has been strongly influenced by the conflict with the Chinese Communists, both governments striving for international recognition of their claim to be the sole legitimate government of China. Since the 1970s the ROC's insistence on this claim has accelerated its growing diplomatic isolation. The

ROC's main foreign ally has been the USA. Since 1949, the relations between the two states passed through phases of different intensity. Immediately after the Nationalists' flight to Taiwan, the USA adopted a policy of indifference towards the survival of the ROC. Following the outbreak of the Korean war in 1950, it began to actively support Taiwan, providing it with military aid and supporting the ROC's position in the United Nations against claims by the PRC. In December 1954, the ROC signed a mutual defence pact with the United States. Attempts by the Communists to take Quemoy and Matsu in the autumn of 1954 and in 1958 were repeatedly frustrated by Nationalists resistance under American encouragement.

During the Nixon administration, American interest in a rapprochement with the PRC became predominant, accordingly its relations with the ROC turned from an asset to an obligation. Even after de-recognition in 1978, relations with the USA continue to be of utmost importance for Taiwan. Although of unofficial character, the Taiwan Relations Act (TRA), passed by the American Congress in 1979, provides a legal basis for relations between both states. The TRA provides for cultural, commercial and other unofficial relations with the people of Taiwan, stressing continued American interest in the safety of Taiwan and its intention to provide it with arms needed for self-defence.

The United States is Taiwan's main supplier of armaments. Recurring differences in the assessment of Taiwan's military needs as well as the continuing efforts of the PRC to forestall further sales of American weapons to the island have induced the ROC to strive for a high degree of self-sufficiency in armament. The ROC has developed a fighter aircraft and several types of missiles, other segments of its defence industry are also expanding.

The gradual emergence of the PRC from its isolation during the 1960s and '70s negatively affected the ROC's international position. On Oct. 25, 1971, the UN General Assembly recognized the PRC as the representative of China to the United Nations, and the PRC replaced the ROC in the General Assembly and the Security Council. The Nationalist delegation withdrew in protest. This event produced a bandwagon psychology among other nations, who terminated diplomatic relations with the ROC in order to recognize the PRC as the legal government of China.

In the early 1980s the ROC maintained diplomatic relations with only 21 nations, among them only South Africa, South Korea, Saudi Arabia and the Vatican possess significant international status. It also lost its membership in most international organizations, the only exception being the **Asian Development Bank**.

Faced with growing international isolation, the ROC's foreign policy concentrated on developing so-called "substantial relations" with countries with whom it did not maintain official relations, stressing economic and trade relations, instead. At present, it maintains 91 diplomatic or representative offices in 65 countries. Relying on its increasing economic might Taiwan has begun to pursue an active foreign policy aimed at re-entering international organizations and strengthening its international presence. The government decided to adopt a flexible approach, walking a thin line between legitimacy and practicality.

The Nationalist government holds fast to its aim of recovering the mainland and an eventual reunification of China. Unable to achieve this by military means in the past, it now conceives of this task primarily as a political endeavour. The government's reaction to the more conciliatory approaches by the PRC, suggesting the establishment of direct contacts and economic relations, have been primarily defensive, symbolized by the "Three No" policy of no contacts, no negotiations, no compromise. Since 1986 the policy towards China has become more flexible, allowing Taiwan residents to visit their relatives on the Chinese mainland and admitting a limited number of inhabitants of the mainland to Taiwan. Direct telephone and telecommunication links were also established. In May 1989, the government decided that a delegation from Taiwan would go to Peking and attend the annual meeting of the Asian Development Bank.

Outline of economic development. During Japanese colonial rule, Taiwan's economy was developed as an integral part of the Japanese empire, providing raw and processed materials for consumption and further manufacture in the Japanese islands. The Japanese developed a transport infrastructure with good roads and ports as well as food processing industries. Intensive development efforts in agriculture had accustomed the peasantry to technological changes. During the last phase of the Pacific War extensive damage to transportation and productive facilities was caused by Allied bombing.

The defeat on the mainland awakened the KMT to the importance of social and economic reform. Its development policies on Taiwan thus not only aimed at economic growth, but also at an equitable distribution of its results. In 1949 the government started a programme of land reform, thereby fulfilling Sun Yat-sen's "land to the tiller" ideal. Its three stages consisted of a compulsory reduction of the annual land rent from the prevailing 50–70 per cent to 37.5 per cent of the main crop. Tenant farmers were given a written lease that was valid for a period of at least six years. By these measures, the livelihood of 300,000 farm families was substantially improved.

The second stage of the land reform programme began in 1951 with the sale of 430,000 acres of public land, at a purchase price of two and a half times the annual yield of the main crop, repayable in 20 six-monthly instalments at 4 per cent interest.

The last stage was launched by the government in 1953. Private and tenanted land had to be sold to the government, which resold it to farmers at the same price while charging a 4 per cent annual interest. No less than 193,823 families benefited from these measures, bringing the total number of landowning families to 400,000. The completion of this programme reduced tenancy considerably. In the 1960s tenants operated only 10 per cent of the land, while 90 per cent was tilled by owners.

Agriculture provided the basis for economic development during the 1950s. Farm yields have shown an annual increase of 4.4 per cent during the last 25 years and cover about 80 per cent of the population's food requirements.

Industrial development also proceeded in several stages. After an initial period (1945–52) of rehabilitation of industrial machinery, the government launched a series of Four-Year Economic Development Plans. During the first phase import substitution policies in the areas of chemical fertilizers, textiles and cement were stressed. With US aid both inflation and exchange rate devaluation were overcome in the late 1950s. Between 1958 and 1963 steps towards a liberalization of trade and foreign exchange were taken. Due to structural changes in the economy the share of agricultural products in Taiwan's exports fell to 50 per cent in 1960. Per capita real income grew at an average annual rate of 3 per cent.

During the second stage, from 1963 to 1973, Taiwan's economy underwent sustained growth. The government encouraged foreign investments and stimulated exports. Export processing zones for manufactured exports, industrial parks and transportation infrastructure were established. Per capita real GNP grew at an average rate of 7 per cent a year. The change of export structure continued and the percentage of agricultural products decreased further to 17 per cent while that of industrial products rose to 83 per cent. Within this category 90 per cent were manufactured products. The electronics industry grew fastest in this period, attracting the largest share

of foreign investment and exporting most of its output. Other important export industries were textiles, exporting about 60 per cent of its output, and chemical industries. The ratio of exports to GNP rose to around 50 per cent.

During the 1970s Taiwan's economy was exposed to the effects of the first oil crisis. The decline in export sales and domestic private investment was offset by the government through an economic stabilization programme and measures to deepen the industrial base and to upgrade its transportation infrastructure. The "10 great projects", implemented in the period 1973–1979, were designed to build a heavy industrial base and to improve the basic utilities, road, rail and port facilities needed in a modern industrial state. Taiwan's ecomony recovered quickly from the recession, between 1973 and 1982 its GNP rose at an average annual rate of 9.5 per cent.

Taiwan's successful economic development has been strongly influenced by the government's effectiveness in promoting economic modernization, primarily through policies designed to restructure economic incentives, to shift resources from low to high value-added products and to achieve equilibrium within the economic system by offsetting scarcities. Government policies also aimed at an equitable distribution of income among the population, with the highest 20 per cent income bracket only four times as great as the lowest 20 per cent.

Recent developments. The economic consequences of de-recognition were limited. Although confidence in the economy was shaken initially, the Taiwan Relations Act removed some of the concern over the island's ability to weather the diplomatic and economic storm. In order to overcome the effects of rapidly rising wage levels, making Taiwan's exports increasingly less competitive in its traditional labour-intensive industries, as well as the tightening export quotas on many of these industries, the government adopted a number of measures to promote investment in capital- and technology-intensive industries. As part of this shift in strategy, the government established the Hsinchu Science and Technology Park. The new strategic industries, which will become the island's growth industries in the near future, include machinery, machine tools, computer, microcomputer, and telecommunication items. In a related development Taiwan's labour-intensive industries began to move abroad in growing numbers, preferred locations being the PRC, Thailand, Indonesia and the Philippines, where Taiwanese investment in 1988 surpassed that of the USA and Japan.

Growing surpluses in Taiwan's foreign trade

and foreign reserves of more than US$70,000 million in 1987, put increasing pressure on the government to liberalize Taiwan's economy and to lower import barriers. Friction has been especially strong with the United States, Taiwan's main export market, where its surplus in the balance of trade exceeded US$10,000 million for several consecutive years. In response, Taiwan intensified its efforts for market diversification, lifting the ban on direct and indirect trade with Communist states in Eastern Europe, and began to look for increased indirect trade with the PRC via Hong Kong. In order to stimulate imports, the government adopted comprehensive tariff reductions and a revaluation of the NT dollar, whose value in relation to the US dollar increased by 18 per cent in 1987.

HH

TAIWAN RELATIONS ACT. When the American administration under President Carter decided to establish diplomatic relations with the People's Republic of China (PRC) on Jan. 1, 1979, formal diplomatic relations with the Republic of China on Taiwan had to be terminated. At the time of establishment of relations with the PRC the American Congress made clear its intention to maintain, on an unofficial basis, trade, cultural and other relations with Taiwan.

Although President and Congress concurred in their intentions to maintain an unofficial relationship with Taiwan on a legal basis, the President's legislative draft was less inclusive than Congress had expected. The Taiwan Relations Act (TRA) enacted by both Houses of Congress (Public Law 96-8) in April 1979, therefore contained a number of clauses not included in the presidential draft.

In the TRA's preamble Congress declared the United States' continuing interest in a peaceful solution of Taiwan's future. Any other solution would endanger peace and security in the western Pacific and be of grave concern to the USA, which would continue to provide Taiwan with arms of defensive character and resist any resort to force or other forms of coercion that would jeoparize the security, or the social and economic system, of the people on Taiwan.

Although the TRA stated unequivocally that "the US will make available to Taiwan such defence articles and defence services in such quantity as may be necessary to enable Taiwan to maintain a sufficient self-defence capability", this passage has given rise to contention. Taiwan's armament requirements, as far as the USA is concerned, are determined by the American President. Due to differing assessments of Taiwan's situation there have been continuing debates concerning arms requirements between Taiwan and the USA as well as between Congress and the Administration.

In the absence of diplomatic missions relations between the two sides are maintained by non-profit corporations. The USA established the American Institute on Taiwan; the Co-ordination Council for North American Affairs serves as its counterpart on Taiwan. Both are staffed with personnel from the diplomatic service on temporary leave. The institutions maintain representative offices in the other nation's capital as well as a number of branch organizations in other cities. In October 1980 both sides concluded an agreement on privileges, exemptions and immunities granting offices and staffs of the two organizations a status equal to that accorded to international organizations and their personnel.

HH

TAKESHITA NOBORU. Takeshita looked set to be Japanese Prime Minister of substance when he became president of the **Liberal Democratic Party** (LDP) in 1987. He had secured control of the **Tanaka** faction, far and away the largest single block of votes in the LDP, and had a reputation as a master of campaigning and political organization. In the event he did not survive a single term but was driven from office by the public outcry over the **Recruit Scandal**. Even without formal office he cannot be less than a formidable power broker within the party and a major influence on the government of the day.

RAB

TANAKA KAKUEI. The name of former prime minister Tanaka Kakuei (prime minister from 1972 to 1974) is synonymous with political corruption by virtue of the Lockheed scandal, an affair in which the Lockheed Aircraft Company, acting through the Marubeni Corporation, sought to influence the Japanese government in its efforts to win the contract to supply aircraft (the Lockheed Tristar) to All Nippon Airways, Japan's principal domestic airline. This led to the payment of substantial sums of money to influential go-betweens. Tanaka was one of these.

RAB

TEAM SPIRIT. Team Spirit is a military exercise between the United States and South Korean forces which began in 1976 and has taken place on an annual basis ever since. The exercises have involved not only 43,000 US military personnel deployed in South Korea but also major reinforcements from elsewhere in the Pacific. In April 1988, a few months before the Olympic Games were to take place in Seoul, the annual exercise included a US naval task force of 34 ships drawn from the Seventh Fleet and involved an amphibious landing by 1,000 marines and M-60 tanks. The exercises usually involve over 200,000 personnel.

The annual exercise has become a source of dispute and tension between North and South Korea. Although the United States and South Korea both emphasize that the exercises are defensive in character and intended simply to enhance deterrence on the Korean peninsula, the exercises are vehemently denounced by North Korea. In 1988, for example, Pyongyang accused Washington of "stirring up war fever". In addition, North Korea, in response to the exercise, usually places its own forces on a higher state of alert and on several occasions, has broken off negotiations with South Korea only to resume them after the exercise was over. In January 1986, for example, two days before the sixth North-South economic meeting, North Korea announced the indefinite postponement of the dialogue because of Team Spirit. The South Koreans claimed that rather than being a nuclear war manoeuvre aimed against North Korea, Team Spirit was simply a training exercise. They also claimed that they routinely inform the North of the impending exercise and have even invited observers.

There has been some evidence, however, that as the dialogue between North and South Korea has improved, at least intermittently, South Korea has recognized that the annual exercise can have a disruptive effect. In January 1989 there were reports in South Korean newspapers that Team Spirit would be scaled down in 1989 and might even be cancelled in 1990. This was denied by a military spokesman who claimed that the authorities had not considered the possibility of reducing the scale of their exercise let alone terminating it. In spite of these denials there appears to have been considerable debate in official circles in Seoul about whether or not the exercises should be modified.

While they are clearly an irritant to the North, the annual Team Spirit exercises are important in reaffirming the United States commitment to South Korea – and will become even more significant if there is a reduction in the US presence on the peninsula. On the other hand, if the dialogue between the two Koreas makes progress then Seoul might well decide that there could be advantages in scaling down the exercise after all.

PW

TERRORISM. The Pacific region in recent years has been relatively free of terrorism, compared to the more troubled areas of the Middle East and Europe. In the 1970s, Japan produced a notorious international terrorist cell known as the Japanese Red Army Faction, but that seems largely to have been suppressed. Japanese terrorists held hostages in the French embassy in the Hague in 1974, until a negotiated release was arranged.

Terror tactics have been used in various parts of Latin America, often in association with guerrilla movements. Currently, such criminal behaviour and intimidation can be found in Peru (often associated with the Shining Path guerrillas) and countries with a severe drugs problem, notably Colombia. Death squads are a disturbing feature of life in both Guatemala and El Salvador. In the latter, some of these have been linked to personalities in the right-wing ARENA coalition which now controls the country.

The United States is leading a high-profile international campaign to combat terrorism, partly because its own citizens have on occasions been the victims of terrorist activities abroad. Terrorism has featured on the agenda of the seven major western industrial nations (which include Canada and Japan). These have agreed to upgrade international co-operation to counter the problem, through such agencies as Interpol and national intelligence organizations. (*See also* **Guerrilla Movements**)

JF

THAILAND. *Population*: 54,700,000 (est. 1988). *Area*: 513,100 sq km. *Gross Domestic Product*: US$48,200 million (1987). *Trade (1988)* imports US$17,600 million, exports 14,700 million. *Top five trading partners*: (imports) Japan, United Kingdom, Singapore, West Germany and Malaysia; (exports) United States, Japan, Singapore, Netherlands and West Germany. *Defence spending*: US$1,714 million (1987–88). *Education spending*: US$1,749 million (1987–88). *Urban population as percentage of total*: 17. *Life expectancy*: 64. *Birth rate*: 29 per thousand.

Geographical background. The Kingdom of Thailand lies at the heart of mainland Southeast Asia. It is bordered to the west and north by Burma, to the north-east by Laos and to the south-east by Kampuchea. Thailand extends southward, along the isthmus of Kra, to the Malay Peninsula, where it borders Malaysia. As of 1988, just under 30 per cent of Thailand's total land area was forest compared with approximately 47 per cent under cultivation.

The capital, Bangkok, is by far the largest city in Thailand with a population approaching 5,500,000 in late 1986. Other principal towns include Songkhla, Chon Buri, Nakhon Si Thammarat and Chiang Mai. Between 1980 and 1987 Thailand's population increased by an average annual rate of 2.1 per cent and by the year 2000 it is estimated that the population will have risen to over 66,000,000.

Socio-political background. Thailand is populated by at least 20 different ethnic-linguistic groups. The Thais are the dominant grouping, but the northern areas of Thailand contain large concentrations of Lao people and a somewhat smaller number of **Hmong (Meo) People** or "hill tribes". **Theravada Buddhism** is the predominant religion, professed by over 95 per cent of the country's total population. Approximately 4 per cent of the population are Muslims, mainly in the southern provinces near Malaysia. There are a small number of Christians and most of the immigrant Chinese community are Confucians.

In 1988 Thailand claimed to have; (i) an 86 per cent literacy rate; (ii) 9,100,000 children in attendance at primary and secondary schools; and (iii) a 28,700,000-strong workforce.

Thailand is a constitutional monarchy with a bicameral National Assembly consisting of: (i) a 261-member Senate appointed by the King on the recommendation of the Prime Minister; and (ii) a 347-member House of Representatives elected for a four-year term by adult suffrage of persons 21 or more years old. The King appoints the Prime Minister, on the advice of the National Assembly, and the Council of Ministers, on the advice of the Prime Minister. Martial law was declared in 1976 and remains in force although some powers have been relaxed. The Armed Forces have traditionally played a prominent role in Thai politics.

Pre-modern history. The first historical Thai (Siamese) kingdom was established in 1238 in Sukothai, in what is today north-central Thailand. Sukothai had initially been under Khmer control, but the growth of the Thai population in the area had made it increasingly difficult for the Khmers to suppress assertions of Thai independence. Under the rule of King Ramkamheng, Thai influence expanded southwards in the late thirteenth and early fourteenth centuries. In the mid-fourteenth century a new Siamese state, Ayuthia, emerged at a point on the Chao Phraya river, hitherto the locus of a Mon civilization, that was attainable by sea-travelling ships. Ayuthia not only subsumed Sukothai, but pursued a successful policy of expansion, conquering the Khmer kingdom of Angkor and taking Burmese land to the west, Thai principalities in the north and Malay territories to the south. During the sixteenth and seventeenth centuries Ayuthia also involved itself in the developing trade between Europe and the Far East, particularly under the rule of King Narai (1657–88). Ayuthia remained as the capital of traditional Siam until 1767, when the ascendant Burmese attacked the city and laid it to waste.

A new Thai state centre was established by a war-lord, General Taksin, at Thonburi, at the mouth of the Chao Phraya river. He was overthrown in 1782 by the house of Chakri, and the capital was moved across the Chao Phraya to Bangkok. The rule of the first Chakri kings in the eighteenth and early nineteenth centuries was marked by attempts to re-impose Siamese authority over southern Laos, western Kampuchea and northern Malaysia. At the same time attempts were also made to strengthen their administrative hold over the various feudalities, or tributary states, which together constituted Siam.

Under the rule of King Chulalongkorn (Rama V, 1868–1910), a major restructuring of the state was undertaken. The restructuring was motivated partly by economic necessity, especially in an attempt to counter the effects of the Bowring Treaty imposed by Britain in 1855 to break the king's export monopoly. However, the reforms also arose out of the ruling elite's interest in Western ideas and technology. It is possible to identify two distinct phases of political re-organization: (i) the Chakri Reformation of 1872–1892, when reforms were introduced in finance, communications, transport, education and personnel administration; and (ii) the radical re-organization of 1892 when a Western-style council of ministers was established. By establishing a modern, bureaucratic monarchy and by yielding Lao and Kampuchean territory to France and Malay territory to Britain, King Chulalongkorn managed to maintain Siam as the sole South east Asian country to avoid colonial control.

Early modern history. King Chulalongkorn's "radical re-organization" of 1892 included the appointment of a 12-member council of ministers. The ministers were all members of the royal family, but their many subordinates in the burgeoning bureaucracy were drawn from the lower strata, having been recruited through the rapidly expanding educational system. In 1911 a civil service school was established, which admitted not only members of the old nobility (the *sakdina* class), but also members from "notable families or of means suitable to permit them to become royal pages". Once the new bureaucratic elite had been established it was only a short time before its members developed a system of (Western influenced) beliefs that conflicted with the old principles of royal absolutism. The process was hastened by the death of Chulalongkorn in 1910, and his replacement by the unpopular King Vajiravudh (Rama VI). In 1911 junior military officers failed in an attempt to overthrow the King in favour of a Republic.

The collapse of the international rice market during the Great Depression of the late 1920s–early 1930s created severe budgetary problems for Vajiravudh's successor, King Prajadhipok (Rama VII), who responded by making deep cuts in civil service and military spending. In 1932, a European-educated civilian-military group carried out a successful and bloodless coup d'etat (commonly referred to as a "revolution"), aimed at removing the country's absolute monarchical system in favour of a system modelled on the European constitutional monarchies. The ideological leader of the coup was Dr Pridi Phanomyang, accompanied by Col. Phahon Phomphayuhasena (representing the older generation of officers) and Maj. (later Field Marshal) Phibun Songkhram (representing the younger generation).

Political history. The 1932 coup initiated a confused and rapid chain of political events. Dr Pridi was quickly denounced as a communist and was forced into exile; a neutral civilian Prime Minister, Mano, was appointed; two constitutions, one provisional and one permanent, were promulgated; and, in 1933, Phibun led another successful coup, removing Mano and installing Col. Phahon (who was Army Commander-in-Chief at the time) as Prime Minister. Phahon suppressed a monarchist rebellion in October 1933 and elections were held the next month for half the seats in a National Assembly, as stipulated under the 1932 Constitution. Following the elections, Phahon introduced into his cabinet a younger circle of military officers led by Phibun (as Defence Minister), who quickly emerged as the country's ruling power bloc. Elections were held in 1937 and 1938, after which Phahon was retired and Phibun became Prime Minister.

Field Marshal Phibun immediately embarked on a militantly anti-Chinese and anti-Western campaign. An admirer of the fascist *Führerprinzip*, he stressed his position as the powerful leader of a modern society, and in 1939 Siam adopted the more nationalist name of Thailand. The Phibun regime collaborated with the Japanese invasion of Thailand in 1941, declaring war on the Allies early the next year. However, when it became evident that the Axis Powers were going to be defeated, Phibun's power base diminished. He was formally overthrown in mid-1944 by a vote of the National Assembly and was replaced by Khuang Aphaiwong, a civilian who enjoyed the support of Dr Pridi (who, during the War, had led the Free Thai Movement which had clandestinely co-operated with the Allies). After the Japanese surrender, Seni Pramoj (the Thai ambassador to Washington at the outbreak of the war and a leading figure in the Free Thai Movement) replaced Khuang as Prime Minister.

The post-war civilian interregnum (1945–47) was as chaotic as the interval immediately following the "1932 Revolution". Conflict and corruption within the bureaucratic polity meant that as many as 10 cabinets were formed by five civilian Prime Ministers. For a short time in mid-1946, Dr Pridi held the post of Premier, but he was forced to resign following the mysterious death of King Ananda (Rama VIII) in June. Finally, in late 1947, following a succession of weak governments, and emboldened by US "Cold War" rhetoric, the Army seized control. Although led by Gen. Phin Chunhawan, commander of the First (Bangkok) Region, the real motivation behind the coup came from Phibun, who officially took power again in April 1948. Vestiges of the brief period of post-war constitutional democracy remained in force until late 1951, when Phibun dissolved the National Assembly, abrogated the Constitution and banned all political parties. He reversed this hardline stance in 1955, in an attempt to outmanoeuvre his opponents within the military elite. He announced that elections would be held to a National Assembly in 1957 and reactivated the political process.

Phibun's belated flirtation with liberalism did little to stem the increasing power of Police General Phao Sriyanon and the Bangkok Army commander Gen. Sarit Thanarat. Both had large economic and military power bases, but Sarit had the advantage of close relations with the United States. Using Phibun's blatantly rigged elections as his opportunity, Sarit seized power in a bloodless coup in 1957, forcing both Phibun and Phao into exile. At first Sarit appointed Pote Sarasin (the secretary-general of SEATO) as Prime Minister, but in late 1958 he assumed full power himself, declaring martial law and dissolving all political parties. Sarit called for a restoration of the "old values", including (for the first time since the 1932 Revolution) an appeal for loyalty to the King.

Field Marshal Sarit died in 1963, and his two protegés, Gen. Thanom Kittikachorn (who had been his Prime Minister) and Gen. Praphat Charusathien, emerged as the new leaders of the ruling military power bloc. A Constitution was promulgated in 1968 and in February 1969 elections were held to a new National Assembly. In the freer atmosphere of the post-election period, liberal elements within the ruling elite began to express discontent with the general atmosphere of repression and the state of the economy. To contain these rising tensions, Praphat and Thanom staged a coup in late 1971, again annulling the Constitution, dissolving the National Assembly and declaring martial law under a military junta called the National Executive Council. During 1972 student-led demonstrations began and at the end of the year, a new interim Constitution was promulgated giving widespread powers to Gen. Thanom. At the same time a new National Assembly was appointed with military and police representatives holding 200 of the 299 seats.

As the student unrest increased and spread to other sections of Thai society during 1973, military leaders gradually withdrew their support from Thanom and Praphat. Finally, in October 1973 the Army Commander-in-Chief, Gen. Krit Siwara, and **King Bhumibol Adulyadej** both withdrew their support from the regime and it quickly collapsed. The King appointed an interim government under Dr Sanya Dharmasakti, the President of the Privy Council. A new Constitution was promulgated in October 1974, which again legalized political parties. Elections to a new House of Representatives held in January 1975 were contested by over 40 parties, none of which achieved a working majority. In February, a coalition government was formed by Seni Pramoj (leader of the **Democrat Party** – DP), which survived for a month before suffering a defeat during a vote of "no confidence". Kukrit Pramoj (Seni's brother) formed a fresh coalition government, headed by his **Social Action Party**, which lasted until Kukrit's resignation in January 1976. The DP greatly increased its representation in an election held that April, and Seni formed another coalition government. The election campaign was marred by serious violence, with over 30 deaths, including three candidates.

Seni's government was overthrown by a military coup on Oct. 6, 1976, when a junta calling itself the "National Administrative Reform Council" (NARC) seized power. The military had moved after a day of serious unrest in Bangkok, as armed police and right-wing extremists (including *Nawapon* members, Red Guards and Village Scouts) stormed the capital's Thammasat University, killing at least 40 students. The attack was the culmination of months of destabilizing political violence carried out by the extreme right. The students had barricaded themselves in the university in early October in protest at the return from exile in September of Field Marshal Thanom.

The first statement issued by the NARC declared that "a group of students had committed *lèse majesté*" as "part of the communist scheme to take over Thailand". Orders issued subsequently proclaimed martial law, annulled the 1974 Constitution, dissolved the National Assembly and the cabinet, and vested the powers and the duties of the Prime Minister and the cabinet in the hands of the NARC Chairman (Adm. Sangad Chaloryu), who was declared Supreme Commander of the armed forces and the civil service. Other orders issued during the night of Oct. 6-7 dissolved all political parties and forbade the formation of new ones and imposed strict press censorship. A new Constitution was promulgated on Oct. 22, under which the NARC took on the role of a Prime Ministerial Advisory Council. A Cabinet was appointed on the same day headed by Thanin Kraivichen, a right-wing Supreme Court judge. In accordance with the new Constitution, King Bhumibol appointed a 340-member (military-dominated) advisory National Administrative Reform Assembly in mid-November.

A military coup was attempted in Bangkok in March 1977 but was suppressed within a few hours; the leader of the coup, Gen. Chalard Hiranyasiri, was shot without trial in mid-April. On Oct. 20, Thanin Kraivichen's government was overthrown by a "Revolutionary Council" of high-ranking military officers, the composition of which was almost identical with the NARC which had carried out the 1976 coup. The "Revolutionary Council", led by Adm. Sa-ngad, stated in a broadcast that they had taken power because there was "disunity among government officials and among the people". Orders were issued abrogating the 1976 Constitution and dissolving the National Administrative Reform Assembly. An interim constitution, the provisions of which were largely similar to the 1976 constitution, was promulgated in November under which the members of the "Revolutionary Council" would form a National Policy Council (NPC), the King would appoint a Prime Minister and a National Legislative Assembly (NLA) on the advice of the NPC Chairman, and the Assembly would appoint a committee to draft a fresh constitution. The King appointed Gen. Kriangsak Chamanan (secretary-general of the NPC and supreme commander of the Armed Forces) as Prime Minister in mid-November; a 360-member NLA (over 60 per cent of whom were military officers) was subsequently appointed by royal proclamation.

In December 1978 the NLA approved a new Constitution (the 12th since 1932), which remained in force as of mid-1989. A ban on political parties and political gatherings was lifted in January 1979 and in April national elections were held for a 301-member House of Representatives. The SAP, led by Kukrit Pramoj, gained the largest number of seats (82). The 225-member Senate appointed by Gen. Kriangsak after the elections consisted almost entirely of members of the armed forces. A joint session of the new parliament in early May asked Gen. Kriangsak to form another administration. A new Cabinet was formed in late May, and of the 43 ministers and deputy ministers, only eight were MPs compared with 17 members of the armed forces or police.

An economic crisis caused by accelerating inflation and an increasingly adverse balance of payments, led to two changes of government in the first three months of 1980. Gen. Kriangsak formed a new Cabinet in early February, but resigned at the end of the month to avoid a parliamentary vote of no confidence and was succeeded by Gen. Prem Tinsulanonda, the Army Commander-in-Chief and Defence Minister. Gen. Prem formed a Government in March, which included an increased number of MPs, drawn in the main from the SAP, the Democrat Party and *Chart Thai*. In March 1981, Gen. Prem formed a new Government after a Cabinet crisis had led to the resignation of 13 members of his previous government.

A group of Army officers seized control of Bangkok on April 1, but the attempted coup collapsed two days later. The coup attempt was organized by a group of about 20 colonels nicknamed the "Young Turks" (after the secret society of officers responsible for the Turkish revolution of 1908), the most prominent of whom were Col. Prachak Sawangchit, commander of the 2nd Infantry Regiment, and Col. Manoon Rupkachorn, commander of the 4th Armoured Regiment. All of them were aged about 40, and had graduated together from the Chulachomklo Military Academy. They advocated greater democracy, measures against corruption and a major shift of wealth to the under-privileged. The coup was defeated by troops loyal to Gen. Prem (who had earlier secured the King's support) on April 3. Some of the coup promoters fled the country, others were arrested but freed in May after the King granted an amnesty.

No single party won an overall majority in elections to the House of Representatives held in April 1983. *Chart Thai* won the largest number of seats, but did not join the new four-member coalition, again led by Gen. Prem. Immediately preceding the election, constitutional changes had been introduced greatly reducing the powers of the (military-dominated) Senate and debarring serving military personnel and civil servants from holding ministerial posts. The amendments met with stiff opposition among elements of the military loyal to the Army Commander-in-Chief and Supreme Commander of the Armed Forces, Gen. Arthit Kamlang-Ek. A devaluation of the Thai *baht* in November 1984 precipitated a further confrontation between Prem and Arthit, with the latter threatening to withdraw military support for the ruling coalition. A compromise was reached, but relations between the two remained tense. A further abortive coup was launched in September 1985, whilst both Prem and Arthit were out of the country. Although the attempt was led by the "Young Turk" leader, Col. Manoon, it soon transpired that senior military leaders had been involved, and those subsequently arrested and charged with insurrection included former Prime Minister, Gen. Kriangsak.

Recent developments. In early May 1986, the government was defeated in a parliamentary vote on proposed vehicle tax legislation, prompting Gen. Prem, the (non-party) Prime Minister, to dissolve the House of Representatives, nine months before the expiry of its term. The vehicle tax issue was not of fundamental importance, but *Chart Thai*, then the main opposition party, had reportedly planned to present a motion of no confidence in Gen. Prem in the event of a government defeat. A general election was held in late July, and the Democrat Party won 100 of the 347 seats. A fresh coalition government was formed, with Gen. Prem as Prime Minister at the head of a cabinet which included representatives of the DP, Social Action Party, *Chart Thai* and *Rassadorn* as well as independents.

In late May 1986, Gen. **Chaovalit Yongchaiyut**, hitherto Army Chief-of-Staff, replaced Gen. Arthit Kamlang-Ek as Army Commander-in-Chief. Gen. Prem had announced in March that he would not permit an extension of Arthit's tenure as Army leader, arousing speculation that troops loyal to Arthit might stage a coup attempt. Prem's concern was such that on the eve of the announcement of Arthit's removal, he left Bangkok for the headquarters of the Second Army Region (his former command region) in the Central Plains city of Nakhon Ratchasima. Once in office, Gen. Chaovalit, a Prem loyalist and a class one graduate of the Chulachomklo Royal Military Academy, pledged his intention to detach the military from politics and to ensure fair elections. He announced plans to delegate power to a committee to implement the annual military reshuffle to "forestall favouritism and forge unity"; nevertheless, the 1986 military reshuffle saw a significant rise in the power of Chaovalit's Chulach-omklo classmates.

In February 1987 the Internal Security Operation Command (ISOC) was re-organized, with Gen. Prem as its nominal director and Gen. Chaovalit as deputy director and effective head. The ISOC had traditionally been responsible for administrating the secret military fund, foreign military aid and all anti-communist forces. However, following its restructuring, the Command took on the role of a civilian policy-making and planning body. The change was seen as an institutionalization of the 1980 prime ministerial Guideline 66/2523 which provided the Army with a legitimate political role. Criticism of the ISOC's restructuring was led by former Prime Minister and "elder statesman" Kukrit Pramoj, who alleged that the changes reduced the power of parliament. In April Kukrit alleged that the ISOC had been infiltrated by communists and that Gen. Chaovalit had been "brainwashed". His remarks were made in the context of speeches made by Chaovalit in early 1987 in which he called for a "peaceful revolution" (patiwat) in Thailand involving structural changes within the political, economic and social spheres. A National Revolutionary Council claimed at its inaugural meeting in late April that it supported Gen. Chaovalit's concept of a "peaceful revolution"; Chaovalit denied any involvement with the Council. In October 1987, the Army formally called for changes to the country's 1978 Constitution at the annual ISOC meeting. Lt.-Gen. Charuey Wongsayant, the newly appointed Army Chief of Staff, said at a press conference that Thailand, at present, had the form of a democratic system, but that the substance was incomplete. Therefore, he went on, the country needed to "alter the rules and regulations" covering "important laws". Rumours that the Army might stage a coup attempt spread through Bangkok in mid-May 1988. The rumours started when Gen. Chaovalit stated in an interview that there was a possibility of a "revolution approved by the people" taking place in Thailand, and confirmed that the Army was strong enough to stage a coup. After a meeting with King Bhumibol, Kukrit Pramoj claimed that the implied threat in Chaovalit's remarks had bordered on illegality.

In November 1987, the House of Representatives approved the first reading of legislation designed to amend the country's 1978 Copyright Act. However, the focus of the parliamentary debate had been less on the proposed legislation than on the issue of a possible Cabinet reshuffle. The call for a reshuffle was voiced most vociferously by dissident deputies of the Democrat Party (the largest component of the ruling coalition).

The dissidents, who called themselves the "January 10 group" after the date on which DP leadership elections had been held in 1987, demanded representation in the Cabinet. Over 30 "January 10 group" members had voted with the opposition during the Copyright Act debate. During further parliamentary deliberation of the Act in late April 1988, DP dissidents again voted against the government, before resigning from the party and forming a new grouping (**Prachachon**). All DP ministers resigned from the Cabinet on the grounds that they had failed to maintain party unity provoking Gen. Prem into another early dissolution of the House (two years ahead of schedule) and the calling of a general election. Some commentators claimed that Gen. Prem had dissolved the House partly to avoid a no confidence debate scheduled for early May during which some opposition MPs had threatened to reveal damaging information about the Prime Minister's personal life. Earlier in April, Gen. Chaovalit had declared that he intended to resign as Army Commander-in-Chief, thereby keeping a promise which he had made upon his appointment to remain in the post for only two years. However, in early May (i.e. in the aftermath of the dissolution of the House) it was announced that Prem had refused to accept Chaovalit's resignation.

A group of 99 academics revived an ancient tradition in late May when they filed a petition with King Bhumibol requesting royal intervention to ensure Gen. Prem's political impartiality in the forthcoming general election. Prem subsequently promised that he would remain impartial in the election but cautioned his academic critics against inappropriately involving the king in political issues.

In the campaigning for the July elections, the competing parties tended to divide into loose pro- or anti-Prem coalitions. Included amongst the latter group was Gen. Arthit's Puangchon Chao Thai. As in the 1986 election, no one political party gained an overall majority, the largest number of seats (87) being won by Chart Thai. Gen. Prem was invited to serve a further term as Prime Minister, but turned the offer down (a decision for which he won widespread praise, even from staunch critics). An alternative arrangement was forged in which Maj.-Gen. **Chatichai Choonhaven** (the Chart Thai leader) was appointed in early August as Prime Minister at the head of a new six-member coalition government. Chatichai was the first Prime Minister to sit in the House of Representatives as an MP since the overthrow of Seni Pramoj in 1976.

The replacement of Prem's quasi-democratic regime with an ostensibly fully democratic government was greeted with some apprenhension in business and military circles. However, confidence in Gen. Chatichai's government has grown during his first 10 months in power. Much of the period has been spent initiating populist measures. The final batch of 16 suspects involved in the September 1985 abortive coup attempt were quickly pardoned, salary increases for the military and the civil service were approved, the minimum wage for private-sector workers was raised and oil prices reduced. In the first half of 1989, Chatichai convened three "mobile" cabinet meetings in the south, north-east and northern regions at which various propositions for investment in the poorer regions were discussed.

Van Chansue, a wealthy Sino-Thai businessman, was appointed Senate speaker (and therefore president of the Thai parliament) in late April 1989. Van was one of 94 senators (the majority being senior military officers and businessmen) appointed in mid-April to replace those who had completed their six-year term. In early May the four main opposition parties gained Supreme Court approval to merge, an exercise that was subsequently undermined by the defection of at least nine opposition MPs to Prime Minister Chatichai's *Chart Thai* Party. Later that month over 120 non-government MPs proposed that the Constitution be amended so that the post of president of parliament be held by the House speaker (as opposed to the Senate speaker).

Foreign relations. An inclination to "bend with the wind" has characterized Thai foreign policy during the nineteenth and twentieth centuries. By conceding to European interests in the late nineteenth century, the Thai state managed, alone amongst South east Asian nations, to maintain its formal independence. During World War II, Thailand elected to become Japan's ally, declaring war on Britain and the USA and using the opportunity to regain Indo-Chinese land previously ceded to France. The period of the "Cold War" saw the anti-communist military regime in Bangkok develop close links with the USA against China and Vietnam. The US policy of containment led to the formation of **SEATO** (the South-East Asia Treaty Organization) in 1954, the headquarters of which were based in Bangkok.

Thailand was a founder member of the **Association of South-East Asian Nations (ASEAN)** in 1967. After communist victory in Indo-China in 1975, Thailand lessened its ties with the USA and established friendlier relations with China. Following the entry of Vietnamese troops into Kampuchea in late 1978, Thailand assumed the role of the front-line ASEAN state and was a prime mover in efforts to diplomatically and economically isolate Vietnam. Large numbers of Kampuchean refugees entered Thailand, where they were established in border camps administered by the member-groups of the tripartite exiled **Coalition Government of Democratic Kampuchea** (CGDK). From 1979 onwards Vietnamese and Kampuchean troops have regularly entered or shelled Thai territory during their operations against the CGDK forces. The Laos–Thailand border has been the scene of periodic border incidents since 1975, often involving shooting exchanges across the Mekong River (which itself constitutes the border for some 800 km). In 1984 a serious territorial dispute arose over three villages on the northern section of the border (west of the Mekong) over which both countries claimed sovereignty. Heavy fighting broke out again in late 1987 and early 1988 at another disputed section of the border. According to some reports, up to 700 Lao and Thai troops were killed during the dispute, which was eventually settled in February 1988.

Following his appointment as Prime Minister of Thailand in August 1988, Maj.-Gen. **Chatichai Choonhaven** announced his intention to transform Indo-China from "a battlefield into a marketplace". Chatichai's apparent abandonment of Foreign Ministry policy (whereby no official contact with Indo-China should take place before a complete Vietnamese troop withdrawal from Kampuchea) caused consternation within the Foreign Ministry itself and also within ASEAN. Chatichai again provoked surprise in some quarters in late January 1989 when he held talks in Bangkok with **Hun Sen**, Premier of the Phnom-Penh regime.

Outline of economic development. Although Thailand, alone amongst South-East Asian states, avoided European colonial penetration, its economic development was nevertheless conditioned by the West's presence in the region. The Bowring Treaty of 1855 effectively ended the Thai royal elite's export monopoly, and allowed Britain, and to a lesser extent France, to incorporate the Thai state into the world economy. In 1896 an Anglo-French treaty placed Thailand (then Siam) firmly into Britain's trade and investment sphere, a relationship that continued until the United States usurped Europe's commanding role in the country in the aftermath of World War II. The USA, keen to gain support in its "Cold War" containment of communism, invested heavily in right-wing, praetorian Thailand, finding its return by utilizing the country as a major strategic base during the Vietnam War. Following America's defeat in Indochina in 1975, US bases and aid were withdrawn, adding greatly to Thailand's difficulties during a period of national and international economic depression.

Accelerating inflation and an increasingly adverse balance of payments caused an economic crisis in Thailand in the late 1970s which led, in turn, to changes in the government during 1980. The primary cause of the crisis was the cost of oil, which had accounted for only 4 per cent of Thailand's total imports by value before the increases of 1973, but rose to 23 per cent in 1977. Oil imports totalled US$1,100 million in 1977 and rose to some US$2,500 million in 1980. The annual inflation rate rose from 8.5 per cent at the beginning of 1978 to just under 15 per cent in 1979, and by February 1980 was over 20 per cent.

To counteract the growing trade deficit and declining foreign exchange reserves, the government had freed the Thai *baht* from its link with the US dollar in March 1978, and pegged it to a weighted basket of currencies, including the dollar, the yen and the deutschemark. At the same time the government raised tariffs on over 140 import items. The economic crisis came to a head in October 1979, when the government doubled the price of electricity and water, which had been subsidized for many years, whereupon many firms raised their prices to cover the increase. After a protest campaign by the trade unions and students the government rescinded the increases in November, but the firms which had raised their prices did not reduce them. Popular discontent further increased in February 1980 when fuel prices were increased.

In late 1980, the World Bank produced an economic report on Thailand which advocated a five-year programme of "structural readjustment" aimed at: (i) curtailing the deterioration in the current account in the short term; (ii) reducing the economy's growing dependence on imported energy resources in the medium term; and also (iii) strengthening the balance of payments situation through enhanced agricultural production incentives and diminished protection for domestically oriented industries. In June 1981 the International Monetary Fund (IMF) approved a two-year standby arrangement authorizing purchases of up to US$940 million in support of the government's programme of economic stabilization. The next month, the *baht* was devalued by over 8 per cent against the weighted basket to which it was linked.

Many of the World Bank's recommendations were adopted as part of the country's fifth Five-Year Plan (1982-86), which came into effect in October 1982. A particular feature of the fifth Plan was the proposed reduction, from 75 to 46 per cent, in the proportion of the country's energy supplies met by imported oil. This was to be made possible by the use of natural gas, which in September 1981 had begun to flow from large deposits exploited by the Union Oil Company of Thailand. Emphasis was also placed on the development of heavy industry. Progress on the Plan was disappointing. For the period 1980-85, average annual GDP growth was less then 4 per cent (almost half that for the 1970s) and as export prices for the country's main commodities (rice, rubber, tapioca) slumped the trade deficit widened. As a proportion of GDP, the nation's foreign debt grew from 21 per cent in 1981 to 37 per cent in 1986.

In late 1984 the *baht* was devalued by almost 15 per cent and a series of other measures were taken to reduce imports and increase exports, although none resulted in any improvement in the balance-of-payments. In June 1985 the IMF approved loans worth some US$580 million of which US$184 million was in compensatory financing, to offset a decline in export income, and the remainder was in the form of a 21-month stand-by arrangement. In the following months, however, there was a sudden improvement in the balance of payments and the stand-by loan was eventually returned in late 1986 undrawn. The rapid expansion of Thailand's exports that started in early 1986 was partly attributable to the depreciation of the Thai *baht* against major non-US currencies in line with the fall of the US dollar during 1985-86. The growth in exports of labour-intensive products was accompanied by an increase in tourism and a rise in foreign investment (particularly Japanese) applications. GDP expanded, in real terms, at a rate of 3.5 per cent in 1986, improving to 6.6 per cent in 1987.

Current economic situation. The resurgence of the Thai economy, which had started in mid-1986 after a period of stagnation, continued in 1987 and 1988, leading to predictions by some commentators that the country was on the verge of joining Singapore, South Korea, Hong Kong and Taiwan as a so-called "newly industrialized country" (NIC).

During 1988, there was a broad-based export surge and a GDP growth rate of 11 per cent was recorded. Investment from Japan, Taiwan and South Korea continued to increase, with direct foreign investment for the period January–August 1988 totalling US$764 million compared with US$488 million for the whole of 1987. Government revenue for fiscal 1987 (September 1987 to September 1988) was close to US$3,600 million over the US$7,980 million target, pitching the budget in surplus by about US$1,940 million. This allowed the government to pay a number of foreign debts ahead of schedule and to increase infrastructural investment.

The months of 1988 were notable for the unexpected rise of gems and jewellery as one of the top export earners, and also for the resurgence of the agricultural sector, which grew by a rate of 8.6 per cent. The agricultural sector's share of the GDP had progressively diminished during the 1970s and 1980s (whilst nevertheless remaining by far the dominant sector in terms of employment), but in 1988 Thai farmers produced a large rice crop against all expectations, allowing the government to export over four million tonnes of rice into a high-price world market.

Reports in early 1989 suggested that the economy was in a position to maintain the high level of manufacturing-led growth achieved in 1988, and that any slowdown would stem from the failure of world commodity prices.

Prospects for development. Most commentators are agreed that, as of early 1989, Thailand was well positioned to take on the mantle of Asia's next "newly industrialized country", behind Singapore, Hong Kong, Taiwan and South Korea. Thailand possesses a large and relatively inexpensive labour force, abundant land and economical building costs. In addition, the potential for a prolonged period of political stability appears greater in the late 1980s than at any time since the overthrow of the absolute monarchy in the 1930s.

The ethos of the current Chatichai regime is resolutely economy-orientated, and, to the chagrin of the Foreign Ministry, the country's foreign policy appears to be formulated to complement economic development. Of all the ASEAN countries, Thailand is the best poised to benefit from the inevitable settlement of the conflict in neighbouring Kampuchea. Chatichai's "battle-fields into marketplace" speech, delivered soon after he became Prime Minister, served notice on hardliners in his government and in the ASEAN ranks that Thailand intended to pursue a pragmatic approach towards trade and investment in Indochina. In the long-term, the government aims to create a Bangkok-centred Mekong community, involving Thailand, Vietnam, Laos, Kampuchea and Burma. In early 1989 talks began aimed at securing Australian funding for the first bridge across the Mekong, linking Thailand with Laos.

Although the future for the Thai economy appears positive, there are a number of factors that could induce a slowdown during the 1990s. The expansion of the economy has placed overwhelming pressure on the country's infrastructure, particularly ports, roads, water and electricity supplies and telecommunications.

Programmes approved in the 1980s should, however, come into fruition during the 1990s. For example, as part of the wider Eastern Seaboard Development Programme, the government in 1986 approved plans to build by 1991 the country's first commercial deep-sea port and export processing zone at Laem Chabang in Chon Buri province. Once in operation, the Laem Chabang port should take some pressure off Klong Toey port in Bangkok, which in late 1988 was almost saturated. In March 1989 the government unveiled plans to transform southern Thailand, an area long associated with tin mining and plantation agriculture, into a major industrial centre by the mid-1990s. The plan proposed the construction of: (i) an "economic corridor" linking newly created ports and industrial zones on the western and eastern coasts; and (ii) an oil refinery at Khlong Sai. It was also proposed to establish large tourism zones in provinces adjacent to the Andaman Sea.

The maintenance of high growth rates will also depend upon Thailand's ability to diversify export production (agriculture remains relatively untapped) and export markets, thereby avoiding over-dependence on a potentially hostile USA. Accusations have already been made of dumping on the US market of Japanese steel produced in Thailand and commentators predict that US President Bush will come under increased congressional pressure to wage a protectionist war against Asian exporters.

DS

THERAVADA BUDDHISM. There are five Theravada countries: Sri Lanka, Burma, Thailand, Laos, and Kampuchea, and their cultures have much in common.

In Thailand and Laos, Theravada Buddhism is the official religion, having been introduced in the fifth century CE. There are 24,000 temples in Thailand and 200,000 monks, and all boys should spend some time in a monastery. Formerly there were some nuns, but there are none in Theravada lands now. Movements for the renewal of Buddhism are the most advanced in Thailand, and it has been seen as compatible with or prefiguring modern science. Buddhist universities guide monks towards teaching and social service. One monk, Buddhadasa, head of a monastery at Chaiya in the south, has sought to draw Buddhists of different groups together by propounding a mixture of Theravada and **Mahayana** teachings. The World Fellowship of Buddhists, founded in 1950, has its headquarters in Bangkok and works for peace and reconciliation in 34 countries of Asia, Oceania, America and Europe.

In Thailand 95 per cent are Buddhists, but only 58 per cent of Laotians. Though traditional tribal religions exist among Thai mountain peoples, such as the Karens, they are much stronger in Laos with an estimated 33 per cent of the population. There are some 1,900 pagodas in Laos, with two monastic orders, and a Buddhist Institute in Vientiane founded in 1947 which supervises Buddhist education.

In Kampuchea Theravada Buddhism dominated from the fourteenth century. There are famous ancient ruins at Angkor Wat, "City of Water", a complex of religious buildings in the jungle dating from the height of Khmer rule in the twelfth century. These buildings were partly Hindu, partly Buddhist, symbolizing the universe according to Hindu cosmology and with some Hindu gods later replaced by figures from Buddhism.

In the early 1970s there were 2,800 monasteries in Kampuchea with 68,000 monks. Most boys spent some time in a monastery to learn the principal Buddhist teachings and lay people returned there for retreats in the rainy season. There was a Buddhist university in Phnom Penh and a vast primary school network attached to the monasteries. Under the *Khmer Rouge* in 1975 many educated people were executed, including members of the Buddhist Sangha, and a new intolerant "religion" took over which has been called "post-Buddhist, quasi-Marxism". It sought to get rid of the impurities of education and urban living, forced the people into the country, and devastated Phnom Penh. After the Vietnamese intervention in 1979 there came a more orthodox Marxist regime, still with restrictions on all forms of religion.

GP

TIANANMEN INCIDENTS. In 1976 the Qing Ming Festival, the traditional time for paying respects at the graves of parents and ancestors, fell on April 4. On that day thousands of wreaths, portraits and poems were placed on the Revolutionary Martyrs' Memorial on Tiananmen Square in Beijing to commemorate the death of Prime Minister **Zhou Enlai**, who had died on Jan. 8. These were implicitly a criticism of the radicals in the party leadership and support for **Deng Xiaoping**, then Prime Minister. Overnight the Beijing authorities had all the wreaths removed. This provoked a massive protest meeting on the square, which was finally dispersed by the army in the evening with several hundred deaths. The affair was condemned as counter-revolutionary, and two days later Deng was replaced by **Hua Guofeng**. After Hua's ouster the incident was officially re-described as revolutionary rather than counter-revolutionary.

In April 1989, following the death of former Party leader **Hu Yaobang**, Chinese students demonstrated in the square, eventually calling for greater democracy and moves against corruption. Party leader **Zhao Ziyang** declined to crush the student movement. Workers and residents of Beijing swelled the ranks to over a million people in May at the time of the Sino-Soviet summit in Beijing. Martial law was declared, but only fully implemented on June 4 when thousands of protesters were killed by troops brought in to restore government control. Zhao was purged and thousands of sympathizers were arrested and some executed in the aftermath of the Tiananmen Massacre.

CIPF

TIN. The Pacific's chief tin deposits are located in the equatorial regions of Asia, Australia and in central America.

Production of tin dropped steadily in the mid-1970s but recovered to exceed 200,000 tonnes for the first time in 1979. It stayed at that level until 1982 when a decline set in again: by 1987 world production of tin had fallen to 136,400 tonnes. In Malaysia, hitherto the world's largest producer, production dropped in 1986 to 29,134 tonnes, its lowest point in modern times. The 1980s proved a difficult time for Malaysia's tin industry. Low prices, high production costs and export controls combined to force the closure of some 200 Malaysian gravel-pump mines between 1981 and 1984. In 1982 alone one-fifth of the industry's workforce was laid-off. Compared with 626 working mines in 1983 there were only 174 left by July 1986. By the end of 1987 the figure had recovered to 221.

Smelter production of primary tin worldwide fell by 1987 to 146,500 tonnes. Indonesia today smelts almost the entirety of its mine production. Malaysia and Japan do likewise and also import tin concentrates. Australia smelts some 30 per cent of its mine production, the rest being sent to Penang in peninsular Malaysia. In Singapore an independent tin smelter has operated since 1977.

Until the mid-1970s consumption of steel has usually exceeded production, putting great pressure on surplus stocks. The trend reversed itself between 1973 and 1983 when production outstripped consumption in each successive year. In 1984–87, however, demand again exceeded supply. In 1987, for example, the consumption of tin touched 167,400 tonnes while production was only 146,500 tonnes.

With such volatility between demand and supply governments worldwide have been concerned to stabilize prices within an agreed range by use of a regulating reserve stock. A series of International Tin Agreements (ITAs) has sought to do this since 1956. These have been administered by the London-based International Tin Council. Lower, middle and upper price sectors are set between two fixed "floor" and "ceiling" levels. So if the market price of tin moves above the "ceiling" tin is sold from the reserve stock until the price falls back below the "ceiling". If the price slips below the "floor" tin is bought by the reserve stock until the price rises above the "floor" figure. The ITA also provides for IMF assistance in supporting the pricing system and the ITC can introduce export controls, exceptionally, if the "floor" price is seriously threatened.

In June 1983, Malaysia, Indonesia and Thailand founded the Association of Tin Producing Countries (ATPC) to protect their own special interests. It was intended to complement the role of the ITC and not to oppose it. Australia too later joined the ATPC.

The ITA itself was placed under growing strain during the 1970s and 1980s as fluctuation in production and demand made it increasingly difficult to control the price of tin. Finally after years of difficulty on Oct. 24, 1985 the ITC informed the London Metal Exchange (LME) that it was no longer able to support the price of tin. The agreement was thrown into disarray but finally the sixth ITA scheduled to expire on June 30, 1987 was extended two years with the Council itself to give up its price-support role and to serve instead only as a source of statistical information.

The crisis in tin trading is having a disturbing influence on the pattern of tin production; Malaysia, where the cost of production is especially high has been forced to introduce drastic cut-backs.

The dramatic reduction in the role of the ITC gave added significance to the actions of the ATPC. After extended negotiations the group introduced export quotas for tin, totalling 96,000 tonnes, effective from March 1, 1987. The aim was to raise the price of tin while reducing the level of surplus stocks as large stocks were thought to depress prices. Stocks have since fallen but prices have not resumed their former heights.

RS

TOKELAU (Union Islands). *Population* (est. 1986): 1800, mostly Polynesians. *Area*: 10 sq km. A territory of New Zealand, since 1948, comprising three islands located some 480 km north of Western Samoa. The main settlement is Nukunonu. *Languages:* English and Polynesian.

The islands were probably originally settled from Samoa. British, American and French explorers, missionaries and traders visited the islands during the nineteenth century. Formal British interest began in 1877, and a protectorate was established in 1889. In 1916 the group became part of the colony of the Gilbert and Ellice Islands, and was then administered by New Zealand from 1925.

The islands are governed by local village councils, and three councils of elders, under a New Zealand administrator based at Apia, Western Samoa. The economy is a subsistence one in agriculture and fishing, requiring regular New Zealand subventions and producing some emigration.

TBM

TONGA (Friendly Islands). *Population* (est. 1988) 95,300, mostly Polynesian. *Area*: 699 sq km. An independent monarchy within the Commonwealth, comprising an archipelago of 169 islands of which 36 are permanently inhabited, in two north–Fiji. *Capital:* Nuku'alofa.

Tonga has been inhabited for at least 3,000 years by Austronesian peoples, developing a stratified social system under a hereditary paramount ruler. European contact dates from 1616. A Methodist mission was established in 1826. In 1900, King George Tupou II negotiated a treaty of friendship with Britain, which developed into a protectorate five years later. In 1970 Tonga achieved complete independence within the Commonwealth.

Government is by the hereditary monarch (since 1965 Taufa'ahau Tupou IV) who is head of state and of government, an appointed 10-member privy council, and a partly-elected (18 out of 29) legislative assembly. Languages spoken are Tongan, an Austronesian language, and English.

There is a successful subsistence economy based on agriculture and fishing, with exports of copra, vanilla and bananas. A tourist industry is developing.

TBM

TRADE. The volume of trade conducted by the countries of the Pacific region is immense. It also makes up a very large proportion of total world trade. In 1987 the combined exports of the countries of the region totalled approximately US$970,000 million, roughly 41 per cent of total world exports. Their imports together totalled approximately US$1,038,000 million in 1987, or roughly 43 per cent of total world imports. This represents a significant increase in the economic importance of the region over the course of the present decade, for in 1980 the combined exports of the countries of the Pacific region made up only 36 per cent of total world exports, and the region's imports formed only 37.5 per cent of world imports.

On the export side, much of the increase can be attributed to the rise in exports from the Asian countries of the Pacific region. Japan, of course, has led the way, but the newly industrializing economies (NIEs) of South Korea, Hong Kong, Taiwan and Singapore have also made significant steps forward. So, too, have Thailand and the People's Republic of China, the latter having doubled its exports since 1980. As regards imports, the single most significant change has been the vast increase in imports into the United States since the beginning of the decade, although the Asian nations of Japan, the People's Republic of China, Taiwan, South Korea and Hong Kong have also considerably enlarged their markets for imported goods.

Distribution. In both value and quantity, trade in the Pacific is dominated by the industrialized countries in the region. In 1987, the combined exports of the United States, Canada, Japan, Australia and New Zealand totalled US$613,494 million, which was 63 per cent of the total exports of all the countries of the region. In 1987, the combined imports of the five industrialized countries of the Pacific totalled US$704,261 million, thus making up 68 per cent of the total imports of the countries of the region.

The 16 Asian countries of the Pacific region excluding Japan (North Korea, South Korea, The People's Republic of China, Mongolia, Hong Kong, Brunei, Indonesia, Malaysia, Macao, The Philippines, Singapore, Thailand, Kampuchea, Laos, Vietnam and Taiwan) were together responsible for exports valued at US$274,619 million in 1987, which was equivalent to 28 per cent of the total exports of the region. Their imports were valued at US$245,793 million, or 24 per cent of the combined imports of the countries of the region.

In 1987, the nine Central and Southern American countries (Chile, Colombia, Costa Rica, Ecuador, El Salvador, Guatemala, Mexico, Panama and Peru) together accounted for less than 5 per cent of the exports of the Pacific region, with a total value of US$45,318 million. With imports totalling US$43,284 million, they together accounted for only 4 per cent of the total imports of the Pacific region.

The remainder of the trade of the Pacific region is accounted for by the USSR with 4 per cent of its exports and 4 per cent of its imports, and by the Pacific Island countries who together make up a fraction of one per cent of the trade of the region as a whole.

Direction. There are several possible ways of classifying Pacific trade, but when focusing particularly on the genesis of trade, two categories seem especially useful. They are: (i) trade between the advanced industrial nations of the region and (ii) trade between the advanced industrial nations of the region and the developing countries of the region. In the former case, trade will take place in a large variety of goods. For example, industrial nations have large demands for many kinds of agricultural commodities which they are freqeuntly unable to satisfy from domestic sources. In the Pacific region Japan is the outstanding example of such a country. Japan's attempts to satisfy its needs for many kinds of marine, meat, poultry, vegetable and grain products, as well as the need for huge amounts of feedstuff to meet the demands of its considerable livestock industry, generates a massive trade in these commodities. Among the sources of supply are, importantly, the United States (fish, grain, meat, soya beans, tobacco etc.), Canada (grain, beef etc.), Australia (meat, grain etc.) and New Zealand (wool, mutton, vegetables etc.). The large continental economies of Australia, Canada and the United States have, of course, a higher degree of self-sufficiency in the area of agricultural commodities. Nevertheless, they too buy these types of goods from each other, and even to some extent from Japan. (For example, Japan sold more than US$404 millions-worth of food products to the United States in 1987, chiefly marine products, fruit and vegetables.)

Advanced industrial countries also buy large quantities of raw materials and fuels from each other. Again we may illustrate this from Japan's experience. From the United States Japan imports a great deal of cotton, metal ores and fossil fuels. From Canada Japan buys large quantities of metal ores, lumber and **coal**. From Australia Japan gets metal ores and coal, both in great quantities, and even from New Zealand Japan obtains lumber and pulp.

However, advanced industrialized countries also sell large quantities of manufactured goods to each other. The economic reasons for this are well understood. Comparative advantage is not spread evenly across the whole range of industrial products, so that because of the acquisition of a technological lead, or because of the utilization of the economies of scale, or because of better management or a variety of other possible reasons, one country can produce some manufactured goods more efficiently than the others and sell these goods to them. Thus, for example, Japan has come to dominate the markets of North America and Oceania in automobiles and a variety of consumer electronics. Added to this, the advanced technology consumer and capital (producer) goods typically produced by the industries of advanced industrial nations find their chief markets where average consumer incomes are high. This is, of course, in other advanced industrial countries. Moreover, there is now a high degree of both vertical and horizontal integration amongst the industries of these countries due to direct and indirect investment across national boundaries, very often with multi-national corporations acting as the vehicle for this process. The result of this is, *inter alia*, that large amounts of goods transferred internally within the multinational corporation as a result of its corporate strategy actually cross national boundaries and are registered as exports or imports. For example, many Japanese electronics and other firms in Australia and the United States have up to now been little more than assembly operations, and their needs for components have largely been sourced from factories in Japan.

For all these reasons, we find that much of the trade between industrial nations, and the industrial nations of the Pacific are no exception, is in manufactured goods. We must add to this that increasingly in recent years there has arisen a massive trade in services of many kinds. American banks and securities houses are well represented in the financial services markets in Tokyo now that many, though not all, of the legal barriers to entry have been removed. The same is true of Japanese banks and securities houses in New York, and along with them the ancillary services of accountants, lawyers and consultants of all kinds. Travel and tourism continues to grow unabated, and so on.

However, when we come to examine the trade between advanced industrial countries and developing countries, we generally find that the pattern of trade is much less complicated because it is much less diverse. Developing countries generally sell agricultural products or raw materials to industrial nations, usually in exchange for manufactured products or services, or sometimes fuels. We would expect to see this overall pattern emerge as we examine in detail the trade in the Pacific region between its developing and developed countries. However, there are in the region a number of countries who are intermediate between the two extremes we have identified. They are sometimes known as the Asian

NIEs and they include in their ranks South Korea, Hong Kong, Singapore and Taiwan. Other countries in the region such as Thailand, Malaysia and Indonesia have also undergone a significant degree of industrial progress in recent years. In the case of all these nations we shall find that the rather over-simplified description of their patterns of trade outlined above will be somewhat complicated and obscured. Nevertheless, the essential truth of the patterns outlined is borne out in the following statistically-based description of trade in the Pacific region.

Trade between the advanced countries of the Pacific region takes place between Australia, Canada, Japan, New Zealand and the United States. As indicated earlier, trade between these countries dominates the trade of the region as a whole. The combined exports of the five made up 63 per cent of the combined exports of all the countries of the region in 1987. For imports, the proportion was 68 per cent.

When we look more closely at the structure of this trade, we find that it is dominated by two great streams of goods and services. One crosses back and forth across the Pacific Ocean between the North American continent and Japan. The other is a north–south flow across the long land frontier between the United States and Canada. More than 41 per cent of all Pacific trade as we have defined it (i.e. the value of the trade of every Pacific trading nation summed together) is accounted for by the flow of goods and services among these three countries. The single largest flow is between the United States and Canada. Exports to each other from these two close neighbours was valued at close to US$129,000 million in 1987, which is the equivalent of 21 per cent of the combined exports of all the countries of the region. The next most significant exchange of goods and services is between the United States and Japan. They exported to each other in 1987 goods and services to the value of more than US$113,000 million. This is the equivalent of more than 18 per cent of the exports of all the Pacific countries together.

Nearly 31 per cent of Japan's trade (exports and imports together) in 1987 was with the United States. A little over 3 per cent of Japan's total trade was with Canada. More than 17 per cent of the trade of the United States was with Japan, whilst nearly 6 per cent of Canada's trade was with Japan in 1987. By contrast, nearly 70 per cent of Canada's trade in 1987 was with the United States, whilst more than 19 per cent of the total trade of the United States was with Canada.

These broad figures reveal several important things. The first, and perhaps most significant, is the remarkable degree of interdependence that exists between the economies of Japan and her two North American trading partners, and particularly between the economies of Japan and the United States. Trade in goods and services is not, of course, the only standard for judging interdependence, since there are also important financial flows in the form of direct and indirect investment by the citizens and the government of one country in the other. But as we shall see later, they too tend to stem from the nature of the trading relations between the countries concerned.

The next point to note is that the figures, used without modification, appear to show that while trade with Japan is important to the United States, trade between it and Canada is quantitatively even more important. Looked at from the Japanese side, the United States is far and away its single most important trading partner, and the degree of Japan's dependence on the United States both as a source of imports and as a market for its exports is striking. The place that the United States occupies in Canada's external economic relations is truly remarkable.

Trade friction. It is necessary to delve a little deeper into the trading relations between these three countries to discover the exact distribution of benefits that emanates from this huge commercial interchange that so dominates Pacific trade. The starting point is the bilateral balance between pairs of countries. In a trading regime where countries buy and sell freely around the world, only chance could produce an exact balance of trade between any given pair of countries. Overall payments must balance because of the nature of the accounting procedure used. When traded exports of goods and services are not equal in value to traded imports of goods and services for a given country in a given acounting period, the imbalance is matched by a compensating change on the capital account. Thus a balance of trade surplus (current account surplus) produces an increase in external financial (capital) assets. This is prefaced by a minus sign in the balance of payments accounts. The assets acquired may be short-term (e.g. foreign currency, financial assets with less than one year's term), or long-term capital assets including equity claims (i.e. ownership) in foreign corporations and other organizations.

The United States has run a large and persistent balance of trade deficit with both Canada and Japan throughout the course of the present decade. For example, American exports to Japan were valued at US$28,249 million in 1987, whilst its imports from Japan were valued at US$88,074

million. More than 40 per cent of United States exports to Japan consist of foodstuffs, raw materials and fuels, and while it sells machinery and equipment (capital goods) in large quantities to Japan, it clearly fails to make inroads into the markets for advanced consumer products whose demand is sensitive to increasing consumer incomes (income elastic). By contrast, imported Japanese cars, consumer electronics and a whole array of other goods have come to fill American stores. This supply of diverse, competitively priced, attractive products has benefited Americans as consumers, but by the same token, it has produced a decline in manufacturing industry in the United States with a consequent decline in manufacturing employment and in the basic industries like coal and steel.

This imbalance of trade has become a rich source of friction between the two nations. The reaction of the United States government during the 1980s has been partly to attempt to limit Japanese imports by, for example, urging voluntary export restraint in areas like the automobile industry. By and large, the Japanese reaction to these demands has been positive, and where compliance has been less than total, it can usually be traced to a large, unsatisfied demand in America for Japanese goods. The United States government has also persistently attempted to lower what it regards as unfair barriers to entry facing American producers trying to sell in Japanese markets. The main vehicle for pursuing this course of action has been the ongoing market-oriented sector-specific (MOSS) talks. For example, one issue the United States negotiators have pursued with dogged persistence at the MOSS talks has been the procurement policy of the Japanese authorities in the case of public sector projects. The New Kansai International Airport was a case in point. The American side felt the Japanese should throw open parts of the construction and installation work to international tender, and after much pressure, including an intervention from President Reagan in the form of a letter to Prime Minister **Nakasone**, the New Kansai International Airport Company announced an open tender policy in April, 1987. The United States is also seeking participation in about another 15 large-scale civil engineering projects in Japan.

Another source of extreme irritation with Japan in the United States is the problem of what the Americans see as agricultural protectionism in Japan. Japan operates a system of import quotas for 23 farm and marine products, including milk, cream, beef and oranges for example. In October 1986, the Americans went so far as to level restrictionist charges against Japan before GATT on 11 of the items. Its 1987 ruling that 10 out of the 11 items were in violation of GATT rules was accepted by Japan in February 1988. However, the United States continues to press Japan at their bilateral talks over the size of the quotas on the imports of oranges and beef. Moreover, the battle over imported rice, where Japan operates a complete embargo, has hardly been joined.

Undoubtedly, American pressure has had its effect. The decision by the Japanese government to introduce a supplementary programme of measures to stimulate the economy in May, 1987 was, in part, in deference to American demands. The measures were worth US$ 1,000 million in extra expenditure, and included an agreement to purchase United States-made super computers for the Tokyo Institute of Technology. The supplementary budget was accompanied by a sustained campaign in Japan, orchestrated by Prime Minister Nakasone, which urged Japanese consumers to buy more foreign goods.

However, the United States is by no means satisfied with the slow pace of the diminution of its trade deficit with Japan. The result was the passage through the House of Representatives in April 1987 of a protectionist trade bill which contained amendments to Section 301 of the 1974 Trade Act calling for stronger retaliatory measures against America's trading partners who are guilty of "unfair" trade practices. The bill also contained the Gephardt amendment which imposes mandatory trade surplus reductions on Japan and others of America's trading partners with whom there are large deficits. In July of 1987, the United States Senate followed the lead of the lower house with its own version of a comprehensive trade bill, which was also passed with an overwhelming majority. The so-called "super 301" section of the bill is an attempt to get Japan and other countries, like the Asian NIEs, who have persistent current account surpluses with the United States to remove trade barriers against American goods within three years.

Naturally, the Japanese government and people are unhappy with this American reaction. There is a good deal of support for the idea that the huge public sector deficit that grew up in the Reagan era is more to blame for the problem. In Japanese eyes, American financial imprudence has priced its goods out of international markets and sucked in imports to the detriment of its manufacturing industries. So much damage was done in the early and mid-1980s that even the rapid appreciation of the yen against the dollar after the Plaza accord of the Group of Seven was an insufficient restorative to allow ailing American industry to recover. Nor do the Japanese feel the United States is being entirely

reasonable over the issue of agricultural trade. Many feel that, despite the problems of Japanese agriculture centering around the persistent overproduction of rice and the absurd producer subsidy programme which is at the root of the problem, the measures proposed by America to free agricultural trade would, if adopted, give the Japanese farm sector too little time to adjust and would result in wholesale disruption within the industry.

There, for the moment, the unhappy situation rests, but a number of observations seem worth making. First of all, the situation is one of considerable danger for the Pacific economy as a whole. Protectionist sentiments in the United States are directed primarily, but not solely, against Japan. Other countries in the Asia-Pacific region, the **Association of South-East Asian Nations (ASEAN)** countries for instance, also run surpluses on their current accounts with the United States, though of course not on the scale of Japan's. They, too, have been subjected to American pressure to open their markets. (It is interesting to note that less is heard about the United States current account deficit with Canada, although it too is large and persistent. We hear more often of Canadian fears over the degree to which their economy is dependent on the United States.) If the drift towards protection continues and is not stemmed by the Uruguay Round of tariff negotiations, then the economies of many Pacific countries who trade heavily with the United States will be damaged and development in some will be seriously impaired.

It is therefore imperative for the economic health of the entire region that the United States and Japan find a way at least of containing their differences, even if they cannot resolve them. Wise counsellors in both countries have suggested a way forward may lie in a higher degree of integration between the two economies. As was pointed out above, this is occurring in any case as Japan acquires more and more American assets. Through the acquisition of financial assets the money markets of Tokyo and New York are already intimately bound together. Through direct investment of one kind and another, Japanese-owned corporations are already quite numerous in the United States, with beneficial effects on employment and possibly for American management techniques. But the wholesale shifting of production capacity across the Pacific and the buying-up of more and more American real estate by Japanese businesses is not a long-term solution. It can provoke resentment in the United States, while the trade deficit remains large. A greater degree of similarity in the fiscal systems of the two countries might help. A little has already been done to remove the features of the Japanese system that have produced the now notorious high rate of personal saving which some commentators feel has been at the root of the failure to import a sufficient quantity of foreign goods into Japan, including American goods. A thorough-going examination of a whole range of measures, including corporate and personal taxation rates and structure and arrangements affecting depreciation rates, might prove profitable in the longer term. So also might an examination of the possibilities for a greater harmonization of the currencies of the two nations. In other words, the two economic giants, on whose actions the health of the world economy so much depends, cannot go on indefinitely without much more positive co-operation in the areas of macroeconomic policy and even industrial policy.

Japanese trade with Australia and New Zealand. Quantitatively, the north–south flow between Japan and Australia and New Zealand does not match the east–west flow between Japan and the North American continent. Nevertheless, it is exceedingly important to all three countries. In 1987, Australia's exports to Japan were valued at US$6,790 million. This was more than one quarter of all Australia's exports and by far its largest overseas market. Although Australia only ranks about fifth in size as a market for Japanese exports, it is nevertheless an important outlet for the products of Japan's heavy and chemical industries, and for a wide range of manufactured consumer goods. Japan is, of course, highly dependent upon Australia for many kinds of metal and mineral raw materials, as well as for large quantities of fossil fuels. The tendency throughout the decade has been for Australia to run a surplus on its balance of trade with Japan, though not of a magnitude that has caused particular concern. More anxiety has been expressed at times about the scale of participation of Japanese business in the Australian mining industry, frequently accompanied as it has been by a large equity involvement.

In 1987, Japan was also New Zealand's largest single export market, although only slightly larger than the United States and Australia. Exports to these three countries accounted for nearly one half of New Zealand's total exports. The pattern of trade between New Zealand and Japan resembles that between Australia and Japan, except that a larger proportion of the former's exports are made up of the products of agriculture. To a certain degree, trade between Japan and her two southern partners resembles the pattern of trade we identified as more often characterizing commercial relationships between developed and developing countries. However, at the present state of development of the three countries and with the present currency alignments, trade between Japan and her two partners in Oceania tends to be symbiotic in nature.

In many important respects, trade across the Pacific between Australia and New Zealand on the one hand and the United States on the other resembles the north–south pattern of trade between Japan and Australia and New Zealand. The tendency is to import from the United States machinery and other manufactured goods not obtained from Japan or Western Europe, in exchange for which Australia and New Zealand export agricultural products and raw materials. In the light of the nature of their trading arrangements, it is clear that both Australia and New Zealand are somewhat vulnerable to fluctuations in the price of food and raw materials. These tend to be determined in volatile world markets and are affected, *inter alia*, by climatic conditions and subject to large swings in demand, whereas manufactured products of the sort sold in such large quantities by the great Japanese corporations are priced on a cost-plus basis and are thus, to some degree, protected from the full effects of price fluctuations. The governments of both countries are aware of the potential dangers of this situation, and have tried to encourage a wider range of industries and exports. However, retrenchment has been the dominant theme in the domestic economies of both nations in recent years, and the need for economic diversification remains as pressing as ever.

It has already been pointed out that the typical pattern of trade between the advanced and the developing countries of the region tends to be less diverse in nature, concentrating as it does on the exchange of the products of the primary sectors of the economies of the developing countries for the products of the manufacturing and service sectors of the advanced countries of the region. The basic truth of this proposition can be confirmed when we examine first the trade structure of the Latin American countries of the Pacific region, and then that of the countries of the Asian Pacific.

South and Central American Pacific nations. When we examine the economies of Chile, Colombia, Costa Rica, Ecuador, El Salvador, Guatemala, Mexico, Panama and Peru, all of which have a Pacific seaboard, we find several striking features possessed in common by each of these countries. The first is the high level of reliance they all have on exports and imports. This is not merely an arithmetic statement about the size of the international sector of their economies as a proportion of total GNP. By the very nature of the South and Central American debt crisis, output and exports have to grow faster than imports to enable them to have any chance of servicing their massive external debts, let alone making inroads into the principal. This level of indebtedness has arisen as the result of borrowing to achieve economic development, much of it borrowing for public sector projects whose return as measured by additional exports has been insufficient to pay for the sums borrowed. The problem has, of course, been made additionally difficult by the high rates of – seemingly endemic – inflation, which make a rapid growth in export volumes virtually impossible. To summarize the nature of the difficulty: (i) the need to generate a surplus of exported goods and services over imported goods and services in order to service and pay-off their external debts, implies that each country must achieve an equivalent surplus of saving over investment in their domestic economies. If saving is to expand, consumption will contract, thus acting as a restraint on domestic growth in the short term; or else investment must contract, thus diminishing the potential for producing more in the future; (ii) since the public sector has been responsible for incurring much of the external debt, to service it requires a large internal transfer of resources to the public sector from the private sector. Raising the level of public revenue implies the raising of taxes at a time when incomes are being severely restrained by the debt crisis itself.

All of the countries of Pacific Latin America are facing these problems to a greater or lesser degree. The structure of their external trade implies that it is to the Pacific economy – and in particular to the advanced countries of the region – that they must look first for any relief. The reason for this is very simple. It is that in every case the bulk of the trade of these countries is with the three countries of Canada, Japan and the United States. For example, in 1987, 34.5 per cent of Chile's exports went to the above three economic giants of the Pacific and 45.8 per cent of its imports originated with them. In the case of Colombia, the proportions were 47.5 per cent and 49.2 per cent. For Costa Rica the figures were 52.1 per cent and 53.3 per cent; for Ecuador 64.5 per cent and 44.9 per cent; for El Salvador 53.9 per cent and 46.6 per cent; for Guatemala 55.8 per cent and 48.4 per cent; for Mexico 79.3 per cent and 82.6 per cent; for Panama 38.5 per cent and 34.5 per cent, and for Peru 39.7 per cent and 36.7 per cent. In all these cases, the major passage of goods and services was in a north–south direction between Latin America and the United States.

Contrast these large flows of goods and services with those that take place among the Latin American Pacific nations; or with those that occur between Pacific Latin America and the Asian Pacific countries. With the exception of the small Central American States whose trade with each other is in the range of 10–20 per cent, Latin American trade with the rest of the Pacific region is small and undeveloped. In other words, it is primarily north–south trade of the classic kind between the advanced and the developing countries of the Pacific region. The scope for future integration of the entire Pacific economy, including the Latin American Pacific countries, would seem to be determined primarily by the success of efforts to diversify and industrialize the economies of this part of the region, which in turn depends on the success with which the twin problems of massive foreign indebtedness and chronic inflation are tackled co-operatively.

Asian–Pacific trade. One of the most important changes to have occurred in the Pacific region in the last decade or so is the growth in the economies of the nations of East Asia. This growth has, to a large extent, been export-led. In the mid-1980s there was a vigorous expansion in the volume of exports of manufactured goods in particular, accompanied by a recovery in the international prices of the primary sector exports of the countries of the region, such as timber, rubber, rice and oil. The result has been a further strengthening of the balance of trade surpluses of many of the countries of the region, and an additional strain placed on their relations with the United States.

In 1987, exports grew fastest in the newly industrializing economies of Hong Kong and Singapore where an already-existing competitive advantage resulting from the productivity gains of the early 1980s in manufacturing industry was reinforced by rapid increases in investment out of export earnings. South Korea, despite revaluing its currency by 6.7 per cent in an effort to reduce its large balance-of-payments surplus with the United States, continued to experience a rapid growth in its exports, particularly to Western Europe and Japan. Similarly, the realignment of Taiwan's currency with the dollar – an appreciation of 15.7 per cent in 1987 – slowed down Taiwanese exports somewhat, but only from a growth rate of 25.3 per cent in 1986 to 15.3 per cent in 1987. Despite a poor performance by their agricultural sectors, exports from Malaysia and Thailand also increased quickly in 1987, largely as a result of direct investment in these two countries by Japan. The same factor was at work in the case of Singaporean exports. The position in Indonesia and Malaysia, for example was further improved by the increase in primary product prices, including oil.

What we have been observing in the countries of the Asian–Pacific region in the last decade or so is a fundamental change in the pattern of comparative advantage over a broad range of manufacturing industry. A wave of rapid industrialization has proceeded from Japan first to the newly industrializing countries of Asia (the Asian NIEs), and thence to the countries of ASEAN. The heavy industries such as iron and steel and shipbuilding were in the vanguard of this process, but they are being followed by industries producing sophisticated consumer products whose technologies are also relatively advanced. Japan has, of course, greatly aided and abetted in this process through its willingness to export the production technologies of these industries to the countries of Asia via its massive direct investment in the region. The incentives to do so were considerable. Standardized and well understood production technologies developed in Japan become mobile and can be sent in pursuit of cheaper sources of labour, provided only that managerial standards, too, can be maintained. As a result, Japan is still able to dominate the consumer markets of Europe and North America through the activities of its multinational corporations in Asia, while at the same time taking some of the potential heat out of its trade friction with the United States. By contrast, there has arisen a series of relatively smaller-scale trade conflicts between the United States and the Asian NIEs and the countries of ASEAN which the former has attempted to tackle on a bi-lateral basis. Thus we have observed a series of adjustments and realignments between the US dollar and the currencies of the countries of the Asian–Pacific, accompanied by a good deal of American activity directed towards negotiating voluntary export restraint agreements and the removal of what the US government regards as unfair barriers against the entry of American goods into Asian markets.

It is the history of recent commercial relations between Japan and the United States repeating itself, and it threatens to stem the tide of development in the region, heavily dependent as it is on the growth of trade. Neither the Uruguay round of GATT negotiations nor bi-lateral trade talks may be entirely effective in containing the problem. The fundamental difficulty for the Pacific economy is that the United States continues to be the key player in its development and its future integration. Without the huge market for imported goods which is the United States market, development in the Asian–Pacific would be markedly slower, if not stalled completely. However, Asian industrialization has removed the heart from the traditional manufacturing base of the United States' economy. The world is less prepared than in the days of the Bretton Woods system to accept the United States currency and its short-term debt instruments as the basis for international settlements. Neither the people of the United States nor its government have come to terms with the new status of their country as a major debtor nation, and protectionist sentiment in the country remains one of the greatest dangers of all. There is a great need for restraint and statemanship. But above all, the forces at work which are altering the economic balance of power in the Pacific need to be more completely and widely understood. With this understanding may come the institutions for co-ordinating the currency realignments and the macro-economic policies of the nations of the region which are essential for future harmonious economic co-existence.

DA

TRADE UNIONS. Trade Unions were instrumental in winning better working conditions and good living wages throughout the industrialized world, often in the face of considerable resistance. But in some advanced countries, such as the United States, workers are beginning to question their contemporary relevance. Union membership has fallen significantly in the United States among the indigenous population, though vigorous campaigns have had to be conducted on behalf of migrant workers, such as Mexican lettuce pickers in California. In Canada, the Pacific coast has had the worst history of labour relations in the country. In an effort to attract investment, the provincial government of British Columbia introduced legislation in 1987 to curb strikes by mandatory "cooling-off" periods. Similarly, Expo 86 in Vancouver opened on time because non-union labour was brought in to get round a strike.

The socialist concept of trade unions is quite different to that in western industrialized countries. The Leninist view in the Soviet Union is that unions are an agency of the Communist Party, with the express aim of enabling workers to increase production. It therefore came as something of a shock when miners in various parts of the Soviet Union struck in 1989 and militated for better working conditions. If *perestroika* continues in the Soviet Union, then some kind of semi-autonomous unions in various sectors cannot be ruled out.

In China, however, the authorities responded forcefully when an attempt was made to establish independent workers' unions during the pro-democracy movement of Spring 1989. Activists of the self-styled Workers' Autonomous Association took part in the sit-ins in Tiananmen Square (*See* **Tiananmen Incidents**) in Beijing. They are believed to have been killed or imprisoned when the crackdown came in June and the organization was declared illegal. The official Chinese unions have a clearly-stated purpose in their constitution, which calls on them to facilitate the role of the working class as the main force in building a "socialist material and spiritual civilization" (adopted October 1983). The leadership of the **Chinese Communist Party** is emphasized in the very first sentence of that constitution.

Japan has an unusual history of labour relations, having formed a partnership between management and the workforce which is one key to the country's colossal economic success. The sense of belonging to individual firms is considerable and workers are highly protected by companies so long as they remain faithful to them – which the vast majority do.

In other parts of the Pacific region, however, trade unions still have important battles to fight. Child labour is still endemic in countries such as Thailand and parts of South America, for example. Unionization of the labour force is sternly resisted by employers.

JF

TRANS-SIBERIAN RAILWAY. A railway running for over 6,500 km across the south of Siberia in the Asian part of the Soviet Union, from Chelyabinsk in the Ural mountains to Vladivostok on the Pacific coast. Constructed between 1891 and 1905, it gave a boost to the settlement and economic exploitation of the sparsely inhabited regions in the east of Russia.

IG

TRUONG CHINH. President of the Socialist Republic of Vietnam from 1981 to 1987; also secretary-general of the Indochinese Communist Party (ICP), then of the Vietnam Workers' Party, 1941–56; and general secretary of the Vietnamese Workers' Party from July to December 1986. Born Dang Xuan Khu in 1907 in Nam Dinh, he joined the local revolutionary youth association and was a member of the Indochinese Communist Party by 1930. He spent the years 1931–36 in Son-La prison (in the north); on his release, he emerged as a leading figure in the ICP and its National Democratic Front in the late 1930s. He later worked hard to establish an underground network during World War II, and became secretary-general of the ICP at its eighth plenum in 1941.

He played a key role in the "August Revolution" of 1945-6, but was later critical of its moderation; and in the late 1940s he emerged as a strong admirer of the Maoist form of guerrilla struggle. He continued as secretary-general when the Vietnamese Workers' Party re-emerged in 1951 and was the leading spirit behind a series of mass mobilization campaigns, culminating in the highly controversial (and sometimes violent) land reform movement of 1954-56. For "excesses" in that campaign, and possibly for other reasons, he was dismissed from the secretariat in October 1956 but retained his place in the Politburo. As deputy prime minister (1958-60) he was able to speed up the co-operativization of agriculture, but in a reshuffle of government and party positions during 1960 he appears to have lost ground to **Le Duan**. Truong Chinh was chairman of the National Assembly from 1960 until 1981, when he became president of the State Council and head of state. His actual influence over affairs waned during the 1970s, but in 1986 he again held the top party position (as general secretary) for five months following the death of Le Duan. He retired from that position and from the Politburo at the party's sixth congress (December 1986) and six months later gave up the presidency. He died following a fall on Sept. 30, 1988.

RBS

TSEDENBAL, MARSHAL YUMJAAGIYN. Former Mongolian statesman, born in 1916. He was leader (first and later general secretary) of the **Mongolian People's Revolutionary Party** between 1940 and 1954 and again between 1958 and 1984; Chairman of the Mongolian Council of Ministers (Prime Minister) from 1952 to 1974; and Chairman of the Presidium of the People's Great Hural (President of Mongolia) from 1974 to 1984. In August 1984 he was ousted as President and party leader, and spent the next four years as a virtual political exile in the Soviet Union; his "retirement" and absence from Mongolia were officially attributed, however, to ill health. Increasingly since then his responsibility has been implied in Mongolian official pronouncements for many of the country's socio-economic problems.

IG

TUNGSTEN. Tungsten is a metallic element mainly obtained from its ores, wolframite and scheelite. The People's Republic of China produces about one third of the world's supply of tungsten and is thought to have some 37.5 per cent of the world's reserves.

Tungsten prices have been highly volatile in recent years because of the unpredictability of Chinese export policy and the strategic importance of the metal. During the early 1970s prices were depressed touching an all-time low of US$3,000 per tonne in 1972. Prices then recovered and between 1979–81 were relatively stable at around $14,000 per tonne. However, prices fell steadily as world consumption fell following the decline in drilling activity, recycling of used tungsten and a greater release of US stocks.

In 1976 the leading tungsten producers – but excluding China – set up the Primary Tungsten Association (PTA) to protect and advance the interests of the tungsten industry. Through the auspices of the UN Conference on Trade and Development (UNCTAD) the PTA is hoping to arrange an international commodity agreement for tungsten under which a systematic control of nationally held stocks will help control prices. To date little progress has been made. The slow growth in the consumption and the constantly falling prices militate against the prospects for an international agreement to regulate the market. Indeed the collapse of the well established agreement on the tin market has disenchanted many countries with the idea of attempting a commodity agreement on tungsten. Certainly, the Chinese influence on the tungsten market continues to increase and any hope of an international agreement on tungsten would need Chinese participation. The annual production of tungsten, in thousands of tonnes, is as follows: China, 12.5; South Korea, 2.5; USA, 0.98; Peru, 0.72; Mexico, 0.5; North Korea, 0.5.

RS

TUVALU. (Formerly Ellice Islands) *Population* (est. 1988): 8,700, mostly Polynesian, except on Nui which is Micronesian. *Area*: 26 sq km. An independent state within the Commonwealth, with Queen Elizabeth II of the United Kingdom as head of state, and a Tuvaluan Governor-General. Tuvalu comprises nine islands in the central-western Pacific, 4,000 km north-east of Australia. *Capital*: Fongafale, on Funafuti atoll.

Settlement probably dates from around 300 CE on Nui, some centuries later on other islands. European contacts – traders, castaways, slave traders, whalers – developed during the nineteenth century. In 1856, the United States claimed the four southern islands. In 1865 the London Missionary Society established a mission converting the islanders to Christianity. In 1892 the Ellice Islands joined with the Gilbert Islands in a British protectorate, which became a colony in 1916. In World War II the United States built airfields on three of the Ellice Islands, when Japan occupied the Gilberts (later Kiribati). In 1974 Ellice islanders voted for separation from the Gilberts, and became independent, as Tuvalu, in 1978.

There is an elected House of Parliament of 12 members, serving four-year terms, a small cabinet holding executive powers, and elected island councils. The languages spoken are English and Tuvalu Samoan.

In 1979 the United States relinquished its claim to the four southern islands and signed a treaty of friendship with Tuvalu, giving the US access to US-built bases and the right to veto military use of the islands by other countries.

There is a subsistence economy (yam, bananas, coconuts, fishing). Many Tuvaluans work overseas. Tuvalu relies heavily on foreign aid, especially from Britain, Australia, New Zealand, the European Community, Japan, and the United Nations Development Programme.

TBM

TUVANS. A turkic-speaking ethnic group found in the East Siberian region of the Soviet Union. The Tuvans, who number around 150,000 people in the Soviet Union, enjoy administrative-territorial autonomy in the Tuva Autonomous Soviet Socialist Republic (established in 1961), which is situated alongside the Mongolian border. The territory of the modern Tuva republic was part of the Chinese province of Outer Mongolia until 1911, was made a Russian protectorate in 1914, and following the civil war in Russia in 1918–21 became the nominally independent state of Tannu-Tuva. It was fully incorporated into the Soviet Union only in 1944. (*See also* **Mongolia**)

IG

U

UNITED DEMOCRATIC PARTY (UDP – THAILAND). The centrist United Democratic Party (*Saha Prachathippatai* – UDP) was formed in 1986 as a result of divisions within the **Social Action Party.** In the July 1986 elections, the party won 38 seats and did not participate in the Prem government. Support for the UDP declined massively during the July 1988 elections, and it won only five seats. Nevertheless, it joined the six-member ***Chart Thai***-led coalition government in August, and the party's leader (appointed in May 1988), Col. Phol Reongpraservit, is one of eight Ministers attached to the Prime Minister's Office.

DS

UNITED DEVELOPMENT PARTY (INDONESIA). The United Development Party (*Partai Persatuan Pembangunan* – PPP) was formed in 1973 as a merger of four Islamic formations, namely the Islamic Scholars' Renaissance (*Nahdatul Ulaama* – NU), the Indonesian Islamic Party (*Partai Islam Indonesia* – Parii), the United Islamic Party of Indonesia (*Partai Sarekat Islam Indonesia* – PSII) and the Islamic Education Unity Party (*Persatuan Terbijah Islamijah* – Perti). Although Islamic in orientation, the PPP generally supports the **Suharto** government in matters other than those relating to religion.

In the 1977 elections to the House of Representatives the PPP obtained 99 elective seats (out of 360) and 29.3 per cent of the total vote (somewhat more than the aggregate share of the four constituent parties in 1971). In May 1982 the PPP's share of the vote slipped to 28 per cent and its representation to 94 elective seats (out of 364), although this outcome was challenged by the party, which claimed in particular that the official results for Jakarta were fraudulent. At a congress in December 1984 the NU decided to withdraw from the PPP and from "practical politics" and to concentrate instead on social and educational activities. In the April 1987 elections the PPP declined further to 61 elective seats (out of 400) and 16 per cent of the valid votes, although it again challenged the results, this time claiming in particular that its loss of majority status in the traditional Muslim stronghold of Aceh was due to electoral fraud perpetrated by **Golkar.**

In March 1988 the PPP chairman, H.J. Naro, became a candidate for the post of Vice-President (reportedly with support from sections of the armed forces) but withdrew at the last moment, thus allowing the Golkar chairman, Lt.-Gen. Sudharmono, to be elected unopposed by the People's Consultative Assembly.

DS

UNITED MALAYS NATIONAL ORGANIZATION (UMNO). UMNO was formally established at a Johore congress in 1946 under the leadership of Datuk Onn bin Jaafar, who was succeeded in 1951 by Tunku Abdul Rahman. Against a background of armed Communist insurgency, UMNO in 1952–54 constructed an Alliance coalition with the two main Chinese and Indian communal parties. Having first come to power in 1955 under the colonial regime, the Alliance led the country to independence in 1957 and won large parliamentary majorities in the 1959, 1964 and 1969 elections, with UMNO as the pre-eminent government party. An eruption of serious inter-communal violence following the 1969 elections precipitated the resignation of Tunku Abdul Rahman in September 1970, when Tun Abdul Razak became UMNO president and thus Prime Minister. Under his leadership the Alliance was converted into a broader-based **National Front.** Tun Abdul Razak died in early 1976 and was succeeded by Dato Hussein bin Onn, who was himself succeeded by Dr **Mahathir Mohamed Seri** in mid-1981. Having won further large parliamentary majorities in 1974, 1978, and 1982, the UMNO-led coalition was again returned to power in August 1986, when UMNO secured 83 of the 148 seats (out of 177) won by the Front.

Meanwhile, internal divisions had surfaced within UMNO in February 1986 and at the party's 38th general assembly in April 1987 Dr Mahathir was challenged for the UMNO presidency (an almost unprecedented event) and was only narrowly re-elected, whereupon his opponents challenged the legality of the election on the grounds that ineligible delegates had been present. The outcome of their legal action was a more fundamental High Court ruling on Feb. 4, 1988, that the existence of 30 unregistered UMNO branches effectively rendered the whole party an "illegal society" under the 1966 Societies Act. Immediately after this ruling Tunku Abdul Rahman announced plans to create a new party called UMNO – Malaysia, while Dr Mahathir on

255

Feb. 16, 1988, announced the formation of the UMNO – *Baru* (Malay for "new"). Supported by a majority of the old UMNO leadership, the "New UMNO" was immediately admitted to the National Front. The original anti-Mahathir UMNO litigants lodged an appeal against the High Court ruling in late February on the grounds that they had only been challenging the April 1987 leadership elections and not the legality of the party as such; the appeal was rejected in August 1988. In late January 1989, Datuk Musa Hitam, a former Deputy Prime Minister and a leading anti-Mahathir dissident, declared himself a member of UMNO – *Baru*. However, other leading anti-Mahathir UMNO dissidents had formed a group around Tunku Razaleigh Hamzah, called *Semangat '46* (Spirit of 1946, referring to the year of the original UMNO's founding).

DS

UNITED NATIONALIST DEMOCRATIC ORGANIZATION (UNIDO – PHILIPPINES).

UNIDO, led by **Salvador Laurel**, was formally launched in April 1982 as an alliance of anti-Marcos groups. For the 1984 legislative elections UNIDO ran a unified opposition campaign in over 180 districts with the PDP-Laban alliance. It did not, however, endorse a "basis for Unity Agreement" signed in late 1984 by a number of prominent opposition leaders. In March 1985 UNIDO formed a National Alliance Council (NAC) with the aim of agreeing on a single candidate for the forthcoming presidential election. An agreement was eventually, and unexpectedly, reached in December 1985 with a recently formed coalition vehicle for supporters of **Corazon Aquino**, that Aquino should stand for the presidency as a UNIDO candidate with Laurel as her running-mate for the vice-presidency. Once Aquino had defeated **Marcos** and had established herself in office, Vice-President Laurel became increasingly estranged from the new President and, correspondingly, the UNIDO machinery moved steadily away from its partnership with Aquino's PDP-Laban towards the right-wing opposition.

DS

UNITED STATES OF AMERICA. *Population*: 248 million (est. 1988 for this and following data). *Area*: 9,363,130 sq km. *Gross Domestic Product*: US$4,489,000 million. *Trade*: imports: $424,081 million; exports: $250,405 million; total: $674,486 million. *Top five trading partners*: Canada (imports: $71,510 million;

exports: $57,354 million; total: $128,864 million); Japan (imports: $88,074 million; exports: $28,249 million; total: $116,121 million); West Germany (imports: $28,028 million; exports: $11,748 million; total: $39,766 million); United Kingdom (imports: $17,998 million; exports: $14,114 million; total: $32,102 million); South Korea (imports: $17,991 million; exports: $8,099 million; total: $26,080 million). *Total Federal Government spending*: $1,054,091 million. *Defence spending*: $269,690 million. *Education spending*: $17,780 million. *Urban population as percentage of total*: 74.5. *Birth rate*: 6.8 per thousand. *Life expectancy* 78.2.

The Pacific dimension. Historically, the USA has developed by westward expansion from a cluster of states on the Eastern seaboard. Its key Pacific state, California, was ceded by Mexico in 1848, becoming the 31st state in 1850. Over the next half century the development and integration of the USA as a continental power, from the Atlantic to the Pacific, proceeded apace, hastened by the growth of a national railway system, the rise of nationally operating business corporations, and the continued influx of immigrants (primarily from Europe). That process of westward expansion has continued in the twentieth century. Hawaii, annexed to the USA in 1898, and Alaska, purchased from Russia in 1867, were admitted as the newest states of the Union in 1959. California, meanwhile, has in the period since World War II become the nation's most populous state (with an estimated 28,000,000 people by 1988) and an economic powerhouse (particularly associated with the growth of new technology industry, as in Silicon Valley) which considered alone would constitute the seventh largest economy in the Western World. Symbolic of the rise in importance of the Western seaboard, Los Angeles has grown from a small settlement in the early years of this century, to the nation's second most populous metropolitan area, and is expected to outstrip New York by the end of the century. While the Pacific states (California, Alaska, Hawaii, Oregon and Washington) contain only one sixth of the total US population, the region is the fastest growing in the country.

At the same time, the USA as a whole has come to experience a significant shift in its global perspective. In 1941 the USA became embroiled in World War II not through German action, but by the Japanese attack on Pearl Harbour. For the first time foreign entanglement had come from the Pacific area. Throughout most of the post-war period, however, military involvements in Korea and Vietnam (and tension with China over the position of Taiwan) notwithstanding, the primary focus of US foreign policy was on Europe, and especially the Soviet threat across the Iron Curtain. The principal trading axis of the USA was also with Europe. During the 1980s Americans have (almost exaggeratedly) come to see the Pacific Rim as the new political and economic focus of the world. In 1983 trans-Pacific trade exceeded trans-Atlantic trade for the first time. In particular the rise to economic power of "Japan Inc." has inspired a tide of apprehension that America (although still by a wide margin the world's largest economy, and immensely the strongest Western military power) is "in decline", that economic supremacy is passing to Japan, and that political leadership will follow. While there are signs that this pre-occupation may now be being counterbalanced by an awareness of the significance of the movement toward European political and economic integration, the USA has now clearly come to define itself as a "bi-polar" nation, a nation of the Pacific as much as of the Atlantic.

Political history. In 1987, Americans celebrated the 200th anniversary of their Constitution. The USA has in that time developed from a small agrarian nation with a population of 4,000,000 people into the world's largest economy with some 250 million people. The political system has experienced dramatic development as well: among other changes, 26 amendments have been added to the Constitution, including the first 10 (Bill of Rights) guaranteeing civil liberties; the 13th and 14th abolishing slavery (1865) and the 15th enfranchising blacks (1867); the 17th allowing direct election of senators (1913), and the 19th enfranching women (1920). Meanwhile 37 new states have joined the original 13.

But in a world where most nations experience political instability, the continuities of America's political system are even more remarkable. Political change has largely been incremental and rarely accompanied by violence. With a few notable exceptions Americans (and especially blacks in the Southern states) have enjoyed continuous civil and human rights as guaranteed in the Bill of Rights and for the last century two major parties (the Democrats and Republicans) have dominated the political process at both federal and state level, with orderly transfers of power from election to election.

America's political system is essentially a reaction to the failings of the wartime Continental Congress (1776-81) and Articles of Confederation (1781-87), and tradeoffs among the different states and their respective interests. Both early governments were essentially an alliance of 13 sovereign states presided over by a president;

powers of taxation, trade regulation, and conscription remained largely in the hands of the states. But an increasing number of political leaders soon realized that a stronger government was necessary if the United States was to overcome such problems as vast national and state debts, foreign threats, local unrest such as Shay's Rebellion (1786), and economic stagnation.

In 1786 Congress called for a convention the following spring to address these and related questions. In May 1787, 55 delegates gathered in Philadelphia and for the next four months hotly debated the structure and powers of a future government. The resulting Constitution was built around several key compromises. The delegates were split into three camps concerning executive powers. Alexander Hamilton and John Adams advocated a powerful executive and state; Thomas Paine and Benjamin Franklin wanted a weak Cabinet system subservient to a weak Congress; while Thomas Jefferson and James Madison succeeded in pushing through the mainstream position calling for a check and balance system between the three branches of national government, as well as between the national and state governments. Hamilton and Adams did succeed in ensuring that the president would be elected indirectly through an electoral college while states were allowed to continue the requirement that only property owners could vote. In addition, the presidency combined several important roles including head of state, head of government, and commander-in-chief to the military.

The delegates were split just as deeply over the structure and powers of Congress. Eventually it was decided that a Senate with two members from each state serving six-year terms would satisfy the small states' concern for equal power with large states, while a House of Representatives with the number of state members based on population ensured that the large states would be adequately represented. The two-year terms for representatives satisfied those concerned with maintaining close ties between Congressmen and their constituents. The Hamiltonians were pleased when it was decided that senators would be elected indirectly by state legislatures, while the Jeffersonian faith in the common man was fulfilled with direct elections for the House of Representatives. Congress was given the powers to regulate trade, coin money, collect taxes, and declare war. The southern states, which had generally been lukewarm at best over independence, were mollified by allowing the continuation of state rights over slavery and any other matters not included in the constitution.

Although a Bill of Rights was not included in the original Constitution, the Jeffersonians succeeded in getting an additional 10 amendments approved by December 1791 that guaranteed Americans full civil rights. Other reforms soon followed. Chief Justice John Marshall presided over several key court cases that clarified and asserted the Supreme Court's right of judicial review and strengthened federal over state powers. By the mid-1820s, property requirements for voting had been abandoned by almost all the states while secret ballots were widely used.

During this time American politics divided into a two-party system, crystallizing in the mid-nineteenth century into the Democrats and Republicans. Following the Civil War (1861–65), when Southern states sought to secede from the Union and were defeated by the more populous North, the Republicans maintained a strong hold over the federal government until the 1930s. The Democrats dominated only in the South. From 1861 to 1933, the Republicans controlled the House for 50 years, the Senate for 54, and the presidency for all but 16 years. It took the great depression after 1929 and the Hoover administration's failure to alleviate mass unemployment and poverty to bring about a shift in power from the Republicans to the Democrats. President Franklin D. Roosevelt forged a winning coalition of progressives, labour, blacks, ethnic groups, and working class behind his New Deal policies designed to stimulate growth, and provide welfare and social security. The policies in effect represented an historic reversal of the Democrats' commitment to "states' rights" and minimalist federal government, and the beginning of the emergence of the main emphasis of the party on "big government" policies. While the New Deal alleviated the worst conditions, it took the massive production stimulus of World War II for the United States to return to steady economic growth and prosperity. Between 1932 and 1988, the two parties split control over the White House, with the Democrats winning eight elections and the Republicans seven. The Democrats, however, have enjoyed a majority in both the House and Senate for all but a few years, retaining their dominance in the South even as that part of the nation has come to support Republican presidential candidates.

Another change starting from the Roosevelt era was the growing power of the presidency. Before Roosevelt, powerful presidents were the exception rather than the rule; Polk, Lincoln, McKinley, and Wilson assumed a powerful hand over government during periods of national crisis, but almost all others were essentially caretakers, reacting to events rather than pursuing new policy initiatives. In contrast, Roosevelt not only changed the orientation of government toward the economy and society from passivity to activism, but also began to build up the institutions of the executive branch to implement his policies. In the aftermath of World War II the powers of the presidency were also greatly strengthened by the rise of US military and foreign policy influence, the exercise of which was concentrated in the White House.

Until the early 1970s, Congress and the nation not only accepted but encouraged the growing power of the presidency in order to deal with national challenges like the great depression, World War II, and the Cold War. The steady enlargement of the president's powers was, however, checked with the Congressional backlash against the Watergate scandal which forced President Nixon to resign in 1974. That year Congress passed the War Powers Act which imposed limits on the president's ability to conduct American military operations overseas without Congressional approval. Since then the Democrat-controlled Congress has frequently checked or even reversed White House policy. For example, the 1984 Boland amendment attempted to reverse the Reagan administration policy toward Central America by forbidding any American military aid to the Contra guerrillas trying to overthrow the left-wing Sandinista regime in Nicaragua. The Reagan administration continued providing military funding to the Contras by covert means, but these efforts were exposed with the Iran–Contra scandal which broke in November 1986.

Economic development. America's economy has developed in a pattern of steady long-term growth interrupted by periods of retrenchment or stimulus. The government's role in the economy has changed greatly over the past 200 years. The federal government gradually assumed a greater role in the economy up to 1932, and an accelerated role since. At first the government role was confined to putting tariffs on imports, which were set at a rate high enough to allow American industries to develop, while low enough to satisfy the needs of everyone else.

Throughout the nineteenth century, the government directly stimulated growth by developing canals, railroads, and highways which gradually transformed the network of small regional markets into a national market in which firms could enjoy economies-of-scale production. It also aided development by giving away land to homesteaders and railroads. Repeated government exploration expeditions into the Western wilderness helped to open that territory to miners, farmers, and industrialists.

But it took the manufacturing needs of the

Civil War before America's economy experienced a genuine industrial takeoff. Steel, textiles, ship-building, and a range of other industries achieved vast production scales to serve military needs, and subsequently retooled to serve civilian markets after the War. A growing flow of foreign immigrants throughout the nineteenth century helped man the factories and stimulate mass demand for products and services, while British and other foreign investments fuelled the financial needs of American entrepreneurs.

In the twentieth century, the American economy benefited greatly from both world wars. Although the United States emerged from World War I as the world's biggest economy, Washington continued to refuse to take an active role in helping manage the global economy despite the fact that Britain was increasingly incapable of bearing the costs of upholding the system. The United States actually pulled down the world trade system with the Smoot Hawley Law of 1930 which erected high tariff barriers – foreign governments followed suit and world trade collapsed. The Roosevelt administration abandoned its predecessor's isolationist policies and instead began negotiating with the other industrial powers to revive world trade. At the same time the Roosevelt administration began using fiscal policies to stimulate the economy.

The production demands of World War II pulled the American economy out of the doldrums and onto a path of steady development. The American-sponsored multilateral Bretton Woods Agreement (1944) and General Agreement on Tariffs and Trade (1947) required almost 50 nations to fix their currencies and dismantle trade barriers to stimulate the world economy. After the war, Washington sent over $11,000 million in aid to Europe, $2,200 million to Japan, and thousands of millions elsewhere in an attempt to help rebuild those countries' shattered economies. The Korean War (1950-53) stimulated the takeoff of the world economy, and both the United States and rest of the relatively open market countries experienced continual economic growth until OPEC's quadrupling of oil prices in 1973.

But the American economy began experiencing development problems well before 1973. The Johnson administration policy (1963-69) of funding both the Great Society and Vietnam War led to inflation and balance of payments problems. Meanwhile, European and, in particular, Japanese firms, generously aided by their governments, were catching up with and often surpassing their American counterparts in industries like textiles, consumer electronics, and steel. President Nixon (1969-74) attempted to reverse

America's relative economic decline by abandoning the Gold Standard and imposing temporary tariffs in August 1971, devaluing the dollar by 15 per cent in December, and finally allowing the dollar to float in 1973. America's economic gains from these interventionist policies were however wiped out by the OPEC oil price rises of 1973 and 1979 which led to stagnant growth, high inflation, unemployment, and high interest rates.

Since the world recession of the early 1980s the US economy has enjoyed the longest period of continuous growth in its history. Despite this, however, a related series of imbalances in the economy have triggered a major debate about future prospects. The federal budget deficit, as a result of tax cuts, increases in real terms in military spending, and the irresistible momentum of built-in inflationary social security benefits, soared during the Reagan administration. Congress and the administration agreed legislation (the Gramm-Rudman Act of 1985) which provided a formula for orderly deficit reduction, but in successive years the targets have not been reached and the Gramm-Rudman process has come to be viewed with widespread scepticism. In April 1989 Congress and the White House agreed a package of measures which would notionally reduce the deficit in fiscal 1990 (beginning Oct. 1, 1989) to $100,000 million, but most independent experts believed the budgetary assumptions were unrealistic, and that a figure of $130,000 million or more was likely. While the deficit level is markedly reduced from its mid-1980s peak the deficit remains a persistent problem and George Bush since becoming President in January 1989 has stuck firmly to Reagan's policy of not raising taxes.

The budget deficit has been financed by an inflow of foreign capital, and in the USA there has been a growing apprehension that foreigners (and especially the Japanese) have been "buying up" the USA. At the same time the USA has run a severe deficit on its trade, a deficit which arguably has arisen more from the weakness of its exporting industries than from the demand of US consumers for foreign goods. (The USA in relation to the size of its economy having the lowest volume of trade of any leading economy.) On its trade with Japan the USA has run particularly significant deficits, with Japan accounting for 40% of the total deficit in 1988. Controversy over Japanese protectionist attitudes has at times assumed a bitter character, with the Reagan and Bush administrations facing congressional pressure (which they have largely resisted) to take punitive action against Japan. Given that the USA has also run severe deficits with most of its other trading partners, including countries themselves in deficit with other nations, the vehemence of the hostility has arguably reflected less as objective assessment of Japanese "unfairness" then anxiety about Japanese aggrandisement.

In the early 1980s the USA was the largest net creditor in the world with an investment surplus of $141,000 million in 1981; by 1986, however, it had become the largest net debtor with a net debt of $263,600 million. While the scale of the debt, relative to that of the US economy, was of little direct significance (there were no difficulties in servicing the debt), this dramatic reversal led to widespread anxiety that the USA might be faltering as a major economic power. Again, Japan was viewed as America's heir apparent. The issue has become one where image and self-definition is as important as reality: to most Americans it is "Japan Inc." that is buying up the USA, although Japanese direct assets in the USA ($33,400 million at the end of 1987) are actually less than those of Britain ($74,900 million) and even the Netherlands ($47,000 million); likewise Japan's emergence as the world's leading net creditor has persuaded many Americans that Japan is "taking over" as banker of the world (and so the West's leading power) although Britain has continued a relative economic decline despite standing as second only to Japan as a net creditor.

Foreign Policy. It is sometimes easy to forget that despite its present role as a global superpower and leader of the Western alliance, the United States managed to heed President Washington's admonition to "avoid entangling alliances" throughout most of its history. Without a neighbouring foreign threat, the government could concentrate its foreign policy on promoting territorial expansion across the continent and into the Pacific Basin while negotiating access for American merchants in overseas markets. America's links with the Pacific began as early as 1784 when the "empress of China" became the first American merchant ship to trade at Canton, and were dramatically symbolized a generation later when in 1805 Lewis and Clark led the first American expedition to cross the continent and gaze out over the Pacific Ocean. It was the government's success at waging both war and diplomacy that eventually transformed these first tenuous trade and exploration efforts into global economic and military power.

Throughout the nineteenth century, the government added new areas of territory to the United States through a series of treaties, some backed by skilful diplomacy, others by war.

Washington did not hesitate to identify and defend American overseas spheres of interests. As early as 1823, the Monroe Doctrine warned the European powers not to attempt any new colonization of Latin America. Commodore Perry's two voyages to Japan (1853–54) during which he succeeded in opening Japan to the world economy marked the beginning of America's status as a Pacific Basin Great Power. The Open Door policy (1898) forced the European powers to allow American business equal access to China's markets.

The Versailles Treaty (1919), following the entrance of the United States into World War I (1917), marked America's tentative emergence as a global power. President Wilson took the lead in pushing the inclusion of notions of democracy and self-determination in the treaty and the creation of the League of Nations. Although in rejecting membership with the League of Nations the Senate followed the traditional pattern of American isolationism, the United States clearly remained a global military power through its negotiation of the Washington (1922) and London (1930) treaties in which the American and British navies remained the world's largest. Yet the government plunged itself into economic isolation in 1930 through the tariff walls erected by Smoot Hawley.

It was the Japanese attack on Pearl Harbour in 1941 that forced Washington into unequivocally fulfilling its responsiblities as a great power, and since America's explosion of an atomic bomb in 1945, as a superpower; a role it has consistently followed to the present day. Washington has led three great foreign policy crusades since 1941: against the Axis powers until their 1945 defeat, and since then the interrelated goals of creating and supporting a liberal world economy and containment of the Soviet Union and communism.

American foreign policy has passed through two phases since 1945 in pursuit of these goals, the first characterized by its ideological fervour, the second by its pragmatism. During the first phase the United States negotiated the creation of a range of institutions designed to promote trade and contain the Soviet Union. Washington directly negotiated such political institutions as the United Nations and Organization of American States, and economic such as the World Bank, International Monetary Fund, and Organization of Economic Co-operation and Development. It has indirectly encouraged others, such as the European Communities and **Association of South-East Asian Nations (ASEAN)**, as well as tied the world in a web of bilateral and multilateral military pacts with West Europe (Nato), Japan, Australia and New Zealand (**ANZUS Pact**), South-east Asia (**SEATO**), and the Middle

East (Centro); it helped launch and fuelled these organizations with massive economic and military aid. This diplomacy was supported by two intensive wars, in Korea (1950–53) and Vietnam (1961–75), and covert espionage activities including toppling unfriendly regimes in Guatemala and Iran.

The second more pragmatic phase started in 1969 with the Nixon presidency. Nixon recognized that the United States had succeeded both in creating a dynamic world economy and in containing the Soviet Union. The decline of the Soviet military threat and rise of an economic threat from erstwhile allies in Western Europe and Japan required new policies. In response to the declining geopolitical threat, Washington negotiated a treaty with Hanoi that enabled the United States to withdraw its troops from Vietnam (1972), and detente with both the Soviet Union and China. The Salt I Arms Control Treaty (1974) was the first significant attempt to slow down the nuclear arms race. In response to the rising geoeconomic threat Nixon abandoned the Bretton Woods system of fixed exchange rates (1971–73) and began to retaliate against unfair foreign trade practices. These policies were continued throughout the 1970s by Presidents Ford and Carter.

The Reagan administration at first (1981–85) reverted to the early post-war ideological "free trade" and "evil empire" orientations to the world economy and Soviet Union, respectively. But by the mid-1980s, after the economic policies had not only clearly failed, but actually accelerated America's relative economic decline and the Cold War policies complicated rather than resolved many international problems, the Reagan administration switched to more pragmatic policies attempting to alleviate the deepening trade deficits and cut an intermediate nuclear arms control treaty with the Soviet Union (1987). The Bush administration has continued these pragmatic policies.

At the same time the Pacific has emerged as co-equal with Europe as a focus of foreign policy concerns. US attitudes toward Japan have shown a degree of ambivalence. On the one hand, the Reagan administration put pressure on Japan to increase its military spending above the threshold of 1 per cent of GNP (compared with the more than 6 per cent spent by the USA) and to share the burden of defending Western interests in the Pacific. At the same time, there has been an undercurrent of apprehension as to the impact of remilitarized Japan, already established as a great economic power, on US interests in the Pacific. While Japan is officially regarded as a close ally, and the Tokyo–Washington axis has become the

most important in the Western alliance, friendship is tempered by doubts as to the fundamental unity of interests between the two countries. It is far from clear how far Japan will seek to expand its foreign policy involvement, and how far it will remain content to achieve an economic ascendancy not reflected in diplomatic, territorial, cultural or military ambitions.

George Bush is arguably the most knowledgeable President in US history in respect of Pacific Basin affairs. His past assignments have included heading the US mission to Beijing in 1974–75 as US relations with China were being opened up. The first year of the Bush administration has, however, witnessed a continuity of established policies towards the region rather than any significant initiatives. The cautious rapprochement with China has remained unaffected by China's own resumption of closer ties with the Soviet Union, or indeed by the crackdown by Chinese hardliners on the reform movement. At the same time, the USA has begun to reassess the nature of its relationships with such states as the Philippines and South Korea which have sought to move from client status to a more equal position as allies. The one-time assured US hegemony in the Pacific has faltered, and the USA faces a complex mosaic of interests in which the distinction between friends and enemies is less clear-cut. At the same time the dramatic developments in the Soviet Union and Eastern Europe especially in 1989 have tended to offset what had arguably become an over-intense preoccupation with the Pacific region.

WN

UNITED STATES–JAPANESE SECURITY RELATIONS.

The most important United States alliance in the Pacific has been that with Japan. The alliance has been of considerable benefit for both parties. For the United States it has ensured that Japan has in effect been part of the global security system constructed by Washington as part of its efforts at containment. For Japan the alliance has provided a security guarantee that has made it possible to focus its effort on economic growth.

The US–Japanese alliance was the product of the Allied occupation of Japan and of the Cold War between the United States and the Soviet bloc. Gen. MacArthur promulgated a new constitution for Japan and was determined to ensure that militarism and totalitarianism were excluded from Japanese life. The aim was to transform Japan into the "Switzerland of East Asia" and Japan was given a constitution which went into effect in 1947 and which contained a clause renouncing war as a legitimate instrument of Japanese policy. In 1948, however, there was a shift of emphasis in United States policy towards Japan, motivated in part by the deteriorating relationship with the Soviet Union. During late 1948 and 1949 a new consensus began to emerge in Washington on policy towards Japan. Greater emphasis was placed on the construction of military facilities in Japan and Okinawa, and on Japanese economic recovery, while the role of US occupation forces was down-played. What really crystallized the evolution of United States policy towards Japan, however, was the **Korean War**. This made it imperative for the United States to co-opt Japan as a Pacific ally and to conclude a long deferred peace treaty. John Foster Dulles, who had been appointed as adviser to the Secretary of State, Dean Acheson, was charged with negotiating the peace treaty.

By 1951 the Japanese government – largely under the impetus of the war in Korea – had come to see the benefits of a continued presence of American troops. Accordingly, the Treaty of Peace with the Allied Powers which was signed on Sept. 8, 1951, was accompanied by a Security Treaty between the United States and Japan. Although the preamble made clear that the United States expected Japan increasingly to seek responsibility for its own defence, in the meantime the United States was prepared to maintain certain of its armed forces in and about Japan. Article 1 of the Treaty stated that "such forces may be utilized to contribute to the maintenance of the international peace and security in the Far East and to the security of Japan against armed attack from without . . .". The Peace Treaty left the United States as the sole UN administrator of the Ryukyu Islands. This enabled it to transform Okinawa into a forward military base which had considerable importance in American strategy, but created a disaffected population on the island and cause some strain in the US–Japan alliance during the 1950s.

Both the Peace Treaty and the US–Japan Security Treaty came into effect on April 28, 1952. During the 1950s, however, the relationship evolved in ways which made it necessary to establish a new framework. Accordingly, the two governments negotiated a new treaty which was signed on Jan. 19, 1960 and entered into force on June 23, 1960. The Treaty, which ushered in a period of much more equal partnership, pledged the signatories to encourage economic collaboration between them and reaffirmed that the United States land, naval and air forces were granted use of facilities and areas in Japan. More important in many ways than the terms of the Treaty, however, was an exchange of notes in

which the United States pledged that it would engage in prior consultation with Japan before there were any increases in its forces in Japan, prior to any changes in arming and equipping these forces, and before they were used for any action outside the territory under Japanese rule.

The 1960s Treaty did not deal with the Ryukyu Islands, and the future of these islands became the key issue in the US–Japan relationship during the 1960s, a decade in which Japan's gross national product almost tripled. Although the American base at Okinawa took on greater importance as a result of US involvement in Vietnam, there was increased willingness by Washington to compromise on its political status. An agreement was finally signed on June 17, 1971 on the transfer to Japan of sovereignty over the Ryukyu Islands, and they reverted to Japanese jurisdiction on May 15, 1972. The United States was granted the use of the Kadena Air Force base on Okinawa, although with the proviso that Japanese approval was necessary for operations to be launched from the base.

Although agreement on what had been a troublesome issue was reached in 1971, in other respects it was a traumatic year for US–Japanese relations. In July, it was announced that President Nixon would be visiting Beijing the following year – an about-turn in United States policy that had been made without any prior consultation with Japan. The difficulties were intensified by a surprise devaluation of the dollar and the imposition of an import surcharge by the United States. The psychological impact of these developments, however, was underlined by the United States military retrenchment that took place during the 1970s.

These developments led to some questioning of the extent to which Japan could rely on the United States' security guarantee. This question became more important during the 1970s as the Soviet presence in the Pacific became more salient. Nevertheless, the security framework enshrined in the US–Japanese bilateral relationship has remained intact. Although Japan expanded its Self Defence Forces, there was no fundamental reappraisal by Japan of its military role, especially after it became clear that United States retrenchment in Southeast Asia would not be followed by disengagement from Northeast Asia.

For its part, the United States has remained somewhat ambivalent about Japan taking on more military responsibility. On the one hand, there have been strong pressures from the US Congress for America's allies in both Asia and Europe to take a larger share of the burden of defence. On the other hand, it was the United

States which imposed on Japan a constitution that forbids it from going to war and which restricts the type of military forces it is allowed to have. Furthermore, there is a reluctance on the part of the United States to do anything which might contribute to the resurgence of Japanese nationalism. There are also concerns that a militarily more powerful Japan will provoke considerable anxiety and fear elsewhere in Asia. Recognizing these competing impulses, Japan has attempted to go some way to meet the burden-sharing demands without doing anything that might be seen as a potential threat to the security of other Asian states. Although Japan's defence budget has increased as its GNP has grown, the percentage of the GNP devoted to defence has remained remarkably low and is still under 2 per cent. Nevertheless, by the late 1980s, Japan was officially spending around 30 billion dollars *per annum* on defence as well as an additional 10 billion on service pensions. These figures compare well with 35 billion spent by the United Kingdom, 32 billion by France and 31 billion by Germany. The funds are devoted to military forces which protect the Japanese islands themselves as well as two sea lanes which stretch out to 1,000 miles. In order to do this, Japan has acquired more anti-submarine aircraft and more destroyers than the United States deploys in the Western Pacific. It has also acquired sophisticated systems such as F-15s and Patriot missiles, as well as the Aegis radar system, and has committed itself to producing under licence 100 P3C anti-submarine aircraft. There have been steps to increase co-operation between Japanese and United States forces, and in 1982 joint exercises were held for the first time. Furthermore, in 1987 the Japanese government agreed to increase its share of the costs of maintaining United States bases in Japan.

If the alliance remains close, however, it has also been subject to considerable stresses and strains. One source of these has been the economic relationship between the two states. Although both sides have adopted corrective measures Japan has consistently run large trade surpluses with the United States. This has contributed to the American trade deficit and has fuelled demands by the United States Congress for protectionist legislation. If trade and security issues become more directly linked then managing the alliance will be even more difficult.

Another issue that has caused some problems has been that of technology transfer. In 1987 it was revealed that Toshiba had sold sensitive technology to the Soviet Union. Although the Japanese government subsequently tightened up its export controls, the disclosure led the Pentagon to cancel several projects involving Japanese companies. Even more serious was the dispute over the FSX fighter aircraft. In June 1988 Japan and the United States agreed to co-produce a fighter. In early 1989, however, there was considerable opposition in Congress to what was seen as a form of technology transfer that would facilitate the creation of a Japanese aircraft industry and thereby add to its industrial competitiveness, especially in relation to the United States. Some critics of the deal also argued that instead of acquiring the new plane, Japan should buy American F-16s – a deal that would do something to ease the trade deficit. In spite of this opposition and complications caused by congressional actions, the deal was approved.

If there are many resentments and frustrations on the American side of the Alliance, there are also some on the Japanese side. Opposition to US bases in Japan has been consistent. In May 1989 the anti-United States sentiment was given a boost when it was disclosed that in 1965 a United States plane carrying a nuclear bomb had been lost at sea 65 miles from Japan. Although the United States assured Japan that there was no threat to its environment, the disclosure touched a very sensitive nerve in Japan. It certainly raised the issue of whether United States ships visiting Japan were violating Japan's non-nuclear principles – a question that Japan has traditionally refrained from asking.

In spite of these strains, there is a basic firmness to the US–Japanese Alliance. In the final analysis, the two states need each other. The link with Japan is crucial to the United States position in the Pacific, while American protection remains something that Japan values. If both sides have a strong interest in maintaining the Alliance in the 1990s, however, it is clear that the tensions and difficulties will require skilful management if the common interests are not to be submerged by mutual acrimony.

PW

UNITED STATES-PHILIPPINES SECURITY RELATIONS. The relationship between the United States and the Philippines goes back to the nineteenth century when the United States, under President Mckinley, having defeated Spain, took possession of the Philippines. The Philippines has had American forces on its territory since 1908 and an American base at Clark Field since 1902.

Ejected by Japan from the Philippines, Gen. MacArthur vowed to return and, after the defeat of Japan, the United States once again took possession of the islands. Although the Philippines became independent in July 1946, the Treaty reserved US use of the bases. On March 14, 1947, the representatives of the United States and the Philippines signed an agreement providing for the establishment for a 99-year period of 23 US ground, naval and air bases on the islands. This agreement provided a basis for massive American presence which has remained one of the key elements in United States strategy in the Pacific. It was supplemented by a more formal political linkage when, on Aug. 31, 1951, the United States, as part of its Pacific containment strategy, signed a mutual defence treaty with the Philippines. In this treaty, which entered into force on Aug. 27, 1952, the signatories undertook to consult in the event of a threat of armed attack on one of the parties and to maintain and develop the means to deter aggression.

Not surprisingly, therefore, the United States played a key role in the Philippines during the 1950s and helped the government contain an insurgency by communist guerrillas, the Huk. There were question marks about the status of the bases, however, and in July 1956 the United States confirmed that it recognized the sovereignty of the government of the Philippines over the United States bases. In response to continued controversy over the bases, however, a memorandum was signed on Oct. 12, 1959. This shortened the leases from the initial 99 years to 25 years from the date of the memorandum and committed the United States to consult the government of the Philippines before either the operational use of the bases or the installation of long range missiles. These arrangements were superseded by an executive agreement of September 1966 between the United States and the Philippines. This amended the 1947 agreement on the bases, and set a fixed term for the bases agreement. This was now set at 25 years, to end Sept. 16, 1991. After this date the agreement is subject to termination at one year's notice by either side.

In a further agreement signed on Jan. 6, 1979, the United States was allowed continued use of the Clark Field air base and the Subic Bay naval base for a further five years and was guaranteed "unhampered military operations involving its forces in the Philippines". In return Filipino sovereignty over the bases was reaffirmed, the agreement was to be reviewed every five years and the United States government committed itself to efforts to obtain large-scale military assistance and sales credit to the Philippines.

The American bases in the Philippines are of crucial importance to United States strategy in the Pacific. They are America's largest bases outside the United States itself and their importance was underlined in the 1970s as the Soviet naval presence in the Pacific became more evident and

the Soviet navy acquired bases and facilities in Vietnam. The bases consist of the Clark Air Base, the Subic Bay Naval Base and several ancillary facilities, including Tabones Training Complex, Wallace Air Station, a radar surveillance site and tactical air training facility, John Hay Air Force base (a rest and recreation centre) and San Miguel Naval Communication System, which is a part of the US Navy's global communication system.

Clark Air Base is home base for a tactical fighter wing and a tactical airlift wing, and also acts as the logistics hub for US air forces in the Western Pacific. It houses maintenance facilities, and large stockpiles of fuel and ammunition. It is also a crucial element in the Pacific and Indian Ocean airlift system. The Subic Bay complex is designed to provide logistic support for naval operations in both the Western Pacific and the Indian Ocean and can help to sustain the operations of several carrier battle groups. The bases are essential to the US strategy of forward deployment in the Pacific and facilitate rapid response in a crisis. The base at Subic took on great importance in supplying US naval forces during the Vietnam War while Clark acted as a transportation hub for the movement of men and material.

In the 1980s the bases took on greater importance as the Soviet Union increased the strength of its Pacific fleet and occupied the former US bases in Vietnam at Danang and Cam Ranh Bay. In the event of a conflict in Southeast Asia, the bases in the Philippines would provide the United States with important assets and access to the South China Sea. They also help the United States to threaten the Soviet lines of communication to Vietnam. The bases are also important in relation to Northeast Asia and US support for Japan and South Korea, while they also enhance the American capacity to conduct military operations in the Indian Ocean and Persian Gulf.

The main difficulty with the bases is maintaining their legitimacy against a background of domestic political turmoil in the Philippines. The fact that President **Marcos** was a strong supporter of the United States, together with the United States' desire to retain the bases, meant that Washington was widely seen in the Philippines as closely linked to the Marcos regime which was becoming increasingly repressive. The Reagan administration, however, skilfully disengaged from Marcos and threw its support behind **Corazon Aquino**, thereby establishing a good relationship with the new government.

Because of uncertainty about the future viability of the bases given anti-American sentiment in the Philippines, attention has been given to possible redeployment options. One possibility would be to redeploy to existing US bases elsewhere in the Pacific, especially those at Guam, Hawaii and Japan (including Okinawa). A second alternative would be to expand the base structure in Micronesia and redeploy there. This would involve enlarging the air and naval bases at Guam, extending the base structure to Saipan and Tinian and developing a new facility on Palau. A third alternative would be to redeploy to new bases on the South China Sea such as Taiwan. None of these alternatives is without its difficulties, however, and all three would mean some reduction in operational effectiveness as compared with the existing arrangements. Some combination of the second and third options would seem most advantageous but even this is a second best solution. It would cost around 8 billion dollars to relocate the bases, and in order to avoid this the United States has consistently furnished the Philippines with both military and economic assistance.

This assistance, however, has not prevented the emergence of considerable anti-American sentiment nor the growth of opposition to the bases. Under left-wing and nationalist pressure the Philippine Congress, in August 1987, introduced a bill that would ban nuclear weapons from the Philippines. This bill, which passed the Senate in May 1988, suggests that there could in the future be some tension between the concerns of the Philippines and a United States policy of neither confirming nor denying the presence of nuclear weapons on particualr US ships. A more immediate problem though was the continued activity of communist guerrilla forces. In November 1987 the guerrillas declared war on United States' forces in the Philippines, prompting these forces to go on alert. Later that month they claimed responsibility for the killings of US servicemen, and have continued to launch attacks on US personnel and property during 1988 and 1989.

At the same time the United States has managed to establish a reasonably good relationship with the Aquino government. It has provided considerable aid to the government to help fight the continuing insurgency, providing 450 million dollars to the Aquino government during its first 20 months. Partly because of the domestic pressures, however, the Philippine government has adopted a tough stance on the bases. In March 1988 the Foreign Minister stated that the bases were unwanted, that they served US interests and that the United States would have to pay significantly more for them. The last set of talks under the old agreement began in April 1988 and quickly became difficult over the issue of compensation. The United States has provided aid to the Philippines rather than rent for the

bases, and was emphatic that compensation was not rent. However agreement was reached in October 1988, in which the United States promised to give the Philippines 481 million dollars in both 1989 and 1990 – a figure that was up significantly from the 180 million per year that it had been providing. There is still uncertainty about the fate of the bases after the current agreement expires in 1991. An additional complication in the negotiations for renewing the bases agreement stems from Soviet statements suggesting that the Soviet Union would leave Cam Ranh Bay if the United States would pull out of the Philippines. Although the United States will be anxious to retain the bases, it will almost certainly have to make more concessions to the Philippines than it has done in the past.

PW

UNITED STATES-REPUBLIC OF KOREA SECURITY TREATY. Among United States military commitments in the Pacific, that to South Korea has been one of the most enduring but also one of the most troublesome. The commitment grew out of American involvement in the **Korean War** and has involved both a mutual security treaty and the deployment of United States forces in South Korea.

The US–Republic of Korea mutual security treaty was signed in Seoul on Aug. 8, 1953, and formally signed in Washington on Oct. 1, 1953. It legally entered into force on Nov. 17, 1954. The Treaty, of indefinite duration, can be ended at 12 months' notice by either party. The key articles in the Treaty are Articles 2, 3 and 4. Article 2 states that if the security or independence of either party is threatened then they will consult together. Furthermore, "separately and jointly, by self-help and mutual aid, the parties will maintain and develop appropriate means to deter armed attack". Article 3 states that an armed attack in the Pacific area on either of the signatories would be regarded by the other as dangerous to its own peace and security and that it would "act to meet the common danger in accordance with its constitutional processes". While much of this language is reminiscent of the North Atlantic Treaty signed by the United States and its European allies in 1949, Article 4 of the US–South Korea Treaty added an extra dimension, stating that "the Republic of Korea grants, and the United States accepts, the right to dispose US land, air and sea forces in and about the territory of the Republic of Korea as determined by mutual agreement".

Article 4 has provided the legal framework for the United States to maintain a significant military presence in South Korea since the war. This has been designed to deter another North Korean attack on South Korea and has tied the United States to the security of South Korea far more closely than a treaty alone would have done. Successive US administrations have reaffirmed the need for this presence. The contingent itself, though, has diminished considerably in size since its peak of 360,000 at the height of the Korean War. By 1957 the presence had diminished to 60,000 and consisted of two infantry divisions as well as tactical air power. It is also widely accepted that although the United States has adhered to its position of neither confirming nor denying the presence of nuclear weapons, there are in fact American tactical nuclear weapons deployed in South Korea.

With the American retrenchment that followed the Vietnam War, the Nixon administration withdrew 20,000 troops from South Korea, although in an effort to overcome South Korean concerns, it agreed to give 1.5 billion dollars to assist South Korea's force modernization plan. The Carter administration, however, announced in 1977 that it intended to withdraw the remaining United States ground troops from Korea. This was to be done in phases and was to be completed by 1992. Part of the rationale for this was concern that in the event of another conflict on the Korean peninsula the United States would be inextricably involved as a result of its military presence rather than through rational calculation. Although the United States pledged that it would augment its air power based in Korea and maintain its communication and intelligence facilities, the troop withdrawal decision aroused both dismay and disapproval. Not only was the South Korean government anxious to avoid what it saw as abandonment by the United States, but Japan was also concerned that the American withdrawal from Southeast Asia, which had taken place in the first half of the 1970s, was being followed by military withdrawal from Northeast Asia. In addition to these international pressures to reconsider the decision, the Carter administration was subjected to strong domestic pressure. The United States Army was extremely unhappy about the decision, while the CIA produced figures which suggested that North Korean military strength was greater than had been believed. These arguments evoked considerable sympathy in Congress and in 1979, with only 3,600 men withdrawn, the administration announced that there would be no further troop cuts. It was also significant that when in October 1979 President **Park** was assassinated, the United States deployed an aircraft carrier and support ships to the vicinity of the Korean peninsula to ensure that the North did not attempt to exploit the situation.

If there was no fundamental change in the size of the US presence in South Korea during the late 1970s there was an important change in the status of these forces. In 1978 South Korea and the United States transferred their forces to a new Combined Forces Command, which was headed by a United States general with a South Korean general as his deputy. The US contingent therefore remained in Korea not as part of the United Nations force but as a result of the mutual Defence Treaty.

During the 1980s in fact collaboration between United States and South Korean forces has increased. In 1975 the two states announced that they were beginning a series of annual exercises, and although these have invariably been described by North Korea as dangerously provocative, they have clearly been part of an exercise in both deterrence of North Korea and reassurance of South Korea. The annual joint exercises, however, became particularly important in 1988 in the run up to the Olympic Games which were held in Seoul. Although these exercises led North Korea to place its forces on full alert, as they had done in the past, they were nevertheless important in inhibiting any North Korean efforts to disrupt the Olympic Games.

The United States commitment to South Korea, therefore, has been maintained and the visible embodiment of that commitment has remained more or less unchanged since the early 1970s. In some respects, it has even been strengthened, and the Reagan administration modernized the equipment of US forces on the peninsula. A wing of 72 F-16s replaced the F-4s while the forces were strengthened by the introduction of the Stinger surface-to-air missiles as well as other precision-guided munitions.

At the same time, South Korea has taken serious steps to modernize its forces. As it has become more prosperous this has become easier and the United States has replaced its earlier grant aid with a policy of commercial sales to South Korea. Yet the United States had provided a solid foundation on which South Korea could build and between 1950 and 1980 it provided its ally with military aid of approximately 5.8 billion dollars. During the 1970s, however, South Korean defence spending rose by an average rate of over 12 per cent annually. During this period too South Korea made great strides in establishing its own defence industry.

It was also significant that, in talks which ended in June 1988, South Korea agreed to pay more of the support costs for US forces in South Korea. Although South Korea already contributed 1.9

billion dollars *per annum* (1.6 billion in terms of rent-free facilities to the upkeep of United States forces deployed in the country, and another 300 million in direct contributions) it agreed to increase its contribution. Secretary of Defence Carlucci welcomed this pledge and made clear that United States forces would stay in South Korea "as long as they are needed and as long as the Korean people want us to stay". As well as wanting cost-sharing, however, the United States has attempted to press South Korea into playing more of a regional role, including sending mine-sweepers to the Persian Gulf. Not surprisingly, Seoul resisted.

The possibility of an American reassessment of the United States presence is not the only source of difficulty in US–South Korean relations. If one challenge to the US commitment to South Korea comes from those in the United States who are concerned about military over-stretch and budget deficits, another comes from anti-American sentiment in South Korea itself. There has been considerable opposition in South Korea to the American presence, on the grounds that the United States has supported a series of repressive governments in Seoul. The sentiment was increased by the rather negative image of South Korea that was given by the United States television networks during the Seoul Olympics. It is also fuelled by American pressure on South Korea to open up its markets, thereby doing something to lessen the 10 billion dollar trade surplus which South Korea enjoyed during 1987. Throughout the latter half of 1988 there were attacks on Americans in South Korea and in early 1989 US troops in both Taegu and Kwangu were warned not to leave their bases in uniform.

Some of these difficulties may be alleviated by the agreement in May 1989 to move the US headquarters out of Seoul into rural areas and this should be completed by the mid-1990s. Discussions about modification of the operational command arrangements for the combined forces which would give South Korea more responsibility were also initiated. The United States also agreed to discuss the Status of Forces Agreement to ensure that South Koreans have the same rights as other US allies with American military bases on their territory. Although the bilateral alliance remains intact, therefore, there are signs of change and a recognition that South Korea will take on increasing responsibility. There is also a growing belief that there will be reductions in US forces in South Korea during the 1990s. Although the basic geopolitical calculations underpinning the alliance have not changed, it increasingly appears to be an alliance in transition.

PW

UNITED STATES–TAIWAN SECURITY RELATIONS. The United States' relationship with Taiwan has endured since the early 1950s. Yet it has undergone considerable alterations in its form as American priorities in the Pacific have changed. The US commitment to Taiwan grew out of the Cold War in Asia, and as the United States' assessments of the security situation have altered so has the commitment diminished. Although the formal commitment was abandoned by the Carter administration, however a residue of the security guarantee remains.

The civil war in China between the ruling **Kuomintang** and the Communists resulted in a communist victory and the proclamation of the People's Republic of China in Beijing on Oct. 1, 1949. By the end of the year the Kuomintang government had moved to Taiwan, and established a new capital. Although there had been some muted sympathy in Washington for **Mao Zedong** and his supporters – who had been described by some congressmen as "agrarian reformers" – this did not last in the climate of the late 1940s. Furthermore, the defeat of **Chiang Kai-shek** caused a profound shock in the United States, provoking a bitter debate about the loss of China and helping to create a climate in which McCarthyism could flourish. In these circumstances, there were powerful political pressures impelling the Truman administration to support Chiang Kai-shek and his desire to return to the mainland.

The United States' commitment to Taiwan developed most rapidly as a result of the **Korean War**, which was interpreted in Washington as part of a wider conflict between the free world and the communist bloc. On June 27, 1950, two days after the war began, Truman announced that he had ordered the Seventh Fleet not only to prevent any attacks on Taiwan by Communist China but also to ensure that the Taiwan government ceased air and sea operations against the mainland. Although his successor, President Eisenhower, announced on Feb. 2, 1953 that the Seventh Fleet would no longer be employed to shield Communist China, the real problem was protecting Taiwan from Beijing.

This became particularly urgent in 1954 as Beijing increased the pressure on Taiwan. In August 1954 the US Secretary of State, John Foster Dulles, declared that the Seventh Fleet would protect not only Taiwan but also other offshore islands that were crucial to its security. In September the Chinese army began the bombardment of Quemoy, in response to which Chiang's forces launched attacks against the mainland. It was against this background that the United States formalized its security relationship with Taiwan. On Dec. 1, 1954, the two governments signed a mutual security treaty in which the United States agreed to defend Taiwan, the Pescadores and "such other territories as may be determined by mutual agreement" against armed attack. This did nothing to defuse the crisis, however, and in January 1955 both chambers of congress passed the Formosa Resolution authorizing the President to use armed force to defend Taiwan and the Pescadores. After the Communist seizure of the Tachen and Nanchi islands in February the crisis receded and did not erupt again until 1958. In this crisis the United States escorted supply ships to Quemoy and effectively prevented it from being seized. The United States' commitment to Taiwan, therefore, was a clear and significant element in the Cold War in Asia. As the Cold War receded, however, and the United States reappraised its relationship with Beijing, it was inevitable that the relationship with Taiwan would be affected.

The reappraisal took place in the early 1970s and stemmed from the desire on the part of the Nixon administration to exploit the Sino-Soviet conflict by establishing closer links with the People's Republic of China, which, it was believed, could help to contain Soviet power in Asia. At the end of Nixon's visit to China in February 1972, Beijing announced that Taiwan continued to obstruct the normalization of relations with the United States, while the United States declared that it was interested in "a peaceful settlement of the Taiwan question by the Chinese themselves" and affirmed its "ultimate objective of the withdrawal of all US forces and military installations from Taiwan".

The process of normalization continued throughout the 1970s, not least because the United States was anxious to play its China card in the competition with the Soviet Union. This policy was strongly pushed by President Carter's National Security Adviser Zbigniew Brzezinski and resulted in the announcement on Dec. 15, 1978 that full diplomatic relations between Washington and Beijing were to be established on Jan. 1, 1979. The implications for Taiwan appeared ominous as the United States acknowledged that there was but one China and that Taiwan was merely a part of it, and announced that the mutual defence treaty of 1954 would be terminated and that the remaining American military personnel in Taiwan would be withdrawn. Although the normalization of China was a long overdue attempt to rationalize American policy, the implications for Taiwan were disturbing. The abandonment of Taiwan was not complete, however, and it was announced that the people of the United States would "maintain cultural, commercial and other unofficial relations with the people of Taiwan". Moreover, the United States made clear that it expected the Taiwan issue to be settled peacefully.

The treaty termination occurred at a time when there was growing concern in the USA, especially among conservatives, that the Carter administration was following a policy of retreat. This was compounded by the emotional significance that many conservatives attached to support for Taiwan. Not surprisingly, therefore, there was opposition to the treaty termination and Senator Barry Goldwater attempted to get the Supreme Court to declare it unconstitutional. Although this did not succeed, the fact that legislation was required to establish the new unofficial relationship presented congressional critics of the Carter administration's policy with an opportunity to amend the policy in ways which reaffirmed the US commitment to Taiwan.

In March 1979 Congress passed the Taiwan Relations Act. The legislation declared that the United States would supply defensive arms to Taiwan and would "maintain the capacity . . . to resist any resort to force or other forms of coercion that would jeopardize the security, or the social or economic system, of the people on Taiwan". It also emphasized that the United States would "consider any effort to determine the future of Taiwan by other than peaceful means, including by boycotts or embargoes, a threat to the peace and security of the Western Pacific area and of grave concern to the United States". In addition, President Carter himself, under pressure from the critics, made clear that the United States could still interpose its naval forces between Taiwan and the mainland should this prove necessary. Some military links such as sales of equipment and naval visits by United States forces were also maintained. The unofficial links were also carefully institutionalized. Although the lack of official relations meant the lack of official embassies, the United States established the American Institute in Taiwan which was staffed with Foreign Service officers who were temporarily on leave. Some military advisers also remained in Taiwan although with the status of civilians.

The implication is that the commitment was maintained, albeit through a series of informal measures. The Reagan administration was more sympathetic to the position of Taiwan than the Carter administration and initially continued arms supplies. Although its policy led to some cooling of the relationship with Communist China, on Aug. 17, 1982, Washington and Beijing agreed that the arms sales would be reduced. In accordance with this agreement the United States refused to sell Taiwan an advanced fighter aircraft and the Harpoon anti-ship missile. To some extent, however, these restrictions were compensated by non-governmental sales and by agreements which enabled Taiwan itself to produce sophisticated equipment under licence. In spite of the demise of the formal US commitment to Taiwan, therefore, the bilateral relationship remains a very real one, although one that is likely to diminish in importance in the future.

PW

UNO SOSUKE. Uno briefly enjoyed tenure as prime minister of Japan in July and August 1989, following the resignation of **Takeshita Noboru** in the wake of the **Recruit Scandal**. Uno's fall from grace was occasioned by the revelations of a self-styled geisha who made public his illicit sexual relationship with her. The result was the worst upper house electoral defeat the **Liberal Democratic Party** has experienced in 40 years. Uno resigned to take responsibility for the defeat.

RAB

V

VANUATU, REPUBLIC OF. (Formerly the New Hebrides.) *Population* (est. 1988): 149,000, mostly Melanesians. *Area*: 14,763 sq km. Independent republic within the Commonwealth, comprising a Y-shaped north-south chain of 13 main islands and many smaller ones, some 800 km west of Fiji. *Capital:* Vila, on Efate, the main island. Official *languages* are Bislama, an English-based Melanesian pidgin, English and French, but many Melanesian languages and dialects are used. *Religion:* mainly Christian.

Many of the islands have been inhabited for at least 3,000 years. European contact dates from 1606 (de Quiros), then 1768 (de Bougainville) and 1774 (Cook). Conflicting French and British claims in the nineteenth century were resolved by establishing a Joint Naval Commission in 1887, leading to a condominium in 1906. The islands escaped Japanese occupation in World War II, and provided a major Allied base. A Representative Assembly (1974–77) led to a constitutional conference in Paris, elections and a constitution (1979), with independence in July 1980, briefly marred by an attempted secessionist revolt in Espiritu Santo. Father Walter Lini, leader of the *Vanuaaku Pati*, has been Prime Minister since that date, through three elections.

There is a single-chamber Parliament of 46 members elected by universal franchise (proportional representation) every four years. The Prime Minister appoints the Council of Ministers. There is a National Council of Chiefs concerned with customary and traditional matters.

Vanuatu has a free market, subsistence economy, with cash crops and fishing, plus a few light industries.

Since independence Vanuatu has established diplomatic relations with numerous countries of widely differing political persuasions, including the Soviet Union. In January 1987 a one-year agreement was signed giving the Soviet Union the right, for a fee of US$1,500,000, to fish in Vanuatu's 200-mile zone, but not to enter the 12-mile territorial waters except for replenishment. From May to August 1987, Vanuatu prevented visits by Australian military ships and aircraft in reaction to an Australian protest that Libya was trying to set up a permanent base in Vanuatu to penetrate and destabilize the region. Relations were resumed after Vanuatu expelled two Libyans who had arrived to establish a diplomatic mission.

In 1988–89 there was a constitutional crisis which led to the president, George Sokomanu, being dismissed and gaoled for six years for attempting to overthrow the government and install his nephew as prime minister. The sentence was quashed on appeal.

TBM

VIETNAM. (Note: *see also* **Vietnam, Democratic Republic of**; **Vietnam, Republic of**; **Vietnam, Socialist Republic of.**)

History and geography. Vietnam occupies the eastern part of the Indochinese Peninsula, embracing the Red River (Tongking) delta and the lower Mekong delta, a series of lowlands along the intervening coast, and also a substantial hinterland of highland and forest areas. As an independent state, originally controlling only the northern part of the present territory, the kingdom of Dai Viet emerged in the tenth century CE after nine centuries of domination by successive Chinese dynasties. But national legend, recorded in the early Dai Viet histories, traces the origins of the Vietnamese people back to a line of Hung Vuong kings long before Chinese rule, and their festival is still commemorated annually on April 7. Archaeologically, the area is known to have been occupied by tribal groups whose distinctive cultures go back to at least the third millennium BCE. Successive Chinese attempts to reconquer Dai Viet (in 1075–1285–recalling those wars the Vietnamese still think of China as the "traditional enemy"; but for much of the period from the tenth to the nineteenth centuries the Vietnamese court sent tribute missions to the Chinese capital, and several centuries of domination left behind an institutional and cultural heritage pervaded by Chinese influence. Vietnamese **Confucianism**, typified by the role of scholar-officials selected in examinations, became especially strong in the fifteenth century; and again during periods of Confucian revival in the late seventeenth century and in the years 1820–tially to the Chinese Mahayana tradition; and other religious sects – notably the Cao Dai and Hoa Hao in southern Vietnam – also reflect Chinese inspiration.

The territorial expansion of Vietnamese power occurred in several stages. The "Indianized" Cham states which had flourished on the coast of what is now Central Vietnam from the sixth century CE were subdued and annexed in a series of wars from the eleventh to the fifteenth centuries. Farther south, the Mekong Delta was formerly part of Cambodia but was conquered by Vietnam in the late seventeenth and eighteenth centuries; Saigon became an important city only after about 1780. Expansion and conquest, however, also brought territorial division among the Vietnamese themselves. The sixteenth and seventeenth centuries were marked by long periods of civil war. Not until 1802 was the whole of present-day Vietnam united for the first time under the Nguyen dynasty, ruling from Hue. That unity lasted less then 60 years. In 1859–expedition, partly in response to persecution of Christian missionaries by the Confucian court, ended in the occupation of Saigon. Under two Treaties of Saigon, in 1862 and 1873, Vietnam ceded to France full sovereignty over the South ("French Cochinchina", now called Nam-Bo). The second of these treaties, which followed an incursion by the French into the Hanoi area, also granted trading concessions and religious freedom in other parts of Vietnam. A more ambitious French military expedition between 1882 and 1885, involving at one stage also a war between France and China, established control over "Tongking" (now Bac-Bo) and central Vietnam or "Annam" (now Trung-Bo). In 1884 the Treaty of Hue recognized a French protectorate over both areas. The French already had a protectorate over Cambodia by then. In 1887 both Vietnam and Cambodia were drawn into the Indochinese Union, to which Laos was added in 1893. Opposition from a number of traditionally oriented resistance movements was overcome by 1900, and French rule lasted in this form until 1945.

Important economic developments occurred during the colonial period, mainly to the advantage of European enterprises and of the more successful Chinese immigrants. The North was important for its minerals and it was also a trade route to south-west China. But while Haiphong grew into a significant port, Hanoi became something of a backwater. In the Centre, too, Hue remained a backwater (as the "imperial capital") while Danang emerged as the principal port. Both those areas had very densely populated lowlands with an impoverished peasantry and were net importers of rice. "Cochinchina" was economically the richest area, producing a substantial rice surplus (much of which was exported) as well as rubber, sugar and tea. Saigon (now Ho Chi Minh City) developed into a major port with a large Chinese community living in nearby Cholon.

Among the Vietnamese, French rule stimulated the growth of nationalism from about 1904, under the influence of French education and of contemporary trends in China and Japan. Early revolutionary and reform movements were especially strong in the Centre and North, where they were responsible for open rebellions in 1908 and 1916–develop in the 1920s, out of which emerged the Indo-Chinese Communist Party. In "Cochinchina" a constitutionalist movement had some success for a time, but it too was overtaken by more radical ideas.

Revolution, war and partition 1945–75. The fall of France to Nazi Germany in 1940, followed by a Japanese military occupation of Indochina in 1940–41, left a much weakened French administration in control for much of World War II. The war also forced a reorientation of the colonial economy. Finally on March 9, 1945, the Japanese overthrew the French regime and seized power. The "emperor" Bao Dai was instructed to renounce treaties with France and to establish an "independent" government, headed by a pro-Japanese nationalist, Tran Trong Kim. But the Communist-led Viet Minh was also increasingly active, as a resistance movement, and the sudden surrender of Japan in August 1945 opened the way for **Ho Chi Minh** to seize the initiative and lead the "August Revolution". On Sept. 2 1945, he proclaimed the independent Democratic Republic of Vietnam. His provisional government in Hanoi survived the invasion of northern Indochina by Chinese nationalist troops, lasting from September to March 1946, and later entered into direct negotiations with the returning French. The Viet Minh attempted to seize power in Saigon, too, but their leadership of the revolution in the South was less firmly established They had to enter into a shaky alliance with the Cao Dai and Hoa Hao religious sects whose leaders were later won over by the French. In September 1945 a British force arrived in Saigon to receive the surrender of Japanese forces. It also countenanced (if it did not actually assist) a recovery of control by the French, which was followed by the arrival of additional troops from France in October. By March 1946 the French had secured control of southern Indochina and were in a position to negotiate a withdrawal of Chinese forces from the North – allowing their own forces to return to Haiphong and then to Hanoi. Ho Chi Minh, having signed a provisional accord on March 6, went to France to attend the Fontainebleau Conference on the future of Vietnam (July–August 1946) but failed to obtain a satisfactory agreement. In December 1946 an apparent Viet Minh attempt at a coup against the French garrison in Hanoi, and seizure of other towns, ended in a retreat from the capital by Ho Chi Minh's government. By 1947–48 the Viet

Minh had lost control of most of "Tongking", while retaining part of northern Central Vietnam. But they were not completely annihilated and refused to surrender.

In the Indochina War which followed (1946–54) the turning point came in 1949–50, when the Viet Minh secured military aid and training from the Chinese Communists. By 1952 the French were on the defensive in northern Vietnam. (Guerrilla warfare in the South was a less serious threat at this stage.) Politically the French responded to this situation by creating in March 1949 an Associated State of Vietnam, headed by the ex-emperor Bao Dai. But increasing dependence on United States military and financial aid after 1951 also led to pressure on France to cede full independence to the Vietnamese. On the battle-field the climax came at Dien Bien Phu, where the Viet Minh (with considerable Chinese assistance) inflicted a major defeat on the French expeditionary forces in May 1954. That was followed by French loss of control over much of the "Tongking" delta, leaving them with no choice but to negotiate an end to the conflict at the Geneva Conference (May–July 1954) and to hand over all of Vietnam north of the 17th parallel to the Viet Minh. In theory the Geneva Agreement involved a regroupment of military forces over the next 300 days, and the creation of military (and temporarily administrative) zones north and south of that line. In practice the North became the Democratic Republic of Vietnam (DRV) with Ho Chi Minh's government re-established in Hanoi; while the South was taken over by Bao Dai's State of Vietnam, to which the French had granted virtual independence in June 1954. However, Franco-American rivalry in Saigon led to a political crisis in 1955, in the course of which Bao Dai's nominees were removed from power by his pro-American prime minister Ngo Dinh Diem. French forces withdrew altogether in 1956. Meanwhile in October 1955, with Washington's encouragement, Diem proclaimed the Republic of Vietnam and ruled it as president until 1963. The Republic itself lasted until 1975, with a new constitution in 1966 under which Nguyen Van Thieu became president (1967–75). Following the collapse of the Republic of Vietnam in April 1975, South Vietnam was formally placed under the rule of a "Provisional Revolutionary Government of South Vietnam" created by the Communist side in 1969. But real power lay with the People's Army of Vietnam and with the Party. In July 1976 the two halves of Vietnam were finally re-unified, with Hanoi as the capital, and the DRV became the Socialist Republic of Vietnam.

In June 1969 the Communist side had, in the meantime, established its own Provisional Revo-lutionary Government of (the Republic of) South Vietnam, which formally took over the South at this point. But effective power lay with the Vietnamese Communist Party and the North Vietnamese armed forces in the South. In November 1975 an agreement was signed in Saigon providing for full re-unification of the country in the following year. This was implemented with the holding of nationwide elections (under firm Party control) in April and the convening of a new National Assembly in Hanoi, which on July 2, 1976, established the Socialist Republic of Vietnam.

RBS

VIETNAM, DEMOCRATIC REPUBLIC OF (NORTH VIETNAM). (Note: *see also* **Vietnam.**) Founded in Hanoi in the "August Revolution" of 1945, the Democratic Republic of Vietnam (DRV) derived its legitimacy from **Ho Chi Minh's** proclamation of independence on Sept. 2 that year. Its first two governments (August 1945–February 1946 and February–November 1946) were both headed by Ho himself and dominated by the Viet Minh, even though the second one was technically a coalition with the two main nationalist parties. A third government, composed mainly of Viet Minh ministers, was driven out of Hanoi by the French in December 1946, but survived in the maquis to govern an expanding "liberated area" after 1949. In January 1950 it was formally recognized by China and the USSR as the only legitimate government of Vietnam. (Shortly afterwards, the United States and Britain recognized the "State of Vietnam" which had been set up by France within the French Union.) Following the Geneva Agreement of 1954, the government of the DRV returned to Hanoi and gained complete administrative control over Vietnam north of the 17th parallel. It remained the government of North Vietnam for the next 21 years, but following the formal re-unification of North and South in July 1976 it was succeeded by the Socialist Republic of Vietnam (*see* **Vietnam, Socialist Republic of**).

RBS

VIETNAM, REPUBLIC OF (SOUTH VIETNAM). (Note: *See also* **Vietnam.**) Established in Saigon in October 1955 by its first president, Ngo Dinh Diem, in the aftermath of the Geneva partition of Vietnam into two military zones. Constitutionally it claimed to replace the State of Vietnam, set up by the French in 1949 under the ex-emperor Bao Dai, which had

been granted formal independence in June 1954. The existence of the Republic of Vietnam (RVN) was never recognized by the government of the Democratic Republic of Vietnam installed in Hanoi in 1954; but with support from the United States it survived until April 1975.

The final declaration of the Geneva Conference had envisaged nationwide elections in 1956, leading to re-unification; but Diem argued that free elections were impossible with a Communist regime in control of the North and he refused to discuss even the modalities for an election. With considerable United States economic assistance and the presence of several hundred American military advisers, he proceeded to build the South into a stable and prosperous state, suppressing any opposition. Communist elements in the south, pursuing a line decided ultimately in Hanoi, began a campaign of political struggle against this regime in 1956-67, which by 1959-60 developed into an armed struggle under the ostensible leadership of the National Liberation Front of South Vietnam (founded in December 1960).

Diem remained president for eight years, until he was overthrown (and killed) in an American-sanctioned coup d'etat in November 1963. By that time the Americans were deeply involved in a counterinsurgency campaign to defend the Saigon regime, against a Communist-led armed struggle which had gathered momentum since 1958-59. But the military regime which took over from Diem was unable to establish a stable government, and further coups and crises followed in January 1964; August–September 1964; January–February 1965; and May–June 1965. New leaders followed in quick succession: Duong Van Minh (November 1963–January 1964); Nguyen Khanh (January 1964–February 1965), Phan Huy Quat (February–June 1965); and Nguyen Cao Ky, as head of a military directorate (June 1965–September 1967). Meanwhile the Communist military-political threat to the regime grew steadily more serious, leading to greater United States involvement. Large numbers of American combat troops were deployed on the ground from April 1965, and a bombing campaign was mounted against North Vietnam; by 1968 there were over 500,000 American troops in South Vietnam, together with smaller contingents from South Korea, Australia and other countries.

A new political crisis in spring 1966, including an open revolt by Buddhist leaders in Danang and Hue, led to the promise of a new constitution. Constituent assembly elections took place in September 1966 and a constitution was approved the following year. In September 1967, General Nguyen Van Thieu was elected president of this "second republic": a post which he continued to

hold until 1975 (being re-elected "unopposed" in 1971). His regime survived the Tet Offensive mounted by Communist forces in January–February 1968, even though the psychological impact in Washington led the United States to decide to limit its further involvement in the war and to embark on a policy of "Vietnamization". The gradual withdrawal of American forces (by then numbering 542,000) began in June 1969 and was speeded up during the next three years. By 1972 the main responsibility for ground fighting rested with the retrained and heavily rearmed forces of the RVN. United States aid programmes also began to bear fruit during 1969-71, and a more successful "pacification" programme increased Saigon's control over much of the countryside. This progress was interrupted by a major Communist offensive in spring 1972, which RVN forces were able to counter with American air support (and with the renewal of American bombing of the North). Nevertheless it ended with a much larger number of North Vietnamese regular forces in control of a significant amount of territory inside South Vietnam.

Washington's determination to complete the withdrawal of its own forces was undiminished, and in January 1973 the United States and North Vietnam signed the Paris Agreement, under which all American troops would leave within two months – but with a ceasefire-in-place which would leave North Vietnamese forces in the South. The agreement also provided for political talks between the RVN government and the southern Communist leadership (since June 1969, constituted as the Provisional Revolutionary Government of South Vietnam). Talks began in April 1973 but had made little progress by the time they broke down in May 1974. Meanwhile the government of Nguyen Van Thieu, although it had received large supplies of military equipment before the ceasefire, found itself in financial difficulties: partly as a result of the oil price increase (1973-74); and partly because the US Congress refused to increase its economic assistance and by late 1974 had actually reduced it. The Communist forces, having strengthened their own position over the previous year, took advantage of Saigon's weakness to launch a final offensive early in 1975. The rapid collapse of RVN forces in the Central Highlands and along the Central Vietnamese coast was followed by the capture of Saigon (in a conventional assault) on April 30, 1975. Thieu having fled in mid-April, it was left to Duong Van Minh to perform the act of surrender which brought the RVN's existence to an end.

The Provisional Revolutionary Government of (the Republic of) South Vietnam formally took over the South at this point. But effective power lay with the Vietnamese Communist Party and the North Vietnamese armed forces in the South. In November 1975 an agreement was signed in Saigon providing for full re-unification of the country in the following year. This was implemented with the holding of nationwide elections (under firm Party control) in April; and the convening of a new National Assembly in Hanoi, which on July 2, 1976, established the Socialist Republic of Vietnam (*see* **Vietnam, Socialist Republic of**).

RBS

VIETNAM, SOCIALIST REPUBLIC OF.
(Note: *see also* **Vietnam**; **Vietnam, Democratic Republic of**: **Vietnam, Republic of**.) *Population*: 65.2 million (1988 est.). *Area*: 329 sq km. *Urban population as percentage of total*: 19. *Birth rate*: 34 per thousand. *Life expectancy*: 63.

Political history. The Socialist Republic of Vietnam (SRV), proclaimed in Hanoi on July 2, 1976, succeeded both the Democratic Republic of Vietnam (DRV) which had been founded in 1945 and had governed North Vietnam since 1954; and the "Republic of South Vietnam", whose provisional revolutionary government had been established by the Communist side in 1969 and had taken over formal responsibility for the government of South Vietnam in May 1975. In practice there was essential continuity with the DRV, which had previously claimed to be the only legitimate authority throughout Vietnam. The DRV constitution of 1959 (replacing that originally adopted in 1946) continued in force. Although a new one was promised, it took until 1979 to publish a draft and the SRV constitution was not finally adopted until the end of 1980. In all three constitutions sovereignty is vested in a national assembly, whose standing committee meets more frequently than the full assembly; and governmental authority belongs to a council of ministers. (A state council was added to the structure in 1980, whose president is head of state.) In broad terms it could be said that the 1959 document owed a great deal to the model of the People's Republic of China; that of 1980 was more in line with the Soviet model, as revised by Brezhnev in 1977.

The constitution does not, however, define the realities of power in Communist Vietnam. It is more useful to recognize four distinct institutional hierarchies of authority, existing side by side but interlocking with one another as follows: (i) the national assembly (closely related to the state council after 1980) has a direct but informal relationship with the **Vietnamese Fatherland Front**, the body charged by the **Vietnamese Communist Party** (VCP) with responsibility for mobilizing the population at large behind Party and government policies; (ii) the council of ministers, headed by the prime minister (with a varying number of deputy prime ministers), which forms the government; (iii) the People's Army of Vietnam (PAVN), embracing all the armed forces, which has a general political department and a hierarchy of political commissars to ensure full obedience to the Party line; and (iv) the Vietnamese Communist Party which has its own Central Committee, Inspection Committee, Politburo and Secretariat, but also permeates the whole power structure and is the real centre of debate and decision-making on major issues. From 1960 until 1980 these hierarchies were headed by four of the most important leaders of the "August Revolution" of 1945 (under the overall leadership of **Ho Chi Minh** himself until 1969).

The period of partition (1954–75) was dominated by the various phases of the Vietnam War, in which the North gave increasing support to the southern Communists and eventually took over many aspects of the struggle on the ground – including sending an increasing number of PAVN troops into the South between late 1964 and the final offensive of 1975. The war also led to an American bombing campaign against North Vietnam (from early 1965 to late 1968 and again in 1972) which inflicted especially severe damage during 1967–68 and in 1972. Such progress as had been made towards "socialist construction" was largely reversed by this destruction. But the economic decentralization policies made necessary by the bombing were to have lasting, and not necessarily damaging, consequences for the running of the country. The war also made North Vietnam heavily dependent on its principal socialist allies.

In 1976 there was a sense that a new start was being made, under a new government (approved by the national assembly in July) and a new Party line (approved by the 4th Congress of the VCP in December). But the range of options which appeared to exist immediately after re-unification seemed gradually to narrow during 1976–77; and by the second half of 1977 the SRV had begun to commit itself to a hard-line economic policy (including rapid "socialist transformation" in the South) and a closer relationship with the Soviet Union. This conditioned all other aspects of policy. The international position of the SRV, and of the DRV before it, has been governed by a Marxist-Leninist tradition going back to the relationship between the Indochinese Communist Party and the Communist International in the 1930s. It has also been profoundly influenced by the party's ambition to forge close relations with the revolutionary movement in neighbouring Cambodia and Laos. The two themes became increasingly intertwined after 1976.

Ho Chi Minh's strategy over several decades had been to maintain good relations with both Soviet and Chinese Communist leaders, balancing one against the other. In the early 1950s Stalin appears to have instructed the Viet Minh to follow the Chinese model and to depend chiefly on Chinese military aid; but from 1955 onwards, Ho welcomed indications that Moscow was interested in cultivating direct contacts with Vietnam and offering direct aid. As Sino-Soviet relations began to deteriorate after 1960, Hanoi was careful not to alienate either Moscow or Beijing; and down to 1977–78 the Vietnamese appear to have succeeded in maintaining friendship with both. But Hanoi's dependence on Soviet military assistance after 1965 was too great to allow the luxury of following the Chinese along a path of openly criticizing the Communist Party of the Soviet Union (CPSU); whilst the Russians were determined to prevent the Chinese from drawing Vietnam into an independent Asian Communist grouping.

During the 1970s, under the leadership of **Le Duan**, the VCP moved steadily closer to Moscow in essential matters; and in 1977 it appeared to have decided to lean even more positively towards the Soviet Union, by becoming associated with the CMEA (Comecon); a body which Vietnam joined as a full member in July 1978. The Vietnamese further alienated Chinese sympathy by embarking on a form of "socialist transformation" in South Vietnam which adversely affected the interests of Chinese residents. By mid-1978 some of the latter were taking to boats in the South China Sea; while even Chinese residents who had lived relatively happily in North Vietnam since 1954 began to stream across the Chinese land border (*see* **Boat People, Vietnamese**). In mid-1978 China announced the suspension of all its aid projects in Vietnam and withdrew its technical advisers. Hanoi's response was to sign a Soviet–Vietnamese friendship treaty in Moscow on Nov. 3, 1978, which appears to have included permission for the Soviet navy to use facilities at Cam Ranh Bay.

By this time Sino-Vietnamese relations were closely bound up with Hanoi's ambitions in Laos and Cambodia. Laos, whose leader **Kaysone Phomvihan** had been closely associated with the Vietnamese Communist movement since 1950s, was ready to sign a Laos–Vietnam friendship treaty in July 1977 and subsequently broke off relations with Beijing. But the **Kampuchean Communist Party** of **Pol Pot**, having taken over Phnom Penh with only minimal Vietnamese help in April 1975, was taking an increasingly anti-Vietnamese line and seeking ever closer relations with Beijing during 1977–78. Tension between the SRV and Democratic Kampuchea mounted during those years and there was serious border fighting between them. Finally, having signed the Soviet treaty, Vietnamese forces invaded Cambodia at the end of 1978, and by Jan. 9, they had captured Phnom Penh. The new government of **Heng Samrin** was then willing to sign its own friendship treaty with Vietnam in February 1979.

Relations with China reached crisis point, however. In response to the occupation of Kampuchea, the Chinese invaded Vietnam's northern border and, in a short but highly destructive campaign from Feb. 17 to March 5, 1979, captured the towns of Cao Bang and Lang Son. They then withdrew by March 16; but incidents continued to occur along the heavily defended border on numerous occasions during the next seven years. The Chinese were worried by the possibility of an active military alliance between Moscow and Hanoi, and began to insist that the Soviet-backed occupation of Cambodia by Vietnamese forces was an obstacle to the normalization of Sino-Soviet relations. A dispute also developed between Vietnam and China over control of the Paracel and **Spratly Islands** in the South China Sea.

These developments inevitably had a profound impact on Vietnam's internal affairs. Economically, the loss of Chinese aid coincided with an American embargo on relations with Vietnam – with Japan and the European Communities following Washington's example. At the same time, it was necessary to allocate greater resources then ever to national defence. Politically, the intimate relationship between the Vietnamese and Chinese Communist Parties meant that Sino-Vietnamese hostility created problems of internal security in Vietnam. The top leadership remained remarkably united under the strain, with only one former Politburo member (**Hoang Van Hoan**) choosing to defect to China. Interior minister Tran Quoc Hoan was dismissed early in 1980, possibly for having failed to prevent Hoan's escape; and Vo Nguyen Giap's retirement at about the same time may have been related to differences arising from the new war. At middle and lower levels, however, there seems to have been a more substantial purge of Chinese-oriented cadres.

Despite a major Soviet effort to make up for Vietnam's loss of Chinese aid projects, the 1980s were to prove a decade of disappointment and uncertainty, when an ageing leadership failed to come to grips with Vietnam's problems and at the same time refused to be pushed aside. The 5th congress of the VCP (March 1982) saw a reaffirmation of what might be called socialist "conservatism".

Concern about the critical situation in Cambodia, and about possible Chinese efforts to undermine the stability of Vietnam itself, led to a tightening of security during 1982–84, including the imposition of more restrictions on Catholic and Buddhist organizations.

In 1986, however, two developments seemed to presage significant change: the death of Le Duan in July; and the advent of Gorbachev's new policies in the Soviet Union (and his new approach to Asian affairs). Le Duan's immediate successor as Party leader was Truong Chinh (July–December 1986); but at the 6th Congress of the VCP in December it was agreed that Truong Chinh, Pham Van Dong and Le Duc Tho would all retire from the Politburo, opening the way for Nguyen Van Linh to succeed as general secretary. In July 1987 Truong Chinh handed over the presidency of the state council to Vo Chi Cong. Pham Van Dong also retired, to be succeeded as prime minister by Pham Hung, and Le Duc Anh took over command on the PAVN from Van Tien Dung, who had been removed from the Party Politburo at the 6th congress and was forced to retire as army commander and defence minister in February 1987. It was noticeable that all these key members of the new team (Nguyen Van Linh, Vo Chi Cong, Pham Hung and Le Duc Anh) had played important roles in the war in the South before 1975. Nguyen Van Linh and also the planning chief Vo Van Kiet (another southern veteran) were known to favour an acceleration of the policy of economic reform, but they met with resistance from "conservatives" (notably the retired Le Duc Tho) who saw the elimination of offical corruption through Party discipline as the most urgent task. When Pham Hung died in March 1988, another conservative, Do Muoi, was appointed prime minister. However, by the spring of 1989 Nguyen Van Linh appeared to be coming out on top.

Foreign relations. In the aftermath of the upheavals of 1978–79, Vietnam has become an extremely close ally of the Soviet Union. Militarily, it allows the Soviet fleet to make use of Cam Ranh Bay, as well as receiving considerable military assistance for its own armed forces. Economically, Vietnam is a full member of the CMEA (Comecon) and has increasingly geared its economic planning to that of the wider socialist community. Important economic and technical agreements were signed in 1983 and again in 1985 (during Le Duan's last visit to Moscow).

The close relationship was reaffirmed when Nguyen Van Linh paid his first visit to the Soviet Union, as Party leader, in May 1987. By then, Hanoi was ready to respond to the principles put forward by Gorbachev in his major speech on Asian policy at Vladivostok in July 1986. Closely tied to Vietnamese–Soviet relations was the pattern of close co-operation which had emerged amongst the "three Indochinese countries" after 1980 (*see* Indochinese Co-operation).

The question of relations between Vietnam and the United States was more complex in the aftermath of the Vietnam War. Visits by United States officials to Hanoi in 1973 (Henry Kissinger) and early 1977 (Leonard Woodcock) failed to establish a basis for normalization: at that stage Hanoi insisted on large amounts of US aid as a disguised form of war reparations, which they said had been promised by President Nixon in a secret letter after the Paris Agreement of January 1973. The Americans insisted that the resumption of open war by Hanoi in 1974–75 had invalidated that promise. In June 1977 the US Senate passed amendments making it illegal for the president to make any offers of aid to Vietnam or to support loans to Vietnam by international lending institutions. The United States did, however, end its objections to the admission of Vietnam to the United Nations, which finally took place on Sept. 20, 1977. Following the Vietnamese occupation of Cambodia, the United States imposed an economic embargo on both countries, and persuaded the EC and Japan to follow suit. Among Western countries, only Sweden was willing to continue developing economic relations with Hanoi in the 1980s.

The other element in Vietnamese–American relations was the question of American soldiers still listed as "missing in action". A number of low-level contacts on that subject occurred, but it was not until the visit of General John Vessey to Hanoi in August 1987 that serious progress began to be made. The Americans were in no hurry to normalize relations, and it remained to be seen whether agreement on the Cambodian question would be followed by more progress in that direction.

Vietnam's relations with its Southeast Asian neighbours were also adversely affected by the Cambodian invasion, after signs of improvement in the period after 1976. The Association of South-East Asian Nations (ASEAN) countries, especially Thailand and Singapore, joined China in supporting the anti-Vietnamese resistance movement and in promoting a boycott of economic relations with Vietnam and Cambodia. As time went on, the Vietnamese tried to drive a wedge into ASEAN solidarity by cultivating better relations with Indonesia (whose government had its own suspicions of China). The visit of the Indonesian foreign minister to Ho Chi Minh City in July 1987 marked the beginning of a slow process of negotiation on the future of Cambodia. The Vietnamese were by then sufficiently confident to promise a unilateral pull-out of their troops by the end of 1990. In 1988-89, even relations with Thailand began to improve, following the appointment of **Chatichai Choonhaven** as prime minister in Bangkok.

The Socialist economic system. The Communist approach to economic development in Vietnam has been based on a two-stage model of "socialist transformation" followed by "socialist construction". The actual pattern of development, however, has been distorted by the consequences of the Geneva partition, which led to the separate development of the South under a non-Communist regime for 20 years. Thus the North passed through the phase of "socialist transformation" during the 1950s and early 1960s, whereas that phase did not begin in the South until after 1975.

In the North the transformation of agriculture began with a programme of land reform (1953-56), based essentially on the Chinese model, but then continued (1958-61) on the basis of a more strictly Stalinist model of co-operativization. Other economic activities in the North were also nationalized or co-operativized during 1954-56. It then became possible to think in terms of initial steps towards "socialist construction" on the basis of centralized planning. A Three-Year Plan, for 1958-60, was followed by the first Five-Year Plan (1961-65). The latter assumed in principle that the completion of agricultural transformation, combined with a substantial amount of economic assistance from China and the Soviet Union, had created conditions for rapid industrialization. Some major projects got under way, but after 1965 progress was interrupted (and then reversed) by the consequences of the war. The US bombing of the North during 1965-68 necessitated a decentralization of economic planning and production (as well as physically destroying much of what had been built up during the preceding decade). Some effort was made to restore the full rigours of collectivization in agriculture under a new agrarian law of 1969 but in the early 1970s the emphasis was once again on maximizing productive effort rather than maintaining socialist purity.

By 1975-76, following political re-unification of the two halves of Vietnam, the economic planners faced the dual problem of reviving "socialist construction" in the North at the same time as carrying out "socialist transformation" in the South. They also had to adjust to a new Soviet attitude to economic co-operation which no longer insisted on direct imitation of the Soviet model. It emphasized instead the principle of an "international division of labour", within which different socialist economies would make distinctive contributions in relation to their existing and potential strength. Therein lay the significance of Vietnam's eventual decision to join Comecon in 1977-78. That organization provided the context within which Vietnamese planners, with Soviet advice, devised a new sequence of five-year plans: for 1976-80, 1981-85 and 1986-90.

In the South the main question during the period 1976-80 was how rapidly to proceed with the transformation of agriculture, trade, and such industry as existed. After moving cautiously at first, the party decided in July 1977 to step up the co-operativization of southern agriculture. In March 1978 "bourgeois" trading activity in Ho Chi Minh City (Saigon) was abolished without warning. That was followed in May by a sudden change of currency which allowed a uniform, strictly controlled, banking and currency system to be imposed on both halves of Vietnam. It was also decided to step up the development of "new economic zones" in hitherto uncultivated forest and upland areas – to which former Saigon traders were invited to move. Not surprisingly these measures contributed to the sharp increase in the exodus of "boat people" from southern Vietnam during 1978-79. But in September 1979 – faced with acute problems generated by the conflict with China and the invasion of Cambodia, including the end of Chinese aid and the need to devote more resources to national defence – the Politburo decided to revert to a policy of encouraging private initiative in order to promote increased production both in agriculture and in the consumer goods industries. Low-level incentives introduced at that time were followed by the evolution of a new product-contract system in 1981-82, which allowed more tasks in agriculture to be carried out by individual households for their own profit. In Ho Chi Minh City during those years there were even experiments with private trading enterprises.

Also by 1981 there was a growing debate throughout the Communist world about the need for reform in economic management of state enterprises. The reformers appear to have lost the first round of the debate at the 6th Party Congress (March 1982), when there was also a backlash against some of the experiments that had been receiving encouragement from Nguyen Van Linh in Ho Chi Minh City. There was no possibility of a resumption of the trend towards co-operativization, however, and by 1985 the impulse to reform was again apparent. The VCP Central Committee's 8th plenum (June 1985) made sweeping decisions with regard to wages and the abolition of subsidies, and set the pattern for an overall transition to socialist accounting methods. A pilot implementation of the latter at Haiphong the following month seemed to work satisfactorily. But nationwide change required a currency reform. Unfortunately the decision to change the currency yet again, announced on Sept. 14, 1985, was badly mismanaged. By the end of the year it was blamed for a rapid onset of inflation, which gathered momentum during 1986-87. Vietnamese who had currency to save turned increasingly to the US dollar as their principal store of value, and also the means of access to a growing black market of illicit imports. As inflation got even worse, the black market rate of exchange rocketed: from 400 *dong* to the US$ in 1985, to 1,000 *dong* by the end of 1987; and 4,500 *dong* by September 1988.

These developments greatly complicated the implementation of reform, but the basic trend continued. A Party directive of April 1986 gave greater autonomy and accounting responsibility to local enterprises; and at the 6th Party Congress (December 1986) Nguyen Van Linh became general secretary. Further changes approved at a Central Committee plenum on April 1987 increased the incentives to peasants and contract workers, ended discrimination against private capitalists, and abolished controls over the movement of goods across provincial boundaries. One year later (April 1988) a Politburo directive on agriculture widened the scope of the product-contract system to allow most tasks to be performed by household units, while allowing peasants to keep nearly half (instead of one quarter) of their output for private sale. Co-operativization was thus virtually abandoned, although the state still had to obtain a portion of each crop to ensure continuing subsidized prices for its own employees. Meanwhile the continuing intention to change over to "socialist business accounting" was reaffirmed at the new Central Committee's 3rd Plenum (August 1987), when it was decided that the new system would be applied first in consumer goods enterprises and in joint Soviet-Vietnamese enterprises. But progress was slow and in 1989 Nguyen Van Linh was still expressing impatience both with the failure to implement decisions and with the continuing low level of economic performance. The 6th Plenum (March 1989) attempted yet again to define a programme of management reform as well as to develop the mechanism of investment and to lay a basis for increased production in what were now the three most essential areas: agriculture, consumer industries, and production for export.

RBS

VIETNAM-CAMBODIA CONFLICT. The war between Vietnam and Cambodia can be understood largely in terms of ideological rivalry, territorial ambition, nationalist sentiments and security concerns. Part of the problem was that Cambodia, in the latter half of the 1970s, became involved in the rivalry between Vietnam and China. Beijing had traditionally attempted to ensure that Cambodia remained free of foreign domination and had encouraged the policy of neutrality followed by **Prince Sihanouk** during the 1950s and 1960s. In 1970, however, Cambodia was dragged into the Vietnam war, and there were incursions by both South Vietnamese and United States forces as well as a US bombing campaign. At the same time the fall of Prince Sihanouk and the coming to power of Lon Nol left the *Khmer Rouge* as the only serious resistance to the new regime. Chinese support for the *Khmer Rouge* appeared to pay dividends when they came to power in 1975. The new regime, however, embarked upon a policy of excess and extermination at home and an aggressive policy towards Vietnam.

There had been tension between the *Khmer Rouge* and Hanoi during the closing stages of the Vietnam War, but these had been contained. The *Khmer Rouge* regime under **Pol Pot**, however, was assertive in pressing old territorial claims and a short time after coming to power took possession of Phu Quoc and Poulo Panjang in the Gulf of Thailand. Although these were quickly regained by Vietnam it was not an auspicious start to the relationship between Hanoi and the *Khmer Rouge* regime.

Fighting on the border between the two seems to have taken place in 1976 and in 1977 the *Khmer Rouge* stepped up the extent of their raids not only on disputed territory but also in areas which were clearly Vietnamese. In the autumn a massacre of the inhabitants of a Vietnamese village provoked a response in which Vietnamese forces penetrated 15 miles into Cambodia. While this operation was successful in military terms it did not deter further *Khmer Rouge* actions against the border. A second element in the response by Vietnam, therefore, was to encourage internal resistance to Pol Pot.

Neither of these tactics, however, seemed sufficient to stop the deterioration of the situation in 1978. Indeed, Vietnamese concerns were intensified by the deteriorating relationship with Beijing, which continued to give strong support to the *Khmer Rouge*. Facing what was clearly a two-front threat, Vietnam decided that the provocations by the Pol Pot regime had become intolerable. On Dec. 25, 1978, Vietnamese troops invaded Cambodia. They rapidly captured the capital Phnom Penh and established the People's Republic of Kampuchea (PRK). The new Vietnamese-installed government was led by **Heng Samrin**.

It was against this background that China – concerned about the credibility of its commitment to the *Khmer Rouge* as well as about the close links between Hanoi and Moscow – invaded Vietnam. There was a clear if tacit linkage between the Vietnamese intervention in Cambodia and the Chinese action against Vietnam. China's action, however, did not succeed in teaching Vietnam the lesson that Beijing had intended. Nor did it succeed in dislodging Vietnam from Cambodia.

The problem for Vietnam in Cambodia or Kampuchea, as it was now known, was that it had difficulty in establishing the legitimacy of the new government which replaced Pol Pot and the *Khmer Rouge*. Furthermore, the very presence of Vietnamese forces stimulated old rivalries and encouraged opposition to the Vietnamese-backed regime of Heng Samrin. The main resistance came from the *Khmer Rouge* which continued to be supported by China. In 1982, however, the anti-government forces in Kampuchea formed a tri-partite coalition – the **Coalition Government of Democratic Kampuchea (CGDK)**. This consisted of the *Khmer Rouge*, and two other groups which were not communist. One was the Kampuchean People's National Liberation Front (KPNLF), the other was FUNCINPEC led by Prince Sihanouk. The coalition was very much an alliance of convenience with Sihanouk remaining very concerned about the *Khmer Rouge* and sharing the view of the PRK government that they should not be allowed to return to power.

At this stage, Vietnam was both unable and unwilling to withdraw without seeing the government that it had established replaced by an anti-Vietnamese opposition that included Pol Pot and the *Khmer Rouge*. Hanoi was faced with a dilemma. It had to keep its troops in Cambodia until the threat of *Khmer Rouge* resurgence was removed, but the longer they remained the more anti-Vietnamese feeling was likely to grow. One solution to this dilemma was to search for a political settlement. The difficulty here, however, was Vietnam's insistence that the "Pol Pot clique" be eliminated or at the very least excluded from any further government. It also made clear that any settlement had to be within the framework of the People's Republic of Kampuchea

which it had established. In other words, Cambodia would not be allowed to move from a communist state towards greater democracy.

In view of this it was not surprising that the situation remained deadlocked. Vietnam had about 140,000 troops in Kampuchea supporting the government, which also received financial and material aid from the Soviet Union. With **Gorbachev**'s desire to improve Sino-Soviet relations, the Soviet Union became somewhat readier to place pressure on Hanoi to become more conciliatory in its approach. Furthermore, in the 1984–85 dry season offensive, Vietnamese and PRK forces launched a successful offensive against CGDK camps close to the border with Thailand. Subsequently, in August 1985, Hanoi announced that it would withdraw all its forces from Kampuchea by 1990. Although this aroused considerable scepticism, it was followed by a series of moves to reduce the Vietnamese presence in Kampuchea. In 1987 it was announced that 20,000 troops were being withdrawn and that Vietnam would leave by 1990 even if the Pol Pot clique still existed. In May 1988 Hanoi announced that 50,000 troops would be withdrawn by the end of the year.

The more conciliatory stance by Vietnam was partly the result of a growing faith in the capacity of the PRK armed forces to contain the resistance, partly a reflection of the Soviet pressure and partly a result of a reappraisal by Hanoi, in early 1988, of its policies towards the United States and China, as well as its internal needs. It also reflected a recognition by Hanoi that its interventionist policy, in certain respects at least, had been counter-productive, isolating it diplomatically and economically. Not surprisingly, therefore, there was a significant shift in Hanoi's defence policy during 1988. As well as the withdrawal of more forces from Kampuchea it also withdrew its 50,000 troop contingent from Laos. This seemed to reflect a move away from the attempt to ensure that there was a favourable constellation of forces in Indochina, a trend that was confirmed in late 1988 by reports that action was being taken to strengthen the forces in the Seventh Military region where the *Khmer Rouge* incursions had taken place prior to Vietnam's invasion of Cambodia. It was also announced that there were plans to cut the size of the armed forces – which currently number 1,250,000 men – by up to 50 per cent. This reflected a new emphasis by Vietnam on economic development and nation-building.

Even with this more flexible approach, however, progress in finding a diplomatic solution to the Kampuchean problem was slow. In December 1987 Prince Sihanouk and the PRK Prime Minister, **Hun Sen** met in Paris for four days of talks and signed a four-point agreement calling for joint efforts to create "a new democratic, independent Kampuchea". In the first half of 1988 considerable progress appeared to be made, but in July in a further meeting at Jakarta, the talks became bogged down over the issues of how to share power until a new government is elected and how to prevent the return to power of the *Khmer Rouge*. Hun Sen had a seven-point peace proposal which called for Prince Sihanouk to head a "national reconciliation council" of the four Cambodian factions to oversee a political settlement and to organize elections for a future government. The sticking point was that Hun Sen insisted that his government should stay in power until the elections took place. Sihanouk demanded the formation of an interim government and armed forces consisting of the four factions. The other difficulty was how to prevent the *Khmer Rouge* from returning to power. This had long been a sticking point and remained a key issue.

Part of the difficulty stemmed from uncertainty about how much support the *Khmer Rouge* would be able to mobilize in the countryside after Vietnamese troops had left. In 1989 the issue of verification of the Vietnamese withdrawal also impeded progress. Nevertheless, the withdrawal seems to be going ahead and although the future of the Kampuchean government remains uncertain, it does appear that the Vietnamese withdrawal of troops will be completed by the autumn of 1989. The prospects for peace, therefore, may be considerably greater than at any time since the Vietnamese invasion. Nevertheless, there are considerable uncertainties about the future of Kampuchea itself and of the impact that internal developments will have on the evolution of its relationship with its neighbours.

PW

VIETNAMESE COMMUNIST PARTY. Successor to the Indochinese Communist Party (ICP) with which it claims full continuity – celebrating Feb. 3, 1930 as the date of its foundation and numbering its conferences from the "first" in 1935. The ICP was revived, as the Vietnamese Workers' (*Lao Dong*) Party in February-March 1951, when it held its "second" Congress. It kept that name until the 4th Congress (December 1976) when it became the **Vietnamese Communist Party** (VCP). **Ho Chi Minh** was effective leader of the party from his return to Vietnam in 1945 till his death in 1969. In 1959 the party decided on a resumption of armed struggle in South Vietnam, which was pursued under the ostensible leader-

ship of a non-communist "National Liberation Front". A supposedly separate "People's Revolutionary Party of South Vietnam" was created in 1961, but actual party control in the South was held by the Central Committee's own southern office (known in English as "Central Office for South Vietnam") which directed the southern struggle in accordance with the line established at the party's 3rd congress (September 1960) and with later Politburo decisions taken in Hanoi. Both in the earlier war against the French and in the war against the Americans, the party exercised day-to-day control over the armed forces through the political commissars assigned to every unit.

From 1960 the VWP also faced the problem of how to react to the growing "dispute" between the **Chinese Communist Party** (CCP) and the Communist Party of the Soviet Union (CPSU). **Le Duan** was later noted for his sympathy with Moscow rather than Beijing, but for most of the 1960s and 1970s the Vietnamese avoided any confrontation with the Chinese. But neither did they imitate the radical "Maoism" of the Great Leap Forward (1958–59) or the Cultural Revolution (1966–76). The Vietnamese refused to follow the CCP into open revolt against Moscow, and although relations with the latter may have been in doubt for a short time in 1964, the Vietnamese made their position clear in 1966 by sending Le Duan to attend the 23rd Congress of the CPSU in March 1966. After 1976 (when its 4th congress was attended by M.A. Suslov) the VCP moved much closer to the CPSU, a process which culminated in an open break with the Chinese and the signing of a Vietnamese-Soviet Friendship Treaty in 1978. The earlier Western impression of a Vietnamese Communist leadership divided between pro-Moscow and pro-Beijing factions was then shown to be erroneous. Only one senior leader, **Hoang Van Hoan** was so thoroughly pro-Chinese that he felt it necessary at that point to defect to the CCP; which he did in July 1979.

The VWP, having grown out of the ICP, placed great emphasis on friendship and co-operation with the People's Revolutionary Parties established in Cambodia (1951) and in Laos (1955). Its relations with the Laotian Communist movement were entirely satisfactory from Hanoi's viewpoint, especially after 1959. Relations with the Cambodian Communists deteriorated following the emergence of the **Kampuchean Communist Party** in the 1960s and the ascendancy of **Pol Pot**. Not until 1979, following the Vietnamese military occupation of Cambodia, did the VCP have a party in power in Phnom Penh with which it could effectively collaborate; the **Kampuchean People's Revolutionary Party**.

The illness and death of Le Duan (July 1968) coincided with the growth of the reform movement in the CPSU and with Gorbachev's bid to develop a new Asian policy on the basis of a rapprochement between the CPSU and the CCP. The leaders of the VCP were cautious about both developments.

RBS

VIETNAMESE FATHERLAND FRONT.

Established in 1955 to replace a National United Front (the *Lien Viet*) founded in 1946, which had formally merged with the Viet Minh in 1951. Firmly under the control of the Vietnamese Workers' Party (now the **Vietnamese Communist Party**), the Vietnamese Fatherland Front (VFF) embraced the various mass organizations of North Vietnam – trade unions, peasant associations, women's associations, youth union – and also non-communist political parties and representatives of the various religions. Its task was to propagate the party line and to mobilize support both for the socialist revolution in the North and for the continuing diplomatic and political struggle against the United States and the Saigon government. At first the new Front had its own branches south of the 17th parallel. But in December 1960 a separate organization was created to mobilize support for what had by then become an armed as well as a political struggle: the National Front for the Liberation of South Vietnam (NLF). Although vigorously denying its Communist inspiration, the latter closely paralleled the VFF in its structure and was equally firmly under the leadership of the party. In February 1977, following re-unification of the country, a conference was held in Ho Chi Minh City (Saigon) to bring about a reintegration of the two Fronts (still under the name VFF). It remains an important organization for communicating party policy to the mass organization and non-Communist groupings; it also plays a key role in vetting candidates for election to the Vietnamese National Assembly.

RBS

VO CHI CONG.

President of the Socialist Republic of Vietnam (SRV) since June 1987, Vo Chi Cong (also known as Vo Toan) was during the 1960s and 1970s a leading figure on the Communist side in South Vietnam. Born in 1912 in Quang Nam province, he played an active part in the revolutionary struggle in Central Vietnam from 1945 and remained south of the 17th parallel after the Geneva partition of 1954–55. In the early 1960s he was identified as a deputy

chairman of the National Liberation Front of South Vietnam and as a leader of the People's Revolutionary Party of South Vietnam (in effect, the southern section of the Vietnamese Workers' Party). He remained in the South until 1973, but after re-unification moved permanently to Hanoi to become deputy prime minister and minister of marine products in 1976. He became a member of the **Vietnamese Communist Party** politburo at the 4th congress (December 1976). He emerged as the senior deputy prime minister in 1986, following the dismissal of the hard-liner To Huu; and for a time it seemed as if he, rather than Pham Hung, would succeed Pham Van Dong as prime minister. Instead, in mid-1987, he was appointed president of the State Council and of the SRV.

RBS

VO NGUYEN GIAP.

Former Vietnamese defence minister and commander of the People's Army of Vietnam from 1948 to 1980. Born in 1912 in Quang Binh province in Central Vietnam, he became involved in radical politics as a student in Hue and joined the Indochinese Communist Party in 1933. He later became a teacher in Hanoi, and a prominent party worker during the period of its legal activities (1936–39). Summoned to join **Ho Chi Minh** in southern China in 1940, he worked closely with Pham Van Dong in building up the Cao Bang base area in the next few years; and in December 1944 (on instructions from Ho) established the first "armed propaganda" unit which was the progenitor of the People's Army of Vietnam (PAVN). He served as interior minister and security chief in the provisional government established by Ho Chi Minh in Hanoi in 1945–46. During the war against the French (1946-54) he became the Viet Minh's military leader, and his stature was greatly enhanced by the victory over their expeditionary forces at Dien Bien Phu in May 1954. After the Geneva partition he opposed a purely "diplomatic" strategy for recovering control over the South, and he played a key role in devising the successive strategies which eventually forced the United States to abandon its support for a separate South Vietnam. He was probably author of the Tet offensive of 1968, which had only limited success, but his precise role in many individual campaigns is impossible to define. It was the PAVN chief-of-staff, Van Tien Dung, who claimed most credit for the final offensive which led to the capture of Saigon in April 1975 and also for the lightning campaign which captured Phnom Penh and much of Cambodia at the beginning of 1979. It was Dung, too, who succeeded as defence minister and armed forces commander when Giap was forced to retire from those positions at the beginning of 1980. Giap left the Politburo at the party's 5th Congress (1982) having been a member since 1951.

RBS

W

WALLIS AND FUTUNA. *Population* (est. 1986): 14,000, Polynesian. *Area*: 274 sq km. Self-governing French overseas territory, 400 km west of Western Samoa, and comprising Uvea (Wallis), and Futuna and Alofi (Hoorn Islands). *Capital*: Mata-Utu, on Uvea.

The islands were settled at least 2,000 years ago. Repeated wars for supremacy occurred between island chiefs. European contact dates from 1616 (Schouten and Le Maire) and the islands were Christianized by Marist missionaries after 1837. In 1887 France added the islands to the dependency of New Caledonia and in 1959 the people voted to become an overseas territory of France.

The economy is based on subsistence farming and fishing, with the export of copra, although this was severely affected by an insect infestation in the 1960s and 70s. Many islanders have migrated to New Caledonia.

TBM

WEE KIM WEE. Wee Kim Wee was sworn in as Singapore's fourth President in September 1985, having been unanimously elected by Parliament the previous month. He replaced C.V. Devan Nair, who had resigned the post in March 1985 after apparently admitting that he was unable to fulfil his duties because of a dependence on alcohol. President Wee is a former journalist and diplomat, and, prior to his election, he was chairman of the Singapore Broadcasting Corporation.

DS

WESTERN SAMOA. *Population* (est. 1986): 180,000, Polynesian. *Area*: 2842 sq km. Independent state comprising group of two large and seven smaller islands forming the western end of the Samoan chain, adjoining American Samoa. *Capital*: Apia, on Upolu Island.

Polynesians, probably from Tonga, settled the islands around 3,000 years ago, and from here settled much of eastern Polynesia. European contact dates from 1768 (de Bougainville), and a London Missionary Society mission from 1830. Rivalry between chiefs, compounded by competition for influence between Britain, the US and Germany, led eventually to the Berlin Treaty of 1889 guaranteeing Samoan independence and neutrality. The treaty was annulled in 1899, and

Germany annexed Western Samoa. A resistance movement developed.

At the outbreak of World War I, New Zealand occupied Western Samoa, and after the war it was given a League of Nations mandate over the islands. After World War II they became a United Nations trust territory, administered by New Zealand. There followed a movement towards independence, which was obtained in 1962 after a referendum. The constitution provides for a 47-member legislative assembly (*Fono*) elected every five years by the heads of extended families. The Prime Minister, since April 1988, is Tofilau Eti Alesana.

Western Samoa has a subsistence economy (agriculture, timber, fishing), helped by foreign aid programmes and a growing tourist industry. There is a steady migration to New Zealand. The British Monarch is head of state.

TBM

WOMEN'S ISSUES. Feminism is a quintessentially American concept, born out of a radical reappraisal of traditional roles and stereotypes. Social scientists believe World War II probably had an influence, in that many women then found themselves with a new function in both economic and social life. The subsequent rise in awareness of women's issues was largely prompted by American writers and activists, though it was also worked on by Europeans and Australasians – including the Australian-born author of the seminal book *The Female Eunuch*, Germaine Greer. In comparison with North America though, Australia remains a male-dominated society. Within the United States, there is also a quite marked contrast between the more liberal coasts and the conservative south. It is also interesting that women's liberation has not resulted in a sharp increase in female American politicians.

Indeed, it is a remarkable paradox that women have reached the top of the political tree in Pacific countries where men still exercise a lot of their traditional authority. Those include Japan – where **Doi Takako** of the Socialist Party has helped to transform both Japanese politics and women voters' perception of themselves – and the Philippines, where **Corazon Aquino** is in the presidential seat, rather than exercising a more familiar female influence from the sidelines, as her predecessor's wife Imelda did. Without her husband's assassination, it is very doubtful whether Corazon Aquino would ever have become so actively involved in politics herself. To that extent, she is in the pattern of other female political leaders like Eva Peron of Argentina and Benazir Bhutto of Pakistan, whose careers stemmed directly from family connections.

Throughout much of Latin America (and indeed, in the Philippines), the concept of machismo still survives, though the power of the matriarchal figure can be considerable. Some Latin societies have challenged set patterns of behaviour, however, including Nicaragua since the Revolution.

In certain sectors of Muslim society in Malaysia and Indonesia, there has actually been a reversal of liberal ideas about the equality of the sexes as a result of Muslim fundamentalism.

JF

WORKERS' PARTY OF SINGAPORE. The Workers' Party was founded in 1957 by David Marshall, Singapore's first Chief Minister (1956-57). Following Marshall's resignation in 1962, it took a low profile until being revived in 1971 by J.B. Jeyaretnam, its current secretary-general. In a by-election held in late October 1981, Jeyaretnam was elected and thus became the first opposition member in parliament for 15 years. Jeyaretnam was re-elected with an increased majority in December 1984, but was subsequently disbarred from his seat in November 1986 when the Singapore Supreme Court upheld his conviction, and that of the party's chairman Wong Hong Toy, on charges of perjury in connection with bankruptcy proceedings brought against the party in 1982. After his release from prison in late 1986, Jeyaretnam sought without success to secure a review of the case, claiming that the fine imposed on him had been politically motivated in that it had exceeded the S$2,000 level specified by the Constitution as being the threshold beyond which a recipient would be automatically disqualified from Parliament for a period of five years.

DS

Y

YAKUTS. An ethnic group found in the Far Eastern Region of the Soviet Union. The Yakuts, who number over 300,000 people, enjoy administrative-territorial autonomy in the vast Yakut Autonomous Soviet Socialist Republic (founded in 1922), which covers 3,103,200 sq km of the Soviet Far Eastern Region.

IG

YANG SHANGKUN. Born in 1904 in Sichuan province, Yang was a student in Shanghai, joined the **Chinese Communist Party** in 1926, and studied in Moscow. On his return he served in various party and army posts, and he took part in the **Long March**. For most of the period 1949-66 he held leading posts within the Central Committee (CC) Secretariat in Beijing. He was branded as a counter-revolutionary in the Cul-

tural Revolution, and only re-emerged to prominence in 1978. After a series of short-term posts in Guangdong province, he returned to Beijing as Secretary-General of the party's Military Affairs Commission, where he was deputy to **Deng Xiao ping**. He also directed CC work on Taiwan. Since 1987 he has been a member of the party Political Bureau, and since 1988 state President.

CIPF

YI KUN MO (Yi Kŭn-mo). Premier, Democratic People's Republic of Korea. Candidate member, Central Committee, **Korean Workers Party**, 1961; member, Executive Committee, Conference of Party Representatives, Korean Workers Party, 1966; Candidate member, Politburo, Korean Workers party, 1971; Premier.

JHG

Z

ZHAO ZIYANG. Born in 1919 into a landlord family, he joined the **Chinese Communist Party** in 1938. He served as a local party leader in central China up till 1949, thus gaining deep experience of local rural conditions. Between the mid-1950s and the Cultural Revolution he occupied increasingly senior party posts in Guangdong province and then the Central-South China Party Bureau.

In 1967 he was denounced, but he again re-emerged in 1971 as chairman of the Inner Mongolian Autonomous Region. In 1972 he was back in Guangdong, becoming First Party Secretary in 1974. In 1976 he assumed the equivalent post in Sichuan province. His success in transforming the agricultural system there marked him out as a future reformer, attracted the attention of **Deng Xiaoping**, and also made him a rival of **Hua Guofeng**. In 1979 he became a full member of the Political Bureau and in 1980 he replaced Hua as Prime Minister.

He was the architect of the economic reform programme in the 1980s, and also supported the gradual liberalization of the political system. Following the fall of **Hu Yaobang** in January 1987, Zhao became acting General Secretary of the party, apparently reluctantly. He was confirmed in this post at the 13th Party Congress in 1987, and he gave up the post of Prime Minister to **Li Peng** in 1988.

In 1989 he refused to approve the violent suppression of the demonstrations on Tiananmen Square (*see* **Tiananmen Incidents**), and after a tearful public meeting with some of the student leaders on the square, he was dismissed as General Secretary, being replaced by Jiang Zemin.

CIPF

ZHOU ENLAI. Born in 1898 into an upper-middle-class family in Zhejiang province, Zhou spent some years studying classics for the state examinations. In 1917, however, he went to study in Japan, returning to China two years later and being arrested after the **May 4th Movement**. Soon afterwards he went to France as a worker-student, where he founded the Chinese Communist Youth League. He returned to China in 1924 and was appointed Director of the Political Department of the joint CCP-Guomindang Whampoa Military Academy headed by **Chiang Kai-shek**.

He barely survived the Shanghai massacre in 1927, and in the same year was elected to the party's Political Bureau, remaining a member continuously until his death. In the early 1930s there was some rivalry between him and **Mao Zedong**, but after that, he was permanently loyal to Mao. During World War II he headed the communist liaison office attached to the nationalist government in Chongqing.

With the founding of the People's Republic of China, Zhou became Prime Minister and, for some time, Foreign Minister. Possessed of wit, courtesy and apparently inexhaustible stamina, he was the first architect of China's foreign policy and its public face. At home he was always a force for realism in policy-making, even in the Cultural Revolution, when he attempted to tone down its worst excesses and protect as many of its targets as possible, although he never appears to have stood up to Mao. He provoked the enmity of the radicals, who nicknamed him "Confucius", but he died in 1976 mourned by millions of Chinese, as witnessed by the Tiananmen protests (*see* **Tiananmen Incidents**).

CIPF

ZINC. Zinc is not found in its free state: the main ore, zinc blends, usually occurs with other minerals such as silver and lead. It is extracted by smelting or by an electrolytic process if electric power is readily available. Canada is a large producer of zinc ore but it is also found in Australia, South Korea, Japan, China, Mexico, Peru and the USA. The annual production of zinc, in thousands of tonnes, is as follows: Canada, 1,207; Australia, 657; Peru, 568; Mexico; 290; USA, 278; Japan, 253; China, 190; North Korea, 150; South Korea, 54.

RS

GENERAL INDEX

The following index is designed to assist cross-referencing by topic. For each country in the region, the index points to all cross references specific to that country ("See also") and also other significant references ("other references") found elsewhere. All main entry terms are indexed. Thus Mao Zedong is indexed; to cross-reference to other Chinese leaders however, turn to the index entry for China.

Southeast Asia